CHICAGO PUBLIC LIBRARY

R0600? 19401

D0065015

BUSINESS/SCIENCE/TECHNOLOGY DIVISION
CHICAGO PUBLIC LIBRARY
400 SOUTH STATE STREET
CHICAGO, IL 60605

Profile of the
U.S. Economy

A SURVEY OF GROWTH AND CHANGE

OTHER PUBLICATIONS

In co-authorship with W. S. *Woytinsky:*
DIE WELT IN ZAHLEN (THE WORLD IN FIGURES), 7 *volumes*
WORLD POPULATION AND PRODUCTION: TRENDS AND OUTLOOK
WORLD COMMERCE AND GOVERNMENTS: TRENDS AND OUTLOOK
LESSONS OF THE RECESSIONS

SO MUCH ALIVE: THE LIFE AND WORK OF W. S. WOYTINSKY (*editor*)
TWO LIVES IN ONE

THE CHICAGO PUBLIC LIBRARY
MAY 8 1967 M

Profile of the
U.S. Economy

A SURVEY OF
GROWTH AND CHANGE

BY

Emma S. Woytinsky

FOREWORD BY
EWAN CLAGUE

EMMA VOITINSKII

FREDERICK A. PRAEGER, *Publishers*
New York · Washington · London

cop. 1
Soc

FREDERICK A. PRAEGER, *Publishers*
111 Fourth Avenue, New York, N.Y. 10003, U.S.A.
77–79 Charlotte Street, London W.1, England

Published in the United States of America in 1967
by Frederick A. Praeger, Inc., Publishers

© 1967 by Emma S. Woytinsky

All rights reserved

Library of Congress Catalog Card Number: 66-13673

Printed in the United States of America

THE CHICAGO PUBLIC LIBRARY

MAY 9 1967 M

R06007 19401

CHICAGO PUBLIC LIBRARY

To

MY WOLIK

IN LOVING MEMORY

If this book has any merit,
it is because of our years of work together

CHICAGO PUBLIC LIBRARY

Foreword

Forty years ago, in Germany, the remarkable husband-and-wife team of Wladimir and Emma Woytinsky pioneered with a new type of economic book when they published the seven-volume work *The World in Figures*. This was a unique combination of statistical tables, graphic charts, and analytical interpretation of key economic factors in the important industrial nations of the world. Paraphrasing Raymond Goldsmith's evaluation in *So Much Alive*, one can say that this astonishingly successful attempt to present statistical material in a way appealing to the general reader, while maintaining high standards of professional scholarship, was characterized by an extraordinary breadth of coverage (included were many countries now called developing nations, which in the 1920's appeared as subjects of the great economic powers, and not as independent masters of their own destinies), as well as by a careful selection of topics, an unusual acumen in the brief methodological introductions to various fields of statistics, and exceptionally vivid graphic illustrations. Recognition of the merit of the work was immediate, and it grew with each succeeding volume.

Later when the Woytinskys established themselves in the United States, they produced another classic—a monumental two-volume combination of statistical data portraying world economic trends in the postwar period: (1) *World Population and Production*, and (2) *World Commerce and Governments*.

In 1960 Wladimir died. Emma at first devoted her attention to the publication of his memoirs, *Stormy Passage*, which has been translated into six languages. Then she wrote her own memoirs, *Two Lives in One*, which provide a warm personal touch to the objective recording of events by her famous husband. She also organized and directed the publication of *So Much Alive*, a memorial volume to her husband, written by his professional colleagues and associates here and abroad.

Emma Woytinsky then decided to return to their traditional work and elected to prepare a statistical survey of the U.S. economy on a broad historical basis. The new survey, PROFILE OF THE U.S. ECONOMY, is unique in American economic literature. Its comprehensiveness is unusual; it covers every major pertinent topic: the basic environmental factors, such as land, water, and air; population; the labor force; health and education; national income and wealth; consumer expenditures; agriculture; mineral industries and power; manufactures; construction and housing; trade and transportation; price indexes; wages and hours of work; public finance; banking; social security. There is a most stimulating chapter on the American economy in the age of science and technology, and another on the election of the President and the Congress.

The uniqueness of this book consists not only in the selection of topics and the appropriate use of statistics in long historical series but also in the charts, maps, and other visual presentations, as well as the brief textual interpretations which help make the subject matter meaningful and significant for the reader.

Nowhere else can one find assembled in a single source the vast amount of material that is so concisely summarized and analyzed in this volume. The United States produces volumes of statistics on all aspects of our economy, more perhaps than any other nation in the world. The problem for most students and professors, and for the general user of statistics, is the difficulty of locating information in the numerous publications in which the statistics appear. Mrs. Woytinsky has rendered a service to all users of statistics—students, professors, and the general public —by assembling the selected data that provide the key to the story without overburdening the reader with unnecessary details.

This volume will be of interest also to readers in other nations, who have less opportunity to know the facts concerning the American people and our economy. Just as many of the past Woytinsky writings have been translated into many languages in many countries, so will PROFILE OF THE U.S. ECONOMY become a sure candidate for wide distribution throughout the world.

EWAN CLAGUE

Washington, D.C.
May, 1966

Author's Preface

In the late 1930's, my husband and I thought of presenting a statistical survey of the United States, beginning with its earliest period and concluding with the 1940 Census, then in preparation. We worked out an outline, wrote many single chapters, and made some attempts to arrange for publication of the volume. War interrupted this work, and we never returned to it. When, after the death of my husband, I decided to pick up the thread of our traditional work, my first thoughts went to that project. Though its outline had to be changed considerably and most, if not all, of the prepared chapters had to be rewritten or abandoned and new chapters introduced, our skeleton plan could nevertheless be preserved in essence. To me, this was of double importance: it gave me a feeling of continuing the work we had planned to accomplish together, and it assured me of the validity of the undertaking. The only question was whether I could possibly prepare this survey alone. I decided to give the project a try, and the readers will decide whether my effort has succeeded.

The United States of the 1960's is quite different from the United States of the 1930's in many respects, and some of the appraisals and prognostications made in that earlier period had to be revised. But in one respect this country has not changed at all: the help and cooperation which a researcher receives here from the government agencies have no counterpart anywhere in the world. The researcher in Washington, D.C., is particularly blessed in this respect: one telephone call, and any figure is checked, any methodological problem is clarified, a new source is indicated, and in a day or two the latest publications arrive, saving time and energy for the researcher. In this country, the government is indeed the servant of the people.

Though all agencies, without a single exception, have been invariably helpful and cooperative, I want to express my special thanks to the Bureau of Labor Statistics (Department of Labor), Social Security Administration (Department of Health, Education, and Welfare), and the National Science Foundation, which graciously agreed to read relevant chapters, comment on them and provide me with additional information not available otherwise.

My warm appreciation goes to Ewan Clague, who helped me immeasurably with advice and knowledge of sources not yet available to the public and, despite his many commitments, has found time to read the entire manuscript; to Gerhard Colm for his comments on the chapter on public finance; to George Garvy for his help on the chapters on national income, consumer expenditures and banking; to Seymour Fiekowsky for his comments on the chapter on public finance; to Jacob Perlman for his comments on the chapter on the American economy in the age of science and technology; to William Wynne for his comments on the chapter on trade, and to Louis Bean for comments on the chapter on elections. Of course, I alone am responsible for any shortcomings or errors in judgment or data that may be found in this volume. As always, editing of the manuscript was in the experienced hands of our permanent editor and close friend, Mary Ross Gannett.

EMMA S. WOYTINSKY

Washington, D.C.
April, 1966

Contents

Profile of the
U.S. Economy

A SURVEY OF GROWTH AND CHANGE

I. *The United States*

1. *How Large Is the United States?*

After nearly 100 years of growth and expansion, the United States came
to extend over an area of 3 million square miles. The size remained unchanged until 1959, when 2 territories—Alaska, with 586,400 sq. mi., and
Hawaii, with 6,424 sq. mi.—became the forty-ninth and fiftieth member
states of the Union, respectively, thereby bringing the U.S. area to 3,615,211
sq. mi. The total area of the original 13 colonies, in 1783, was 889,000 sq.
mi., including the sparsely inhabited and partially unexplored hinterland.
It stretched from the Atlantic coast in the east to the Mississippi River in
the west, and from the St. Lawrence River in the north to Spanish possessions along the Mexican Gulf in the south (see Table I.1 and Figure I.1).
The United States then had only 5 cities with more than 10,000 inhabitants,
and all of them hugged the Atlantic coast: New York, Philadelphia, Boston,
Charleston, and Baltimore.

Soon after the Union was formed, 3 new states were admitted: Vermont
(1791), Kentucky (1792), and Tennessee (1796). In 1803, Ohio became
the seventeenth state. In the same year, the purchase of Louisiana from
Napoleon—for $15 million—doubled the territory of the nation, adding all
of the Mississippi Basin down to the Gulf of Mexico, and hastened the
westward expansion of settlements. More than 90 years elapsed before this
territory was settled and organized politically. The first state west of the
Mississippi River to enter the Union was Louisiana (1812).

In 1816–19, 4 new states were organized in the western territories of the
original 13 colonies: Indiana (1816), Mississippi (1817), Illinois (1818),
and Alabama (1819). In 1820, Maine became a state, and in the following
year, Missouri, the second state west of the Mississippi River, was admitted
into the Union. Acquisition of Florida from Spain (1819) gave the United
States its natural southeastern border.

3

FIGURE I.1

MAJOR ACQUISITIONS OF TERRITORY BY THE UNITED STATES

U.S. Department of Commerce, Bureau of the Census

TABLE I.1

AREA AND POPULATION OF THE UNITED STATES, 1790

States	Area (In Sq. Mi.) Based on Modern Maps	Population (In Thousands) Based on 1790 Census
The original 13 states		
New Hampshire	9,431	142
Massachusetts[a]	31,306	475
Rhode Island	1,248	69
Connecticut	4,965	238
New York[b]	49,294	426
New Jersey	8,244	184
Pennsylvania	45,126	434
Delaware	2,370	59
Maryland (inc. District of Columbia)	12,397	320
Virginia[c]	66,797	748
North Carolina	52,426	394
South Carolina	30,989	249
Georgia	59,265	83
Western territories (from the present western boundaries of the original 13 states to the Mississippi River)		
Kentucky	40,598	74
Tennessee	42,022	36
Other[d]	432,500	-
TOTAL	889,000	3,929

[a]Includes area of Maine, which became a state in 1820. The territory added here is that determined by the settlement of a border dispute with Great Britain (1842).
[b]Includes Vermont, which became a state in 1791.
[c]Includes West Virginia, which separated from Virginia in 1863.
[d]Later, 7 states were organized in this area: Michigan and Wisconsin in the north; Alabama and Mississippi in the south; Ohio, Indiana, and Illinois in the middle.

Meanwhile, the United States continued to expand its settlements and political organization westward. Arkansas became a state in 1836, Michigan in 1837, Iowa in 1846, Wisconsin in 1848. On the route to the Pacific coast lay thinly settled territories nominally controlled by Mexico—a relic of the early Spanish colonization of this area. The Republic of Texas joined the Union in 1845. After the United States briefly clashed with Mexico, most of the territory of the present Mountain and Pacific states was ceded to the United States, in 1848. The territory of present-day Washington and Oregon had been acquired 2 years earlier, without warfare, following the old frontier disputes with Great Britain. California became a state in 1850, Oregon in 1859. However, not all of the Central region had yet been organized into states—the political organization envisaged by the Constitution. Minnesota became a state in 1858, Kansas in 1861, Nebraska in 1867.

In 1867, shortly after the Civil War, Alaska was purchased from Russia for $7.2 million. The political organization of the West proceeded step by step: Nevada was admitted into the Union in 1864; Colorado in 1876; the Dakotas, Montana, and Washington in 1889; Idaho and Wyoming in 1890; Arizona and New Mexico in 1912; Alaska and Hawaii in 1959.

The present United States occupies a 1,200-mi.-deep land belt stretching from the Atlantic to the Pacific. The distance between the 2 coasts is approximately 3,400 mi. along the Canadian and Alaskan borders, and 2,400 mi. at the south, along the Mexican border and the Gulf.

Before World War I, the area of the outlying possessions was 126,000 sq. mi., of which 115,600 lay in the Philippine Islands. On July 4, 1946, the Islands were granted independence and became the Republic of the Philippines. Overseas possessions now include Guam (212 sq. mi.); the Virgin Islands (133 sq. mi.); American Samoa, Midway, and other islands (118 sq. mi.); and the Trust Territory of the Pacific Islands (687 sq. mi.). The free Commonwealth of Puerto Rico, associated with the United States by a popular vote on March 3, 1952, and the Congressional Act of July 25, 1952, has a territory of 3,435 sq. mi. The Canal Zone, under jurisdiction of the United States by treaty with the Republic of Panama covers 553 sq. mi. (This treaty is to be revised in the near future.)

The main importance of these outlying territories and trusteeships to the United States lies in their strategic location. The Panama Canal is the only water lane between the Atlantic and Pacific coasts, with Puerto Rico and the Caribbean area protecting the Canal, while the Pacific Islands secure the route across the Pacific.

About half the area of the United States is a broad plain, sloping southward and drained by the Mississippi and its tributaries. It is flanked in the west by rugged mountains and in the east by lower ridges of the Appalachian system, separated by a lowland belt from the Atlantic coast and the Gulf of Mexico. In contrast to settlement in other countries, the movement of population did not follow the course of rivers and valleys but pushed westward from the Atlantic coast, crossing mountains, rivers, and plains.

The borders of the United States include some 12,383 mi. of seacoast (Atlantic Ocean, 2,069 mi.; Gulf of Mexico, 1,631 mi.; Pacific Ocean, 7,623 mi.; Arctic coast of Alaska, 1,060 mi.) and 3,770 mi. of Great Lakes shoreline—Superior, Huron, Michigan, Erie, and Ontario. The Atlantic Ocean is a moat stretching for more than 3,000 mi. between the United States and Europe. The distance between Pacific ports and Japan is more

TABLE I.2
THE UNITED STATES AND SELECTED COUNTRIES,
BY AREA, 1963

Country	Area (In Thousands of Sq. Mi.)	
	Total	Agricultural Land[a]
United States	3,615	1,700
Canada	3,852	241
Brazil	3,286	500[b]
Argentina	1,072	580[b]
Mexico	762	367
United Kingdom	94	77
West Germany	96	55
France	211	134
Italy	116	80
U.S.S.R.	8,650	2,182
China (Mainland)	3,692	...
India	1,176	671
Japan	143	26
Australia	2,971	1,798[c]

[a]Arable land and land under permanent crops, permanent
  meadows, and pastures.
[b]Incomplete data.
[c]Of which 104,000 sq. mi. is arable land, with 53,000
  being permanent pastures; the largest part of the rest
  is rough grazings.

than 5,000 mi. (Yokohama-Seattle, 4,900 mi.; Yokohama–San Francisco, 5,220 mi.; Yokohama–Los Angeles, 5,570 mi.).

In area, the United States is the fourth largest country in the world (see Table I.2). The U.S.S.R. holds first place, followed by Canada and then China. If one excludes the Arctic wastes and sterile deserts and plains in the last 3, the U.S.S.R. would still be the world's largest country, with the largest arable territory, and the United States would rank next.

The area of the United States dwarfs those of the great powers in the Eastern Hemisphere (France, 211,000 sq. mi.; Italy, 116,000; Federal Republic of Germany, 96,000; the United Kingdom, 94,000). In the Western Hemisphere, Brazil is the only nation except Canada whose land resources can be compared to those of the United States.

The United States is almost twice as *wide* from east to west as it is *long* from north to south. In contrast, many countries stretch lengthwise, from north to south, as do Argentina, Chile, and Mexico in the Western Hemisphere, and Great Britain, Sweden, Norway, Italy, and Japan in the Eastern Hemisphere.

FIGURE I.2

THE CLIMATIC ZONES OF THE UNITED STATES

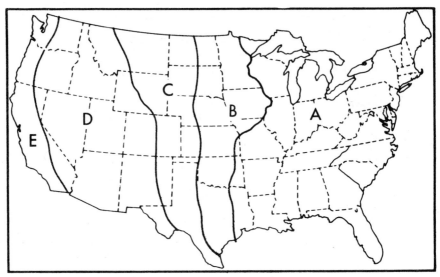

U.S. Department of Agriculture

2. *Our Place in the Sun*

The United States lies almost wholly in the northern part of the temperate zone, corresponding roughly to that of western Europe and the Mediterranean basin. It includes several "climatic regions," each of which in turn has a variety of conditions.

Climatic contrasts are more sudden and striking between the Atlantic and the Pacific regions than between north and south. The principal climatic regions, and consequently the chief economic divisions, are therefore separated by north-south lines rather than crosswise lines (see Figure I.2).

More than seven-tenths of the population is concentrated in the humid east (A). As the weather moves from west to east, much of the air that reaches the Atlantic seaboard passes over wide stretches of the land. Greatly chilled in winter and heated in summer, this air brings extremes of cold and heat to the eastern areas, like those in the interior of the continent. Change from winter to summer is abrupt. There is a striking difference in winter temperatures between north and south; the difference in summer temperatures is much smaller (see Appendix Table I). Annual rainfall is greatest along the Atlantic coast (50 inches and more) and decreases as one goes west (see Figure I.3).

The interior subhumid lands (B), in the opinion of the Department of Agriculture, are "so well endowed physically—in surface configuration, soil, and climate—for agricultural use" that "no other region of the earth of

FIGURE I.3

PRECIPITATION PATTERNS IN THE UNITED STATES

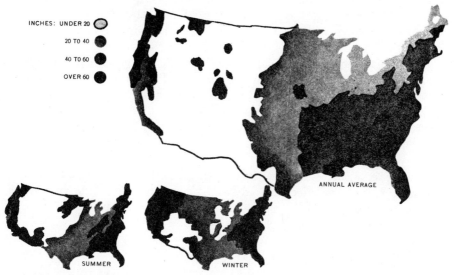

U.S. Department of the Interior, Geological Survey

equal size" can measure up to them. The only important handicap is drought. Yet, although rainfall exceeds evaporation by only a narrow margin, it is concentrated in the early warm season, thus assuring adequate moisture to growing crops in their stalk-forming period. Differences between the most northern and southern temperatures are great, with winters about 50° higher in the south than in the north. Thus, the growing season may last only 3–4 months in North Dakota but 8–9 months in Texas.

In the Great Plains (C), rainfall is scanty and unpredictable, varying from less than 10 in. in the dry years to about 30 in. in the wet ones. Occasionally, masses of moist tropical air moving from the south collide so forcefully with dry polar air coming from the north that violent storms and heavy precipitation occur. Drought periods of 35 days and more are normal, but longer periods are frequent. Dry farming is practiced extensively.

The bulk of the west (D) is screened from the Pacific by successive parallel mountain ranges that act as barriers to the eastward-moving moist air, which accounts for the heavy rainfall on the western slopes of these ranges and the aridity on the slopes and valleys to the east. Within as small a distance as 40 mi., some valleys may get only 4 in. of precipitation, while the mountain slopes may receive more than 40 in. (see Figure I.3 for precipitation patterns in the United States).

A narrow zone of summer-dry climate, more than 1,000 mi. long but only 150–200 mi. wide, stretches along the Pacific coast (E). Rainfall is heavy in the north, where the climate resembles that of Norway and the British Isles, while in southern California rainfall is lighter, and climatic conditions are more like those in Spain, Italy, and Greece. Winters are mild, because air from the Pacific is warmer than the air refrigerated by passage over snow-covered land; summer temperatures are moderated by the proximity to the sea.

The climate of Alaska is relatively mild in the south, with precipitation of about 55 in. January temperatures correspond to those in central Maryland and southern Illinois. In the north, winters are very severe, and extremely cold weather prevails in the interior and the Arctic area. The growing season ranges from 160 days along the southeastern coast to 80–90 days in the interior. The unusual length of daylight compensates for the short growing season.

In Hawaii, rainfall variations are extreme, from less than 20 in. to almost 250 in. per year. The effect of trade winds dominates the entire area in all seasons. Temperature shows a very moderate difference between winter and summer, and there are no sudden changes.

3. *Land, Water, Air*

Land, water, and air are the basic environmental resources, and no human being can live without them. The United States is well provided with all 3, but in the course of its development, each has become a major many-faceted national problem.

Land. About 60 per cent of the area of the United States consists of lowlands and plains less than 650 feet high; some 30 per cent, of highlands with altitudes ranging from 650 to 2,000 ft.; and the remainder, of higher mountains, suitable chiefly for grazing and timber production with occasional cultivable spots.

Mountains and highlands are predominantly in the west, fringed by a narrow strip of lowlands along the Pacific coast. The east, particularly along the Atlantic coast and the Gulf of Mexico, consists of lowlands and plains, but this area is crossed by a vast Appalachian system stretching almost parallel to the Atlantic and covering, with some minor eastern highland ranges, nearly a sixth part of the country.

Of the total land area, nearly 59 per cent is in private hands; 39 per cent is owned by the Federal Government, the states, and municipalities; the remaining 2 per cent represents trusts and tribal Indian lands. Although the Federal Government owns 34 per cent of the total, the percentage varies greatly from state to state. In Alaska, 99.8 per cent of the land is Federally owned; in Nevada, 86.2 per cent; in Utah, 67.3, and in Idaho, 64.5 per cent. On the other hand, the Federal Government owns only 2.6 per cent of the land in Delaware, 1.7 per cent in Texas, and 0.3 per cent in Connecticut (see Table I.3). Nearly nine-tenths of the Federally owned area is made up of forests or grazing lands; the rest consists

TABLE I.3

TOTAL LAND AND LAND OWNED BY THE FEDERAL GOVERNMENT, BY STATE, 1964

State	Total Land (In Millions of Acres)	Per Cent Federally Owned	State	Total Land (In Millions of Acres)	Per Cent Federally Owned
Alaska	365.5	99.8	Mississippi	30.2	5.1
Nevada	70.3	86.2	North Dakota	44.5	4.6
Utah	52.7	67.3	Vermont	5.9	4.3
Idaho	52.9	64.5	Kentucky	25.5	4.2
Oregon	61.6	52.2	Missouri	44.2	3.8
Wyoming	62.3	48.2	Louisiana	28.9	3.6
Arizona	72.7	44.7	Alabama	32.7	3.3
California	100.2	44.5	Oklahoma	44.1	3.0
Colorado	66.5	36.0	Maryland	6.3	2.9
New Mexico	77.8	34.3	Delaware	1.3	2.6
Montana	93.3	29.6	New Jersey	4.8	2.1
Washington	42.7	29.4	Pennsylvania	28.8	2.0
District of Columbia[a]	-	28.3	Texas	168.2	1.7
New Hampshire	5.8	12.2	Indiana	23.2	1.6
Florida	34.7	9.7	Nebraska	49.0	1.5
Arkansas	33.6	9.2	Illinois	35.8	1.2
Michigan	36.5	8.9	Massachusetts	5.0	1.2
Virginia	25.5	8.4	Rhode Island	0.7	1.1
South Dakota	48.9	7.0	Kansas	52.5	1.0
Minnesota	51.2	6.5	Ohio	26.2	0.8
Hawaii	4.1	6.2	New York	30.7	0.7
West Virginia	15.4	6.2	Maine	19.8	0.6
North Carolina	31.4	6.1	Iowa	35.9	0.4
Tennessee	26.7	5.9	Connecticut	3.1	0.3
South Carolina	19.4	5.8			
Georgia	37.3	5.5			
Wisconsin	35.0	5.2	TOTAL	2,271.3	33.9

[a]Less than 50,000.

of national parks and historical sites, military fields, flood-control and reclamation projects, and so on.

In 1959, the total land area was divided nearly equally between farm-land and non-farmland (49.4 and 50.6 per cent, respectively). The precise relationship depends partly on the census definition of a farm. In the 1950 census, places with 3 or more acres were counted as farms if the annual *value* of home-garden products amounted to $150 or more; in the 1959 Census, places with less than 10 acres were counted as farms if yearly *sales* of agricultural products amounted to at least $250.

In 1959 (the year of the last agricultural census for which data are available), a little over one-third of all farmland was cropland, and almost half was grassland pasture, including cropland used only for the pasture; almost 15 per cent was woodland, either pastured or not pastured, and 3 per cent was in roads, farmsteads, and so on. Non-farmland is divided into three groups: grazing land; forest land not grazed; and land occupied by cities and towns, rural homesites not on farms, highways and railroads, airports, wildlife refuges, and desert, swamp, and other wasteland (see Table I.4).

Much of the land has suffered from ruthless exploitation in the past: destructive cutting practices in forests; the frequent use of land susceptible to erosion for crops requiring clean cultivation, such as cotton, corn, or

TABLE I.4

UTILIZATION OF FARM AND NONFARM LAND, 1880, 1950, AND 1959[a]

	Millions of Acres			Per Cent		
	1880	1950	1959	1880	1950	1959
In farms	536	1,161	1,123	28.2	51.1	49.4
Cropland	188	409	392	9.9	18.0	17.3
Grassland pasture	122	486	532	6.4	21.4	23.4
Woodland pasture	190	135	93	10.0	6.0	4.1
Woodland not pastured		85	71		3.7	3.1
Farmsteads, roads, and other	36	46	35	1.9	2.0	1.5
Not in farms	1,367	1,112	1,148	71.8	48.9	50.6
Grazing land	883	402	319	46.4	17.7	14.0
Forest and woodland not grazed	368	335	438	19.3	14.7	19.5
Other land	116	375	391	6.1	16.5	17.1
TOTAL LAND AREA	1,903	2,273	2,271	100.0	100.0	100.0

[a]Includes Alaska and Hawaii in 1950 and 1959.

tobacco; the vast expansion of wheat fields in the Great Plains, with the resulting ruin of the grass cover. A program of soil conservation unlike any previously undertaken anywhere began in 1935 with the establishment of the Soil Conservation Service. The program is carried on cooperatively with the farmer, based on plans worked out with him for his land. Many different methods are used—terracing, contouring, strip-and-cover cropping, crop rotation, stubble-mulching, gully-planting, woodland improvement, and so on. In 1950, the conservation work covered about 850 million acres of land in farms and ranches. In 1964, 1,058 million a. in farms were organized in 2,971 conservation districts. Twenty-four states, Puerto Rico, and the Virgin Islands are completely covered by such districts.

Water. It has always been accepted that the United States is well supplied with water from rainfall, rivers, and ground sources. But while there is as much water now as there ever was, the nation's needs for it have grown to an extent that the relatively fixed water supply can barely satisfy them. In one form or another, every state has some kind of water problem, whether availability, quality, salinity, or an excess that causes floods (see Figure I.4).

Industry takes half of all water used; to it, water is the most important raw material serving as a power source, coolant, cleansing agent, ingredient of many products, transportation device. It takes more water to manufacture 1 yard of rayon than to grow, process, and weave a yd. of cotton, silk, or wool. A paper plant uses 200 gallons of water to produce a dollar's

FIGURE I.4

MAJOR WATER PROBLEMS IN THE UNITED STATES

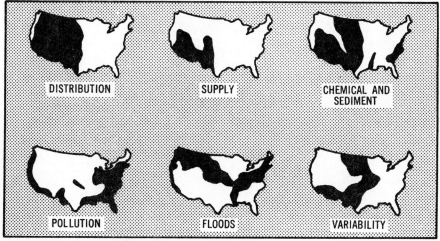

U.S. Department of the Interior, Geological Survey

worth of paper; a steel plant, 1,400 gal. of water for a dollar's worth of steel.

Agriculture is another insatiable user of water, mostly for irrigation. In a certain sense, it "consumes" more water than industry because 60 per cent of irrigation water is not recoverable; moreover, water that does return to various watercourses is loaded with chemicals difficult to remove.

Municipal uses of water are rapidly increasing with the growth of the population and rising standards of sanitation.

In 1960, for the first time, the nation's use of water—323 billion gal. a day—exceeded the dependable supply of 315 billion gal. (see Table I.5). By 1980, consumption of water is expected to reach almost 600 billion gal. a day (see Figure I.5); by the year 2000, our water requirements may amount to 1,000 billion gal. a day, or more. Yet, the maximum supply

TABLE I.5

SUPPLY AND USE OF WATER IN THE UNITED STATES,
1900-1960, AND PROJECTIONS FOR 1970 AND 1980

Supply and Type of Use	Billions of Gallons a Day						
	1900	1920	1940	1950	1960	1970	1980
Estimated dependable supply	95.0	125.0	245.0	270.0	315.0	395.0	515.0
Use rate of fresh water							
Agricultural	22.2	58.4	74.1	104.6	141.0	165.9	166.0
Industrial	15.0	27.2	52.0	84.0	159.9	218.3	394.0
Municipal	3.0	6.0	10.1	14.1	22.0	27.0	37.0

FIGURE I.5

USE, DEMAND, AND SUPPLY OF WATER IN THE UNITED STATES

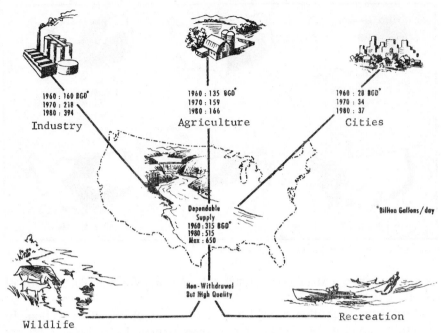

1960 : 160 BGD*
1970 : 218
1980 : 394
Industry

1960 : 135 BGD*
1970 : 159
1980 : 166
Agriculture

1960 : 28 BGD*
1970 : 34
1980 : 37
Cities

Dependable
Supply
1960 : 315 BGD*
1980 : 515
Max : 650

*Billion Gallons/day

Non-Withdrawal
But High Quality

Wildlife

Recreation

Department of the Interior, Geological Survey

which can be developed through conservation measures, is 515 billion gal. a day by 1980. It is estimated that the most that the nation can ever have available as a result of engineering works is about 650 billion gal. a day.

But quality of water is an even more serious problem than quantity of it. Theoretically, it is possible to reuse water infinitely. Reuse is being practiced on a large scale already, and growing reuse of water that has gone through the water mains and sewers of cities is inevitable. Just as inevitable is the disposal of treated waste from municipalities, communities, factories, and farms into the watercourses. Thus the basic question is of water-pollution control. Thousands of communities, with a population of scores of millions, still dump raw, untreated sewage into the streams to be carried to the next user. Extensive farm use of fertilizers, insecticides, and other chemicals discharges great quantities of pollutants into watercourses. The crowding of people in cities intensifies problems of waste disposal and of processing billions of pounds of detergents which resist decomposition and reappear in drinking water even after treatment. In addition to these types of waste, a new source of water pollution has come into being: radioactive wastes.

Water pollution is no longer a local affair; streams carrying waste recognize no city or state boundaries. Pollution control requires the cooperative efforts of local and Federal governments, and a determined participation of industry. The Water Quality Act of 1965, passed with overwhelming majorities in both Houses of Congress, holds the promise of nationwide intensive efforts to reclaim the clean streams and lakes this country once had.

Air. Another vital natural resource—air—is also becoming a serious national concern. Many features of modern life, such as industrialization, urbanization, and human mobility, tend to result in air pollution. The major source of it is the motor vehicle, which accounts for about half of the total air pollution. As the number of motor vehicles—cars, trucks, buses—continues to grow, the photochemical smog they produce increasingly pollutes the air, especially in areas with congested population and intensive traffic. Atmospheric sampling has revealed that smog formation occurs from coast to coast, and the peculiar damage to vegetation caused by smog has been detected in at least 27 states and the District of Columbia. It is believed that acceptable concentration limits for air pollutants have been exceeded in many instances.

Air is polluted by substances—such as particles of smoke, dust, fumes—released by activities of men in concentrations sufficient to interfere with safety or health of human beings or with the use and enjoyment of property. These gaseous discharges—carbon monoxide, sulphur dioxide, fluorine, phosphorous compounds, and other gases and contaminants created in the air by the interaction of such substances—come from various sources: exhaust pipes of cars and trucks, factory smokestacks and home chimneys, incinerators, burning municipal dumps, trains, airplanes, and ships.

The degree of concentration of the pollutants in the air depends on the amounts discharged, the chemical and physical reactions they undergo before and after dispersion, and climatic conditions. With increasing urbanization, more and more people live in crowded areas, with relatively smaller air resources. Nearly 20,000 air samplings taken in 232 cities during 1957–63 showed that "suspended particulate matters" (particles of smoke, dust and fumes, and droplets of viscous liquid remaining in the air) ranged, on the average, from 80 micrograms in communities of 10,000–25,000 people to 128 micrograms in communities of 400,000–700,000, and 182 micrograms in communities with 3 million or more. For the 232 cities, the average was 115 micrograms, the minimum 5, and the maximum 1,706. Corresponding figures for 60 nonurban stations were: average, 36; minimum, 1; maximum, 843.

It is estimated that 6,000 communities in the United States are affected by air pollution: all 212 Standard Metropolitan Statistical Areas and about 40 per cent of the communities with a population of 2,500–50,000 (see Figure I.6.). The economic damage caused by air pollution is estimated to exceed $11 billion annually; the damage consists of injury to livestock and crops, corrosion of structures and materials, reduction of

FIGURE I.6

AREAS WITH AIR POLLUTION PROBLEMS IN THE UNITED STATES

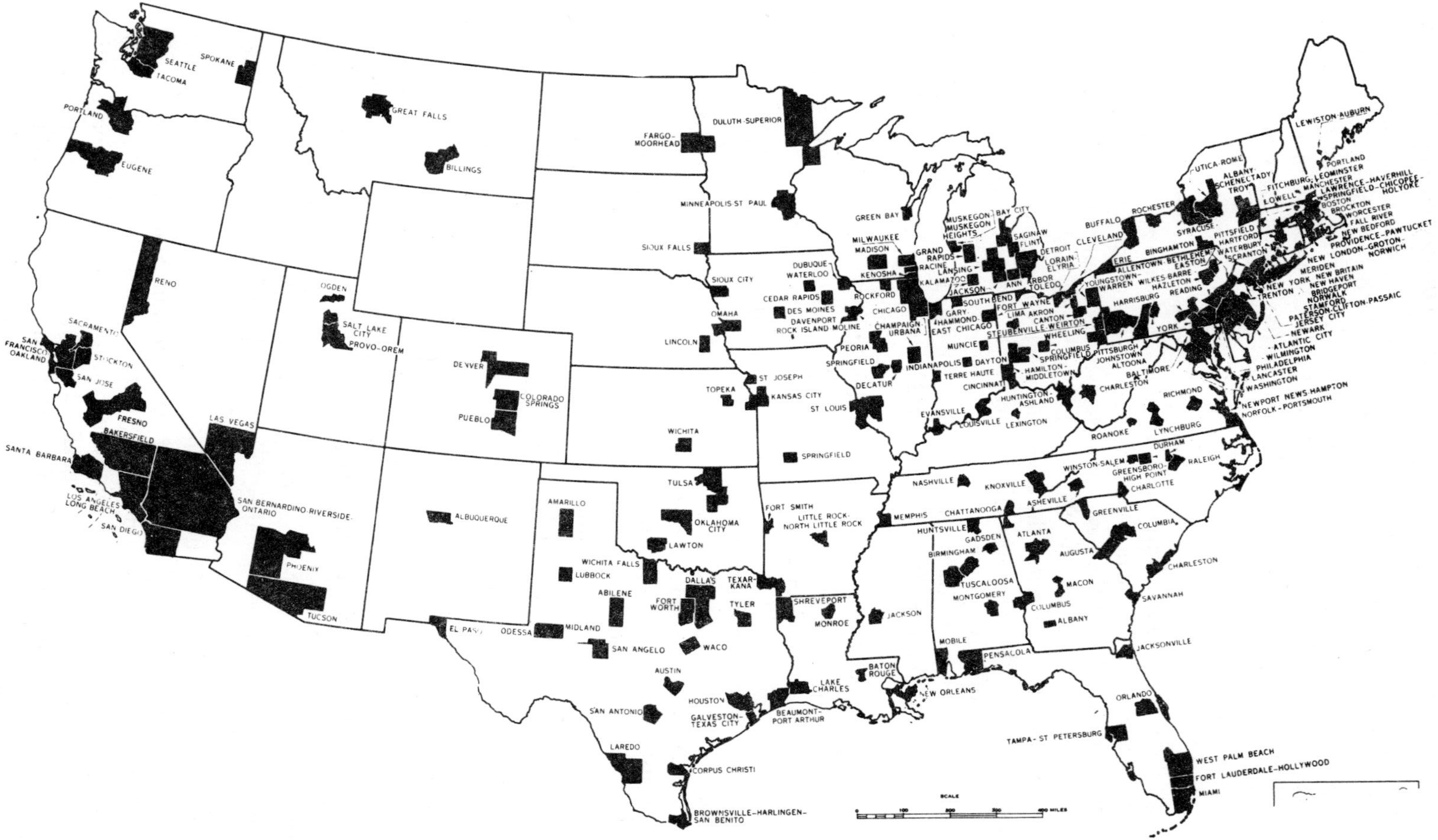

U.S. Department of Commerce, Bureau of the Census

FIGURE I.7

TOTAL REFUSE PRODUCTION IN THE UNITED STATES

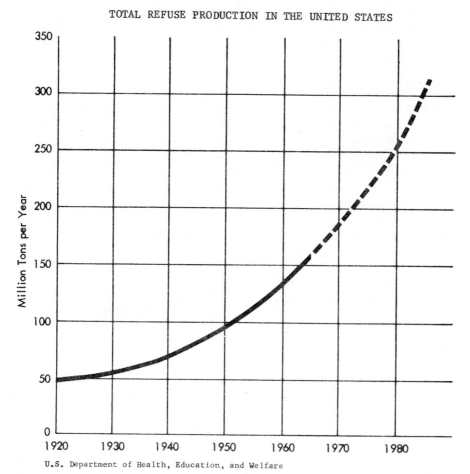

U.S. Department of Health, Education, and Welfare

property values, and so on. The harmful effect on human health cannot be calculated in money.

In 1955, the National Air Sampling Network was created, with the objective of determining the extent and nature of air pollution, studying trends in levels of atmospheric contaminants, and investigating relationships between air pollution and socio-economic, geographic, topographic, and other factors. The Network comprises 250 stations: 215 urban and 35 nonurban. Since 1956, this network and the National Radiation Surveillance Network have been collecting data on radioactivity in the atmosphere.

Production of solid waste in the United States, which contributes to both air and water pollution and creates rodent and insect problems, has reached such proportions that it outstrips the waste-disposal facilities of virtually every community in the nation. It averaged 50 million tons in 1920, 70 million in 1940, and 140 million t. in 1960. By 1980, it is estimated that it will reach 250 million t., 5 times as much as in 1920 (see Figure I.7.).

The Clean Air Act Amendments and Solid Waste Disposal Act of 1965 provide the basis for uniform national measures against air pollution. This is of utmost importance in control of ubiquitous automotive smog, which individual municipalities and even single states cannot handle. It is expected that within 2 years all new motor vehicles will be equipped with pollution-control systems. Other measures comprise research in more effective disposal arrangements of air pollutants and solid waste, in factors governing their dispersion and ways of preventing air pollution. As in the fight against water pollution, it is believed that only productive cooperation of all public authorities with the private sector, largely responsible for a major share in these problems, would help to rid the country of poisoned air and mountains of refuse.

II. *We, the People*

4. *Population of the United States, 1790–1960*

The first census, in 1790, counted 3.9 million inhabitants in the United States. We were then a small nation, not only in comparison with the great powers, such as Russia (more than 30 million inhabitants), France (25 million), Austro-Hungary (22 million), Italy (15 million), and Great Britain (15 million), but even in comparison with Spain (nearly 10 million).

Since that time, the population of the United States has increased steadily. Up to 1860, the rate of its growth was amazingly stable—an increase of about 35 per cent in each decade, so that the number of people about doubled every 22 years: from 1790 to 1812, from 1812 to 1834, and from 1834 to 1856 (see Table II.1 and Figure II.1).

By the middle of the last century, the United States had a population of 23.2 million—about as many inhabitants as Great Britain and almost twice as many as Spain. In Europe at that time, only Russia and France had larger populations (the German principalities were not yet united under Prussia).

After the Civil War, the rate of population growth in the United States dropped to 25 per cent per decade and remained at this level until almost the end of the century. This rate of growth was about twice as high as that in Russia and Germany, 2½ times as high as that in Great Britain and Belgium, 4 times as high as that in Italy, 5 times as high as that in Spain. In absolute numbers, the population of the United States increased much more between 1850 and 1900 than in the preceding 50 years (by 52.8 million, as compared with 17.9 million in the first half of the century).

TABLE II.1

POPULATION OF THE UNITED STATES, 1790-1965

Census Year	POPULATION			
	Number of Persons (In Thousands)	Per Sq. Mi. of Land Area	Increase over Preceding Census	
			Number of Persons (In Thousands)	Number of Persons (Per Cent)
1790	3,929	4.5	-	-
1800	5,308	6.1	1,379	35.1
1810	7,240	4.3[a]	1,931	36.4
1820	9,638	5.5	2,399	33.1
1830	12,866	7.4	3,228	33.5
1840	17,069	9.8	4,203	32.7
1850	23,192	7.9[a]	6,122	35.9
1860	31,443	10.6	8,251	35.6
1870	39,818	13.4	8,375	26.6
1880	50,156	16.9	10,337	26.0
1890	62,948	21.2	12,792	25.5
1900	75,995	25.6	13,047	20.7
1910	91,972	31.0	15,978	21.0
1920	105,711	35.6	13,738	14.9
1930	122,775	41.2	17,064	16.1
1940	131,669	44.2	8,894	7.2
1950	150,697	50.7	19,028	14.5
1960	178,464	60.1	27,766	18.4
1950[b]	151,326	42.6[d]	19,161	14.5
1960	179,323	50.5	27,997	18.5
1963[c]	189,417	52.4	10,094	5.6
1964[c]	192,119	53.1	2,702	1.6
1965[c]	194,572	53.8	2,453	1.3

[a]Decline in the average density of population from the preceding census is due to the territorial expansion of the United States through acquisition of thinly populated areas: Louisiana purchase in 1803 and accession of Texas, Oregon, and other formerly Mexican territories in 1840.
[b]Includes Alaska and Hawaii.
[c]Estimated population.
[d]Decline due to addition of Alaska.

After 1900, the rate of population growth slowed down. As a result of the Depression in the 1930's, which stopped the immigration (see Sec. 5) and cut down the birth rate (see Sec. 14), the population increased only 7 per cent between 1930 and 1940. In the last 2 decades, however, the rate of growth has accelerated rapidly: to 14.5 per cent between 1940 and 1950, and 18.4 per cent between 1950 and 1960.

The census of 1960 reported 178.5 million inhabitants of the conterminous United States; 226,167 in Alaska; and 632,772 in Hawaii. The population abroad, chiefly members of the armed forces, their families, and other civilians, numbered 1.4 million; in outlying areas (Virgin Islands, Guam,

FIGURE II.1

GROWTH OF POPULATION IN THE UNITED STATES, 1790-1960

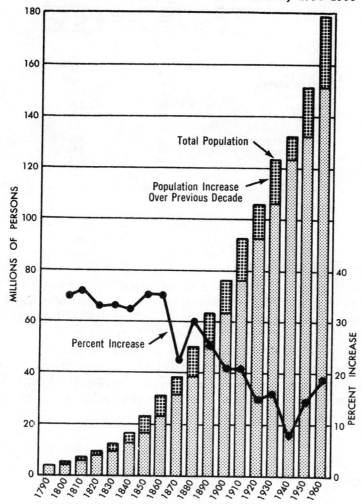

U.S. Department of Commerce, Bureau of the Census

other Pacific Islands, and in the Panama Canal Zone), an additional 238,000 were counted. The Commonwealth of Puerto Rico had 2.4 million inhabitants.

The United States ranks fourth among the countries of the world in population. Among Occidental nations, it is second only to the U.S.S.R. Its population exceeds that of the United Kingdom, France, and Italy combined (see Table II.2).

The population of the United States is increasing by about 2.5–2.7 million a year, and this increase is expected to continue throughout the next decade or two.

TABLE II.2

POPULATION OF SELECTED COUNTRIES, 1962-63

| Country | Number of Inhabitants | |
	In Millions	Per Sq. Mi.
China	647[a]	...
India	460	392
U.S.S.R.	225	26
United States	189	53[b]
Indonesia	100	174
Pakistan	99	270
Japan	96	672
Brazil	76	23
United Kingdom	54	571
West Germany	55	579
Italy	50	434
France	48	227

[a]1953.
[b]1963; without Alaska and Hawaii, 60.

5. Where We Came From

The large growth in population in the nineteenth century (see Table II.1) was due to the stream of immigrants, which in turn was speeded up by progress in water transportation. From 1820 to 1900, 19 million immigrants from all parts of Europe entered the United States. In the 50 years from 1790 to 1840, hardly more than a million crossed the ocean in sailing vessels; from 1840 to 1964, almost 42.2 million arrived on steamships. Although not all these immigrants have stayed in the United States, they represented the largest and most momentous migration in the history of mankind (see Table II.3 and Figure II.2).

TABLE II.3

IMMIGRATION INTO THE UNITED STATES, 1820-1964
(In Thousands)

Year	Number of Immigrants	Year	Number of Immigrants
1820	8	1911-1915	4,460
1821-1830	143	1916-1920	1,276
1831-1840	599	1921-1925	2,639
1841-1850	1,713	1926-1930	1,468
1851-1860	2,598	1931-1935	220
1861-1870	2,315	1936-1940	308
1871-1880	2,812	1941-1945	171
1881-1890	5,247	1946-1950	864
1891-1900	3,688	1951-1955	1,088
1901-1905	3,833	1956-1960	1,428
1906-1910	4,962	1961-1964	1,154
	TOTAL	1820-1964	42,995

FIGURE II.2

IMMIGRATION TO THE UNITED STATES, 1820-1962

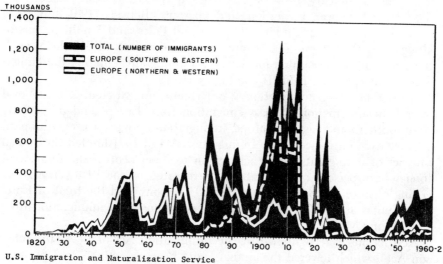

U.S. Immigration and Naturalization Service

The yearly number of immigrants increased from decade to decade, from about 5,000 a year shortly after the Revolutionary War to 1 million a year before the outbreak of World War I. This increase was interrupted in the 1860's by the Civil War, after which it resumed climbing, though temporarily slowed down by each economic setback, as, for example, the financial panics of 1873 and 1883. In 1914–18, the influx of immigrants was stopped by World War I, and shortly thereafter it was restricted by the Immigration Acts of 1921, 1924, and 1927. Immigration dropped almost to zero in the 1930's; during the worst Depression years, more persons left the United States than entered its ports.

The part that various European countries have played in the immigration to the United States has changed as time has gone on. The first stock of the original settlers on the Atlantic coast consisted largely of British and Dutch colonists. Immigrants from Great Britain, especially from Ireland, prevailed before 1840. The potato famine in Ireland in 1847 brought that country's emigration to the United States to an unprecedented high point. As a result of political troubles in Germany in 1848, Prussians thronged American harbors, and subsequently the Germans continued to be one of the largest immigrant groups. Immigration from the Scandinavian countries increased slowly but steadily. All in all, immigration from northern and western Europe predominated between 1790 and 1890: of the 15.7 million persons who came to this country, 10 million were from northwestern Europe, 4 million from Germany, and only 1.7 million from other countries.

Toward the end of the nineteenth century, immigration from southern and eastern Europe increased spectacularly. More and more people came from Austro-Hungary, from poverty-stricken Italy, and from Czarist Russia, harassed by war, revolution, and pogroms. Between 1901 and 1920, 3.2 million Italians, 2.5 million Russians and Poles, and 3 million Austro-Hungarians landed on these shores. At the outbreak of World War I, these 3 countries accounted for half of all immigrants entering the United States (see Appendix Table II and Figure II.2).

Until that time, immigration was virtually unrestricted. After World War I, in anticipation of mass emigration from Europe and particularly from southern and eastern Europe, immigration quotas for each European country were introduced. The Immigration Act of 1921 limited the annual number of immigrants from each nation to 3 per cent of the number of foreign-born persons of that nationality reported by the 1910 census. The ceiling of immigration was set at 357,803 persons, and the total of European quotas at 357,747. No limitation was imposed on immigration from Canada and Mexico.

Restrictions were tightened by the Immigration Act of 1924 (the Johnson Act), which lowered the annual quota for each country to 2 per cent of the number of persons born in that country who were residing in the United States in 1890. This act reduced the over-all ceiling of immigration to 153,714 persons in each fiscal year and set particularly small quotas for the countries of southern and eastern Europe. The Immigration Act of 1927 cut the over-all maximum to 150,000 and re-allocated quotas for particular countries in such a way as to keep the existing composition, by origin, of the U.S. population. The quotas for southeastern Europe were again cut.

The Immigration Act of 1952 based the annual quota on a flat one-sixth of 1 per cent of the population of the census of 1920. Quotas were further revised by Presidential proclamation in 1953 and annually since 1957; the total in 1961 amounted to 156,487.

On December 1, 1965, a new immigration law became effective. Under it, all "quota" countries are entitled to the existing number of immigrant visas until July 1, 1968. After that date, national-origin quotas will be abolished, and visas will be accorded in order of request for them and with a new system of preferences: the relatives of U.S. citizens and lawfully resident aliens, persons with special skills or coming for labor needed in this country, and refugees. A maximum of 20,000 per annum is set for any country in the Eastern Hemisphere, and of 170,000 for that area as a whole. For the first time in U.S. history, a numerical limit is set on immigration from the Western Hemisphere: 120,000 per annum.

Before World War II, immigration to the United States from Europe was at a low ebb. After the war, immigration increased, but it has never regained the level of the early 1900's.

In addition to quota immigrants, there are nonquota immigrants, such as persons born in Canada and Latin America, their wives, their children under age 21, ministers of religious denominations, and some other categories. Also, the Displaced Persons Act of 1948 and the Refugee Relief Acts of 1953, 1958, and 1959 allowed nonquota admission of certain refugees and their wives and children (cf. Sec. 9).

6. *Where We Live*

A large part of the population of the United States is concentrated in the northeastern corner of the country, between the Canadian border and the Great Lakes in the north, the Mississippi River in the west, the Ohio River in the south, and the Atlantic coast in the east. This densely populated area includes most of the original territory of the United States (cf. Figure I.1). In 1960, 81 million persons, almost half the total population, were living here within an area of 420,000 sq. mi.—that is, within about one-ninth of the land area of the country. This region has an average of 193 inhabitants per sq. mi.

TABLE II.4

U.S. POPULATION BY GEOGRAPHIC DIVISION, 1960

	Number of Persons	
	In Thousands	Per Sq. Mi.
New England	10,509	166.5
Middle Atlantic	34,168	340.1
East North Central	36,225	148.0
West North Central	15,394	30.2
South Atlantic	25,972	97.0
East South Central	12,050	67.0
West South Central	16,951	39.5
Mountain	6,855	8.0
Pacific[a]	21,198	23.6
UNITED STATES	179,323	50.5

[a]Includes Alaska and Hawaii.

Another densely populated region is the southeastern corner of the United States, bounded by the Mississippi and Ohio Rivers, the Atlantic coast, and the Mexican Gulf. In 1960, this corner had a population of 38 million within 460,000 sq. mi. (83 inhabitants per sq. mi.). The population density here is nearly half that of the northeast and 4 times that of the area west of the Mississippi.

The western part of the country may be divided, according to density of population, into 3 regions, which correspond to distinct climatic zones and extend from the Canadian border to the Mexican: the Central states (from Minnesota and North Dakota to Texas and Louisiana), with a population of 32 million within 960,000 sq. mi. (33 persons per sq. mi.); the Pacific states, with 21 million people on 917,000 sq. mi. (24 persons per sq. mi.); and between these 2 regions, the immense strip of Mountain states, with 865,000 sq. mi., almost one-fourth of all the land area of the country and with only 7 million inhabitants (8 persons per sq. mi.) (see Table II.4).

FIGURE II.3

U.S. POPULATION DENSITY, BY COUNTY, 1960

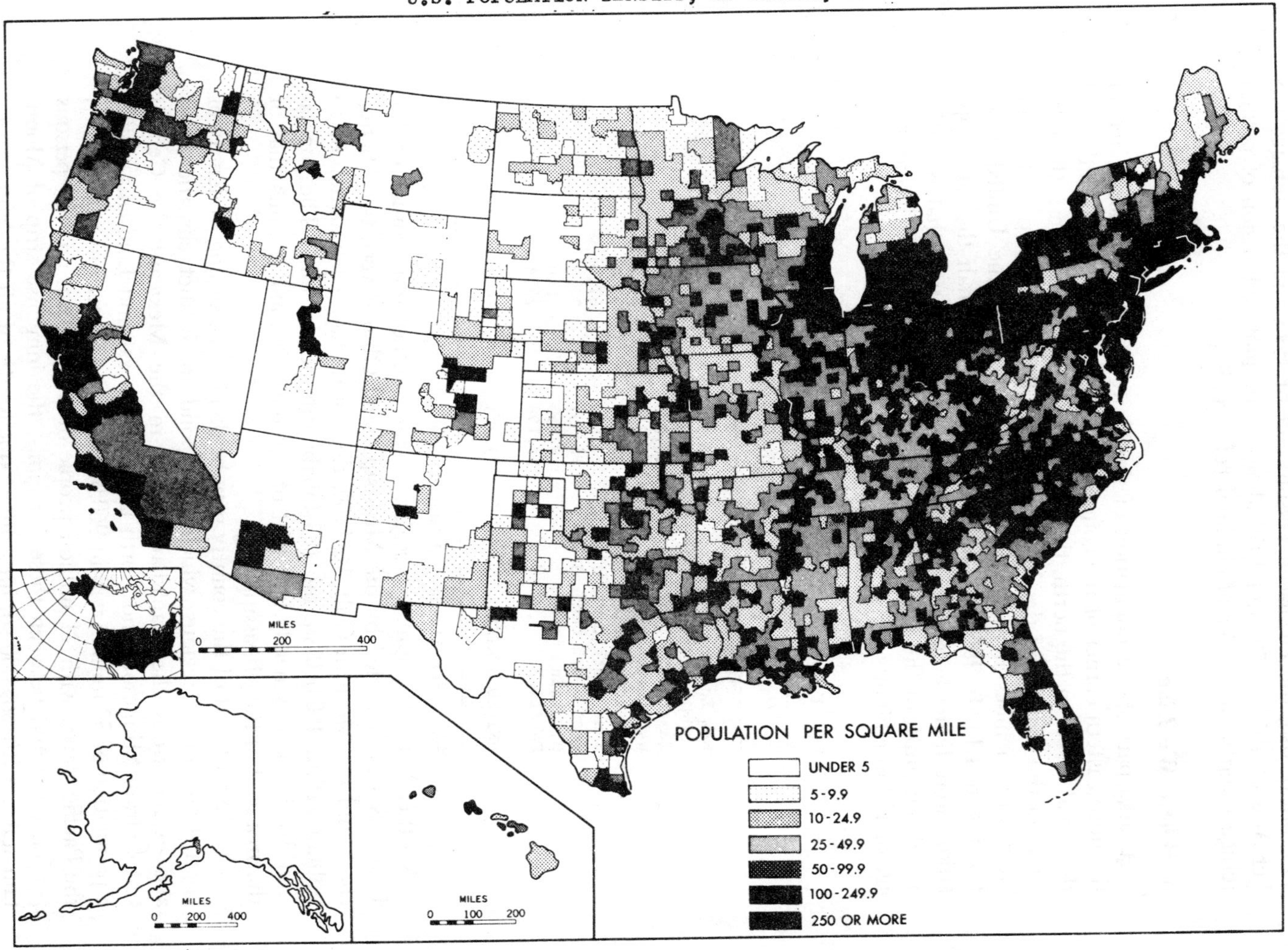

POPULATION PER SQUARE MILE

UNDER 5
5-9.9
10-24.9
25-49.9
50-99.9
100-249.9
250 OR MORE

MILES
0   200   400

MILES
0   200   400

MILES
0   100   200

U.S. Department of Commerce, Bureau of the Census

The uneven distribution of the population is due partly to historic factors (colonization of the continent by immigrants from Europe) and partly to natural and climatic conditions (rainfall, temperature, river courses, and the like). In turn, the uneven distribution of the population is one of the main factors in the structure of our economy. The northeastern region is the stronghold of American industry. However, the older metropolitan centers are too distant from the frontier states, and these states are too rich in natural resources to justify their economic dependence on New York, Philadelphia, or Chicago. Therefore, new industrial centers have developed in Texas, California, Washington, and other western states.

Contrasts in the density of population in geographic divisions and individual states are shown in Appendix Table III and Figure II.3. While Rhode Island had 812 people per sq. mi. in 1960, and New Jersey 807, Oregon had only 18 inhabitants per sq. mi.; Utah, 11; Wyoming, 3; and Alaska, 0.4.

In comparison with other great nations, the United States, with its 65 inhabitants per sq. mi. in 1964, is sparsely populated. China has 3 times as many inhabitants per sq. mi., and India 6 times as many. The population density of Japan, crowded on its islands, is 11 times that of ours. The United Kingdom and the Federal Republic of Germany each have 9 times our density of population—571 and 567 inhabitants per sq. mi., respectively. However, some states of the United States are nearly as heavily populated as Europe's most densely populated countries: Rhode Island, for example, with 812 inhabitants per sq. mi., exceeds Belgium (783) and is not far behind the Netherlands (909). In contrast, the U.S.S.R. has even fewer inhabitants per sq. mi. than the United States: 26 as against 65 (see Sec. 8).

7. How We Move Around

Initially, the civilization of the United States was rooted in a narrow strip along the North Atlantic coast and did not penetrate much beyond the Appalachian Mountains. From there it spread gradually over the continent. Its expansion is best illustrated by the uneven population growth of different regions and divisions.

Colonization of the East Central states—from Ohio to Mississippi—began shortly after the founding of the United States. In 1800, the population of this region was less than 400,000, approximately 7 per cent of the total population of the United States, and in 1850 it was nearly 8 million, or 33 per cent of the total.

In the second half of the nineteenth century, the western frontier of the United States receded farther. The outstanding feature of the internal migration was the rapid development of the midwestern region, from the Mississippi to the semi-arid plains at the foot of the Rocky Mountains. The population of this region increased from 400,000 in 1830, to 900,000 in 1840, to 3.9 million in 1860, to 9.5 million in 1880, and to 16.9 million in 1900. The share of this predominantly agricultural region in the total population of the country increased from 8 per cent in 1850 to 22 per cent in 1900.

Because of the lack of roads, travel to the West was difficult and dangerous at the beginning of this period, and only small groups of settlers penetrated into the wilderness, following old Indian trails. The census of 1850 found 73,000 white settlers in the area now described as the Mountain states, and 105,000 within the present borders of California and Oregon. Settlement of Mormons in Utah and the discovery of gold in California accelerated the colonization of these states. At the end of the nineteenth century, approximately 2 per cent of the population of the United States lived in the Mountain states, and somewhat more than 3 per cent in the Pacific states.

In the twentieth century, the growth of these regions accelerated. The population of the Mountain states increased from 1.7 million in 1900 to 6.9 million in 1960, while that of the Pacific states rose from 2.4 million to 21.2 million during the same period. The growth of California was spectacular—from 1.5 million to 15.7 million.

The Middle Atlantic states have been the gateway through which most immigrants entered the country. The share of these states in the total population was about 25 per cent in the first half of the nineteenth century, declined to 20 per cent by 1880, and, with slight ups and downs, has remained at that level. By contrast, the New England states, with a somewhat larger population in 1790, registered a much slower growth. Their share in the total population of the country dropped from 28 per cent in 1790 to 10 per cent in 1860, then to about 7 per cent in 1900, and was 6 per cent in 1960.

The Southern states, which included exactly half the total population in 1790, failed to keep pace with the growth of the North. In 1870, two-thirds of the U.S. population was concentrated in northern and western states, and only one-third was in the South. This relationship remained about the same through 1964, when the Southern states accounted for about 31 per cent of the total population (see Table II.5 and Appendix Table IV).

The general trend of internal migration is measured by shifts of the U.S. center of population, a point about which the total population of the country is conceived to balance—i.e., in order to reach it, all the residents on any one side of it would have to cover the same total distance as those living on the other side of that point. In 1790, the center of population was not far from the Atlantic coast, near Baltimore, Md. Ten years later, it had shifted to Washington, D.C., the new capital of the nation. It continued to move westward, remaining almost precisely at the same parallel (39°N). By 1880, it had reached Cincinnati, and in 1960, it was in Illinois, several miles northeast of Louisville (see Figure II.4).

TABLE II.5

GROWTH OF U.S. POPULATION, BY GEOGRAPHIC DIVISION, 1790-1964
(In Thousands)

	1790	1850	1900	1950	1960	1964
New England	1,009	2,728	5,592	9,314	10,509	11,070
Middle Atlantic	958	5,899	15,455	30,164	34,168	36,055
East North Central	-	4,523	15,986	30,399	36,225	37,619
West North Central	-	880	10,347	14,061	15,394	15,751
South Atlantic	1,852	4,679	10,443	21,182	25,972	28,311
East South Central	109	3,363	7,548	11,477	12,050	12,678
West South Central	-	940	6,532	14,538	16,951	18,263
Mountain	-	173	1,675	5,075	6,855	7,697
Pacific	-	106	2,417	15,115	21,198	23,891
UNITED STATES	3,929	23,192	75,995	151,326	179,323[a]	191,334

[a]Includes Alaska and Hawaii.

The high mobility of its population is characteristic of the United States. About 20 per cent of the entire population move from one residence to another each year, and over 6 million persons move from one state to another. Between March, 1963, and March, 1964, the population moved as shown in Table II.6.

FIGURE II.4

CENTER OF POPULATION FOR CONTERMINOUS UNITED STATES, 1790-1960

U.S. Department of Commerce, Bureau of the Census

TABLE II.6

MOBILITY OF CIVILIAN POPULATION, MARCH, 1963-MARCH, 1964

	Number (In Thousands)	Per Cent
Living in same house	148,125	79.9
Living in different house	36,327	19.6
Living in different house in same county	24,089	13.0
Living in different county, same state	6,191	3.3
Living in different state	6,047	3.3
Living abroad, at beginning of period	859	0.5
TOTAL CIVILIAN POPULATION, AGED 1 YEAR AND OVER, MARCH, 1964	185,312	100.0

8. *Cities and Rural Communities*

As late as 1860, four-fifths of the population of the United States lived in open country or in villages. In spite of the growing proportion of urban population, country people predominated through World War I. The 1920 census was the first to record more people in urban communities than in rural areas—that is, in places with less than 2,500 inhabitants (see Table II.7 and Appendix Table V).

In 1790, the United States had only 12 communities with a population of more than 5,000, and 12 others with a population from 2,500 to 5,000. Together, these 24 communities accounted for 202,000 persons, or some 5 per cent of the nation's population. Fifty years later, there were 85 towns and cities with a population of more than 5,000, and 46 smaller towns, each with from 2,500 to 5,000 inhabitants. The urban population was then 1.8 million, or 10.5 per cent of the total. A century later, in 1940, there were 1,077 places with more than 5,000 inhabitants, and 965 with from 2,500 to 5,000. The urban population then totaled 74.4 million, or 56.5 per cent of the total. In 1950, and again in 1960, the definition of

TABLE II.7

URBAN AND RURAL POPULATION
OF THE UNITED STATES, 1790-1960
(In Millions)

	1790	1840	1890	1900	1920	1940	1960
Rural	3.7	15.2	40.8	45.8	51.6	57.2	54.1
Urban	0.2	1.8	22.1	30.2	54.2	74.4	125.3
TOTAL	3.9	17.1	62.9	76.0	105.7	131.7	179.3

FIGURE II.5

URBAN AND RURAL POPULATION, 1790-1960

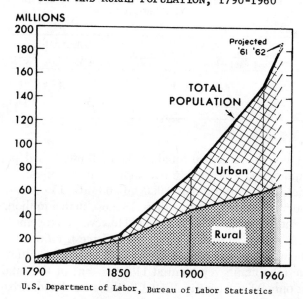

U.S. Department of Labor, Bureau of Labor Statistics

urban population was broadened to include not only incorporated places with 2,500 or more inhabitants, but also the densely settled fringe of urbanized areas, whether incorporated or not. According to the current census classification, there were, in 1960, 3,293 places with 5,000 inhabitants or more, and 2,152 places with 2,500 to 5,000. The urban population in 1960 comprised 125.3 million, or 70 per cent of the total population of the United States. Corresponding data for the previous urban classification were 113.1 million, or 63 per cent, as shown in Figure II.5.

In the second half of the nineteenth century, the growth of cities was greatly stimulated by the development of industries and the influx of immigrants. The industrial workers among them usually settled not far from the port of entry, along the Atlantic coast.

Not until the 1930's did the growth of the proportion of urban population slow to nearly a standstill: the proportion was 56.2 per cent of the total population in 1930, and 56.5 per cent of the total in 1940. This change in the trend was due largely to the decline in the rate of population growth (cf. Sec. 4), the drop in immigration (cf. Sec. 5), and mass unemployment (which held back the flow of young people from the farms to the cities). However, the upward trend was re-established later and has continued with increased strength since 1950. In the intercensal years 1950–60, the South and the Northeast, in particular, have experienced the greatest decline in rural-farm population.

The growth of the proportion of urban population has been accompanied by a rapid development of large cities. In 1900, there were 38

TABLE II.8

PERCENTAGE DISTRIBUTION OF URBAN AND RURAL POPULATION,
BY REGION, 1960

| Inhabitants | U.S. Total | The North | | | | The South | | | The West | |
		New England	Middle Atlantic	North Central East	North Central West	South Atlantic	South Central East	South Central West	Mountain	Pacific
Rural	30.1	23.6	18.6	27.0	41.2	42.8	51.6	32.3	32.9	18.9
Urban	69.9	76.4	81.4	73.0	58.8	57.2	48.4	67.7	67.1	81.1

cities with more than 100,000 inhabitants; of these, 6 had populations of 500,000 or more, and 3 of these 6 had more than 1 million. In 1930, there were 93 cities with more than 100,000 inhabitants, 13 of which had more than 500,000 inhabitants, and 5 of these 13 more than a million. The respective figures from 1960 are: 132, 21, and 5. However, a movement toward the outlying areas of the large, especially of the largest, cities has taken place. Many of them lost population in the intercensal years: cities with 1 million or more inhabitants represented 11.5 per cent of the total population in 1950, but only 9.8 per cent in 1960. On the other hand, urban communities with 2,500–10,000 inhabitants, inclusive of unincorporated urban areas with less than 2,500 population, slightly increased their percentage of total population, from 15 to 15.6; communities with 10,000–100,000 inhabitants, from 19.6 to 25.8 per cent (see Appendix Table V).

The trend toward the development of small suburban communities, densely populated (some with 1,500 persons or more per sq. mi.), a kind of "metropolitan ring," brought the growth of central cities nearly to a standstill between 1950 and 1960. Further intensification of this development may be expected.

The ratio of rural to urban population varies from state to state, and from one geographic region to another (see Table II.8 and Figure II.6). In New England and the Middle Atlantic states, 35.8 million lived in urban communities in 1960, as compared with 8.9 million in rural areas. In the East North Central and the Pacific states, 43.6 million persons are concentrated in urban communities, while 13.8 million live in rural areas. As late as 1920, rural population predominated in 33 states; in 1940, in 28 states; but in 1960, only in 11 states (Alaska, Arkansas, the Carolinas, the Dakotas, Idaho, Kentucky, Mississippi, Vermont, and West Virginia; see Figure II.6). Among these predominantly rural states, only the Dakotas have about as many farm people as rural nonfarm inhabitants (410,000 as compared with 413,000). In each of the other 9 states, the nonfarm population exceeds the number of farm people by a considerable margin—7.3 million, as compared to 2.9 million for the group as a whole.

Despite the decline in the rural population, it still carries considerable political weight and probably will continue to do so for some time, until

FIGURE II.6

PER CENT OF URBAN POPULATION, BY STATE, 1960

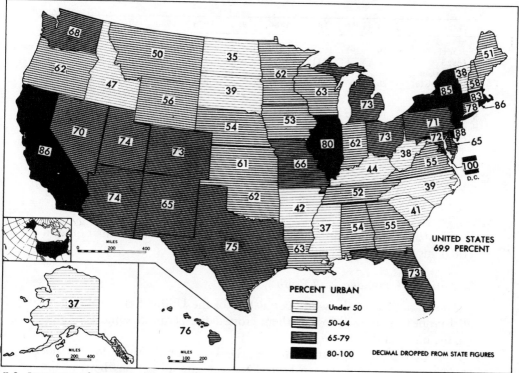

U.S. Department of Commerce, Bureau of the Census

the overdue reapportionment of electoral districts is fully implemented (see Sec. 99).

Some of the large cities of the United States can look back to a century or more of steady growth; others are comparatively young. Table II.9 shows the disparities in the rate of growth of the 10 largest cities in the United States. The ranking of some has changed within the last two decades. Los Angeles, for example, has moved ahead of Philadelphia and Detroit; Houston, fourteenth in rank in 1950, was seventh in 1960; Boston and Pittsburgh no longer rank among the top 10 cities in number of inhabitants (see Table II.9).

The United States, unlike many other large countries, is highly urbanized even though the country as a whole is sparsely populated. Only the United Kingdom substantially exceeds the United States in this respect (80.8 and 69.9 per cent urbanization, respectively). Western Germany (1960) has approximately the same degree of urbanization as the United States. Much depends, of course, on what is considered an "urban" or a "rural" area, and definitions vary greatly in different countries. Neverthe-

TABLE II.9

POPULATION OF THE TEN LARGEST U.S. CITIES, 1790-1960
(In Thousands)

City	1790	1840	1860	1880	1900	1920	1930	1940	1950	1960
New York	49	391	1,175	1,912	3,437	5,620	6,930	7,455	7,892	7,782
Chicago	-	4	112	503	1,699	2,702	3,376	3,397	3,621	3,550
Los Angeles	-	-	4	11	102	577	1,238	1,504	1,970	2,419
Philadelphia	28	94	566	847	1,294	1,824	1,951	1,931	2,072	2,003
Detroit	-	9	45	116	286	994	1,569	1,623	1,850	1,670
Baltimore	14	102	212	332	509	734	805	859	950	939
Houston	-	-	-	-	45	138	292	385	596	938
Cleveland	-	6	43	160	382	797	900	878	915	876
Washington, D.C.	3[a]	24	75	178	279	438	487	663	802	764
St. Louis	-	16	161	351	575	773	822	816	857	750

[a]1800.

less, "urban" is likely to include a heavy concentration of population and "rural" usually comprises village areas.

9. Nativity, Language, and Faith

The forefathers of the white population of the United States came from all European nations. Most of them crossed the ocean at some time during the nineteenth century.

The Census of Population divides the U.S. population into 2 major categories: native and foreign born. "Natives" are all persons born in the United States, the Commonwealth of Puerto Rico, or a possession of this country; also, a small number of persons who, though born abroad or at sea, have at least 1 native American parent. All others are considered "foreign born." Nativity and parentage data for the total population are available only in the censuses of 1900 and 1960; for intervening years, tabulations were prepared for only the white population. However, comparatively few nonwhite foreign-born persons immigrated to this country after 1900.

Since the beginning of this century, the native population has comprised an increasingly large proportion of the total population: 86 per cent in 1900, 95 per cent in 1960.

In 1960, persons born of native white parents constituted 79.2 per cent of the total population, as compared with 60.5 per cent in 1910. The proportion of white persons born in this country of 1 or 2 foreign parents declined from 23.1 per cent in 1910 to 15.0 per cent in 1960. The proportion of foreign-born white persons is also decreasing: 16.3 per cent in 1910, 5.9 per cent in 1960. The trend to greater national homogeneity resulted from the decline in immigration since the beginning of World War I (see Sec. 5 and Table II.10).

The foreign-born population and native population of foreign or mixed

TABLE II.10

NATIVITY AND PARENTAGE OF THE WHITE POPULATION
1890-1960

Nativity and Parentage	In Millions					Per Cent				
	1890	1910	1930	1950	1960	1890	1910	1930	1950	1960
Native parentage	34.5	49.5	70.4	101.1	125.8	62.6	60.5	63.8	74.8	79.2
Foreign white stock	20.6	32.2	39.9	33.8	33.1	37.4	39.5	36.2	25.2	20.8
Foreign born	9.1	13.3	14.0	10.2	9.3	16.6	16.3	12.7	7.6	5.8
Foreign parentage	8.1	12.9	17.4	14.8 ⎫ 23.8		14.7 ⎱	15.8	15.8	11.0 ⎱ 15.0	
Mixed parentage	3.4	6.0	8.5	8.8 ⎭		6.2 ⎰	7.3	7.7	6.5 ⎰	
WHITE, TOTAL	55.1	81.7	110.3	134.9	158.8	100.0	100.0	100.0	100.0	100.0

foreign-American parentage are combined in statistics into a single category designated "foreign stock" (all first- and second-generation Americans). In 1960, this group comprised 33 million white persons and 1 million nonwhite. While it represented more than one-third of the white population of New England and the Middle Atlantic states, in the southern states its share was very small: 9.3 per cent in the West South Central states, 8.0 per cent in the South Atlantic states, and only 2.2 per cent in the East South Central states (see Table II.11). The Bureau of the Census stated in 1909 that the nationality composition of the white population in the southern states had probably changed little since 1790, whereas in the rest of the nation it had changed greatly. This may be true even today.

TABLE II.11

RATIO (PER CENT) OF PERSONS OF FOREIGN WHITE STOCK
TO TOTAL WHITE POPULATION, BY GEOGRAPHIC DIVISION, 1890-1960

Geographic Division	1890	1900	1910	1920	1930	1940	1950	1960
New England	47.3	54.6	49.7	61.7	60.7	51.9	45.4	37.4
Middle Atlantic	48.2	51.0	55.2	55.5	54.5	46.4	41.1	34.8
East North Central	45.2	46.0	45.6	43.7	40.4	31.9	26.9	21.1
West North Central	42.4	43.8	42.5	38.9	33.8	26.2	20.8	16.3
South Atlantic	9.4	8.9	9.0	9.0	8.3	6.7	7.3	8.0
East South Central	6.9	6.3	5.2	4.3	3.5	2.2	2.3	2.2
West South Central	16.0	15.6	14.2	14.2	13.2	9.9	9.7	9.3
Mountain	46.2	45.9	41.8	37.7	33.0	24.4	19.4	15.7
Pacific	49.4	49.2	47.6	46.1	43.3	34.7	28.2	23.9
UNITED STATES	37.4	38.7	39.5	38.4	36.2	29.1	25.0[a]	20.8

[a] Includes Alaska and Hawaii.

Vast differences still exist within the country, differences based not only on geographic features, but also on history and cultural heritage: the immigrants did not settle evenly in the country. The early arrivals, predominantly English, settled along the Atlantic coast. The Scottish and Irish, coming later, moved farther into the interior. The Germans and Scandinavians opened new lands in Wisconsin, Minnesota, and the Dakotas. Newcomers from eastern and southern Europe settled largely in the cities. Mexicans and Orientals established themselves along the Mexican border and the Pacific coast, respectively.

In 1940, English was the mother tongue of at least 96 per cent of the white third-generation Americans, that is, of persons born here whose parents also were born in this country. It was also the mother tongue of 53 per cent of second-generation Americans, born here of foreign or mixed

TABLE II.12

MOTHER TONGUE OF FOREIGN-BORN POPULATION, 1960
(In Thousands)

English	1,853	Lithuanian	99
German	1,279	Japanese	95
Italian	1,226	Czech	92
Spanish	767	Chinese	90
Polish	582	Serbo-Croatian	88
Yiddish	504	Portuguese	87
French	330	Danish	80
Russian	277	Finnish	53
Hungarian	213	Arabic	50
Swedish	212	Romanian	38
Greek	173	Slovenian	32
Norwegian	141		
Slovak	125	Other	314
Dutch	124	Not reported	709
Ukrainian	107	TOTAL	9,738

parentage, and of 23 per cent of all foreign-born Americans. According to the 1960 census, there were 9.7 million foreign-born persons in the United States. Their mother tongue (the principal language spoken at home before arrival here) comprised all the European and several Asian languages, as shown in Table II.12.

Spanish has shown the greatest increase among the foreign born: 3.9 per cent in 1940, 7.9 per cent in 1960. Its centers have been Texas, Arizona, and New Mexico, and lately Florida (the Cuban refugees). In New Mexico, many public documents are issued in both English and Spanish, and both languages are used in the legislature.

Practically all national religious bodies compile reports on their memberships, but not all groups count their members in the same way. Most Protestant bodies count persons who have attained full membership, among whom all but a small minority are more than 13 years of age; Roman Catholics count all baptized persons, including infants; Jews regard as members all Jews in communities having congregations. The Roman Catholic Church is the single largest religious organization in this country, but the total membership of the Protestant denominations considerably exceeds the number of Catholics.

The report of the Bureau of the Census on religious affiliation of the population in the United States, published in 1958, was the first report containing nationwide statistics on religion of the population. According to it, the South is predominantly Protestant (82.8 per cent of the population); Roman Catholics are concentrated in the Northeast, predominantly in the large cities; and persons of the Jewish faith are also concentrated in the large northeastern cities.

In the country as a whole, the Protestants represent two-thirds of the population 14 years and over (119.3 million), and the Roman Catholics slightly over one-fourth, while Jewish persons account for a little over 3 per cent. "No religion" was reported for 3.2 million, and 1.1 million did not report.

In all the groups, the number of women somewhat exceeds that of men, except in the group "no religion," where there are about 3 times as many men as women. Nine out of 10 nonwhite persons are Protestants: the largest group is the Baptists, followed by the Methodists. The census reported that in 6.4 per cent of all marriages, the husband and wife belonged to different religious groups (see Appendix Table VI).

10. White and Nonwhite Population

Almost nine-tenths of the inhabitants of the United States are white (see Figure II.7A). The nonwhite minority includes a large and relatively homogeneous Negro population and a small number of Indians, Japanese, Chinese, Filipinos, and others of nonwhite races.

Of the 158.8 million white inhabitants in 1960, 70 per cent lived in urban areas, predominantly in central cities and on their fringes; an even larger percentage of the 18.9 million Negroes (73 per cent) was concentrated in central cities, but fewer of them lived on the urban fringe. Only a few Indians lived in cities; most of them were in rural reservations. The Japanese, Filipinos, and Chinese are city folk, especially the Chinese: out of 237,000 Chinese, 227,000 lived in urban areas (see Table II.13). On the whole, the nonwhite population prefers urban areas, and between rural nonfarm areas and rural farm areas, it prefers the former.

American Negroes are the only group of the population whose forefathers did not seek America of their own volition as the Promised Land of Freedom. They are descendants of slaves sold by tribal chiefs or kidnaped by pirates and imported from Central and West Africa and the West Indies in Colonial times and the early decades of the United States. Be-

FIGURE II.7.A

RACIAL COMPOSITION OF THE POPULATION
IN THE UNITED STATES, 1790-1960

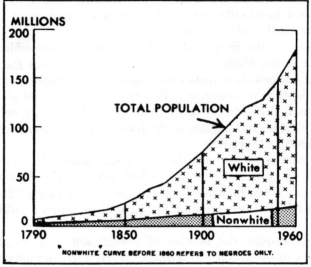

U.S. Department of Health, Education, and Welfare

tween 1615, when the first party of slaves was brought to North America, and 1808, when the slave trade was prohibited by Congress, 330,000–350,000 Negroes were thus imported.

Some 50,000 additional slaves were acquired by the United States in Louisiana, Florida, and Texas, and many more were smuggled into the

TABLE II.13

DISTRIBUTION OF WHITE AND NONWHITE POPULATION
BY URBAN AND RURAL AREA, 1960

Area and size of places	White	Negro	Indians	Japanese	Chinese	Filipinos	Other
				(In Thousands)			
Urbanized areas	83,770	11,258	85	317	208	103	108
Central cities	47,627	9,702	64	240	176	76	89
Urban fringe	36,143	1,555	20	77	33	27	18
Other urban	26,658	2,550	61	64	18	27	42
Places of 10,000 or more	14,561	1,493	28	39	13	13	25
Places of 2,500 to 10,000	12,097	1,057	33	25	6	13	17
Urban total	110,428	13,808	146	381	227	130	150
Places of 1,000 to 2,500	5,996	439	22	16	2	10	12
Other rural	42,408	4,625	356	67	9	37	56
Rural total	48,403	5,064	378	83	11	47	68
UNITED STATES	158,832	18,872	524	464	237	176	218

country through the southern ports between 1808 and the Civil War. In the Colonial period, the Negroes were mostly used as servants on tobacco and sugar plantations. Historically, this accounts for the concentration of Negroes in the South.

In 1790, Negroes represented about 20 per cent of the population of this country, and nearly 50 per cent of that of the South. After the importation of slaves was outlawed, and white immigration from Europe began to increase, the proportion of Negroes in the population began to decline: their numbers could grow only by natural increase and their death rate was high. In 1850, Negroes accounted for 15.7 per cent of the population; in 1900, for 11.7; in 1940, for 9.8; in 1960, for 10.5 (see Figure II.7A). With immigration from Europe at a low ebb after World War I, and with the decline in the death rate and the higher fertility rate, the Negro population increased by 26.7 per cent between 1950 and 1960, as compared with 17.5 per cent for the whole population (see Figure II.7B for the contrast in rates of natural increase).

Two trends have been characteristic of the distribution of Negroes over the country since the middle of the nineteenth century: migration from rural to urban areas in the South, and migration from the South to industrial states in the North. The northward migration began in the last quarter of the nineteenth century, after the Civil War. The Negro population of the United States increased from 6.6 million in 1880 to 18.9 million in 1960. Of these additional 12.3 million, nearly 6 million moved northward from the South, where they were born. The shortage of labor, especially of common labor, during both World Wars, contributed to the acceleration of migration of Negroes to New York, Philadelphia, Chicago, Detroit, and cities in the West.

Yet despite this movement, the bulk of the Negro population still resides in the South. In 1940, more than 78 per cent lived in the South, in an area that comprised less than one-third of the country's population; in 1960, 60 per cent remained in that area (see Table II.14). Excluding Oklahoma, Kentucky, and West Virginia (on the fringe of this area), the other 14 southern states had, in 1960, 47.7 million inhabitants, of whom 10.9 million, or 23 per cent, were Negroes. They constituted 46 per cent of the population of Mississippi, 35 per cent of South Carolina's, 32 per cent of Louisiana's, 30 per cent of Alabama's and Georgia's. In the North and West, including Oklahoma, Kentucky, and West Virginia, with a total population of 131.7 million, only 7.6 million, or 5.8 per cent, were Negroes.

Not only have the western states a far lower percentage of Negroes than the southern states, but unlike other regions of the country, they have never known slavery. The first year in which Negroes were recorded statistically in the West was 1850, with a figure of 1,200; in 1860, there were 4,500 Negroes. Of these, 26 were slaves in 1850, and 29 in 1860, as compared with 3.4 million and 4.1 million slaves, respectively, in the South

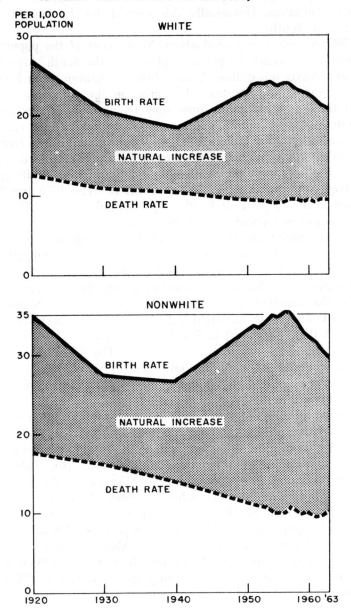

FIGURE II.7.B

RATES OF NATURAL INCREASE
OF WHITE AND NONWHITE POPULATION, 1920-63

PER 1,000
POPULATION

WHITE

BIRTH RATE

NATURAL INCREASE

DEATH RATE

NONWHITE

BIRTH RATE

NATURAL INCREASE

DEATH RATE

1920   1930   1940   1950   1960 '63

U.S. Department of Health, Education, and Welfare

TABLE II.14

DISTRIBUTION OF NEGROES IN THE UNITED STATES
BY GEOGRAPHIC DIVISION, 1880-1960

Geographic Division	1880	1900	1920	1940	1960	1880	1900	1920	1940	1960
	(In Thousands)					(Per Cent of Population)				
New England	40	59	79	102	243	1.0	1.1	1.1	1.2	2.3
Middle Atlantic	189	326	600	1,268	2,785	1.9	2.1	2.7	4.6	8.2
East North Central	183	258	515	1,069	2,885	1.6	1.7	2.4	4.0	8.0
West North Central	202	238	279	351	562	3.3	2.3	2.2	2.6	3.7
South Atlantic	2,941	3,729	4,325	4,699	5,845	38.7	35.7	30.9	26.4	22.5
East South Central	1,925	2,500	2,524	2,781	2,699	34.5	33.1	28.4	25.8	22.4
West South Central	1,088	1,694	2,064	2,425	2,768	32.6	25.9	20.1	18.6	16.3
Mountain	5	16	31	36	123	0.8	1.0	0.9	0.9	1.8
Pacific	7	15	48	135	962	0.6	0.6	0.9	1.4	4.5
UNITED STATES	6,581	8,834	10,463	12,866	18,872	13.1	11.6	9.9	9.8	10.5

and 3.6 million and 3.4 million, respectively, in the whole United States (see Table II.15).

But some Negroes in the United States, even in the South were free: in 1860, there were 258,000 free Negroes in the South and 488,100 in the country as a whole. Some of them owned slaves and received, along with white slave-owners, payment for emancipating their charges.

The Indian population numbered some 846,000 when the first European colonists settled in what is now the United States (see Figure II.8). Wars and theretofore unknown diseases took a heavy toll, and the Indians began to decline in numbers, until there were only 243,000 in the latter part of the nineteenth century. Since that time, the Indian population has increased steadily, and the 1960 Census enumerated 524,000, including the Indians in Alaska. Of these, more than half lived on reservations and

TABLE II.15

NEGROES AND NEGRO SLAVES IN THE UNITED STATES
BY REGION, 1790-1860

Year	United States		Northeast		North Central		South		West	
	Total	Slave	Total	Slave	Total	Slave	Total	Slave	Total	Slave
				(In Thousands)						
1790	757.2	697.7	67.4	40.4	-	-	689.8	657.3	-	-
1800	1,002.0	893.6	83.1	36.4	0.6	0.1	918.3	857.1	-	-
1810	1,377.8	1,191.4	102.2	27.1	6.9	3.3	1,268.6	1,161.0	-	-
1820	1,771.7	1,538.0	110.7	18.0	18.3	11.3	1,642.7	1,508.7	-	-
1830	2,328.7	2,009.0	125.2	2.8	41.5	25.9	2,161.9	1,980.4	-	-
1840	2,873.7	2,487.4	142.3	0.8	89.3	58.6	2,642.0	2,428.0	-	-
1850	3,638.9	3,204.3	149.8	0.2	135.6	87.4	3,352.2	3,116.6	1.2	b
1860	4,441.8	3,953.7	156.0	a	184.2	114.9	4,097.1	3,838.8	4.5	b

[a] 18 slaves.
[b] 26 slaves in 1850; 29 in 1860.

FIGURE II.8

APPROXIMATE LOCATION OF AMERICAN INDIAN TRIBES TODAY

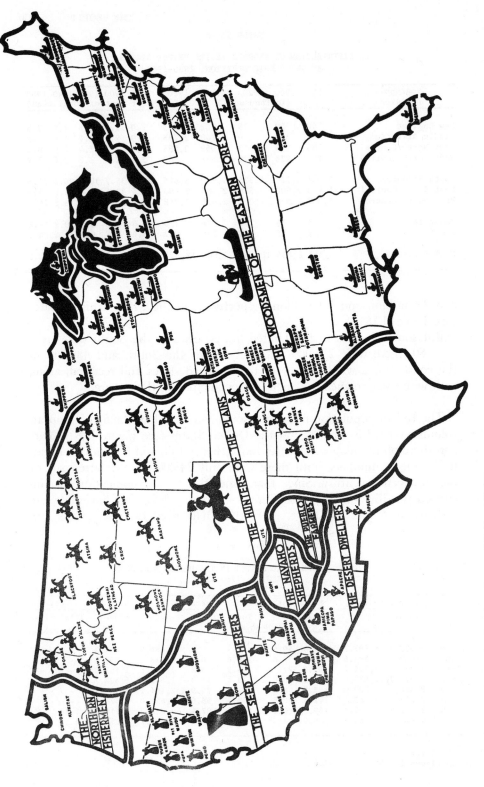

U.S. Department of the Interior, Bureau of Indian Affairs

FIGURE II.9

INDIAN POPULATION IN STATES WITH INDIAN RESERVATIONS, 1960

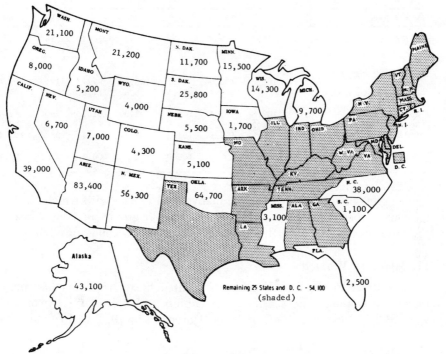

U.S. Department of Health, Education, and Welfare

many others in areas adjacent to the reservations. Nine out of 10 Indians live in 1 of the 25 states that have Federal reservations, mainly in Arizona, Oklahoma, New Mexico, California, North Carolina, the Dakotas, Montana, and Washington (see Figure II.9). The largest group of Indians in states without Federal reservations (16,500) lives in New York State.

Recently, there has been a considerable movement of Indians away from the reservations, and many off-reservation Indians have begun to settle in large cities, especially in states with Federal reservations. The majority of Indian reservations cannot support their rapidly growing population. Efforts are needed to intensify agriculture through better conservation practices and land use in general and by consolidation of scattered land tracts, to induce industry to open plants in Indian communities or adjacent to them, and to raise the educational level of those who wish to remain on the reservations as well as those who aspire to enter the larger society of America.

More than 400 treaties have been negotiated between Indian tribal groups and the United States; of these, 371 were ratified, while others have never been ratified by the Senate. In 1871, this practice was terminated

TABLE II.16

NUMBER OF MEN AND WOMEN, AND SEX RATIO BY NATIVITY
AND COLOR IN THE UNITED STATES, 1850-1960

Sex and Race	1850	1870	1890	1910	1930	1940	1950	1960
Men (in thousands)	11,838	19,494	32,237	47,332	62,137	66,062	75,187	88.331
Women " "	11,354	19,065	30,711	44,640	60,638	65,608	76,139	90,992
Men per 100 women:								
Native	103.1	100.6	103.9	102.2	100.8	99.7	99.0	97.4
Foreign-born	-	-	-	131.1	116.6	111.8	103.8	102.7
White	105.2	102.8	105.4	106.6	102.9	101.2	99.0	97.4
Negro	99.1	96.2	99.5	98.9	97.0	95.0	94.3	93.4
Indians	-	-	102.6	103.5	105.1	105.5	108.7	102.1
Total population	104.3	102.2	105.0	106.0	102.5	100.8	98.7	97.1

by Congressional action. There are many tribal groups with which treaties
have never been negotiated, such as the Pueblo groups in New Mexico,
the Hopi in Arizona, and the Mohave Indians in Arizona and California.

11. *Men and Women*

In contrast to the Old World, the United States for years had more
men than women. The sex ratio (the number of men per 100 women)
was 104.3 in 1850, and 104.7 in 1860. It dropped to 102.2 in 1870, and in-

FIGURE II.10.A

SEX RATIO OF THE POPULATION
OF THE UNITED STATES, 1860-1960

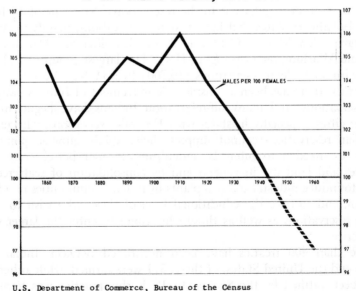

U.S. Department of Commerce, Bureau of the Census

creased to 106 in 1910. Since that year, every census has reported a decline
in the sex ratio, but not until 1950 did the census, for the first time, count
more women than men in the population of this country: 98.7 men per
100 women. In 1960, the ratio declined to 97.1 (see Table II.16 and Figure
II.10A).

In the western states and the Dakotas, however, the sex ratio remains
rather high. In 1960, the highest ratio was registered in the last 2 states to
join the Union—Hawaii, 114.8, and Alaska, 132.3—while in Nevada it was
107.0; in Wyoming, 104.9; in Montana, 103.8. In contrast, the figure for
Pennsylvania was 94.8; New York, 93.8; and Massachusetts, 93.4. In only
2 regions—the Mountain and Pacific states—did the 1960 census report
more men than women: 101.2 and 100.4, respectively (see Table II.17).

TABLE II.17

SEX RATIOS BY GEOGRAPHIC DIVISION, 1960

Geographic Division	Men	Women	Men per 100 Women
	(In Thousands)		
New England	5,121	5,388	95.0
Middle Atlantic	16,605	17,563	94.5
East North Central	17,863	18,362	97.3
West North Central	7,609	7,785	97.7
South Atlantic	12,792	13,179	97.1
East South Central	5,909	6,141	96.2
West South Central	8,364	8,587	97.4
Mountain	3,449	3,406	101.2
Pacific	10,619	10,579	100.4
UNITED STATES	88,331	90,992	97.1

Among Negroes, the sex ratio has been consistently below the national
average, and now, as earlier, there are more women than men. Among
other nonwhite groups—the American Indians, Japanese, and Chinese—the
sex ratio is high. In the foreign-born population, the surplus of men over
women is impressive (see Figure II.10B).

Both the surplus of men over women and the changes in the sex ratio
depend largely on the flow of immigration. Single men are more inclined
to leave their native country than are single women. Frequently, married
men came to the United States alone and did not send for their families
until they had gained a footing. But more men than women have crossed
the seas and continents, and the surplus of men over women increased as
immigration mounted and began to decline when it slowed down. The
drop in the sex ratio between 1860 and 1870 reflected the casualties in the
Civil War.

With the sharp decline in immigration since 1920, the sex ratio also declined, and this decline was accentuated by the World War II casualties,
and the fact that many men in the armed forces stationed abroad are ex-

FIGURE II.10.B

SEX RATIOS OF SELECTED POPULATION GROUPS, 1960

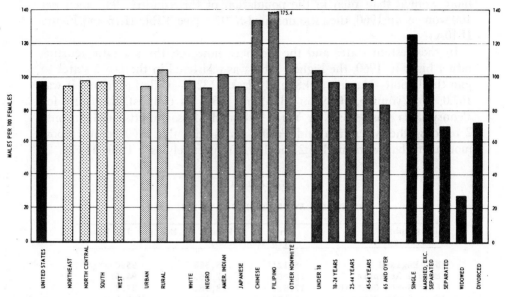

U.S. Department of Commerce, Bureau of the Census

cluded from census reporting. The decline in immigration has remained an important factor in lowering the sex ratio. So also has the differential in mortality—i.e., the fact that women, on the average, live longer than men.

While men constitute the majority of international and national migrants, more girls than boys move from farm homes to the city. In 1960, there were 107.2 men per 100 women on the farms and 103.3 per 100 in rural nonfarm areas, but there were only 94.0 in urban areas.

The ratio of men to women differs in the age groups of the population, and the difference among the farm people is exactly the opposite of that in the city population. Among children under 5, the ratio of boys to girls is practically the same in the urban, rural nonfarm, and rural farm populations (103.4, 104.0, and 104.2 to 100, respectively, in 1960). At age 14, the relative surplus of boys begins to diminish in urban areas but increases on farms. In the 15–24 age group, there is a conspicuous surplus of women in urban areas and a relatively larger surplus of men on the farms. The disparity lessens in the 25–34 age group but widens at the higher ages and is particularly sharp in the highest age groups.

The surplus of women in urban areas in 1960 amounted to 3.8 million in round numbers, while in the rural nonfarm and rural farm populations, the surplus of men was 660,000 and 470,000, respectively (see Appendix Table VII).

On the international scene, the sex ratio varies greatly: countries which experienced large immigration in the past years—Australia, New Zealand, Canada—still have more men than women, as have Argentina, Cuba, Israel, Venezuela, and some African countries, e.g., Algeria, Tunisia, Sudan, and the Union of South Africa. European ratios are closer to that in the United States, but in many countries they are considerably lower, as, for example, the Federal Republic of Germany, East Germany, Finland, Spain, Portugal, Austria, and Hungary. In many instances, outflow of population and war losses have played a more important role than biological factors. In contrast, Asian countries have a considerably higher sex ratio, ranging from 100.8 in Korea to 100.4 in Thailand to 111.5 in Ceylon and 111.1 in Pakistan, possibly reflecting the greater care that is taken of male children among some peoples (see Appendix Table VIII).

12. *The Young and the Old*

The relative number of persons in various age groups of the population depends on the changes in the birth rate, the death rate in the various age groups, and the flow of international migration. Should the total population remain about the same over a long period of time, and should the same number of babies be born each year, the number of persons to reach the age of 5, 10, or 15 years, and so on, would depend entirely on the death rate in each age group. The number of babies less than 1 year of age would be smaller than the number of births in a year; the number of persons aged 99 to 100 years would be almost zero; and between these, the number of persons in each age group would be somewhat smaller than that in the age group immediately below. Such an age distribution might be represented as a pyramid, wide at the bottom (the babies and children), and gradually narrowing to the highest age groups at the top (see Figure II.11).

The foundation of the pyramid will appear particularly wide in comparison with the middle and upper part if the death rate—especially infant mortality—is high. The slopes of the pyramid will become steeper if the death rate declines. If the population in a country grows rapidly and the annual number of births increases, the base of the age pyramid is broad. On the other hand, if the number of births declines, there may be fewer children under 5 years than in the 5–9 and 10–14 age groups that survived from the larger baby crops in the preceding 5-year periods. In this case, the population pyramid narrows at the bottom. If the birth rate continues to decline for a number of years and the mortality rate is very high, the shape of the pyramid may change so that it may resemble the steeple on a Russian church or an upside-down onion.

Changes in the age distribution of a population are sometimes measured by the median age, that is, by the middle point in age that divides equal numbers of older and younger persons. The median age of the population in this country was 20.2 years in 1870, 24.1 in 1910, 26.5 in 1930, 29 in

FIGURE II.11

POPULATION OF THE UNITED STATES, BY SEX AND SINGLE YEARS OF AGE, 1950 AND 1960

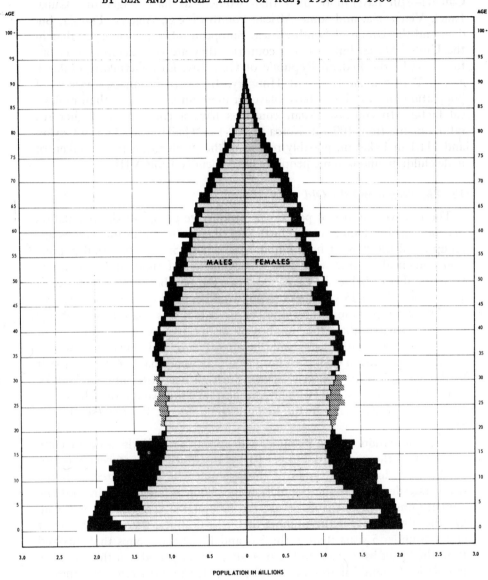

U.S. Department of Commerce, Bureau of the Census

FIGURE II.12

PERSONS AGED 65 YEARS AND OVER, 1920-70

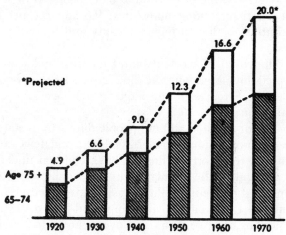

U.S. Department of Health, Education, and Welfare

1940, and 29.5 in 1960. This pattern indicates the continuous aging of the U.S. population.

Changes in the age distribution of the population are very important for many reasons. A decline or increase in the number of children changes the pattern of family life, affects the economy, and has great bearing on education and housing policy. An increase in the number of old people makes the problems of old-age security and medical care increasingly acute.

Changes in the age distribution of the U.S. population from 1870 to 1960 reflect the history of the country: its rapid growth before World War I, with large numbers of immigrants entering its ports; the drop in general and infant mortality; fluctuations in the birth rate, which slowed down in the 1930's under the impact of the Depression, and has increased vigorously since World War II; decline of immigration due to imposed restrictions; and the increasing proportion of old people.

The number of children under 5 years of age dropped from 11.5 million in 1930 to 10.6 million in 1940, increased to 16.2 million in 1950 and 20.3 million in 1960. With a modest drop in the rate of fertility, this age group is expected to reach 22 million by 1970. During the same period, the number of persons aged 65 years and over was 6.7 million in 1930, 9 million in 1940, 12.3 million in 1950, and 16.6 million in 1960. The U.S. Bureau of the Census projection for 1970 raises this figure to 20 million (see Figure II.12 and Appendix Table IX), and 28 million before the end of this century (cf. Table III.14).

The proportion of children under 5 years is considerably greater among nonwhite persons than among white—14.6 per cent as against 10.9 per cent in 1960. But conversely, the proportion of older people is higher among the white population than among nonwhites: 9.6 and 6.1 per cent, respectively. This contrast is due to higher fertility and mortality rates among the nonwhites.

With the differential in mortality rates for men and women (see Sec. 16), women predominate among the older groups of the population, while children under age 5 represent the largest single age group among both sexes, white and nonwhite.

The proportion of children and old people differs from state to state. As a rule, there are proportionately more children and fewer old people in the South than in the North. Thus, in 1960, children under age 15 constituted 28.7 per cent of the population in Massachusetts, 27.6 per cent in New York, and 29.8 per cent in Illinois, as compared with 35.7 per cent in South Carolina, 34.4 per cent in Mississippi, and 33.6 per cent in Georgia. In contrast, persons aged 65 years and over represented, respectively, 10, 10.1, and 9.6 per cent in Massachusetts, New York, and Illinois, as against 8.7, and 7.4 per cent in South Carolina, Mississippi, and Georgia.

Comparison with foreign countries suggests that many European countries have population patterns similar to that of the United States.

13. *Households and Families*

The 1960 census enumerated 53 million households in the United States. Of these, 45 million, or 85 per cent, were husband-wife families. The remaining households comprised relatives other than married couples and individuals living alone or with unrelated persons, such as lodgers, resident employees, and so on.* The number of households increased by 3 million between 1960 and 1964.

The average size of the household decreased consistently—from 5.8 persons in 1790 to 4.9 persons in 1890, 3.8 persons in 1940, and 3.3 persons in 1960, as well as in 1964. Because of this, the number of households expanded proportionately faster than the population: between 1920 and 1964, for example, the number of households increased 2.3 times while the population increased 1.8 times (see Table II.18 and Figure II.13). This decline in the average size of a household is due not only to the declining birth rate until the 1940's, but also to the fact that more young and old people began to make their homes apart from relatives, a trend that has

---

* A household consists of all the persons who occupy a housing unit—a house, an apartment, or even a single room if it has an independent entrance and housekeeping facilities. A family consists of two or more persons living together and related to each other by blood, marriage, or adoption. An individual living alone constitutes a household but not a family. The definitions of a "household" and a "family" have been changed in several census enumerations and differed from 1950 to 1960, but these changes have not significantly affected the comparability of results for large areas of the country or the nation as a whole.

TABLE II.18

NUMBER AND AVERAGE SIZE OF HOUSEHOLDS
IN THE UNITED STATES, 1790-1964

| Year | Number of Households | | | Average Size |
| | Total | Nonfarm | Farm | of Household |
	(I n	T h o u s a n d s)		
1790	558	...	...	5.8
1850	3,598	...	...	5.6
1890	12,690	7,923	4,767	4.9
1900	15,964	10,274	5,690	4.8
1910	20,256	14,132	6,124	4.5
1920	24,352	17,600	6,751	4.3
1930	29,905	23,300	6,605	4.1
1940	35,089	27,946	7,143	3.8
1950	43,554	37,279	6,275	3.5
1960	53,021	49,459	3,562	3.3
1964	55,996	52,651	3,345	3.3

FIGURE II.13

POPULATION AND HOUSEHOLDS
IN THE UNITED STATES, 1890-1960

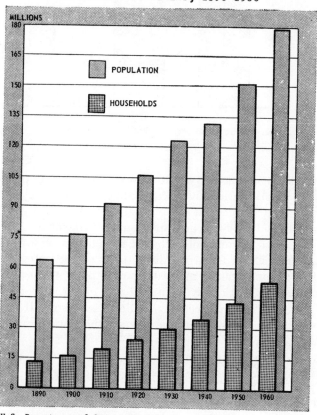

U.S. Department of Commerce, Bureau of the Census

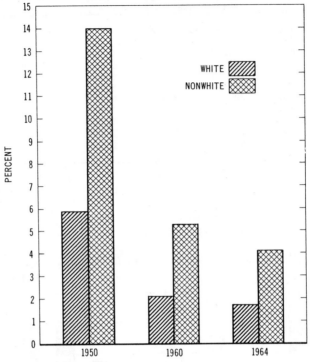

U.S. Department of Commerce, Bureau of the Census

been favored by economic and social changes. More young people go away to college and learn to live away from their parents; they also tend to marry earlier than before and establish their own homes. On the other hand, pensions and social security payments enable many old people to maintain independent households; the life span has increased and widowed older people frequently remarry. This situation is reflected in the sharp decline of the proportion of married couples, both white and nonwhite, that share the homes of relatives: from 6 and 14 per cent, respectively, in 1950 to 2 and 4 per cent, respectively, in 1964 (see Figure II.14).

Farm households are larger, on the average, than rural nonfarm or urban households: 3.8, 3.5, and 3.3 persons in 1960, respectively. The average is highest for nonwhite farm households, with 5.3 persons, as opposed to white urban households with 3.1 persons per household.

Since the turn of the century, the increase in households has been almost exclusively among the nonfarm population, where the number has risen from 14 million in 1910 to 27.9 million in 1940, and 49.5 million in 1960; the respective numbers of farm households have been 6.1 million, 7.1 mil-

TABLE II.19

DISTRIBUTION OF FAMILIES BY SIZE, 1950 and 1960

Number of Members in Family	1950				1960			
	Total	Urban	Rural nonfarm	Rural farm	Total	Urban	Rural nonfarm	Rural farm
	(I n		T h o u s a n d s)					
2 members	12,886	8,992	2,464	1,430	14,756	10,722	3,008	1,026
3 members	9,535	6,544	1,823	1,168	9,754	7,081	2,018	656
4 members	7,697	5,142	1,520	1,036	8,990	6,467	1,938	585
5 members	4,142	2,566	860	716	5,756	3,999	1,328	430
6 members	2,034	1,134	451	448	3,037	2,002	760	276
7 or more	2,159	981	512	667	2,836	1,671	805	361
ALL FAMILIES	38,453	25,359	7,630	5,465	45,128	31,940	9,856	3,332

lion, and 3.6 million. The greatest drop in the number of farm households was from 1950 to 1960—by 2.7 million, or about 43 per cent.

Another noteworthy change in the pattern of households in the last decade occurred with regard to the number of primary individuals as heads of households (that is, household heads living alone or with non-relatives). Their number increased from 4.7 million in 1950 to 8.4 million in 1960, or from 10.9 per cent to 15.8 per cent of all households. The rate of increase differed in rural and urban areas (35 and 97 per cent, respectively) and among the nonwhite and the white population (43 and 87 per cent, respectively).

Of the 179.3 million inhabitants of the United States in 1960, 164 million, or 92 per cent, lived as members of families; 13.4 million, or 7 per cent, as unrelated individuals, and 1.9 million, or 1 per cent, as inmates of institutions.

In 7 out of 8 of the 45.1 million families (or 39.6 million) enumerated by the 1960 census, both husband and wife were present in the household. Of the remaining 5.5 million families with the spouse of the head present, 1.3 million had a male head and the remaining 4.2 million, a female head (separated, divorced, or widowed, or a mother reported as never married).

Of the husband-wife families, 23.5 million had children under age 18 living with them—55.8 million children in all. The proportion of these families was highest, 86 per cent, where the head was in the 25–44 age group and lowest, 14 per cent, where he was 55 years or older.

An additional 8.5 million children under age 18 lived with 1 parent only or with neither parent; 90 per cent of the white youngsters lived with both parents, as compared with 66 per cent of the nonwhite.

In 1950, every fourth family had 3 members, and about 1 out of 10 included 6 or more persons. The change from 1950 to 1960 was twofold: in 1960, about every fifth family had 3 members; about every seventh family, 6 or more persons (see Table II.19).

On farms, there are proportionately about twice as many large families—

6 persons or more—as in urban areas: 19 per cent, as compared with 11.5 per cent, respectively, in 1960. Among the nonwhite families, 24.4 per cent in rural nonfarm areas and 34.6 per cent in rural farm areas had families of 7 or more members, as compared with 6.8 and 8.6 per cent, respectively, for the white families (see Appendix Table X).

Of the 45.1 million families in 1960, 23.5 million had one breadwinner; 13.6 million, 2 earners and 3.2 million, 3 earners or more (including persons temporarily out of work at the time of enumeration); 4.8 million families had no working member.

Most heads of families in which no member was working were widowed or were elderly persons who had retired from the labor force. Some derived income from pensions, investments, or public-assistance payments. Both husband and wife were working in one-third of the husband-wife families in the 45–64 age group with children under 18 years.

Of the 45.1 million family heads, almost 10 million had completed up to 7 years of elementary schooling, and 7.8 million, 8 years. Close to 9 million had completed 1 to 3 years of high school, and 10.3 million, 4 years. Some 4 million had 1 to 3 years of college, and 4.2 million had 4 years or more.

According to the sample survey conducted by the Bureau of the Census in March, 1964, there were at that time 56 million households in the United States. On the average, the annual increase in the number of households between the 1960 census and the 1964 sample survey has been 900,000, which represents the difference between the annual number of new households formed and the number of those dissolved because of death, divorce, or other reasons. The average size of the household remained stable: 3.3 persons.

The entire increase in the number of households occurred among the nonfarm population, from 49.5 million in 1960 to 52.5 million in 1964, while the number of farm households declined from 3.6 million to 3.3 million in the same time span.

III. *The Life Cycle*

14. *Our Baby Crop*

Birth registration is comparatively new in the United States. In 1915, 10 states (including New York, Pennsylvania, Massachusetts, and Michigan) and the District of Columbia began to collect birth statistics, and not until 1933 did birth registration become nationwide. Figures for Alaska were included in 1959 and for Hawaii, in 1960. In 1963, birth registration completeness was 98.9 per cent for the country as a whole—99.4 per cent for the white population and 96.8 per cent for the nonwhite.

Birth rates in registration states averaged 29.5 per 1,000 population in 1915 and declined continuously thereafter, until the lowest point (18.4) was reached in 1933, in the depth of the Depression. Under the impact of the improved economic conditions and the upsurge in birth numbers during and especially after the war, the trend was reversed, but it has never regained the 1915 level. The birth rate for the country as a whole was 19.4 in 1940; jumped to 26.6 in 1947, the peak of the "baby boom"; fluctuated for several years at around 24–25 per 1,000; and has declined slightly in recent years. In 1964, it was 21.2 per 1,000 population (see Figure III.1A).

Approximately 3 million babies were born in 1915 and about that many a decade later. Since then, the *number* of births has been declining but not as rapidly as the birth *rate*. At the trough of the Depression, about 2.3 million babies were born. In comparison with 1915, the decrease in numbers was 23 per cent, while the birth rate, calculated on the basis of a much larger population, had fallen 35 per cent (see Figure III.1B).

During World War II, the number of births began to increase—to 3.1 million in 1943, and 3.8 million in 1947, after the end of hostilities and

FIGURE III.1.A

VITAL STATISTICS RATES IN THE UNITED STATES, 1915-64

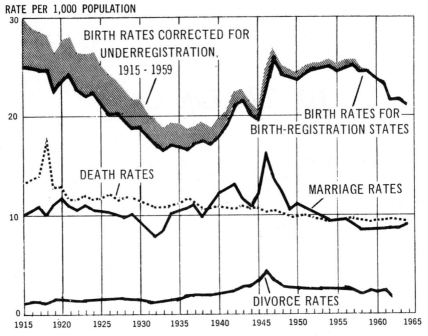

U.S. Department of Commerce, Bureau of the Census--Data from U.S. Department of
Health, Education, and Welfare, Public Health Service

the demobilization of the armed forces. In the 1950's, it averaged 4.1–4.2
million, and it remained at about that level in the 1960's until 1965, when
it dropped to 3.8 million. During the 1950's, almost 41 million children
were born, about 8.8 million more than in the previous decade.

The long-standing differential between white and nonwhite birth rates has
continued. It was even accentuated after the peak year 1947, when the white
birth rate began to decrease, but the nonwhite continued to rise for another decade, until 1957, when it reached its peak—35.3 per 1,000. Subsequently it, too, declined. In 1963, it was 29.7, exceeding the white birth
rate by about 43 per cent (see Table III.1).

A major factor determining the future of a people is the "fertility rate,"
the number of babies born in a year per 1,000 women of child-bearing age
(the other factors being the mortality rate and migration). Fertility may
also be measured in terms of the number of children per family classified
by the duration of marriage, or per 1,000 women classified by age.

Like the crude birth rate, the fertility rate was high at the beginning of
this century (and much higher in the nineteenth century). Despite the

FIGURE III.1.B

LIVE BIRTHS AND BIRTH RATES, 1910-62

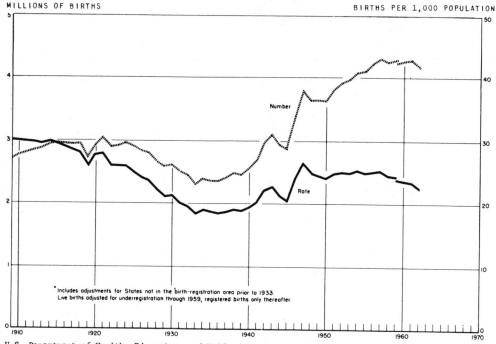

MILLIONS OF BIRTHS   BIRTHS PER 1,000 POPULATION

*Includes adjustments for States not in the birth-registration area prior to 1933.
Live births adjusted for underregistration through 1959, registered births only thereafter.

U.S. Department of Health, Education, and Welfare, Public Health Service

baby boom of the last decade, the rate has never again reached the level
of 1910, when 126.8 babies were born per 1,000 women aged 15 to 44
years; it came closest in 1957 (122.7); in 1963, it was 108.4 for all women
(103.7 for white, 144.8 for nonwhite); it dropped to 104.8 in 1964 and 96.7
in 1965 (see Table III.2).

Thus throughout this century, as before, the fertility rate of nonwhite
women was considerably higher than that of white women. In the 1950's,
the fertility rate went up for both groups, but more heavily for the nonwhite than for white women. Since the peak year of 1957, it began to
decline, yet it remains higher by about 39 per cent for nonwhite than for
white women (see Figure III.2A).

Nearly 1 out of 10 women between the ages of 45 and 49 who had ever
married was childless in 1910, 1 out of 5 in 1950, and there was only a
slight further decline in 1960. At the other extreme, 1 out of 9 women in
this age group in 1910 had ever borne 10 or more children; 1 out of about
50, in 1950 and 1960. The figures for the white women are very close to
the above, but for nonwhite women, corresponding figures are quite different: 1 out of 4 had 10 children or more in 1910; 1 out of 20, in 1950 and
1960 (see Appendix Table XI).

TABLE III.1

NUMBER OF LIVE BIRTHS AND BIRTH RATE PER 1,000
POPULATION IN THE UNITED STATES BY RACE, 1910-65

Year	Live Births (In Thousands)[a]			Rate		
	Total	White	Nonwhite	Total	White	Nonwhite
1910	2,777	2,401	...	30.1	29.2	...
1915	2,995	2,594	...	29.5	28.9	...
1920	2,950	2,566	383	27.7	26.9	35.0
1925	2,909	2,506	403	25.1	24.1	34.2
1930	2,618	2,274	344	21.3	20.6	27.5
1933	2,307	1,983	325	18.4	17.6	25.5
1935	2,377	2,042	334	18.7	17.9	25.8
1940	2,559	2,199	360	19.4	18.6	26.7
1945	2,858	2,471	388	20.4	19.7	26.5
1947	3,817	3,347	469	26.6	26.1	31.2
1950	3,632	3,108	524	24.1	23.0	33.3
1955	4,104	3,488	617	25.0	23.8	34.7
1956	4,218	3,573	645	25.2	24.0	35.4
1957	4,308	3,648	660	25.3	24.0	35.3
1958	4,255	3,598	657	24.6	23.3	34.3
1959[b]	4,245	3,622	673	24.0	23.1	34.2
1960[b]	4,258	3,601	657	23.7	22.7	32.1
1961	4,268	3,601	667	23.3	22.2	31.6
1962[c]	4,167	3,394	642	22.4	21.4	30.5
1963[c]	4,098	3,326	634	21.7	20.7	29.7
1964[c]	4,027	...	...	21.2	...	...
1965[cd]	3,767	...	...	19.4	...	...

[a]Includes adjustments for states not in the birth-registration area before 1933. Includes Alaska from 1959 and Hawaii from 1960.
[b]Live births adjusted for underenumeration through 1959; registered births thereafter.
[c]Data by color exclude residents of New Jersey.
[d]Preliminary.

TABLE III.2

LIVE BIRTH RATE PER 1,000 WOMEN AGED 15-44 YEARS, 1910-65

Year	Total	White	Nonwhite
1910	126.8	123.6	n.a.
1920	117.9	115.4	137.5
1930	89.2	87.1	105.9
1940	79.9	77.1	102.4
1950	106.2	102.3	137.3
1957	122.7	117.5	162.8
1960	118.0	113.2	153.6
1961	117.2	112.2	153.5
1962	112.1	107.5	148.7
1963	108.4	103.7	144.8
1964	104.8	...	...
1965[a]	96.7	...	...

[a]Preliminary.

FIGURE III.2.A

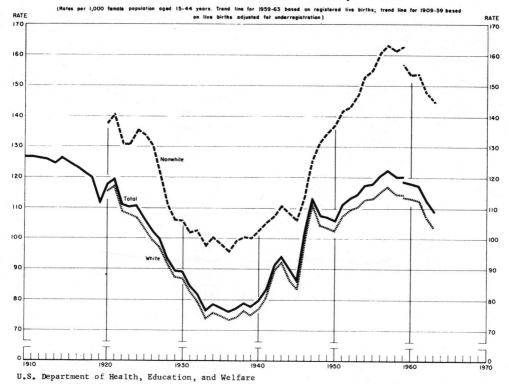

FERTILITY RATES IN THE UNITED STATES, 1910-63

(Rates per 1,000 female population aged 15-44 years. Trend line for 1959-63 based on registered live births; trend line for 1909-59 based on live births adjusted for underregistration)

U.S. Department of Health, Education, and Welfare

Women in both color groups in urban areas have fewer children than in rural areas. In 1960, the average number of children per 1,000 white women aged 35 to 44 years who had ever been married ranged from 2,408 for urban women to 3,262 for rural-farm women; the respective figures for nonwhite women were 2,641 and 5,524.

There are various other differentials in fertility rates according to religious affiliation, income, and occupation; and there are also differences among rates in different states. Thus, in 1960, Baptist and Roman Catholic women recorded proportionately more children than women in other religious groups. Again, the relative number of children ever born to women between the ages of 15 and 44 was greater in families with incomes below $2,000 than in higher income groups; more children were born to wives of farmers, farm laborers, and foremen or service workers, including workers in private households, than to wives of professional, technical, or clerical workers. Likewise, in 1960, the number of children born per 1,000 women between the ages of 15 and 44 was higher among those who had less than 8 years of schooling than those with 4 or more years of college: 3,118, as compared with 1,592.

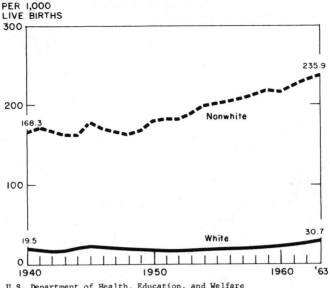

PER 1,000
LIVE BIRTHS

Nonwhite

White

U.S. Department of Health, Education, and Welfare

The rate of children born out of wedlock per 1,000 unmarried women aged 15 to 44 years was 7.1 in 1940; it had doubled by 1950 (14.1) and tripled by 1960 (21.6). In 1963, it was 22.5. Two out of 5 mothers of babies born out of wedlock were under 20 years; about 2 per cent were under 15 years of age. The increase in the number of illegitimate births was considerable for both white and nonwhite groups: for the white, the number of illegitimate live births rose from 41,200 in 1938 to 102,200 in 1963; for the nonwhite, from 46,800 to 150,700, respectively. The illegitimacy ratio (per 1,000 total live births) for the nonwhite group in 1963 was nearly 8 times that of the white: 235.9 as against 30.7 (see Figure III.2B). This wide difference is partly due to a relatively greater underreporting of illegitimate births in the white group and the greater ability of its members to move from the community before the birth of the child. The District of Columbia has the highest ratio of illegitimacy for the white group: in 1963, 118.6; the ratio for the nonwhite was highest that year in West Virginia (342.8), followed by Tennessee (328.8), and Delaware (318.2).

Birth rates and rates of annual population increase vary from country to country. In the Western Hemisphere, the United States and Argentina show an annual increase of population of 1.6 per cent; Canada and Australia, 2.1 per cent. Many Latin countries have a rate of 3 per cent or more: Mexico 3.1 per cent; Brazil and Venezuela, 3.4 per cent. On the other hand, European countries have very low rates of annual population increase: Italy, 0.6; Portugal, Czechoslovakia, the United Kingdom, Denmark, Finland, Spain, and Greece 0.6–0.8 per cent. Japan has cut its rate of population increase drastically, to the level of Bulgaria: 0.9 per cent. India's increase rate is 2.3 per cent and that of Israel, Thailand, South Korea, and the Philippines fluctuates around 2.8–3.3 per cent. The U.S.S.R., with 1.7 per cent, is close to the U.S. pattern (see Appendix Table XII for birth rates in selected countries).

15. How Many Marriages and Divorces?

In some states, marriages and divorces are recorded only at the county level, but more and more states now require that these events be recorded at the state level. In 1957, a marriage-registration area covering 30 states and 5 independent areas was inaugurated; a divorce-registration area for 14 states and 3 independent areas was established a year later. Completeness of records by state offices varies, but there has not been a nationwide test as yet.

The number of marriages and divorces varies from year to year. Marriage rates (per 1,000 population) depend on the age composition of the population, changes in the custom of early or late marriage, completeness of registration, the spread of common-law marriage, and on nondemographic factors such as business conditions, but also on the divorce rate, since a formal divorce is often followed by remarriage of one or both partners. The peak year for both marriages and divorces in this country was 1946, immediately after the demobilization (see Table III.3 and Figure III.3).

TABLE III.3

MARRIAGES AND DIVORCES, NUMBER AND RATE
PER 1,000 POPULATION, 1910–65

Year	Marriages (In Thousands)	Rate	Divorces (In Thousands)	Rate
1910	948	10.3	83	0.9
1915	1,008	10.0	104	1.0
1920	1,274	12.0	171	1.6
1925	1,188	10.3	175	1.5
1930	1,127	9.2	190	1.6
1935	1,327	10.4	218	1.7
1940	1,596	12.1	264	2.0
1946	2,291	16.4	610	4.3
1950	1,667	11.1	385	2.6
1955	1,531	9.3	377	2.3
1960	1,523	8.5	393	2.2
1961	1,548	8.5	414	2.2
1962	1,580	8.5	413	2.2
1963	1,651	8.8	428	2.3
1964	1,720	9.0	445	...
1965	1,789	9.2	481	...

FIGURE III.3

MARRIAGE AND DIVORCE RATES IN THE UNITED STATES, 1935-63

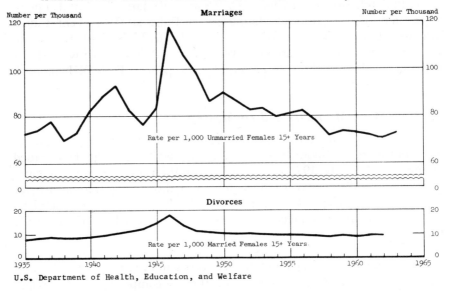

U.S. Department of Health, Education, and Welfare

These marriage and divorce rates are crude, being based on total population, including children and other nonmarriageable persons. More refined and telling are marriage rates based on figures for women between the ages of 15 and 44 (since 99 per cent of all first marriages and 90 per cent of all marriages occur within this age span) and divorce rates based on married women aged 15 years and over. The corresponding rates are shown in Table III.4.

TABLE III.4

MARRIAGE AND DIVORCE RATES, 1940-65

Year	Marriage Rate per 1,000 Women Aged 15-44	Divorce Rate per 1,000 Married Women 15 Years and Over
1940	49.8	8.8
1950	48.7	10.3
1952	44.7	10.1
1954	43.0	9.5
1956	45.4	9.4
1958	40.9	8.9
1960	42.2	9.2
1962	42.5	9.4
1963	43.7	...
1964	44.8	...
1965[a]	45.9	...

[a]Preliminary.

TABLE III.5

PER CENT OF MARRIED PERSONS, BY AGE GROUP, 1890-1960

	Men			Women		
Year	14 years	15-19	20-24	14 years	15-19	20-24
1890	...	0.5	18.9	0.2	9.5	46.7
1910	0.1	1.1	24.0	0.4	11.3	49.7
1940	0.1	1.7	27.4	0.3	11.6	51.3
1950	0.6	3.1	39.9	0.7	16.7	65.6
1960	0.6	3.8	45.9	1.1	15.7	69.5

The median* age at first marriage has gone down slowly but almost uninterruptedly during the last century for men, from 26.1 years in 1890 to 24.3 in 1930, and 22.8 in 1963. For women, the corresponding figures are: 22.0, 21.3, and 20.4 years. This decrease occurred despite the fact that today the average young person stays in school several years longer than at the beginning of this period. Economic prosperity, more widespread family planning and spacing of births, and the recent development of wives working for a time after marriage to supplement the family income have been contributing factors.

Several changes can be observed in the marital status of men and women over the 3 decades 1930 through 1960:

1. The proportion of single, never-married persons has declined for both sexes: in 1930, 28.4 per cent of all women and 35.8 per cent of all men were reported as single; in 1960, the figures were 19.0 and 24.9 per cent, respectively.

2. The sharpest break in this respect occurred in a single decade, between 1940 and 1950: the proportion of unmarried women dropped from 27.6 per cent to 20.0, and of men, from 34.8 per cent to 26.4 per cent.

3. The trend has been toward earlier marriages. The percentage of males and females married between the ages of 20 and 24 has risen from 18.9 to 45.9 between 1890 and 1960 for men and from 46.7 to 69.5 for women (see Table III.5).

4. The proportion of divorced men and women increased greatly between 1890 and 1960: from 0.2 per cent to 2.1 per cent for men, and from 0.4 per cent to 2.9 per cent for women.

5. On the average, there are 3 divorced women to every 2 divorced men, and 4 widows to every widower.

6. In all age groups, among both white and nonwhite persons, a greater proportion of women than men are widowed. The greater longevity of women is one reason for this difference; another is that widowers remarry much more frequently than do widows (see Appendix Table XIII).

---

* The median is the value which divides the distribution into 2 equal parts—one-half of the cases falling below this value and one-half exceeding this value.

Beginning with 1950, census data have included the classification "spouse absent," with the subdivision "separated" and "other." The "separated" category indicates that the marriage is in difficulties, though final steps to dissolve it have not been taken. The "other" group may include husbands or wives working away from home, military personnel stationed abroad, and so on. In 1960, 2.1 million marriages out of 42.4 million were reported with "spouse absent"; of these, 0.9 million were "separated."

The proportion of "separated" marriages is much higher among nonwhite than white married couples: in 1960, it was 5.4 per cent for nonwhite males and 8.4 per cent for nonwhite females, as against 1.0 and 1.3 per cent, respectively, for the white. Generally, the percentage of married white persons is higher than that of married nonwhite (see Table III.6).

These differences can be explained partly by the fact that many mar-

TABLE III.6

PER CENT OF SEPARATED MARRIAGES, 1960

| | White | | Nonwhite | |
	Men	Women	Men	Women
Urban				
Married	70.8	64.9	64.7	61.1
Separated	1.0	1.4	6.0	9.5
Rural nonfarm				
Married	69.9	70.8	57.2	58.7
Separated	0.9	1.0	4.1	5.4
Rural farm				
Married	67.1	72.5	57.2	59.5
Separated	0.5	0.4	2.8	3.8
TOTAL				
Married	70.3	66.7	62.6	60.6
Separated	1.0	1.3	5.4	8.4

riages among nonwhites are not formalized, and by the greater economic instability of the nonwhite population, a factor that is not conducive to taking on permanent obligations. Marriages among the nonwhite are also less durable than among white persons. The proportion of the persons ever married and still living with their first spouse can be considered a good indicator of marriage durability: in 1960, only 48 per cent of nonwhite married women aged 45–49 years and over lived with their first husbands, as compared with 73 per cent of white women in the same age and marital group.

In 1956, 16 states reported detailed data on the number of remarriages by age group. Only 8 out of 10 marriages were first marriages for both the bride and the groom; the rest were remarriages, varying in frequency from

TABLE III.7

PER CENT OF FIRST AND SUBSEQUENT MARRIAGES
BY AGE OF SPOUSE, 1956

Age	Bride				Groom			
	First	Second	Third	Fourth or more	First	Second	Third	Fourth or more
Under 15 years	99.7	0.3	...	...	100.0	...	...	...
15 years	99.4	0.5	...	...	100.0	...	...	...
17 years	99.0	1.0	...	...	99.8	0.2	...	...
19 years	97.0	2.9	0.1	...	99.4	0.6	...	...
21 years	93.4	6.4	0.2	...	97.9	2.0	...	...
23 years	85.3	13.9	0.7	...	94.9	4.9	0.1	...
25 years	74.3	23.6	1.9	0.2	90.2	9.5	0.3	...
27 years	63.6	33.1	3.1	0.3	83.3	16.0	0.8	...
29 years	52.9	42.0	4.4	0.7	73.6	24.8	1.5	0.2
31 years	45.2	46.9	6.8	1.0	64.3	31.7	3.7	0.3
33 years	39.0	52.2	7.9	0.9	58.4	37.2	4.0	0.5
35 years	34.1	55.3	9.4	1.2	50.0	44.1	5.3	0.5
37 years	29.0	59.2	10.1	1.7	43.5	48.9	6.6	1.0
39 years	24.8	61.8	11.4	1.9	38.6	52.6	7.6	1.1
41 years	22.8	61.9	13.3	2.0	34.2	55.2	8.9	1.7
43 years	19.8	64.8	13.2	2.2	31.5	57.3	9.6	1.6
45-49 years	17.4	65.6	14.6	2.3	24.5	62.0	11.8	1.7
50-54 years	12.9	67.7	16.2	3.2	18.4	65.2	13.8	2.6
55-59 years	10.4	68.8	18.0	2.8	14.1	68.8	14.4	2.7
60-64 years	7.7	69.7	18.5	4.1	9.7	70.1	17.1	3.2
65-69 years	6.2	69.5	20.1	4.2	7.1	71.3	18.4	3.3
70-74 years	5.1	67.7	22.7	4.4	4.5	73.1	18.1	4.3
75 years and over	4.6	56.5	32.7	6.2	2.3	66.3	25.0	6.5
TOTAL	78.9	18.1	2.7	0.4	79.9	17.3	2.4	0.4

age group to age group. At the age of 31, more than half of all brides (and at 35, half of the grooms) were being married for the second or third time. In the 45–49 age group, more than three-fourths of all marriages were re-marriages. Below that age, these were largely remarriages of divorced persons. With advancing age, a considerable proportion of all marriages were remarriages of widowed persons. Men undertake marriage later than women and also appear to decide more slowly to break up a marriage. Thus, in 1956, at the age of 21, only 1 man out of 50 was remarried, as against 1 out of 16 women; at the age of 25, only 1 man out of 10 was remarried, as compared with 1 out of 4 women (see Table III.7).

Marriage licenses for areas representing nearly two-fifths of the total U.S. population show that June is the favorite month for marriage (see Table III.8).

Marriage rates in other countries vary greatly, ranging from less than 20 per 1,000 persons of marriageable age (15 years and over) to more than 100. Some differentials in rates are due to definitions of "marriage"—a religiously sanctioned act, a civil registration, a "consensual marriage"—

TABLE III.8

MARRIAGES AND MARRIAGE RATES, BY MONTH,
1963 AND 1964

Month	Number (In Thousands) 1963	1964	Rate Per 1,000 Population 1963	1964
January	100	107	6.3	6.6
February	105	121	7.3	8.0
March	101	109	6.3	6.7
April	119	130	7.7	8.3
May	131	133	8.2	8.2
June	213	229	13.7	14.6
July	143	152	8.9	9.4
August	170	169	10.6	10.4
September	151	159	9.7	10.1
October	135	133	8.4	8.2
November	141	134	9.0	8.5
December	143	144	8.9	8.8
TOTAL	1,651	1,720	9.0	8.8

and to differences in the lower and upper age limits used in computing the marriageable population. Nevertheless, despite their shortcomings and diversity, the international data afford an approximation of marital status abroad. Marriage rates in the United States are rather close to those in Canada, the Netherlands, United Kingdom, Australia, and New Zealand. Low rates in many Latin countries can be explained by the negative attitude of the people toward the official registration and licensing of marriages: common-law, or "consensual," marriage requires no payment to the priest and can be dissolved without encountering the Catholic Church's prohibition of divorce (see Appendix Table XIV).

16. *How Many Deaths?*

Almost no official registration of deaths existed in the United States prior to 1900, and dependable, though still incomplete, death statistics did not become available for all the states until 1933. Today, death registration is believed to be nearly as complete as birth registration.

It is believed that the death rate per 1,000 population was about 25–28 at the beginning of the nineteenth century (but much higher in epidemic years). By the end of that century, it had declined to a little above 17, and each subsequent decade has lowered the figure. Over the last 10 years, the range between 9.3 and 9.6 has been determined largely by the prevalence of influenza; in 1954, when there were practically no epidemics of respiratory diseases, the rate was 9.2. In general, the death rate is higher among men than among women (see Table III.9 and Figure III.1A).

Each year, about 1.7–1.8 million persons die in the United States (some 47,000–48,000 a day). The death rate has not changed much in recent years, but the number of deaths has been increasing with the increase in population.

TABLE III.9

DEATHS AND DEATH RATES PER 1,000 POPULATION,
BY SEX AND COLOR, 1900-1964

Year	Number of Deaths (In Thousands)	Death Rate per 1,000 Population						
		Total			White		Nonwhite	
		Both Sexes	Male	Female	Male	Female	Male	Female
1900	1,310	17.2	17.9	16.5	17.7	16.3	25.7	24.4
1910	1,356	14.7	15.6	13.7	15.4	13.6	22.3	21.0
1920	1,382	13.0	13.4	12.6	13.0	12.1	17.8	17.5
1930	1,393	11.3	12.3	10.4	11.7	9.8	17.4	15.3
1940	1,417	10.8	12.0	9.5	11.6	9.2	15.1	12.6
1950	1,452	9.6	11.1	8.2	10.9	8.0	12.5	9.9
1960	1,712	9.5	11.0	8.1	11.0	8.0	11.5	8.7
1961	1,702	9.1	10.7	7.9	10.7	7.8	10.9	8.4
1962	1,757	9.5	10.9	8.1	10.8	8.0	11.2	8.5
1963	1,813	9.6	11.1	8.2	11.0	8.1	11.5	8.7
1964	1,801	9.4	10.8	8.0	10.8	8.0	11.2	8.3

The sharpest decline in death rates has been in infancy. At the beginning of this century, 1 baby boy in 6 died before reaching the age of 1; in 1920, 1 baby in 10; in 1930, one in 14; in 1963, 1 in about 40 (see Table III.10). An infant faces the greatest danger in his first hours of life: more than one-third of all infant deaths occur on the first day. The so-called neonatal death rate (death occurring under 28 days of age per 1,000 live births) was 18.2 in 1963 and was estimated at 17.6 in 1965.

No less impressive is the improvement for children aged 1–4 years: their rate dropped from nearly 20 deaths per 1,000 at the beginning of this century to 1 per 1,000 in 1963.

The death rate is lowest in the 5–14 age group and increases thereafter with age. For persons aged 25–44 it is still very low compared with the next age group, 45–54; then in the higher age groups it rises sharply (see Figure III.4).

TABLE III.10

DEATH RATES BY SEX AND AGE GROUP, 1900-1963
(Per 1,000 Population)

Age	Male						Female					
	1900	1920	1940	1960	1962	1963	1900	1920	1940	1960	1962	1963
Under 1 year	179.1	103.6	61.9	30.6	28.3	28.5	145.4	80.7	47.7	23.2	22.3	21.8
1-4 years	20.5	10.3	3.1	1.2	1.1	1.1	19.1	9.5	2.7	1.0	0.9	0.9
5-14 years	3.8	2.8	1.2	0.6	0.5	0.5	3.9	2.5	0.9	0.4	0.4	0.6
15-24 years	5.9	4.8	2.3	1.5	1.5	1.5	5.8	5.0	1.8	0.6	0.6	1.0
25-34 years	8.2	6.4	3.4	1.9	1.9	1.9	8.2	7.1	2.7	1.1	1.0	2.3
35-44 years	10.7	8.2	5.9	3.7	3.6	3.8	9.8	8.0	4.5	2.3	2.3	5.3
45-54 years	15.7	12.6	12.5	9.9	9.6	9.8	14.2	11.7	8.6	5.5	5.3	9.2
55-64 years	28.7	24.6	26.1	23.1	22.7	23.0	25.8	22.4	18.0	12.0	11.6	11.8
65-74 years	59.3	54.5	54.6	49.1	49.1	51.1	53.6	50.5	42.2	28.7	28.3	28.8
75-84 years	128.3	122.1	121.3	101.8	98.7	101.3	118.8	115.9	'03.7	76.3	73.3	72.6
85 years and over	268.8	253.0	246.4	211.9	220.2	223.0	255.2	244.7	227.6	190.1	196.8	201.6
ALL AGES	17.9	13.4	12.0	11.0	10.9	11.1	16.5	12.6	9.5	8.1	8.1	8.2

FIGURE III.4

DEATHS BY AGE GROUP IN THE UNITED STATES, 1960-64

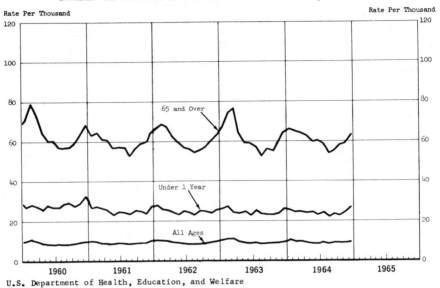

U.S. Department of Health, Education, and Welfare

The age distribution of the population affects the death rate. With the increase of higher age groups within the population, the death rate also rises. Age-adjusted rates remove this effect by weighting death rates in each group by the size of that group in some selected population distribution. Using the 1940 population pattern as a standard, the age-adjusted death rate for 1963 was 7.5, rather than 9.5.

In all age classes, the death rate among men is somewhat higher than among women. The differential begins with the first days and months of life; mortality among boys at birth is about one-fourth higher than among girls (25.1 per 1,000 living, as compared with 19.0).

The death rate among the nonwhite population is higher than among white people, but the differential has narrowed appreciably in recent decades. In 1920, the death rate of the white population was 12.6 per 1,000 and that of the nonwhite, 17.7. The corresponding rates for 1930 were 10.8 and 16.3; for 1950, 9.5 and 11.2; for 1963, 9.5 and 10.1.* However, the differential is still considerable for deaths among the infants under 1 year (per 1,000 live births): 22.9 for the white and 43.2 for the nonwhite babies in 1960, and 22.4 and 40.0, respectively, in 1963 (see Figure III.5). Infant mortality among the reservation Indians in 1960 was estimated at 46 per 1,000 live births, twice that of the general population.

* Exclusive of residents of New Jersey.

FIGURE III.5

INFANT MORTALITY RATES
IN THE UNITED STATES, BY COLOR, 1933-63

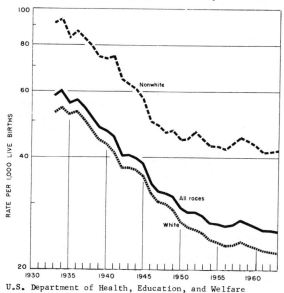

U.S. Department of Health, Education, and Welfare

A successful struggle has been waged against communicable diseases, ailments of children (whooping cough, scarlet fever, diphtheria, and others) and all diseases associated with nutrition and environmental sanitation. Tuberculosis, diarrhea, enteritis, and syphilis have been almost conquered; within the last 60 years the death rate from tuberculosis fell from 194 per 100,000 population to 5. However, medical science has not been equally successful with regard to chronic diseases associated with aging and certain diseases of infancy. In some instances, there has even been an increase in the death rates for specific diseases, for example, the death rate for arteriosclerotic heart disease, including coronary thrombosis, rose from 213 in 1950 to 290 in 1963 (per 100,000 population). Fifty years ago, the death rate from cancer was 76 per 100,000 population; today it is 152; from heart diseases, 137 and 367, respectively (see Appendix Table XV). This rise is due partly to the fact that more and more people live to ages at which such ailments are more common.

More than half of all deaths (some 54 per cent) in the last decade are attributable to a single cause: cardiovascular disease. Following this is malignant neoplasms (cancer, 15–16 per cent). About 40 per cent of all deaths of white persons were from heart diseases, as compared with 28 per cent for the nonwhite.

FIGURE III.6

MAJOR CAUSES OF DEATH IN THE UNITED STATES, 1960-64

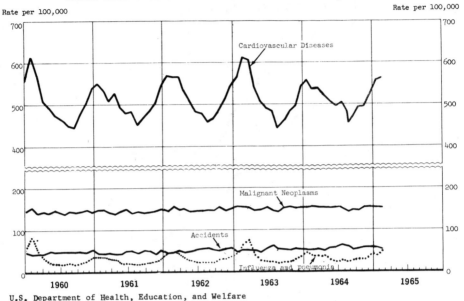

U.S. Department of Health, Education, and Welfare

Among the major causes of death in the United States, accidents rank third, after cardiovascular diseases and cancer (see Figure III.6). According to the U.S. Public Health Service, as many as 45 million Americans were injured in accidents in 1963; 38 million of them received medical attention, and 101,000 died. In the first 34 years of life (age group 1–34), accidents are the principal killer. The death rate from accidents went down from 72 per 100,000 population in 1940 to 52 in 1960, but has remained rather constant in recent years. The rate for accidents while at work has been slightly declining, but that of home and other accidents has been increasing. Of the 45 million injuries in 1963, about 20 million happened in or around the home: more than 11 million inside, and 9 million outside but on the home premises. Men have a higher incidence of accident injuries in all age groups than women, and nonwhites a higher rate than whites, but the difference by sex is greater than by color: for every age group below 75 years, the highest rates are for nonwhite men. Infancy is an especially dangerous time.

The urban population has higher mortality rates than the rural, and the crude death rate increases with the size of the city. This phenomenon, which has been observed for more than a hundred years, is partly explained by the fact that the proportion of residents aged 65 years and over is greater in cities than in rural areas. In 1950, death rates per 1,000 population in urban areas were 10.5, and in rural areas 8.3; in 1960, the figures

TABLE III.11

DEATH RATE PER 1,000 POPULATION, BY GEOGRAPHIC DIVISION, 1940-64

Geographic Division	1940	1950	1960	1961	1962	1963	1964
New England	11.7	10.4	10.6	10.3	10.6	10.6	9.9
Middle Atlantic	11.2	10.5	10.5	10.4	10.5	10.6	10.3
East North Central	11.0	10.0	9.6	9.3	9.6	9.8	9.6
West North Central	10.3	10.1	10.1	9.8	10.1	10.3	10.3
South Atlantic	10.5	8.9	9.1	8.8	9.0	9.2	9.1
East South Central	10.4	9.1	9.5	9.3	9.6	9.9	9.6
West South Central	9.7	8.4	8.7	8.4	8.7	8.7	8.6
Mountain	10.2	8.6	8.1	7.8	7.7	7.8	8.0
Pacific	11.5	9.3	8.7	8.4	8.4	8.5	8.4
UNITED STATES	10.8	9.6	9.5	9.3	9.5	9.6	9.4

were 10.3 and 8.4, respectively. In cities of 1 million persons or more, the death rate in 1960 was 11.5.

There are considerable variations in death rates from one geographic division to another and from state to state. Differences in racial composition, the age structure of the population, internal migration, climatic, economic, and social conditions influence the rates. Regional changes in death rates between 1940 and 1964 are shown in Table III.11.

The average death rate in the United States is lower than in many foreign countries, but some European countries, among them the Netherlands and Norway, have lower rates. Israel has the exceptionally low death rate of 6.1 per 1,000 population.

Infant mortality rates vary much more sharply from country to country, ranging from 15.8 deaths of infants under 1 year of age per 1,000 live births in the Netherlands and 13.6 in Sweden to 104 in Ecuador and 170 in Brazil (see Table III.12). Infant mortality in this country, though lowest in 1964, is still higher than in 12 other countries.

17. Life Expectancy

The impact of changing economic, environmental, and health conditions may be measured by the future longevity of the people, i.e., the average number of years of life remaining to a person at a given age. Without forecasting the length of life of the respective generations, this measure shows their expectation of life if the death rates for the various age groups do not change in the future.

On the basis of death rates for the various age groups in 1900–1902, life expectancy at birth of white male children was estimated at 48.2 years. White males born in 1929–31 might expect to live 59.1 years and those born in 1949–51, 66.3 years. For white males, life expectancy at age 20 increased from 42.2 years in 1900–1902 to 49.5 years in 1949–51 and 50.1

TABLE III.12

CRUDE DEATH RATES AND INFANT MORTALITY RATES
IN SELECTED COUNTRIES, 1962-64[a]

Country and Year	Crude Death Rates	Infant Mortality Rates[b]	Country and Year	Crude Death Rates	Infant Mortality Rates[b]
United States, 1964	9.4	24.2	Romania, 1964	8.0	55.8
Canada, 1964	7.6	26.3	Spain, 1964	8.7	37.9
Mexico, 1964	9.8	67.7	Sweden, 1964	10.0	13.6
Costa Rica, 1964	8.9	66.7	Switzerland, 1964	9.2	20.5
Guatemala, 1962	17.3	91.3	United Kingdom, 1964	11.3	30.7
Honduras, 1963	9.6	47.0	Yugoslavia, 1964	9.4	77.5
Argentina, 1964	8.0	60.7			
Bolivia, 1963	6.0	86.0	U.S.S.R., 1963	7.2	30.9
Chile, 1963	12.8	111.0			
Colombia, 1963	11.7	88.2	Japan, 1964	6.9	23.2
Peru, 1963	8.2	94.8	India, 1962	8.8	81.0
Ecuador, 1963	13.5	104.0	Indonesia, 1961	10.2	81.7
Brazil, 1955-60	11-16	170.0	Israel, 1964	6.1	26.9
Venezuela, 1963	7.2	47.9	Philippines, 1963	7.1	72.8
			Ceylon, 1963	8.5	52.1
Austria, 1964	12.3	20.9	China (Taiwan), 1964	5.7	26.4
Belgium, 1964	12.1	27.2	Burma, 1963	17.8	128.1
Czechoslovakia, 1964	9.6	21.2	Thailand, 1962	7.9	44.7
Denmark, 1964	9.8	19.1	Pakistan, 1962	16-17	96.6
Finland, 1964	9.3	16.9			
France, 1964	10.7	23.4	United Arab Republic, 1963	15.3	133.9
West Germany, 1963	11.4	26.9			
Greece, 1963	7.9	39.8	Union of South Africa:		
Hungary, 1964	9.9	39.8	White, 1962	9.0	28.9
Ireland, 1964	11.4	26.8	Colored, 1962	15.1	119.6
Italy, 1964	9.6	35.5	Asians, 1962	7.4	55.7
Netherlands, 1964	7.7	15.8	Bantu, 1956	11.5	...
Norway, 1964	10.0	16.7			
Poland, 1964	7.6	47.8	Australia, 1964	9.0	19.1
Portugal, 1964	10.2	73.1	New Zealand, 1964	8.8	19.1

[a]Crude death rate: Number of deaths, exclusive of stillbirths, per 1,000 persons; infant mortality rate: deaths of infants under 1 year of age per 1,000 live births.
[b]1963 for Belgium, Canada, China (Taiwan), Costa Rica, Japan, Mexico, Netherlands, Portugal, Romania and Switzerland; 1961 for Ceylon.

years in 1963; at age 40, from 27.7 years to 31.2 and 31.6 years, respectively (see Table III.13).

At all ages, life expectancy is higher for women than for men. In 1949–51, a newborn white female could expect an average life of 72 years; in 1963, 74.4 years. At the age of 20, her life expectancy would be 54.6 and 56.4 years, respectively. The reason for this difference is that in all age groups the death rate among males is higher than among females (see Sec. 16 and Figure III.7).

Life expectancy of nonwhite persons, predominantly Negroes, is appreciably shorter than that of white persons in the same age and sex groups. The difference is most striking for the newborn and much smaller for older persons. However, the differential has declined considerably: in 1900–1902, life expectancy of a newborn Negro male child was only 32.5 years, 15.7 years less than for the white male; in 1963, his life expectancy was 60.9 years, 6.6 years less. At the age of 40, life expectancy of a non-

TABLE III.13

LIFE EXPECTANCY OF THE POPULATION
IN THE UNITED STATES BY SEX, AGE, AND RACE,
1900-1963

Date	Male, at age of						Female, at age of					
	0	1	10	20	40	65	0	1	10	20	40	65
WHITE												
1900-02	48.2	54.6	50.6	42.2	27.7	11.5	51.1	56.4	52.2	43.8	29.2	12.2
1909-11	50.2	56.3	51.3	42.7	27.4	11.3	53.6	58.7	53.6	44.9	29.3	12.0
1919-21	56.3	60.2	54.2	45.6	29.9	12.2	58.5	61.5	55.2	46.5	30.9	12.8
1929-31	59.1	62.0	55.0	46.0	29.2	11.8	62.7	64.9	57.7	48.5	31.5	12.8
1939-41	62.8	65.0	57.0	47.8	30.0	12.1	67.3	68.9	60.8	51.4	33.3	13.6
1949-51	66.3	67.4	59.0	49.5	31.2	12.8	72.0	72.8	64.3	54.6	35.6	15.0
1960	67.4	68.2	59.6	50.1	31.6	12.9	74.1	74.6	66.0	56.2	37.1	15.9
1963	67.5	68.2	59.6	50.1	31.6	12.8	74.4	74.8	66.2	56.4	37.3	16.0
NONWHITE[a]												
1900-02	32.5	42.5	41.9	35.1	23.1	10.4	35.0	45.5	43.0	36.9	24.4	11.4
1909-11	34.1	42.5	40.7	33.5	21.6	9.7	37.7	45.2	42.8	36.1	23.3	10.8
1919-21	47.1	51.6	46.0	38.4	26.5	12.1	46.9	50.4	44.5	37.2	25.6	12.4
1929-31	47.6	51.1	44.3	36.0	23.4	10.9	49.5	52.3	45.3	37.2	24.3	12.2
1939-41	52.3	56.1	48.5	39.7	25.2	12.2	55.5	58.5	50.8	42.1	27.3	14.0
1949-51	58.9	61.2	53.0	43.7	27.3	12.8	62.7	64.4	56.2	46.8	29.8	14.5
1960	61.1	63.2	54.9	45.5	28.4	12.7	66.3	67.9	59.6	49.9	32.1	15.2
1963	60.9	62.9	54.5	45.1	28.1	12.2	66.5	68.0	59.6	50.0	32.1	15.0

[a]Negroes only for 1900-31; in 1962, excludes data for New Jersey, since this state
did not require reporting of color.

FIGURE III.7

LIFE EXPECTANCY AT BIRTH IN THE UNITED STATES,
BY SEX AND COLOR, 1940-70

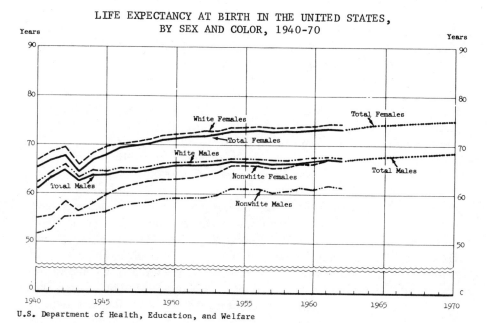

U.S. Department of Health, Education, and Welfare

white male in 1963 was 28.1 years, that is, 3.5 years less than for a white male.

In 1961, life expectancy at birth for the white population for the first time exceeded 70 years. Since 1900, life expectancy for the total population has increased by more than 22 years; for the white population, by 23 years; for the nonwhite population, by more than 30 years.

Expectation of life at birth is strongly affected by the high mortality during the first year of life. Among those who survive the hazards of birth and infancy, the increase in life expectancy is greater for the nonwhite than the white because of the higher infant mortality among the nonwhite population. It is believed that unless there is a major breakthrough in the prevention or treatment of cancer and heart diseases, life expectancy in this country will increase only slowly during the rest of the century.

Life expectancy in the United States is close to that in the advanced countries of Europe, in Canada, Australia, and New Zealand. The U.S.S.R. in 1960–61 reported a life expectancy at birth of 70 years for both sexes. Japan's and Israel's figures are not much different from those for some European countries. Life expectancy in Yugoslavia is substantially lower, but the saddest data are those of India; there, in 1957–60, life expectancy at birth for males was only 41.9 years, and for females, 40.6 years (see Appendix Table XVI).

18. *The Future Population of the United States*

For estimating the future population of the United States, the Bureau of the Census has applied a "component" method, that is, a method combining separate projections for each of the components of population change—births, deaths, and net immigration—with estimates of the current population, age group by age group. The latest projections for 1980, with extension for the year 2000, published in July, 1964, are based on the estimate of the current population, inclusive of the armed forces abroad. Changes that occurred between April 1, 1960, the date of the last census, and the new bench mark of July 1, 1963, have been taken into account. Most calculations have been made by electronic computer.

Of all the components in population change, the fertility rate is the most uncertain. The 2 other components are less difficult to appraise in their impact on the future population: a slight decline in mortality over the next several decades and a net immigration of 300,000 per year have been accepted as reasonable assumptions. But for the fertility component, 4 alternative assumptions have been used (see Table III.14 and Figure III.8): A. The high fertility rates of the post–World War II period will continue; B. A modest drop is to be expected in the levels of fertility in the last decade; assumptions C and D were developed in close relation one to another, with assumption D representing the lowest fertility experienced before the war, exclusive of that in the Depression years. Series C repre-

TABLE III.14

PROJECTIONS OF THE POPULATION OF THE UNITED STATES
BY AGE GROUPS, 1960-2000[a]

Year and Series	All Ages	Under 5 Years	5-9 Years	10-14 Years	15-19 Years	20-24 Years	25-34 Years	35-44 Years	45-64 Years	65 and Over
1960	180.7	20.4	18.8	16.9	13.5	11.1	22.9	24.2	36.2	16.7
1965: A	195.1	21.2								
B	194.7	20.8	20.4	18.9	17.0	13.6	22.4	24.5	39.1	18.1
C	194.1	20.2								
D	194.1	20.2								
1970: A	211.4	24.0	21.3							
B	209.0	22.0	20.8	20.5	18.9	17.1	22.2	23.0	41.9	19.6
C	206.1	19.7	20.3							
D	205.9	19.4	20.3							
1975: A	230.4	27.3	24.0	21.3						
B	225.9	25.2	22.0	20.9	20.5	19.1	31.1	22.5	43.4	21.2
C	220.1	22.3	19.7	20.3						
D	218.9	21.3	19.5	20.3						
1980: A	252.1	30.6	27.3	24.1	21.4					
B	245.3	28.3	25.2	22.1	20.9	20.6	36.5	25.3	43.3	23.1
C	236.5	25.2	22.4	19.8	20.4					
D	233.1	23.2	21.3	19.5	20.4					
1985: A	275.6	33.0	30.6	27.4	24.1	21.5				
B	266.3	30.5	28.4	25.3	22.1	21.0	40.0	31.1	43.0	25.0
C	254.0	27.0	25.3	22.4	19.8	20.5				
D	248.0	24.2	23.2	21.4	19.6	20.5				
1990: A	301.2	35.6	33.0	30.6	27.4	24.2	42.4			
B	288.2	32.0	30.5	28.4	25.3	22.2	41.9	36.4	44.5	27.0
C	271.4	27.4	27.0	25.3	22.5	19.9	41.4			
D	262.2	24.3	24.3	23.2	21.4	19.7	41.4			
1995: A	320.7	39.3	35.6	33.1	30.6	27.5	45.9			
B	311.8	34.3	32.0	30.5	28.4	25.4	43.6	39.8	49.8	28.1
C	289.2	28.4	27.5	27.0	25.3	22.6	40.7			
D	276.3	24.6	24.3	24.3	23.3	21.5	40.5			
2000: A	361.9	43.7	39.2	35.7	33.1	30.7	51.9	42.2		
B	338.2	37.7	34.3	32.0	30.5	28.5	47.9	41.7	57.4	28.2
C	308.5	30.6	28.4	27.5	27.1	25.4	42.8	41.2		
D	290.9	25.8	24.7	24.4	24.3	23.4	41.5	41.2		

[a]As of July 1; includes Alaska, Hawaii and armed forces abroad. Series A results do not differ substantially from those obtained under the assumption that the average annual level of fertility in 1960-63 will persist throughout the projection period.

sents a mean between the corresponding fertility rates in B and D.* In general, the Bureau of the Census holds that possible variations in mor-

* In its previous projections, the Bureau of the Census used alternative assumptions, based on calendar-year gross-reproduction rates. For these latest projections, it used data on fertility history of cohorts of women, that is, women born in specific years, as they progress through the childbearing ages. For cohort fertility, see P. K. Whelpton, *Cohort Fertility, Native White Women in the United States* (Princeton, N.J.: Princeton University Press, 1954).

FIGURE III.8

POPULATION PROJECTIONS
TO 2000 IN THE UNITED STATES

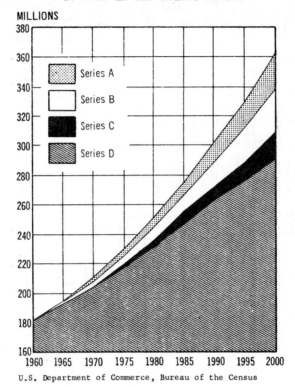

U.S. Department of Commerce, Bureau of the Census

tality and net immigration are less important for determining the size of the future population of this country than variations in fertility.

In its projections, the Bureau of the Census makes the basic assumptions that there will be no major war, widespread epidemic, or similar catastrophe, and that there will be no severe economic depression. The Bureau also stresses that its projections are speculative and that the degree of uncertainty concerning the future level of fertility remains large. As it states: "Annual fertility has fluctuated widely in certain past periods, and a 10 per cent rise or fall in annual rates is not unprecedented in the light of the postwar experience." The Bureau therefore does not recommend any one series as the "best" series, but, of course, it expects that the range of the alternative fertility rates will turn out to be realistic.*

* It is interesting to note in this connection that an earlier projection of the U.S. population for the period 1945–75 and continuing up to 2000, by P. K. Whelpton, prepared under the auspices of L. E. Truesdell and published by the Bureau of the Census in 1947, gave 163.9 million population for 1980, and 163.3 million for 2000.

IV. *Health and Education*

19. *Health Conditions*—20. *We Learn the Three R's*—21. *Our Schools*

19. *Health Conditions*

On the average, illness and injury cause a civilian in the United States to lose 6 working days a year, and a child between 6 and 15 years to lose about as many school days. In 1965, a sample survey conducted by the U.S. Public Health Service reported that for the nation as a whole, including Alaska and Hawaii, this average resulted in a loss of nearly 400 million working days and 214 million school days. In 1964, 1.4 million persons were absent from work on an average day on account of illness or injury.

Curtailment of activity is caused by chronic conditions, such as arthritis, rheumatism, impairment of vision, etc., and by acute conditions, such as respiratory difficulties, infectious and parasitic diseases, and diseases of the digestive system.

The incidence of acute conditions is highest among children under 5 years and decreases with age: in 1962, the rate per 100 was 222 for all ages; 367 for children under 5 years, as against 128 for persons 65 years and over. In contrast, the average prevalence of chronic conditions due to degenerative diseases is highest among older persons: in 1959–61, the rate per 1,000 persons with heart conditions was 7.9 in the age group under 44 years, 55.3 for the group aged 45–64, and 153.8 for older people; the corresponding figures for arthritis and rheumatism were 15.5, 147.8, and 281.5; for high blood pressure, 8.8, 69.4, and 137.5; for visual impairment, 7, 26.7, and 108.4.

Among the civilian population interviewed by the Public Health Service in 1959–61, approximately 14 million persons had chronic conditions that limited them in their major activity; 4 million of them were unable to carry on major activities—to work or keep house or attend school—and the rest experienced greater or lesser limitations in their regular activities. The

77

proportion affected varied with age and was largely concentrated in the higher age groups: one-fourth reported heart conditions and another fourth, arthritis, rheumatism, and impairment of vision as the causes of their chronic limitations.

Between 1900 and 1963, the number of physicians in the United States more than doubled, from 119,749 to 289,200; that of dentists more than tripled, from 29,665 to 105,952. The rate of physicians per 100,000 population was 157 in 1900; it had declined to 131 by 1938 and remained at that level, with small ups and downs; in 1963, it was 149. In contrast, the rate of dentists increased from 39 to 59 in 1930; in 1963 it was 56.

Most physicians prefer to settle in the more prosperous, industrialized eastern and western states. In 1963, the number of physicians per 100,000 population was 207 in New York State, 178 in California, 169 in Colorado,

TABLE IV.1

THE NUMBER OF PHYSICIANS PER 100,000 POPULATION
IN SELECTED COUNTRIES, 1961

Israel	239	France	106
U.S.S.R.	192	Spain	99
Austria	183	Sweden	95
Czechoslovakia	180	Poland	93
Italy	163	Mexico	59
United States	148	Brazil	38
West Germany	144	Turkey	35
Switzerland	136	Iran	28
Belgium	135	Ceylon	21
United Kingdom	117	India	19
Australia	114	Thailand	13
Canada	108	Pakistan	11
Japan	107		

and 180 in Connecticut, as against 79 in Alabama, 76 in Mississippi, and 73 in South Dakota. The District of Columbia is in a class by itself, with 357 physicians per 100,000 persons. The distribution of dentists has followed about the same pattern.

Few countries have more physicians in proportion to their population than the United States; in fact, the majority of mankind has insufficient medical personnel (see Table IV.1).

Between 1909 and 1963, the number of hospitals in the United States increased from 4,359 to 7,138, with the largest relative increase occurring in hospitals of the Federal Government. The number of beds per 1,000 population (excluding armed forces abroad) increased from 4.7 to 9.0; during World War II, it reached a record high with 12.1 beds (see Table IV.2 and Figure IV.1). Of the total number of beds, 1.7 million, two-thirds, are operated publicly, mostly by the state or local authorities; about

TABLE IV.2

HOSPITALS AND HOSPITAL BEDS,
BY OWNERSHIP OR CONTROL, 1909-63

Year	Number of Hospitals				Number of Beds				
	Total	Govern- mental	Non- profit	Proprie- tary	In Hospitals (In Thousands)				Per 1,000 Population[b]
					Total	Govern- mental	Non- profit	Proprie- tary	
1909	4,359	303	...	...	421	189	...	...	4.7
1914	5,047	387	...	...	532	245	...	...	5.4
1918	5,323	413	...	...	612	281	...	...	5.9
1923	6,830	1,736	3,332	1,762	756	472	238	46	6.8
1928	6,852	1,813	5,039	a	893	568	326	a	7.4
1933	6,437	1,776	4,661	a	1,027	694	333	a	8.2
1938	6,166	1,728	2,757	1,681	1,161	815	290	56	8.9
1943	6,655	2,284	2,956	1,415	1,649	1,276	323	50	12.1
1948	6,335	1,900	3,084	1,351	1,411	1,012	349	50	9.7
1953	6,978	2,230	3,369	1,379	1,581	1,118	410	54	9.9
1958	6,818	2,259	3,524	1,035	1,572	1,067	459	46	9.1
1961	6,923	2,362	3,588	973	1,670	1,129	494	47	9.1
1963	7,138	2,453	3,663	1,022	1,702	1,126	523	53	9.0

[a]Included with nonprofit hospitals.
[b]Excludes armed forces abroad.

three-tenths are run by nonprofit organizations, such as church or other religious groups or nonprofit corporations. Hospitals are unevenly distributed over the country, and medical facilities are largely concentrated in metropolitan areas; many sparsely populated rural sections of the country have neither enough doctors nor enough hospital beds.

FIGURE IV.1

OWNERSHIP OF HOSPITAL BEDS IN THE UNITED STATES, 1935-62

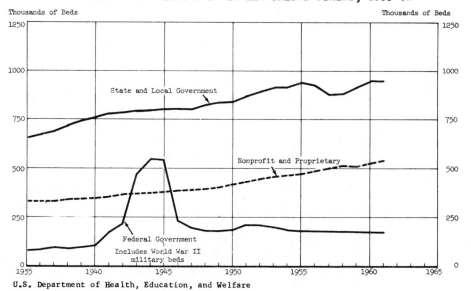

U.S. Department of Health, Education, and Welfare

With the growth of cities, the rise in the standard of living, and changes in medical practices, the use of hospitals, measured by admissions per 1,000 civilian population, increased steadily, from 58.6 in 1935 to 142.8 in 1963 (see Table IV.3). The average length of stay per patient declined from 15 to 9.2 days, respectively. Hospital expenses rose substantially, more sharply than the cost of living in the postwar period, partly because of increased payroll expenses, and new and expensive services and equipment. Between 1946 and 1963, hospital cost per patient day in general hospitals quadrupled, from $9.37 to $38.91 (see Figure IV.2A). Because the average stay in the hospital has been shortened, total expense per patient stay increased less, from $86 to $298 for all treatments, or by 248 per cent, instead of 314 per cent. During this period, hospital daily service charges have risen nearly 5 times as much as the Consumer Price Index for all items (see Figures IV.2B and C).

The mental hospitals of the United States had 784,000 beds in 1963, or 46 per cent of all hospital beds. The number of resident patients was close to 600,000, of whom about 10 per cent were veterans. The rate of patients per 100,000 population was 206.8 in 1909 and 368.4 in 1940; it rose during the war years to 409 and has been gradually declining ever since. In 1962, it was 321.8 and in 1964, 291.8 (see Table IV.4).

Stay in mental hospitals is usually of long duration, and many patients spend 4 or more years there. The mental hospitals of state and local governments admitted 285,244 mentally sick persons in 1963 and released 247,228, either directly discharging them or placing them on extramural care. That year, 49,039 patients died in mental hospitals, so that by the end of 1963 the remaining resident patients numbered about 505,000. In addition, the institutions for the mentally retarded had 185,000 patients in 1963 and 187,000 in 1964. General hospitals with psychiatric services had 8,700 patients, and outpatient psychiatric clinics treated 378,000 patients in 1964.

Mental hospitals and institutions for the mentally retarded are maintained chiefly through public funds: Federal, state, county, and municipality.

The nation's expenditures for health and medical care, including public-health services, industrial in-plant services, medical-facilities construction, veterans' hospitals, direct payments and insurance benefits, etc., amounted to $3.6 billion in 1929, $12.2 billion in 1950, and $36.8 billion in 1964. Of these totals, public expenditures represented 14.1, 25.4, and 25.5 per cent, respectively.

In terms of gross national product, total expenditures for health and medical care increased from 3.6 per cent in 1929 to 4.6 per cent in 1950 and 5.8 per cent in 1964. Per capita consumer expenditures for medical care and voluntary health insurance amounted to $131.2 in 1964: $39.9 for hospital services, $35.8 for physicians' services, $28.4 for drugs and appliances, $12.4 for dental services, $7.7 for other medical help, and $6.8 net cost of insurance (see Secs. 40, 83, and 93).

TABLE IV.3

HOSPITAL USE IN THE UNITED STATES, ANNUAL RATE
PER 1,000 POPULATION, 1935-63

| Year | General and Special Hospitals[a] | | |
	Admissions	Total Days	Average Length of Stay (In Days)
1935	58.6	882.0	15.0
1940	74.3	1,019.2	13.7
1945	120.2	1,986.8	16.5
1950	109.8	1,165.3	10.6
1955	125.4	1,237.5	9.9
1956	120.1	1,248.4	9.7
1957	132.4	1,264.6	9.6
1958	133.9	1,273.5	9.5
1959	130.5	1,252.2	9.6
1960	136.3	1,264.8	9.3
1961	136.4	1,269.1	9.3
1962	139.8	1,294.8	9.3
1963	142.8	1,313.7	9.2

[a] Includes all types of hospitals other than
mental and tuberculosis.   Beginning 1959,
includes Alaska and Hawaii.

FIGURE IV.2.A

HOSPITAL EXPENSES PER PATIENT DAY, 1946-63

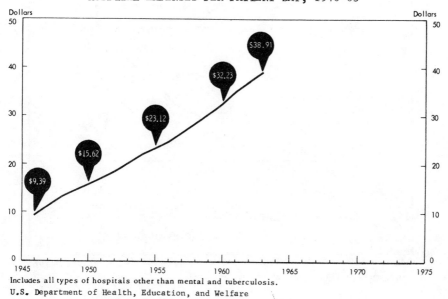

Includes all types of hospitals other than mental and tuberculosis.
U.S. Department of Health, Education, and Welfare

CONSUMER PRICES AND MEDICAL CARE COST, 1945-63

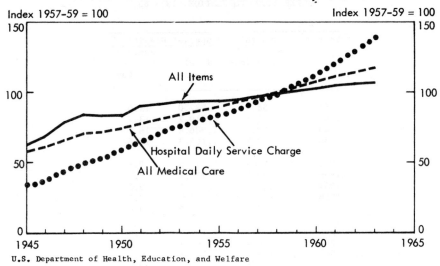

U.S. Department of Health, Education, and Welfare

FIGURE IV.2.C

RISE IN HOSPITAL COSTS IN THE UNITED STATES, 1946-62

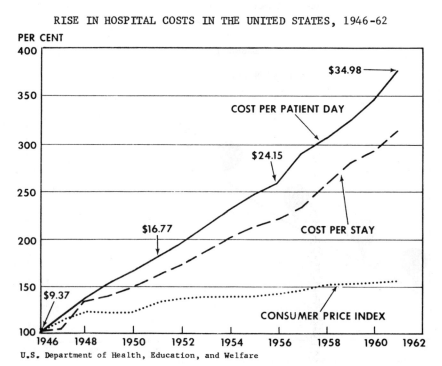

U.S. Department of Health, Education, and Welfare

TABLE IV.4

PATIENTS IN MENTAL HOSPITALS AND INSTITUTIONS,[a]
1935-64

Year	Patients in Mental Hospitals					Patients in Institutions for Mentally Retarded			
	Total		Hospitals			Total		Institutions	
	Number	Rate	Federal	State and County	Private	Number	Rate	Public	Private
1935	421.7	331.4	22.5	388.5	10.7	97.4	76.6	93.2	4.2
1940	485.0	368.4	33.8	440.5	10.2	104.8	79.6	101.2	3.6
1945	521.8	409.0	45.4	463.3	13.1	119.2	93.5	113.4	5.8
1950	580.5	384.9	53.9	512.5	14.1	135.1	89.9	128.1	7.0
1955	633.5	388.7	60.0	558.9	14.6	151.1	93.1	143.5	7.6
1960	611.4	343.2	62.1	535.5	13.8	171.5	96.3	163.7	7.8
1961	603.0	332.9	62.6	527.5	12.9	169.7	93.7	162.5	7.2
1962	591.3	321.8	61.9	515.6	13.8	182.1	99.1	173.6	8.5
1963[b]	580.0	310.9	62.5	504.6	12.9	184.9	99.1	174.4	10.5
1964[b]	552.6	291.8	61.8	490.8	-	187.0	98.8	179.3	7.7

[a]Patients, in thousands; rate per 100,000 civilian population, except 1935, total population.
[b]Preliminary.

The United States is the only great industrial country without a compulsory nationwide health-insurance program or compulsory nationwide sickness benefits. Medical care is provided for veterans, and there are some provisions for medical help to Federal employees. But, in general, health services are provided mostly through private facilities and personal physicians; these are supplemented by public hospitals and institutions (especially for mental diseases, where public medical care was established because of the need for custody). A large part of the population has some protection against prohibitive medical costs through various plans carried by insurance companies and paid for either individually or by the employer, or by both employer and employee. In 1964, over 163 million people had some form of hospital insurance; some of them had, in addition, coverage for surgical expenditures and/or physicians' visits in hospitals. However, there is a correlation between the income level and health-insurance coverage. In 1962–63, 34 per cent of persons with family income of less than $2,000 had hospital insurance; 29 per cent carried surgical insurance; in families with income of $4,000–$6,999 comparable percentages were 79 and 74; with income of $7,000 and more, the percentages were 88 and 83.*

---

* Some persons may carry both types of insurance.

TABLE IV.5

PHYSICIANS' AND DENTISTS' VISITS PER YEAR PER PERSON[a],
1963-64

	Physicians	Dentists
Residence of patients		
Urban	4.8	1.8
Rural nonfarm	4.3	1.9
Rural	3.3	0.9
Family income		
Under $2,000	4.3	0.8
$2,000-$3,999	4.3	0.9
$4,000-$6,999	4.5	1.4
$7,000 and over	4.9	2.3

[a]Consultation with a physician in person (in office
or home) or by telephone: examination, diagnosis,
treatment or advice; a visit to a dentist's office
for advice or treatment.

According to household interviews conducted by the National Health
Survey, the urban population and higher-income groups get more medical
care than rural people and the lower-income groups (see Table IV.5).

Yet medical costs represent a larger percentage of the personal income
of low-income groups than of families in higher-income brackets.

According to the Public Health Service, an estimated 890 million medical visits and 248 million dental visits—5 medical visits and 1.4 dental
visits per person per year—were made between July, 1962, and June,
1963. However, 15 per cent of the American people have not been to a
doctor in the past 2 years, and 18 per cent have never seen a dentist. This
lack of medical and dental care is the result both of the unequal distribution of medical services throughout the country and of the unequal distribution of personal income.

In July, 1965, the Congress enacted legislation providing medical care
for persons aged 65 and over, as part of the social security system. The
plan covers hospitalization and various medical services for approximately
19 million older people. It started operating in July, 1966. The legislation
also introduced a supplementary plan of voluntary medical insurance. The
basic plan is financed by a special tax on earnings, to be paid by employers,
employees, and the self-employed; the voluntary plan is financed by monthly
premiums of $3 paid by those who join it and matched by the U.S. Treasury
(see Sec. 93).

20. We Learn the Three R's.

The first public schools were founded in the United States early in the
nineteenth century. State-supported public education was introduced in
the 1850's and became almost universal in the 1870's. The first basic

TABLE IV.6

PERCENTAGE OF ILLITERACY, BY RACE, 1947 AND 1959

	Population (In Thousands)	Illiterate (Per Cent)		Population (In Thousands)	Illiterate (Per Cent)	
		White	Nonwhite		White	Nonwhite
		1947			1959	
14-24 years	24,257	0.6	4.4	25,118	0.5	1.2
25-34 years	22,481	0.8	7.2	22,700	0.7	4.2
35-44 years	19,898	1.3	9.7	23,443	0.9	6.1
45-54 years	16,625	2.0	13.8	20,135	1.3	10.2
55-64 years	12,652	4.2	19.1	15,070	2.3	13.0
65 years and over	10,515	4.9	32.4	14,907	5.1	25.5
TOTAL, 14 years and over	106,428	1.8	11.0	121,373	1.6	7.5

goal of public education was to teach the entire population to read and write. Despite all the advances in education, there are still some illiterate persons, though their number is very small. They are concentrated predominantly among nonwhite persons raised in the South. Among young people, literacy has been substantially achieved (see Table IV.6).

Today the country is no longer concerned with mere ability to read and write, but with what is called the "functional illiteracy" of persons who have had only a few years of schooling (see Figure IV.3). Completion of

FIGURE IV.3

PER CENT OF FUNCTIONAL ILLITERATES IN THE UNITED STATES, BY STATE, 1960

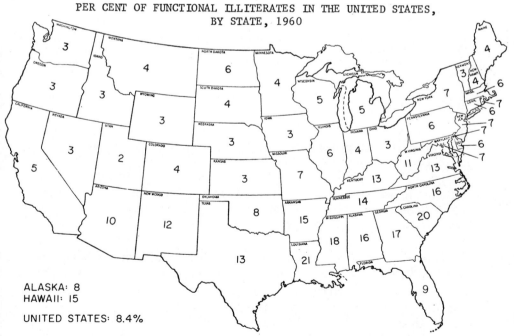

ALASKA: 8
HAWAII: 15

UNITED STATES: 8.4%

U.S. Department of Commerce, Bureau of the Census

at least 5 years in an elementary school is considered the minimum needed to meet the requirements of employment in the modern economy and to participate in the political and cultural life of the nation. Actually, persons who have less than 8 years of formal schooling find many employment opportunities and chances for betterment of income closed to them.

The 1960 Census reported that almost 24 million persons aged 25 years and over had completed less than 8 years of schooling (12.6 million men and 11.2 million women). According to the Current Population Survey of March, 1962, by the Bureau of the Census, the number of persons 14 years and older with less than 5 years of schooling was 8.2 million; over one-fourth of them were nonwhite.

Young people have a higher educational attainment than older groups in terms of the median number of school years completed (see Table

TABLE IV.7

MEDIAN SCHOOL YEARS COMPLETED BY PERSONS 25 YEARS
OLD AND OVER, BY AGE GROUP, 1940-62

Age	Median Number of Years Completed			
	1940	1950	1960	1962
25-29 years	10.3	12.1	12.3	12.4
30-34 years	9.5	11.6	12.2	12.3
35-39 years	8.8	10.7	12.1	12.2
40-44 years	8.6	9.8	11.8	
45-49 years	8.5	8.9	10.6	11.2
50-54 years	8.4	8.7	9.7	
55-59 years	8.3	8.5	8.8	8.9
60-64 years	8.3	8.4	8.6	
65-69 years	8.2	8.2	8.4	8.4
70-74 years	8.1	8.2	8.3	
75 years and over	8.0	8.1	8.2	

IV.7). In 1960, an adult aged 25–29 years had 12.4 median number of years of formal schooling and had therefore graduated from high school; in contrast, the group aged 69 and over was represented by an elementary-school education only, with 8.4 median number of school years completed. Comparing 3 generations separated from one another by 25 years, we find that only 18 per cent of those aged 70–74 years in 1962 had graduated from high school and 48 per cent of those in age group 40–44 years, as against 64 per cent of those aged 20–24.

The pattern of educational attainment differs somewhat for boys and girls. While both start their education on equal terms, so to speak, more boys terminate their education on graduating from elementary school and take jobs or apprenticeships. Proportionately more girls than boys graduate from high school, and proportionately more girls go on to college. Many of these, however, drop out of college before graduation to take clerical jobs

TABLE IV.8

YEARS OF SCHOOL COMPLETED BY PERSONS AGED 25 YEARS AND OVER, 1940 AND 1960[a]

	Total	Elementary School			High School		College	
		Less Than 4 Years	5-7 Years	8 Years	1-3 Years	4 Years	1-3 Years	4 Years
1940								
White	100.0	10.9	17.4	29.8	15.8	15.3	5.9	4.9
Nonwhite	100.0	41.8	29.9	11.9	8.7	4.5	1.9	1.3
Total	100.0	13.7	18.5	28.2	15.2	14.3	5.5	4.6
1960								
White	100.0	6.7	12.8	18.1	19.3	25.8	9.3	8.1
Nonwhite	100.0	23.5	23.6	12.8	18.8	13.4	4.4	3.5
Total	100.0	8.3	13.9	17.6	19.2	24.6	8.8	7.7

[a] Conterminous United States.

or to marry; therefore, relatively more boys than girls graduate from college—9.7 and 5.8 per cent, respectively. Interestingly, there is no comparable sex difference with respect to college education among nonwhite persons.

The educational differential between white and nonwhite persons is still considerable but is decreasing with each decade. In 1940, only 8.7

FIGURE IV.4

DISTRIBUTION OF THE POPULATION 25 YEARS OLD AND OVER, BY YEARS OF SCHOOL COMPLETED, AND COLOR, 1940-60

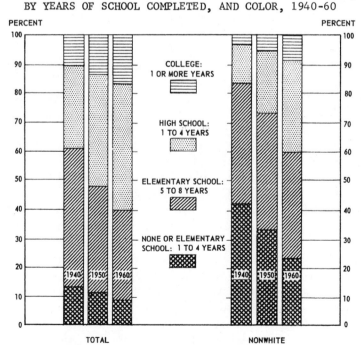

U.S. Department of Commerce, Bureau of the Census

per cent of the nonwhite persons 25 years and older had completed 1 to 3 years of high school, and only 4.5 per cent had graduated; for 1960, the corresponding figures were 18.8 and 13.4 per cent. For white persons, the percentages in 1940 were 15.8 and 15.3, respectively; for 1960, 19.3 and 25.8. The trend in college education is similar (see Table IV.8 and Figure IV.4). It is important, however, to bear in mind that educational institutions for white persons surpass those for nonwhite in academic standards, so that an equal number of years of schooling does not mean equal education for the 2 groups.

Of the 2,008 institutions of higher education in the United States in 1960, 106 were Negro institutions with 89,000 students (42,000 male and 47,000 female). There was a sprinkling of white students registered, while many Negro students were attending other institutions of higher learning. Of the 107 Negro institutions of higher education in 1964, 47 were publicly controlled and the remaining 60 were private; among the students, girls predominated with 58,300, as compared with 47,200 boys.

Desegregation of public elementary and secondary schools has proceeded at a turtle's pace in the South. Of the nearly 6,000 school districts, 1 out of 5 was desegregated between 1956 and November, 1964. Of the total Negroes enrolled, only 8 per cent were attending schools together with white students: 273,000 out of 3.4 million. Intravariation among Southern states was very great, from less than 0.05 per cent in Alabama to 88.1 per cent in West Virginia (see Table IV.9). In the single school district of Washington, D.C., there were 124,000 Negro and 17,500 white students. Of these, 106,000 Negro pupils attended school together with white students: 86 per cent of the total Negro enrollment.

The educational level is higher in urban areas than in rural nonfarm and, particularly, rural farm areas. In 1960, the median number of years of school completed in urban areas by a male in the age group 25 years and over was 11 and by a female, 11.2 years; corresponding figures for the rural nonfarm areas were 9 and 10 years, respectively; for the rural farm areas, 8.6 and 9.2 years. As in past censuses, the median educational level in 1960 was higher for women than for men.

In all age groups, the educational attainment was highest in the West and lowest in the South. Utah, Alaska, and Nevada ranked highest among the states in terms of per cent of population aged 25 years and over who were high-school graduates: 56, 55, and 53 per cent, respectively, as compared with 30, 29, and 28 per cent for Mississippi, Arkansas, and Kentucky. The differential in the educational attainment of the white and nonwhite groups also was largest in the South.

There is also a direct correlation between the income, educational level, and occupation of parents and the extent of the education their children receive. Among families with annual income of $5,000, 1 child out of 2 graduates from high school, but only 1 in 5 goes on to college. In families

TABLE IV.9

DESEGREGATION OF PUBLIC ELEMENTARY AND SECONDARY
SCHOOLS IN THE SOUTH, BY STATE, 1964[a]

State	School Districts		Enrollment				Negro Students in Schools with White Students	
	Total	Deseg-regated	Total		In Desegregated Districts		In	Per Cent
			White	Negro	White	Negro	Thousands	Enrolled
			(In Thousands)					
Alabama	118	8	550	203	152	89	0.1	[b]
Arkansas	412	24	334	115	93	29	1	0.8
Delaware	78	43	83	19	78	14	11	57.8
Florida	67	21	1,002	246	812	175	7	2.7
Georgia	196	11	753	355	196	134	1	0.4
Kentucky	204	164	620	56	540	56	35	62.5
Louisiana	67	3	489	321	62	86	4	1.1
Maryland	24	23	565	167	360	167	86	51.7
Mississippi	150	4	308	296	35	22	0.1	[b]
Missouri	1,542	203	818	102	...	94	44	43.1
North Carolina	171	84	829	349	549	201	5	1.4
Oklahoma	1,118	200	542	44	325	37	14	31.7
South Carolina	108	16	372	261	156	84	0.3	0.1
Tennessee	152	61	724	174	459	135	9	5.3
Texas	1,380	291	2,087	344	1,500	225	25	7.3
Virginia	130	81	734	234	585	189	12	5.1
West Virginia	55	44	427	21	390	21	19	88.1
TOTAL	5,972	1,281	11,236	3,398	6,493	1,758	273	8.0

[a]Data reported by Southern Education Reporting Service in Nashville. Its definition of
desegregation: change in schools from segregated white and Negro status to biracial or
multiracial status, either in practice or principle.
Enrollment data for Alabama Arkansas and Virginia: 1963; for Florida, Kentucky,
Louisiana, Missouri, Tennessee, Texas, West Virginia - some data estimated.
[b]Less than 0.05 per cent.

with annual income of $10,000 or more, 9 children out of 10 graduate from
high school, and 3 out of 5 go to college.

Where the father has had a college education, 89 per cent of the children have spent some time in college. Similar relationships are observed
when fathers are professional people or own or manage businesses and
the like: their children are much more likely to go to college than the sons
and daughters of factory workers or manual laborers.

In March, 1962, the U.S. population included 57.4 million high-school
graduates and 9.7 million college graduates. Among the nonwhite population, there were 3.3 million high-school graduates and 444,000 college
graduates. Half the nation's labor force had at least a complete high-
school education, and 1 out of 8 or 9 workers or foremen had some college
education.

For 1980, the Bureau of Census projects 76 million persons with high-
school education and 27 million with college education, or 58.0 and 20.5
per cent of the population aged 25 years and over, respectively (see Figure
IV.5).

FIGURE IV.5

PROJECTED EDUCATIONAL ATTAINMENT IN THE UNITED STATES
FOR 1970 AND 1980

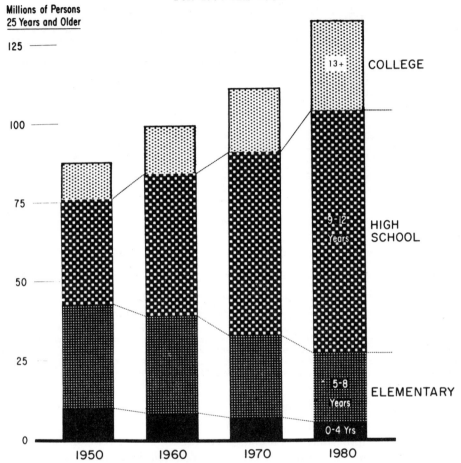

U.S. Department of Commerce, Bureau of the Census

The difference in the level of educational attainment represents one of the major factors in the lifetime income of an individual. In 1961, this difference was between $125,000 for a person with less than 8 years of school and $361,000 for a college graduate. In 1963, the median income showed the same pattern (see Table IV.10 and Figure IV.6).

Each year, approximately 1 million young people leave high school before completing their course of study. The greatest number of dropouts occurs when attendance ceases to be compulsory (at the age of 16 in most states). Most withdrawals from school take place at the switch from junior to senior high school (from the ninth to the tenth grade). Thus, students aged 16 and 17 are affected most. The percentage of dropouts is higher for nonwhite youngsters than for white; 35.6 and 21.0, respectively, in the

TABLE IV.10

LIFETIME AND ANNUAL MEAN INCOME OF MALES 25 TO 64 YEARS OLD,
BY EDUCATIONAL ATTAINMENT, 1949, 1956, AND 1961

	Lifetime Income (In Thousands of Dollars)			Annual Income (In Dollars)		
	1949	1956	1961	1949	1956	1961
Elementary school:						
Less than 8 years[a]	79.7	108.3	124.9	2,232	2,979	3,483
8 years	106.9	148.0	168.8	2,988	4,079	4,750
High school:						
1-3 years	121.9	169.5	193.1	3,279	4,634	5,305
4 years	148.6	208.3	224.4	3,820	5,553	6,102
College:						
1-3 years	173.2	243.6	273.0	4,480	6,505	7,392
4 years or more	241.2	340.1	360.6	6,236	8,716	9,530

[a]Includes males reporting no years of schooling completed.

14–24 age group in 1960; higher for rural residents than urban, 23 per cent
for rural farm people, 28 per cent for rural nonfarm, and 21 per cent for
urban people.

FIGURE IV.6

MEDIAN MONEY INCOME OF FAMILIES,
BY YEARS OF SCHOOL COMPLETED AND COLOR OF HEAD, 1963

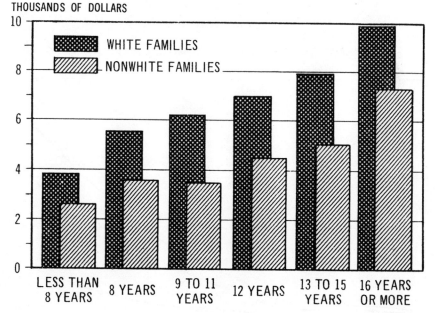

U.S. Department of Commerce, Bureau of the Census

TABLE IV.11

EXPENDITURES FOR EDUCATION, 1930-64
(In Millions of Dollars)

School Year Ending	All Levels		Elementary and Secondary		Higher Education		All Expenditures as Per Cent of Gross National Product
	Total	Public	Total	Public	Total	Public	
1930	3,234	2,655	2,601	2,366	632	289	3.3
1940	3,352	2,756	2,594	2,364	758	392	3.5
1950	9,335	7,312	6,672	5,883	2,662	1,430	3.5
1956	16,812	13,352	12,632	11,005	4,180	2,348	4.1
1960	24,617	19,282	18,385	15,628	6,232	3,654	5.0
1961	27,300	21,300	20,000	17,100	7,300	4,200	5.2
1962	29,430	22,870	21,200	18,220	8,230	4,650	5.7
1963	31,980	24,760	22,960	19,660	9,020	5,100	5.8
1964	33,700	27,100	24,100	21,300	9,600	5,800	5.4

Education accounts for almost half the total expenditures of local governments and is the second-highest expenditure at all levels of government budgets. In 1963, public expenditures on all levels amounted to about $25 billion (private, to nearly $7 billion); in 1964, to almost $27 billion. In 1960, direct general expenditures for education represented 15 per cent of the total expenditures of all government levels (following the 36.9 per cent spent for defense), 32.5 per cent of all state expenditures, and 44.4 per cent of the expenditures of local governments. Expenditures

FIGURE IV.7

EDUCATIONAL EXPENDITURES IN THE UNITED STATES, 1935-63

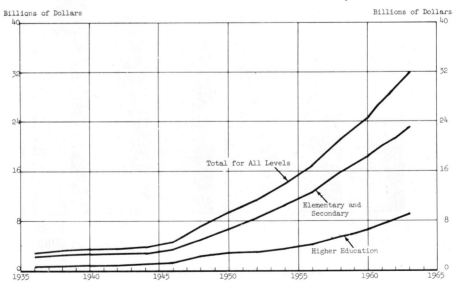

U.S. Department of Health, Education, and Welfare

TABLE IV.12

EXPENDITURE PER PUPIL IN PUBLIC ELEMENTARY
AND SECONDARY SCHOOLS, 1900-64
(In Dollars)

	Total Expenditure[a]	Current Expenditures
1900	20.2	16.7
1920	64.2	53.3
1940	105.7	88.9
1950	258.9	208.8
1960	472.2	375.4
1962	518.0	419.0
1963	538.0	433.0
1964	558.0	455.0

[a] Includes capital outlay and interest, allocated per pupil.

for education took 3.3 per cent of the gross national product in 1930 and 5.4 per cent in 1964 (see Table IV.11 and Figure IV.7).

Half or more than half of all expenditures for the public-school system goes for teachers' salaries: $1.4 billion out of $2.3 billion in 1940; $8.4 billion out of $15.6 billion in 1960. Expenditures per pupil have been increasing continuously (see Table IV.12 and Figure IV.8).

In 1964, current expenditures per pupil ranged from $273 in Mississippi

FIGURE IV.8

PUBLIC SCHOOL EXPENDITURES PER PUPIL
IN AVERAGE DAILY ATTENDANCE, 1935-63

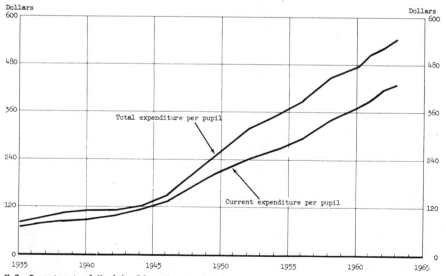

U.S. Department of Health, Education, and Welfare

and $277 in Alabama to $554 in Wyoming, $551 in Illinois, and $790 in New York. In between were Maine with $371, Iowa, with $464, and Rhode Island, with $514. In the outlying areas, the range in 1962 was from $147 in Puerto Rico to $395 in the Canal Zone.

In 1964, the salary of a classroom teacher in the public schools averaged $6,035 a year for elementary schools and $6,503 for high schools, with many variations on both levels. The annual salary of a full-time faculty member in institutions of higher education varies greatly according to rank, type of institution, type of control (public or private), and so on. The average salary for university professors in 1964 was from $12,543 to $13,426; for associate professors, from $9,460 to $9,471; salaries for assistant professors and instructors were considerably lower. Administrative officers—presidents and deans—had substantially higher salaries, ranging from $25,679 to $30,894 for presidents and $16,101 to $17,542 for deans. Corresponding salaries were lower in liberal-arts and teachers' colleges.

TABLE IV.13

ENROLLMENT IN ELEMENTARY AND SECONDARY SCHOOLS
AND PER CENT OF POPULATION ATTENDING SCHOOLS, 1870-1964

Year	Total	Public	Private	Public	Private
		(In Thousands)		(Per Cent)	
1870	6,872	6,872	...	57.0	...
1880	9,863	9,863	...	65.5	...
1890	14,479	12,723	1,757	68.6	...
1900	16,855	15,503	1,352	71.9	6.5
1910	19,372	17,814	1,558	73.5	7.0
1920	23,278	21,578	1,699	78.3	6.5
1930	28,329	25,678	2,651	81.3	8.9
1940	28,045	25,434	2,611	84.4	8.9
1950	28,492	25,111	3,380	81.6	11.2
1956	35,872	31,163	4,709	83.6	12.6
1958	39,000	33,700	5,300	83.5	13.2
1960	42,013	36,087	5,926	82.2	13.5
1962	44,256	38,252	6,003	82.5	12.9
1963	46,617	40,217	6,400	83.8	13.3
1964	47,700	41,000	6,700	84.0	13.7

21. Our Schools

Practically the entire school-age population of the United States except the chronically sick and the residents of institutions for the handicapped are enrolled in schools: kindergartens, elementary schools, and secondary schools, both public and private. It took a century to achieve universal education (see Table IV.13).

The only break in the consistent growth of enrollment occurred during 1934–38; this was due to the decline in the school-age population. With the baby boom of the postwar years, the upward trend was resumed; in the last 2 decades, universal enrollment became a reality. Until the end

FIGURE IV.9

PUBLIC AND NONPUBLIC SCHOOL ENROLLMENT
IN THE UNITED STATES, 1935-63

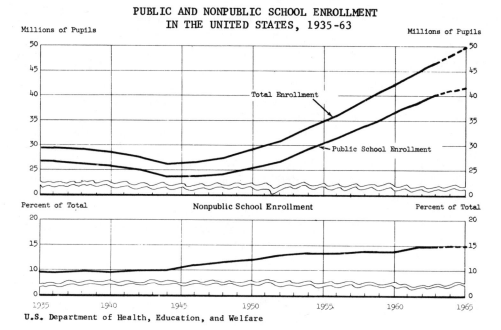

U.S. Department of Health, Education, and Welfare

FIGURE IV.10

PER CENT OF THE POPULATION 16 AND 17 YEARS OLD
ENROLLED IN SCHOOL, BY STATE, 1960

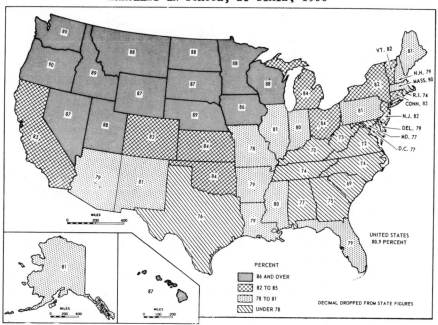

U.S. Department of Commerce, Bureau of the Census

of World War II, less than 1 child in 10 attended a private school. Since 1946, the proportion of pupils in private schools has risen and in recent years about 1 child in 7 has been attending a private school (see Figure IV.9).

In 1960, about 2 out of 3 children in the 5 to 6 age group attended kindergarten or elementary school; at ages 7 to 15, during which years attendance is compulsory in nearly every state, 95 out of 100 children were enrolled in school. More than 8 out of 10 youngsters in the 16–17 age group were enrolled in schools—nearly twice as many as half a century ago. In some states—e.g., Oregon, Washington, Nebraska, Idaho—about 9 out of 10 youngsters of that age group attended schools (see Figure IV.10). The school enrollment for that age was lowest in South Carolina, and almost as low in Kentucky, Virginia, and West Virginia.

According to the projections of school population made by the Department of Health, Education, and Welfare, enrollment will increase considerably by 1975 (see Table IV.14 and Figure IV.11).

TABLE IV.14

PROJECTION OF SCHOOL ENROLLMENT, 1964-75
(In Millions)

Year	Total	Public Schools		Private Schools	
		Kindergarten and 1-8 Grades	9-12 Grades	Kindergarten and 1-8 Grades	9-12 Grades
1964	47.8	29.7	11.2	5.5	1.4
1966	49.6	30.7	11.6	5.6	1.5
1968	51.0	31.2	12.4	5.7	1.7
1970	52.3	31.5	13.3	5.2	1.7
1975	55.3	32.7	14.7	6.0	1.9

Though data for different countries are not fully comparable because of differences in the extent of census coverage, definitions, scope of territory, academic standards, precision in processing, margin of error, and so on, they nevertheless provide a general approximation of the level of school enrollment. From continent to continent, the figures vary, from 21.3 per cent of the total population in North America inclusive of Central America and the Caribbean, and 19.9 per cent in Oceania, to 15.9 per cent in Europe as a whole, 13.1 per cent in South America, 10.5 per cent in Asia, and 7.8 per cent in Africa. Enrollment in individual countries also varies greatly from region to region.

The highest enrollment in per cent of total population is in the United States, the Netherlands, Japan, and New Zealand (28.2, 25.8, 25.2, and 24.6 per cent of the total population, respectively). At the other end of the spectrum is Saudi Arabia, with a 2.2 per cent enrollment (see Table IV.15). Though these figures, reported by UNESCO, would place Italy and Germany next to Argentina, they are meaningful only if Argentina

FIGURE IV.11

FALL ENROLLMENT IN THE UNITED STATES, 1953-75

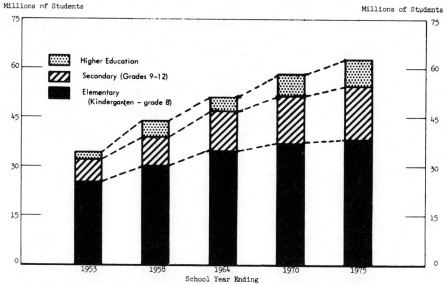

U.S. Department of Health, Education, and Welfare

is compared with a similar country, such as Brazil, or India with Pakistan, or New Zealand with the United States.

In the United States, the rate of school enrollment has traditionally been

TABLE IV.15

ESTIMATED SCHOOL ENROLLMENT, IN SELECTED COUNTRIES,[a] 1960-61

Country	Per Cent of Total Population	Country	Per Cent of Total Population
United States	28.2	Argentina	18.2
Netherlands	25.8	Sweden	17.9
Japan	25.2	West Germany	17.6
New Zealand	24.6	Italy	16.5
France	23.3	Switzerland	15.9
Australia	22.6	Spain	15.0
Poland	22.5	Turkey	13.5
Belgium	22.3	United Arab Republic	13.3
Czechoslovakia	22.3	Brazil	13.0
United Kingdom	22.0	Portugal	12.9
Israel	21.3	Indonesia	11.2
Romania	20.9	Guatemala	10.4
U.S.S.R.	20.5	India	9.8
Yugoslavia	19.1	Pakistan	7.4
Philippines	19.0	Saudi Arabia	2.2

[a] Includes all schools: preschool, elementary, secondary, vocational, teacher training schools, higher and special education.

TABLE IV.16

PER CENT OF PERSONS ENROLLED IN SCHOOLS IN THE UNITED STATES,
BY COLOR, AGE, AND SEX, 1964

Age Group (In Years)	Total		Male		Female	
	White	Nonwhite	White	Nonwhite	White	Nonwhite
5- 6	84.0	79.6	84.0	79.6	83.9	79.5
7-13	99.0	99.1	98.8	98.6	99.1	99.6
14-17	93.5	90.7	94.7	92.3	92.2	89.0
18-19	42.3	37.1	52.4	40.6	33.7	34.0
20-24	17.9	9.1	25.6	10.0	11.2	8.3
25-29	5.4	4.3	8.3	6.6	2.6	2.5
30-34	2.6	2.8	3.6	3.9	1.6	1.8
TOTAL	58.6	59.5	62.3	62.4	55.0	56.8

lower among nonwhite persons than among the white. At the beginning of this century, 3 out of 10 nonwhite youngsters of school age were enrolled, as compared with 5 or 6 out of 10 white boys and girls. The differential, however, has narrowed with each decade, particularly since 1940. Today, the difference is small at the level of elementary schooling, but increases in secondary schools and especially at college age. Of 10 children aged 5–6 years, 8 are in kindergarten; every healthy child in the 7–13 age group is enrolled in school (see Table IV.16). On the whole, the enrollment pattern of nonwhite youngsters in 1962 was only about a decade or so behind that of white children.

With improvement of transportation facilities and country roads, particularly important for rural children, and with better child health care and a generally higher standard of living, both school attendance and the length of school terms have shown an upward tendency (see Table IV.17).

School attendance varies among states and age groups, and between urban and rural areas, boys and girls, and white and nonwhite children.

TABLE IV.17

SCHOOL ATTENDANCE AND AVERAGE LENGTH OF SCHOOL TERM, 1880-1962

Year	Average Number of Days Attended Per Enrolled Pupil	Average Length School Term (In Days)
1880	81.8	130.3
1900	99.0	144.3
1910	113.0	157.5
1920	121.2	161.9
1930	143.0	172.7
1940	151.7	175.0
1950	157.9	177.9
1960	160.2	178.0
1962	162.3	179.1

THE CHICAGO PUBLIC LIBRARY

The rate of attendance was highest in 1960 in the Pacific states, with 96.7 per cent of the pupils enrolled, in contrast to 88.8 per cent in the South Atlantic states. The rate was 98.6 per cent in California, 96.4 per cent in Vermont, 85.8 per cent in Mississippi, and 85.2 per cent in Arizona.

Secondary and higher education got a comparatively slow start: at the turn of this century, only 11.4 per cent of the boys and girls aged 14–17 were enrolled in high school, and only 4 per cent of those aged 18–21 attended college. Since then, enrollment has increased rapidly; it doubled in each of the following decades and is still growing. In 1964, high-school enrollment comprised 93.5 per cent of all youngsters aged 14–17. College enrollment included 40 per cent of all persons aged 18–21 years and is expected to reach 49 per cent by 1970 (see Table IV.18).

The number of teachers in public elementary and secondary schools was 1.4 million in 1961, and 1.9 million in 1964. The latest figure (1958) for teachers in nonpublic schools was 163,000. Most teachers on these levels are women; men teachers represent about 30 per cent of the total.

In 1962, colleges had 425,000 faculty members, and men constituted about 78 per cent of the total teaching body.

Federal-state cooperation in vocational education has been carried on and has been gradually expanded by additional legislation since 1917, when the Smith-Hughes Act authorized the Federal Government to assist the states financially in developing programs in this field. Programs in agriculture, trade and industries, home economics, and technical subjects, as well as in training teachers for such programs, have been operating in all states, with expenditures shared by the Federal, state, and local governments.

In 1918, a total of 164,000 students were enrolled in vocational courses; of these, 118,000 studied trade and industries. In 1930, enrollment almost reached the million mark (982,000); in 1949, the 3-million mark was crossed, and in 1963 there were more than 4 million students in vocational classes (see Table IV.19 and Figure IV.12).

Expenditures have increased every year, from $3 million in 1918 to $55 million in 1940, $129 million in 1950, and $309 million in 1963. The share of the Federal Government has fluctuated; it was 26.7 per cent in 1918, rose to 36.3 per cent in 1940, and has since declined. In 1963, it amounted to 17.7 per cent, as compared with 36.4 per cent paid by state governments and 45.9 per cent by local governments (see Figure IV.12).

Every state has programs for vocational education. In 1963, California and Texas had the 2 largest concentrations of students in vocational courses: 454,706 and 416,561, respectively. These 2 states were followed (figures in thousands of students) by New York (245), North Carolina (174), Georgia (162), Michigan (153), Florida (152), Ohio (138), Wisconsin (133), and Washington (127).

The Vocational Education Act of 1963 provides the first major redirec-

TABLE IV.18

ENROLLMENT IN SECONDARY SCHOOLS AND INSTITUTIONS
OF HIGHER EDUCATION, 1890-1975

Year	Grades 9-12 and Postgraduate (In Thousands)		Per Cent of Population Aged 14-17 years	Higher Education (In Thousands)		Per Cent of Population Aged 18-21 years
	Public Schools	Private Schools		Public Schools	Private Schools	
1890	203	95	6.7	157		3.0
1900	519	111	11.4	91	147	4.0
1910	915	117	15.4	167	189	5.1
1920	2,200	214	32.3	315	282	8.1
1930	4,399	341	51.4	533	568	12.4
1940	6,635	488	73.3	797	698	15.7
1950	5,758	695	76.8	1,355	1,304	25.5
1960	8,531	1,068	86.1	1,832	1,384	37.5
1962	9,617	1,152	89.7	2,597	1,610	38.9
1964	11,200	1,400	93.5	3,084	1,726	40.4
Projections[a]						
1966	11,600	1,500	-	3,380[b]	1,840[b]	43.2
1968	12,400	1,700	-	-	-	...
1970	13,300	1,700	95.6	4,764	2,145	48.9
1975	14,700	1,900	99.5	6,206	2,410	...

[a] Prepared by the U.S. Department of Health, Education and Welfare under the assumption that recent enrollment trends will continue to 1975 and that the distribution between public and private schools will remain constant at current levels. Population projections used are from the Bureau of the Census.

[b] 1965.

TABLE IV.19

ENROLLMENT IN VOCATIONAL SCHOOLS BY TYPE OF PROGRAM, 1918-63
(In Thousands)

	1918	1930	1940	1950	1960	1962	1963
Agriculture	15	188	584	765	796	823	828
Home economics	31	175	819	1,430	1,588	1,725	1,840
Trade and industry	118	619	758	805	938	1,009	1,002
Distribution and marketing	-	-	129	365	304	322	310
Practical nursing	-	-	-	-	40	49	54
Technical education	-	-	-	-	101	149	185
TOTAL	164	982	2,291	3,365	3,768	4,077	4,217

FIGURE IV.12

ENROLLMENT IN VOCATIONAL EDUCATION,
BY TYPE OF PROGRAM, AND EXPENDITURES BY LEVEL OF GOVERNMENT, 1935-63

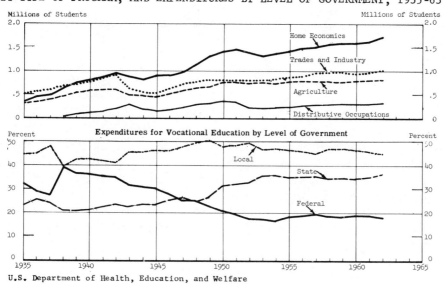

U.S. Department of Health, Education, and Welfare

tion of vocational education since its inception. It not only authorizes much larger funds for development of the program, but also broadens it to include business and office occupations not covered under previous legislation, provides for an experimental 4-year program for residential vocational schools and payments for student-work programs. The act permits greater flexibility in the use of Federal funds and provides funds for the construction of area school facilities on a 50–50 basis, with state participation. It also requires periodic re-evaluation of the program in the light of current manpower needs and job opportunities.

V. *America at Work*

22. Who Is in the Labor Force?—23. Who Is Not in the Labor
Force?—24. How Many Are Employed?—25. Who Is Unemployed?—26. Mobility of Labor— 27. The Future of Manpower

22. *Who Is in the Labor Force?*

The 1940 Census introduced a new concept, the "labor force"; prior
censuses had reported "gainful workers," that is, persons who declared that
they belonged to a gainful occupation, whether they were working at the
time of the count or were seeking work. In contrast, the "labor force" is
defined on the basis of activity during the reference week (the last week
before census-taking) and comprises all persons aged 14 years and over
who were employed, unemployed (that is, were without work but were
seeking it, or not seeking it because of a special reason such as sickness),
or were in the armed forces. All these together represent the nation's total
labor force; without the armed forces, they represent the civilian labor
force.

Certain categories previously counted among "gainful workers," such as
the retired, the permanently disabled, or inmates of institutions, are now
excluded from the labor force. On the other hand, it includes persons
seeking work without previous work experience, namely, new workers,
who were not counted before 1940. It also includes unpaid family members who work 15 hours or more in a family business or on a family farm,
and the students who have a part-time job while attending school.

Because of differences in the definitions, the data on the labor force in
the Censuses of 1940, 1950, and 1960 are not completely comparable with
the statistics for gainful workers. Nevertheless, the Bureau of the Census
believes that the old series represent a generally reliable measure of long-
term trends, and it has adjusted them so as to make them usable for comparison with the figures of the last 3 Censuses.

TABLE V.1

TOTAL AND CIVILIAN LABOR FORCE, 1929-65

| Year | Total Labor Force | | Civilian Labor Force |
	Number (In Thousands)	Per Cent of Population[a]	Number (In Thousands)
1929	49,440	56.2	49,180
1933	51,840	55.8	51,590
1939	55,600	55.4	55,230
1943	64,560	61.6	55,540
1949	63,721	57.4	62.105
1953	67,362	57.8	63,815
1959	71,946	57.6	69,394
1960	73,126	58.3	70,612
1963	75,712	57.3	72,975
1964	76,971	57.4	74,233
1965	78,357	57.5	75,635

[a]Aged 14 years and over (see Figure V.1).

FIGURE V.1

STATUS OF THE LABOR FORCE, 1947-64
(Monthly Data. Seasonally Adjusted)

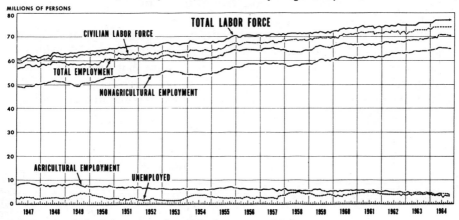

U.S. Bureau of the Budget--Data from U.S. Department of Labor

The labor force of this country* increased from 49.4 million in 1929 to 64.7 million in 1950, 77.0 million in 1964, and 79.6 million in 1966 (July) (see Table V.1 and Figure V.1).

The 2 major factors in the growth of the nation's labor force have been the increase in the population of working age and the growing participation of women in work outside the home. The population aged 14 years

* Data on the labor force are obtained by a sample survey of households, made by the Bureau of the Census for the Bureau of Labor Statistics (BLS), from about 35,000 households in 357 areas throughout the country. Data refer to the activity or status of surveyed persons for the week nearest the 15th day of the month.

TABLE V.2

CIVILIAN LABOR FORCE IN THE UNITED STATES,
BY SEX AND COLOR, 1890-1964

Year	Millions of Persons Aged 14 Years and Over				Per Cent of Population			
	Male		Female		Male		Female	
	White	Nonwhite	White	Nonwhite	White	Nonwhite	White	Nonwhite
1890	16.1	2.0	2.8	0.9	84.0	86.6	15.8	37.7
1900	20.1	2.6	3.8	1.2	85.4	88.5	17.3	41.2
1920	28.8	3.2	6.7	1.5	84.1	87.5	20.7	40.6
1930	33.3	3.7	8.6	1.8	81.7	86.1	21.8	40.5
1940	36.5	3.8	11.2	1.8	79.7	80.0	24.5	37.3
1950	39.1	4.1	14.4	2.1	79.2	76.6	28.1	37.1
1960	42.3	4.7	20.5	3.1	80.5	79.4	35.5	46.3
1962	42.6	4.7	21.2	3.2	78.6	76.4	35.6	45.6
1963	43.1	4.8	21.8	3.3	78.1	75.8	35.9	45.6
1964	43.5	4.9	22.4	3.4	76.0	74.2	36.7	46.6

and over tripled between 1890 and 1960, increasing from about 42 million in 1890 to 101 million in 1940 and 134 million in 1964. But whereas the male labor force about tripled during that period, from 18 to 48 million, the female labor force expanded more than 6 times, from 3.7 to 25.8 million (see Table V.2).

In recent years, participation of males in the labor force—that is, the percentage of all persons in a given age group who are in the labor force—has increased substantially in the 20–64 age group, but many boys under 20 and men of 65 years and over either have not entered the ranks of the labor force or have withdrawn—the former, by remaining in school longer;

TABLE V.3

CIVILIAN LABOR FORCE PARTICIPATION
RATES BY AGE, SEX, AND COLOR, 1948-64

Age in Years, and Color	Male						Female					
	1948	1953	1958	1960	1962	1964	1948	1953	1958	1960	1962	1964
White												
14-19	50.7	46.4	43.5	43.6	40.8	41.0	32.8	30.5	29.7	30.7	29.7	29.0
20-24	84.4	87.4	86.7	87.8	86.5	85.7	45.1	44.1	46.1	45.7	47.1	48.8
25-34	96.0	97.5	97.2	97.7	97.4	97.5	31.3	31.7	33.6	34.1	34.1	35.0
35-44	98.0	97.9	98.0	97.9	97.9	97.6	35.1	38.8	41.4	41.5	42.2	43.3
45-54	95.9	96.4	96.6	96.1	96.0	96.1	33.3	38.7	46.5	48.6	48.9	50.2
55-64	89.6	87.7	88.2	87.2	86.7	86.1	23.3	28.5	34.5	36.2	38.0	39.4
65 and over	46.5	41.3	35.7	33.3	30.6	27.9	8.6	9.4	10.1	10.6	9.8	9.9
Nonwhite												
14-19	58.3	50.3	44.0	45.0	38.4	37.7	30.5	25.4	24.8	25.8	24.0	22.8
20-24	85.6	92.3	88.7	90.4	89.3	89.4	47.1	45.1	48.3	48.8	48.6	53.6
25-34	95.3	96.7	96.3	96.2	95.3	95.9	50.6	48.1	50.8	49.7	52.0	52.8
35-44	97.2	97.3	96.4	95.5	94.5	94.4	53.3	54.9	60.8	59.8	59.7	58.4
45-54	94.7	93.9	93.9	92.3	92.2	91.6	51.1	51.0	59.8	60.5	60.5	62.3
55-64	88.6	86.7	83.3	82.5	81.5	80.5	37.6	35.9	42.8	47.3	46.1	48.4
65 and over	50.3	41.1	34.5	31.2	27.2	29.6	17.5	11.4	13.3	12.8	12.2	12.7

the latter, by retiring earlier. Though the number of men aged 65 years and over in 1964 was considerably larger than in 1950 (7.8 million as against 5.8 million), there were fewer men in these age groups in the labor force in 1964 than in 1950 (2.1 million as compared with 2.5 million).

The participation rate declined considerably more among nonwhite workers than among white. Thus while the white males nearly maintained their participation rate in the age groups of 35–44 and 45–54 throughout 1948–64, there was a gradual but noticeable decline among nonwhites. The participation rate for both white and nonwhite women showed a decline in the 14–19 age group (a sharper decline for the nonwhite than white girls), but increased for higher age groups (see Table V.3).

Between 1950 and 1960, the population aged 14 years and over increased

FIGURE V.2.A

WOMEN IN THE LABOR FORCE IN THE UNITED STATES,
1920-60, AND PROJECTION FOR 1970
(Per Cent of All Workers)

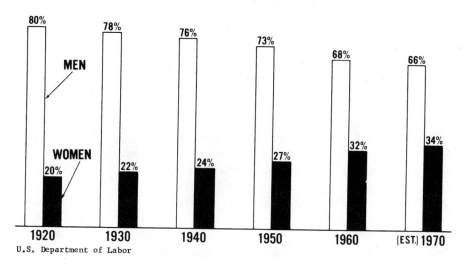

U.S. Department of Labor

by more than approximately 14 million, and the labor force, by about 7.5 million (2.6 million men and 4.9 million women). Thus women, who represented only one-third of all workers, accounted for nearly two-thirds of the increase in the labor force. It is expected that their share in the labor force will slightly increase by 1970 (see Figure V.2A). These figures reflect the growing tendency among married women to enter the labor market once their children reach school age, and, in particular, college age. Women between the ages of 35 and 44 and especially those aged 45 years and over have entered the labor force in ever-increasing numbers. Today, approximately 3 out of 5 women workers are married, and among married women, 1 in 3 is working (see Figure V.2B). Though many mar-

FIGURE V.2.B

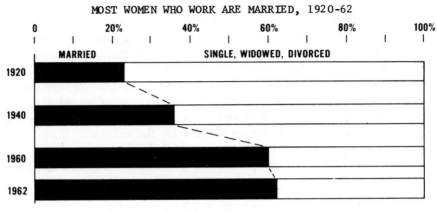

MOST WOMEN WHO WORK ARE MARRIED, 1920-62

U.S. Department of Labor

ried women have part-time jobs, nearly three-fourths of all working women are full-time workers.

Almost the entire increase in women's employment during the last decade has been among married women; there has been relatively little change in the number of employed single, widowed, and divorced women.

In 1964, the rate of participation in the labor force was 78 per cent for white males and 76 per cent for nonwhite males. The situation for women was the reverse: 36.4 and 46 per cent, respectively. This relation persisted in urban, rural nonfarm, and rural farm areas (see Table V.4).

Nonwhite women have always participated in the labor force in greater proportion than white women. In 1964, 1 out of 3 white women was in the labor force, as compared with almost 2 out of 3 nonwhite women. Proportionately, almost as many nonwhite as white women had full-time year-round jobs: 32 and 38 per cent, respectively.

TABLE V.4

RATE OF PARTICIPATION IN THE LABOR FORCE, BY SEX, RACE, AND TYPE OF AREA, 1964

| | White | | Nonwhite | |
	Men	Women	Men	Women
Urban	79.2	36.2	75.0	45.8
Rural nonfarm	74.3	28.5	62.3	31.5
Rural farm	78.9	22.7	70.6	24.4

23. *Who Is Not in the Labor Force?*

In 1940, 44.2 million persons aged 14 years and over of the U.S. non-institutionalized civilian population were reported as not being part of the labor force. With the growth of the population, their number increased to 46.2 million in 1950, 52.2 million in 1960, and 57.9 million in 1965. In the period 1960–64, nearly 2 out of 3 of these were women keeping house; about 1 out of 5 was in school. The remainder comprised "others": persons unable to work because of chronic physical or mental illness or old age, or voluntarily idle persons; occasional workers not reported as unemployed;

FIGURE V.3

WHO IS IN THE LABOR FORCE AND
WHO IS NOT IN THE LABOR FORCE, 1961

Annual Average, 1961

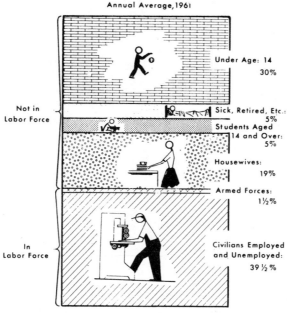

U.S. Department of Labor, Bureau of Labor Statistics

family members doing only incidental work less than 15 hours a week; and so on (see Figure V.3).

In the postwar period, the total proportion of the population aged 14 years and over not in the labor force has ranged from 41 to 43 per cent. The 2 important trends in that part of the U.S. population not at work are the growing numbers of young and old persons and the continuing decrease of nonworking women. Longer schooling and the steady shift of young people from farm to city, where work by youngsters is less common than in rural areas, account for their growing nonparticipation in the labor force. Liberalized retirement provisions of the social security system and

TABLE V.5

PERSONS NOT IN THE LABOR FORCE, BY SEX,
ANNUAL AVERAGES, 1957-64

Year	Number (In Millions)			Per Cent		
	Total	Males	Females	Total	Males	Females
1957						
Keeping house	33.9	0.1	33.8	68.2	0.9	85.6
In school	7.0	3.5	3.5	14.1	34.3	8.9
Unable to work	1.8	1.1	0.8	3.6	10.8	2.0
Other	7.0	5.5	1.4	14.0	54.0	3.5
Total	49.7	10.2	39.5	100.0	100.0	100.0
1960						
Keeping house	34.5	0.1	34.5	66.1	0.9	84.8
In school	8.2	4.1	4.1	15.7	35.6	10.1
Unable to work	1.8	1.1	0.7	3.4	9.6	1.7
Other	7.8	6.3	1.5	14.8	53.9	3.4
Total	52.2	11.5	40.7	100.0	100.0	100.0
1962						
Keeping house	35.3	0.1	35.2	63.7	0.8	83.2
In school	9.6	4.8	4.7	17.3	36.6	11.1
Unable to work	1.8	1.1	0.7	3.2	8.4	1.7
Other	8.7	7.0	1.7	15.7	53.4	4.0
Total	55.4	13.1	42.3	100.0	100.0	100.0
1963						
Keeping house	35.3	0.1	35.2	62.6	0.7	82.2
In school	10.1	5.1	5.0	17.9	37.5	11.7
Unable to work	1.8	1.1	0.7	3.2	8.1	1.6
Other	9.2	7.3	1.9	16.3	53.7	4.4
Total	56.4	13.6	42.8	100.0	100.0	100.0
1964						
Keeping house	35.5	0.1	35.3	62.1	0.7	81.7
In school	10.5	5.2	5.3	18.4	37.4	12.3
Other	11.2	8.6	2.6	19.6	61.9	6.0
Total	57.2	13.9	43.2	100.0	100.0	100.0

various pension plans in many industries have encouraged the earlier withdrawal of old workers from the labor force. (For growing entrance of women into the labor force, see Sec. 22.)

Men not in the labor force are divided into 2 major groups—those in school (37 per cent) and "others" (about 62 per cent). In contrast, only 6 per cent of women not in the labor force are in the 2 categories—"unable to work" and "others" (see Table V.5). More than 80 per cent of the women not in the labor force are working in their own households. While about the same number of girls as boys attend school (5.2 and 5.3 million, respectively) and thus are not in the labor force, schoolgirls represent only about 12 per cent of all nonworking females.

The age distribution of men and women not in the labor force also differs greatly. Among the men, the 2 greatest concentration points are in

TABLE V.6

PERSONS NOT IN THE LABOR FORCE, BY AGE AND SEX
ANNUAL AVERAGE, 1963

Sex and Age (in Years)	Number (In Thousands)				
	Total	Keeping House	In School	Unable to Work	Other
Male	13,590	136	5,079	1,119	7,258
14-15	2,798	8	2,273	4	513
16-17	1,842	5	1,518	3	315
18-19	748	1	617	3	127
20-24	727	3	549	28	146
25-34	290	3	98	60	130
35-44	289	8	18	96	167
45-54	439	12	4	160	262
55-64	1,066	19	1	235	811
65 and over	5,391	77	1	527	4,786
Female	42,822	35,185	5,021	701	1,914
14-15	3,031	105	2,350	2	574
16-17	2,289	264	1,663	7	355
18-19	1,355	603	620	7	125
20-24	3,265	2,825	319	24	97
25-34	7,062	6,929	30	31	70
35-44	6,872	6,724	29	36	82
45-54	5,368	5,236	10	44	79
55-64	5,067	4,885	1	76	105
65 and over	8,514	7,613	2	473	426

the age groups 14–17 and 65 and over, followed by somewhat lesser concentrations in the 16–17 and the 55–64 groups. Of the 13.9 million males not in the labor force in 1964, 4.8 million were youngsters and almost 5.5 million were older men, that is, 35 and almost 40 per cent, respectively. The remainder are in age groups ranging from 18–19 years to 60–64 years (see Table V.6 for 1963 detailed data).

Of the 43.8 million women not in the labor force in 1964, the greatest single concentration is likewise in the age group 65 years and over (8.6 million); otherwise, the strongest concentration is in the 25–44 age group (13.9 million). The remainder are distributed among other age groups.

The line between participation and nonparticipation in the labor force is not very rigid. During any year, individuals shift from one status to another, from work to retirement and vice versa, from occasional unreported work to a part-time job or even permanent work. On the average, however, such shifts cancel each other out, without affecting the over-all figures.

24. How Many Are Employed?

In 1929, the nation had a civilian labor force of 49.2 million; of these, 47.6 million were employed. Then the number of employed persons began to decline, until 1933, when it reached its lowest point—38.8 million were employed of a labor force of 51.6 million. Thereafter, the number of employed persons fluctuated from year to year, but the trend was upward. In 1943, under the impact of war, 54.5 million persons were employed; the 60-million mark promised by President Franklin D. Roosevelt was reached in 1951, and in mid-1964, for the first time, more than 70 million persons held jobs. All in all, 12 million persons were added to the employment rolls between 1947 and 1964 (see Figure V.1). However, part-time work has accounted for a good part of the increase.

In 1964, more than 42 million male and 23.3 million female workers were employed in nonagricultural industries, and 4.8 million in agriculture; the corresponding figures for the end of 1965 are: 43.6, 25.1 and 4.1. The nonagricultural sector of the economy has increasingly provided employment: the number of its workers amounted to 37.2 million in 1929, 52.5

TABLE V.7

EMPLOYED PERSONS BY TYPE OF INDUSTRY AND CLASS
OF WORKER, 1947-65, ANNUAL AVERAGES

Type of Industry and Class of Worker	Persons Aged 14 Years and Over (in Thousands)								
	1947	1950	1958	1959	1960	1961	1962	1963	1965
Agriculture	8,266	7,507	5,844	5,836	5,723	5,463	5,190	4,946	4,585
Wage and salary workers	1,677	1,733	1,671	1,689	1,866	1,733	1,666	1,676	1,492
Self-employed	4,973	4,346	3,087	3,027	2,802	2,744	2,619	2,437	2,307
Unpaid family workers	1,616	1,427	1,086	1,121	1,054	985	905	834	786
Nonagricultural industries	49,761	52,450	58,122	59,745	60,958	61,333	62,657	63,863	67,594
Wage and salary workers	43,290	45,977	51,332	52,850	53,976	54,284	55,762	57,081	60,765
Self-employed	6,045	6,069	6,185	6,298	6,367	6,388	6,271	6,195	6,213
Unpaid family workers	427	404	605	597	615	662	623	587	616
TOTAL EMPLOYMENT	58,027	59,957	63,966	65,581	66,681	66,796	67,846	68,809	72,179

million in 1950, 60.0 million in 1960, and nearly 68 million in 1965. In contrast, agriculture has offered work to fewer and fewer people: 10.5 million in 1929, 7.5 million in 1950, 5.7 million in 1960, and 4.6 million in 1965 (see Table V.7 and Figure V.1). The entire loss in agricultural employment occurred among farmers and unpaid family workers. The number of wage and salary earners in agriculture, 1.6–1.7 million, experienced only slight fluctuations from year to year.

In the growing nonfarm sector of the economy, not all branches expanded equally. There were even some losers: mining now engages some 300,000 fewer workers than in 1947; transportation and public utilities have 135,000 fewer workers on their payrolls. In contrast, the ranks of employees in trade have grown by one-third, from more than 9.0 million to 12.6 million; in services, from 5.1 million to 8.9 million; in government, from 5.5 million to 10.0 million. The greater part of the last increase has been in state and local government, where the number of employees has more than doubled; from 3.6 million to 7.7 million (see Table V.8). The Federal Government actually added only about 0.5 million employees in the course of these 18 years.

The most striking change in employment since World War II is that for the first time, services, defined broadly (trade, transportation and public utilities, finance, teaching, government, etc.), have come to employ more people than production of goods (agriculture, mining, manufacturing, construction). The United States has become unique among the countries

TABLE V.8

EMPLOYEES ON NONAGRICULTURAL PAYROLLS, BY INDUSTRY[a]
1939-65

Industry Division	Annual Averages (In Thousands)						
	1939	1947	1950	1960	1963	1964	1965
Mining	854	955	901	712	635	633	628
Contract construction	1,150	1,982	2,333	2,885	2,983	3,056	3,211
Manufacturing	10,278	15,545	15,241	16,796	17,005	17,259	17,984
Transportation and public utilities	2,936	4,166	4,034	4,004	3,914	3,947	4,031
Wholesale trade	1,684	2,361	2,518	3,004	3,119	3,173	3,263
Retail trade	4,742	6,595	6,868	8,388	8,685	8,959	9,322
Finance, insurance, real estate	1,462	1,754	1,919	2,669	2,873	2,964	3,043
Service and miscellaneous	3,517	5,050	5,382	7,392	8,230	8,569	8,903
Government:							
Federal	905	1,892	1,928	2,270	2,358	2,348	2,379
State and local	3,090	3,582	4,098	6,250	6,841	7,248	7,667
TOTAL	30,618	43,881	45,222	54,370	56,643	58,156	60,432

[a]Payroll data of nonagricultural establishments are not comparable with the monthly data of the BLS "household" survey: they exclude unpaid family workers, domestic service in private homes, proprietors and other self-employed persons, all of whom are covered by the household survey. They also exclude persons on unpaid leave; on the other hand, the "payroll" counts a person employed by two or more establishments at each place of employment, while the household survey counts him only once, according to his single major activity.

of the world in that it needs fewer people to produce food, clothing, houses, automobiles, and all other goods than are engaged in servicing the nation in trade, transportation of goods and people, communications, teaching, managing real estate and money, caring for people in hospitals and homes, and performing endless other tasks, large and small (see Figure V.4).

The shift from production industries to services has been accompanied by a shift from blue-collar workers to white-collar workers (see Figure V.5). The 1960 census was the first in which white-collar workers outnum-

FIGURE V.4

EMPLOYMENT IN GOODS-PRODUCING INDUSTRIES
AND SERVICE INDUSTRIES, 1919-63

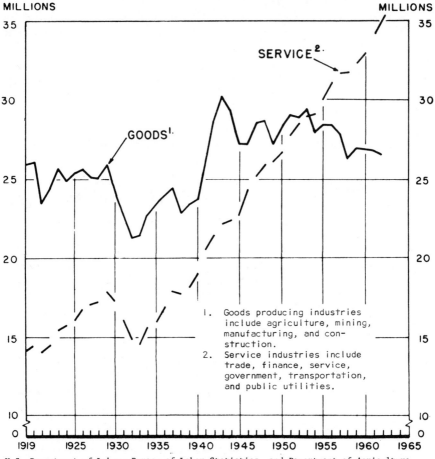

U.S. Department of Labor, Bureau of Labor Statistics, and Department of Agriculture

The figure caption notes within the chart read:

1. Goods producing industries include agriculture, mining, manufacturing, and construction.
2. Service industries include trade, finance, service, government, transportation, and public utilities.

bered manual workers: 43 per cent of employed persons, as against 36 per cent. Also, within each of these groups, the occupations requiring the most education and training—professional and technical—have increased more rapidly than others. Among blue-collar workers, those in skilled jobs have accounted for almost all the increase in employment, while employment in unskilled work has declined. The number of all blue-collar workers—craftsmen, foremen, operatives, laborers (except mine and farm)—increased only slightly between 1947 and 1965, from 23.6 million to 26.5 million. During those years, the number of white-collar workers rose from 20.2 million to 32.1 million; that of service workers outside private households (nurses, hospital attendants, barbers, beauty operators, janitors, etc.), from 4.3 million to 7.1 million.

FIGURE V.5

TRENDS IN EMPLOYMENT FOR
MAJOR OCCUPATION GROUPS, 1947-61

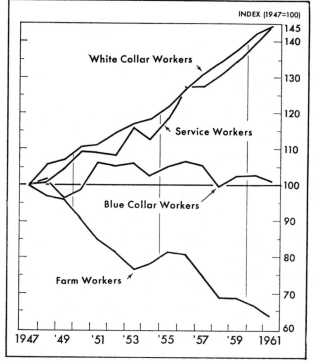

U.S. Department of Labor

Even in manufacturing, the nonproduction workers—executives, sales personnel, office workers, engineers and scientists, administrative personnel—have grown in number, while the number of production workers has slightly fallen (see Table V.9).

Individual branches of manufacturing differ greatly in this respect. More than 1 person out of 5 employed in the production of aircraft and parts was in the professional category, in contrast to only 1 in 100 among textile or apparel workers. In manufacturing as a whole, professionals constituted about 1 worker out of every 13.

Other important changes in employment have arisen from shifts in the location of industries—from east to west and south. The Pacific and the South Atlantic states have been the most rapidly growing areas. Between 1947 and 1964, employment increased in the Pacific states from 4.2 million to 7.3 million (74 per cent); in the Mountain states, from 1.2 to 2.1 million (75 per cent); in the South Atlantic states, from 5.3 to 8.0 million (51 per cent), whereas in the West North Central region, employment rose from 3.4 to 4.4 million (30 per cent); in New England, by 12 per

TABLE V.9

PRODUCTION AND NONPRODUCTION WORKERS
IN MANUFACTURING, 1947-64

Year	Number (In Thousands)		Per Cent of Total	
	Production Workers	Nonproduction Workers	Production Workers	Nonproduction Workers
1947	12,990	2,555	83.6	16.4
1950	12,523	2,718	82.2	17.8
1955	13,288	3,594	78.7	21.3
1960	12,586	4,210	74.9	25.1
1961	12,083	4,243	74.0	26.0
1962	12,488	4,365	74.1	25.9
1963	12,555	4,440	73.9	26.1
1964	12,769	4,490	74.0	26.0

cent, and in the Middle Atlantic states by only 9 per cent. The Federal Government's large-scale defense and space programs in the Western and South Atlantic states are largely responsible for the rapid rise in employment in those areas (see Table V.10).

Some industries employ comparatively few women; some hire nonwhite workers, others do not; in some occupations, mostly in service-type jobs, there is an above-average concentration of young or old workers, as in retail trade, the entertainment industries, hotels, real estate, and so on. Construction, mining, steel, and other metal industries employ very few women compared with the food and textile industries, finance, teaching, etc. Thus while women constitute 26 per cent of all employed persons in manufacturing, they account for only 2 per cent in mining, 5 per cent in construction, 6 per cent in primary-metal industries, and 7 per cent in the

TABLE V.10

EMPLOYEES IN NONAGRICULTURAL ESTABLISHMENTS,
BY GEOGRAPHIC DIVISION, ANNUAL AVERAGES, 1947-64[a]

Geographic Division	Number (In Thousands)						
	1947	1950	1960	1961	1962	1963	1964
New England	3,333	3,345	3,707	3,727	3,799	3,814	3,835
Middle Atlantic	10,813	10,876	11,914	11,829	12,051	12,073	12,162
East North Central	10,066	10,368	11,639	11,361	11,656	11,859	12,076
West North Central	3,414	3,608	4,197	4,190	4,275	4,340	4,409
South Atlantic	5,269	5,564	7,213	7,277	7,557	7,814	8,035
East South Central	2,148	2,247	2,759	2,764	2,858	2,947	3,017
West South Central	3,059	3,333	4,270	4,287	4,418	4,526	4,623
Mountain	1,170	1,276	1,873	1,927	2,004	2,064	2,098
Pacific	4,171	4,331	6,463	6,575	6,857	7,066	7,263
United States	43,443	45,222	54,203	53,989	55,515	56,643	58,188

[a]National totals differ from the sum of regional figures because methods of computation vary slightly within the areas.

lumber industry, all of which involve hard physical labor and health haz-ards. On the other hand, women account for 34 per cent of the persons employed in the instruments industry and related-products industries; 45 per cent in tobacco manufacture; 50 per cent in finance, insurance, and real estate; and 78 per cent in apparel and related-products industries.

Nonwhite persons, almost exclusively Negroes, are employed in agricul-ture and many major industries, but in all of these they are concentrated in jobs requiring physical strength. Many are employed in road-making, building construction, and personal services. In agriculture, nonwhite males account for 12 per cent of total employment; in logging, for more than 28 per cent; in mill work, for 18–19 per cent; in hotels and lodging places, for 40 per cent.

The most common occupation of the nonwhite women is domestic service (52 per cent of the total employed in that industry), hotels and lodging homes (20 per cent), agriculture (21 per cent), cleaning (29 per cent), teaching and government service (12 per cent). Their proportion in manufacturing is very small, ranging from 1 to 8 per cent.

25. Who Is Unemployed?

Persons who are not working but are seeking work are counted as un-employed. This concept of unemployment includes not only workers who have lost their jobs but also those who have quit their jobs to look for other employment, new entrants into the labor market without previous work experience, persons whose job-seeking has been interrupted by temporary illness, and persons who would be looking for work if they believed that jobs were available in their occupations or in their communi-ties.*

There are 2 basic sources of unemployment statistics in this country— the Current Population Survey, which covers about 35,000 households on the employment status of persons aged 14 and over, and data compiled by the unemployment-insurance offices on unemployed workers receiving unemployment benefits. The Survey data are much more inclusive, because the unemployment insurance claims exclude workers who have exhausted their benefit rights, new workers who have not yet established eligibility for unemployment insurance, and those who work in establishments not covered by unemployment insurance, such as agricultural workers, state and local government employees, occasional domestic servants, unpaid family workers, the self-employed, and persons who work for nonprofit organizations. On the other hand, if the Current Population Survey were to enumerate all unemployed persons rather than those in a selected 35,000 households, its data might differ from those obtained by their

---

* Statistics of most other countries do not count some of these groups (new workers, housewives seeking temporary work, young people who work during out-of-school time) as unemployed.

TABLE V.11

AVERAGE NUMBER OF UNEMPLOYED AND
UNEMPLOYMENT RATES, 1900-1965

Year	Average Number (in Thousands)	Per Cent of Civilian Labor Force	Year	Average Number (in Thousands)	Per Cent of Civilian Labor Force
1900	1,420	5.0	1934	11,340	21.7
1901	710	2.4	1935	10,610	20.1
1902	800	2.7	1936	9,030	16.9
1903	800	2.6	1937	7,700.	14.3
1904	1,490	4.8	1938	10,390	19.0
1905	1,000	3.1	1939	9,480	17.2
1906	280	0.8	1940	8,120	14.6
1907	600	1.8	1941	5,560	9.9
1908	2,960	8.5	1942	2,660	4.7
1909	1,870	5.2	1943	1,070	1.9
1910	2,150	5.9	1944	670	1.2
1911	2,290	6.2	1945	1,040	1.9
1912	1,960	5.2	1946	2,270	3.9
1913	1,680	4.4	1947	2,142	3.6
1914	3,110	8.0	1948	2,064	3.4
1915	3,840	9.7	1949	3,395	5.5
1916	1,920	4.8	1950	3,142	5.0
1917	1,920	4.8	1951	1,879	3.0
1918	560	1.4	1952	1,673	2.7
1919	950	2.3	1953	1,602	2.5
1920	1,670	4.0	1954	3,230	5.6
1921	5,010	11.9	1955	2,654	4.0
1922	3,220	7.6	1956	2,551	3.8
1923	1,380	3.2	1957	2,936	4.3
1924	2,440	5.5	1958	4,681	6.8
1925	1,800	4.0	1959	3,813	5.5
1926	880	1.9	1960	3,931	5.6
1927	1,890	4.1	1961	4,806	6.7
1928	2,080	4.4	1962	4,007	5.6
1929	1,550	3.2	1963	4,166	5.7
1930	4,340	8.7	1964	3,876	5.2
1931	8,020	15.9	1965	3,456	4.6
1932	12,060	23.6			
1933	12,830	24.9			

sampling method; the margin of error between these 2 procedures, however, is believed to be small and inconsequential.

Unemployment is a familiar phenomenon in the economic life of any industrially advanced country, and its fluctuations reflect a direct correlation with the pulse of the economy. In the United States, 1 worker out of 4 was jobless in 1933, but only 1 in 100 in 1944, and 1 in 22–25 in 1965 (see Table V.11).

Unemployment, however, results also from many factors other than general deterioration of economic conditions—seasonal fluctuations in some industries and services, such as construction, retail trade, government; sickness; labor turnover; mobility of the population in general;

structural changes in the country's economy; automation; and so on. Not all unemployment is avoidable, and not all is detrimental. When a worker loses a few weeks of work in successful search for more suitable employment, the loss benefits him and the economy as a whole.

Three groups in the labor force are hit particularly hard by unemployment.

Young people between the ages of 14 and 25 lose jobs more easily than adult workers: they enter the labor market without work experience, frequently change in search for better jobs, and, having no seniority, are dismissed before older workers. Today the situation is aggravated by the fact that the unskilled and semiskilled jobs that ordinarily provide the first opportunities for young entrants are increasingly scarce; yet with the greater spread and longer duration of unemployment in general, there is greater competition for such jobs. As a result, 1 out of 7 boys or girls in the 14–19 age group and 1 out of 5 in the 16–17 age group are unemployed, as compared to 1 out of 50 for men in the 35–44 group and 1 out of 25 women in that age group.

Mature workers have their special unemployment problems. Though normally protected by seniority rights in case of layoffs, they find it much more difficult than young workers to obtain employment once they have lost their jobs: they are not as willing to move to other communities, away from their homes and friends; they are less adaptable to new work requirements and may find that their skills have become obsolete; they have to face age discrimination on the part of the prospective employer, in part because they may affect his pension costs adversely. Thus they swell the group of long-term unemployed. In 1965, about 1 out of 4 unemployed men had been unemployed 15 weeks or longer; this ratio was as low as 1 out of 10 for teenagers, but as high as 2 out of 5 for men 45 years and over.

Nonwhite workers are the hardest hit by unemployment because of 2

TABLE V.12

UMEMPLOYMENT RATES BY COLOR AND SEX, 1948-64[a]

Color and Sex	1948	1950	1952	1954	1956	1958	1960	1962	1963	1964
White										
Male	3.1	4.5	2.2	4.4	3.1	6.1	4.8	4.6	4.7	4.2
Female	3.4	4.9	2.9	4.9	3.8	6.2	5.3	5.5	5.8	5.5
Both sexes	3.2	4.6	2.4	4.5	3.3	6.1	5.0	4.9	5.1	4.6
Nonwhite										
Male	5.1	8.9	4.5	9.2	7.3	13.7	10.7	11.0	10.6	9.1
Female	5.2	7.8	4.8	8.2	8.0	10.8	9.5	11.1	11.3	10.8
Both sexes	5.2	8.5	4.6	8.9	7.5	12.6	10.2	11.0	10.9	9.8

[a]Persons aged 14 years and over.

FIGURE V.6

UNEMPLOYMENT RATES FOR WHITE
AND NONWHITE WORKERS, 1948-64

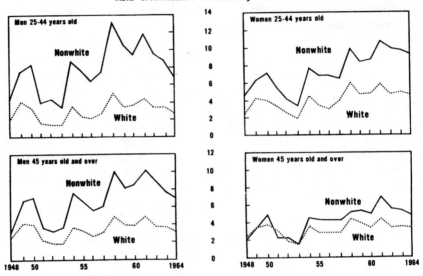

U.S. Department of Labor, Bureau of Labor Statistics

additional disadvantages—race discrimination and their generally lower educational attainment. In 1964, unemployment among nonwhite workers, of whom Negroes represent some 90 per cent, was more than double that of white workers: 9.8 per cent, as compared with 4.6 per cent (see Table V.12 and Figure V.6). The high unemployment rate among nonwhite workers also depends to some extent on the fact that they are concentrated in the occupations with the highest unemployment rates, such as farm work and semiskilled production jobs. Even within these occupations, they often perform the lowest-paid unskilled work. Moreover, they spend more time looking for work between jobs than white workers and are subject to more frequent periods of unemployment.

The difference in the proportion of white and nonwhite workers with year-round full-time jobs has been appreciable: only half the nonwhite men worked steadily at full-time jobs during 1961, as compared with two-thirds of the white. This difference has been recorded since the late 1940's, when such data first became available. However, recent years have witnessed a drastic change in this situation. The uninterrupted expansion of the national economy, combined with deliberate efforts of government and private employers have almost closed this gap. In 1965, 91.4 per cent of white male workers and 88.3 per cent of nonwhite males in nonagricultural industries were on full-time schedules; the respective figures for women were 74.9 and 70.5 per cent.

Lack of adequate education affects all workers, white and nonwhite. The higher the required skill and educational qualifications, the lower the rate of unemployment, and in some professional and technical occupations there is even a shortage of labor. Unemployment rates are very low, between 1 and 2 per cent, among professional and technical workers and among managers and officials. Generally, each step up the educational ladder marks a drop in the rate of unemployment. Within the professional and technical occupations, the trend is toward increased demand for workers at the top of the skill range for each group and toward narrowing opportunities for those with lesser qualifications within the group. In this connection, the groups most dramatically affected by unemployment are the "dropouts" from high school. Their rate of unemployment is considerably higher than that for teenagers who have high school diplomas. Even when they find employment, it is in the least desirable jobs; most often they work as laborers in jobs that provide no training and little security.

One of the most alarming features in the postwar profile of unemployment is the fact that after each of the successive recessions between 1954 and 1963, unemployment has stabilized at a higher level than it did in the preceding recovery. Thus, the 1955–57 unemployment rate of 4.1 per cent was above the 1951–53 rate of 2.7 per cent; the 1959–60 rate of 5.5 per cent was higher than the 1955–57 rate, and the 1962–63 rate again was higher in recovery years than before the recession. In fact, the rate in the good year 1962 settled at the level of the recession of 1954 (5.6 per cent of the civilian labor force).

Because of the diversity of the American economy, unemployment is not distributed evenly throughout the country. There are some areas with unemployment rates of 6–7 per cent or more and others where unemployment affects less than 3 per cent of the civilian labor force. Major areas with persistent unemployment are located in a few states—predominantly in Pennsylvania, West Virginia, New Jersey, Rhode Island, and Massachusetts. Three of the nation's chief industrial centers—Detroit, Pittsburgh, and Providence-Pawtucket—have persistent unemployment. Practically all areas dependent on coal mining suffer from unemployment. Generally, the eastern part of the country is more seriously affected by unemployment than the less industrialized western part. In 1963–64, the per cent of unemployed within the total working force ranged from an average of 2.6 per cent in Iowa and 3.0 per cent in Nebraska to 6.8 per cent in New Jersey and Rhode Island, 7.8 per cent in Alaska, and 8.8 per cent in West Virginia. Puerto Rico stands out with the highest unemployment rate: 12 per cent.

In a dynamic economy, unemployment, like employment, is fluid. There is a constant movement among the unemployed—some move into jobs or out of the labor force, while others lose their jobs or quit, and non-

TABLE V.13

DURATION OF UNEMPLOYMENT, 1947-64

Duration of Unemployment (In Weeks)	Number of Unemployed (In Thousands)						
	1947	1957	1960	1961	1962	1963	1964
Less than 5 weeks	1,255	1,485	1,798	1,897	1,754	1,847	1,787
5-10 weeks	511	650	823	964	812	879	797
11-14 weeks	143	240	353	411	323	354	319
15-26 weeks	234	321	502	728	534	535	490
27 weeks and over	164	239	454	804	583	553	482
TOTAL	2,356	2,936	3,931	4,806	4,007	4,166	3,876

workers begin to look for jobs and thus swell the ranks of the unemployed. Even among the long-term unemployed, the movement into and out of the group affects about 25 per cent every month. Thus unemployment— voluntary or involuntary idleness—is spread among many more persons during the year than are unemployed at any given time.

Half of the unemployed remain without work for less than 5 weeks; unemployment lasts from 5 to 10 weeks for about one-fifth and from 11 to 26 weeks for another fifth or somewhat less. The last 10–12 per cent constitute the hard core of unemployment—they are without jobs for 27 weeks or more and are outside the regular state insurance coverage (see Table V.13 and Figure V.7).

FIGURE V.7

SHORT- AND LONG-TERM UNEMPLOYMENT, 1957-65
(Seasonally Adjusted Quarterly Averages)

U.S. Department of Labor, Bureau of Labor Statistics

In spite of existing unemployment, much overtime work exists in various industries. Employers consider it more practical to resort to higher-paid overtime work than to hire additional workers and take on obligations of training, pensions, and so on. Workers, in turn, are willing to work extra hours and increase their earnings. Thus in 1962, only two-fifths of all employed workers had a regular 40-hour week; about one-fourth worked 48 hours or more; still another fourth worked less than 35 hours and some workers had a 41–48-hour week. While unemployment was averaging 5.6 per cent of the work force, the average overtime in manufacturing reached a 6-year peak of 3 hours a week (see Sec. 89).

Many workers have a second job, which sometimes is a part-time job,

TABLE V.14

DISTRIBUTION OF WORKERS WITH TWO OR MORE JOBS, BY INDUSTRY
AND CLASS OF WORK, 1956-64

	(In Thousands)					
	1956 July	1959 December	1960 December	1962 May	1963 May	1964 May
Agriculture	866	321	332	364	386	405
Wage and salary workers	295	104	97	102	146	139
Self-employed workers	402	199	208	210	195	230
Unpaid family workers	169	18	27	52	45	36
Nonagricultural industries	2,787	2,645	2,680	2,978	3,535	3,321
Wage and salary workers	2,569	2,451	2,489	2,764	3,361	3,135
Self-employed workers	200	182	184	194	169	175
Unpaid family workers	18	12	7	20	5	11
TOTAL, holding 2 or more jobs	3,653	2,966	3,012	3,342	3,921	3,726
Per cent of total employed persons	5.5	4.5	4.6	4.9	5.7	5.2

but often a primary one. In agriculture, self-employed farmers and unpaid family workers often have nonfarm jobs, and farm laborers in particular are likely to take a second job. Predominant among multiple-job holders, however, are wage and salary workers in nonagricultural industries. In July, 1956, 3.7 million employed persons had 2 jobs or more (5.5 per cent of total employed); in May, 1964, 3.7 million (5.2 per cent). The distribution of workers with multiple jobs by industry and class of work is shown in Table V.14.

Unemployment has been greater in this country than in most other industrial countries, even when account is taken of the broader definition of who is counted as unemployed. In 1962, the United States had a slightly lower rate of unemployment than Canada (5.6 per cent against 5.9 per cent), but a much higher rate than various advanced industrialized countries in Europe, such as West Germany (0.7 per cent), the United Kingdom (2.1), Netherlands (0.8), and others, many of which actually experienced shortage in important branches of the economy. In the fourth quarter of 1965, the unemployment rate in the United States dropped to 4.2 per cent; the number of unemployed was below 3 million for the first time since October, 1957. The disparity between the U.S. unemployment rate and that in Western European countries is narrowing more and more, as the continuous high level of the nation's economic activities generates new demands for labor, and various branches of the U.S. economy begin to face shortages in labor supply.

26. *Mobility of Labor*

Economic life in the United States is characterized by greater mobility of population, especially of labor, than exists in other industrially advanced countries. Many factors contribute to such movements of workers from one area to another as are caused by changes of place of work within the same industry and shifts to new occupations. The American economy could not be as dynamic as it is and could not effect great technological readjustments within comparatively short periods of time except for this adaptability of labor to changing economic requirements and conditions.

Job change is one of the most important factors causing people to move: toward areas with greater work opportunities or better jobs, or changing employers. In 1964, 1 out of 5 Americans (aged 1 year and over) changed residence. During the last decade, 23 states had an excess of domestic in-migration over out-migration, largely from the South. There is a close relationship between expanding employment and the influx of workers. Thus, between 1955 and 1960, 3.1 million migrants took up residence in the Pacific states as nonagricultural-employment payrolls increased by 900,000; the corresponding figures for the South Atlantic states were 3.2 million and 824,000, respectively. In the same period, the areas of high unemployment showed an outflow of population (3.2 per cent for all areas as a whole, 7.3 per cent for Detroit and 7.6 per cent for Wilkes-Barre, Pa., as compared with an inflow to areas of low unemployment (3.3 per cent for all areas as a whole, 7 per cent for Jacksonville, Fla., and 8.8 per cent for Denver, Colo.).

Another visible relation is between income and mobility of workers. With diminishing income, the worker's readiness to change residence increases (see Table V.15).

The unemployed are more mobile than the employed; those with part-time employment show a greater willingness to move than do full-time workers. Thus workers with 50–52 weeks in one job had a migration rate of 4.3 per cent in 1962; those with 27–49 weeks, 9.9 per cent; and those with 26 weeks or less, 13.4 per cent.

TABLE v.15

MOBILITY OF WORKERS BY LEVEL OF INCOME, 1962

Annual Money Income (In Dollars)	Over-all Mobility Rate (Per Cent)
Under 1,000	22.0
1,000-1,999	30.5
2,000-2,999	28.8
3,000-3,999	25.5
4,000-4,999	23.2
5,000-5,999	18.5
6,000-6,999	18.4
7,000-9,999	15.6

Some geographic shifts of the labor force are caused by changing patterns in the industries that work for national defense. An example of such change is the revolutionary revision in the weapons system; tanks and other military hardware represented half of all military goods produced in 1953, but only 12 per cent of the contract awards in 1961. These changes brought about major geographical shifts of industries from the North East Central region to the Pacific and Mountain states. Along with such changes in the U.S. procurement, the demand for workers in one region declines and in another grows, causing in-and-out movements of labor (see Figure V.8).

FIGURE V.8

PER CENT CHANGE IN NONAGRICULTURAL EMPLOYMENT, BY STATE, 1947-62

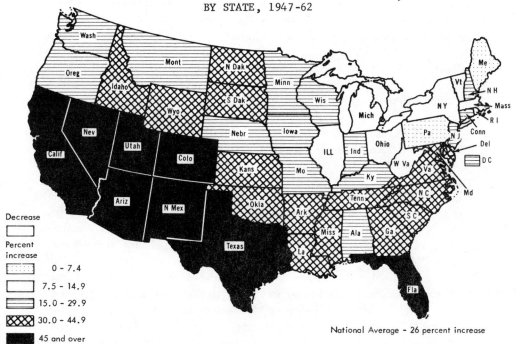

Decrease

Percent increase

0 - 7.4

7.5 - 14.9

15.0 - 29.9

30.0 - 44.9

45 and over

National Average - 26 percent increase

U.S. Department of Labor, Bureau of Labor Statistics

FIGURE V.9

WORKERS CHANGING JOBS, BY AGE AND SEX, 1961

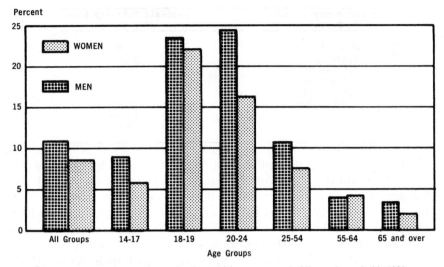

1/ Persons 14 years of age and over who changed jobs, as a percent of those who worked in 1961.

U.S. Department of Labor, Bureau of Labor Statistics

In 1961, 8 million workers changed their jobs—some for better work, others for less desirable employment; some voluntarily, others after having lost their jobs; some changed more than twice within a single year; some found jobs within 1–14 weeks, others looked for jobs 15 weeks or more (see Appendix Table XVII). Young persons change jobs 4 or 5 times as frequently as older workers, men more often than women (see Figure V.9), nonwhite men more often than white men. Among women, the pattern is rather different; nonwhite women have a lower rate of job mobility than the white.

Most of the intraoccupational shifts take place in unskilled work. More than half of farm laborers changed jobs more than twice in 1961, the usual reason being the ending of a temporary job. The highest rate of change among major occupational groups was among the nonfarm laborers, where 1 out of 6 workers was involved in job changing; among blue-collar workers, 1 out of 7; and in clerical and sales occupations, 1 out of 10 had more than one job during 1961. The construction industry has a unique pattern of job shifts: 1 out of 4 male workers changed jobs at least once during 1961, and 1 out of 8 made more than 1 job change. In manufacturing as a whole, 1 out of 10 male workers and 1 out of 11 or 12 female workers changed jobs; half of them found employment in other industries. For women, the highest job-change rate was in trade, 12 per cent, and the most common reason was improvement in status. All in all, in growing industries, mobility of labor is greater in response to new opportunities offered, while in declining industries workers hesitate to move on their own initiative.

A new factor affecting labor mobility has gained prominence since the last war—private pension plans. In 1945, such plans covered 6.5 million workers; today at least half of the employees in nonagricultural establishments are thus covered. According to a sample survey made in 1964 in 212 Standard Metropolitan Statistical Areas, 69 per cent of the plant workers there, exclusive of construction and extractive industries, were protected by retirement pensions of one sort or another; for office workers (except administrative, executive, and professional employees), coverage amounted to 79 per cent. In many pension plans, workers must perform 15–20 years of service to qualify, and they have to be prepared to forego pension rights if they resign. Young workers without accrued rights are, naturally, less restrained in their mobility than older workers. Recently, however, new features (transfer of pension credits, earlier retirement, vesting) have been introduced into pension plans that ensure workers of their accrued pension rights.

27. The Future of Manpower

Because of the unprecedented rise in the birth rate after World War II, the labor force is expected to expand greatly when the young people born in the late 1940's and in the 1950's enter the labor market.*

The most consequential factor in the development of the labor force is the rate of growth of the population of working age. While the potential labor force of the United States is expected to increase by 12.9 million between 1960 and 1970, the 14–24 age group will stand out as the most rapidly increasing; it will account for an increase of 6.7 million, half of the total, as compared with a rise of less than half a million between 1950 and 1960. Actually, the projected increase of young workers has been scaled down somewhat, because it is expected that more young people than before will attend colleges and graduate schools.

The number of workers aged 45 years and over will increase slightly less than in the previous decade, by 4.7 million instead of 5.4 million. This difference is due partly to the tendency to retire earlier than before, a tendency made possible by social security benefits and the expansion of private pension plans.

The influx of women into the labor force is expected to continue, though perhaps at a slightly lower rate: in the 1950's, the addition of women to the labor force exceeded that of men—4.8 million as compared

* The projections of the Department of Labor on the labor force in 1970 and 1975 are based on various assumptions, such as that the economy of this country will continue to operate at a relatively high level, that there will be no major war, that the rate of participation in the labor force will not change significantly. These projections can be made with reasonable accuracy because the potential workers have already been born, death rates change rather slowly over time, and immigration is limited.

with 3.5 million—but it is expected that in the 1960's, 6.7 million women will join the labor market, as compared with 6.2 million men. Moreover, in the 1970's, men will account for a considerably greater portion of the increase in the labor force than women: 9.2 million and 6.2 million, respectively (see Figure V.10).

Between 1970 and 1980, the development of the labor force is expected to be less dramatic than in the 1960's. About 3.5 million young workers in the 14–24 age group will be added to the labor force, while the greatest expansion will be in the next older group, 25–34—from 17 to

FIGURE V.10

PROJECTION OF THE LABOR FORCE,
BY SEX, FOR 1970 AND 1975

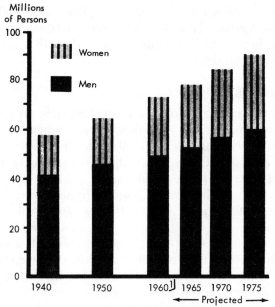

⅃⅃ Alaska and Hawaii included beginning 1960.
U.S. Departments of Commerce and Labor

almost 25 million. In 1960, that group represented 20.7 per cent of the total labor force; its share is expected to fall to 19.7 per cent in 1970, but to rise to 24.6 per cent by 1980 (see Table V.16).

The participation rates of the male labor force are expected to continue to decline: from 84.4 per cent in 1950 and 79.7 per cent in 1960 to 77.2 per cent in 1980. In contrast, the women's participation rates would follow their own trend, rising as they did from 33.1 per cent in 1950 and 36.1 per cent in 1960 to 40.6 per cent by 1980. Their participation rates are estimated to increase for all age groups, except the very last (65 years and over).

TABLE V.16

PROJECTIONS OF LABOR FORCE AND PARTICIPATION RATES
BY AGE AND SEX, FOR 1970 AND 1980

Age and Sex	Labor Force, Annual Averages (In Millions)				Labor Force Participation Rates (Per Cent)			
	1950	1960	1970	1980	1950	1960	1970	1980
Male, 14 years and over	46.1	49.6	55.8	65.0	84.4	79.7	77.0	77.2
14-19	3.4	3.8	5.2	5.7	53.2	46.3	44.4	44.8
20-24	5.2	4.9	7.5	9.1	89.0	88.9	86.6	87.2
25-34	11.0	10.9	12.1	17.6	96.2	96.4	96.2	96.2
35-44	10.0	11.5	10.9	12.1	97.6	96.4	96.7	96.7
45-54	8.1	9.6	10.7	10.2	95.8	94.3	95.0	96.0
55-64	5.8	6.4	7.4	8.2	87.0	85.2	84.3	83.7
65 and over	2.5	2.4	2.1	2.1	45.8	32.2	25.1	21.8
Female, 14 years and over	18.7	23.5	30.2	36.4	33.1	36.1	39.9	40.6
14-19	2.0	2.4	3.4	3.7	31.5	30.1	30.1	31.0
20-24	2.7	2.6	4.3	5.4	46.1	46.1	50.3	52.6
25-34	4.1	4.2	4.9	7.3	34.0	35.8	38.6	40.3
35-44	4.2	5.3	5.6	6.4	39.1	43.1	47.5	50.0
45-54	3.3	5.1	6.7	6.8	38.0	49.3	55.3	59.5
55-64	1.8	3.0	4.3	5.3	27.0	36.7	43.8	47.3
65 and over	0.6	1.0	1.1	1.3	9.7	10.5	9.8	9.9

With the present supply of labor, the main problems will be the extent and character of the demand for labor. Agriculture, despite its growing output, is the only sector of the economy that will experience a decline in

FIGURE V.11
GROWTH OF PRODUCTIVITY IN AGRICULTURE AND
OTHER SECTORS OF THE ECONOMY, 1947-61

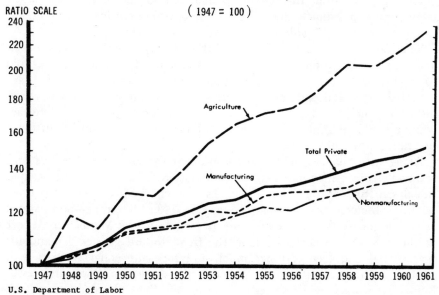

U.S. Department of Labor

TABLE V.17

PROJECTION OF NONAGRICULTURAL LABOR FORCE,
BY INDUSTRY, FOR 1970 AND 1975

Industry Division	Nonagricultural Labor Force (In Millions)		
	Actual	Projected	
	1960	1970	1975
Service-producing industries	34.0	43.7	48.8
Wholesale and retail trade	11.4	14.0	15.6
Government	8.5	11.5	12.8
Service and miscellaneous	7.4	10.2	11.9
Transportation and public utilities	4.0	4.4	4.5
Finance, insurance, real estate	2.7	3.5	3.9
Goods-producing industries	20.4	24.0	25.4
Manufacturing	16.8	19.2	20.3
Contract construction	2.9	4.0	4.4
Mining	0.7	0.7	0.7
TOTAL	54.3	67.7	74.2

the labor force. Greatly expanded use of machinery and fertilizers and other advances in technology have resulted in a steadily increasing rate of productivity, which has far outstripped that in manufacturing (see Figure V.11). It is estimated that work opportunities in agriculture will decline from 5.4 million in 1960 to 4.2 million in 1970, and less than 4 million in 1975 (see Sec. 45). Manufacturing is expected to provide some 5 million jobs within this 15-year period, but to absorb the increase in labor supply at a much slower rate than service-producing industries, estimated to employ 15 million new workers within these years.

Transportation as a whole offers little prospect for labor absorption, and employment in one of its branches, the railroads, is likely to continue to decline, whereas air transportation, trucking, and warehousing are expected to expand and provide additional jobs. These and other service industries, such as trade, government, finance, insurance, real estate, accounting, and auditing, will provide a total of many more jobs than manufacturing (see Table V.17).

Along with changes in the composition of the labor force by age and sex, and changes in employment patterns (see Sec. 22, 23, 26), the occupational structure of the labor force has also changed. Some occupations became obsolete, new occupations appeared on the scene—occupations requiring greater skill and education. According to the Manpower Report of the U.S. Department of Labor, the trend toward greater demand for professional and technical personnel, and for white-collar workers, will continue throughout the entire period under discussion; fewer and fewer blue-collar workers will be needed, and among them the demand will be

TABLE V.18

EMPLOYMENT BY MAJOR OCCUPATION GROUP,
ACTUAL AND PROJECTED, 1960-75

	Number of Employed Persons (In Millions)			Per Cent of Employment		
	Actual	Projected		Actual	Projected	
	1960	1970	1975	1960	1970	1975
Farmers, managers, laborers, foremen	5.4	4.2	3.9	8.1	5.3	4.5
Laborers, except farm and mines	3.7	3.7	3.7	5.5	4.6	4.3
Operatives and kindred workers	12.0	13.6	14.2	18.0	16.9	16.3
Craftsmen, foremen, kindred workers	8.6	10.3	11.2	12.8	12.8	12.8
Service workers	8.3	11.1	12.5	12.5	13.8	14.3
Sales workers	4.4	5.4	5.9	6.6	6.7	6.7
Clerical and kindred workers	9.8	12.8	14.2	14.7	15.9	16.2
Professional, technical, kindred workers	7.5	10.7	12.4	11.2	13.3	14.2
Managers, officials, proprietors, except farm	7.1	8.6	9.4	10.6	10.7	10.7
TOTAL	66.7	80.5	87.6	100.0	100.0	100.0

for craftsmen and skilled workers, with little need for additional manual laborers. In contrast, the number of service, sales, and clerical workers is expected to rise from 22.5 million in 1960 to 29.3 million in 1970, and 32.6 million in 1975, or from 33.8 per cent of total employment in 1960 to 36.4 per cent in 1970 and 37.2 per cent in 1975 (see Table V.18).

Geographic trends in the increase of the labor force, noticeable in the last decade, are expected to continue. The rate of growth will be greatest in the Pacific and Mountain states, and in 4 of them—California, Alaska, Arizona, and Nevada—may amount to 50 per cent or more. Outside these regions, Florida is likely to have the highest rate of increase in the labor force—67 per cent—while the large industrial states, New York and Pennsylvania, may increase their labor force by only 13 and 9 per cent, respectively. In many other states—in New England, the East South Central and West South Central regions, and in North Dakota—the increase may be only 5 per cent, while Arkansas and West Virginia may experience a decline in the labor force. As always, it is possible that projections made by the Department of Labor early in 1960 may deviate substantially in both directions during the 1970's.

VI. *How Rich Is This Nation?*

28. The Gross National Product and the National Income of
the United States—29. Components of the GNP and the National Income—30. Personal Income—31. Disposable Income,
Consumer Expenditures, and Savings—32. Assets and Debts of
the American People—33. Rich States, Poor States—34. The
National Wealth of the United States

28. The Gross National Product and the
National Income of the United States

The *gross national product* (GNP) represents the over-all measure of
the nation's total output of goods and services at current market prices.
In other terms, it is the value of expenditures by which the nation's goods
and services are currently acquired. These expenditures consist of 4 major
items: (1) personal consumption expenditures; (2) gross private domestic
investment; (3) net export of goods and services; (4) government purchases of goods and services. The GNP also includes some items not
bought in the market; the most important among these is the imputed
value of owner-occupied dwellings. No account is taken, however, of such
items as the value of the housewife's services, or the householder's work
in making home repairs, or of home dressmaking and the like. Only the
end products of a year's economic activity are included. For example, since
the output of bread is included, that of the wheat used to make it is not.

The *national income* is the sum of earnings of labor and property from
the current production of goods and services by the national economy.
It consists of 4 major items: (1) salaries and wages, including payments
in kind, such as the value of meals given to employees as a part of their
pay, and also social security contributions by employers, payments under
workmen's compensation laws, industrial pensions, and pensions of Government employees and members of the armed forces; (2) the net income
of unincorporated businesses, including that of farmers in terms of their
money income, the produce they raise and consume, and government pay-

TABLE VI.1

GROSS NATIONAL PRODUCT AND NATIONAL INCOME
OF THE UNITED STATES, 1929-65
(In Billions of Dollars)

Year	Gross National Product	National Income	Year	Gross National Product	National Income
1929	103.1	86.8	1947	231.3	199.0
1930	90.4	75.4	1948	257.6	224.2
1931	75.8	59.7	1949	256.5	217.5
1932	58.0	42.8	1950	284.8	241.1
1933	55.6	40.3	1951	328.4	278.0
1934	65.1	49.5	1952	345.5	291.4
1935	72.2	57.2	1953	364.6	304.7
1936	82.5	65.C	1954	364.8	303.1
1937	90.4	73.6	1955	398.0	331.0
1938	84.7	67.4	1956	419.2	350.8
1939	90.5	72.6	1957	441.1	366.1
1940	99.7	81.1	1958	447.3	367.8
1941	124.5	104.2	1959	483.7	400.0
1942	157.9	137.1	1960	503.8	414.5
1943	191.6	170.3	1961	520.1	427.3
1944	210.1	182.6	1962	560.3	457.7
1945	212.0	181.5	1963	589.2	481.1
1946	208.5	181.9	1964	628.7	514.4
			1965	675.6	554.6

ments to them; (3) interest, including that paid on mortgages and debts, public and private, net rent and royalties, such as net rents on residential dwellings and other buildings, and the estimated rental value to homeowners of their homes; (4) net profits of corporations, adjusted for profits and losses arising merely from changes in the price of inventories held.

The total value of these 4 items represents the *net* value of all goods and services produced in the nation. However, apart from wage costs, interest, and profits at all stages of production and distribution, the current prices of goods and services reflect 2 additional items: (1) business taxes, such as excise taxes, import duties, corporate taxes, property taxes, and so on; (2) depreciation and depletion charges on capital—that is, essentially, the costs of capital maintenance, which are included in the price of the product.

When these items are added to the national income and adjustments are made for the re-evaluation of inventories and debts, the total represents the gross national product at current prices.

According to the estimates of the Department of Commerce, the national income of the United States amounted to $86.8 billion in current prices in 1929 and to $40.3 billion in 1933, at the bottom of the Depression. Since then, it has climbed steadily, except in 1938 and during the postwar recessions of 1945, 1949, and 1954. The defense program and war production raised national income to $104.2 billion in 1941 and $182.6 billion in 1944. After the war, it rose to $241.1 billion in 1950,

TABLE VI.2

GROSS NATIONAL PRODUCT, 1929-64
(In Billions of 1954 Dollars)

1929	181.8	1950	318.1
1933	126.6	1960	439.9
1939	189.3	1963	492.6
1945	314.0	1964	516.0

reached the $400-billion mark in 1959, and with $514.4 billion in 1964 exceeded half a trillion dollars for the first time. In 1965, it amounted to $554.6 billion.

The gross national product topped national income by $15–$20 billion in the 1930's; because of the increase in business taxes, the difference widened to more than $30 billion by 1945 and more than $40 billion in 1950. By 1964–65, it exceeded national income by more than $100 billion (see Table VI.1).

In constant dollars of 1954, the GNP increased not 6 times as it did in current dollars between 1929 and 1964 ($103.1 billion and $628.7 billion) but less than 3 times (see Table VI.2).

Between 1929 and 1964—i.e., in the preceding 35 years—the U.S. population has increased by less than 60 per cent, while the per capita gross national product and national income nearly quadrupled in current dollars (see Table VI.3).

29. Components of the GNP and the National Income

Part of the gross national product is used for public purposes, such as national defense, internal security and public administration, education, construction and maintenance of highways and bridges, health services, etc. This share is made up of the expenditures of the Federal, state, and local governments. The remainder of the GNP comprises the expenditures by private individuals for direct consumption and by corporations for

TABLE VI.3

PER CAPITA GROSS NATIONAL PRODUCT AND NATIONAL INCOME, 1929-64
(In Dollars)

Year	Gross National Product	National Income	Year	Gross National Product	National Income
1929	857	717	1958	2,553	2,110
1933	446	315	1959	2,726	2,262
1935	569	453	1960	2,782	2,994
1940	761	616	1961	2,820	2,319
1945	1,526	1,309	1962	2,974	2,431
1950	1,876	1,595	1963	3,111	2,527
1955	2,405	1,998	1964	3,212	2,677

TABLE VI.4

GROSS NATIONAL PRODUCT OF THE UNITED STATES,
BY MAJOR COMPONENT, 1929-65
(In Billions of Dollars)

Item	1929	1933	1939	1945	1950	1960	1962	1964	1965[a]
Personal consumption	77.2	45.8	66.8	119.7	191.0	325.2	355.1	398.9	428.5
Durable goods	9.2	3.5	6.7	8.0	30.5	45.3	49.5	58.7	64.8
Nondurable goods	37.7	22.3	35.1	71.9	98.1	151.3	162.6	177.5	189.0
Services	30.3	20.1	25.0	39.8	62.4	128.7	143.0	162.6	174.7
Gross private domestic investment	16.2	1.4	9.3	10.6	54.1	74.8	83.0	92.9	104.9
New construction	8.9	1.4	4.9	4.4	28.6	41.0	44.6	48.6	51.9
Producers' durable equipment	5.6	1.5	4.0	7.3	18.7	30.3	32.5	39.4	45.5
Change in business inventories	1.7	-1.6	0.4	-1.0	6.8	3.6	6.0	4.8	7.4
Nonfarm	1.8	-1.4	0.3	-0.6	6.0	3.3	5.3	5.4	7.1
Farm	-0.1	-0.2	0.1	-0.4	0.8	0.2	0.7	-0.6	0.3
Net exports of goods and services	1.1	0.4	1.1	-0.6	1.8	4.1	5.1	8.6	7.2
Government purchases of goods and services	8.5	8.0	13.3	82.3	37.9	99.6	117.1	128.4	135.0
Federal	1.3	2.0	5.1	74.2	18.4	53.5	63.4	65.3	66.7
National defense	-	-	1.2	73.5	14.1	44.9	51.6	49.9	49.6
State and local	7.2	6.0	8.2	8.1	19.5	46.1	53.7	63.1	68.2
GROSS NATIONAL PRODUCT	103.1	55.6	90.5	212.0	284.8	503.8	560.3	628.7	675.6

[a]Preliminary.

capital formation, including accumulation of inventories, maintenance of industrial plant, and new investment.

Personal consumption expenditures for goods and services constitute the main item, averaging 64–65 per cent of the GNP in 1955–64, as compared with about 75 per cent in 1929 and 1939 and 77 per cent in 1934. About 45–47 per cent of personal expenditure goes for purchase of nondurable goods, such as food, fuel, clothing, etc.; services absorb somewhat less, and the remainder is used for the purchase of durable goods.

The remaining third of the GNP is accounted for by expenditures for (a) gross private domestic investment (some 15 per cent), such as new construction, purchase of producers' durable equipment, and inventories, (b) government purchases of goods and services (about 20 per cent), such as national defense, compensation of public employees, government enterprises, and net government purchases abroad. The Federal Government accounts for the largest part of government purchases, and national defense currently takes nearly 75 per cent of that sum. Net exports of goods and services, though very important for many branches of the national economy (see Sec. 75–77), represent a minor part of the GNP: they may amount to 1 per cent or less of the total, or they may represent a negative value (see Table VI.4 and Figure VI.1).

FIGURE VI.1

GROSS NATIONAL PRODUCT, BY MAJOR COMPONENT, 1947-64
(Quarterly Data in Current Prices.
Seasonally Adjusted Annual Rates)

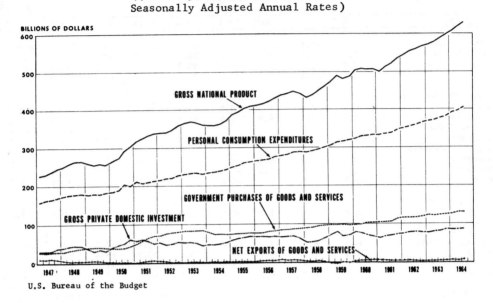

U.S. Bureau of the Budget

TABLE VI.5

NATIONAL INCOME OF THE UNITED STATES,
BY MAJOR COMPONENT, 1929-65
(In Billions of Dollars)

Item	1929	1933	1939	1945	1950	1960	1962	1964	1965[c]
Compensation of employees	51.1	29.5	48.1	123.1	154.6	294.2	323.6	365.3	391.9
Wages and salaries	50.4	29.0	45.9	117.5	146.8	270.8	296.1	333.5	357.4
Supplements[a]	0.7	0.5	2.2	5.6	7.8	23.4	27.5	31.8	34.5
Proprietors' income	15.1	5.9	11.8	31.4	37.5	46.2	50.1	51.1	54.6
Business and professional	9.0	3.3	7.4	19.2	24.0	34.2	37.1	39.1	40.3
Farm	6.2	2.6	4.4	12.2	13.5	12.0	13.0	12.0	14.3
Rental income of persons	5.4	2.0	2.7	5.6	9.4	15.8	16.7	18.2	18.6
Corporate profits[b]	10.5	-1.2	6.3	19.2	37.7	49.9	55.7	64.5	73.1
Net interest	4.7	4.1	3.5	2.2	2.0	18.4	11.6	15.2	16.5
NATIONAL INCOME	86.8	40.3	72.6	181.5	241.1	414.5	457.7	514.4	554.6

[a]Employer contributions to social-insurance, private-pension, and welfare funds.
[b]Includes inventory-valuation adjustment.
[c]Preliminary.

FIGURE VI.2

NATIONAL INCOME, 1947-64
(Quarterly Data. Seasonally Adjusted Annual Rates)

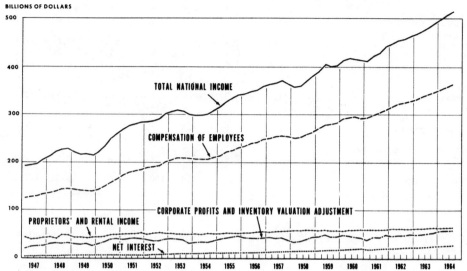

BILLIONS OF DOLLARS

TOTAL NATIONAL INCOME

COMPENSATION OF EMPLOYEES

CORPORATE PROFITS AND INVENTORY VALUATION ADJUSTMENT

PROPRIETORS' AND RENTAL INCOME

NET INTEREST

U.S. Bureau of the Budget

In national income, labor's share—that is, salaries and wages, including employers' contributions to social security, pensions of various types, remunerations and bonuses of executives, etc.—accounted for about 58 per cent of the total in 1929, 66–68 per cent in 1939–45, and exceeded 70 per cent in 1960–65. In other industrial countries, labor's share fluctuates within the same range: Canada, 69 per cent; France, 61; West Germany, 64, Australia, 64; the United Kingdom, 75; Sweden, 70 per cent. In some advanced countries, however, labor's share is smaller: Belgium, 58 per cent; Denmark, 59; New Zealand, 60; Austria and the Netherlands, 61. In the underdeveloped countries, labor receives a substantially lower share of national income: Peru, 37 per cent; the Philippines, 42; Greece, 41; and Brazil, Ceylon, and Taiwan, 47–49 per cent.

In the United States, the course of proprietors' income has run in the opposite direction from that of labor: it represented 17 per cent of national income in 1929 and 1945, was about 15.5 per cent in 1950, and declined to about 11 per cent in the 1960's. The chief decline was for farmers, whose share in national income fell from 6.5 per cent in 1945 to 3 per cent or less in the 1960's.

The share of corporate profits (after taxes) has fluctuated between 11 and 13 per cent of national income, except in the Depression years, when there were losses instead of gains, and in the prewar years. The share of net interest and that of rental income of persons ranges between 2.5 and 3.5 per cent of national income (see Table VI.5 and Figure VI.2).

TABLE VI.6

PERCENTAGE DISTRIBUTION OF NATIONAL INCOME, BY LEGAL FORM OF ORGANIZATION, 1929-63

	1929	1933	1939	1945	1950	1960	1962	1963
Income originating in business	89.0	81.9	84.9	77.8	87.4	83.4	82.5	82.2
Corporate business	51.5	43.2	49.7	45.5	54.7	54.6	54.0	53.8
Sole proprietorships and partnerships	27.3	26.3	26.5	26.8	25.9	21.2	21.1	20.7
Other private business	9.4	10.9	7.4	4.6	5.7	6.3	6.3	6.4
Government enterprises	0.9	1.6	1.3	0.9	1.1	1.3	1.1	1.3
Income originating in general government	4.9	11.7	10.4	19.4	8.6	11.4	12.0	12.2
Income originating in households and institutions	5.1	5.6	4.3	2.6	3.5	4.7	4.8	4.9
Income originating in the rest of the world	0.9	0.8	0.4	0.2	0.5	0.6	0.7	0.7
NATIONAL INCOME	100.0	100.0	100.0	100.0	100.0	100.0	100.0	100.0

A little more than half the national income, 54–55 per cent, originates in corporate business; its share fluctuated only slightly during the 1950's. In contrast, the share of sole proprietorships and partnerships has gone down slowly but continuously, from 27 per cent of national income in 1929 to 21 per cent in 1963. Another sector of private business (mutual financial institutions, cooperatives, nonprofit organizations, individually owned property, etc.) experienced a relative decrease from about 9.4 per cent of national income in 1929 to 4.6 per cent in 1945; it now approaches 7 per cent.

Income originating in general government (compensation of employees) has grown more substantially, from 4.9 per cent of national income in 1929 to 10.4 per cent in 1939 and 19.4 per cent in 1945, the peak year; it now amounts to 12–13 per cent. Net national income originating in the rest of the world is insignificant (see Table VI.6).

In terms of industrial origin, there have been changes in the relative importance of different sectors of the economy in production of national income.

The share of agriculture (including forestry and fisheries) has been declining for a long time: it exceeded 10 per cent of national income in the 1920's, accounted for about 8–8.5 per cent in the 1930's, and was on about the same level during the war years (because of special efforts to produce more food for this country, the Allies, and the future needs in postwar years), then dropped to about 7.5 per cent in 1950, and now fluctuates around 4 per cent, accounting for $20 billion out of about $555 billion in 1965 (see Table VI.7).

The share of mining also has fallen. Mining output contributed $2 billion to the national income of $87 billion in 1929 and $1.6 billion

TABLE VI.7

NATIONAL INCOME OF THE UNITED STATES,
BY INDUSTRIAL ORIGIN, 1929-64
(In Billions of Dollars)

Industrial Division	1929	1933	1939	1945	1950	1960	1962	1964
All industries	36.3	13.0	28.0	74.5	110.7	169.2	184.0	204.7
Agriculture[a]	8.5	3.9	6.0	15.2	17.6	16.9	18.5	17.6
Mining	2.1	0.6	1.6	2.8	5.2	5.7	5.7	6.2
Contract construction	3.8	0.8	2.3	4.3	11.9	20.8	22.8	26.2
Manufacturing	21.9	7.7	18.1	52.2	76.2	125.8	137.0	154.7
Services	44.5	21.6	35.6	69.8	105.4	190.1	209.8	235.5
Wholesale and retail trade	13.5	5.6	12.6	28.0	40.9	64.4	70.3	78.1
Transportation	6.6	3.0	4.6	10.5	13.4	18.2	19.1	21.0
Finance, insurance, real estate	12.8	5.9	8.0	13.0	22.0	45.9	50.7	57.0
Communications and public utilities	2.8	2.0	2.8	4.2	7.3	17.2	19.0	21.4
Other services	8.8	5.1	7.6	14.1	21.8	44.4	50.7	58.0
Government	5.1	5.3	8.5	36.8	23.6	52.9	60.7	70.0
Rest of the world	0.8	0.3	0.3	0.4	1.2	2.4	3.3	4.1
NATIONAL INCOME	86.8	40.3	72.6	181.5	241.1	414.5	457.7	514.4

[a]Includes forestry and fisheries.

out of $72.8 billion in 1939 (2.2–2.3 per cent), but in the 1960's it accounts for only $5–$6 billion, or 1.2 per cent.

Manufacturing's share in national income amounted to 25 per cent in 1929 and in 1939, climbed to 32 per cent by 1950, and represented 30 per cent in 1964. The share of all industries, as a group, declined from 46 per cent in 1950 to about 40 per cent in 1964.

Services, including government, maintained their share of about 55–60 per cent of national income throughout most of the period, with slight ups and downs. Within this broad group, there were considerable changes: the share of transportation declined from 7.5 per cent in 1929 to 6.3 per cent in 1939 and 4 per cent in the 1960's; that of government increased from some 6 per cent in 1929 to 12 per cent in 1939, rose to about 20 per cent in 1945, and fell back to about 13–14 per cent in the 1960's.

International data on the industrial origin of gross domestic product are not uniform and are of varying reliability; however, they still provide a general picture of the position of various industries in selected countries (see Table VI.8).

The United States and the United Kingdom are the only 2 countries in the world in which agriculture's share in gross domestic product is as low as 4 per cent; it accounts for 6 per cent in West Germany, 7 per cent in Belgium, and 8 per cent in Canada. In contrast, agriculture generates 16 per

TABLE VI.8

PERCENTAGE DISTRIBUTION OF GROSS DOMESTIC PRODUCT
IN SELECTED COUNTRIES, 1963

Country	Agriculture[a]	Manufacturing, Mining	Construction	Public Utilities	Transport, Communications	Trade	Other Services
United States	4	30	5	2	6	16	37
Canada	8	30	5	3	9	13	32
Argentina	17	34	4	2	8	15	20
Chile	9	23	4	1	8	22	33
Colombia	32	20	5	1	7	12	23
Ecuador	38	17	4	1	4	12	24
Austria	11	39	9	3	7	9	22
Belgium	7	33	7	2	7	11	33
France	9	38	8	2[b]	5	13	27
West Germany	6	44	8		6	12	24
Italy	16	34	8	3	7	9	26
Norway	9	27	8	3	18	12	23
United Kingdom	4	38	7	3[c]	8	12	30
Yugoslavia	28	40	8		7	11	6
India	45	20[d]	-	-	16[f]	-	19
Israel	11	24	8	2	8	20	27
Pakistan	53	14	3	-	3	9	18
Philippines	34	21	4	3[e]	-	11	27
Japan	13	32	7	10[e]	-	16	22

[a] Includes forestry and fishing, except for Argentina, where forestry is included in manufacturing.
[b] Included in mining.
[c] Electricity and gas included in manufacturing and mining; water and sanitary services included in other services.
[d] Includes construction and public utilities.
[e] Includes transportation and communications.
[f] Includes trade.

cent of gross domestic product in Italy; 28 per cent in Yugoslavia; 32–34 per cent in Colombia and the Philippines; and 53 per cent in Pakistan.

Manufacturing and mining together account for about one-third of the gross domestic product in the United States but for a greater share in some other industrially advanced countries: 38 in the United Kingdom and France, and 44 per cent in West Germany.

The distribution of the gross national product by main items of expenditure varies from country to country. In most industrialized countries, private consumption ranges between 57 and 66 per cent of the total: 62–66 per cent in the United States, Canada, France, the United Kingdom, and Australia; 57 in West Germany; 58 in Sweden and Norway. Expenditures of general government, however, are lower in most countries than in the United States and Sweden (19 per cent of the GNP), except the United Kingdom, with 17 per cent, and Israel, with 22 per cent. In Canada, West Germany, and Italy, they absorb 15–16 per cent of the GNP. By contrast, the share of fixed capital formation, in the terminology

TABLE VI.9

PERCENTAGE DISTRIBUTION OF GROSS DOMESTIC PRODUCT
BY MAIN ITEMS OF EXPENDITURES IN SELECTED COUNTRIES,
1962-63

Country	Consumption Private	Consumption Govern- ment	Fixed Capital Form- ation	Increase in Stocks	Exports Less Imports Goods	Exports Less Imports Services	Net Factor Income from Abroad
United States	63	19	16	1	5	4	
Canada	63	15	22	1	20 a	20 a	-2
Argentina	64	16	24	2			-1
Chile	79	10	13	-	12	12	-2
Colombia	78	7	19	1	11	14	-2
Mexico	81	5	14	a	11	10	-1
Belgium	68	12	20	-	35	36	1
France	65	14	20	1	14	14	-
West Germany	57	16	25	1	19	18	-
Italy	62	16	23	1	16	18	-
Norway	58	16	30	-	40	43	-1
Sweden	58	19	23	-	28	31	1
United Kingdom	66	17	16	1	19	20	1
Israel	71	22	31 [b]	-	23	45	-2
Japan	53	10	33	5	11	12	-
Philippines	76	10	13	1	24	23	-1
Australia	63	11	25	1	18	16	-2
New Zealand	62	13	23	3	25	24	-2

[a] Exports less imports are -1.

[b] Includes increase in stocks.

of the United Nations, or gross private domestic investment, as it is classified in this country, generally exceeds substantially our share of 16 per cent—again with the exception of the United Kingdom, where it is the same. But it accounts for 23–25 per cent in Italy, West Germany, and Australia, and is as high as 30 per cent in Norway and 33 per cent in Japan. Foreign trade plays a much more important role in the GNP of other countries than in that of the United States. Net factor income from abroad* is either negligible or represents 1 per cent of GNP for most countries. For countries such as Canada, Australia, New Zealand, Israel, and some other countries, the percentage is negative (see Table VI.9).

30. Personal Income

Personal income consists of current income from all sources received by individuals, unincorporated businesses, and nonprofit institutions: wages, salaries, and other labor income, rent, dividends, proprietors' income, and transfer payments (social security benefits, government pensions, veterans' pensions, and so on, minus contributions to social insurance), and also nonmonetary items, such as the rental value of owner-occupied homes, values of food consumption on farms, and various unpaid services.

* All income from abroad (rent, interest, dividends, profits from enterprises abroad, earnings from working abroad, etc.) less the payments made to the rest of the world.

FIGURE VI.3

COMPONENTS OF PERSONAL INCOME, 1930-64

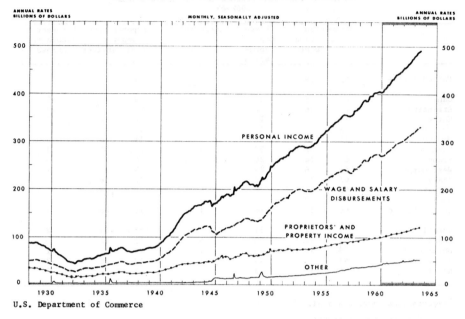

U.S. Department of Commerce

TABLE VI.10

PERSONAL INCOME, BY MAJOR COMPONENT, 1929-65
(In Billions of Dollars)

Item	1929	1933	1939	1945	1950	1960	1962	1964	1965
Wages and salaries	50.4	29.0	45.9	117.5	146.7	270.8	296.1	333.5	357.4
Goods industries	21.5	9.8	17.4	45.8	64.6	112.5	120.8	133.9	143.9
Distributive industries	15.6	8.8	13.3	24.8	39.9	68.1	72.5	81.1	86.5
Service industries	8.4	5.2	7.1	12.2	19.9	41.5	46.8	54.1	58.1
Government	4.9	5.1	8.2	34.9	22.4	48.7	56.0	64.3	68.9
Other labor income	0.6	0.4	0.6	1.8	3.8	12.0	13.9	16.5	18.2
Proprietors' income	15.1	5.9	11.8	31.4	37.5	46.2	50.1	51.1	54.6
Business and profes-sional	9.0	3.3	7.4	19.2	24.0	34.2	37.1	39.1	40.3
Farm	6.2	2.6	4.4	12.2	13.5	12.0	13.0	12.0	14.3
Rental income of persons	5.4	2.0	2.7	5.6	9.4	15.8	16.7	18.2	18.6
Dividends	5.8	2.0	3.8	4.6	8.8	13.4	15.2	17.2	18.9
Personal interest income	7.2	5.7	5.5	6.3	9.2	23.4	27.7	34.3	37.1
Transfer payments	1.5	2.1	3.0	6.2	15.1	28.5	33.3	36.6	39.2
OASI[a]	-	-	-	0.3	1.0	11.1	14.3	16.0	18.0
Unemployment insurance	-	-	0.4	0.4	1.4	2.8	2.9	2.6	2.2
Veterans' benefits	0.6	0.5	0.5	2.8	4.9	4.6	4.8	5.3	5.6
Other	0.9	1.6	2.0	2.7	7.9	10.0	11.2	12.7	13.4
Personal contributions for social insurance	-0.1	-0.2	-0.6	-2.3	-2.9	-9.3	-10.3	-2.4	-13.2
PERSONAL INCOME	85.9	47.0	72.8	171.1	227.6	401.0	442.6	495.0	530.7

[a]Old-age and survivors' insurance; first payments: $1 million in 1937, $14 million in 1939.

Total personal income amounted in 1929 to $86 billion; it plummeted to $47 billion in 1933, the worst Depression year, increased to $73 billion on the eve of World War II and continued the upward trend ever since, except for a slight decline in 1949. It exceeded $400 billion in 1960 and reached $536 billion in the third quarter of 1965 (see Figure VI.3). The rate of increase of its different components varied: in the 36 years from 1929 through 1965, the labor income increased 7 times, from $50 billion to $357 billion; the proprietors' income, more than 3 times, from $15 billion to $55 billion; and dividends and personal-interest income about 4 times, from $13 billion to $56 billion. Social-insurance payments (old-age survivors' benefits and unemployment compensation) began in the late 1930's and amounted to $20 billion in 1965 (see Table VI.10).

Per capita personal income for the nation as a whole was $1,496 in 1950; $2,215 in 1960; and $2,724 in 1965. The growth of per capita personal income by 23 per cent between 1960 and 1965 reflected the increase in real purchasing power since consumer prices have been advancing in this period by about 1.5 per cent a year.

There is a wide interstate variation in the level of per capita personal income, ranging in 1964 from $1,438 in Mississippi to $3,460 in Delaware

FIGURE VI.4

PER CAPITA PERSONAL INCOME, BY STATE, 1964

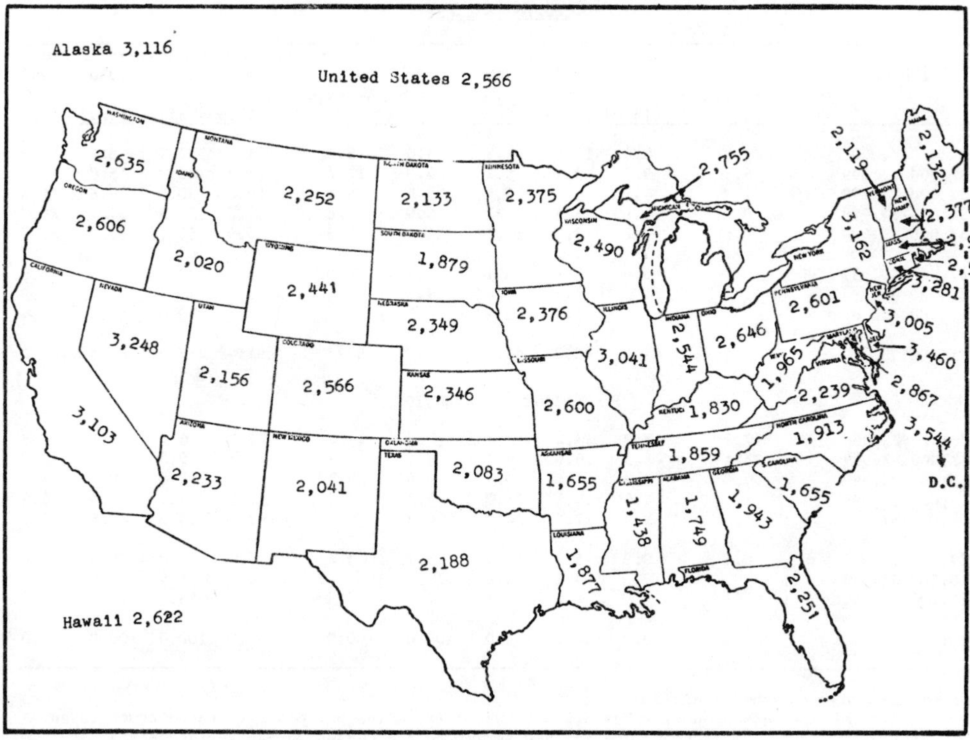

Alaska 3,116

United States 2,566

Hawaii 2,622

and $3,544 in the District of Columbia. Nine states had a per capita personal income above $3,000; 12 reported an income from $2,500 to $3,000; and 11 states, an income under $2,000 (see Figure VI.4; cf. Table VI.24). In 1965, only 5 states were in that last income group.

The number of consumer units (families and unattached individuals) increased from 38.4 million in 1935–36 to 48.8 million in 1950 and 57.9 million in 1962, or by 27 per cent in the first period and 18 per cent in the second. The aggregate family personal income (before taxes) rose from $62.7 billion in 1935–36 to $217.3 billion in 1950 and $420.4 billion in 1962 (see Table VI.11).

Average personal income per consumer unit rose from $2,340 in 1929 to $4,440 in 1950; $6,820 in 1960; and $7,510 in 1963—before taxes. With adjustment for the rise in prices, the increase has been much less: in 1963 dollars, the average family personal income amounted to $4,300 per consumer unit in 1929; $5,580 in 1950; $7,030 in 1960; and $7,510 in 1963.

In 1962, there were 46.9 million families and 11 million unattached individuals in the United States. In current dollars, the average (mean)

TABLE VI.11

CONSUMER UNITS[a] AND FAMILY PERSONAL INCOME, BY INCOME
LEVEL, 1935-62[b]

Income Level	Consumer Units					Aggregate Family Personal Income				
	1935-36 Average	1941	1950	1960	1962	1935-36 Average	1941	1950	1960	1962
	(In Millions)					(In Billions of Dollars)				
Under $2,000	29.8	24.4	11.4	7.3	6.9	28.5	25.5	13.2	8.2	7.7
$2,000-$2,999	5.1	9.2	8.1	5.2	4.9	12.2	22.7	20.3	13.0	12.4
$3,000-$3,999	1.7	4.1	8.6	5.9	5.6	5.8	14.0	30.0	20.8	19.8
$4,000-$4,999	0.6	1.6	7.1	6.2	5.9	2.8	7.2	31.5	27.7	26.7
$5,000-$7,499	0.6	1.2	8.5	13.9	14.0	3.6	6.9	51.2	86.2	87.2
$7,500-$9,999	0.2	0.4	2.8	8.1	9.1	2.0	3.2	23.4	69.9	78.6
$10,000-$14,999	} 0.3	} 0.5	1.5	6.0	7.2	} 7.8	} 11.9	18.3	71.2	84.9
$15,000 and over			1.0	3.6	4.2			29.3	85.3	103.4
ALL UNITS	38.4	41.4	48.8	56.1	57.9	62.7	91.4	217.3	382.3	420.4
	PERCENTAGE DISTRIBUTION									
Under $2,000	77.7	58.9	23.2	13.1	12.0	45.4	27.9	6.1	2.1	1.8
$2,000-$2,999	13.1	22.3	16.6	9.2	8.5	19.5	24.8	9.3	3.4	3.0
$3,000-$3,999	4.4	9.8	17.6	10.6	9.8	9.2	15.3	13.8	5.5	4.7
$4,000-$4,999	1.7	4.0	14.4	11.0	10.2	4.5	7.9	14.5	7.3	6.4
$5,000-$7,499	1.6	2.8	17.5	24.8	24.3	5.8	7.6	23.6	22.5	20.7
$7,500-$9,999	0.6	0.9	5.6	14.5	15.7	3.2	3.5	10.8	18.3	18.6
$10,000-$14,999	} 0.9	} 1.3	3.1	10.6	12.3	} 12.4	} 13.0	8.4	18.6	20.2
$15,000 and over			2.0	6.2	7.2			13.5	22.3	24.6
TOTAL	100.0	100.0	100.0	100.0	100.0	100.0	100.0	100.0	100.0	100.0

[a]Families and unattached individuals.
[b]The Office of Business Economics has discontinued this series but plans to reconstruct it on another basis. The aim is to relate the new series to the Census Bureau series on the distribution of cash incomes and the Bureau of Labor Statistics surveys of income.

TABLE VI.12

AVERAGE FAMILY PERSONAL INCOME, 1955-62

	1955	1957	1959	1962
Number of families (in millions)				
Total	42.7	43.7	44.8	46.9
Nonfarm	37.6	38.8	40.1	42.6
Farm-operator	5.1	4.9	4.6	4.3
Average income (in dollars)				
Total	6,303	6,992	7,435	8,151
Nonfarm	6,626	7,352	7,802	8,469
Farm-operator	3,917	4,111	4,264	5,015

family personal income per family increased from $6,303 in 1955 to $8,151 in 1962; that of unattached individuals, from $2,663 to $3,472, respectively. The average number of persons per family was 3.6 in 1955 and 3.7 in 1962; and their per capita family personal income was $1,755 and $2,211, respectively.

The average family personal income of nonfarm families is considerably higher, by about two-thirds or more than that of farm-operator families: $8,469 as against $5,015 in 1962 (see Table VI.12).

TABLE VI.13

AVERAGE FAMILY PERSONAL INCOME BY REGION, 1961
(In Dollars)

	United States	North- east	North Central	South	West
All families, income after taxes	5,595	6,436	5,536	4,600	6,217
Urban	5,957	6,604	5,863	5,036	6,386
Rural nonfarm	4,700	5,710	4,697	3,977	5,438
Rural farm	4,424	5,057	4,878	3,592	6,149

However, such contrasts are not uniform throughout the nation. As the Survey of Consumer Expenditures, conducted jointly by the Bureau of Labor Statistics and the Department of Agriculture, has shown, the average income of the farm family in the South was far behind that of an urban family in 1961, but in the West, the discrepancy was very small (see Table VI.13).

The rise in average family personal income since World War II is reflected, except in the postwar recession years, in an upward shift of families on the income ladder. Millions of families moved from lower to higher income rungs, and new families appeared on the bottom rung, while their ranks have become thinner. There were 13.1 million families

TABLE VI.14

PERCENTAGE DISTRIBUTION OF WHITE AND NONWHITE
FAMILIES, BY INCOME LEVEL, 1947-62

Size of Income	White Families					Nonwhite Families				
	1947	1950	1955	1960	1962	1947	1950	1955	1960	1962
Under $1,000	9.0	10.0	6.6	4.1	3.2	28.8	28.1	19.0	13.4	9.2
$1,000-$1,999	14.9	12.2	8.7	6.9	5.8	33.5	25.3	20.7	18.3	16.3
$2,000-$2,999	22.3	17.3	10.4	8.1	6.9	18.8	23.5	17.6	14.8	17.6
$3,000-$3,999	20.8	21.3	14.3	9.4	8.2	8.4	13.5	17.2	14.0	13.5
$4,000-$5,999	20.5	24.0	29.4	23.8	20.1	7.5	6.2	16.9	19.1	19.6
$6,000-$6,999	9.5	5.5	9.9	11.2	10.5	3.0	1.5	4.8	6.7	7.3
$7,000-$9,999		6.1	13.9	21.3	23.8		1.7	3.1	8.7	10.8
$10,000-$14,999	3.0	3.5	5.3	11.2	15.6	0.1	0.3	0.6ᵃ	4.3	4.1
$15,000 and over			1.5	4.1	5.9				0.6	1.6
TOTAL	100.0	100.0	100.0	100.0	100.0	100.0	100.0	100.0	100.0	100 0
Median income, (in dollars)	3,157	3,445	4,605	5,835	6,548	1,614	1,869	2,549	3,233	3,465

ᵃLess than 0.05 per cent.

in the income group under $3,000 in 1947; 7.7 million in 1955; and 6.1 million in 1962. In the next income group, $3,000-$3,999, there were 7.9, 5.9, and 3.8 million families, respectively. At the same time, the groups of middle-income families ($6,000-$9,999) expanded from 5.2 million in 1947 to 11.8 million in 1955 and 16.2 million in 1962. Corresponding figures for the income bracket $10,000-$14,999 are 1.2, 3.0, and 6.9 million.

In 1947, families with income over $3,000 received 85 per cent of total personal income in the country; in 1955, 94.6 per cent; and in 1962, 97.1 per cent (see Appendix Table XVIII).

There is a great though somewhat narrowing contrast in the distribution of white and nonwhite families by the size of money income. In 1962, one-sixth of white families had income under $3,000, as compared with more than two-fifths of the nonwhite. In the upper income groups, contrasts are also sharp: every fifth white family had an income exceeding $10,000, but only 1 in 16 nonwhite families was in that income bracket (see Table VI.14).

Despite the progress that has been made, inequality in income and contrasts between wealth and poverty still exist in our "affluent" society, though what is called "poverty" in this country might perhaps be considered a rather satisfactory level of income in many other countries.

Inequality in the distribution of income can be shown by arraying all consumer units by family personal income in 5 (or 10) equal groups and measuring the share of each group (quintile or decile) in the aggregate family personal income. When the consumer units are divided into quintiles, each comprising the same number of consumer units, the following features become apparent:

(1) There has been almost complete stability in the relative distribu-

TABLE VI.15

FAMILY PERSONAL INCOME OF CONSUMER UNITS,
BY EACH FIFTH AND TOP FIVE PER CENT OF UNITS, 1935-62

Size of Income	Per Cent of Income					Average Income, (In Dollars)				
	1935-1936	1941	1950	1960	1962	1935-1936	1941	1950	1960	1962
Lowest fifth	4.1	4.1	4.8	4.6	4.6	337	450	1,056	1,562	1,662
Second fifth	9.2	9.5	10.9	10.9	10.9	749	1,044	2,418	3,731	3,966
Third fifth	14.1	15.3	16.1	16.4	16.3	1,146	1,694	3,579	5,577	5,938
Fourth fifth	20.9	22.3	22.1	22.7	22.7	1,708	2,463	4,911	7,731	8,241
Highest fifth	51.7	48.8	46.1	45.4	45.5	4,216	5,396	10,254	15,493	16,505
TOTAL	100.0	100.0	100.0	100.0	100.0	1,631	2,209	4,444	6,819	7,262
Top 5 per cent	26.5	24.0	21.4	19.6	19.6	8,654	10,617	19,066	26,721	28,482

tion of family personal income from 1947 through 1962. The lowest fifth of the families and unattached individuals accounted for 4.1 per cent of the total personal income in 1935–36, 4.8 per cent in 1950, and 4.6 per cent in 1962; the highest quintile, for 51.7, 46.1, and 45.5 per cent, respectively. The same observation is valid for the 3 middle quintiles, or the remaining 60 per cent of all consumer units.

(2) The top 5 per cent of consumer units accounted for 21.4 per cent in 1950 and 19.6 per cent in 1962—a rather slight decline (see Table VI.15 and Figure VI.5).

FIGURE VI.5

FAMILY PERSONAL INCOME RECEIVED
BY EACH FIFTH OF FAMILIES AND UNATTACHED INDIVIDUALS IN 1962

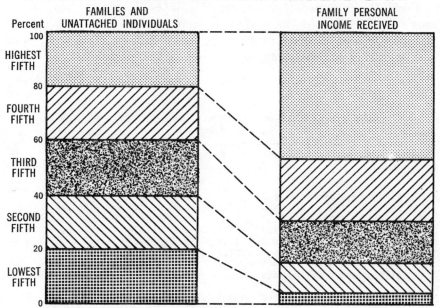

U.S. Department of Commerce, Bureau of the Census

On the whole, this indicates that small gains have been made in the redistribution of national income and that a substantial proportion of consumer units is still at the bottom of the income scale.

The Federal income tax affects the relative distribution of personal income. Thus, in 1962, the aggregate personal income of the lowest fifth of consumer units was 4.6 per cent before the tax and 4.9 per cent after payment of the tax. On the other hand, the share of the highest fifth, who paid a progressively higher income tax, declined from 45.5 per cent before the tax to 43.7 per cent after the tax. The corresponding figures for the top 5 per cent of the consumer units were 19.6 per cent before and 17.7 per cent after.

Among the 57.9 million consumer units in 1962, 4.3 million were farm-operator families and 11 million were unattached individuals. These 2 groups were heavily represented in the income bracket under $3,000: 1.7 and 5.7 million, respectively. For the farm-operator families, food and fuel produced and consumed on the farm is valued at farm prices; valuation at retail prices might have moved some of them into the next bracket.

The lowest fifth of income recipients includes some retired persons who live independently and supplement their social-security benefits—and, in some cases, their accumulated savings—by small current income, but who are not necessarily people of low-income status. Some short-run difficulties, such as temporary sickness or unemployment or a business reverse may push some consumer units into the low-income groups and cause hardships at a given time, without making these families or individuals chronically "poor" people.

The 1960 census report on income of families and unattached individuals in 1959 differs in some respects from the preceding data of the Office of Business Economics. First, the census data are "frequently based not on records but on memory," which may lead to understatement of

TABLE VI.16

INCOME DISTRIBUTION OF FAMILIES, BY RACE AND RESIDENCE, 1960
(Per Cent)

Money Income	Total	White	Nonwhite	Urban	Rural Nonfarm	Rural Farm
Under $1,999	13.1	11.0	32.4	9.4	18.3	32.2
$2,000-$2,999	8.3	7.6	15.5	6.9	10.5	15.0
$3,000-$3,999	9.5	9.1	13.5	8.5	11.5	12.7
$4,000-$4,999	11.0	10.9	11.4	10.7	12.5	10.4
$5,000-$5,999	12.3	12.7	8.6	12.6	12.5	8.2
$6,000-$6,999	10.7	11.2	5.7	11.8	10.1	5.9
$7,000-$9,999	20.1	21.2	8.7	22.6	15.5	9.0
$10,000-$14,999	10.5	11.2	3.4	12.2	6.5	4.6
$15,000 and over	4.6	5.0	0.8	5.3	2.5	2.2
UNITED STATES	100.0	100.0	100.0	100.0	100.0	100.0

income because "the tendency is to forget minor or irregular sources of income." Other errors in reporting are due to misunderstanding of income questions or to misrepresentation as well as to "the failure, on occasion, to obtain from the respondent any report on other money income." The census covers only money income and disregards the fact that "many farm families receive an important part of their income in the form of rent-free housing and of goods produced and consumed on the farm."

The definitions of income differ in these 2 offices of the Department of Commerce, for the Bureau of the Census obtains the data from households, while the estimates of the Office of Business Economics come from business, government, and other sources. Yet census data provide some information not available otherwise on income distribution by sex, race, urban and rural area, age, and so on.

Contrasts revealed by the 1960 census in the distribution of 45.1 million families by income size in relation to race and to the type of area in which they lived are in line with those reported by the OBE (see Table VI.16).

Thus, while 1 in 9 white families had income under $2,000 in 1959, nearly a third of the nonwhite families were in that income bracket. Almost one-half of all white families reported an income above $6,000 that year, as compared with less than one-fifth of all nonwhite families. Regional differences in average income were relatively greater among nonwhite than among white families. Median income of nonwhite families ranged from $2,600 in the South to $5,400 in the West; the corresponding figures for the white families were $5,200 and $6,700.

The census data, too, confirm that urban families have higher income than rural residents, and that rural nonfarm families have higher incomes than farm people. The median income of urban families was $6,166; of rural nonfarm families, $4,750; and of rural farm families, $3,228.

Of the 4.1 million boys aged 14–19 years who reported some money earnings in 1960, 7 out of 10 earned less than $1,000; nearly 1 in 4 had income of $1,000—$2,999; and the remainder, income exceeding $3,000. In the next age group, 20–24 years, about 1 out of 6 earned less than $1,000; 2 out of 5 had income under $3,000; somewhat more than 1 in 20 earned more than $6,000.

31. Disposable Income, Consumer Expenditures, and Savings

Personal income represents private purchasing power and a base for taxation by the Federal and, in some cases, state and local governments. What is left after personal taxes constitutes *disposable income*.

With the development of the American economy and the growth of the population, disposable income has increased uninterruptedly, except in the Depression years; from $83 billion in 1929 to $207 billion in 1950 and $436 billion in 1964.

TABLE VI.17

DISPOSABLE INCOME IN CURRENT AND CONSTANT DOLLARS, 1929-64

| Year | Personal Income | Taxes[a] | Disposable Income | | Per Capita Disposable Income | |
| | | | In Current Prices | In 1964 Prices | In Current Prices | In 1964 Prices |
			(In Billions of Dollars)		(In Dollars)	
1929	85.9	2.6	83.3	155.1	682	1,273
1933	47.0	1.5	45.5	117.9	364	938
1940	78.3	2.6	75.7	175.6	576	1,329
1945	171.1	20.9	150.2	243.8	1,075	1,743
1950	227.6	20.7	206.9	264.4	1,369	1,743
1955	310.9	35.5	275.3	313.3	1,661	1,896
1960	401.0	50.9	350.0	365.3	1,936	2,021
1963	464.8	60.9	403.8	408.1	2,125	2,155
1964	495.0	59.2	435.8	435.8	2,248	2,248

[a] Includes nontax payments and other government revenues from individuals, such as fines, penalties, and so on.

While total disposable income more than quintupled, in current dollars, between 1929 and 1964, per capita disposable income increased much less, because of the growth of the population. In 1964 dollars, disposable income increased less than 3 times over that period, and per capita income less than doubled; between 1950 and 1964, the per capita income increased by less than 30 per cent (see Table VI.17 and Figure VI.6).

The largest part of disposable income is spent for consumer goods and services, and the remainder is set aside as savings. Consumer expenditures usually absorb more than nine-tenths of disposable income and in some years, 97–98 per cent. When the disposable income shrinks to a level that cannot satisfy the essentials of life, consumers draw on savings, if available,

FIGURE VI.6

PER CAPITA DISPOSABLE INCOME, 1947-64
(Quarterly Data.
Seasonally Adjusted Annual Rates)

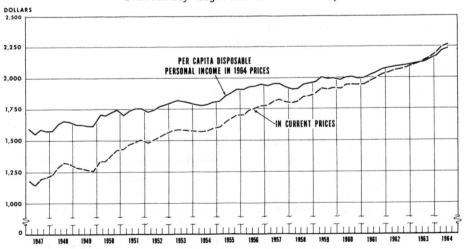

U.S. Bureau of the Budget--Data from U.S. Department of Commerce and Council of Economic Advisers

TABLE VI.18

COMPONENTS OF PERSONAL SAVING, 1946-63
(In Billions of Dollars)

Personal Saving	Annual Average 1946-49	Annual Average 1950-55	1955	1960	1962	1963
Gross investment in tangible assets	16.8	27.6	33.0	36.8	39.2	41.0
Nonfarm homes	7.1	13.4	17.3	18.9	17.9	18.3
Other construction and producers' durable equipment	9.7	13.3	14.8	17.1	20.1	21.5
Inventories of noncorporate enterprises	-	0.9	0.9	0.8	1.2	1.2
Depreciation	6.6	11.1	12.8	16.5	17.4	18.1
Nonfarm homes	2.1	3.2	3.9	5.7	6.5	7.0
Noncorporate nonfarm enterprises	2.5	4.1	4.7	5.9	5.9	6.0
Farm enterprises	1.8	3.4	3.7	4.2	4.2	4.3
Other	0.2	0.4	0.5	0.7	0.8	0.9
Net investment in tangible assets	10.2	16.5	20.2	20.3	21.8	22.9
Increase in financial assets	9.2	17.3	22.5	20.1	37.9	41.1
Currency and bank deposits	2.4	5.2	3.3	2.8	18.0	17.5
Savings and loan association shares	1.3	3.3	5.2	8.3	10.0	11.8
Securities	1.5	2.5	6.3	-0.1	-0.9	0.5
Private insurance and pension reserves	4.0	6.4	7.9	9.2	10.8	11.2
Increase in debt (consumer debt, mortgage debt, securities loans, other)	9.8	16.3	24.5	22.6	32.9	38.5
Errors and omissions	0.1	-0.1	0.7	-3.9	-1.1	-2.1
TOTAL PERSONAL SAVING	9.4	17.6	17.5	21.7	27.8	27.5

or resort to loans, which appear as dissavings.* Between 1946–49 and 1963, net personal savings have grown from $9.4 billion to $27.5 billion, in spite of the simultaneous growth of debts to corporations and financial intermediaries from $9.8 billion to $38.5 billion (see Table VI.18).

During World War II, when the entire economy of the United States was geared to production of military hardware and other war necessities, personal consumption expenditures fell to the unprecedented level of 75 per cent of disposable income. The remainder accumulated in the hands of consumers, partly in the form of government bonds (see Table VI.19).

The Securities and Exchange Commission calculates personal savings in a different way from the above estimates by the Office of Business Economics. It shows the increase in financial assets held by individuals minus the increase in their debt. In contrast to the OBE figures, its estimate of gross savings includes consumer durable goods and government insurance funds. On the whole, the SEC estimates are in fair agreement with those of OBE, though some years the difference may be substantial (see Table VI.20).

* Personal savings consist of tangible assets (homes, producers' durable equipment, inventories, etc., less depreciation) and financial assets (currency, bank deposits, securities, etc.), less debts.

TABLE VI.19

CONSUMPTION EXPENDITURES AND SAVINGS, 1929-64

Year	Consumption Expenditures (In Billions of Dollars)	Disposable Income Savings	Consumption Expenditures (Per Cent)	Savings
1929	79.1	4.2	95.0	5.0
1933	46.4	-0.9	102.0	-2.0
1940	71.8	3.8	94.8	5.2
1942	89.3	27.6	76.6	23.4
1944	109.1	37.3	74.6	25.4
1945	120.7	29.6	80.0	20.0
1950	193.9	13.1	93.2	6.8
1955	259.5	15.8	94.3	5.7
1960	333.0	17.0	95.1	4.9
1963	383.4	20.5	94.9	5.1
1964	409.5	26.3	94.0	6.0

The role of savings in the development of the national economy is very significant. Although they originate in many parts of the economy, personal and corporate savings are the most consequential. The first are channeled into the purchase of Government securities and corporation stocks, home mortgages, personal savings accounts and other forms of bank deposits, etc. The corporate savings ordinarily turn into investments of physical assets, and when expansion outruns the available savings, use is made of the capital market by issuing bonds, stocks, or other forms of loans. The capital market is provided by savings deposited at commercial banks, trust and insurance companies, and the like. It is estimated that consumer savings have on the average supplied over $13 billion annually to the credit market through the period of 1954-62.

TABLE VI.20

FINANCIAL SAVINGS OF INDIVIDUALS, 1940-64
(In Billions of Dollars)

	1940	1950	1960	1962	1963	1964
Currency and bank deposits	2.9	3.5	2.7	18.0	17.5	17.8
Savings shares[a]	0.3	1.7	8.3	10.0	11.8	11.3
Securities	-0.4	0.9	-0.5	-0.9	0.5	5.2
Private insurance and pension reserves	1.8	4.8	9.5	10.8	11.2	12.3
Government insurance and pension reserves[b]	1.3	1.1	3.4	3.0	4.4	5.4
Less increase in debt:	1.7	10.7	15.4	19.6	23.2	22.9
Mortgage debt	0.9	6.8	10.9	13.4	15.9	16.2
Consumer debt	1.0	3.7	4.2	5.0	6.3	6.5
Securities loans	-0.2	0.2	0.3	1.1	0.9	0.2
TOTAL FINANCIAL SAVING	4.2	1.3	8.0	21.2	22.3	29.1

[a] Includes shares in loan associations, and shares and deposits in credit unions.
[b] Includes social-security funds, and state and local retirement systems.

TABLE VI.21

FINANCIAL ASSETS AND LIABILITIES OF INDIVIDUALS, 1950-64
(In Billions of Dollars)

	1950	1955	1960	1961	1963	1964
Financial assets, total	...	738	975	1,112	1,241	1,372
Currency and deposits	130	156	181	190	225	243
Currency	23	26	26	26	89	97
Demand deposits	50	56	54	54		
Time and savings deposits	57	75	101	110	136	146
Savings shares	15	35	66	76	98	109
Securities	...	385	505	608	650	730
U.S. savings bonds	50	50	46	46	48	49
Other U.S. Government[a]	18	18	27	26	27	29
State and local government	13	19	31	32	34	36
Corporate and other[a]	...	298	401	504	541	615
Private insurance and pension reserves	68	104	152	167	190	206
Insurance reserves	57	77	96	102	112	118
Insured pension reserves	6	11	19	20	23	25
Noninsured pension reserves	6	16	37	45	55	63
Government insurance and pension reserves	40	58	71	72	79	84
Liabilities, total	58	118	185	200	242	265
Mortgage debt	38	79	130	142	171	187
Consumer debt	18	34	51	52	63	70
Securities loans	3	5	5	6	8	8
Net equity (assets-liabilities)	...	620	790	913	999	1,107

[a]Estimated market value.

32. Assets and Debts of the American People

The gross financial assets (the market value of accumulated assets) of individual Americans is a respectable amount: $1,372 billion at the end of 1964! Securities holdings represented 53 per cent (or $730 billion) of the total; currency and bank deposits amounted to about $243 billion; savings shares, $109 billion; and private and government insurance and pension reserves, $290 billion. The liabilities totaled $265 billion and consisted of mortgage debt (about 70 per cent of total debt), consumer debt (more than 26 per cent), and securities loans. The net equity (assets minus debts) amounted to $1.1 trillion (see Table VI.21).

Though these figures look very impressive, they tell a less cheerful story when the assets are distributed among American families. According to the Survey Research Center of the University of Michigan, about one-third of the families (35 per cent) had no liquid assets* at all in 1964; 15 per cent owned less than $500 each; and 23 per cent possessed from $500 to $2,499.

* Includes U.S. savings bonds, checking and savings accounts in banks, and shares in savings and loan associations and credit unions; currency is excluded.

TABLE VI.22

SHORT- AND INTERMEDIATE-TERM CONSUMER CREDIT, 1929-64
(In Millions of Dollars)

Year	Total	Installment Credit					Noninstallment Credit		
		Total	Automobile Paper	Other Consumer Goods	Repair Loans	Personal Loans	Total	Charge Accounts	Other
1929	7,116	3,524	1,384	1,544	27	569	3,592	1,996	1,596
1933	3,885	1,723	493	799	15	416	2,162	1,286	876
1939	7,222	4,503	1,497	1,620	298	1,088	2,719	1,414	1,305
1941	9,172	6,085	2,458	1,929	376	1,322	3,087	1,645	1,442
1943	4,901	2,136	355	819	130	832	2,765	1,440	1,325
1945	5,665	2,462	455	816	182	1,009	3,203	1,612	1,591
1947	11,598	6,695	1,924	2,143	718	1,910	4,903	2,381	2,522
1950	21,471	14,703	6,074	4,799	1,016	2,814	6,768	3,367	3,401
1953	31,393	23,005	9,835	6,779	1,610	4,781	8,388	4,274	4,114
1956	42,334	31,720	14,420	8,606	1,905	6,789	10,614	4,995	5,619
1959	51,542	39,245	16,420	10,630	2,809	9,386	12,297	5,104	7,193
1962	63,164	48,034	19,540	12,605	3,246	12,643	15,130	5,684	9,446
1963	69,890	53,745	22,199	13,766	3,389	14,391	16,145	5,871	10,274
1964	76,700	59,300	24,550	15,200	3,500	16,050	17,400	6,300	11,100

FIGURE VI.7

CONSUMER CREDIT OUTSTANDING, 1947-64
(Short- and Intermediate-Term.
End-of-Month Data)

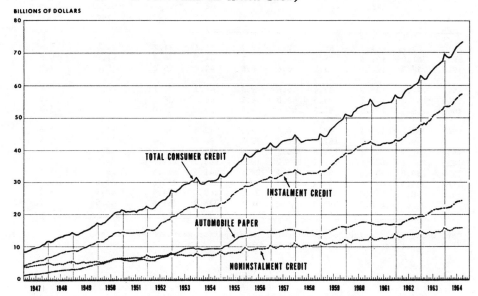

U.S. Bureau of the Budget--Data from Board of Governors of the Federal Reserve System

On the other end of the scale, 12 per cent of the families owned from $5,000 to $24,999, and 1 per cent, $25,000 and over.*

In the case of individual debt, short- and intermediate-term consumer credit (installment credit, charge accounts, single-payment loans, and others) has multiplied about tenfold between 1929 and 1964, from $7.1 billion to $76.7 billion. Within these 35 years, installment credit developed spectacularly. For instance, in 1929, both installment and noninstallment credits were of about equal size: $3.5 billion and $3.6 billion, respectively. In 1964, the corresponding figures were $59.3 billion and $17.4 billion. The most important single item of installment credit is automobile paper, which showed little change in amount between 1939 and 1947 ($1.5 billion and $1.9 billion, respectively) but increased to $14.4 billion by 1956 and again to $24.6 billion in the following decade (see Table VI.22). The consumer credit renews itself continuously by repayments and new transactions, yet never stops growing; in less than 2 decades, between the end of 1947 and the fourth quarter of 1964, it increased nearly 7 times, from $11.6 billion to $76.7 billion (see Figure VI.7).

* Savings kept in the form of owner-occupied homes, business assets, retirement funds, old-age pensions, and life insurance funds were mentioned very infrequently by the interviewed families in 1964. These families did not consider such assets as reserve funds.

TABLE VI.23

NET PUBLIC AND PRIVATE DEBT,[a] 1929-64

Year	Total Public Debt[b]	Total Private Debt	Cor- porate Debt	Individual and Noncorporate Debt				
				Total	Farm	Nonfarm		
						Total	Mortgage	Commercial and Financial	Consumer

Year	Total Public Debt[b]	Total Private Debt	Cor-porate Debt	Total	Farm	Total	Mortgage	Commercial and Financial	Consumer
1929	29.7	161.2	88.9	72.3	12.2	60.1	31.2	22.4	6.4
1933	41.0	127.5	76.9	50.6	9.1	41.5	26.3	11.7	3.5
1939	58.9	124.3	73.5	50.8	8.8	42.0	25.0	9.8	7.2
1941	72.6	139.0	83.4	55.6	9.3	46.3	27.1	10.0	9.2
1943	169.3	144.3	.95.5	48.8	8.2	40.5	26.1	9.5	4.9
1945	266.4	139.9	85.3	54.6	7.3	47.4	27.0	14.7	5.7
1947	237.7	179.7	108.9	70.8	8.6	62.3	38.8	11.9	11.6
1950	239.4	250.9	142.1	108.8	12.3	96.6	59.4	15.8	21.4
1953	256.7	329.8	179.5	150.3	16.9	133.6	83.8	18.4	31.4
1956	268.1	439.4	231.7	207.7	19.5	188.2	121.3	24.4	42.5
1959	298.8	547.4	283.3	264.1	23.0	241.1	160.8	28.7	51.5
1962	329.6	689.0	347.4	341.6	30.2	311.4	210.6	37.6	63.2
1963	340.7	752.8	374.6	378.2	33.2	345.0	234.2	40.9	69.9
1964	352.7	810.9	395.3	415.6	36.8	378.8	257.6	44.5	76.7

[a]Net debt: duplications of government and corporate debt are eliminated.
[b]Federal, state, and local government debt.

In view of the controversy, theoretical and political, about the issue of public debt in this country, it may be worth-while to compare it with the total private debt of the American people—individual, corporate, and non-corporate. Apart from the years of World War II and a few postwar years, private debt has always been larger than public debt. Beginning with 1943, public debt expanded rapidly and left private debt far behind. The resurgence of the latter started in 1946, the first postwar year, and by 1950 it overtook public indebtedness. Since then, it has not ceased to rise; by the end of 1964 it was again, as in 1940–41, approximately twice as large as the public debt (the combined government debt: Federal, state, and local) (see Table VI.23).

The corporate debt represents about half the total private debt; the remainder consists of the debt of individuals and noncorporate debt— farm and nonfarm. About two-thirds of the individual and noncorporate debt is mortgage, with farm mortgages amounting to only 6–7 per cent of all mortgage debt (see Sec. 46).

33. Rich States, Poor States

The 2 largest states—New York and California—together receive al-most one-fourth of all personal income in the United States. Along with 8 other states—Illinois, Pennsylvania, Ohio, Texas, Michigan, New Jersey, Massachusetts, and Florida—they account for six-tenths of the total. At the other extreme, the whole group of 21 states lowest in personal income

FIGURE VI.8

MEDIAN FAMILY INCOME, BY STATE, 1960

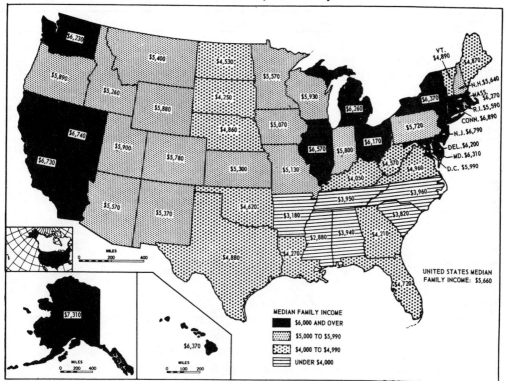

U.S. Department of Commerce, Bureau of the Census

(each with less than $4 billion) has considerably less than either New York or California.

Geographically, the "rich" states represent 2 blocks on the map: one in the northeast, the old stronghold of American industry, stretching from the Atlantic coast along the Canadian border and Great Lakes; the other in the Far West, the new center of dynamic, booming industrial expansion. Similarly, the "poor" states form 2 blocks: the larger group covers the whole southern and southeastern corner of the country, along the Mexican Gulf; the minor group is located in the north, midway between the 2 oceans. The states with the largest income also have the largest populations.

According to the Census of 1960, the median family income* in the United States was $5,660. For the distribution of states by median family income, see Figure VI.8.

---

* The *median income* is the amount which divides all families and unrelated individuals into 2 equal groups, the one with income above the median and the other, with that below the median.

TABLE VI.24

PER CAPITA PERSONAL INCOME, BY STATE, 1950-64
(In Dollars)

State	1950	1960	1964	State	1950	1960	1964
District of Columbia	2,201	2,993	3,544	Nebraska	1,469	2,135	2,349
Delaware	2,146	3,002	3,460	Kansas	1,379	2,060	2,346
Connecticut	1,915	2,854	3,281	Montana	1,614	1,935	2,252
Nevada	1,938	2,801	3,248	Florida	1,293	1,969	2,251
New York	1,887	2,779	3,162	Virginia	1,214	1,849	2,239
Alaska	2,231	2,772	3,116	Arizona	1,295	2,019	2,233
California	1,838	2,722	3,103	Texas	1,334	1,920	2,188
Illinois	1,829	2,634	3,041	Utah	1,282	1,912	2,156
New Jersey	1,786	2,652	3,005	North Dakota	1,262	1,746	2,133
Massachusetts	1,664	2,511	2,965	Maine	1,185	1,869	2,132
Maryland	1,594	2,395	2,867	Vermont	1,182	1,882	2,119
Michigan	1,686	2,320	2,755	Oklahoma	1,128	1,841	2,083
Ohio	1,615	2,335	2,646	New Mexico	1,158	1,815	2,041
Washington	1,670	2,307	2,635	Idaho	1,283	1,765	2,020
Hawaii	1,405	2,292	2,622	West Virginia	1,098	1,671	1,965
Oregon	1,600	2,236	2,606	Georgia	1,015	1,609	1,943
Pennsylvania	1,568	2,254	2,601	North Carolina	1,010	1,559	1,913
Missouri	1,439	2,203	2,600	South Dakota	1,211	1,854	1,879
Colorado	1,457	2,282	2,566	Louisiana	1,089	1,606	1,877
Indiana	1,514	2,186	2,544	Tennessee	992	1,535	1,859
Rhode Island	1,637	2,180	2,514	Kentucky	965	1,535	1,830
Wisconsin	1,472	2,162	2,490	Alabama	870	1,462	1,749
Wyoming	1,634	2,311	2,441	South Carolina	855	1,381	1,655
New Hampshire	1,314	2,079	2,377	Arkansas	807	1,337	1,655
Iowa	1,447	2,024	2,376	Mississippi	731	1,167	1,438
Minnesota	1,396	2,073	2,375				

Differentials in per capita personal income are wide among both regions and states. Per capita income is highest in the Far West, $3,006 in 1964, about 17 per cent above that year's national average of $2,566; it is lowest in the Southeast, $1,917—25 per cent below the national average. The spread in per capita income is even greater from state to state, ranging in

TABLE VI.25

PER CAPITA PERSONAL INCOME IN RELATION TO NATIONAL AVERAGE,
BY STATE, 1964

UNITED STATES	100				
District of Columbia	138	Pennsylvania	101	North Dakota	83
Delaware	135	Missouri	101	Maine	83
Connecticut	128	Colorado	100	Vermont	83
Nevada	127	Indiana	99	Oklahoma	81
New York	123	Rhode Island	98	New Mexico	80
Alaska	121	Wisconsin	97	Idaho	79
California	121	Wyoming	95	West Virginia	77
Illinois	119	New Hampshire	93	Georgia	76
New Jersey	117	Iowa	93	North Carolina	75
Massachusetts	116	Minnesota	93	South Dakota	73
Maryland	112	Nebraska	92	Louisiana	73
Michigan	107	Kansas	91	Tennessee	72
Ohio	103	Montana	88	Kentucky	71
Washington	103	Florida	88	Alabama	68
Hawaii	102	Virginia	87	South Carolina	64
Oregon	102	Arizona	87	Arkansas	64
		Texas	85	Mississippi	56
		Utah	84		

TABLE VI.26

DISTRIBUTION OF PERSONAL INCOME BY REGION, 1929 and 1963
(Per Cent)

	1929	1963
New England	8.32	6.48
Mideast	32.06	24.75
Great Lakes	23.61	21.14
Plains	8.87	7.95
Southeast	11.67	16.19
Southwest	4.97	6.87
Rocky Mountain	1.88	2.32
Far West	8.62	14.30
UNITED STATES	100.00	100.00

1964 from more than $3,200 in the District of Columbia, Delaware, Connecticut, and Nevada to $1,438 in Mississippi (see Table VI.24). In 32 states, per capita income was below the national average; the regions and states were arrayed in relation to the national average, $2,566 in 1964, as shown in Table VI.25.

Changes in personal income by states and regions depend on many factors: shift of industries, movement of population, significant alterations in the defense or national-highway programs, ups and downs in construction activities, and so on. In the course of the 15 years 1948–63, some states, in particular, California, Nevada, Arizona, New Mexico, and Florida, have experienced increases in personal income much more rapidly than other states. The regional distribution of personal income has shown a clear shift from the North and East to the South and West. In 1929, the 4 northern and eastern regions (New England, Middle Atlantic, Great Lakes, and Plains) accounted for nearly three-fourths of total personal income in the country; in 1963, their share amounted to only three-fifths (see Table VI.26).

Regional differences in average income levels had been very sharp in the early 1930's, but they narrowed during World War II and the following years, though the Rocky Mountain region, Great Plains, Southwest, and especially the Southeast are still below the national average of per capita personal income (see Figure VI.9).

34. The National Wealth of the United States

The *national wealth* of a country consists of 2 types of assets—reproducible assets (structures, equipment, and inventories) and nonreproducible assets (chiefly land and subsoil assets). The most complete estimate of the national wealth of the United States is that prepared by Raymond W. Goldsmith;* it covers the period from 1900 through 1958 and evaluates all

* This section uses the estimates of Mr. Goldsmith, as they appear in his study *The National Wealth of the United States in the Postwar Period* (published for the National Bureau of Economic Research; Princeton, N.J.: Princeton University Press, 1962).

FIGURE VI.9

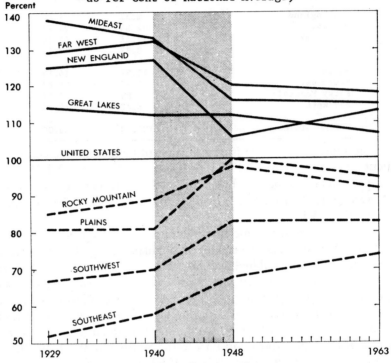

REGIONAL DIFFERENCES IN PER CAPITA
PERSONAL INCOME IN THE UNITED STATES, 1929-63
(Regional Per Capita Incomes Expressed
as Per Cent of National Average)

U.S. Department of Commerce, Office of Business Economics

tangible assets of this country plus net foreign assets, that is, the net balance of this country's claims against foreign countries. The tangible assets are evaluated at their reproduction cost; the nonreproducible assets, at market value.

The estimates are approximate, and despite the author's efforts to check each component in various ways, the margin of error cannot be defined exactly. Nevertheless, the estimates provide a valuable understanding of the magnitude of each tangible asset and of its importance in relation to others.

The national wealth of the United States, measured in current dollars, is estimated at $88 billion for 1900, $439 billion for 1929, and $1,703 billion for 1958. In constant dollars of 1947–49, the increase in national wealth becomes much more modest—not nearly 20 times between 1900 and 1958 as in the preceding figures, but only 4 times: $315 billion in 1900, $778 billion in 1929, and $1,244 billion in 1958. Between 1945 and 1958, national wealth, in current dollars, almost tripled; in constant dol-

FIGURE VI.10

TOTAL NET WEALTH, EXCLUDING MILITARY,
SELECTED YEARS, 1900-1958

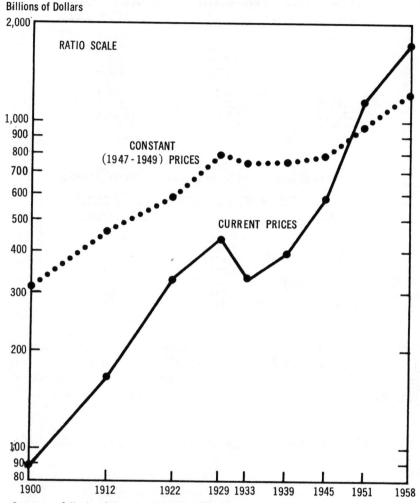

Courtesy of National Bureau of Economic Research:
R.W. Goldsmith, The National Health of the United States
in the Postwar Period (New York, 1962).

lars, the increase was only 58 per cent. Estimates on both valuation bases
are represented in Table VI.27 and Figure VI.10.

Over a period of time, a substantial part of the increase in total national
wealth has been absorbed by the growth of the population, as is evident
from figures for per capita wealth (see Table VI.28).

The average annual increase in national wealth through the postwar
years 1945–58 was 8.5 per cent in current dollars; in constant dollars,
about 3.5 per cent. The annual rate of growth of reproducible tangible

TABLE VI.27

NATIONAL WEALTH OF THE UNITED STATES, 1900-1958
(In Billions of Dollars)

Year	Current Dollars	Constant Dollars (1947-49)
1900	87.7	314.6
1929	439.2	778.0
1933	330.3	742.2
1939	395.6	748.4
1945	576.2	788.1
1950	1,067.1	949.2
1955	1,401.9	1,131.6
1958	1,702.8	1,244.4

TABLE VI.28

PER CAPITA NATIONAL WEALTH IN THE UNITED STATES, 1900-1958

End of Year	Current Dollars	Constant Dollars (1947-49)
1900	1,144	4,094
1929	3,587	6,352
1933	2,621	5,886
1939	3,015	5,699
1945	4,097	5,608
1958	9,781	7,097

wealth only (i.e., excluding land and subsoil assets) was approximately 4 per cent in constant dollars. Per capita, the annual rate of growth of national wealth in current dollars was about 7 per cent; in constant dollars, this rate was about 1.4 per cent for aggregate wealth and 2.2 per cent for reproducible assets only.

The main components of national wealth are structures (residential and

TABLE VI.29

ESTIMATED VALUE OF MAIN COMPONENTS OF
NATIONAL WEALTH, 1900-1958
(In Billions of Current Dollars)

Year	Structures	Equipment	Inventories	Consumer Durables	Land	Other
1900	34.9	6.5	6.8	6.1	31.0	2.4
1929	189.9	38.4	31.5	42.2	113.5	23.7
1933	159.5	29.2	18.7	25.7	81.2	16.0
1939	188.5	34.2	25.3	32.5	88.6	26.4
1945	285.6	48.6	42.9	46.3	121.6	31.3
1950	507.3	110.0	79.4	111.3	201.8	57.3
1955	683.7	156.8	102.6	150.8	256.2	52.2
1958	833.7	199.9	111.8	178.8	310.8	67.8

nonresidential), producer durables (equipment), inventories, consumer durables, and land.

The values of some components of national wealth have increased faster than those of others: structures, equipment, and consumer durables experienced a higher rate of growth than inventories, and inventories a higher rate than land.

Structures account for nearly half the total national wealth, producer durables for some 12 per cent, consumer durables for about 11 per cent, inventories for approximately 7 per cent, land (including forest and subsoil assets) for about 18 per cent; the remainder includes comparatively small assets such as livestock, monetary gold and silver, and net foreign assets (see Table VI.29).

The values of the various components of national wealth have changed in different directions and at different rates, and these changes are reflected in the components' shares of the total. Agricultural land, for example, represented 18.3 per cent of national wealth in 1900, 8.7 per cent in 1929, and 6 per cent in 1958. In contrast, the share of consumer durables, only 6.9 per cent in 1900, rose to 10.5 per cent in 1958. In general, the share of nonreproducible assets has shrunk and that of reproducible wealth, especially producer and consumer durables, has increased markedly —from 7.4 and 6.9 per cent, respectively, in 1900 to 11.8 and 10.5 per cent in 1958 (see Table VI.30).

The distribution of national wealth by type of ownership has undergone various changes since the turn of this century, but there have been no significant changes in the postwar years. Three major groups—nonfarm households, business, and government—own most of the nation's tangible assets. Nonfarm households have consistently owned 33–35 per cent of all tangible wealth. Business, which comprises agriculture and both unincorporated business and corporations, accounted for 61 per cent of the nation's tangible wealth in 1900, but only 47 per cent in 1958. The components within this last group have developed differently; agriculture, which represented 28 per cent of the nation's assets in 1900, had shrunk to some 11 per cent by 1958; ownership of unincorporated business also has declined in value but much less drastically, from 8 per cent to 6 per cent over the same period. On the other hand, corporations now own 30 per cent of all tangible wealth, as compared with less than 25 per cent in both 1900 and 1945. The government owns a little more than 15 per cent of the total national wealth; of this, one-third, 5.2 per cent, is owned by the Federal Government, and two-thirds, 10.2 per cent, by state and local governments (see Table VI.31). Military assets, excluded from all figures in this section, amounted, in current prices, to $73 billion in 1945 and $89 billion in 1958. They are held by the Federal Government.

The structure of the national wealth of the United States is rather similar on the whole to that of the industrially advanced countries for

TABLE VI.30

PERCENTAGE DISTRIBUTION OF NATIONAL WEALTH
BY TYPE OF TANGIBLE ASSET, 1900-1958

End of Year	Total	Structures		Producer Durables	Inventories	Consumer Durables	Land			Livestock	Monetary Metals	Net Foreign Assets
		Residential	Non-residential[a]				Agricultural	Residential	Non-residential[b]			
1900	100.0	19.9	20.0	7.4	7.8	6.9	18.3	5.0	12.0	3.6	1.9	-2.7
1929	100.0	21.8	21.4	8.7	7.2	9.6	8.7	5.5	11.7	1.5	1.1	2.8
1933	100.0	22.5	25.8	8.8	5.7	7.8	7.6	5.7	11.3	1.0	1.4	2.5
1939	100.0	23.1	24.6	8.7	6.4	8.2	6.6	5.8	10.0	1.3	5.0	0.4
1945	100.0	26.5	23.1	8.4	7.5	8.0	8.1	3.9	9.1	1.7	4.2	-0.4
1950	100.0	25.1	22.5	10.3	7.4	10.4	6.6	3.7	8.6	1.6	2.5	1.3
1955	100.0	25.1	23.7	11.2	7.3	10.8	6.0	3.7	8.6	0.8	1.9	1.1
1958	100.0	24.1	24.8	11.8	6.6	10.5	6.0	3.6	8.7	1.1	1.5	1.4

[a]Private nonresidential and public civilian structures.
[b]Private nonresidential and public civilian land.

TABLE VI.31

PERCENTAGE DISTRIBUTION OF TANGIBLE WEALTH
BY TYPE OF OWNERSHIP, 1900-1958

End of Year	Total	Government		Private					
		Federal	State and Local	Nonfarm House-holds	Nonpro-fit Organiza-tions	Agri-culture	Unincor-porated Business	Corpora-tions	Net Foreign Assets
1900	100.0	2.8	5.3	31.9	1.7	27.9	8.2	24.9	-2.7
1929	100.0	2.0	7.8	34.3	1.7	14.7	8.3	28.4	2.8
1933	100.0	2.9	11.1	33.1	1.9	12.4	7.6	28.7	2.5
1939	100.0	7.8	10.6	33.3	1.7	11.5	7.6	27.0	0.4
1945	100.0	8.1	10.0	33.8	1.6	15.0	6.8	24.8	a
1950	100.0	7.0	9.3	34.5	1.8	12.8	6.9	27.8	a
1955	100.0	6.0	9.7	35.7	2.0	10.7	6.6	29.2	a
1958	100.0	5.2	10.2	35.4	2.1	10.7	6.4	30.0	a

aAllocated among sectors.

which comparable data are available. Since World War II, the share of land has tended to decline generally and that of producer durables, to rise. Net foreign assets, however, represent a much larger share of national wealth in many other countries than in this country, where they amounted to only 1.5 per cent of the total in 1958.

VII. *Consumer Expenditures*

35. *Allocating What We Spend*

In our economic system, production is controlled by the market, which
in turn is controlled by consumers' demands for goods and services and
their capacity and willingness to pay the prices required by the producers.
The basic principle of budgeting is to obtain the greatest amount of
satisfaction for a given amount of money. Accordingly, the most urgent
needs come first, and others are satisfied insofar as purchasing power remains. The allocation of expenditures over time varies with changes in
prices, the size and composition of the household, the quality of merchandise offered in the market, the fashion, the season and weather, and—
most of all—with changes in income.

The distribution of consumer expenditures among various commodities
and services is determined by the way in which each of us distributes
what he spends. Although the behavior of each individual consumer is
unpredictable, the pattern of aggregate consumer expenditures is fairly
consistent. When the price of an indispensable commodity goes up, consumers increase their outlay for that particular commodity and cut other
expenditures. When the price of an article of relative luxury rises, some
consumers do without it and thus free a part of their purchasing power
for other purposes. Increase in income encourages spending for coveted
articles of comfort and luxury; when income is declining, the demand for
luxuries diminishes long before that for essentials. All in all, outlays for
luxuries are more sensitive to variations in income changes and business
conditions than expenditures for necessities.

In the United States as a whole, outlays for food, including beverages and tobacco, and for housing and household operation make up somewhat more than half the total expenditures. Services of a personal character (medical care, recreation, education, personal care and personal business, religious activities) absorb about one-fifth; clothing, including jewelry, accessories, and watches, about one-tenth. The remainder goes for transportation, purchased and owner-operated, including the purchase of an automobile.

Within these broad limits, patterns of consumer spending undergo changes in the course of time, as we can see from the surveys made in the last 50 years.* In 1917–19, food accounted for 45 per cent of total expenditures of low-income families, 40 per cent in 1934–36, 33–34 per cent in 1950, and 28–30 per cent in 1960–61. In the budget of high-income families, the proportion of expenditures for food was 22–24 per cent in 1950 and 20 per cent or less in 1960–61. Another substantial shift in the spending pattern of consumers took place with respect to transportation. In 1917–19, wage-earners and clerical workers allocated only 3.1 per cent of their budget for transportation; by 1934–36, this share nearly tripled— to 8.5 per cent. Within the next 15 years, it became a very important item in the consumer budget, rising to 13.4 per cent of total expenses, and in 1960–61, to 14.7 per cent. Other items in consumer expenditures were not static either, their share changing even within the period between the 2 last surveys, 1950 and 1960–61 (see Table VII.1).

Though many factors affect the distribution of consumer expenditures, the main determinant is income after taxes. In 1950, expenditures for food and housing accounted for nearly 70 per cent of total expenditures by families in the income group between $1,000 and $2,000, as compared to 56 per cent by families with income of $10,000 and more; in 1960–61, for 72 and 46–47 per cent, respectively. Interestingly, while the lower-income families reduced the share of their food expenses from 36 to 31 per cent within this period, they raised the share of expenses for shelter from 16 to 22 per cent, respectively; no such change has been recorded for shelter expenses by upper-income families. The proportion of family expenses for clothing by families with income of $10,000 or more was about double of that used by families with income below $2,000: 12.3 per cent, as compared with 6.1 per cent. Corresponding figures for recreation, reading, and education expenditures were 8.2 and 3.4 per cent (see Appendix Table XIX).

* The surveys of consumer expenditures by the Department of Labor used in this chapter are: the 1917–19 survey of workers' families in cities of all sizes; the 1934–36 survey of wage-earners and clerical workers in cities of 50,000 and more; the 1950 survey of families in urban areas of 48 states (for Wharton School, University of Pennsylvania); the 1960–61 survey, conducted jointly by the Department of Labor and Department of Agriculture, of urban, rural nonfarm, and rural farm families, and single consumers.

TABLE VII.1

DISTRIBUTION OF AVERAGE ANNUAL EXPENDITURES FOR CURRENT CONSUMPTION
BY ALL URBAN FAMILIES AND SINGLE CONSUMERS, 1950 and 1960-61

Item	Expenditures Per Family (In Dollars)		Per Cent of Expenditures	
	1950	1960-61	1950	1960-61
Food	1,130	1,311	29.7	24.3
Tobacco	68	95	1.8	1.8
Alcoholic beverages	65	90	1.7	1.7
Housing	1,035	1,588	27.2	29.5
Shelter, utilities	596	992	15.6	18.4
Household operations	178	319	4.7	5.9
Furnishings and equipment	261	277	6.9	5.1
Clothing	437	558	11.5	10.4
Personal care	85	155	2.2	2.9
Medical care	197	355	5.2	6.6
Recreation	168	217	4.4	4.0
Reading, education	58	109	1.5	2.0
Automobile, purchase and operation	443	700	11.6	13.0
Other transportation	67	93	1.8	1.7
Other expenditures	55	119	1.4	2.2
TOTAL	3,808	5,390	100.0	100.0

The spending patterns of average urban, rural nonfarm, and rural farm families differ, but the difference has become less pronounced than it had been before. Rural nonfarm families, three-fourths of whom live in urban places, are more like city families in their spending habits. As farming merges more and more with the monetized economy, the spending patterns on the farm and in the city come ever closer together; as the proportion of farm population becomes smaller and smaller, the national pattern of family outlays moves closer to the urban pattern.

Farm families spend a lesser part of their budget on food and housing than city people, but a higher proportion of their expenditures goes for medical care: farming is a strenuous occupation, and farm families rarely receive medical care as a fringe benefit of employment. Clothing expenditures are relatively more important for farm families because they are larger. The proportion of spending allocated to personal care is about the same for all groups of the population; that for recreation, reading, and education is somewhat higher for urban families (see Table VII.2 and Figure VII.1).

Consumers often spend *more* than their current income, meeting the deficit in many ways—by parting with some of their assets, selling their car or government bonds if these are available, buying on credit, borrowing cash, increasing their mortgage debt if possible, etc. If for one reason or another, the family expects to receive additional income in the near future,

TABLE VII.2

EXPENDITURES FOR CURRENT CONSUMPTION
OF URBAN, RURAL NONFARM, AND FARM FAMILIES
AND SINGLE INDIVIDUALS, 1960-61[a]

Item	Expenditures Per Average Family (In Dollars)				Per Cent of Expenditures			
	Total	Urban[b]	Rural Nonfarm	Rural Farm	Total	Urban[b]	Rural Nonfarm	Rural Farm
Food and beverages	1,313	1,401	1,133	893	26.0	26.0	26.4	24.9
Tobacco	91	95	85	64	1.8	1.8	2.0	1.8
Housing, total	1,461	1,588	1,189	917	28.9	29.5	27.7	25.5
Shelter, fuel, light, refrigeration, water	907	992	727	541	17.2	18.4	16.9	15.1
Household operation	288	319	222	156	5.7	5.9	5.2	4.3
House furnishings and equipment	266	277	240	220	5.3	5.1	5.6	6.1
Clothing, materials, services	518	558	408	427	10.3	10.4	9.5	11.9
Personal care	145	155	123	106	2.9	2.9	2.9	2.9
Medical care	340	355	297	310	6.7	6.6	6.9	8.6
Recreation	200	217	165	123	4.0	4.0	3.8	3.4
Reading and education	98	109	68	64	1.9	2.0	1.6	1.8
Transportation	770	793	737	613	15.2	14.7	17.1	17.1
Automobile	693	700	700	588	13.7	13.0	16.3	16.4
Other	77	93	37	25	1.5	1.7	0.9	0.7
Other expenditures	111	119	91	77	2.2	2.2	2.1	2.1
ALL EXPENDITURES	5,047	5,390	4,296	3,594	100.0	100.0	100.0	100.0

[a]For rural families, 1961.
[b]Includes families in Anchorage. Alaska, 1959.

it maintains its standard of living even in temporary financial straits. Thus, while current income level largely determines the amount of expenditures,

FIGURE VII.1

PATTERNS OF FAMILY EXPENDITURES, 1961

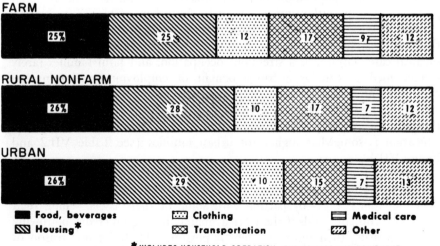

U.S. Department of Agriculture

TABLE VII.3

AVERAGE CONSUMER BUDGET, BY TYPE OF CONSUMER, 1960-61
(In Dollars)

	All	Urban	Rural Nonfarm	Rural Farm
Money income after taxes	5,557	5,906	4,700	4,424
Other money receipts	81	82	76	98
TOTAL	5,638	5,988	4,776	4,522
Additional disbursements:				
Personal insurance	299	324	241	200
Gifts and contributions	280	303	221	220
Net change in assets and liabilities	+199	+177	+176	+519
Available for current consumption	4,862	5,184	4,138	3,583
Current expenditures	5,047	5,390	4,296	3,594
Dissaving	-186	-207	-158	-10

it is not the only factor in consumer budgeting. Expected income may also affect the consumption pattern, enabling the consumer to borrow money and increase current expenditures. Table VII.3 shows how the average consumers manage their budget.

In higher-income brackets, families increase their assets and put a part of their current earnings aside. In 1960–61, the "break-even" point for urban families was after-tax income of $5,000–$5,999; in 1961, for rural nonfarm and rural farm families, of $4,000–$4,999. Beyond that point, consumers reported savings measured by net increase of assets over liabilities (see Table VII.4).

TABLE VII.4

CONSUMERS' REPORTED SAVINGS BY INCOME GROUP, 1961
(In Dollars)

Income Group	Average Income Before Taxes			Net Savings (+), or Dissavings (-)		
	Urban	Rural Nonfarm	Rural Farm	Urban	Rural Nonfarm	Rural Farm
Under 1,000	690	634	43	- 617	- 341	- 2,034
1,000-1,999	1,533	1,546	1,596	- 208	- 123	- 490
2,000-2,999	2,628	2,596	2,613	- 197	- 112	- 272
3,000-3,999	3,767	3,712	3,654	- 260	- 26	- 79
4,000-4,999	4,951	4,878	4,715	- 56	+ 27	+ 575
5,000-5,999	6,079	5,961	5,852	+ 18	+ 80	+ 773
6,000-7,499	7,537	7,400	7,197	+ 131	+ 363	+ 1,045
7,500-9,999	9,787	9,490	9,105	+ 420	+ 673	+ 2,409
10,000-14,999	13,623	13,565	12,786	+ 868	+1,536	+ 4,423
15,000 and over	27,999	27,976	23,809	+4,774	+4,918	+11,143
ALL GROUPS	6,691	5,168	4,732	+ 177	+ 176	+ 519

The striking figures in Table VII.4 are for the rural family with income before taxes of $43 in 1961 and a negative change in assets and liabilities of $2,034. As the Department of Agriculture comments: "Having these resources to call upon indicates that many of the families in this income class at the time of the survey were below their normal income position."

Regional differences exist both in the average level of income and in the way consumers budget their expenditures. While all families spent, on the average, $5,038 for current consumption in 1961, those in the Northeast spent $5,861, and those in the South, $4,190. An average farm family in the West spent more for family living than a rural nonfarm family in the North Central area and almost as much as an urban family in the South. In all regions, the differences in spending between farm and urban families are greater than differences in income (see Table VII.5).

TABLE VII.5

MONEY INCOME AND CURRENT CONSUMPTION EXPENDITURES
OF FAMILIES, BY REGION, 1961
(In Dollars)

	Total	Northeast	North Central	South	West
Money income after taxes:					
Urban	5,957	6,604	5,863	5,036	6,386
Rural nonfarm	4,700	5,710	4,697	3,977	5,438
Rural farm	4,424	5,057	4,878	3,592	6,149
ALL FAMILIES	5,595	6,436	5,536	4,600	6,217
Expenditures for current consumption:					
Urban	5,381	5,998	5,236	4,608	5,711
Rural nonfarm	4,296	5,342	4,190	3,615	5,030
Rural farm	3,594	4,053	3,811	3,157	4,522
ALL FAMILIES	5,038	5,861	4,896	4,190	5,563

Consumer expenditures in metropolitan areas are higher than in the country as a whole: the average in 1960 for all consumer units was $5,630, as compared with $5,038 nationwide. Expenditures by wage and clerical families in metropolitan areas for current consumption, $6,044, are higher than those made by all consumer units, which includes groups such as the unemployed, the retired, and the single consumer, though occasionally the situation is the reverse: the corresponding figures for Cleveland, Ohio, are $6,086 and $6,493. But in most other cases, average current expenditures of wage-earners and clerical employees in 1960 exceeded those of all consumer units as a group (see Table VII.6).

About 10 per cent of all surveyed families were Negroes (8 per cent among rural farm families). The average size of white families was 3.2 persons; of Negro families, 3.8 persons; and 5 persons of Negro rural-farm families. Again, an average head of a white family was 48 years old, had 10 years of school completed, and 1.2 children under 18 years of age; an average Negro family head was 44 years old, had 8 years of school education, and 1.9 children of that age group (corresponding figures for Negro farm-family heads were 52, 5, and 2.4, respectively). Average after-tax income of Negro families was less than two-thirds that of white families in

TABLE VII.6

CURRENT EXPENDITURES, ALL CONSUMER
UNITS AND WORKERS' FAMILIES, 1960
(In Dollars)

Area and Population Group	Current Expenditures	
	All Consumer Units	Wage and Clerical Families
Population 1,250,000 or more		
Baltimore, Md.	5,302	5,589
Boston, Mass.	6,045	,6431
Chicago, Ill.	6,156	6,694
Cleveland, Ohio	6,493	6,086
Detroit, Mich.	5,599	5,759
Los Angeles, Calif.	6,154	6,693
New York, N.Y.	6,336	6,699
Northern New Jersey	6,326	6,501
Philadelphia, Pa.	5,667	5,983
Pittsburgh, Pa.	5,486	5,851
St. Louis, Mo.	5,236	5,909
San Francisco, Calif.	5,705	6,732
Washington, D.C.	5,813	5,470
Population 250,000 to 1,250,000		
Atlanta, Ga.	5,118	5,724
Buffalo, N.Y.	5,627	6,434
Dallas, Tex.	5,587	5,465
Indianapolis, Ind.	4,902	5,404
Seattle, Wash.	5,877	6,365
Population 50,000 to 250,000		
Austin, Tex.	4,425	4,696
Cedar Rapids, Iowa	5,334	6,108
Champaign-Urbana, Ill.	5,365	5,602
Orlando, Fla.	5,657	5,423
Portland, Me.	4,441	5,239
ALL AREAS	5,630	6,044

the country as a whole and less than that on the farm. Because of the larger size of the family and its lower income, food and clothing took higher proportions of the budget among Negro families. It is also significant that rented dwellings absorbed a considerably larger share of their income than that of white families: 9.8 per cent as compared with 4.9 per cent; no difference in this respect was established among the farm people.

TABLE VII.7

PERSONAL CONSUMPTION EXPENDITURES,
BY TYPE OF PRODUCT, 1929-64
(In Billions of Dollars)

Type of Product	1929	1933	1939	1945	1949	1959	1963	1964
Food, beverages, tobacco	21.2	12.8	20.9	43.5	56.6	85.2	95.9	100.1
Clothing, accessories, jewelry	11.2	5.4	8.4	19.6	23.3	31.9	36.8	40.0
Personal care	1.1	0.7	1.0	2.0	2.3	5.0	6.5	7.0
Housing	11.4	7.9	9.1	12.5	19.3	43.7	55.5	59.5
Household operation	10.7	6.5	9.6	15.5	25.9	45.3	53.8	58.0
Medical care	2.9	2.0	2.8	5.0	8.1	17.9	23.4	25.2
Personal business	4.2	2.8	3.3	4.7	6.2	13.9	18.2	19.8
Transportation	7.6	4.0	6.4	6.8	20.8	41.2	49.1	51.6
Recreation	4.3	2.2	3.5	6.1	10.0	17.4	21.6	23.8
Private education and research	0.7	0.5	0.6	0.9	1.5	3.4	4.9	5.3
Religious and welfare activities	1.2	0.9	0.9	1.7	2.2	4.4	5.3	5.8
Foreign travel and remittances	0.5	0.2	0.2	1.2	0.6	2.0	2.8	2.9
TOTAL CONSUMPTION	77.2	45.8	66.8	119.7	176.8	311.2	373.8	398.9

36. Our Consumption Bill

Except for dislocations caused by wartime conditions, the annual variations in the distribution of the nation's spending for current consumption among the main groups of needs are determined mainly by 2 factors: the level of economic well-being in the country and the change in prices. The Depression, in the early 1930's, caused a deep drop in expenditures for recreation and clothing, from $15.5 billion in 1929 to $7.6 billion in 1933. At the same time, as the result of the decline in agricultural prices, expenditures for food fell from $21.2 billion to $12.8 billion. The total of all other expenditures went down no less sharply, from $40.5 billion to $25.4 billion.

In wartime, rising agricultural prices accounted for the substantial increase in expenditures for foodstuffs, from $20.9 billion in 1939 to $33.7 in 1943 and $43.5 in 1945. Expenditures for transportation also experienced a great change during the war, when production of private automobiles ceased and gasoline was rationed. Their share in total consumer expenditures fell drastically, from 9.6 per cent in 1939 to 5.5 per cent in 1943; after the return to a peacetime economy, it more than doubled, rising to 11.7 per cent in 1949 and 13.2 per cent in 1959.

Total consumer expenditures ranged from $77 billion in 1929 to $120 billion in 1945, $311 billion in 1959, and $399 billion in 1964 (see Table VII.7; cf. Table VII.1).

Spending patterns for current consumption vary from country to country, and fully comparable figures exist for only a few countries. Neverthe-

TABLE VII.8

PERCENTAGE DISTRIBUTION OF CONSUMPTION EXPENDITURES
IN SELECTED COUNTRIES, 1962

Country	Food	Beve- rages, Tobacco	Cloth- ing	Utili- ties	House- hold[a]	Health	Trans- port	Other[b]
United States	21	5	9	17	11	8	14	15
Puerto Rico	28	8	10	12	12	7	13	10
Canada	22	8	9	20	7	8	14	12
Belgium	27	7	10	18	13	6[c]	9	10
Denmark	24	10	10	10	10		13	23
Finland	36	9	14	11	9	4	7	10
France	31	9	12	10	10	9	8	11
Greece	43	7	15	12	8	2	7	6
Italy	43	10	10	11	7	5	9	5
Netherlands	31	7	16	14	14	6	4	8
Norway	29	8	15	11	11	4	10	12
Sweden	27	9	13	15	9	4	14	9
United Kingdom	28	13	11	15	10	2	10	11
Yugoslavia	45	10	19	5	7	5	5	4
Ceylon	50	10	10	7	9	2	7	5
Israel	32	5	10	14	11	7	6	15
Japan	44		9	17		...	...	30[d]

[a]Includes household operation (taxes, insurance, mortgage, interest, repairs),
furnishings, and equipment.
[b]Recreation, entertainment, education, miscellaneous.
[c]Included with "other."
[d]Includes expenditures for health and transportation.

less, the data of the United Nations on the ways in which individual countries distribute their expenditures for consumption provide some insight into the importance of various consumption items in the life of different countries, and permit some comparison with the U.S. consumption patterns. Thus, expenditures for food, particularly in combination with those for beverages and tobacco, represent a smaller part of the consumer budget in this country than in many others. Even in Australia and Canada, where the share of expenditures for food in total budgeting approaches that in the United States—23 and 22 per cent, respectively, as compared to 21 per cent in this country—beverages and tobacco account for an additional 10 and 8 per cent, respectively, in contrast to 5 per cent in the United States. In some countries, food takes almost or fully half of total consumer expenditures: 43 per cent in Italy and Greece, 50 per cent in Ceylon. But even in the United Kingdom, food, beverages, and tobacco together account for 41 per cent of consumer expenditures; in France, for 40 per cent; 44 in Japan; and in Finland, for 45. Obviously, the larger the share of the consumer budget spent for food, the less is left for other items (see Table VII.8).

37. What We Spend for Food, Beverages, Tobacco

Expenditures for food, beverages, and tobacco include not only the value of goods produced on farms but, more important, the cost of proc-

TABLE VII.9

APPARENT PER CAPITA CONSUMPTION OF MAJOR FOOD COMMODITIES
IN THE UNITED STATES, 1930-64
(In Pounds)

Commodity	1930	1940	1950	1960	1964
Meats (carcass weight)	129	142	145	161	173
Beef	49	55	63	85	100
Pork	67	74	69	65	64
Fish	10	11	12	11	11
Poultry products:					
Eggs (number)	331	319	389	334	314
Chicken	16	14	21	28	31
Dairy products:					
Milk fat solids	32	33	29	25	23
Nonfat milk solids	36	38	44	43	42
Cheese	5	6	8	8	9
Fluid milk and cream	337	331	349	322	306
Ice cream (product weight)	10	11	17	18	18
Fats and oils (fat content)	45	46	46	45	47
Butter	18	17	11	8	7
Margarine	3	2	6	9	10
Shortening	10	9	11	13	14
Fruits:					
Fresh	134	142	107	97	89
Canned, incl. juices	13	26	35	37	35
Frozen, incl. juices	1	1	/4	/9	8
Dried	5	6	4	3	3
Vegetables:					
Fresh	112	117	115	106	98
Canned	28	34	42	45	46
Frozen	-	1	3	10	12
Potatoes	132	123	106	101	99
Fresh melons	33	27	25	26	23
Sugar (refined)	110	96	101	98	96
Corn products:					
Cornmeal	28	22	12	7	7
Corn syrup	7	8	9	10	14
Wheat flour	171	155	135	118	116
Beverages:					
Coffee (Green bean basis)	13	16	16	16	16
Tea	0.7	0.7	0.6	0.6	0.7
Cocoa beans	3	5	4	4	4
Peanuts (shelled)	3	5	5	5	5

essing, marketing, and distributing services (retail trade, hotels, restaurants, and other eating places), and indirect taxes (sales tax, tax on alcoholic beverages and tobacco). The value of preparation of meals at home is not included.

Along with housing, food is the major item of current expenditures in all budgets. Significant changes have occurred within recent decades, particularly since World War II, in the character of food consumption and, as a result, in the structure of expenditures for food. The United States

FIGURE VII.2

CHANGE IN OUR EATING HABITS, 1910-60

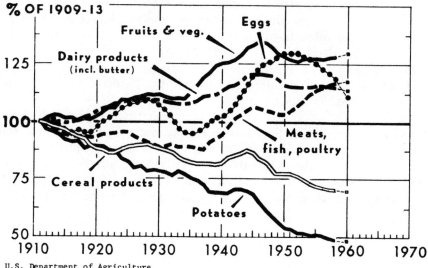

U.S. Department of Agriculture

population has shifted to a large degree from home-prepared to factory-prepared food: precooked hams; frozen cakes and bread; frozen fruit, juices, and vegetables; precooked TV dinners, chicken pies, and pizzas; and so on. This tendency is becoming as characteristic of farm families as it is of urban people.

Food fully or partly processed or prepared comprises work and services that increase the convenience and save time for homemakers but also increase the cost. Nevertheless, the share of expenditures for food (without alcoholic beverages and tobacco) has gradually declined: from about 30 per cent of total expenditures for all urban families and single consumers in 1950 to 24 per cent in 1960–61. Interestingly, the share of expenditures for beverages and tobacco has remained unchanged (1.7 and 1.8 per cent, respectively).

Another new feature in the eating habits of the American people is the growing popularity of meals away from home, noticeable not only in urban centers but in rural areas as well. Carrying meals to work in paper bags or lunch boxes has been a common feature among the American workers. Though this custom still persists, in-plant feeding has become a matter-of-course service in many factories. Dozens of millions of meals are served in plant cafeterias every working day, and this service represents a multi-billion-dollar business.

The amount of food consumed per capita is now some 60–65 pounds less per year than it used to be. Calorie- and weight-conscious consumers have reduced expenditures for cereals, potatoes, and bakery products, while more beef and poultry is consumed than some decades ago. Consumption of butter has also declined, while that of fruit, vegetables, canned and frozen juices has risen substantially (see Table VII.9 and Figure VII.2).

In 1963, outlays for alcoholic beverages amounted to more than $11 billion, and for tobacco, to some $8 billion. The combined national income of Switzerland, Norway, and Denmark, $18.8 billion in 1960, about equals this country's expenditures for drinking and smoking. Sweden's national income would suffice to pay only two-thirds of our annual bill for tobacco and alcoholic beverages.

As income rises, the percentage of the budget used for alcoholic beverages increases, from 1.1 per cent for income under $2,000 to 1.9 per cent for income exceeding $15,000. An inverse correlation exists for expenditures for tobacco: they amount to 1.8 per cent for income under $2,000 and drop to 1 per cent at the $15,000 level.

Expenditures for alcoholic beverages have increased much more rapidly

TABLE VII.10

EXPENDITURES FOR
ALCOHOLIC BEVERAGES AND TOBACCO, 1929-1963
(In Billions of Dollars)

	Alcoholic Beverages	Tobacco
1929	0.6	1.7
1933	0.7	1.2
1939	3.4	1.8
1949	7.7	4.3
1959	9.6	6.9
1963	11.1	8.1

than those for tobacco: between 1929 and 1963, they rose from $0.6 billion to $11.1 billion, or nearly 20 times, as compared with the increase from $1.7 to $7.9 billion, or less than 5 times, for tobacco (see Table VII.10).

38. Shelter and Household Operation

Consumer expenditures for housing include: (a) the rental value of homes occupied by owners and the space rent for tenant-occupied dwellings; and (b) the cost of household operation, comprising purchases of furniture and household equipment; fuel, electricity, gas, water; telephone, telegraph, postage; cleaning preparations, paid domestic service, and many other items.

The 1960 Census of Housing reported 58.3 million housing units, of which 5.3 million were vacant. Of the occupied dwellings, 32.8 million, or 61.9 per cent, were owner-occupied (or had been bought on long-term credit), and 20.2 million, or 38.1 per cent, were occupied by tenants. Except for the break in the line caused by the Depression and reflected in the 1940 Census, the percentage of home ownership has risen steadily: 45.6 per cent in 1920, 47.8 in 1930, and 43.6 per cent in 1940; after the war, the percentage rose rapidly, to 55 per cent in 1950 and 62 per cent in 1960. However, the nonwhite families, with 38 per cent of homeowners among them, still have a long way to go before they reach the percentage of home ownership of white families: 64 per cent.

TABLE VII.11

PERCENTAGE DISTRIBUTION OF EXPENDITURES FOR HOUSING
BY MAJOR ITEM, 1929-64

	1929	1933	1939	1945	1949	1959	1964
Shelter	51.8	55.0	48.7	44.6	42.6	49.1	50.6
Owner-occupied[a]	26.4	26.7	22.3	23.2	24.1	32.2	33.5
Tenant-occupied[b]	20.2	22.9	21.3	16.4	14.1	13.2	13.7
Rental value (farms)	4.1	4.3	3.9	3.8	3.1	2.2	1.9
Other	1.1	1.1	1.2	1.2	1.3	1.5	1.5
Household operation	48.2	45.0	51.3	55.4	57.4	50.9	49.4
Furniture	5.4	3.2	5.1	5.6	6.0	5.3	5.0
Household appliances	3.4	2.8	4.1	1.3	6.9	5.6	4.9
China, glass, utensils, other	8.0	5.8	7.4	8.3	9.0	6.6	6.9
semidurable furnishings	3.2	2.7	3.6	5.5	5.2	3.0	3.2
Cleaning preparations, paper products, etc.	2.2	2.3	2.7	2.6	3.6	3.7	3.5
Stationery, writing supplies	0.6	0.5	0.8	1.5	1.1	1.2	1.2
Electricity	2.8	4.5	4.5	4.3	4.2	5.3	5.4
Gas	2.4	3.4	2.9	2.5	2.3	3.3	3.3
Water	1.3	1.9	1.8	1.5	1.2	1.3	1.5
Other fuel and ice	7.2	8.0	7.5	7.8	6.8	4.7	3.9
Telephone, telegraph, cable, and wireless	2.6	3.0	3.1	4.2	3.8	4.7	5.0
Domestic service	7.7	5.1	6.0	7.6	5.2	4.0	3.3
Other	1.4	1.7	1.8	2.8	2.2	2.5	2.2
TOTAL	100.0	100.0	100.0	100.0	100.0	100.0	100.0

[a]Nonfarm dwellings--space rental value.
[b]Nonfarm dwellings--space rent.

Nationally, more than half (53 per cent) of urban families and about two-thirds of rural nonfarm families were homeowners in 1960–61. The homeowners spent a smaller share of their total expenditures for shelter, utilities, and other items of household operation than the renters.

As for the workers' families, the trend is also toward rising home ownership. In 1901, only 19 per cent of workers' families owned their homes; by 1917–19, the percentage rose to 27; by 1934–36, to 30 per cent; by 1950, to 51; and by 1960, 54 per cent of wage and blue- and white-collar workers were homeowners.

The share of current expenditures allocated to housing, including household operation, follows the same guideline that determines the budget share for food consumption. In 1960–61, the ratio for urban families tapered down from 39 per cent at the bottom of the income scale to less than 30 per cent at its upper end.

For the country as a whole, the shares of consumer expenditures for owner-occupied and tenant-occupied dwellings were not too different: 22.3 and 21.3 per cent, respectively, in 1939. But with expansion of home ownership, the expenditures for purchases of houses and their improvement and maintenance raised the national share for owner-occupied dwellings within the total budget to more than double that for tenant-occupied housing units: 33.5 and 13.7 per cent, respectively, in 1964 (see Table VII.11).

In comparison with 1950, consumers spent in 1960–61 proportionately less for furnishings and equipment: 5.1 per cent of total expenditures, instead of 6.9 per cent (cf. Table VII.1). This is partly due to the fact that such purchases in 1950 reflected the pent-up demand during the war years. Also, there is more builder-installation of equipment in new houses, which shows itself up in higher purchase prices of houses or in rents but not in consumer expenditures for major appliances, such as refrigerators, washing machines, dishwashers, and so on.

In recent decades, the share of total expenditures for household operation has been returning to the proportion that existed before World War II. Purchases of furnishings and household equipment account for about 20 per cent of all expenditures for housing; utilities and communications, for another 20 per cent; cleaning preparations, paper products, and writing supplies, for some 5 per cent. Domestic service now accounts for only 3.3 per cent of total housing expenditures, as compared with 7.7 per cent in 1929, and 7.6 per cent in 1945. Expenditures for electricity doubled between 1929 and 1964, with the extension of the electric network through the rural areas and a wave of acquisitions of refrigerators, washing machines, and other appliances in the 1930's and air conditioners, television and hi-fi sets, and dishwashers after World War II. The importance of expenditures for other fuel declined from 7.2 per cent of the consumer budget in 1929 to 3.9 per cent in 1964 (see Table VII.11).

39. Clothing and Personal Care

The U.S. population spent on clothing, in the broad sense of this term,* $12.3 billion out of the total consumption bill of $77 billion in 1929, and $47.0 billion out of $399 billion, respectively, in 1964. Clothing needs of the nation have taken a proportionately smaller share of total expendi-

---

* Includes accessories, jewelry, watches, clothing materials, upkeep, toilet preparations, and so-called personal care (beauty parlors, barbershops, etc.).

TABLE VII.12

PERCENTAGE DISTRIBUTION OF EXPENDITURES
FOR CLOTHING[a] AND PERSONAL CARE IN THE UNITED STATES, 1929-64

	1929	1933	1939	1949	1959	1964
Footwear	14.9	16.2	14.2	13.0	12.3	11.4
Clothing:						
for women and children	37.9	37.0	38.3	39.7	38.8	38.9
for men and boys	24.5	24.2	24.3	22.6	20.9	21.0
standard clothing issued to military	0.1	0.2	0.2	0.8	0.1	0.1
Cleaning, dyeing, alteration, repair, etc.	3.8	3.8	4.2	5.7 }	7.8	7.1
Laundering in establishments	3.9	4.1	3.3	3.3 }		
Jewelry and watches	4.5	2.8	3.8	5.1	5.5	5.5
Other	1.2	0.9	1.0	0.8	1.1	1.1
Personal care:						
Toilet articles and preparations	4.8	5.2	5.2	4.9	7.5	8.4
Barbershops, beauty parlors, baths	4.3	5.6	5.5	4.1	6.1	6.4
TOTAL EXPENDITURES	100.0	100.0	100.0	100.0	100.0	100.0

[a] Includes accessories and jewelry.

tures in recent decades: 12 per cent in 1964, in contrast to 16 per cent in 1929. This is due to some extent to a decreased emphasis on formal clothing—on replacement of business suits for men and formal attire for women by coordinated "separates," slacks, sport jackets, and so on, and on the current custom of not wearing hats. This new attitude is equally characteristic of city and farm people. On the other hand, there has been some increase in expenditures for clothing upkeep, dry cleaning, storage, and, particularly, for items of personal care.

In the nation as a whole, about one-seventh or one-eighth of the total expenditures for clothing per se goes today for footwear, seven-tenths for clothing, and one-twelfth for cleaning and alterations; the remainder is used for jewelry and watches. This relationship has been, on the whole, remarkably steady (see Table VII.12). As income rises, the percentage of family budget used for clothing increases (see Table VII.13).

Farm families spend less on clothing, on the average, than city families of equal size. Since farm families tend to be larger (as are also low-income families in cities), clothing expenditures are less per capita for farm people than for urban people, by some 30 per cent in 1955.

Since a rural family comprises, on the average, 3.8 persons, as compared with 3.1 persons for the average urban family, its requirements for clothing are correspondingly greater. The same is valid for the nonwhite families, which allocate a larger share of their budget, 12.5 per cent, for clothing needs than the average white family, 10 per cent.

TABLE VII.13

PERCENTAGE OF FAMILY BUDGET USED FOR CLOTHING,
BY INCOME GROUP, 1960-61

Income	Urban Families	Rural Nonfarm Families	Rural Farm Families
	10.4	9.5	11.9
Under $1,000	4.7	2.5	10.4
$1,000-$1,999	6.1	6.4	10.4
$2,000-$2,999	8.2	7.8	10.8
$3,000-$3,999	9.0	8.0	11.7
$4,000-$4,999	9.7	8.4	11.0
$5,000-$5,999	9.9	9.2	11.9
$6,000-$7,499	10.3	10.7	12.8
$7,500-$9,999	11.1	11.0	13.0
$10,000-$14,999	11.9	11.8	13.4
$15,000 and over	12.3	11.7	13.5

In the budget of a standard city worker's family, with 2 youngsters, clothing expenditures, as estimated by the Department of Labor, vary from city to city, ranging from $506 in Houston to $598 in Cleveland and averaging $550–$560 in Washington, D.C.; New York; Boston; Kansas City, Mo.; and Scranton, Penn. By the same estimate, retired couples 65 years or older and living by themselves are expected to spend about two-fifths of the above amounts for their clothing needs: from $197 in Houston to $235 in Cleveland.

FIGURE VII.3

PRIVATE AND PUBLIC EXPENDITURES
FOR MEDICAL CARE, 1935-64

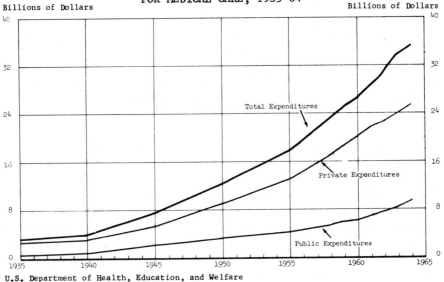

U.S. Department of Health, Education, and Welfare

40. *Health, Education, and Recreation*

Between 1950 and 1964, the composition of the United States population changed dramatically. It increased by 40 million and expanded particularly at both its extremes: by 18 million children aged 14 and under and 5.3 million persons aged 65 years and over. These two age groups require more medical care than other age groups of the population. No wonder, therefore, that consumer expenditures for health nearly tripled from $8.1 billion in 1949 to $25.2 billion in 1964; as did expenditures for public-health services, from $3 billion to $9 billion, respectively (see Figure VII.3). Of the $25.2 billion spent by consumers in 1964, more than four-tenths went

TABLE VII.14

PERSONAL CONSUMPTION EXPENDITURES
FOR MEDICAL CARE, 1929-64
(In Millions of Dollars)

	1929	1933	1939	1949	1959	1964
Drug preparations and sundries	604	427	612	1,555	3,462	4,352
Ophthalmic products and orthopedic appliances	131	92	172	454	717	1,054
Physicians	959	617	866	2,463	5,032	6,756
Dentists	482	276	386	920	1,918	2,439
Other professional services	250	138	167	453	917	1,235
Privately controlled hospitals and sanitariums	403	363	492	1,734	4,601	7,618
Medical care and hospitalization insurance	108	70	153	531	1,277	1,757
TOTAL	2,937	1,983	2,848	8,110	17,924	25,211

for payments to physicians, dentists, and for other professional services; about three-tenths for hospital expenses; and the remainder for drugs and health insurance (see Sec. 19 and Sec. 93; see Table VII.14).

In view of the rise in costs of medical help, various schemes of insurance for hospitalization, surgical services, and other expenses have been developed. By the end of 1964, nearly eight-tenths of the population had been estimated to have hospital-expense protection; more than seven-tenths of the population had insurance for surgical services (cf. Sec. 83).

The highest proportion of those covered in 1962–63, 76 per cent, was in the age group 25–64 years; the lowest, 54 per cent, among persons aged 65 years and over. When the insured were classified by income levels, the picture changed substantially. Only one-third of families in the low-income

TABLE VII.15

PERCENTAGE OF POPULATION COVERED BY HEALTH INSURANCE,
BY INCOME LEVEL, 1962-63

Age	All Incomes	Under $2,000	$2,000-$3,999	$4,000-$6,999	$7,000 and Over
Under 15	68.7	21.9	42.8	78.2	87.6
15-24	66.1	41.6	49.4	73.7	82.6
25-44	76.3	30.9	52.7	81.8	90.0
45-64	75.7	37.9	63.1	83.5	90.5
65 and over	54.0	39.0	58.4	66.4	70.3
ALL AGES	70.3	34.1	51.9	79.0	87.3

group had hospitalization insurance, though usually such families have more children and, often, elderly persons in need of support, than families in the higher-income brackets (see Table VII.15). As income rises, so rises hospitalization coverage and, likewise, the coverage of surgical services (cf. Sec. 83 and Sec. 93).

Expenditures for medical care reflect the same pattern as those for food. Urban families with income under $1,000 spend nearly one-tenth of their budget for medical care, while middle-income families, with income above $4,000, use only one-sixteenth of their expenditures for that purpose. Cash expenditures of nonwhite families for medical care are, generally, smaller than those of white families at similar income levels.

Expenditures for medical care show a direct correlation with the age of consumers. In 1960–61, according to the Survey of Consumer Expenditures and Income, expenditures for medical care represented 5.7–5.8 per cent of the budget when the head of the family was under 44 years, 9.4 per cent at the age of 65–74, and 12 per cent at the age of 75 and over, though the size of the family in older age groups was smallest of all: 1.6 persons per family.

In 1962, per capita expenditures for medical care and voluntary health insurance amounted to $119, of which $37 went for hospital services, $34 for physicians, $30 for drugs and appliances, and $12 for dentists. The remainder was used for other medical services.

The nation's bill for recreation approximates that for medical care: $23.8 billion in 1964. But it includes some items outside the realm of recreation proper—books and maps ($1.9 billion), which might be listed under expenditures for education; and magazines, newspapers, and sheet music ($2.8 billion), which might be distributed among expenditures for business, education, or recreation. The 2 largest groups of expenditures are (1) for radio and television, including repair; records; and musical instruments; and (2) sport equipment; boats; pleasure aircraft; and durable and nondurable toys; each absorbing about $6 billion. Admission charges for

TABLE VII.16

CONSUMER EXPENDITURES FOR RECREATION AND
PRIVATE EDUCATION, 1929-64
(In Millions of Dollars)

	1929	1933	1939	1945	1949	1959	1964
Recreation	4,331	2,202	3,452	6,139	10,010	17,381	23,824
Books, maps, magazines[a]	847	571	780	1,485	2,081	3,269	4,650
Sport supplies, toys[b]	555	274	513	953	2,006	4,344	5,808
Radio, television[c]	1,038	209	448	432	1,877	4,065	5,952
Flowers, seeds, plants	221	90	191	378	451	599	859
Theaters, spectator sports[d]	913	573	821	1,714	1,872	1,571	1,767
Clubs	302	208	199	281	454	721	850
Participant amusements[e]	207	121	183	284	428	991	1,461
Other	248	156	317	612	841	1,821	2,477
Private education and research	664	479	620	936	1,507	3,417	5,304
Higher education	219	203	259	377	692	1,432	2,544
Elementary and secondary	162	121	195	299	399	1,105	1,731
Other[f]	283	155	166	260	416	880	1,029

[a]Includes newspapers, and sheet music.
[b]Boats, pleasure aircraft, wheel goods, durable and nondurable toys.
[c]Includes records, musical instruments, repairs.
[d]Includes movie theaters, opera, football, baseball, horse and dog races, and so on.
[e]Dancing, riding, skating, swimming places, bowling alleys, sightseeing buses, and so on.
[f]Correspondence schools, musical and dancing instruction, expenditures of foundations for education and research.

movies, legitimate theaters, operas, and spectator sports and dues and fees to clubs exceed $2.5 billion. Another item, which has grown in importance from $221 million in 1929 to $859 million in 1964, is the expenditure for flowers, seeds, potted plants, and so on (see Table VII.16).

Private expenditures for education (including tuition fees, payments for commercial and correspondence schools, dancing and musical instruction, and outlays of various foundations) represent a supplement to public expenditures for elementary and secondary schools, colleges and universities, and vocational training (see Sec. 21). In 1964, the outlays of the Federal, state, and local governments for education amounted to $27.1 billion and of nonpublic schools, to $6.6 billion, while expenditures for private education by consumers absorbed $5.3 billion (cf. Sec. 20).

In the budget of consumers, the share of expenditures for education rises with income, from 0.3–0.5 per cent for low-income families to 2.9 per cent at the top of the income scale. Because of the vast network of public schools, however, educational opportunities are distributed more evenly among all groups of the population than these figures might suggest.

41. Automobiles and Other Transportation

In the national consumption bill, expenditures for transportation come immediately after those for food and shelter, including household opera-

TABLE VII.17

PERCENTAGE DISTRIBUTION OF CONSUMER
EXPENDITURES FOR TRANSPORTATION, 1929-64

	1929	1933	1939	1945	1949	1959	1964
User-operated	78.3	76.1	80.6	58.3	86.1	92.2	93.0
New cars and net purchases of used cars	34.0	19.5	26.2	5.2	41.5	41.8	44.2
Tires, tubes, parts, accessories	8.5	7.0	7.6	9.5	6.0	5.7	5.8
Repair, rental, parking, etc.	10.2	9.8	9.4	14.0	11.4	11.5	11.0
Gasoline and oil	23.8	36.8	34.3	26.4	24.3	28.1	27.2
Tolls, insurance	1.8	3.0	3.0	3.2	2.8	5.1	4.8
Purchased	21.7	23.9	19.4	41.7	13.9	7.8	7.0
Local bus, street and electric railway	10.8	14.5	10.7	19.2	6.8	3.2	2.4
Taxicab	2.9	2.4	2.4	5.4	2.3	1.5	1.1
Railway[a]	6.4	5.0	4.0	10.7	2.6	1.1	0.8
Intercity bus	0.7	1.2	1.5	5.0	1.4	0.5	0.6
Airline	...	0.1	0.2	0.8	0.5	1.4	1.9
Waterway and other	0.9	0.7	0.5	0.5	0.2	0.1	0.1
ALL TRANSPORTATION	100.0	100.0	100.0	100.0	100.0	100.0	100.0

[a]Includes commuter transportation and sleeping- and parlor-car fares.

tion, thus pushing out expenditures for clothing from its traditional third place to the fourth place. In 1950, the share of expenditures for transportation was just slightly above that for clothing: 13.4 and 11.5 per cent of total expenditures. But while the share of expenditures for clothing slowly declined, to 10 per cent in 1964, that for transportation has risen to some 13 per cent of total consumption expenditures.

Actually, expenditures for transportation are almost synonymous with expenditures for the automobile, its purchase and operation. The only period in recent decades when expenditures for purchased transportation— by rail, bus, airplane, and so on—almost equaled those for owner-operated transportation was during the last war: then, expenditures were about equally divided between user-operated and purchased transportation into 41.7 and 58.3 per cent, respectively. At all other times, people relied on the automobile for transportation. Even in the Depression years, workers economized on everything—food, clothing, housing—but managed to keep their cars and use them in going to work, looking for jobs, and so on. In its 1935–36 Survey of Consumer Expenditures, the Bureau of Labor Statistics said that "automobile ownership has been one of the most depression-proof elements in the level of living of families in all parts of the United States."

In a sense, the automobile has become not only an indispensable means of transportation in this country but also a symbol of "conspicuous con-

TABLE VII.18

CONSUMER EXPENDITURES FOR AUTOMOBILE TRANSPORTATION,
BY INCOME LEVEL, 1960-61
(Per Cent of Total Expenditures)

	Urban Families	Rural Nonfarm Families	Rural Farm Families
Under $1,000	2.2	4.0	13.2
$1,000-$1,999	3.4	10.4	12.8
$2,000-$2,999	6.5	15.0	13.7
$3,000-$3,999	11.3	16.8	16.0
$4,000-$4,999	13.8	18.4	18.1
$5,000-$5,999	14.1	17.1	17.6
$6,000-$7,499	13.9	17.1	17.3
$7,500-$9,999	14.5	17.5	17.7
$10,000-$14,999	14.4	15.2	18.8
$15,000 and over	10.9	12.7	15.7
ALL FAMILIES	13.0	16.3	16.4

sumption": one no longer exhibits expensive clothing or furniture but displays a new luxurious model of a car (see Sec. 72).

Three out of 4 families owned a car in 1964. Among farm families, for whom some means of automotive travel is frequently the only means of transportation, the percentage is even higher: 82 per cent of rural nonfarm families and 91 per cent of rural farm families own a motor vehicle. Of total consumer expenditures for transportation, the proportion spent for user-operated transportation somewhat exceeded 78 per cent in 1929, 86 per cent in 1949, and was 93 per cent in 1964 (see Table VII.17). Thus, total expenditures for local and intercity transportation, including commutation, and for travel by rail, air, water, bus, streetcar, and taxicab today account for only 7 per cent of consumer expenditures for transportation.

The spending pattern for *automobile* transportation by income level is different from that for other important items of the consumer budget, as the latest survey of the Department of Labor, 1960-61, has shown. In contrast to expenditures for food and clothing, those for the automobile continue to increase with rising income, and only at the highest level of $15,000 and over, do they drop by several points (see Table VII.18).

The total transportation bill of the nation exceeded $51.5 billion in 1964 (see Table VII.19). Of this amount, $48.0 billion went for user-operated transportation: $22.8 billion for purchase of new and used cars; $14.0 billion for gasoline and oil; and $5.6 billion for repair and other services; the remainder was spent on tires, parts, tolls, and insurance.

While expenditures for user-operated transportation multiplied 8 times between 1929 and 1964, those for purchased transportation slightly more than doubled, rising from $1.7 billion to $3.6 billion. Within this last

TABLE VII.19

CONSUMER EXPENDITURES FOR TRANSPORTATION, 1929-64
(In Millions of Dollars)

	1929	1933	1939	1945	1949	1959	1964
User-operated	5,960	3,035	5,128	3,992	17,910	37,980	47,954
New cars and purchases of used cars	2,588	779	1,679	357	8,637	17,154	22,814
Tires, tubes, parts	648	280	484	652	1,216	2,362	2,970
Repair, other services	776	392	596	957	2,373	4,805	5,646
Gasoline and oil	1,814	1,466	2,181	1,809	5,031	11,571	14,023
Tolls and insurance	134	118	188	217	653	2,088	2,501
Purchased	1,652	952	1,237	2,853	2,883	3,204	3,601
Local bus, street and electric railway	820	578	684	1,316	1,407	1,244	1,271
Taxicab	220	96	153	372	465	602	593
Railway[a]	490	200	257	734	545	448	395
Intercity bus	52	46	98	339	319	299	324
Airline	3	3	12	55	116	579	987
Waterway and other	67	29	33	37	31	32	31
ALL TRANSPORTATION	7,612	3,987	6,365	6,845	20,793	41,184	51,555

[a]Includes commuter transportation and sleeping- and parlor-car fares.

group, 2 types of transportation clearly lost favor among consumers, who spent less on them in 1964 than in 1929: water transportation, for which expenditures fell from $67 million to $31 million; and railroads, with a decline from $490 million to $395 million. In contrast, consumer expenditures for taxicabs increased from $220 million to $593 million in the same period and for airline transportation, from $3 million to $987 million (see Table VII.19).

Installment credit has greatly contributed to the growth of automobile ownership in this country. Fewer than half of all automobile buyers pay cash; today, 54–56 per cent of all car buyers use installment credit; this percentage rises to 62 among the purchasers of new cars. Commercial banks and various financial companies hold credits for car purchases, exceeding $22 billion. To low-income groups, installment credit is especially important, though interest they pay on loans increases their expenditures for transportation (see Secs. 32, 72, and 83).

VIII. *Agriculture*

42. *Agriculture in the Nation's Life and Economy*

For more than a century, the United States was an agricultural country;
in 1790, 95 per cent of the population lived in rural areas, and even in
1910, rural people, nonfarm and farm, were the majority (54 per cent).
With every decade, however, expanding industries and services drew more
and more people to towns and cities; the average annual net out-migration
from the farms reached its peak in the war years (see Figure VIII.1A).
While rural people still formed a majority in 39 states in the 1930's, two
decades later they exceeded the urban population in only 19 states; in
1960, in only 11 (see Sec. 7).

The same development took place among the population staying and
working on farms. There were 32 million people on farms in 1920, 23
million in 1950, and 12.4 million in 1965. Farm employment, totaling 13
million workers (family labor and hired labor) in 1920, dropped to 10
million in 1940, 8.4 million in 1955, and 5.6 million in 1965 (see Table
VIII.1 and Figure VIII.1B).

Yet despite the continuous decline in farm population and labor, American agriculture is turning out more and better products than at any time
in the nation's history. Its technical advance in the last 25 years has been
nothing short of phenomenal. Farm production per man-hour has tripled;
it has more than doubled since 1950. Crop production per acre is up 70 per
cent, output per breeding animal is higher by 90 per cent. Farm output
per unit of all farm inputs has become about 50 per cent greater than in
the 1920's, with most of the increase occurring after 1940. Between 1950

187

FIGURE VIII.1.A

AVERAGE ANNUAL NET OUTMIGRATION
FROM THE FARM POPULATION

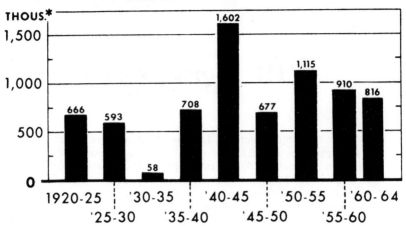

*NET CHANGE THROUGH MIGRATION AND RECLASSIFICATION OF RESIDENCE FROM FARM TO NONFARM.

U.S. Department of Agriculture

and 1965, output increased 35 per cent, as compared to 3 per cent increase in input (see Figure VIII.2).

The United States leads the world in agricultural production. It is the largest producer of meat, poultry, eggs, and cheese; of corn, oats, hops, and sorghum; of tobacco, cotton lint, cottonseed, and soybeans (see Table VIII.2).

The United States is also the world's largest exporter of agricultural products, accounting for one-sixth of the world's total. Only a fifth of its harvested acreage, however, produces for export—71 million a. out of 301 million in 1964, a smaller area than is harvested in 4 states—Illinois, Iowa, and the Dakotas.

TABLE VIII.1

FARM POPULATION AND FARM EMPLOYMENT, 1910-65

| Year | Farm Population | | Farm Employment (In Millions) |
	Millions of Persons	Per Cent of Population	
1910	54.4	34.9	13.6
1920	32.0	29.7	13.4
1930	30.5	24.6	12.5
1940	30.5	22.9	10.0
1950	23.0	15.3	9.9
1955	19.1	11.6	8.4
1960	15.6	8.7	7.1
1962	14.3	7.7	6.7
1963	13.4	7.1	6.5
1964	13.0	6.8	6.1
1965	12.4	6.4	5.6

FIGURE VIII.1.B

FARM AND NONFARM POPULATION
IN PER CENT OF TOTAL POPULATION, 1910-60

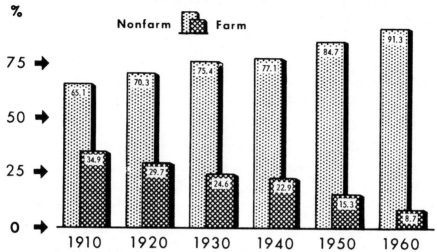

U.S. Department of Agriculture

Historically, agriculture has supported the industrial development of this country. Exports of cotton, tobacco, wheat, and meat paid for machinery and tools imported from Europe. They also enabled it to import many fabricated goods then not produced domestically.

FIGURE VIII.2

FARM OUTPUT AND INPUTS, 1940-65

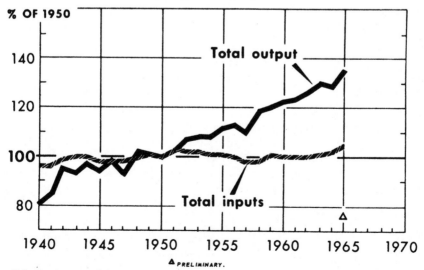

U.S. Department of Agriculture

Agriculture has created many jobs away from the farms. Ten million persons are engaged in storing, transporting, processing, and merchandizing agricultural products. For example, meat packing and poultry dressing, plus preparation of meat, employ more than 300,000 persons on payrolls totaling nearly $1.5 billion. The dairy and baked-goods industries each employ an equal number of workers, with similar payrolls.

Farmers as a group spend some $30 billion a year on goods and services needed in their work (tractors, trucks and cars, feed and seed, fertilizer, fuel, etc.) and $15 billion for food, clothing, appliances, drugs, furniture, and other manufactured goods. They now purchase about two-thirds of all farm inputs.

TABLE VIII.2

RANKING OF THE UNITED STATES AND OTHER COUNTRIES
IN OUTPUT OF MAJOR AGRICULTURAL PRODUCTS, 1962
(Production in Millions of Metric Tons)

Product	World Output	Largest Producer		Second Largest Producer		Third Largest Producer	
Meat[a]	...	United States	13.0	U.S.S.R.	7.6	West Germany	2.7
Poultry meat	...	United States	4.4	United Kingdom	0.3	Italy	0.2
Milk (cow)	303	U.S.S.R.	60.8	United States	57.1	France	24.2
Cheese	...	United States	0.8	France	0.3	Italy	0.3
Butter	...	U.S.S.R.	0.9	United States	0.7	West Germany	0.5
Corn	216	United States	92.6	U.S.S.R.	23.3	Brazil	9.0
Wheat	262	U.S.S.R.	70.6	United States	29.7	Canada	15.4
Oats	51	United States	15.0	Canada	7.6	U.S.S.R.	5.6
Barley	100	U.S.S.R.	19.5	United States	9.4	France	6.0
Hops[b]	74	United States	16.0	West Germany	13.0	United Kingdom	10.0
Sorghum	25	United States	12.0	India	8.0	U.S.S.R.	3.0
Tobacco	4	United States	1.0	India	0.3	U.S.S.R.	0.2
Cottonseed	22	United States	5.5	U.S.S.R.	2.8	India	1.9
Cotton (lint)	12	United States	3.2	U.S.S.R.	1.5	India	0.9
Soybeans	31	United States	18.4	China	10.4	Indonesia	0.4
Eggs	14	United States	4.0	United Kingdom	1.0	Japan	1.0

[a]Beef, veal, pork, mutton, and lamb from commercial and farm slaughter.
[b]Thousands of metric tons.

An American farmer provides food, fiber, and other agricultural products for himself and an average of 33 other persons (see Table VIII.3 and Figure VIII.3). But the efficiency of American agriculture becomes particularly impressive when comparison is made between the amount of labor used in it here with that used in other countries where the results are incomparably smaller. The contrast with agriculture in Asia is especially striking. Some 14 million persons are engaged in agriculture in Japan, and more than 130 million in India. In the U.S.S.R., 39 million were employed in agriculture in 1964, or 37 per cent of the total civilian employment of 106 million. Even so, neither in the U.S.S.R. nor in many other

TABLE VIII.3

PERSONS SUPPLIED PER FARM WORKER,
1850-1964

Year	Persons Supplied	Year	Persons Supplied
1850	4.53	1950	15.47
1880	5.57	1955	19.48
1900	6.95	1960	25.85
1920	8.27	1962	28.57
1940	10.69	1963	30.75
1945	14.55	1964	33.25

countries where it absorbs a much larger part of the national labor force can agriculture begin to compare with the productivity of American farmers. Many of these countries do not even produce an adequate supply of foodstuffs and other agricultural products for their own needs, and must import food for the urban populations.

Agricultural production in the United States includes practically all the field crops, vegetables, and fruits of the temperate and subtropical zones. In many places, comparatively small areas of specialized farming are surrounded by communities with a different type of agriculture. Along with diversification goes regional specialization, with 8 major agricultural regions.

In the heart of the country lies the Corn Belt, which is also the Hog Belt. In the Northeast, the dairy region stretches up to the Canadian borders. Cotton production is concentrated in the Southeast. The subtropical region along the Gulf of Mexico specializes in sugar cane and

FIGURE VIII.3

PERSONS SUPPLIED BY ONE FARM WORKER, 1830-1964

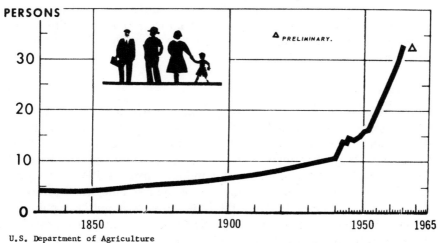

U.S. Department of Agriculture

FIGURE VIII.4

MAJOR TYPES OF FARMING IN THE UNITED STATES, 1959

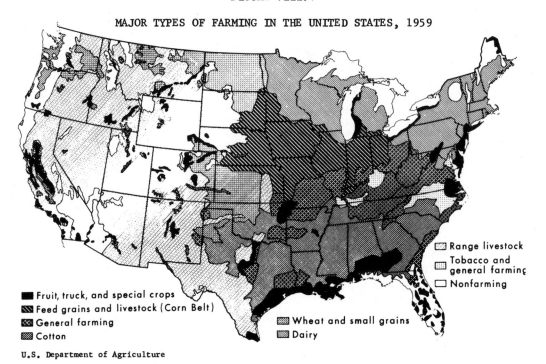

Range livestock

Tobacco and general farming

Nonfarming

Fruit, truck, and special crops

Feed grains and livestock (Corn Belt)

General farming

Cotton

Wheat and small grains

Dairy

U.S. Department of Agriculture

citrus fruit, and the subtropical area along the Pacific, in fruit, truck gardening, and special crops. The bread basket (wheat and small grains) is in the Great Plains, on the Columbia Plateau, and southwest of the Corn Belt. Millions of cattle and sheep graze on vast, treeless, untillable expanses in the West. Deciduous fruit is raised wherever climate and soil permit, while the areas on the Pacific fringe and the shores of the Great Lakes specialize in these products. General farming, scattered throughout the country, occupies a large area in the Southeast. Tobacco cultivation is found in many eastern and central States (see the map of prevailing types of agriculture, Figure VIII.4).

43. *Farms*

The number of farms in the United States increased steadily until 1920, when it exceeded 6 million. Since that year and except for the early 1930's, when some farms were subdivided to accommodate the returning unemployed members of farmers' families, there has been an uninterrupted decline, which is still continuing—6.1 million farms in 1940, 5.4 million in 1950, and 3.7 million in 1959, the year of the last agricultural census for which data are available (data for the 1964 census have not been published as yet). The South has been the greatest loser; the number of its farms dropped by 45 per cent between 1940 and 1959, as compared with 32 per cent for the West and 34 per cent for the North. Of the 2.4 million farms that disappeared between 1940 and 1959, about 2.3 million, or almost 95 per cent, were small farms, largely sharecropper units in the South.

The shrinking number of farms has been caused largely by consolidation into larger units, and perhaps slightly by the "statistical" elimination of tiny farms because of changes in census definition.* The total land in farms, on the other hand, has been on the increase—from 204 million a. in 1850 to 536 million in 1880; 839 million in 1900; 956 million in 1920; and 1,120 million in 1959 (cf. Table I.4). With growth of the acreage and decline in number of farms, the average farm size has increased steadily: 146 a. in 1900, 148 a. in 1920, 216 a. in 1950, and 303 a. in 1959. This trend has prevailed in all parts of the country. It is estimated that there were 3.4 million farms in 1965, averaging 341 a. per farm.

The value of all farms (land and buildings) increased from census to census until 1910. Then it skyrocketed during World War I, exceeded $66 billion in 1920, fell to less than half that amount during the Depression years of the 1930's, and in 1940 was just a little more than half the record high of 1920. Then the value of farms began to climb steeply, reached $75 billion by 1950, and amounted to $129 billion in 1959 and $159 billion in 1965 (48 states).

Before 1900, the value of livestock averaged 15 per cent of the value of land and buildings; in 1964–65, the ratio fluctuated between 10 and 11 per cent. The total value of farm machinery and implements increased from $750 million in 1900 to $3.6 billion in 1920, dropped to $2.2 billion in 1934, and rose to $3.1 billion in 1940. In 1950, it was $11.3 billion; in 1959, $18.5 billion; and in 1964, it exceeded $24 billion.

The average value per farm was less than $3,000 at the turn of the century, exceeded $10,000 in 1920, and dropped to little more than half that amount in the Depression years. In 1950, it was $14,000 and in 1959, almost $35,000. The average value per acre, $69 in 1920, fell to $32 in 1940, and reached $115 by 1959 (see Table VIII.4).

Variations in the average value per farm in different parts of the United States reflect local differences in the types of farms and in farming and marketing conditions. The highest average value per farm is in the Pacific states, nearly $90,000 in 1959; next, that in the Mountain states ($73,000). Farms in the East North Central and the West South Central states had an annual average value just above the national average of $35,000. The average value of farms is lowest in the South Atlantic and East South Central states (see Appendix Table XX). The lowest value per farm

---

* In previous agricultural censuses, places of 3 a. or more which sold products for $150 or more were considered farms. The 1959 census regarded as farms all places of 10 a. or more that had sales of $50 or more and those of less than 10 a. with sales of $250 or more. This resulted in a smaller number of farms counted, but, according to the Department of Agriculture, of the farms that disappeared, less than 1 per cent can be attributed to the change in definition.

TABLE VIII.4

NUMBER, ACREAGE, AND VALUE OF FARMS
IN THE UNITED STATES, 1860-1959

Item	1860	1880	1900	1920	1940	1950	1959
Number and area							
Number of farms (in thousands)	2,044	4,009	5,737	6,448	6,097	5,382	3,704
Land in farms (in millions of acres)	407	536	839	956	1,065	1,161	1,124
Value of farms (in millions of dollars)							
Land and buildings	6,645	10,197	16,615	66,316	33,642	75,261	128,988
Implements and machinery	246	407	750	3,595	3,060	11,314	18,457
Livestock	1,089	1,577	2,864	8,013	4,553	12,900	17,700
Size and value per farm (average)							
Acreage per farm	199	134	146	148	174	216	303
Value per farm (in dollars)	3,251	2,544	2,896	10,284	5,518	13,983	34,826
Value per acre (in dollars)	16	19	20	69	32	65	115
Distribution of farms by acreage (in thousands)							
Under 10 acres	...	139	267	289	506	485	241
10-49 "	...	1,036	1,664	2,011	1,780	1,478	811
50-99 "	...	1,033	1,366	1,475	1,291	1,048	658
100-179 "	...	...	1,912	1,980	1,310	1,103	772
180-259 "	...	1,696			486	487	414
260-499 "	...	...	378	476	459	478	471
500-999 "	...	76	103	150	164	182	200
1,000 acres and over	...	29	47	67	101	121	136

was in Alabama, Tennessee, and Mississippi ($12,780; $13,288; and $14,292; respectively); the highest in California ($131,212). Highest average value per a. of land and buildings is near metropolitan centers, in irrigated and specialty-crop areas of the West, and in the most productive areas of the Corn Belt; lowest value per a. is in the western range areas (see Figure VIII.5).

Comparatively small farms prevail in the East, and large farms are characteristic of the West, especially in the Mountain states. The increasing value of land per a. reflects the continuing demand of farmers for additional land.

Of the 3.7 million farms counted in 1959, 2.4 million, or about two-thirds, were considered "commercial" farms, and the remaining were represented as "part-time" (884,800), "part-retirement" (404,100), and "abnormal" (3,060) farms.*

* The Census considers farms as "commercial" if they sell products worth $2,500 or more, or if they sell products worth $50 to $2,499 when the farm operator is under 65 years of age, has worked less than 100 days off the farm, and the total income from the nonfarm sources of all members of his family, including himself, is less than the total value of products sold. "Abnormal" farms are public and private institutional farms, community enterprises, experiment-station farms, grazing associations, ostrich farms, frog farms, etc.

FIGURE VIII.5

AVERAGE VALUE OF LAND AND BUILDINGS
PER ACRE, BY STATE, 1959

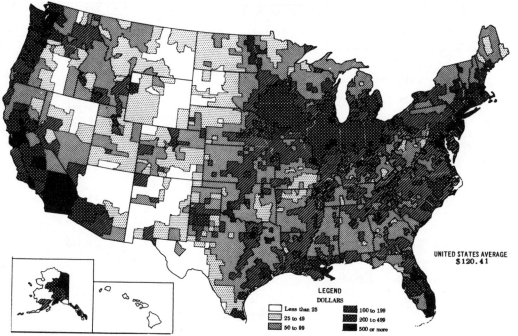

UNITED STATES AVERAGE
$120.41

LEGEND
DOLLARS

☐	Less than 25	▨	100 to 199
▨	25 to 49	▨	200 to 499
▨	50 to 99	■	500 or more

U.S. Department of Commerce, Bureau of the Census

In 1959, the least productive commercial farms, each selling from $50 to $2,499 worth of produce, accounted for 15 per cent of all commercial farms, but for only 1.5 per cent of all sales and less than 4 per cent of total acreage. The most efficient farms, each selling products for $40,000 and more, represented only 4 per cent of all commercial farms, but occupied more than one-fourth of all acreage and accounted for almost one-third of total sales (see Table VIII.5).

TABLE VIII.5

DISTRIBUTION OF COMMERCIAL FARMS
BY VALUE OF SALES, 1959[a]

Value of Products Sold	Number of Farms (In Thousands)	Land (In Millions of Acres)	Average Size (In Acres)	Average Value (In Dollars)
$ 50-$ 2,499	349	37	106	9,848
$ 2,500-$ 4,999	618	119	192	20,738
$ 5,000-$ 9,999	654	189	288	33,791
$10,000-$19,999	483	215	445	56,845
$20,000-$39,999	210	166	791	93,526
$40,000 and more	102	252	2,466	220,687
ALL COMMERCIAL FARMS	2,416	977	303	33,173

[a] Conterminous United States.

TABLE VIII.6

DISTRIBUTION OF FARMS BY TOTAL VALUE,
VALUE OF SALES AND VALUE OF REAL ESTATE, 1959

Class of Farm and Gross Value of Sales of Farm Products[a]	Percentage Distribution			Value of Real Estate	
	Farms	Total Value	Value of Sales	In Billions of Dollars	Per $1,000 of Sales (In Dollars)
Commercial farms with sales (in dollars):					
50- 2,499	9.4	3.2	1.5	4.3	9,287
2,500- 4,999	16.7	10.0	7.5	13.3	5,856
5,000- 9,999	17.6	17.2	15.5	22.8	4,839
10,000-19,999	13.0	21.4	22.0	28.4	4,246
20,000-39,999	5.7	15.7	18.5	20.9	3,698
40,000 and more	2.8	19.4	31.2	25.8	2,710
Other farms:					
Part-time	23.8	8.0	2.3	10.6	15,068
Part-retirement	10.9	3.4	1.1	4.5	13,157
Abnormal	0.1	1.7	0.4	2.2	20,726
ALL FARMS	100.0	100.0	100.0	132.9	4,363

[a]Conterminous United States.

FIGURE VIII.6

PER CENT OF ALL FARMS OPERATED BY TENANTS, 1959

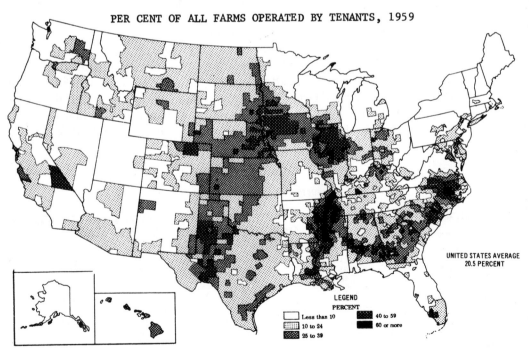

UNITED STATES AVERAGE
20.5 PERCENT

LEGEND
PERCENT

Less than 10   40 to 59
10 to 24   60 or more
25 to 39

U.S. Department of Commerce, Bureau of the Census

On the other hand, these 102,000 most efficient commercial farms are so large that the value of their real estate per $1,000 in sales is very small: $2,710 as compared with $9,287 for the least prosperous commercial farms, $15,068 for part-time farms, and $20,726 for experimental or institutional farms. The economic border between commercial farms was the $10,000 gross sale figure. Below it were about 67 per cent of all farms, with about 30 per cent of total sales in 1959 (see Table VIII.6).

In 1959, livestock farms accounted for 28 per cent of all commercial farms, dairy and poultry farms for 22 per cent, cash-grain farms for more than 16 per cent, cotton and tobacco farms for some 10 per cent each, and general farms for about 9 per cent. The remainder of the farms produced other field crops, vegetables, fruits, and nuts.

44. Farmers

Farm tenure in the United States has undergone great changes between 1880, the first year in which the census provided information on tenure,

TABLE VIII.7

DISTRIBUTION OF FARM OPERATORS BY TYPE OF TENURE, 1880-1959
(In Thousands)

Year	All Farms	Full Owners	Part Owners	Managers	Tenants
1880	4,009	2,984		1,025	
1900	5,737	3,202	451	59	2,025
1920	6,448	3,367	559	68	2,455
1940	6,097	3,084	615	36	2,361
1950	5,382	3,090	825	24	1,444
1954	4,783	2,745	868	21	1,149
1959	3,708	2,117	834	21	736

and 1959, the year of the last census for which data are available. For half a century or a little more, tenancy and sharecropping spread steadily—from 25.6 per cent of all farms in 1880 to 42.4 per cent in 1930. Soon afterward, the percentage of tenant-operated farms began to decline and by 1959 had dropped to 19.8 per cent of all farms (see Figure VIII.6, in which the term "tenants" includes "managers," raising the U.S. average from 19.8 per cent to 20.5 per cent).

As tenancy has declined in recent decades, farm ownership, full or part, has again become the dominant feature of American agriculture. Full owners constitute 57.1 per cent of all farm operators; part owners, 22.5 per cent. In 1959, full owners outnumbered tenant operators nearly 3 to 1, and part owners outnumbered tenants for the first time. The distribution of farm operators by type of tenure is shown in Table VIII.7.

This development has been encouraged by the great advance in agricultural technology and the introduction of more efficient farm-management practices. For economical operation, modern farm machinery

FIGURE VIII.7

MOST FREQUENT METHOD OF RENTING FARMS, 1959

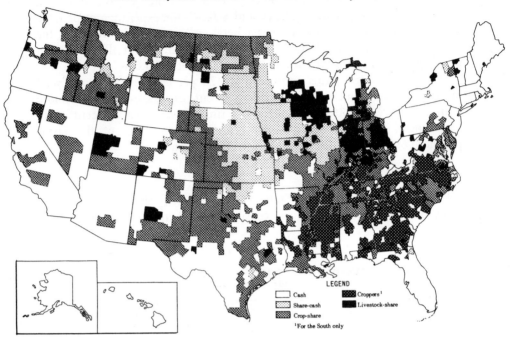

LEGEND

☐ Cash   ▨ Croppers [1]

▧ Share-cash   ■ Livestock-share

▨ Crop-share

[1] For the South only

U.S. Department of Commerce, Bureau of the Census

requires a larger land area than many farms had in the past. This fact has induced many farm operators to use their limited capital to expand their area by part ownership, rather than be the outright owners of less land. Tenants, too, follow that practice by dividing their financial resources between renting and part ownership.

The group of part owners comprises a wide range of combinations of ownership and tenancy, extending all the way from 99 per cent ownership and 1 per cent tenancy to the opposite.

The type of tenancy varies from locality to locality, but in most counties, when staple crops (grains, cotton, tobacco) are grown, a share of the farm produce is paid as rent. This arrangement permits the landlord and tenant to share the risk of production, and it has an additional advantage for the landlord in that it offers him immediate returns from higher yields assured by new production methods. To a lesser degree, share-cash and cash-rentals and other arrangements are also used. Share-cash leases predominate in areas of high productivity in the North Central states, where tenants are engaged in some livestock production (see Figure VIII.7).

The average real estate value per farm greatly differs between various tenure arrangements, mostly because of the differences between the average farm size in the different tenure groups. The average farm value (land

TABLE VIII.8

DISTRIBUTION OF FARMS BY TYPE OF OWNERSHIP, 1959
(Per Cent)

Type of Farms	Full Owners	Part Owners	Tenants
Commercial	51.7	84.6	81.3
Part-time	31.7	12.2	15.1
Part-retirement	16.6	3.2	3.6
Abnormal		Less than 0.05 per cent	
ALL FARMS	100.0	100.0	100.0

and buildings) of part owners amounted to $56,660 in 1959; of tenants, to $36,200; and of full owners, to $22,500. On the one hand, the low value of the full owners' farms is due to the large number of small part-time and part-retirement farms included in that group; on the other, it is explained by a tendency to operate the more productive land, with high valuation, under a leasing arrangement. More than 4 out of 5 part-owners and tenants operate commercial farms, in contrast to full owners, of whom only about 1 out of 2 operate a commercial farm; 1 out of 3, a part-time farm; and 1 out of 6, a part-retirement farm (see Table VIII.8).

For half a century, the average size of full-owner farms was 135 a., with some ups and downs, and only recently has it increased to 164 a., the average size of part-owner farms nearly tripled between 1910 and 1959. For the country as a whole, the average part-owner farm in 1959 was almost 4 times as large as the average full-owner farm and nearly 3 times as large as the average tenant farm. Manager-operated farms are very large: about 15 times as large, on the average, as the average for all farms. The average tenant farm, close to 100 a. early in the century, now exceeds 200 a.

Full-owner and part-owner farms are more or less evenly distributed throughout the nation, though there is some concentration of the former

TABLE VIII.9

PERCENTAGE DISTRIBUTION OF FARM OPERATORS
BY TYPE OF TENURE AND FARM ACREAGE, 1900-1959

Year	Full Owners		Part Owners		Managers		Tenants	
	Farms	Acreage	Farms	Acreage	Farms	Acreage	Farms	Acreage
1900	55.8	51.4	7.9	14.9	1.0	10.4	35.3	23.3
1910	52.7	52.9	9.3	15.2	0.9	6.1	37.0	25.8
1920	52.2	48.3	8.7	18.4	1.1	5.7	38.1	27.7
1930	46.3	37.6	10.4	24.9	0.9	6.4	42.4	31.0
1940	50.6	35.9	10.1	28.2	0.6	6.5	38.8	29.4
1950	57.4	36.1	15.3	36.4	0.4	9.2	26.9	18.3
1954	57.4	34.2	18.2	40.7	0.4	8.6	24.0	16.4
1959[a]	57.1	30.8	22.5	44.8	0.6	9.8	19.8	14.5

[a] Includes Alaska and Hawaii.

in the southern Appalachian area and the eastern part of the North Central states. Tenant farms have always been heavily concentrated in the South, where about half of all tenant farms have been located, most commonly small cotton and tobacco farms; and in the North Central states, with 42 per cent of all tenant farms, mainly in cash-grain areas of Illinois and Iowa. In the Northeast and West, tenancy has been less common but more stable. In 1959, only 1 out of 16 farms in the Northeast was a tenant farm, and 1 out of 8 in the West.

While full owners accounted for 57 per cent of all farms in 1959, they held only 31 per cent of the farmland; part owners, 22.5 per cent of all farmers, operated 45 per cent of the land. Managers constituted 0.6 per cent of the farm operators but handled almost 10 per cent of all farmland. The tenants, some 20 per cent of all farm operators, worked on 14.5 per cent of the land (see Table VIII.9).

The Census classifies farm operators by race as white and nonwhite, the latter comprising Negroes, Indians, Orientals, and all other nonwhite

TABLE VIII.10

NONWHITE FARM OPERATORS, 1900-1959

Year	All Nonwhite Farm Operators	Negroes	
		Number	Per Cent
1900	769,528	746,717	97
1910	924,450	893,377	97
1920	954,284	925,710	97
1930	921,400	882,852	96
1940	689,215	...	...
1950	585,917	559,980	96
1954	483,650	467,656	96
1959	290,831	272,541	94

races. From 1900 to 1920, Negroes consistently represented 97 per cent of all nonwhite operators; subsequently, their percentage had decreased slightly (see Table VIII.10). There was a heavy exodus of nonwhite farm operators from farming in the 1950's; in fact, it was proportionately greater than that of white operators. In the past, nearly all Negro farm operators were concentrated in the South, especially in the Mississippi Delta and the Coastal Plains. Within less than a decade, the South lost more than half of its nonwhite farm operators. In the West, most of the nonwhite operators are Indians and Orientals.

Among white farm operators, the acreage of the average farm is smallest for the full owners and largest for the manager-operated farms. Among the nonwhite operators, the average for the tenant farm is smallest. The same relationship characterizes average farm value, based on land and buildings (see Table VIII.11).

Another difference exists in the value of farm products sold by white

TABLE VIII.11

AVERAGE ACREAGE AND VALUE OF FARMS BY
COLOR OF OPERATORS AND TYPE OF TENURE, 1959

Type of Farm Operators	Number of Farmers (In Thousands)		Average Farm (In Acres)		Average Value of Land and Buildings (In Dollars)	
	White	Nonwhite	White	Nonwhite	White	Nonwhite
Full owners	-2,016.8	97.4	168.5	67.6	17,921	6,255
Part owners	792.4	40.7	627.9	130.6	46,096	9,436
Managers	20.5	0.5	3,567.4	72,437.5	255,504	107,072
Tenants	592.4	141.0	266.1	39.3	24,332	5,284
ALL FARMERS[a]	3,422.4	284.6	312.6	186.7	25,370	6,240

[a]Includes (in thousands) 2.3 white and 5.0 nonwhite farm operators in Hawaii and Alaska from whom data on tenure were not collected.

and nonwhite farm operators. Though it provides only a rough approximation of the level of net farm income (since production expenses vary widely), it does indicate the relative income of operators in different tenure groups. Among the white full owners in 1959, only 1 in 6 was in the lowest commercial-farm class, which sold farm products valued for $50–$2,499; among the part owners, 1 out of 16; and among the tenants, 1 in 10. The respective figures for nonwhite farm operators are: 3 out of 5 for full owners; more than 2 out of 5 among the part owners; and nearly every other tenant. The contrast is as great, if not greater, in the group selling farm products valued at $10,000–$19,999: 1 out of 6 white full owners was in this group, and more than 1 out of 4 part owners and tenants. For the nonwhite farm operators, the distribution was drastically different: 1 out of 30 full owners; 1 out of 20 part owners; and 1 out of 60 tenants were reported in that high class of commercial farming in 1959 (see Table VIII.12).

Agriculture has become more and more an occupation for older people. In 1910, 28.9 per cent of all farmers were under 35 years of age and 23.6

TABLE VIII.12

PERCENTAGE DISTRIBUTION OF COMMERCIAL FARM OPERATORS IN THE
UNITED STATES BY TENURE, COLOR, AND VALUE OF PRODUCTS SOLD, 1959

Value of Products Sold (In Dollars)	White			Nonwhite		
	Full Owners	Part Owners	Tenants	Full Owners	Part Owners	Tenants
50- 2,499	16.5	6.4	9.8	63.8	42.8	46.2
2,500- 4,999	30.8	19.6	20.7	21.7	30.3	36.7
5,000- 9,999	27.2	28.8	29.3	7.4	15.7	14.7
10,000-19,999	16.2	26.2	25.8	3.3	5.3	1.7
20,000-39,999	6.3	12.6	10.5	2.4	2.9	0.5
40,000 and more	3.0	6.5	3.9	1.2	2.8	0.3

per cent were aged 55 years and over; the corresponding percentages for 1959 were 12.7 and 38.7.

The average age of all farm operators in the United States was 48 years in 1940 and 50.5 years in 1959. This increase in age is due to the fact that proportionately more young men in rural areas have been leaving for the city and entering nonfarm employment. Average age is lowest among tenants (42.9 years), followed by part owners (48.3), and full owners (54.1).

The drift away from farms has taken place despite the fact that the standard of farm life has improved considerably in the last 2 decades. In 1940, only 1 farm in 3 was provided with electricity; now nearly all farms have electricity. In 1956, 2 farms out of 3 had a telephone and freezer, and 80 per cent of all farms were located on hard-paved or gravel roads, in contrast to one-third so located in 1950 and one-half in 1940.

The commercial farmer of 1965 differs greatly from an old-time farmer. He is a skilled technician, familiar with complex machinery, hybrid seeds, improved variety of crops, water control, fertilizers, insecticides, weed-killing. He is able to plan, keep records, maintain expensive machinery, negotiate loans with the government and make decisions about what, how, and when to produce. One out of 3 farmers turning out $40,000 or more of farm products for sale has attended college, and 1 out of 8 farmers in the lower group, with products of $20,000 to $39,999 gross sale, also has attended college.

45. Farm Labor

The special conditions of farm work make it difficult to obtain satisfactory statistics on agricultural workers for an entire year: large seasonal variations occur in the number of farm workers and there is double counting of those who move from farm to farm with changes in seasonal work, of farm operators who work as hired labor for other operators, and on some farms, of unpaid family workers who also work as hired labor on other farms.

Except on manager-operated farms, most farm work is done by the farm operator himself and by his family; usually he needs hired labor only at seasonal peaks, particularly for tobacco, cotton, fruit, and vegetable crops. Since seasonal ups and downs occur at different times in various parts of the country, many farm workers move with the demand for labor—from the South to the North and back to the South, in line with maturing crops. In the fall, for example, the South needs fruit packers several weeks earlier than the North, but at peak times, there may even be a shortage of farm workers.

Throughout the nineteenth century, farm labor represented an important part of the nation's labor force; even in 1930, more than 1 worker in 5 was on a farm. But with technological advances in agriculture, modern machinery, electricity, new biological techniques, and application of

TABLE VIII.13

FARM LABOR AS PER CENT OF TOTAL POPULATION
AND TOTAL EMPLOYMENT, 1820-1965

| Year | Employed Persons Aged 10 Years and Over[a] | | | Total Population (In Millions) | Farm Labor as Per Cent of Total Population |
	All Occupations (In Millions)	Agricultural Pursuits (In Millions)	Farm Labor as Per Cent of Total Labor Force		
1820	2.9	2.1	70.4	9.6	21.9
1840	5.4	3.7	68.5	17.1	21.6
1860	10.5	6.2	59.0	31.4	19.7
1880	17.4	8.6	49.4	50.2	17.1
1900	29.1	10.7	36.8	76.0	14.1
1920	41.6	11.1	26.7	105.7	10.5
1930	48.8	10.5	21.5	122.8	8.6
1930[a]	48.6	10.2	21.0	122.8	8.3
1940	51.7	8.8	17.0	131.7	6.7
1950	59.7	7.5	12.6	151.3	5.0
1960	66.7	5.7	8.5	179.3	3.2
1965	72.2	4.6	6.4	195.2	2.3

[a]Beginning 1930, persons aged 14 years and over.

chemistry, farm operators began to dispense with much of the labor necessary in the past. In 1820, farm labor represented more than 70 per cent of the persons employed in all occupations; in 1965, 6.4 per cent. In comparison with total population, farm labor represented 21.9 per cent in 1820, and 2.3 per cent in 1965. Despite the tremendous growth of the population of the United States, there are fewer workers on farms now than there were a hundred years ago (see Table VIII.13).

The number of persons working on farms fluctuates from month to month and is greatest in June and July, when the hired working force is nearly double that in winter: 1.1 million wage and salary workers in February, 1959; 2.1 million in June; also, 0.6 and 1.8 million unpaid family workers, respectively. In 1965, total farm employment (family and hired labor) amounted to 3.8 million in February and 5.6 million in June–July.

Of all hired workers in 1960, only 12 per cent were year-round (250 days or more) workers. The type of farm determines how many year-round workers it needs. A large dairy farm, for example, requires more such help than does a cotton, fruit, or vegetable farm, which mainly employs casual (under 25 days a year) or seasonal (25–149 days) workers. The peak seasonal demand is met partly by migrants from Mexico and the Caribbean* and also by students and housewives who seek farm work only for the summer. In 1960, 261,000 workers were of Spanish-American ances-

* Their number was cut considerably in 1964–65 by government order.

try; two-thirds of them were born in the United States, and nearly 9 out of 10 had their home base in the South or West. In recent years, nearly 30 per cent of all hired farm workers have been females.

The outlay for hired labor on all farms totaled $2.6 billion in 1959. Commercial farms accounted for nearly 97 per cent of that amount, though only 12.5 per cent of them reported regular hired workers—that is, workers employed 150 to 249 days. Of the farms that so reported, manager-operated farms averaged 8.5 workers; part-owner farms, 2.2; tenant farms, 1.7; and full-owner farms, 1.9 regular workers per farm.

In recent years, the total farm-wage bill has been stabilizing at somewhat less than $3 billion a year; the average bill per farm for hired labor is increasing as the number of farms declines. About 15 per cent of the total wage bill consists of perquisites—board, lodging, food, etc.

In 1960, annual cash earnings from farm work averaged $2,255 for year-round workers, $1,113 for regular workers, $357 for seasonal workers and $55 for casual workers. Some of the casual workers averaged about 2 months of wage work during that year, of which only 12 per cent was farm work. All in all, about 1.5 million different people, 40 per cent of the total, spent the equivalent of the two 6-day weeks in cultivating and harvesting crops.

Since 1940, total man-hours of work on all farms has decreased from 20.5 billion to about 9 billion. In the last 30 years, farm production per man-hour has tripled, but substituting machines for muscles has been more successful in crop than in livestock production: 200 per cent increase per man-hour for crop production and only 70 per cent increase for livestock production. For example, some 3 decades ago, 209 man-hours of labor were required to produce a bale of cotton; now 47 hours is the average for the country as a whole; respective figures for 100 bushels of corn are 108 and 11 hours. In contrast, within the same period, man-hours for producing a hundredweight of beef declined only from 4.2 to 2.7; per cwt. of milk, from 3.4 to 1.3. There are still regional differences in the degree of mechanization: labor used per bale of cotton in California was 27 hours in 1955–59, 70 hours in the mid-South, and 114 hours in the southeastern states. There is every reason to believe that efficiency of agriculture will continue to rise, and the use of agricultural labor will continue to decline.

46. Farm Income and the Balance Sheet of American Agriculture

Gross farm income comes from 4 main sources: cash receipts from farm sales; government payments; value of home consumption; and gross rental value of farm dwellings. Net farm income is obtained by deducting production expenses from gross income and making adjustment for inventory changes.

Between 1940 and 1964, cash receipts from marketing more than quadrupled, government payments more than doubled, and the rental value of dwellings almost tripled. The only item of income that declined in value was home consumption, which decreased by nearly $100 million because of the drastic drop in the farm population in that period—from 30.5 million persons to 14.3 million.

The realized net income of farm operators reached its peak in 1947 ($17.1 billion) and has since tended to decline, largely because the costs of production have been rising faster than receipts from marketing and other income sources. In the 1960's, it fluctuated around $11–$12 billion; in 1964, it amounted to $13 billion; and was estimated at $14 billion for 1965 (see Table VIII.14).

In 1964, the net income per farm (excluding changes in inventories) was lowest in Nevada ($553) and highest in Arizona ($16,969), the state with the largest acreage per farm in the country: 5,558 a. Between these 2 extremes were 5 states with realized net income per farm under $2,000; 12

TABLE VIII.14

REALIZED NET INCOME OF FARM OPERATORS, 1910-64
(In Millions of Dollars)

Year	Realized Gross Farm Income[a]	Production Expenses	Realized Net Income of Farm Operators
1910	7,477	3,531	3,946
1920	15,944	8,837	7,107
1930	11,472	6,944	4,528
1940	11,059	6,858	4,201
1947	34,146	17,032	17,114
1957	34,001	23,294	10,707
1960	37,915	26,242	11,673
1962	41,069	28,526	12,543
1963	42,073	29,572	12,501
1964	42,190	29,249	12,941

[a]Excludes net change in farm inventories and includes government payments.

with income under $3,000; 17 states with income of $4,000 and over. Among the latter, Florida and California had a net income per farm of some $11,000. For the country as a whole, the net income per farm was $3,401 in 1962; $3,499 in 1963; and $3,727 in 1964 (see Figure VIII.8). In 1965, it was $4,280.

Livestock and livestock products return more cash to farm operators than crops—$19,764 and $17,135, respectively, in 1964. Meat alone accounted for almost a third of cash receipts from all farm marketings, and dairy products, poultry, and eggs about a fifth. Among crops, feed crops are the single largest source of cash, followed by cotton, vegetables, and food grains (see Table VIII.15). Government payments range between 4.5 and 5.5 per cent of total cash receipts.

TABLE VIII.15

CASH RECEIPTS FROM FARM MARKETINGS OF CROPS AND
OF LIVESTOCK AND PRODUCTS, 1940-64
(In Millions of Dollars)

Item	1940	1950	1955	1960	1962	1964
All crops	3,469	12,356	13,523	15,103	16,162	17,135
Cotton (lint and seed)	638	2,434	2,580	2,340	2,552	2,532
Tobacco	242	1,061	1,225	1,154	1,321	1,414
Food grains	479	1,941	1,990	2,460	2,445	2,159
Oilbearing crops	126	935	1,131	1,364	1,803	1,996
Feed crops	600	2,143	2,555	3,025	2,960	3,343
Vegetables	559	1,436	1,683	1,845	2,029	2,272
Fruits and tree nuts	446	1,188	1,276	1,576	1,523	1,723
Sugar crops	79	216	198	251	308	386
Other crops	300	1,002	885	1,088	1,221	1,310
All livestock and products	4,913	16,105	15,967	18,909	20,025	19,764
Hogs	836	3,214	2,694	2,869	3,150	3,006
Cattle and calves	1,375	5,680	5,246	7,388	8,177	7,758
Sheep and lambs	180	387	316	327	324	326
Wool	106	130	91	108	115	118
Dairy products	1,521	3,719	4,217	4,740	4,841	5,008
Poultry and eggs	828	2,839	3,224	3,282	3,230	3,335
Other[a]	67	136	179	195	188	213
FARM MARKETINGS, TOTAL	8,382	28,461	29,490	34,012	36,187	36,899

[a]Horses, mules, goats, rabbits, fur animals, bees, beeswax, honey, and mohair.

FIGURE VIII.8

REALIZED NET FARM INCOME PER FARM,
BY STATE, IN DOLLARS, 1964

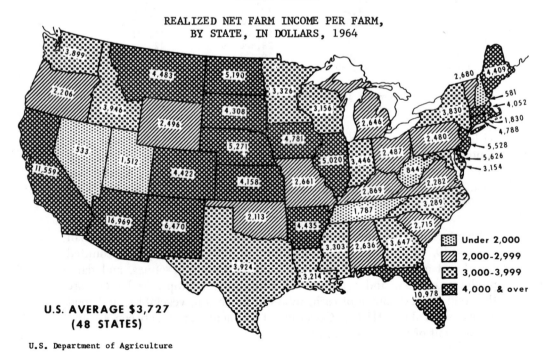

U.S. AVERAGE $3,727
(48 STATES)

U.S. Department of Agriculture

In terms of cash receipts, the importance of different commodities varies from state to state. In 1964, for example, dairy products occupied first place in 11 states (New England states minus Maine, where potatoes and broilers pushed them into third place; and New York, New Jersey, Pennsylvania, Ohio, Michigan, and Wisconsin). Cotton was still king in 7 states (Louisiana, Alabama, Mississippi, Tennessee, Arizona, Arkansas, and Texas); wheat was most important as a source of cash only in North Dakota, Montana, and Washington; tobacco, in the Carolinas and Kentucky; potatoes, in Maine; oranges, in Florida; hogs, in Indiana; corn, in Illinois; and broilers in Delaware, Maryland, and Georgia. Cattle occupied first place in the remaining 17 states.

Of total production costs, purchased feed and livestock accounted for 30–31 per cent; repairs, petroleum, and fuel for about 13–14 per cent; wages for some 10 per cent; taxes and interest on mortgages, about as much.

TABLE VIII.16

INCOME OF FARM POPULATION
FROM FARM AND NONFARM SOURCES, 1950-64

Year	Total Income	Income from:		Per Capita Income from:	
		Farming	Nonfarm Sources	Farming	Nonfarm Sources
		(In Millions of Dollars)		(In Dollars)	
1950	20,366	14,103	6,263	612	272
1955	17,579	11,382	6,197	597	325
1960	18,654	11,444	7,210	733	461
1961	19,033	12,109	6,924	819	468
1962	19,158	12,161	6,997	850	490
1963	18,692	11,988	6,704	898	502
1964	17,881	11,124	6,757	859	522

In addition to income from farming, the farm population derives income from nonfarm sources, such as nonfarm business and professional income, nonfarm work, rents from nonfarm real estate, dividends, interest, unemployment compensation, pensions, and social-security benefits. Nonfarm income of farm people amounts to about half the income earned from farming, or one-third of total income, and per capita income from nonfarm sources is more than half that from farming (see Table VIII.16).

The balance sheet of agriculture, considered as a single enterprise, consists of assets and liabilities. Assets are of two kinds: physical assets (real estate, livestock, machinery, crops stored on and off farms, household furnishings, and equipment) and financial assets (deposits, currency, U.S. savings bonds, investment in cooperatives). Real estate debts and other debts constitute the liabilities.

Real estate represents about two-thirds of the value of all assets in

TABLE VIII.17

BALANCE SHEET OF AGRICULTURE IN THE UNITED STATES, 1940-65[a]
(In Billions of Dollars)

Item	1940	1950	1955	1960	1964	1965[c]
Assets	52.9	132.5	165.1	203.9	228.9	237.6
Physical assets:						
Real estate	33.6	75.3	98.2	129.9	150.7	159.4
Livestock[b]	5.1	12.9	11.2	15.6	15.7	14.4
Machinery and motor vehicles	3.1	12.2	18.6	22.3	24.1	25.2
Crops stored on and off farms	2.7	7.6	9.6	7.8	9.8	8.9
Household furnishings and equipment	4.2	8.6	10.0	9.6	8.6	8.6
Financial assets:						
Deposits and currency	3.2	9.1	9.4	9.2	9.2	9.6
United States savings bonds	0.2	4.7	5.0	4.7	4.2	4.2
Investments in cooperatives	0.8	2.1	3.1	4.8	6.6	7.3
Claims	52.9	132.5	165.1	203.9	228.9	237.6
Liabilities:						
Real-estate debt	6.6	5.6	8.2	12.1	16.8	18.9
Non-real-estate debt:						
to government agencies and banks	1.9	4.5	6.2	7.9	11.4	11.5
to private creditors	1.5	2.3	3.2	4.9	6.7	7.1
Proprietors' equities	42.9	120.1	147.5	179.0	194.0	200.1

[a]Excludes Hawaii and Alaska.

[b]Beginning 1961, excludes horses and mules.

[c]Preliminary.

agriculture; livestock, crops stored, machinery and motor vehicles, about one-fifth; household furnishings, about 4 per cent; and financial assets, some 9 per cent. The claims on farms consist of liabilities, or debts now about 15 per cent, and the remainder, of proprietors' equities (the value of the residual rights in agricultural assets belonging to the proprietors—owners, operators, tenants, and landlords) (see Table VIII.17). Proprietors may be individuals, corporations, or government agencies.

Farmers mortgage their real estate for various reasons: to purchase additional land or a new farm, to renew equipment or finance some nonfarm activity. In 1910, farm mortgage debt amounted to $3.2 billion. By 1921, it had more than tripled ($10.2 billion); it fell to less than $10 billion by 1925, and continued to decline through the years of the Depression and the war to the rock-bottom level of $4.8 billion in 1946. After that year, mortgage debt rose slowly but steadily to a record $18.9 billion on January 1, 1965.

About 2.4 million American farms, or some 39 per cent of the total, were mortgaged in 1940; they accounted for 47 per cent of total value of farm land and buildings and 43 per cent of total farm acreage. In 1950, the num-

FIGURE VIII.9

FARM REAL ESTATE, 1910-64

(Value per Acre, Transfers, and Foreclosures)

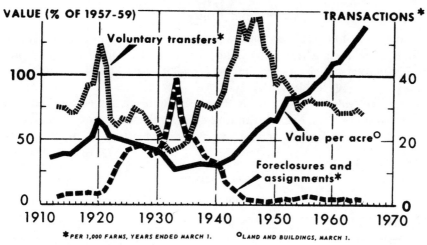

U.S. Department of Agriculture

ber of mortgaged farms was smaller by about 900,000 (1.5 million farms, or 27.5 per cent of all farms). Since 1950, all figures concerning mortgages on farms—acreage, value of mortgaged farms, debt per acre, debt per farm, equity per mortgaged farm—have been rising in all regions of the country, the North as well as the South and the West. There are certain variations from region to region, however: the largest number of mortgaged farms is in the North, the lowest in the West; debt per farm is highest in the West —$6,676 in 1950, as compared with $4,113 in the North and $2,508 in the South. (After 1950, such data are not available on a national scale.)

The large increase of mortgage debt, by about 45–50 per cent between 1960 and 1965, does not seem to have raised the question about the re-payment ability of the farmers: 3 major institutional lenders report a low rate of delinquencies and foreclosures. Only 1.5 foreclosures per 1,000 of all farms were reported, as compared with 28.5 for voluntary sales and about 12.5 per 1,000 for transfers due to inheritances, gifts, and other estate settlements (see Figure VIII.9). A 1960 Sample Survey of Agricul-ture indicates that most farmers were either debt-free or were lightly in-debted at the end of 1960; other sources report that despite the growth of debt since 1960, collections were excellent. Indebtedness is highly concen-trated: less than one-fifth of all farm operators accounted for seven-tenths of total debt; it has grown in size and concentration after 1960, but most debtors have met their commitments in due time.

A factor that has greatly contributed to the growing mortgage debt has been the rapidly expanding consolidation of farms (cf. Sec. 43). When farms are consolidated into larger units, credit is often needed for the purchase of land and machinery. It is estimated that about half of farmland bought in recent years has been for the enlargement of existing farms.

47. *Field Crops, Vegetables, and Fruits*

More than four-fifths of the cropland harvested in the United States is in 8 crops: corn, wheat, oats, barley, sorghum, soybeans, cotton, and hay. In recent years, their acreage has exceeded 93 per cent of the total area in field crops (see Table VIII.18).

The farm value of these crops fluctuates more or less within the same percentages. In terms of farm value, one crop, tobacco, is important though it takes up only a small acreage. It provides one-third as much in cash

TABLE VIII.18

ACREAGE IN FIELD CROPS, 1954-64

Crop	Millions of Acres			Per Cent		
	1954	1959	1964[a]	1954	1959	1964[a]
Corn	78.1	79.6	66.9	23.7	25.8	22.8
Wheat	51.4	49.6	49.2	15.6	16.1	16.8
Oats	37.9	26.6	20.4	11.5	8.6	6.9
Sorghum	17.6	17.9	11.9	5.3	5.8	4.1
Soybeans	16.4	22.1	30.7	5.0	7.2	10.5
Barley	12.6	14.2	10.7	3.8	4.6	3.6
Cotton	18.9	14.9	14.1	5.7	4.8	4.8
Hay, all	72.0	62.4	67.9	21.8	20.3	23.1
Other crops	25.0	20.9	21.5	7.6	6.8	7.2
ALL FIELD CROPS	329.9	308.2	293.3	100.0	100.0	100.0

[a]Harvested acreage of 1964 crops not fully comparable with 1954 and 1959 data.

receipts as corn, for example, but occupies only about one-fiftieth of the corn acreage (see Appendix Table XXI).

Soybeans have registered a more spectacular growth in acreage and production in recent decades than any other crop. Unimportant early in this century, occupying only 50,000 a. in 1907 and 0.7 million a. in 1929, soybeans then attracted more and more acreage and increased in output: 3.4 million a. and 62 million bushels harvested in 1936–40; 11.3 million a. and 230 million bu. in 1946–50, and some 31 million a. and 700 million bu. in 1964. Corresponding figures for the farm value of this crop are $53 million in 1936–40, $581 million in 1946–50, and $1.8 billion in 1964, exceeding tobacco ($1.3 billion in 1964). Yield per a., however, has not increased as rapidly, rising only from 18.1 bu. in 1936–40 to 22.8 bu. in 1964.

In general, production of all crops has greatly profited from the technological revolution in agriculture after World War II (see Sec. 40 and

FIGURE VIII.10

CROP PRODUCTION, 1950-65

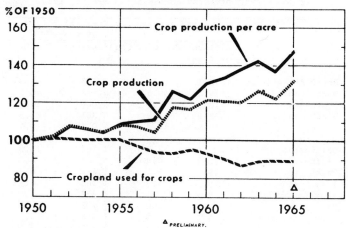

U.S. Department of Agriculture

Sec. 43), but some crops have benefited particularly. Acreage harvested in wheat totaled 76 million a. in 1949 and only 49.2 million a. in 1964, but the harvest was larger in 1964 than in 1949: 1,290 and 1,098 million bu., respectively. The figures for corn in 1949 and 1964, respectively, were 77 and 57 million a. and 2,946 and 3,549 million harvested bu. Cropland used for all crops in 1965 was smaller by 40 million a. than in 1950 but crop production was larger by more than 30 per cent (see Figure VIII.10).

Corn stands first in value of crops in 11 states, predominantly in the North Central region but also in Delaware and Maryland. Wheat is the first crop in value in 5 states (North Dakota, Kansas, Oklahoma, Montana, and Washington); cotton lint in 9 states (all South Central states except Kentucky, where tobacco occupies the first place, and Oklahoma, where wheat is more important); 2 Mountain states (New Mexico and Arizona), and 1 Pacific state (California). Tobacco is the most important crop for Connecticut, Virginia, the Carolinas, and Kentucky. Hay, in all its varieties, raises more cash than any other crop in 13 states (New Hampshire, Vermont, Massachusetts, New York, New Jersey, Pennsylvania, Wisconsin, West Virginia, Wyoming, Colorado, Utah, Oregon, and Nevada). Potatoes are most important in Maine, Rhode Island, and Idaho; peanuts in Georgia; and oranges in Florida.

Distinction should be made, however, between the importance of a certain crop for a particular state and the state's lead in production of that crop. Potatoes occupy first place in the value of crop production in Rhode Island, but the state is absent from a list of the 4 major producers of potatoes—Idaho, Maine, California, and New York, in the order given.

TABLE VIII.19

HARVESTED ACREAGE AND FARM VALUE OF CROPS,
BY GEOGRAPHIC DIVISION AND SELECTED STATES, 1964

	Harvested Acreage		Farm Value of 78 Crops[a]	
	Millions of Acres	Per Cent	Millions of Dollars	Per Cent
North Atlantic	12.1	4.1	1,123	5.3
North Central	174.4	59.5	8,522	40.6
South Atlantic	18.5	6.3	3,000	14.3
South Central	52.6	17.9	4,301	20.5
Western	35.8	12.2	4,072	19.4
California	6.6	2.2	2,102	10.0
Illinois	20.3	6.9	1,448	6.9
Texas	19.9	6.8	1,411	6.7
Iowa	20.3	6.9	1,363	6.5
Florida	1.3	0.4	833	3.9
Minnesota	17.3	6.0	792	3.8
North Carolina	4.5	1.5	914	4.4
Indiana	10.8	3.7	714	3.4
Nebraska	16.4	5.6	636	3.0
Kansas	19.1	6.5	626	3.0
Missouri	11.9	4.0	624	3.0
All other states, except Alaska and Hawaii	144.7	49.9	9,555	45.6
UNITED STATES	293.3	100.0	21,018	100.0

[a] Includes fruits and nuts, and vegetables, as compared to
acreage for 59 crops and vegetables.

Four states stand out in the value of crop production: California,
Illinois, Texas, and Iowa. Together they account for 30 per cent of the
country's total value of crop production, though their cropland is less than
one-fourth of the total acreage in crops. Following in cash receipts from
crops are North Carolina, Florida, Minnesota, Indiana, Nebraska, Kansas,
and Missouri, with nearly 25 per cent of the total value of crop production in 1964 (see Table VIII.19). In cash receipts that year, California
led for all commodities, all crops, hay, greenhouse and nursery products,
eggs, turkeys, tomatoes, sugar beets, and barley. Texas ranked first in
cash receipts from marketing cotton lint, cottonseed, rice, and sorghum
grain; Illinois, from marketing corn and soybeans; Iowa, from all livestock
sales (cattle and calves, and hogs); Wisconsin led in dairy products;
Kansas in wheat; North Carolina, in tobacco; Idaho, in potatoes; Georgia,
in peanuts, forest products, and broilers; Florida, in oranges; Colorado, in
sales of sheep and lambs; and Washington, in apples. The 25 commodities
in which these 10 states were leading ranked, in their turn, by value of
farm marketings.

FIGURE VIII.11

YIELD PER HARVESTED ACRE, PROJECTED TO 1975

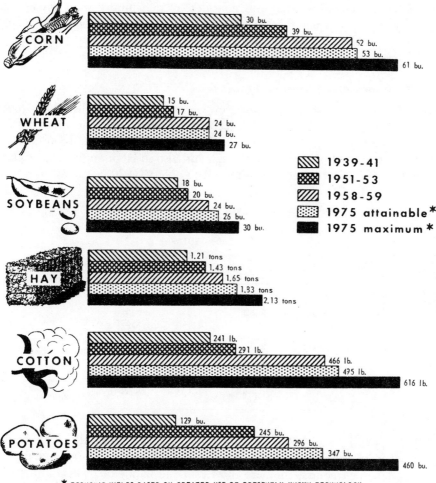

CORN
30 bu.
39 bu.
52 bu.
53 bu.
61 bu.

WHEAT
15 bu.
17 bu.
24 bu.
24 bu.
27 bu.

▨ 1939-41
▧ 1951-53
▨ 1958-59
▨ 1975 attainable*
■ 1975 maximum*

SOYBEANS
18 bu.
20 bu.
24 bu.
26 bu.
30 bu.

HAY
1.21 tons
1.43 tons
1.65 tons
1.83 tons
2.13 tons

COTTON
241 lb.
291 lb.
466 lb.
475 lb.
616 lb.

POTATOES
129 bu.
245 bu.
296 bu.
347 bu.
460 bu.

* ECONOMIC YIELDS BASED ON GREATER USE OF PRESENTLY KNOWN TECHNOLOGY

U. S. DEPARTMENT OF AGRICULTURE

A study by the Department of Agriculture, *Our Farm Production Potential, 1975*, shows that a substantial increase in yield of every major crop per harvested a. is to be expected solely from greater use of presently known technology. Two levels of increase in future yields—"economically attainable" and "economic maximum"—are considered in this study; the different rates of adoption of presently known technology by farmers accounts for a gap between these two levels (see Figure VIII.11 for actual and projected yields of corn, wheat, soybeans, cotton, hay, and potatoes).

The conclusion of the study is that present technological knowledge is sufficient to meet the needs for food and fiber of the projected U.S. population of 230 million in 1975 and to provide for a relatively high level of exports. The rapidly increasing rate at which farmers adopt known technology and a possibility that further advances might occur in this field point to the fact that what was considered "maximum" yield when the study was prepared might be exceeded by 1975. As a matter of fact, yields of some crops, such as wheat and corn, equaled or approached the "attainable" level for 1975 as early as 1958–59.

48. *Livestock and Livestock Products*

Until 1926, cash receipts from crops were consistently higher than from livestock and livestock products, except in an occasional year. Since 1926, the animal branch of American agriculture has become more important in terms of cash receipts from marketings, and also in labor employed, capital invested, and in human consumption (see Table VIII.20).

TABLE VIII.20

CASH RECEIPTS FROM MARKETING OF CROPS
AND LIVESTOCK, 1910-64
(In Millions of Dollars)

Year	Total	Crops	Livestock
1910	5,780	2,929	2,851
1920	12,600	6,644	5,956
1925	11,021	5,545	5,476
1930	9,055	3,868	5,187
1940	8,382	3,469	4,913
1950	28,461	12,356	16,105
1960	33,999	15,090	18,909
1962	36,187	16,162	20,025
1964	36,899	17,135	19,764

Livestock and dairy farms combined account for one-half of all commercial farms in the United States (cf. Sec. 43). Because of the large input of capital they require, they are mostly in the hands of owners and part owners, rather than tenants. Every second operator of a livestock or dairy farm is a full owner, and 3 operators out of 10 are part owners. The relationship is somewhat different on livestock ranches, located primarily in the grazing areas of the Great Plains and the West. Full owners operate about 40 per cent of these, part owners 47 per cent, managers over 3 per cent, and tenants work on the remaining 10 per cent.

The value of livestock and poultry on farms is considerably smaller than that of all farm motor vehicles and other farm machinery: $15.7 million and $24.1 million, respectively, in 1964; and $14.4 million and $25.2 million in 1965 (see Table VIII.17).

The 2 types of domestic animals—productive, which supply foodstuffs (cattle, hogs, and stock sheep), and workstock, which supply draft power (horses and mules)—once followed the same long-term trend of increase

FIGURE VIII.12.A

CATTLE ON FARMS, BY CYCLES

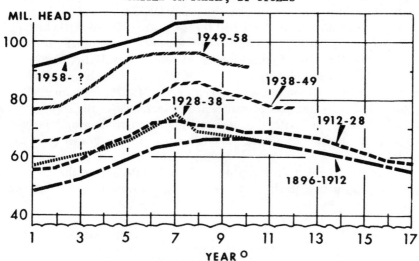

U.S. Department of Agriculture

in numbers. After the mid-1920's, however, cattle and hogs continued to grow in number, while the numbers of sheep and, in particular, horses and mules began to decline. Draft animals no longer are needed on farms, and in 1960 the census stopped counting them. In addition to this long-

FIGURE VIII.12.B

CATTLE ON FARMS, JANUARY 1

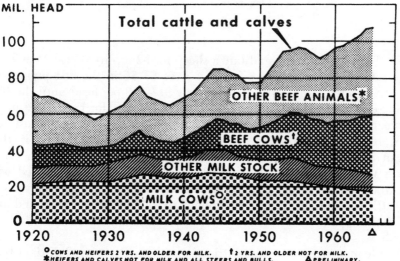

U.S. Department of Agriculture

term trend, there are short cyclical movements in the development of herds of each type of livestock; the longest of these, stretching over a number of years, is for cattle (see Figure VIII.12A for cattle cycles, beginning of 1896, and Figure VIII.12B for the distribution of cattle by type).

Comparison of inventory numbers of livestock from census to census is affected by the date of enumeration; at some dates, births increase the inventory; at others, marketings, farm slaughter, etc., substantially lower the count of livestock on farms (see Table VIII.21; data for January 1).

Not only has the number of cattle greatly increased in the course of the last few decades, but with the new techniques in feeding and breeding, productivity in terms of weight (and also quality) has grown even more rapidly.

All through the nineteenth century and the first decades of the twentieth, prices for productive stock were very low in contrast to those for work-

TABLE VIII.21

LIVESTOCK ON FARMS, 1867-1965
(In Millions of Heads)

Year	Cattle	Hogs	Stock Sheep	Horses	Mules
1867[a]	28.6	34.5	45.0	6.8	1.0
1927	58.2	55.5	38.1	15.4	5.8
1937	66.1	43.1	45.3	11.3	4.5
1947	80.6	56.8	31.8	7.3	2.8
1957	92.9	51.9	26.3	3.6[b]	-
1963	103.7	58.9	25.7	-	-
1964	106.9	58.1	24.3	-	-
1965	107.7	53.1	23.3	-	-

[a]First reporting year.
[b]Includes mules.

stock. Up to 1900, one could buy a sheep for $2; up to World War I, for $3–$4. Corresponding figures for hogs were $5–$6 in the first period and about $10 later. Even cattle brought only $17–$20 per head until the turn of the century, and $40 during World War I. Prices for horses and mules fluctuated considerably but ranged between $55 and $80 in the last century, exceeded $100 during World War I and immediately after it, then began to decline for a while but still were over $100 per head. Cattle prices were exceptionally high in the mid-1950's, which coincided with the trough in the cattle cycle of this country. In 1963, the average value of all cattle was $142 per head, but dropped to $114 in 1965; of hogs and pigs, $27.50, dropping to $24.80; of stock sheep, $14.40, rising to $15.80.

While many countries raise cattle of an all-purpose type, 2 distinct types are raised in the United States: beef cattle and dairy cattle (milk cows).

TABLE VIII.22

SLAUGHTERING BY TYPE OF ANIMALS, 1900-1964
(In Millions of Heads)

Year	Total[a]	Cattle	Calves	Hogs	Lambs and Sheep
1900	78.8	10.8	4.1	51.9	12.0
1910	85.5	14.1	6.9	48.2	16.3
1920	97.5	13.5	8.5	61.5	14.0
1930	108.3	12.1	7.8	67.3	21.1
1940	123.3	15.0	9.1	77.6	21.6
1950	121.6	18.6	10.5	79.3	13.2
1960	135.1	26.0	8.6	84.2	16.2
1962	135.5	26.9	7.9	83.5	17.2
1963	138.7	28.1	7.2	87.4	16.2
1964[b]	140.7	31.6	7.6	86.6	14.9

[a]Inspected, noninspected, retail, and farm slaughter.
[b]Preliminary.

The number of beef cattle has increased spectacularly in recent times—from 30 million head in 1939 to 76 million in 1959 and 90 million in 1965. The decrease in the number of milk cows is likely to continue in the near future.

With the growth of the population and increasing consumption of meat, slaughtering of animals and production of meat likewise increased (see Table VIII.22).

Beef is the preferred meat in this country—production of it has more than tripled since the turn of the century, while that of pork, lamb, and mutton has less than doubled (see Table VIII.23).

TABLE VIII.23

PRODUCTION OF MEAT, BY TYPE, 1900-1964
(In Millions of Pounds of Dressed Weight)

Year	Total	Beef	Veal	Pork	Lamb and Mutton
1900	12,847	5,628	397	6,329	493
1910	13,998	6,647	667	6,087	597
1920	15,334	6,306	842	7,648	538
1930	16,016	5,917	792	8,482	825
1940	19,083	7,182	981	10,044	876
1950	22,075	9,534	1,230	10,714	597
1960	28,242	14,751	1,108	11,614	768
1962	28,989	15,320	1,016	11,844	809
1963	30,559	16,423	927	12,439	770
1964[a]	32,565	18,300	1,010	12,540	715

[a]Preliminary.

FIGURE VIII.13

MILK PRODUCTION, MILK COWS,
AND MILK PER COW, 1947-65

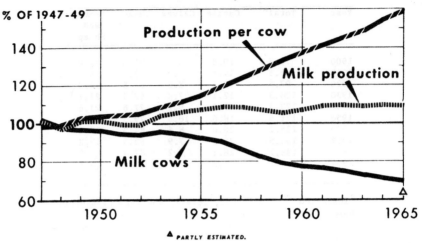

U.S. Department of Agriculture

Per capita consumption of beef is increasing at a very fast rate. It was 63.4 pounds in 1950, 85.8 lbs. in 1960, 94.2 lbs. in 1963, and it exceeded 100 lbs. in 1964 and 1965. Within the same lapse of time, per capita consumption of veal fell from 8 to 5 lbs., and of pork, from 69 to 65 lbs. in 1964 and 59 lbs. in 1965. Consumption of lamb and mutton was 4.2 lbs. in 1964.

In contrast to beef cattle, dairy cattle have been declining in numbers since the end of World War II, from 27.8 million head in 1945 to 23.9 million in 1950 and 17.6 million in 1965. However, milk production per cow has increased so that total output continues to rise. A record quantity

TABLE VIII.24

PRODUCTION OF MILK AND BUTTER, 1889-1964
(In Millions of Pounds)

Year	Milk Produced	Butter Churned on Farms	Butter Made in Factories
1889	44,807	1,024.2	214.5
1899	62,486	1,071.6	421.0
1909	64,211	994.7	627.1
1919	67,124	707.7	938.5
1929	98,988	542.1	1,618.1
1939	106,792	428.7	1,781.7
1950	116,602	261.5	1,386.0
1955	122,945	162.1	1,382.9
1960	122,951	62.2	1,372.9
1962	126,021	41.6	1,537.0
1964	126,598	26.1	1,420.0

FIGURE VIII.14

PRODUCTION OF BROILERS AND TURKEYS, 1954-65

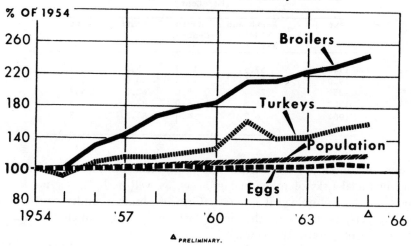

U.S. Department of Agriculture

of milk was produced in 1964 by the smallest number of milk cows in 60 years. Average production of milk per cow was 5,314 lbs. in 1950; and 7,880 lbs. in 1964. In 1961, the scientists of the Department of Agriculture projected the rate of milk production at 7,900 lbs. for 1975, but at the rate at which it has risen in recent years, this figure will be exceeded very shortly (see Figure VIII.13).

Butter used to be churned on farms but now is made predominantly in factories (see Table VIII.24).

The United States has by far the largest herd of milk cows of any country in the world and accounts for nearly 20 per cent of the world's production of milk. Yet the Low Countries and Denmark surpass it in the efficiency of their milk cows: in 1946, milk output per cow amounted to 8,419 lbs. in Denmark; 8,312 in Belgium, and 9,211 lbs. in the Netherlands.

No other major farm product has grown more rapidly than commercial broilers—from some 34 million in 1934 to 2,161 million in 1964, or an increase by some 60 times in 30 years (see Figure VIII.14). Advanced technology and efficient management have reduced production costs, and the price of broilers has been declining since the middle of the 1950's.

Production of commercial broilers has shifted from the Middle Atlantic states, which accounted for nearly half the total before World War II, to the South (see Table VIII.25).

In contrast to broilers, production of chickens has been declining (see Table VIII.26).

The rapid development of broiler production has been stimulated by a

TABLE VIII.25

PRODUCTION OF COMMERCIAL BROILERS, BY REGION, 1940-64
(Per Cent)

Year	North and Middle Atlantic	North Central	South	West
1940	57.5	11.7	25.2	5.6
1950	42.4	13.6	36.9	7.1
1959	24.4	8.0	62.7	4.9
1962	6.8	6.0	82.5	4.8
1964	6.2	4.6	84.8	4.3

system of contract arrangements that has reduced the capital requirements and financial risks of individual growers, as well as by lower production costs due to technological progress. Growing broilers under contract has been eagerly accepted in the South, which has had much unemployed labor and comparatively low wages.

Production of turkey, the all-American bird, nearly tripled between 1940 and 1964, rising from 33.3 million to 99.5 million birds.

Eggs also are an important product for poultry farms. Egg production was more or less stabilized around 30 billion a year in the early part of this century, increased to 38–40 billion in the late 1930's, and rose rapidly during World War II. Since that time, it has been relatively stable, fluctuating between 62 and 64 billion a year (64.6 billion in 1964). The number of layers, about 400 million during the war, is back at the previous figure of about 300 million, but increase in the average production per layer, from 137 eggs a year in 1950 to 217 eggs in 1964, has more than offset this drop in numbers. For egg production, too, advances have been made in the breeding and feeding of hens; seasonality of egg production has been considerably reduced; production is now spread more or less evenly throughout the entire year, instead of being concentrated in the spring

TABLE VIII.26

PRODUCTION OF CHICKENS
AND COMMERCIAL BROILERS, 1940-64
(In Millions of Birds)

Year	Chickens	Commercial Broilers
1940	556	143
1950	535	631
1959	311	1,737
1962	322	2,026
1963	318	2,104
1964	320	2,161

months. Egg production is widely distributed in this country, though about half of the total is produced in the North, about 30 per cent in the South, and the rest in the Western states. The United States is the world's largest producer of eggs, accounting for some 30 per cent of the world's total, 226.5 billion in 1964.

49. Agricultural Surpluses and Government Price Support

The greatly expanded agricultural production in this country far exceeds the demand of the domestic and foreign markets and the requirements for normal carryover. Resulting surpluses depress the prices of farm products, while costs of farm production (machinery, tractors, fertilizer, insurance, building materials, etc.) have risen considerably. Thus farmers have found themselves under double pressure—lower prices for their products and higher prices for purchased goods and services.

Various government programs have been introduced in the last 3 decades to support farm prices and prevent or at least limit the accumulation of surpluses.

In 1933, the Commodity Credit Corporation (CCC) was established to support prices of agricultural commodities through loans, purchases, and other operations. Among its many programs are those of price support, storage facilities, supply and foreign purchases, commodity export, and the International Wheat Agreement. The most far-reaching and important of these is price support.

This program is based on the so-called parity; a ratio of the prices received by farmers to prices paid by them (including interest rates, taxes, and wage rates). The ratio varies from year to year, and from commodity to commodity; it ranged for wheat, for example, from 75 to 90 in 1956–63, not more than 90 per cent and not less than 75 per cent of the parity price at the beginning of the new marketing year. Agricultural commodities are divided into "basic" and "nonbasic," and support is mandatory for some commodities and nonmandatory, or permissive, for others. In 1964, price support was mandatory for feed crops (corn, oats, barley, grain, sorghum), wheat, cotton, rice, most types of tobacco, peanuts, milk, butterfat, wool, mohair, tung nuts, and honey. Also supported under permissive provisions were flaxseed, soybeans, cottonseed, dry edible beans, and crude pine gum.

In most cases, the CCC price support is made to depend on marketing quotas and on restrictions on land in cultivation for the specific commodity. Support prices are announced in advance of the planting or marketing season and are not changed during the season.

CCC acquires large volumes of surplus commodities either through direct purchase or by taking over commodities as collateral for nonrecourse loans to farmers. Since 1933, CCC has paid out approximately $94 billion in the form of loans, purchase costs, carrying charges, direct payments for price support, commodity export payments, and other programs. Loans

TABLE VIII.27

INVENTORY OF THE COMMODITY CREDIT CORPORATION
ON OCTOBER 22, 1965

	Unit	Estimated Total Stock (In Thousands of Units)	Estimated Acquisition Cost (In Millions of Dollars)
Cotton			
Upland	Bl.	10,138	1,598.6
Extra-long staple	Bl.	125	32.5
Grains and feeds			
Wheat	Bu.	492,842	989.6
Corn[a]	Bu.	526,144	640.3
Barley	Bu.	14,092	12.0
Oats	Bu.	40,359	24.2
Grain sorghum	Bu.	481,817	552.6
Rye	Bu.	5,169	5.5
Flaxseed	Bu.	3,766	11.2
Rice, rough	Cwt.	742	3.8
Dairy			
Butter	Lb.	63,253	37.3
Cheese	Lb.	239	0.9
Milk, dried	Lb.	145,293	21.4
Beans, dry edible			
Pea	Cwt.	5	0.04
Oils and peanuts			
Peanuts, shelled	Lb.	1,773	0.3
Peanuts, other	Lb.	5,711	0.9
Linseed oil	Lb.	80,000	9.4
Tung oil	Lb.	14,676	3.5
Honey	Lb.	2,216	0.3

[a]Excludes deliveries to CCC for loans maturing July 31, 1965.

and purchases constitute by far the most important support methods. Of the $56.3 billion in price support extended by CCC in that period, loans account for almost $42 billion, or 74 per cent. Wheat, corn, and cotton account for more than four-fifths of all loans; tobacco, sorghum grain, and soybeans represent about 13–14 per cent of the total; the remainder is spread through a long list of commodities.

In the years of its operations from 1933 through 1964, CCC has collected approximately $64.5 billion, as repayments on loans, proceeds from sales, interest, and other sources of revenue.

Commodities acquired by the CCC move into consumption in various ways. Some are sold on domestic or foreign markets; others are used for food for the armed forces and veterans' hospitals, disaster relief at home and abroad, needy Indians on reservations, foreign relief programs. Some are bartered for strategic or critical materials produced abroad. Substantial quantities have been donated to the school-lunch programs and needy people in the United States.

Surplus commodities are also used for foreign aid in various programs under the Public Law 480, such as the Food for Peace program. In 1964, surplus commodities worth $1.6 billion were shipped overseas under P.L. 480.

FIGURE VIII.15

STORAGE CAPACITY OF THE COMMODITY CREDIT CORPORATION

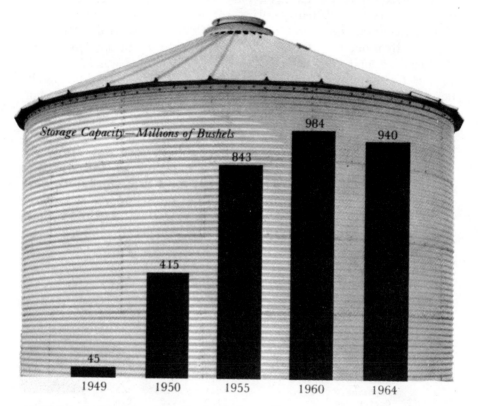

Storage Capacity—Millions of Bushels

			984	940
		843		
	415			
45				
1949	1950	1955	1960	1964

Department of Agriculture, Commodity Credit Corporation

On the average, five 10,000-ton ships leave this country's ports everyday with Food for Peace cargoes. Three-fourths of the food donated under this last program are assigned for children; some 40 million children in 90 countries receive free school lunches. Amounts resulting from sale of surplus commodities to developing countries against their currencies are earmarked, to a substantial degree, for projects within those countries. For example, more than 80 per cent of the rupees realized from such sales to India has been set aside as loans and grants for her economic- and social-development projects.

Huge inventory stocks of the CCC require extensive storage facilities. As of the end of 1964, the CCC owned storage bins with a total capacity approaching a billion bushels, located in the major grain-producing areas, largely in the Corn Belt (see Figure VIII.15). Approximately 11,500 approved private grain-warehouse facilities, with a total capacity of about 4 billion bu., are eligible for storage of either CCC-owned grain or grain placed under loans by farmers. With the financial aid from the CCC, the farmers have built additional on-farm space to store some 800 million bu. At one time, wheat was stored in moth-balled ships but this practice has been discontinued. Butter is stored in commercial freezer storage.

The inventory of the CCC on October 22, 1965, represented a value of $3.9 billion, with 4 items—upland cotton, wheat, corn, and grain sorghum—accounting for almost 96 per cent of the total (see Table VIII.27).

In less than one year, the situation has changed drastically. On August 19, 1966, the total value of price supported commodities was $2.7 billion, or almost one-third smaller than in October, 1965. The same 4 commodities again accounted for about the same percentage of total value, but

TABLE VIII.28

PRICE-SUPPORTED FARM MARKETING, BY COMMODITY, 1950-64
(Per Cent)

	1950	1955	1960	1964
Under price support	42.8	45.9	44.7	44.7
Mandatory support	36.6	39.0	37.7	36.4
Basic commodities	23.0	24.3	22.6	21.2
Cotton	7.5	7.9	6.2	6.2
Wheat	6.1	5.7	6.5	4.8
Corn	4.3	5.1	5.3	4.9
Tobacco	3.7	4.1	3.4	3.8
Rice	0.7	0.9	0.7	1.0
Peanuts	0.7	0.6	0.5	0.5
Nonbasic commodities	13.6	14.7	15.1	15.2
Dairy products	13.0	14.3	13.9	13.6
Other	0.6	0.4	1.2	1.6
Nonmandatory support	6.2	6.9	7.0	8.3
Soybeans	2.1	2.8	3.5	4.8
Cottonseed	1.0	0.8	0.6	0.7
Oats	0.8	0.8	0.6	0.4
Other	2.3	2.5	2.3	2.4
Without price support	57.2	54.1	55.3	55.3
TOTAL MARKETING	100.0	100.0	100.0	100.0

while the stocks of cotton have grown in both volume and value, those of wheat, corn, and grain sorghum have been substantially reduced in both respects.

The states with the largest production of price-supported commodities have been the chief beneficiaries of CCC loans. The 4 Southern cotton-producing states—Arkansas, Louisiana, Oklahoma, and Texas—received $8.4 billion, or 22 per cent, of the total $38.2 billion in loans in 1933–62: $5 billion for support of cotton and the rest largely for wheat and grain sorghum. Texas alone obtained $5.4 billion. The 7 West North Central states—Minnesota, Iowa, Missouri, the Dakotas, Nebraska, and Kansas—accounted for $13.4 billion, or nearly 35 per cent of all loans; 2 crops, corn and wheat, shared almost equally in that amount, with $4.8 and $5.2 billion, respectively.

Almost half of all farm marketing is price supported (see Table VIII.28).

None of the programs used so far—price support, acreage allotments, retiring of the soil in general, direct payments to producers, production control, and so on—has been wholly successful. Some have even created troublesome new problems—for example, when restriction of the acreage in wheat or corn was made a condition to obtaining CCC loans, that land was used to raise feed crops, which in turn became one of the most difficult surpluses to handle. On the other hand, storage expenses represent a drain on the country's resources; they absorb more than $1 million a day.

The fundamental cause of the U.S. agricultural "problem" of surpluses is the technological revolution, which has penetrated into every branch of agriculture and has found the American farmers ready and able to take advantage of every new improvement, every promising technique. Though this problem defies easy solutions, it has provided America with an abundance of foodstuffs, fiber, and other products and is enabling the nation to use its agricultural surpluses not only for various relief programs at home but also to help peoples in many other countries.

50. *Agricultural Exports and Imports of the United States*

Despite its diversity and tremendous volume, our agricultural production cannot meet all the nation's demand for various foodstuffs and other

FIGURE VIII.16.A

TOTAL EXPORTS AND AGRICULTURAL EXPORTS
OF THE UNITED STATES, 1880-1960

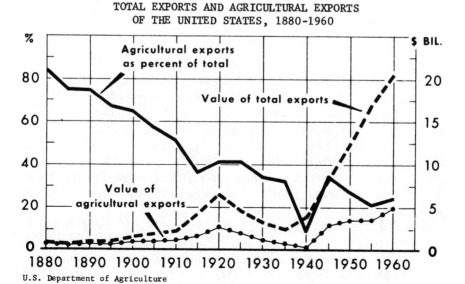

U.S. Department of Agriculture

agricultural products. On the other hand, our surpluses induce our farmers to seek outlets abroad.

Agricultural exports represent about one-fourth of the country's total value of exports, compared to over 80 per cent in the 1880's (see Figure VIII.16A). Agricultural imports amounted to nearly half our imports up to the 1950's and now account for about one-fourth. Some agricultural imports are supplementary, that is, they consist of products similar to those produced domestically or are interchangeable with such commodities to a significant degree. Other imports are complementary; about 95 per cent of these consist of rubber, bananas, coffee, cacao, tea, spices, raw silk, jute, and wool for carpets (see Table VIII.29).

TABLE VIII.29

VALUE OF AGRICULTURAL EXPORTS AND IMPORTS
OF THE UNITED STATES, 1930-64
(In Millions of Dollars, Except Per Cent)

Year, Begin-ning July	Agricultural Exports		Foreign Products (Re-exports)	Agricultural Imports				Excess of Domestic Exports Over Supplementary Imports
	Domestic Products			Total	Supple-mentary	Comple-mentary	Per Cent of All Imports	
	Total	Per Cent of All Exports						
1930	1,496	32	51	1,900	889	1,010	49	607
1934	787	39	21	839	419	420	50	368
1940	738	20	48	1,239	572	667	51	166
1946	2,854	34	191	1,887	1,031	856	45	1,823
1950	2,986	30	53	3,177	1,552	1,625	45	1,434
1952	4,053	26	70	4,699	1,971	2,728	45	2,082
1954	2,936	19	62	4,176	1,694	2,482	40	1,242
1956	3,496	21	65	4,086	1,583	2,503	34	1,913
1958	4,003	21	76	3,929	1,824	2,105	31	2,179
1960	4,517	24	73	4,010	1,979	2,031	26	2,538
1962	5,142	24	63	3,762	2,049	1,713	24	3,093
1963	5,078	24	62	3,907	2,208	1,699	24	2,870
1964	6,074	25	84	4,096	2,225	1,871	23	3,849

Historically, cotton and tobacco have been the 2 single most important export products of American agriculture. Since the end of World War II, however, the relative position of various agricultural products within U.S. exports has undergone a considerable change, largely under the impact of exports sponsored by certain Government programs (donations, grants, Public Law 480, disaster relief, etc.), which in 1964–65 accounted for about one-third of total agricultural exports: $2.1 billion out of $6.1 billion. Wheat (and wheat flour) is the one product that is largely exported under such programs (see Figure VIII.16B).

Grains and preparations now constitute the single most important group of products in U.S. agricultural exports, about $2.7 billion in 1964. Unmanufactured cotton has been next, though lately, exports of it have fallen to about 10 per cent of the total. Oilseeds and vegetable oils, and

FIGURE VIII.16.B

U.S. AGRICULTURAL EXPORTS BY COMMODITY GROUP, 1965

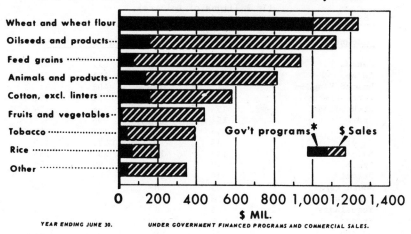

YEAR ENDING JUNE 30.   UNDER GOVERNMENT FINANCED PROGRAMS AND COMMERCIAL SALES.

U.S. Department of Agriculture

feed grains, of slight importance until the late 1940's, now account together for 30 per cent or more of total agricultural exports.

Among the imported commodities, the group of tropical products—
coffee, cacao, tea, and spices—stands out, with some 32–35 per cent of the
total value of our agricultural imports. Animals and animal products and
sugar and related products are the next 2 groups with a large share in
total agricultural imports, each with about 14–16 per cent.

FIGURE VIII.17

U.S. AGRICULTURAL EXPORTS AS PER CENT OF SALES
OF AGRICULTURAL COMMODITIES, 1965

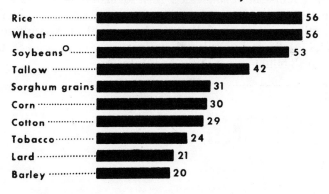

FISCAL YEAR.
* EXPORTS COMPARED WITH FARM SALES FOR CROPS AND WITH PRODUCTION FOR LARD AND TALLOW.
° INCLUDING OIL.

U. S. DEPARTMENT OF AGRICULTURE

TABLE VIII.30

VALUE OF AGRICULTURAL EXPORTS, BY COUNTRY OF DESTINATION, 1955-64
(In Millions of Dollars)

Country	Average 1955-59	1961	1962	1964
Canada	341	491	512	619
Japan	385	554	481	750
United Kingdom	427	431	408	417
West Germany	322	371	391	406
Netherlands	256	318	366	424
India	154	260	296	529
Italy	145	236	176	242
Egypt	38	97	171	136
Belgium	129	120	132	153
Spain	119	154	99	127
Brazil	36	112	95	107
South Korea	83	87	92	98
Pakistan	58	96	91	168
Yugoslavia	105	87	86	105
France	88	112	86	146
Poland	41	64	85	47
Turkey	43	70	81	39
Other	1,163	1,364	1,383	1,583
TOTAL	3,933	5,024	5,031	6,096

The share of exports in total farm sales varies from product to product: in 1965, 56 per cent of the wheat and flour, and rice sold was exported, 53 per cent of the soybeans, and 20 per cent of the barley; also 42 per cent of the tallow produced and 21 per cent of the lard (see Figure VIII.17).

The most important customers for U.S. agricultural products are shown in Table VIII.30. The prospect for continued expansion of our agricultural exports looks promising. Improved economic conditions and rising incomes in the industrialized countries, especially Japan, Canada, and the nations of Western Europe, have increased their demand for livestock products and stimulated our exports of feed grains, soybeans and protein meals, and many other products as well. The Department of Agriculture believes that the U.S. exports in agricultural products may increase to $7 billion or perhaps even $8 billion a year in the near future.

IX. *Mineral Industries and Power*

51. *Our Mineral Resources and Output—52. Miners—53. Mineral Fuels—54. Iron Ore and Ferroalloys—55. Metals and Nonmetallic Minerals—56. Exports and Imports of Mineral Products —57. Power*

51. *Our Mineral Resources and Output*

The value of the mineral output of the United States was $301 million in 1880, rose to $914 million in 1900, and to $6,084 million in 1920. In 1964, it amounted to $20,472 million (see Table IX.1 and Figure IX.1); in 1965, to $21,300. In constant dollars of 1954, the rise was only about 7–8 times, from $2,586 million in 1900 to $20,105 million in 1964, instead of what amounts to more than 20 times in current dollars. For the nation as a whole, the 5 most important products, in order of value, are: petroleum, natural gas, coal, cement, and stone, together accounting for almost 75 per cent of the value of total mineral production in 1964.

Mineral fuels represent two-thirds of the value of our mineral output; metals, some 10–11 per cent; nonmetallic products other than fuels, about 20–22 per cent. Petroleum leads among the mineral fuels; coal once came next, but since 1961, natural gas has occupied second place. Among the metals, iron ore and copper ore each represent more than one-third of the total value. The remainder includes aluminum, zinc, lead, and other metals. The most important nonmetallic minerals are cement, stone, sand, and gravel.

Among the 18 states with the largest mineral output, 7 are petroleum and natural gas states; 4 other states are also important producers (see Table IX.2).

The 18 states listed in Table IX.2 accounted for 84 per cent of the value of all mineral production in the United States in 1964 (see Figure IX.2 for the distribution of the value of mineral production by state).

FIGURE IX.1

VALUE OF MINERAL PRODUCTION IN THE UNITED STATES, 1925-64

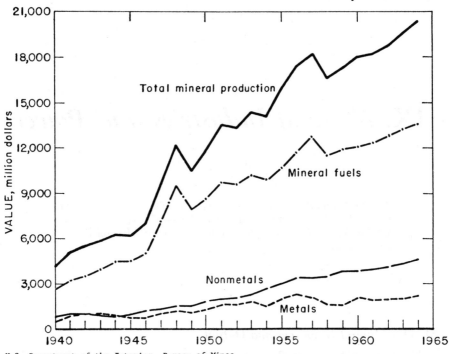

U.S. Department of the Interior, Bureau of Mines

TABLE IX.1

VALUE OF U.S. MINERAL PRODUCTION, 1880-1965

Year	Total	Mineral Fuels	Non-metals	Metals
MILLIONS OF CURRENT DOLLARS				
1880	301	120	56	125
1900	914	406	188	319
1920	6,084	4,193	1,025	866
1940	4,198	2,662	784	752
1950	11,862	8,689	1,822	1,351
1960	18,032	12,142	3,868	2,022
1962	18,838	12,784	4,117	1,937
1963	19,615	13,296	4,317	2,002
1964	20,472	13,585	4,622	2,265
1965[a]	21,300	14,000	4,800	2,500
MILLIONS OF CONSTANT DOLLARS OF 1954				
1900	2,586	1,664	315	607
1920	6,332	4,710	533	1,089
1940	9,104	6,789	897	1,418
1950	12,345	9,342	1,533	1,470
1960	15,671	10,632	3,268	1,771
1962	16,021	10,885	3,484	1,652
1963	16,627	11,268	3,659	1,700
1964	20,105	13,464	4,631	2,010

[a]Preliminary.

FIGURE IX.2

VALUE OF MINERAL PRODUCTION IN THE UNITED STATES,
BY STATE, 1963

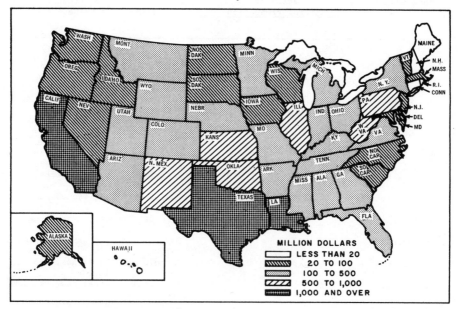

U.S. Department of the Interior, Bureau of Mines

The principal producing states, in order of quantity of output of specific minerals in 1964, are as follows:

Petroleum	Texas, Louisiana, California, Oklahoma
Natural gas	Texas, Louisiana, Oklahoma, New Mexico
Coal, bituminous and lignite	West Virginia, Pennsylvania, Kentucky, Illinois
Anthracite	Pennsylvania
Iron ore	Minnesota, Michigan, California, New York
Copper ore	Arizona, Utah, Montana, New Mexico
Lead ore	Missouri, Idaho, Utah, Colorado
Zinc ore	Tennessee, New York, Idaho, Colorado
Uranium ore	New Mexico, Colorado, Utah, Washington
Molybdenum	Colorado, Utah, Arizona, New Mexico
Potassium salts	New Mexico, California, Utah, Michigan
Phosphate rock	Florida, Tennessee, Idaho, Montana
Sand and gravel	California, Michigan, New York, Ohio
Stone	Pennsylvania, California, Illinois, Texas
Cement	California, Pennsylvania, Texas, Michigan

The United States ranks first in the world in the volume and diversity of its mineral resources and mineral output. It accounts for 27 per cent

TABLE IX.2

MINERAL PRODUCTION AND PRINCIPAL PRODUCING STATES, 1964

Rank and State	Value of Mineral Production		Principal Mineral Products, in Order of Value
	Millions of Dollars	Per Cent	
1. Texas	4,533	22.1	Petroleum, natural gas, natural gas liquids, cement
2. Louisiana	2,785	13.6	Petroleum, natural gas, natural gas liquids, sulphur
3. California	1,561	7.6	Petroleum, natural gas, cement, sand and gravel
4. Pennsylvania	902	4.4	Coal, cement, stone, iron ore
5. Oklahoma	881	4.3	Petroleum, natural gas, natural gas liquids, cement
6. West Virginia	823	4.0	Coal, natural gas, natural-gas liquids, stone
7. New Mexico	720	3.5	Petroleum, potassium salts, natural gas, copper
8. Illinois	591	2.9	Coal, petroleum, stone, sand and gravel
9. Michigan	555	2.7	Iron ore, cement, copper, sand and gravel
10. Arizona	534	2.6	Copper, sand and gravel, cement, molybdenum
11. Kansas	513	2.5	Petroleum, natural gas, cement, natural gas liquids
12. Wyoming	505	2.5	Petroleum, natural gas, uranium, iron ore
13. Minnesota	497	2.3	Iron ore, sand and gravel, stone, cement
14. Ohio	455	2.2	Coal, stone, cement, lime
15. Kentucky	444	2.2	Coal, petroleum, stone, natural gas
16. Utah	391	1.9	Copper, petroleum, coal, uranium
17. Colorado	316	1.5	Petroleum, molybdenum, coal sand and gravel
18. New York	288	1.4	Cement, stone, sand and gravel, salt
Other states	3,178	15.8	
UNITED STATES	20,472	100.0	

of the world's production of petroleum. For natural gas, exact comparable data for world production are not available, but the known marketed production in all countries of the world represents only a small fraction of that in the United States. Our share in the world output of bituminous coal is about 24 per cent; of iron ore, 15 per cent; copper ore, 23 per cent; molybdenum, 70 per cent; sulphur elemental, 46 per cent; cement, 16 per cent; magnesium, about 50 per cent; uranium ore (U_3O_3 content), 46 per cent; potash (equivalent K_2O), 22 per cent; nitrogen, 29 per cent; feldspar, 36 per cent; mica, 56 per cent; vanadium, 57 per cent. The United States is first in the production of aluminum and fourth in that of gold, after South Africa, the U.S.S.R., and Canada (see Table IX.3).

And yet, despite the great development of its mining industry, this

TABLE IX.3

POSITION OF THE UNITED STATES IN WORLD
PRODUCTION OF MINERALS, 1963[a]

Production (In Millions of Specified Units)	World	Largest Producer		Second Largest		Third Largest	
Petroleum (barrels)	10,328	U.S.	2,805	U.S.S.R.	1,646	Canada	275
Natural gas (billions of cubic feet)	...	U.S.	15,547	U.S.S.R.	4,105	Canada	1,364
Coal (short tons[b])	2,218	U.S.	501	U.S.S.R.	452	China[b]	320
Sulphur, native (long tons)	8.1	U.S.	4.9	Mexico	1.5	U.S.S.R.	1.0
Mica (pounds)	400	U.S.	219	India[c]	75	S. Africa	5
Potash (K$_2$O equivalent) (short tons)	12.0	U.S.	2.9	W. Germany	2.1	E. Germany	2.0
Nitrogen (short tons)	17.0	U.S.	4.6	W. Germany	1.6	U.S.S.R.	1.4[d]
Phosphate rock (long tons)	50.4	U.S.	19.8	U.S.S.R.[e]	7.3	Tunisia	2.3
Iron ore (long tons)	510	U.S.S.R.	135	U.S.	74	France	57
Copper ore, metal content (short tons)	5.2	U.S.	1.2	U.S.S.R.	0.8	Chile	0.7
Lead ore, metal content (short tons)	2.8	Australia	0.5	U.S.S.R.	0.4	U.S.	0.3
Zinc ore, metal content (short tons)	4.0	U.S.	0.5	U.S.S.R.	0.4	Mexico	0.3
Aluminum (short tons)	6.1	U.S.	2.3	U.S.S.R.	1.1	Canada	0.7
Cadmium, metal (pounds)	26.3	U.S.	39.9	U.S.S.R.	4.9	Canada	2.4

[a]For mineral fuels, 1964.
[b]Bituminous coal and anthracite; for China, includes lignite.
[c]Exports.
[d]Japan also produced 1.4 million tons.
[e]Apatite.

country cannot depend upon its resources for many important minerals, among them tin, nickel, manganese, beryllium, tungsten, bauxite, columbium, chromite, industrial diamonds, quartz crystals, asbestos, and mercury; antimony, arsenic, graphite, copper ore, natural nitrates, platinum, and several others (see Sec. 56).

Income originated in mining in the United States is relatively small and has been declining for many decades, from about 2.2–2.3 per cent of total national income in the 1920's to 1.2 per cent or less in our time (see Sec. 28). This figure, however, represents only a fraction of the gross value of mineral products produced in the United States, which includes income originated not only in mining proper but also in the processing and refining of petroleum and nonferrous metals and in the processing of iron ore, and which comprises various depreciation deductions for equipment, payments of mines to railroads, utilities, etc.

The share of mining proper in national income in this country is much smaller than in many other countries—3 per cent in Belgium and the United Kingdom, 4 per cent in Canada, 5 per cent in Chile, 12 per cent in Peru, and 14 per cent in South Africa.

52. *Miners*

The record year of employment in the mining industry was 1920, when an average of 1.2 million persons were on the payrolls. After that year, employment declined (figures in thousands): 1,097 in 1929; 854 in 1939; 930 in 1949; 734 in 1959; 635 in 1964.

The chief factor in this drastic drop in the number of employed persons, by nearly half between 1920 and 1964, has been the sharp and uninterrupted reduction of the labor force in the coal industry, one of the 2 major industries in mining (figures in thousands): 730 employees in 1920, 503 in 1929, 422 in 1939, 434 in 1949, 198 in 1959, and 144 in 1964. The explanation is obvious. First, increasing mechanization has resulted in a growing productivity of labor and a declining need for manpower. For example, mechanical loading of coal did not begin until 1923, when 0.3 per cent of the total tonnage produced was mechanically loaded; in 1964, 87.4 per cent was mechanically loaded; in those years, 3.3 and 63.7

TABLE IX.4

EMPLOYMENT IN METAL AND NONMETALLIC MINING, 1939-63
(In Thousands)

Year	Metal Mining			Nonmetallic Mining and Quarrying
	Total	Iron Ores	Copper Ore	
1939	102.6	22.6	26.8	76.2
1949	97.7	33.7	25.9	95.0
1959	83.7	27.7	23.3	120.4
1963	77.6	23.1	26.4	122.1

TABLE IX.5

EMPLOYMENT IN MINERAL INDUSTRIES, 1963
(In Thousands)

	All Employees	Production Workers	Other Employees
All mineral industries	614.2	481.3	132.9
Bituminous coal and lignite	134.1	118.6	15.5
Anthracite	11.8	10.3	1.5
Oil and gas extraction	268.7	191.8	76.9
Crude petroleum	124.9	71.4	53.5
Natural gas	18.0	11.7	6.3
Metal mining	77.6	62.0	15.6
Iron ores	23.1	18.1	5.0
Copper ores	26.4	21.4	5.0
Lead and zinc ores	9.4	7.8	1.6
Gold and silver ores	4.2	3.6	0.6
Nonmetallic minerals	122.1	98.6	23.5
Stone	45.6	38.3	7.3
Sand and gravel	41.0	33.2	7.8

per cent, respectively, of the total was mechanically cleaned. Output per man per year rose from 579 net tons of bituminous coal and lignite in 1920 to 936 in 1939; 1,010 in 1949; and 3,784 in 1964. Second, demand for coal has been declining because of the vigorous expansion in new fuels— petroleum and natural gas (see Sec. 53).

In contrast, employment in industries producing crude petroleum and natural gas increased from 198,000 in 1939 to 331,000 in 1959; subsequently it has declined slightly, to 289,000 employees in 1964. Metal and nonmetallic mining employ considerably fewer workers and salaried personnel than the mineral-fuel industries (see Table IX.4).

The 1963 census of mineral industries reported smaller employment in mineral industries than the 1958 census: 614,217 as against 733,908; the mineral-fuel industries were mostly responsible for the reduction in the force (see Table IX.5).

Texas, the chief center of production of petroleum, the most valuable single mineral product in this country, ranks first in the number of mineral establishments and employees. Pennsylvania and West Virginia, the coal states, occupy the second and third places, respectively. In the value of shipments, Texas towers over all other states, accounting for more than one-fourth of the total. Louisiana ranks next, followed by California and Oklahoma (see Table IX.6).

The ranking of states by the number of persons engaged in mining differs from the ranking by the value of output. Thus Kentucky ranks eleventh in output and seventh in employment; it employs about 20 per cent fewer men than California, but the value of its mineral output is only one-third that of California. Generally, petroleum states rank higher

TABLE IX.6

NUMBER OF ESTABLISHMENTS AND WORKERS, AND VALUE OF SHIPMENTS
IN STATES WITH THE LARGEST OUTPUT OF MINERALS, 1963

State[a]	Number of Establish- ments	Number of		Value of Products	
		All Employees	Production Workers	Millions of Dollars	Per Cent
		(In Thousands)			
Texas	7,734	110.6	75.5	5,648	26.1
Louisiana	1,457	45.3	34.8	3,414	15.8
California	1,732	34.2	24.4	1,562	7.2
Oklahoma	2,517	32.2	21.3	1,051	4.9
West Virginia	2,695	47.6	42.4	902	4.2
Pennsylvania	3,396	49.1	41.2	887	4.1
New Mexico	869	17.6	13.7	876	4.0
Illinois	1,443	22.1	18.0	653	3.0
Kansas	1,813	14.1	11.5	602	2.8
Wyoming	529	8.6	6.5	556	2.6
Kentucky	2,086	25.1	25.2	544	2.5
Minnesota	329	13.1	9.9	502	2.3
Utah	383	10.7	9.1	421	1.9
Arizona	260	15.2	12.8	386	1.8
Colorado	858	11.3	8.4	335	1.5
Michigan	691	12.3	10.3	322	1.5
Ohio	1,540	17.7	14.3	317	1.5
Mississippi	371	5.3	4.0	266	1.2
Virginia	947	15.6	13.9	225	1.0
Florida	216	6.5	5.2	214	1.0
Montana	413	7.5	6.1	189	0.9
Alabama	377	9.1	8.1	170	0.8
New York	519	9.9	6.6	166	0.8
Arkansas	423	4.8	4.0	155	0.7
Indiana	723	7.4	6.0	144	0.7
Tennessee	502	6.8	6.0	128	0.6
Georgia	164	5.6	4.9	106	0.5
UNITED STATES	38,637	614.2	481.3	21,653	100.0

[a]States are arrayed by the value of mineral production in 1958. This ranking
changes slightly from year to year (cf. Table IX.2).

in the value of output than in employment, while the opposite is characteristic of the coal states.

53. *Mineral Fuels*

Coal. The coal reserves of the United States are estimated at 1,660
billion short tons; somewhat more than half is in low-grade bituminous
coal and lignite. Recoverable resources, with present techniques and the
assumption of 50 per cent recovery, amount to 830 billion short tons. Almost 70 per cent of the total reserves lies in the Rocky Mountains; about 85
per cent of present output comes from the remaining 30 per cent of the
reserves, east of the Mississippi River and north of Tennessee and North
Carolina (see Figure IX.3).

The most important coal mines are located in the Appalachian region,
stretching from western Pennsylvania, Ohio, and West Virginia southward across Kentucky and Tennessee to Alabama. This region provides
more than two-thirds of the bituminous coal mined in the United States.

FIGURE IX.3

GEOGRAPHIC DISTRIBUTION OF COAL FIELDS IN THE UNITED STATES

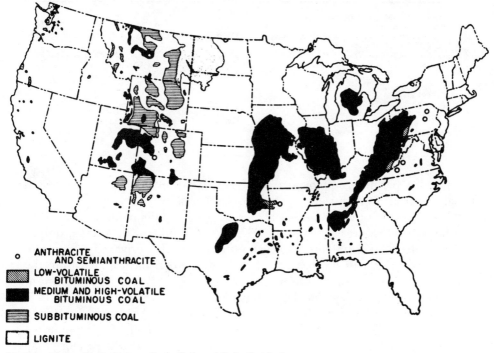

○ ANTHRACITE
     AND SEMIANTHRACITE

▨ LOW-VOLATILE
     BITUMINOUS COAL

■ MEDIUM AND HIGH-VOLATILE
     BITUMINOUS COAL

▤ SUBBITUMINOUS COAL

☐ LIGNITE

Courtesy of Twentieth Century Fund: W.S. and E.S. Woytinsky,
World Population and Production (New York, 1953).

West of the Appalachian region, significant amounts of coal are mined
in Illinois, western Kentucky, and Indiana; small quantities in Iowa,
Missouri, Kansas, Oklahoma, Colorado, Utah, Wyoming, and Montana.
Bituminous coal predominates in all these areas. Anthracite is found in
eastern Pennsylvania and Alaska. High-grade bituminous coal, approaching anthracite in quality, is dug in western Pennsylvania and West Virginia.

Until 1958–59, coal mining employed more wage-workers than all other
mines and quarries combined. The significance of this industry, from the
point of view of the labor market, is enhanced by its concentration in a
comparatively small area, while other kinds of mining are spread widely
over almost the entire country. More than one-fourth of the output in
bituminous coal and lignite comes from West Virginia, another fourth
from Illinois and Kentucky combined, and nearly one-sixth from Pennsylvania.

The number of coal mines increased sharply between 1940 and 1950,
and though it has now declined, it still exceeds that in 1940: clearly, many
new small mines have been opened. Because of the great increase in pro-

TABLE IX.7

EMPLOYMENT AND OUTPUT IN COAL MINING, 1940-64

	1940	1950	1960	1963	1964
Bituminous coal and lignite:					
Number of mines	6,234	9,429	7,865	7,940	7,630
Average number of men employed	439,075	415,582	169,400	141,646	128,698
Output (in thousands of short tons)	460,772	516,311	415,512	458,928	486,998
Average tons per man: per day	5.19	6.77	12.83	15.83	16.84
per year	1,049	1,239	2,453	3,240	3,784
Anthracite:					
Average number of men employed	91,313	72,624	19,051	13,498	13,144
Output (in thousands of short tons)	51,485	44,077	18,817	18,267	17,184
Average tons per man: per day	3.02	2.83	5.60	6.27	6.11
per year	562	597	986	1,354	1,308

ductivity per man, employment has fallen drastically; output has decreased also, but at a much slower pace (see Table IX.7).

The output of bituminous coal crossed the 500-million-ton mark in 1916; the next record was achieved in 1947, with 630 million t.; in 1964, output amounted to 487 million. However, output of coal is expected to rise considerably in the 1970's, because of the growing demand for coal from the electric power industry, the most important market, and also because of increasing export demand. The estimates range from 595 million t. by 1970 to 800–900 million for 1980.

The 3 major consumers of bituminous coal and lignite are industry, coke producers, and electric-power utilities. Together, they take more than

TABLE IX.8

CONSUMPTION OF BITUMINOUS COAL AND LIGNITE, BY CONSUMER CLASS, AND RETAIL DELIVERIES IN THE UNITED STATES, 1923-64
(In Millions of Net Tons)

Year	Total	Electric Power Utilities	Rail-roads	Coke	Steel and Rolling Mills	Cement Mills	Other[a]	Retailers	Bunkers[b]
1923	519.0	39.0	131.5	84.4	c	c	259.1	c	5.1
1928	498.8	41.4	112.4	77.2	c	c	263.6	c	4.3
1933	317.7	27.1	72.5	40.1	14.1	2.8	81.4	77.4	2.3
1938	336.3	36.4	73.9	46.6	11.9	4.4	94.2	66.5	2.3
1943	593.8	74.0	130.3	102.5	15.9	5.8	142.1	120.1	3.0
1948	519.9	95.6	94.8	107.3	14.2	8.5	110.1	86.8	2.6
1953	426.8	112.3	27.7	112.9	8.8	8.2	95.2	60.0	1.8
1958	366.7	152.9	3.7	76.6	7.3	8.3	81.4	35.6	1.0
1960	380.4	173.9	2.1	76.6	7.4	8.2	76.5	30.4	0.9
1961	374.4	179.6	d	73.9	7.5	7.6	77.3	27.7	0.8
1962	387.8	190.8	d	74.3	7.3	7.7	78.8	28.2	0.7
1963	409.2	209.0	d	77.6	7.4	8.1	82.8	23.5	0.7
1964	431.1	223.0	d	88.7	7.4	8.7	82.9	19.6	0.7

[a]Other manufacturing and mining industries.
[b]Foreign and lake vessels.
[c]Includes steel and rolling mills, cement mills, and retail deliveries to other consumers.
[d]Canvass discontinued.

FIGURE IX.4

CONSUMPTION OF COAL IN THE UNITED STATES,
BY CONSUMER CLASS, 1955-64

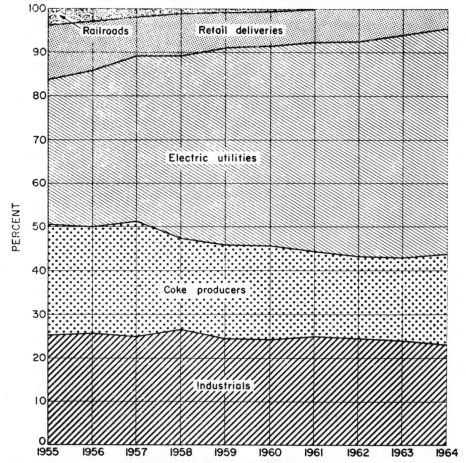

U.S. Department of the Interior, Bureau of Mines

nine-tenths of the total consumption; of this, the electric utilities alone account for half. Retail deliveries—in other words, residential users—take the remainder. The railroads, which accounted for one-fourth of total consumption as recently as the early 1920's, now take less than 1 per cent, and canvass of their use has been discontinued (see Table IX.8 and Figure IX.4).

Production of coke has fluctuated greatly because of ups and downs in the iron industry. Blast furnaces are the leading consumer, taking nine-tenths of total consumption. Since coke is a major item used in steel-making, great efforts have been made by the industry to lower the rate of its consumption per ton of pig iron. These efforts have been successful,

TABLE IX.9

CONSUMPTION OF COKE, BY USE, 1937-63

	Total Apparent Consumption (In Millions	In Blast Furnaces of Short Tons)	Other Uses	Blast Furnaces (Per Cent of	Other Uses Total)
1937-39	42.4	28.0	14.4	66.0	34.0
1947-49	69.9	55.9	14.0	80.0	20.0
1957-59	60.6	54.1	6.4	89.4	10.6
1960	56.9	51.0	5.9	89.6	10.4
1961	52.1	46.8	5.3	89.8	10.2
1962	51.8	46.2	5.6	89.2	10.8
1963	55.0	48.9	6.1	88.9	11.1

and it is expected that this rate will be further reduced as technology advances. Consumption of coke has declined not only in steel-making but in residential and other uses as well (see Table IX.9).

In the 1860's, the output of anthracite exceeded that of soft coal, but by the end of the nineteenth century its share in total coal output had dropped to a little more than 25 per cent; in 1964, it amounted to only 3 per cent (see Table IX.10).

The heyday of anthracite production was in the 1920's; the record year was 1927, when 80 million t. were produced. Then production began to decline, except for some slight expansion during the war years, from 51.5 million t. in 1939-40 to 63.7 million t. in 1944. With every passing year, output has become smaller and smaller: 31 million t. in 1953; 21 million t. in 1958; 17 million t. in 1964 (see Table IX.7 and IX.10).

Anthracite is used for household heating, on the one hand, and by the electric utilities and iron and steel plants, on the other. In the past, space-heating use absorbed about half the output, but lately this demand has

TABLE IX.10

AVERAGE ANNUAL OUTPUT OF BITUMINOUS COAL
AND ANTHRACITE COAL, 1861-1964
(In Millions of Short Tons)

Year	Total	Anthracite	Bituminous
1861-1970	26.1	13.7	12.4
1871-1880	57.2	24.6	32.6
1881-1890	122.8	40.0	82.8
1891-1900	203.0	54.5	148.5
1901-1910	396.9	73.9	323.0
1911-1920	577.7	90.9	486.8
1921-1930	577.2	77.1	500.2
1931-1940	437.0	52.4	384.6
1941-1950	1,232.0	111.5	1,120.5
1951-1960	966.0	56.9	909.2
1962	439.0	16.9	422.1
1963	477.5	18.6	458.9
1964	504.2	17.2	487.0

TABLE IX.11

APPARENT CONSUMPTION OF ANTHRACITE BY SELECTED CONSUMER CATEGORIES, 1955-64
(In Thousands of Tons)

	1955	1957	1959	1961	1963	1964
Domestic use[a]	13,019	10,670	7,562	5,070	4,055	3,334
Electric utilities	3,209	3,363	2,629	2,509	2,155	2,239
Iron and steel industry	1,194	1,955	1,832	1,593	1,887	1,506[b]
Colliery fuel	419	279	129	45	161	144
Cement plants	199	221	159	153	184	153
Railroads	457	361	292	...	...	....
Briquet plants	264	156	43	28	c	c
TOTAL	18,761	17,005	12,646	14,906[d]	12,773[d]	12,636[d]

[a]Retail dealer deliveries; excludes local sales.
[b]Incomplete.
[c]Concealed to avoid disclosure of individual company data.
[d]Includes amounts not broken down by consumer category.

contracted sharply. However, data for consumption in the producing regions are lacking. Only incomplete data are available (see Table IX.11).

Petroleum. Proved reserves of crude petroleum recoverable under existing economic and operating conditions amounted to 31 billion barrels on December 31, 1964. Despite the ever-increasing output of crude oil, the proved reserves have continued to increase as methods of exploration and oil extraction have been improved (see Table IX.12).

TABLE IX.12

OUTPUT AND PROVED RESERVES OF CRUDE OIL, 1900-1964
(In Millions of Barrels)

	Output	Proved Reserves (On December 31)		Output	Proved Reserves (On December 31)
1900	63.6	2,900	1950	1,973.6	25,268
1910	209.6	4,500	1960	2,574.9	31,613
1920	442.9	7,200	1962	2,676.2	31,389
1930	898.0	13,600	1963	2,752.7	30,970
1940	1,353.2	19,024	1964	2,800.0	30,991

The cumulative output of crude petroleum from 1859, when it was first discovered in Pennsylvania, through 1964 amounted to 76.3 billion bar. Texas alone accounts for almost half the proved total reserves (14.3 billion bar. on December 31, 1964); Louisiana is next, with 5.2 billion bar.; California ranks third, with 4.1 billion bar. Figures IX.5A and IX.5B show the location of major oil and natural-gas fields in the United States.

There are nearly 600,000 oil wells in the United States. They are distributed over a score of states, but the major concentrations are as follows (figures in thousands): 199 in Texas, 81 in Oklahoma, 53 in Pennsylvania,

FIGURE IX.5.A

FIELDS OF OIL IN THE UNITED STATES

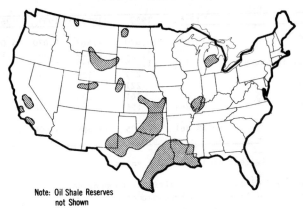

Note: Oil Shale Reserves
not Shown

U.S. Department of the Interior, Geological Survey

FIGURE IX.5.B

FIELDS OF NATURAL GAS IN THE UNITED STATES

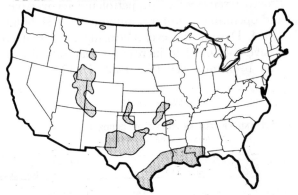

U.S. Department of the Interior, Geological Survey

47 in Kansas, 41 in California, 30 in Illinois, 29 in Louisiana. Average output per well per day is larger in some of the states which have only a small number of wells than in those which are almost blanketed by them (see Table IX.13).

Since its discovery in 1859, crude petroleum has been produced in ever increasing quantities; the average annual output rose from 3 million bar. in 1861–70 to 137 million in 1901–10, 772 million in 1921–30, and 2,787 million in 1964 (see Table IX.14).

Texas has been the major producer; California was next until 1958, when Louisiana for the first time matched its output. Louisiana has occupied second place ever since, but its cumulative output is only about

TABLE IX.13

OIL WELLS: OUTPUT PER
WELL PER DAY, 1964

	Average Number of Wells	Average Output Per Well, Per Day (In Barrels)
Texas	199,119	13.6
Gulf Coast	19,562	26.7
Oklahoma	80,511	6.8
Pennsylvania	53,065	0.3
Kansas	46,715	6.2
California	40,916	20.2
Illinois	29,500	6.4
Louisiana	29,452	52.6
Gulf Coast	15,114	91.3
Kentucky	15,226	3.6
New Mexico	17,570	18.1
Wyoming	8,019	49.1
Colorado	1,981	47.3
Utah	840	93.2
Alaska	56	549.4
UNITED STATES	588,657	12.9

TABLE IX.14

AVERAGE ANNUAL OUTPUT OF CRUDE PETROLEUM, 1861-1964
(In Millions of Barrels)

1861-70	3	1941-45	1,589
1871-80	13	1946-50	1,885
1881-90	29	1951-55	2,339
1891-1900	55	1956-60	2,567
1901-1910	137	1961	2,622
1911-20	305	1962	2,676
1921-30	772	1963	2,753
1931-40	1,066	1964	2,787

half that of California, while the cumulative output of Texas is about double that of California (see Table IX.15).

Petroleum is used in many finished products, and the total demand for all types of oil continues to rise. Gasoline is the major product; distillate fuel oils used for heating and diesel-locomotive fuel rank next (see Table IX.16).

Though this country's output of crude petroleum has grown uninterruptedly, its share in the world output—which has expanded even more rapidly—declined from 64 per cent in 1930 to 27 per cent in 1964. Its share in the world's oil reserves has fallen even more drastically. As recently as 1939, the United States was estimated to possess one-half of the world's petroleum reserves: 17 billion barrels out of 34 billion. Today, its share amounts to less than one-tenth of the world reserves: 31 billion bar.

TABLE IX.15

CUMULATIVE OUTPUT OF
CRUDE PETROLEUM, 1859-1964
(In Millions of Barrels)

Texas	27,673
California	13,225
Oklahoma	9,026
Louisiana	7,485
Kansas	3,751
Illinois	2,528
Wyoming	2,479
New Mexico	1,962
Pennsylvania	1,242
Arkansas	1,199
Mississippi	911
Colorado	759
Ohio	701
Other	3,342
UNITED STATES	**76,283**

as against 327 billion. Within this period of time, huge oil fields have
been discovered in Kuwait, with only 320,000 population but with oil

TABLE IX.16

PETROLEUM RUNS TO STILLS AND REFINERY PRODUCTS
IN THE UNITED STATES, BY TYPE, 1920-64
(In Millions of Barrels)

Product	1920	1930	1940	1950	1960	1962	1963	1964
Input	437	971	1,334	2,190	3,119	3,252	3,361	3,437
Crude petroleum	434	928	1,294	2,095	2,953	3,070	3,171	3,241
Domestic	373	867	1,252	1,919	2,582	2,660	2,758	2,804
Foreign	61	61	42	176	371	410	412	437
Natural gas liquids	3	43	40	95	167	183	190	195
Output	...	931	1,333	2,190	3,119	3,252	3,361	3,437
Gasoline	116	432	597	998	1,510	1,571	1,603	1,675
Kerosene	55	49	74	119	136	156	165	168
Distillate fuel oil	211	82	183	399	667	720	765	741
Residual fuel oil	[a]	291	316	425	332	296	276	268
Military jet fuel	-	-	-	-	88	102	99	108
Lubricants	25	34	37	52	59	61	63	64
Asphalt	-	18	29	58	99	110	112	115
Still gas	-	-	76	84	129	131	130	131
Coke	-	10	8	17	60	79	81	84
Liquefied gases	-	-	-	29	78	77	56	59
Other finished products	-	15	13	16	36	42	117[d]	130[d]
Other unfinished oils[b]	-	-	-	-7	-21	-28	-32	-27
Shortage (or overage)[c]	-	-	-	-1	-53	-64	-74	-79

[a] Included in distillate fuel oil.
[b] Negative quantities (net excess of unfinished oils rerun over unfinished oils produced).
[c] Negative quantities.
[d] Includes petrochemical feedstocks formerly distributed among other petroleum products.

FIGURE IX.6.A

ESTIMATED WORLD RESERVES OF CRUDE PETROLEUM,
END OF 1964

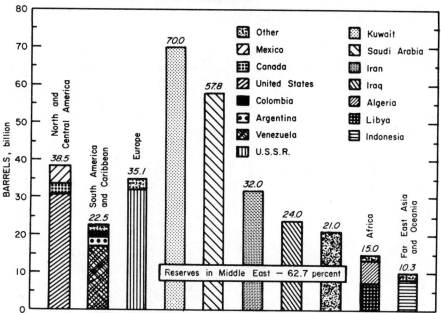

U.S. Department of the Interior, Bureau of Mines

reserves more than twice as large as those of this country. Saudi Arabia, with 6 million population, ranks next, with 58 billion bar. of petroleum reserves (see Figure IX.6A). Nearly one-fifth of domestic demand is now supplied by imports.

Natural gas is found in 31 states, of which five—Texas, Louisiana, Oklahoma, Kansas, and New Mexico—account for nine-tenths of total proved reserves (see Figure IX.5B). Estimates of proved reserves have followed the same course as those of crude petroleum. Between 1945 and 1964, estimated reserves nearly doubled, reaching 281 trillion cubic feet, despite large withdrawals during that period. The increase is due one-third to discoveries of new fields, and two-thirds to revisions of old estimates when new pools are found in old fields and the area of existing fields has been extended (see Figure IX.6B). Gas-reserve experts have estimated that the remaining volumes of gas yet to be discovered range from 500 trillion to 1,800 trillion cu. ft.

In 1961, withdrawals of natural gas from gas and oil wells amounted to 13.3 trillion cu. ft. in 1963 and 15.5 trillion in 1964. Marketed production, i.e., consumption,* of natural gas has grown rapidly from 6.3 trillion cu.

* Gas *consumption* represents 99.9 per cent of total marketed production, the remainder comprising loss in transmission, storage, and export.

FIGURE IX.6.B

AVERAGE ANNUAL ADDITIONS TO THE RESERVES OF
NATURAL GAS IN THE UNITED STATES, 1947-64

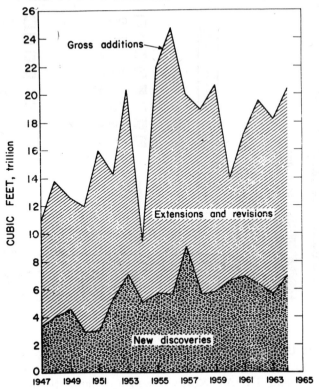

American Gas Association

ft. in 1950 to 9.4 trillion in 1955, 12.8 in 1960, and 15.5 trillion in 1965.
The chief producers are shown in Table IX.17.

The country is served through a network extending from producing
wells to burner tips that consists of 695,000 mi. of pipe of varying
diameters. The interstate pipeline systems receive gas from 24 of the 31
producing states and deliver gas to 46 of the 47 states that use natural
gas and to the Dictrict of Columbia. Mexican and Canadian systems are
connected with the U.S. pipelines, which provide facilities for both import and export of natural gas. Alaska is supplied with locally produced
gas, and only Maine, Vermont, and Hawaii are currently without natural-
gas service (see Figure IX.7).

In 1964, residential consumers numbered more than 37 million and
used one-fourth of the annual output; industry consumed two-thirds, including the field of natural gas (pumping, drilling, extraction loss, etc.).
The 2.8 million commercial consumers used some 8–9 per cent (see
Figure IX.8).

FIGURE IX.7

MAJOR NATURAL GAS PIPELINES, JUNE, 1965

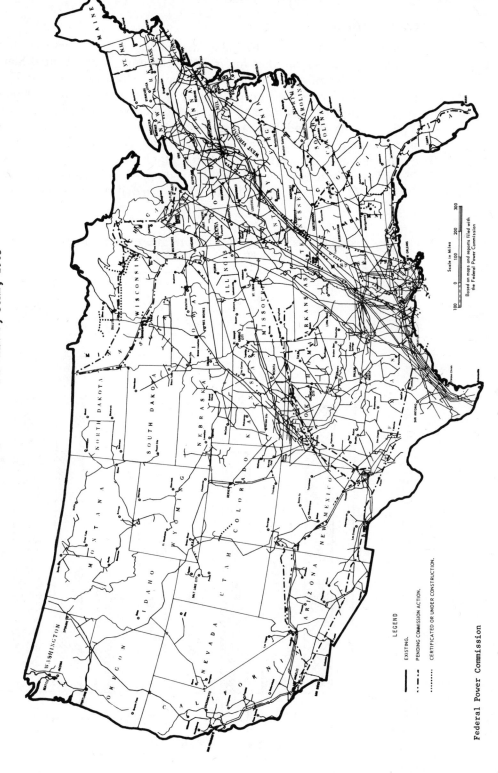

LEGEND

EXISTING. ————

PENDING COMMISSION ACTION. — — —

CERTIFICATED OR UNDER CONSTRUCTION. ....

Scale in Miles

100   0   100   200   300

Based on maps and reports filed with
the Federal Power Commission

Federal Power Commission

CONSUMPTION OF NATURAL GAS IN THE UNITED STATES,
BY PRINCIPAL USE, 1964

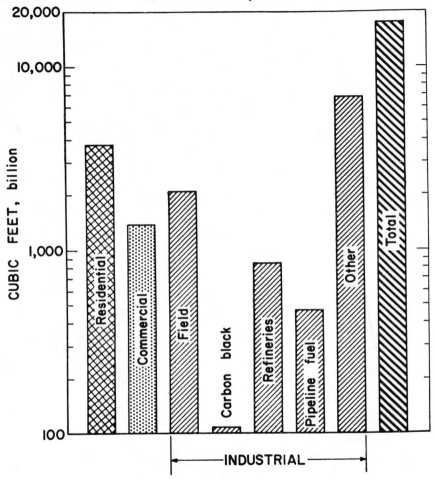

U.S. Department of the Interior, Bureau of Mines

TABLE IX.17

OUTPUT OF NATURAL GAS, BY STATE, 1930-64

| | (In Billions of Cubic Feet) | | | | | | |
	1930	1940	1950	1960	1961	1963	1964
Texas	518	1,064	3,126	5,893	5,964	6,205	6,525
Louisiana	278	343	832	2,998	3,272	3,928	4,175
Oklahoma	348	258	482	824	893	1,234	1,323
New Mexico	9	64	213	799	790	808	879
Kansas	38	90	364	634	649	733	768
California	335	352	558	518	556	646	664
West Virginia	144	189	190	209	211	210	204
Wyoming	43	27	62	182	195	209	232
Mississippi	a	6	114	172	173	177	181
Colorado	3	3	11	107	108	106	114
Pennsylvania	89	91	91	114	100	93	82
Other states	138	173	239	321	343	398	400
UNITED STATES	1,943	2,660	6,282	12,771	13,254	14,747	15,547

aLess than 500 million cubic feet.

FIGURE IX.9

PRODUCTION OF IRON ORE AND IMPORTS FOR CONSUMPTION
IN THE UNITED STATES, 1920-63

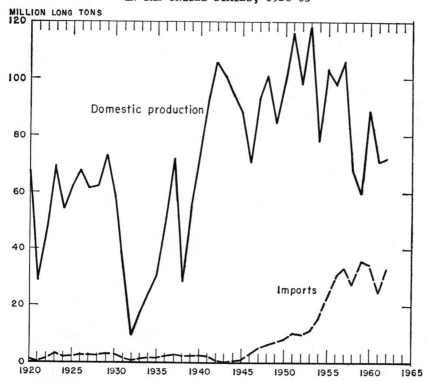

U.S. Department of the Interior, Bureau of Mines

TABLE IX.18

IRON ORE: OUTPUT, IMPORTS, EXPORTS, AND EMPLOYMENT, 1880-1964

Year	Output	Imports	Exports	Employment
	(Thousands of Long Tons)			
1880	7,120	493	-	35,000
1890	16,036	1,247	-	33,341
1900	27,800	898	51	...
1910	57,015	2,591	749	...
1920	67,604	1,273	1,145	50,590
1930	58,409	2,775	752	30,975
1932	9,847	582	83	12,649
1935	30,540	1,492	661	14,987
1940	73,695	2,479	1,386	25,128
1945	88,376	1,198	2,063	26,777
1950	98,045	8,281	2,551	31,087
1955	102,999	23,472	4,517	23,311
1961	71,329	25,805	4,957	22,710
1962	71,829	33,409	5,898	21,010
1963	73,549	33,263	6,812	23,108
1964	84,836	42,408	6,963	...

1963, and again increased to 85 million in 1964 (see Figure IX.9). Interestingly, employment in 1880, when merely 7.1 million t. of iron ore were produced, was greater than in 1963: 35,000 and 23,110 men, respectively. The number of days worked in those 2 years was about the same: 231 and 245; for the length of the working day, summary records are available only for 1890, when the average for 21 industries was 10 hours; today, the average is 8 hours.

There is growing concern in the United States about the possible exhaustion of iron-ore deposits. Efforts are therefore being made to prolong their life by using lower-grade ores after beneficiation (upgrading of low iron content ore to ore of higher Fe) and to utilize the large reserves of taconite, which contains a large percentage of impurities but which can

TABLE IX.19

WORLD AND U.S. OUTPUT OF IRON ORE, 1871-1964

	Output of Iron Ore (In Millions of Long Tons)		U.S. Output as Per Cent of World Output
	World	United States	
1871	30.7	3.4	11.1
1900	91.8	28.0	30.5
1917	148.0	76.8	51.9
1929	202.6	75.5	37.3
1938	167.0	28.4	17.0
1948	216.0	102.6	47.5
1958	398.7	67.7	17.0
1962	499.4	71.8	14.4
1963	509.9	73.6	14.4
1964	513.0	84.8	16.5

be improved by concentration. In the past, there was no clear trend in imports and exports of iron ore, but since the beginning of the 1950's the imports have increased rather sharply and in 1964 exceeded the exports by about 6 to 1: 42,408 l. t. versus 6,963 (see Table IX.18).

The U.S. share in the world output of iron ore depends on 2 variables: sharp fluctuations in production here and the development of the iron-ore industry in other countries (see Table IX.19).

Ferroalloys. Production of steel, especially of high-grade steel, requires that various ferroalloys be added to ordinary carbon steel. U.S. production depends for the quality of its steel on the supplies of many essential ferroalloys from foreign sources.

Each ferroalloy has distinct properties; one imparts specific hardness or malleability to steel, another ensures resistance to corrosion, or greater toughness, etc. The chief alloying elements are manganese, chromium, nickel, cobalt, tungsten, molybdenum, and vanadium.

TABLE IX.20

WORLD AND U.S. OUTPUT OF MOLYBDENUM, 1953-64

	World	United States	U.S. Share
	(In Millions of Pounds)		(Per Cent)
1953-57, average	72.3	59.2	81.9
1960	89.5	68.2	76.2
1961	87.9	66.6	75.8
1962	75.1	51.2[a]	68.3
1963	91.6	65.0	71.0
1964	94.5	65.6	69.3

[a]Mine closed part of the year by a strike.

Manganese is unique because it is indispensable in the production of any steel, regardless of type; there is no adequate substitute for it. Our deposits of this alloying element in western states are of such low grade that their exploitation in peacetime is uneconomical: it is cheaper to use foreign ore. Of 2.2 million short tons of manganese consumed in the United States in 1964, only about 26,000 t., or about one-tenth of 1 per cent, was home produced. During both world wars, domestic ore was used of necessity.

Chromium contributes strength to steel and, if added in large quantities, makes it resistant to corrosion and oxidation. The United States has only negligible deposits of metallurgical-grade chromite and depends on imports. The same is true of 2 other important alloying elements: nickel and cobalt. Nickel makes steel stronger, and cobalt is unique in cementing tungsten carbides. The United States has tungsten mines in the West producing about 9–10 per cent of the world's total; the demand is met 40–50 per cent by imports. Tungsten makes steel hard, even at red heat, and it has also other important uses in industry.

TABLE IX.21

WORLD AND U.S. OUTPUT OF VANADIUM, 1953-63

	World	United States	U.S. Share
	(In Short Tons)		(Per Cent)
1953-57, average	4,189	3,385	80.8
1960	7,236	4,971	68.7
1961	8,727	5,343	61.2
1962	8,286	5,233	63.2
1963	7,004	3,862	55.1

Of *molybdenum*, on the other hand, the world's largest deposit is located in Colorado (the Climax mine), and the United States produces 75–80 per cent of the world's total and considerably more in some years (see Table IX.20).

The United States obtains *vanadium* chiefly as a by-product of uranium mining, and also from some other ores. This country's production of recoverable vanadium represents a substantial part of the world's output (see Table IX.21).

55. *Metals and Nonmetallic Minerals*

Pig iron, steel, aluminum, copper, lead and zinc, gold and silver are the most important metals produced in the United States. The leading

FIGURE IX.10.A

MAJOR LOCATIONS OF RAW MATERIALS FOR THE STEEL INDUSTRY
IN THE UNITED STATES

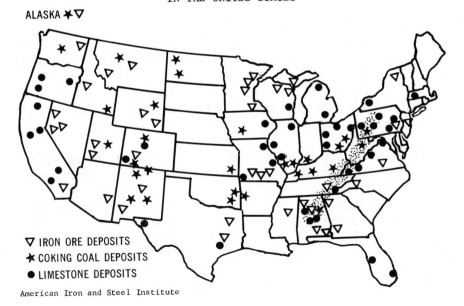

ALASKA ✶▽

▽ IRON ORE DEPOSITS
✶ COKING COAL DEPOSITS
● LIMESTONE DEPOSITS

American Iron and Steel Institute

FIGURE IX.10.B

STEEL-MAKING COUNTIES IN THE UNITED STATES

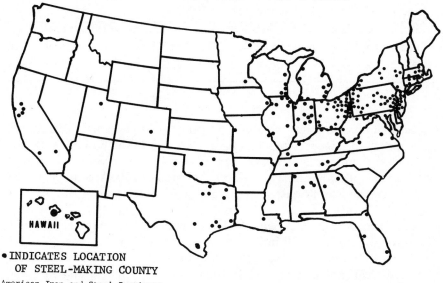

• INDICATES LOCATION
OF STEEL-MAKING COUNTY

American Iron and Steel Institute

nonmetallic mineral products, other than fuels, are cement, stone, clay, sand, and gravel.

Pig iron and steel. Making 1 t. of pig iron requires 1.5–2 t. of iron ore (depending on its metal content); up to a t. of coke; and certain amounts of scrap, fluxes, and other materials. In 1964, the following metalliferous materials were consumed per t. of pig iron produced in the United States (figures in sh. t.): 1.5 of ores and agglomerates (sinter, pellets, etc.), about 0.05 of scrap, approximately 0.1 of miscellaneous materials, and 0.2 of fluxes—in all, 1.8 t. of charge, and 0.7 t. of coke. Because of the necessity to transport such heavy raw materials, iron and steel plants have always been located as close as possible to iron-ore and coal deposits. The distance to major markets has also been a factor in location.

In this country, the location of the industry was predetermined by the large iron-ore deposits in the Lake Superior region (see Sec. 54); by the position of Pittsburgh, in the center of the finest metallurgical-coke area; and by the proximity to eastern industrial concentrations with an insatiable demand for iron and steel. There are several other centers of iron and steel industry in the United States: in the district of Birmingham, Ala.; at Sparrows Point, Md.; in the west (California, Utah, Colorado); and at Trenton, N.J. (see Figures IX.10A and B).

Production of iron and steel developed gradually in the United States, but this country overtook the United Kingdom as early as 1890 and has since been the largest single producer, even in its worst Depression year, 1932 (see Table IX.22). The share of the United States in the world's

TABLE IX.22

OUTPUT OF PIG IRON AND STEEL IN THE
UNITED STATES, 1880-1964
(Millions of Tons)

	1880	1890	1900	1910	1920	1929	1932	1939	1945	1949	1953-57[a]	1963	1964
Pig iron	4.3	10.3	15.4	29.9	40.0	46.5	9.5	35.9	53.3	52.9	72.6	71.8	85.5
Steel	1.2	4.3	10.2	26.1	42.1	56.4	13.7	47.1	71.2	69.6	109.0	109.3	127.1

[a]Average.

output of iron and steel was about 60 per cent after World War I, but subsequently declined as production increased in both the old centers of this industry and many new areas. In 1964, the United States, with 85.5 million t. of pig iron and 127 million t. of steel ingots, accounted for 24 per cent of the world's output of pig iron and 26 per cent of that of steel (see Table IX.23).

Pennsylvania ranks first, with 63 blast furnaces and more than 21 million t. of pig iron and 30 million t. of steel produced in 1964. It is followed by Ohio, with 49 blast furnaces, 15.4 and 21.6 million t. of pig iron and steel, respectively, and Indiana, with 23 furnaces and 11.5 and 17.8 million t., respectively. Together, these 3 states account for more than

TABLE IX.23

OUTPUT OF PIG IRON AND STEEL IN SELECTED COUNTRIES, 1918-64
(Per Cent of World Output)

Country	1918	1929	1934	1939	1944	1949	1953-57	1959	1960	1963	1964
Pig iron											
United States	59.3	43.7	26.3	32.0	52.6	43.3	36.5	25.1	24.1	23.9	24.4
United Kingdom	13.7	7.8	9.8	8.0	6.3	8.4	6.9	5.7	6.2	5.3	5.5
France	1.9	10.5	9.8	7.3	2.7	7.3	5.6	5.6	5.6	5.2	5.1
Belgium	-	4.0	4.8	3.0	0.6	3.2	2.7	2.7	2.5	2.5	2.7
Germany[a]	17.8	13.5	13.9	17.3	14.1	6.2	9.7	9.6	10.0	8.2	8.6
Russia (U.S.S.R.)	0.8	4.0	16.8	15.1	7.9	14.8	17.5	19.0	18.1	20.9	19.7
Japan	1.2	1.6	4.0	4.6	5.3	1.4	3.0	4.4	4.8	7.3	7.7
Other[b]	5.4	14.9	14.6	12.7	10.5	15.4	18.1	27.9	28.7	26.7	26.3
WORLD	100.0	100.0	100.0	100.0	100.0	100.0	100.0	100.0	100.0	100.0	100.0
Steel											
United States	57.5	47.6	32.2	34.7	47.8	44.3	37.9	27.8	26.0	25.7	26.4
United Kingdom	12.3	8.1	10.9	9.6	7.2	9.3	7.6	8.1	7.1	5.9	6.0
France	2.3	8.0	7.5	5.7	1.8	5.8	4.6	5.6	5.0	4.6	4.5
Belgium	-	3.4	3.5	2.2	0.4	2.4	2.2	2.1	2.1	2.0	2.0
Germany[a]	19.3	13.4	14.4	16.2	10.6	5.8	9.0	9.6	9.9	8.2	8.6
Russia (U.S.S.R.)	0.5	4.1	11.8	13.5	8.2	14.5	14.1	20.0	20.4	20.8	19.2
Japan	1.0	1.9	4.1	5.3	4.3	2.0	3.7	5.4	6.4	8.2	9.1
Other[b]	7.2	13.4	15.6	12.8	19.7	15.9	20.9	21.4	23.1	24.6	24.2
WORLD	100.0	100.0	100.0	100.0	100.0	100.0	100.0	100.0	100.0	100.0	100.0

[a]Since 1949, West Germany.
[b]Includes data for China's output.

FIGURE IX.11

PRODUCTION OF PIG IRON AND STEEL, AND STEEL-PRODUCING CAPACITY
IN THE UNITED STATES, 1915-62

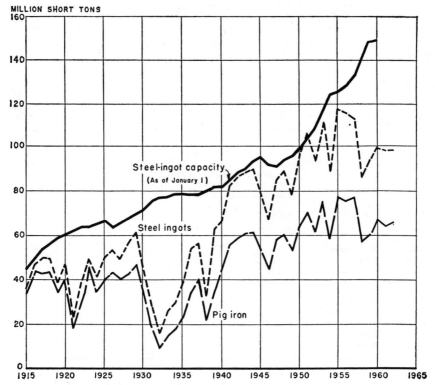

U.S. Department of the Interior, Bureau of Mines

half the total output of pig iron and steel. Only slightly more than two-thirds of the 1960 steel-producing capacity was utilized in 1963 (see Figure IX.11).

The steel industry is expanding the use of oxygen in steel-making. In 1964, basic oxygen converters produced 15.4 million t. of steel, as compared with 1.9 million t. in 1959, and 5.6 million t. in 1962. The Council of Economic Advisers estimates that oxygen steel will account for 45 per cent of our annual steel output in 1970 as against 12 per cent in 1964.

It took the United States 65 years to produce the first billion t. of steel ingots, 18 years to produce the second billion, and 10 years to produce the third billion (see Sec. 63 for further description of the iron and steel industry).

Copper. Since the later part of the nineteenth century, the United States has been the world's largest producer of copper. The main copper deposits are in Arizona, which supplies more than half this country's

TABLE IX.24

MINE PRODUCTION OF RECOVERABLE COPPER, BY STATE, 1953-64
(In Thousands of Short Tons)

	1953-57 Average	1959	1960	1962	1963	1964
Arizona	449	430	539	644	661	691
Utah	241	145	218	218	203	200
Montana	81	66	92	94	80	104
New Mexico	68	40	67	83	83	86
Nevada	74	57	77	83	82	67
Michigan	44	55	56	74	75	69
Other	33	32	30	33	29	30

TABLE IX.25

PRODUCTION OF COPPER IN
THE UNITED STATES, 1953-64
(In Thousands of Short Tons)

	1953-57 Average	1959	1960	1962	1963	1964
Primary (new) copper produced from domestic ores	990	825	1,080	1,228	1,213	1,247
Smelters	997	799	1,143	1,282	1,258	1,301
Refineries	980	797	1,121	1,214	1,219	1,260
From foreign ores	368	302	398	398	377	396
Secondary copper from old scrap only	453	471	429	416	422	474

annual output and leads all other states by a wide margin. Other important deposits are in Utah and Montana, followed by New Mexico and Nevada. Production of recoverable copper increased from 705,000 short tons in 1930 to 909,000 in 1950, 1.1 million in 1960, 1.2 million in 1964, and 1.4 million in 1965 (see Table IX.24).

The industry obtains copper both from ores, domestic and foreign, and from metal recovered from scrap (see Table IX.25).

The two chief consumers of copper in the United States are wire mills, which take nearly three-fifths of the total, and brass mills, with two-fifths. Foundries, smelters, and chemical plants account for the small remainder.

Lead and zinc. Lead and zinc are commonly found together in mineral deposits. The world's greatest deposits of lead and zinc are in the "lead belt" in southeastern Missouri and the zinc deposit, also containing lead ore, in the Tri-State region (Kansas, Oklahoma, and southwestern Missouri). Other important deposits in the United States are the lead and zinc deposits at Coeur d'Alene, Idaho, Bingham, Utah (this deposit also contains copper), Franklin, N.J., and in the zinc belt in eastern Tennessee and southwestern Virginia.

TABLE IX.26

MINE PRODUCTION OF RECOVERABLE LEAD, BY STATE, 1953-64
(In Thousands of Short Tons)

	1953-57 Average	1959	1960	1962	1963	1964
Missouri	125	105	112	61	80	120
Idaho	69	62	43	84	76	71
Utah	46	37	39	38	45	40
Colorado	19	13	18	17	17	21
Other	80	39	34	36	33	35
UNITED STATES	339	256	247	237	253	287

TABLE IX.27

SMELTER PRODUCTION OF LEAD AND ZINC IN THE UNITED STATES, 1953-64
(In Thousands of Short Tons)

	Lead					Zinc				
	1953-57 Average	1959	1960	1962	1964	1953-57 Average	1959	1960	1962	1964
Primary metal from:										
Domestic ores[a]	334	225	229	246	294	494	348	334	448	532
Foreign ores[a]	168	116	154	130	155	437	450	465	431	422
Scrap	4	1	5	2	...	66	58	69	59	63
Antimonial lead	16	12	2	27	...	-	-	-	-	-

[a] For lead: includes production from base bullion.

Missouri is the leading producer of recoverable lead in this country, except 1962, when, because of a prolonged strike in mines in that state, Idaho moved into first place. The combined output of Missouri, Idaho, Utah, and Colorado in 1964 exceeded 252,000 sh. t., or 90 per cent of the country's total (see Table IX.26).

As with copper, the United States meets its need for lead and zinc not only from ore but also from domestic waste in various alloys. In 1964, output of primary refined lead from ores, domestic and imported, amounted to 449,000 sh. t., and that of secondary lead, to 542,000 t. (see Table IX.27).

Mine production of recoverable zinc is distributed more broadly among the states than that of lead (see Table IX.28). Production of zinc, as of lead, fluctuates within more or less narrow limits, and in 196ŗ it exceeded, for the first time, the average output in 1953–57 (see Table IX.27).

The United States ranks first in the production both of recoverable metal content in its ores and of smelter zinc. Canada's ore production approaches ours, but U.S. smelter output exceeds that of Canada by a wide margin. It also exceeds the combined output of Canada and the U.S.S.R. The chief uses for lead in the United States are for storage batteries (38 per cent of total consumption), for gasoline antiknock addi-

TABLE IX.28

MINE PRODUCTION OF RECOVERABLE ZINC, BY STATE, 1953-64
(In Thousands of Short Tons)

	1953-57 Average	1959	1960	1962	1963	1964
Tennessee	43	90	91	72	96	116
Idaho	59	56	37	63	63	59
New York	56	43	66	54	54	61
Colorado	39	35	31	43	58	54
Montana	66	27	13	38	32	29
Arizona	26	37	36	33	25	25
Utah	38	35	36	34	36	31
Illinois	19	27	30	27	20	14
Virginia	19	20	20	27	24	31
Pennsylvania	-	17	14	24	27	21
New Mexico	19	5	14	22	13	31
Washington	27	17	21	22	22	24
Other	110	15	27	47	61	80
UNITED STATES	522	425	435	506	529	576

TABLE IX.29

OUTPUT OF GOLD AND SILVER IN THE UNITED STATES, BY STATE, 1953-63
(In Thousands of Troy Ounces)

	1953-57 Average	1959	1960	1961	1962	1963
Gold						
South Dakota	548.6	577.7	554.8	557.9	577.2	576.7
Utah	424.5	239.5	368.3	343.0	311.9	285.9
Alaska	235.3	178.9	168.2	114.2	165.3	99.6
Arizona	130.8	124.6	143.1	146.0	137.2	140.0
California	217.8	145.3	123.7	97.6	106.3	86.9
Washington	72.8	118.4	129.0	117.3	93.7	98.6
Nevada	79.7	113.4	58.2	54.2	62.9	98.9
Colorado	97.9	61.1	61.3	67.5	48.9	33.6
Other	51.9	44.0	60.2	50.6	39.1	33.8
UNITED STATES	1,859.3	1,602.9	1,666.8	1,548.3	1,542.5	1,454.0
Silver						
Idaho	14,575.6	16,636.5	13,646.5	17,576.3	17,772.4	16,710.7
Arizona	4,748.6	3,898.3	4,775.0	5,120.0	5,453.6	5,373.1
Utah	6,385.2	3,734.3	4,783.0	4,797.6	4,628.4	4,790.5
Montana	6,178.4	3,420.4	3,607.0	3,490.4	4,560.7	4,241.6
Colorado	2,692.4	1,340.7	1,659.0	1,965.0	2,087.8	2,307.3
Missouri	292.0	330.8	15.6	11.8	490.9	131.7
Michigan	257.6	-	-	-	401.5	339.0
Washington[a]	408.2	606.5	628.7	625.2	350.2	374.4
New Mexico	253.6	158.9	303.9	282.8	301.5	256.5
Other	1,927.4	1,067.6	1,347.3	834.9	751.0	718.2
UNITED STATES	37,719.0	31,194.0	30,766.0	34,704.0	36,798.0	35,243.0

[a]Includes production in Pennsylvania, not reported separately.

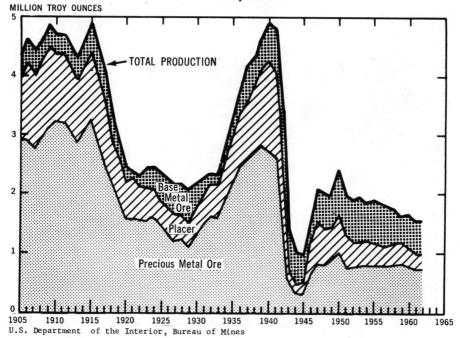

FIGURE IX.12.A

PRODUCTION OF GOLD IN THE UNITED STATES,
BY SOURCE, 1905-62

U.S. Department of the Interior, Bureau of Mines

tives (about 15 per cent), in lead pigments, ammunition, type metal, etc. Zinc is used primarily as refined metal in slab, for making pigments and salts and in galvanizing iron and steel.

Gold and silver. Gold and silver are used primarily for monetary purposes—silver predominantly in Asia, gold in the rest of the world. Considerable quantities also are used for jewelry and in various industries.

In the United States, gold is obtained from a deposit in South Dakota, as a by-product from copper ore in Utah and Arizona, and from placers in Alaska. The share of these states in the country's total production fluctuates; South Dakota, the nation's major producer, accounts for some 40 per cent of the total (see Table IX.29).

About two-thirds of silver is obtained as a by-product from base-metal ores mined chiefly for copper, lead, zinc, and gold; all the remainder comes from ores in which silver is the principal product. Idaho is the chief producer; in recent years its output has been approaching one-half of the country's total (see Table IX.29). Much of the secondary silver is recovered from old jewelry, plate, worn-out coins, and other industrial and monetary sources.

Figures IX.12A and IX.12B illustrate the distribution of gold and silver production in the United States, by source, from the early 1900's to 1963.

FIGURE IX.12.B

PRODUCTION OF SILVER IN THE UNITED STATES,
BY SOURCE, 1910-62

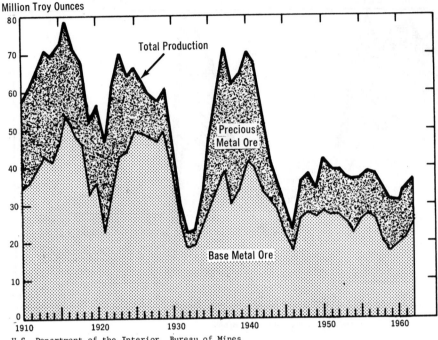

U.S. Department of the Interior, Bureau of Mines

Aluminum. Aluminum is produced in 2 stages: first, alumina is recovered from bauxite ore, then aluminum is produced from alumina.

Bauxite, the basic material, is obtained in this country almost exclusively (98 per cent in 1964) from a comparatively small deposit of high-grade ore in Arkansas. The vast deposits of low-grade ore in Alabama and Georgia have been exploited only in emergencies when cost was not a factor, but in peacetime it is more economical to use imported ores than to operate these mines. Thus the output of bauxite in the United States amounted to 492,000 long tons in 1940, skyrocketed to 2.8 million in 1944. Production contracted again after the war and in 1964 amounted to 1.6 million l. t.

The world's largest producer of bauxite is Jamaica, followed by the U.S.S.R. and Surinam. The U.S. share in the world's output was less than 5 per cent in 1964.

As the demand for aluminum has increased in all industrialized countries of the world, production of that metal has followed a consistent upward trend, particularly since World War II. In the United States, the output of aluminum increased by leaps and bounds—from 131,000 sh. t. in 1939, to 0.8 million t. in 1944, and to 2.5 million in 1964. This coun-

TABLE IX.30

OUTPUT OF BAUXITE AND ALUMINUM IN THE WORLD
AND THE UNITED STATES, 1929-64

Year	Bauxite			Aluminum		
	World United States[a]	United States as Per Cent		World United States		United States as Per Cent
	(In Millions of Long Tons)	of World		(In Millions of Short Tons)		of World
1929	2,115	366	17.3	269	100	37.2
1939	4,301	375	8.7	660	131	19.8
1943	13,770	2,824[b]	45.3	1,915	771	40.3
1953-57, average	17,400	1,705	9.8	3,355	1,521	45.3
1959	22,690	1,700	7.5	4,480	1,954	43.7
1960	27,020	1,998	7.4	4,985	2,014	40.7
1961	28,890	1,228	4.3	5,205	1,904	36.5
1962	30,535	1,369	4.5	5,595	2,118	38.1
1963	29,835	1,525	5.0	6,095	2,313	38.0
1964	33,145	1,601	4.8	6,730	2,553	38.0

[a] Dried-bauxite equivalent.
[b] 1944.

try's share in the world output increased from one-fifth of the total in 1939 to nearly two-fifths in 1964 (see Table IX.30).

Cement. About seven-tenths of the portland cement produced in the United States is made of clay, limestone, and shale; nearly one-fourth is a mixture of cement rock and limestone; and the remainder consists of various combinations of limestone and marl or shale. Output of cement has fluctuated as follows (figures in thousands of bar. of 376 lbs.): 172 in 1929; 125 in 1939; 130 in 1943; 209 in 1949; 350 in 1959; and 369 in 1964.

Portland cement is produced in 41 states and Puerto Rico. Until 1959, Pennsylvania was the major producer, but it now has ceded first place to California; their combined output approaches 25 per cent of the nation's total. Texas and Michigan rank next. Slightly more than three-fourths of plant capacity was utilized in 1964.

Stone, sand, and gravel. Production of stone, in all its varieties, has increased vigorously because of the great expansion of roadbuilding, and construction in general. Since 1950, the output of stone has more than doubled (figures in millions of sh. t.): 141 in 1929, 147 in 1939, 224 in 1949, 584 in 1959, and 726 million sh. t. in 1964. Pennsylvania, Texas, Illinois, and California are major producers. For the same reason—expansion of construction—output of sand and gravel also has increased (figures in millions of sh. t.): 223 in 1929, 226 in 1939, 319 in 1949, 730 in 1959, and 868 in 1964.

56. *Exports and Imports of Mineral Products*

For consumption, the United States imports predominantly ores and concentrates of various base metals of which it has inadequate or no

TABLE IX.31

EXPORTS AND IMPORTS OF METALS AND
NONMETALLIC MINERALS, 1936-65
(In Millions of Dollars)

Year	Exports			Imports		
	Total	Nonmetallic Minerals	Metals and Manufactures	Total	Nonmetallic Minerals	Metals and Manufactures
1936-40	943	466	477	380	137	243
1941-45	1,732	848	884	765	246	519
1946-50	2,202	1,176	1,026	1,434	633	801
1951-55	2,634	1,418	1,216	3,027	1,196	1,831
1956-60	3,402	1,539	1,863	4,366	2,110	2,255
1959	2,494	1,177	1,317	4,658	2,229	2,429
1960	3,218	1,158	2,060	4,572	2,201	2,371
1961	3,035	1,115	1,920	4,753	2,335	2,418
1962	2,794	1,172	1,622	5,206	2,539	2,667
1963[a]	3,086	1,307	1,779	5,217	2,554	2,663
1964	3,513	1,323	2,190	5,704	2,763	2,941
1965	3,617	1,418	2,199	6,869	3,015	3,854

[a] Beginning with 1963, the Bureau of Census has discontinued this classification. The 1963-65 data are therefore not completely comparable.

deposits, and unwrought metals and scrap. Exports usually consist of re-fined and manufactured metals. Imported mineral commodities accounted for 17 per cent of the value of all U.S. imports in 1963–64.

Until the 1950's, the value of exported nonmetallic-mineral products exceeded that of imported products. More recently, the value of imports for consumption has grown rapidly and in 1962 was more than double the average in 1951–55. Imports of metals and manufactures, exclusive of machinery and vehicles, began to outrank exports as early as the first

TABLE IX.32

VALUE OF MINERAL IMPORTS, BY COMMODITY, 1950-64
(In Millions of Dollars)

	1950	1960	1962	1963	1964
Crude petroleum	369	895	1,072	1,837	523
Iron ore	44	322	325	323	156
Bauxite	16	78	122	115	64
Copper ore	36	49	1	11	6
Manganese ore	42	82	66	68	22
Nickel, including matte and oxide	18	30	9	15	13
Chromite	23	24	24	20	11
Tin	47	31	14	3	5
Uranium, ores and concentrates	...	276[a]	252	...	...
Asbestos	47	63	64	62	35
Diamonds					
Gems	102	166	144	224	126
Industrial	37	52	51	50	31

[a] 1961.

half of the 1950's, but have not increased as rapidly as those of nonmetallic minerals including mineral fuels (see Table IX.31).

The great increase in the value of mineral imports is due largely to the growing role of crude petroleum, iron ore, and bauxite: but uranium ores, diamonds, and some other mineral commodities are also increasing their share in our imports (see Table IX.32).

The Commerce Department has calculated the share of imported mineral commodities in the new supply (domestic output plus imports)* in a given year. For crude petroleum, iron ore, and bauxite, the percentages, in terms of value, were 12, 34, and 89, respectively. Imports of some other mineral commodities are especially important: in terms of new supply, imported manganese ore, for example, accounts for more than 99 per cent; uranium, for 65 per cent; chromium, for 88 per cent, and so on.

Mineral fuels, iron ore, and molybdenum play a leading role in our exports of minerals (see Table IX.33), while the value of our imports of crude petroleum and products substantially exceed that of our exports.

TABLE IX.33

EXPORTS OF SELECTED MINERAL COMMODITIES, 1950-64
(In Millions of Dollars)

	1950	1960	1962	1963	1964
Petroleum and products	592	439	401	445	419
Bituminous coal	207	332	351	430	441
Anthracite	63	29	25	44	22
Iron ore and concentrates	16	58	63	76	80
Molybdenum	...	40	23	41	49

The list of our chief suppliers of mineral products reads like a *Who's Who* for the mineral industry of the world. We import:

iron ore from Canada and Venezuela;

copper from Chile, Canada, and Peru;

lead metal from Australia, Mexico, Canada, and Yugoslavia;

lead ore and concentrates from the Union of South Africa, Peru, Canada, Australia, Bolivia, and Honduras;

zinc metal from Canada, Belgium, Luxembourg, Mexico, Congo, and Peru;

zinc ores and concentrates from Canada, Mexico, Peru, Australia, South Africa, and Honduras;

manganese ore from Brazil, Ghana, South Africa, India, British Guiana, and Mexico;

* Output values represent those of mine shipments, sales, or marketable production; those of imports are generally values in the foreign country and do *not* include U.S. import duties, cost of transportation, insurance, and so on. Total import values thus tend to be understated in relation to domestic output.

bauxite from Jamaica, Surinam, and the Dominican Republic;
aluminum from Canada, Norway, and France;
nickel from Canada;
asbestos from South Africa, Canada, Australia, Bolivia, and Finland;
diamonds (gems) from the United Kingdom, Venezuela, British West
    Africa, and South Africa.

The list is far from inclusive; many other mineral products of various importance move in and out of our harbors and over our land borders. Moreover, numerous minerals used in the manufacture of machinery and vehicles thus participate in the foreign trade of the United States.

57. *Power*

The chief sources of energy in the United States are neither coal, as in West Germany, the United Kingdom, France, Belgium, and the U.S.S.R., nor water power, as in the Scandinavian countries, Italy and Canada, but petroleum and natural gas. Several Latin American countries (Mexico, Venezuela, Argentina) also use petroleum as fuel, but extensive use of natural gas as fuel constitutes the unique feature of the U.S. energy economy, not duplicated anywhere in the world. In the last decade, nuclear technology has made great progress, and 17 nuclear plants are already in operation. Others are nearing completion and are scheduled to be in service between now and 1968.

The role of coal in generating energy was unchallenged in this country throughout the nineteenth century. As late as 1920, coal supplied over 80 per cent of total energy (from mineral fuels and water power). But petroleum began to make inroads into the supremacy of coal and, in association with the growing role of natural gas, relegated coal—bituminous, lignite, and anthracite—to the fuel ranking third as a producer of mineral energy. In terms of British thermal units, coal supplied 27.2 per cent of total energy (from mineral fuels and water power) in 1964, as compared with 33.8 per cent provided by crude petroleum and slightly more (34.7 per cent) by natural gas. Water power has remained a minor source: its share amounted to 4.2 per cent (see Appendix Table XXII and Figure IX.13).

Consumption of energy from mineral fuels has been on the increase along with the growth of the national economy, but its components developed differently. In 1925, natural gas (dry and wet) provided only 6.4 per cent of total consumption of energy (from mineral fuels and water power) in this country; in 1964, its share was 33.4 per cent. Corresponding figures for crude petroleum, 22.2 and 36.5 per cent, show a much less spectacular rise, while the share of coal dropped from 70.4 per cent to 22.5 per cent of total consumption. Thus, the bulk of consumption of energy comes from stations operating mostly on liquid fuel and only partly on solid fuel. Though in the last decade or so, hydroelectric installa-

FIGURE IX.13

PRODUCTION OF ENERGY FROM MINERAL FUELS AND WATERPOWER
IN THE UNITED STATES, IN TERMS OF BRITISH
THERMAL UNITS, 1900-1963

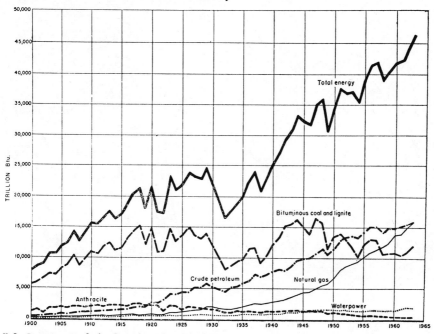

U.S. Department of the Interior, Bureau of Mines

tions have grown spectacularly in the West, the share of water power has
not increased in the last 4 decades: 3.3 per cent in 1925; 3.6 per cent in
1964 (see Appendix Table XXIII).

The electric-power industry was born in this country in the 1880's, when
it became commercially possible to harness the water wheels and especially the steam engines to electric generators. From a very modest beginning, with the Edison Electric Company serving 500 customers with some
10,000 lamps at the end of 1882, the electric-power industry has grown
phenomenally, almost doubling its capacity with each decade. As recently
as 1928, it operated only a few scattered transmission lines, concentrated
in the East and along the Pacific coast. As the demand for electric power
grew, new plants cropped up throughout the country—some privately
owned, others built by municipalities, cooperatives, or state and Federal
agencies. Between 1940 and 1960, the country became crisscrossed by
3,600 separate electric power systems (see Figure IX.14). Today electric
power production is one of this country's largest industries, with gross
capital assets of $69 billion.

Total installed generating capacity grew from 20 million kilowatts in

FIGURE IX.14

THE UNITED STATES POWER SYSTEM, 1928-60

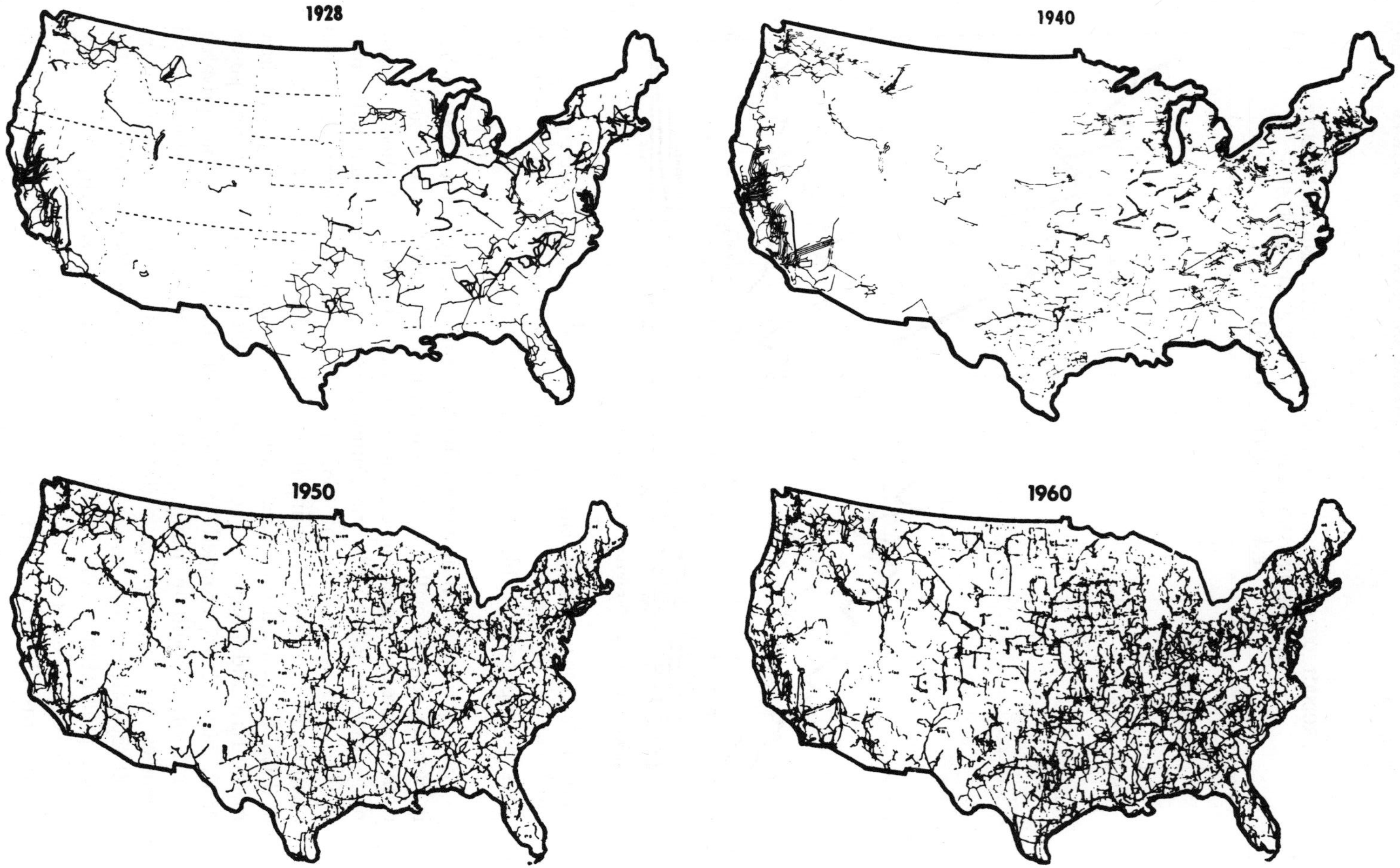

1928

1940

1950

1960

Edison Electric Institute

TABLE IX.34

INSTALLED GENERATING CAPACITY,
BY TYPE OF PRIME MOVER AND CLASS OF OWNERSHIP, 1902-64
(In Millions of Kilowatts)

	1902[a]	1922	1932	1942	1952	1962	1963	1964
Electric utilities	1.2	14.2	34.4	45.1	82.2	191.1	210.5	221.6
Hydropower	0.3	4.1	9.3	12.8	20.4	37.3	40.2	42.0
Steam	0.9	10.0	24.6	31.2	59.7	150.8	167.1	176.3
Internal combustion	-	0.1	0.5	1.0	2.1	3.0	3.2	3.3
Privately owned	1.1	13.4	32.0	37.4	64.8	144.6	158.4	167.5
Publicly owned	0.1	0.8	2.4	7.6	17.4	46.5	52.1	54.1
Municipal	0.1	0.7	1.8	3.3	6.0	12.9	14.2	15.0
Federal	-	-	0.2[b]	3.2	9.7	24.3	27.3	28.2
Other[c]	-	0.1	0.3	1.0	1.7	9.2	10.6	10.9
Industrial establishments	1.8	7.1	8.5	12.2	15.1	17.7	18.2	18.2
TOTAL CAPACITY	3.0	21.3	42.8	57.2	97.3	208.8	228.8	239.8

[a]The first data available.
[b]Includes cooperatives.
[c]Power districts, state projects, and, after 1940, cooperatives.

1920 to 80 million in 1950 and 240 million in 1964. Thermal plants accounted for about three-fourths of the 1964 total (see Table IX.34 and Figure IX.15).

The geographic pattern in the relative share of various prime movers in generating electric capacity is clear; coal prevails in eastern states and the East North Central States; gas in the West South Central states, water power in the Pacific and Mountain states and the East South Central state.

Production of electric energy for public use has increased spectacularly, doubling between 1942 and 1952, and more than doubling in the next decade (see Table IX.35).

More than half the electric energy comes from the conversion of coal (54 per cent in 1963);* less than three-tenths, from oil and natural gas (6 and 21 per cent, respectively); and almost one-fifth, from water power (19 per cent). The Federal Power Commission believes that the fossil fuels will continue to provide increasing amounts of energy in the future but that their share in the total supply will decline as a result of nuclear fuel competition. It expects that by 1980, the share of coal will drop to 47 per cent, though coal will remain the "workhorse" for electric generation. The share of both oil and natural gas will also decline (from 6 to 4 per cent and from 21 to 17 per cent, respectively). In contrast, generation of energy from nuclear power will grow in this period from 0.1 per cent to 19 per cent; the remaining 13 per cent of energy will come from hydropower.

* Includes 0.4 per cent of total generated by nuclear-fueled plants, and minor amounts from wood and waste.

FIGURE IX.15

INSTALLED CAPACITY OF ELECTRIC
UTILITY GENERATING PLANTS IN THE UNITED STATES, 1920-64

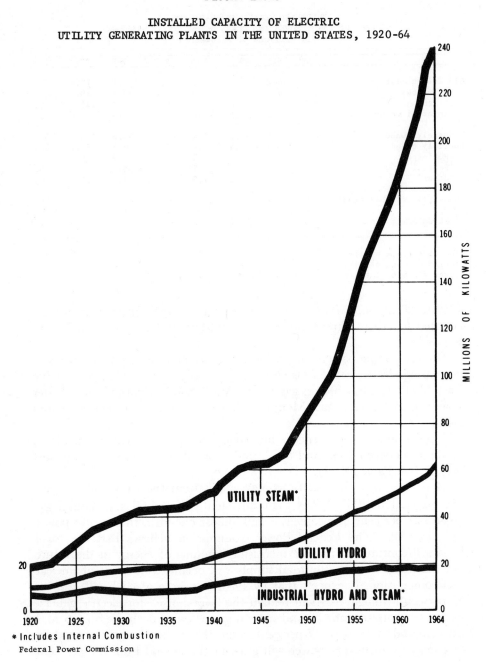

* Includes Internal Combustion

Federal Power Commission

Three areas—Middle Atlantic, East North Central, and Pacific—account for about half the generating capacity and production of electric energy. In 1963, their combined capacity amounted to about 104 million

TABLE IX.35

PRODUCTION OF ELECTRIC ENERGY FOR PUBLIC USE, 1902-64
(In Billions of Kilowatt-Hours)

	1902	1922	1932	1942	1952	1963	1964
Electric utilities	2.5	43.6	79.4	186.0	399.2	916.8	982.7
Hydropower	-	16.9	32.9	63.9	105.1	165.8	176.3
Steam	-	26.6	45.9	120.5	290.4	746.0⎱	806.5
Internal combustion	-	0.2	0.6	1.6	3.7	5.0⎰	
Privately owned	2.3	41.7	74.5	158.1	322.1	701.3	755.8
Publicly owned	0.2	2.0	4.9	27.8	77.1	215.5	227.0
Municipal	0.2	1.6	3.5	7.6	17.5	46.3	50.2
Federal	-	0.1	0.4	16.9	52.5	124.3	129.9
Other[a]	-	0.3	0.9	3.3	7.1	45.0	46.8
Industrial establishments	3.5	17.6	20.0	47.2	63.8	94.6	99.7
Hydropower	...	4.4	3.1	5.3	4.6	...	...
Steam	...	13.2	16.8	39.2	54.3	...	...
Internal combustion	...	b	b	2.7	4.9	...	...
TOTAL PRODUCTION	6.0	61.2	99.4	233.1	463.1	1,011.4	1,082.4

[a]Cooperatives, power districts, state projects.
[b]Included with steam.

kilowatts, out of the total 211 million; their production, to 467 billion kilowatt-hours out of 917 billion. California, with 17 million kw. of installed capacity and 79 billion of kw-hrs produced, outranked all other states; New York State followed next, with 16 million kw. and 65 billion kw-hrs (for the distribution of installed capacity and energy production by area, see Table IX.36).

Total electric-power production (of electric utilities and industrial establishments) crossed the 1-trillion-kw-hr mark for the first time in 1963. Since electricity cannot be stored, production and use must be simultaneous. This raises the problem of peak loads, which do not occur at the same time of the day, week, month, or season. The 1963 peak load of electric utilities in the contiguous United States was 167.7 million kw.; the dependable total capacity would exceed peak demand by some 22 per cent if all capacity could be operated continuously. But this country has 3,600 systems, greatly varying in size, type of ownership, and range of power-supply functions performed.

Actually, in the pluralistic and complex character of its organization, the U.S. electric-utility industry greatly differs from the power industries of the world. However, taken as a whole, it is fairly well interconnected through regional networks, or "grids," though a more complete coordination would make it easier to take advantage of the load diversity existing among the utility systems. Two recent blackouts, particularly the large-scale East Coast power failure on November 9, 1965, have demonstrated that the system is not foolproof. Evidently, this poses before the electric power industry, as its most urgent task, the need to devise safeguards which would make impossible the repetition of such occurrences.

The Federal Power Commission estimates that the peak load will reach

TABLE IX.36

INSTALLED GENERATING CAPACITY AND PRODUCTION
OF ELECTRIC ENERGY, BY GEOGRAPHIC DIVISION, 1950-63[a]

Geographic Division	Installed Capacity (In Thousands of Kilowatts)				Energy Production (In Billions of Kilowatt-Hours)			
	1950	1955	1960	1963	1950	1955	1960	1963
New England	4,052	5,271	7,045	7,931	16.2	22.6	28.8	33.6
Middle Atlantic	13,225	18,213	25,536	31,585	63.4	86.1	112.7	137.2
East North Central	16,083	25,976	36,780	42,585	75.3	125.9	165.1	191.3
West North Central	5,024	7,930	11,538	14,879	19.2	30.5	43.7	56.4
South Atlantic	8,857	15,131	22,696	29,308	43.6	71.2	103.6	129.4
East South Central	4,464	11,657	16,614	21,626	24.6	66.5	87.7	103.1
West South Central	4,717	9,449	16,401	21,702	22.5	40.8	64.6	85.4
Mountain	3,445	6,106	8,700	10,963	16.5	24.2	36.6	42.4
Pacific	9,054	14,733	23,256	29,970	47.8	79.2	112.4	138.1
UNITED STATES	68,919	114,472	168,568	210,549	329.1	547.0	755.4	916.8

[a]Installed capacity of electric utilities as of December 31; production for years ending December 31. Excludes Alaska and Hawaii.

TABLE IX.37

SALES OF ELECTRIC ENERGY, 1950-63
(In Billions of Kilowatt-Hours)

	1950	1955	1960	1962	1963
Residential	72.2	128.4	200.8	232.0	249.8
Commercial	52.1	78.8	132.9	152.7	163.7
Industrial	144.5	260.6	321.3	359.0	382.7
Other	22.1	29.0	31.5	31.8	33.8
TOTAL	290.9	496.8	686.5	775.4	830.1

493 million kw. in 1980, thus tripling the 1963 figure and greatly magnifying the problem of meeting such high electric-load requirements. It also expects that by 1980, nearly all the electric systems of the nation will be interconnected and will operate in exchanging power, in accordance with load diversity patterns.

Industry is the chief consumer of electric energy in the United States. Many industrial plants produce their own electric energy but industry as a whole still accounts for almost half of total energy sales by electric utilities. In 1963, industry purchased 383 billion kw-hrs out of total sales of 830 billion. Residential consumers account for some 30 per cent of total sales (see Table IX.37).

Water power, as compared with mineral fuels, has the advantage of being a source of electricity that does not consume reserves, is not causing air pollution or thermal pollution of streams, does not require fuel for generation, and is very reliable in operation. Because hydroelectric plants are able to start operating quickly and make rapid changes in power output, they are well adapted for serving peak power loads. In many cases, the development of hydroelectric power makes possible such associated benefits as recreation, water supply, flood control, and improvement of fish and wildlife.

As of January 1, 1964, the total potential capacity of hydroelectric power of the United States was estimated at 156 million kw. About 41 million kw., or 26 per cent of the total potential, has been harnessed for the production of electricity. The Mountain and Pacific states, without Alaska, account for more than half of both developed and undeveloped water power: 21 million kw. out of 40 million, and 62 million out of 116 million, respectively (see Table IX.38 and Figure IX.16). Alaska's water-power resources (21.6 million kw.) are almost untouched. The estimate of undeveloped hydroelectric power includes almost 11 million kw. now under construction and scheduled for completion during the next few years.

A new source of power that has just begun to be utilized holds enormous promise for the future: nuclear power.

TABLE IX.38

DEVELOPED AND UNDEVELOPED WATER POWER, BY GEOGRAPHIC DIVISION, 1939, 1950, AND 1964
(In Thousands of Kilowatts)

| Geographic Division | Developed Water Power (Capacity of Actual Installations Only) Electric Utilities and Industrial Plants | | | | | | Estimated Undeveloped Water Power January 1, 1964 |
| | 1939 | | 1950 | | January 1, 1964 | | |
	Total	Utilities	Total	Utilities	Total	Utilities	
New England	1,115	833	1,239	971	1,497	1,235	3,128
Middle Atlantic	1,633	1,563	1,678	1,602	4,218	4,130	5,179
East North Central	790	703	901	828	911	818	1,351
West North Central	537	501	629	577	2,287	2,245	4,515
South Atlantic	2,224	1,803	2,767	2,297	4,600	4,424	9,903
East South Central	1,270	1,140	2,729	2,721	4,294	4,286	4,570
West South Central	140	139	466	463	1,125	1,125	3,453
Mountain	1,583	1,581	2,286	2,282	4,845	4,843	26,652
Pacific	2,783	2,741	5,979	5,933	16,454	16,390	56,983[a]
UNITED STATES	12,075	11,004	18,675	17,675	40,230	39,494	115,734

[a]Includes undeveloped resources of Alaska: 21,617,000 kilowatts.

FIGURE IX.16

DEVELOPED AND UNDEVELOPED HYDROELECTRIC POWER IN THE
UNITED STATES, BY REGION, JANUARY 1, 1964

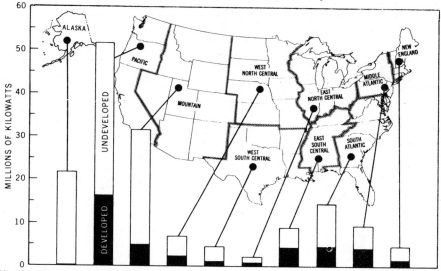

Federal Power Commission

The Federal Power Commission estimates that the United States will probably require 2.8 trillion kw-hrs of electricity by 1980, or slightly more than 3 times the amount produced in 1960. This estimate does not in-

FIGURE IX.17

PROJECTIONS OF ELECTRIC ENERGY REQUIREMENTS
FOR 1970 AND 1980 IN THE UNITED STATES

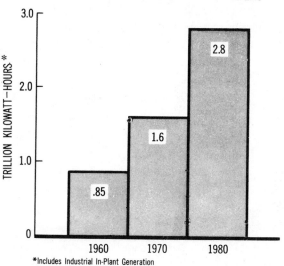

*Includes Industrial In-Plant Generation

Federal Power Commission

TABLE IX.39

INSTALLED CAPACITY AND PRODUCTION OF ELECTRIC ENERGY
IN SELECTED COUNTRIES, 1963

	Installed Capacity (In Millions of kws)	Production (In Billions of kw-hrs)	Kw-hr Per Capita
United States	228.6	1,011.2	5,340
U.S.S.R.	93.0	385.8	1,716
United Kingdom	44.6	163.3	3,035
Japan	34.4	155.4	1,621
West Germany	33.8	137.4	2,385
Canada	26.4	121.6	6,427
France	25.5	85.9	1,796
Italy	21.4	69.1	1,369
China (Mainland)	12.7	29.0	40
Sweden	11.2	40.0	5,256
East Germany	8.9	45.1	2,630
Poland	8.6	33.4	1,087
Spain	8.5	25.2	811
Norway	8.4	40.2	10,950
Switzerland	7.7	22.0	3,789
Other countries	109.7	403.7	255
WORLD	683.2	2,768.4	882

clude the needs of Alaska and Hawaii, whose electric systems are not connected with those of the other 48 states. Interconnection with Alaska is considered a possibility for the future. To produce the 2.8 trillion kw-hrs required by 1980 will necessitate an installed capacity of 525 mil-

FIGURE IX.18

WORLD OUTPUT OF ELECTRIC ENERGY, 1962

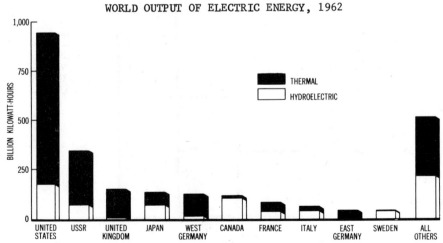

Federal Power Commission

lion kw., compared with about 230 million kw. of capacity in 1963 (see Figure IX.17). This estimate is not intended to be a precise forecast but is rather presented by the Federal Power Commission as a goal contingent upon the economic growth of the country and a well-interconnected and coordinated utility industry.

With its installed capacity of 228.6 million kw., the United States has one-third of the world's total capacity of 683 million kw. It leads other countries by a substantial margin in production, accounting for 35–40 per cent of the world's electric energy. In 1963, its production about equaled the combined production of the 6 producers ranking next in electric energy: the U.S.S.R., the United Kingdom, Japan, West Germany, Canada, and France. On the other hand, countries with abundant hydro-electric resources, like Canada and Norway, are ahead of the United States in the use of power per capita. Sweden's per capita consumption of power is about the same as this country's (see Table IX.39 and Figure IX.18).

X. *Manufactures*

58. *Manufactures in the Nation's Economy*

Despite the very high level of industrialization in the United States, manufacturing industries account for less than one-third of the gross national product—28 per cent, or less than the percentages in Japan (31), Italy (33), or the United Kingdom (35).

Several factors have been instrumental in keeping manufactures from dominating the economic scene in this country. From its beginning, the United States has had very strong and efficient agricultural production, which has supported the development of industry by participating substantially in the country's exports and thus ensuring imports of necessary machinery and raw materials. On the other hand, transportation facilities, the distributive services, and credit institutions have played a greater role here than in some other industrial countries because of great distances, regional and industrial diversification, mass production, and mass consumption. With respect to the size of the labor force, widespread mechanization and the spread of automation and their concomitant, a steadily rising productivity of labor, have reduced, and continue to reduce, manufacture's share in employment of the economically active population. Moreover, as technology increasingly penetrates the national economy and the standard of living rises, employment tends to expand in service industries, though here, too, automation effects some decrease in the number of employed persons.

In summary, the role of manufactures in the national economy in 1964 may be characterized by the following figures: 30 per cent of all non-

TABLE X.1

MANUFACTURING INDUSTRIES[a]
IN THE UNITED STATES, 1899-1963

Year	Establish-ments	Proprietors and Firm Members	Salaried Employees	Production Workers	Total Payroll	Wages	Value Added by Manufacture
			(In Thousands)			(In Millions of Dollars)	
1899	205	...	348	4,502	2,259	1,893	4,647
1909	265	272	750	6,262	4,105	3,205	8,160
1919	270	250	1,372	8,465	12,427	9,664	23,842
1929	207	133	1,290	8,370	14,284	10,885	30,591
1931	171	...	...	6,163	...	6,689	18,601
1933	139	72	770	5,788	6,238	4,940	14,008
1935	168	82	1,059	7,204	9,655	7,311	18,553
1937	167	99	1,217	8,569	12,830	10,113	25,174
1939	174	124	1,719	7,808	12,706	8,998	24,487
1947	241	189	2,376	11,918	39,696	30,244	74,290
1954	287	198	3,753	12,373	62,993	44,595	117,032
1958	299	186	4,359	11,666	78,326	49,575	141,500
1962	...	...	4,636	12,130	94,291	59,129	179,290
1963	...	...	4,740	12,325	99,725	62,162	190,395

[a] The definition of manufacturing industries has undergone changes which somewhat affect the comparability of figures. Data for 1939-63 include employees in manufacturing establishments who were engaged in distribution and construction work. It is not known to what extent earlier figures include such data.

agricultural employment, 29 per cent of all wages and salaries, and 29 per cent of the national income. In that year, more than half of all corporate profits came from manufactures, and more than half of the corporate income tax was borne by manufacturing industries.

The first Census of Manufactures, in 1809, was followed by censuses at 10-year intervals until 1899, with the exception of 1829. Beginning with 1904, the census was taken at 5-year intervals; from 1921 through 1937, at 2-year intervals. The first postwar census was taken in 1947, the next in 1954, 1958, and finally 1963. Only summary data from the 1963 census have been published so far.

Between the quinquennial censuses of manufactures, as established by present legislation, the Annual Survey of Manufactures carries forward the measuring of manufacturing activity for intercensal years. These surveys do not cover the entire field of manufactures but are based on a very large sample—60,000 establishments out of the total of less than 300,000. These are large plants which together engage about two-thirds of all employees in manufacturing, and a representative selection of the more numerous small factories; government-owned and -operated establishments are excluded.

Both the Census and the Annual Survey of Manufactures include only establishments with 1 or more employees at any time during the year. They do not report on establishments with no employees, of which there were 51,800 in 1958; these represented less than half of 1 per cent of all value added by manufacturing industries in that year. The last intercensal surveys were carried out in 1962 and later in 1964, but 1964 data are not yet available.

The number of manufacturing establishments, exclusive of hand and neighborhood industries, has fluctuated but has changed comparatively little since the first decade of this century. In 1909, 264,810 establishments were recorded; in the Depression years, many went out of business, and the number dropped to 139,245. By 1947, the number of manufacturing establishments rose to 240,807 and in 1958 with 299,036 establishments, somewhat exceeded the 1909 figure (1963 data are not available). The number of proprietors and firm members is smaller than that of establishments because of multiple ownership.

The number of salaried employees and production workers has developed differently. By the end of the last century, there were 348,000 employees and 4.5 million production workers in manufacturing establishments; in 1963, 4.7 million white-collar employees and 12.3 million production workers. Thus the number of salaried employees increased more than 13 times, while that of production workers about tripled. Total payroll increased from $2.3 billion to $99.7 billion, in current dollars (see Table X.1).

Of the total 298,182 establishments with 15.4 million employees in 1958,* 1,363 had 1,000–2,499 employees each; and 498 establishments,

TABLE X.2

DISTRIBUTION OF MANUFACTURING ESTABLISHMENTS
BY NUMBER OF EMPLOYEES, PAYROLL, AND VALUE ADDED,
1947, 1954, AND 1958
(Number of Employees and Establishments in Thousands;
Money Figures in Millions of Dollars)

Item and Year	All Establishments[a]	\multicolumn{8}{c}{Employee-Size Class}
		1–19	20–49	50–99	100–249	250–499	500–999	1,000–2,499	2,500 and Over
Establishments:									
1947	241	158	40	19	14	6	3	1	1
1954	287	196	43	21	16	6	3	1	1
1958	298	204	46	22	16	6	3	1	b
Employees:									
1947	14,294	1,034	1,244	1,301	2,229	1,930	1,869	2,146	2,542
1954	15,645	1,195	1,360	1,475	2,430	2,118	1,963	2,227	2,876
1958	15,394	1,202	1,443	1,513	2,497	2,150	1,893	2,046	2,649
Payroll:									
1947	39,696	2,390	3,242	3,440	5,937	5,244	5,219	6,237	7,986
1954	62,963	3,766	4,797	5,449	9,171	8,218	8,046	9,767	13,749
1958	73,750	4,650	6,058	6,416	10,938	9,709	9,176	10,852	15,950
Value added:									
1947	74,290	4,944	6,039	6,581	11,772	10,432	10,110	11,598	12,812
1954	116,848	7,207	8,351	9,662	17,143	15,835	15,451	18,927	24,272
1958	141,270	9,214	11,089	12,024	21,162	19,291	18,103	21,449	28,938

[a]Excludes administrative offices and auxiliary units; also excludes Alaska and Hawaii.
[b]Less than 500.

* Excludes 854 establishments in Alaska and Hawaii.

TABLE X.3

MANUFACTURING ESTABLISHMENTS IN SELECTED COUNTRIES, 1960-62

	Number of Manufacturing Establishments	Persons Engaged (In Thousands)	Average Number Per Establishment
United States	299,036	16,025	53.6
Canada	36,682	1,295	35.3
Belgium	39,790	1,229	30.9
France	503,525	4,858	9.6
West Germany[a]	550,443	9,338	17.0
Italy	600,750	4,492	7.5
Netherlands[b]	100,644	1,160	11.5
Norway	19,229	341	17.7
Spain	117,122	1,613	13.8
Sweden	72,023	991	13.8
Switzerland	91,968	890	9.7
United Kingdom	92,785	7,781	83.9
Japan	553,170	8,950	16.2
Israel	10,021	152	15.2
Taiwan	52,152	446	8.6
Australia[c]	58,080	1,105	19.0
New Zealand[a]	8,981	188	20.9

[a]Establishments with 2 or more workers.
[b]1950.
[c]Establishments with 4 or more workers.

2,500 employees and over. Thus, the 1,861 giant establishments, a little over one-half of 1 per cent of the total number, accounted for 4.7 million, or 30 per cent of all employed persons. They also accounted for 35 per cent of total payroll (see Table X.2).

The average number of employees per establishment in the United States, 53.6 in 1958, is higher than in most industrialized countries. The predominance of small plants in France, Italy, Switzerland, and elsewhere is particularly striking in comparison with this country (see Table X.3).

Other yardsticks (than the size of employment) for measuring the manufacturing activities in a country or a specific industry include the cost of materials used, the amount of power consumed, the value of finished products, etc. The most frequently used measurements are value of shipments and value added by manufacturing, but the value of shipments (or sales) contains duplications resulting from the use of products of some establishments as materials by others. If a factory produces motors and sells them to an automobile plant, the value of its product is counted twice—in *its* report and in the automobile-plant report. In addition, the value of parts of motors and of materials used in making them may be listed 3 or 4 times. For this reason, the total value of manufacturing shipments is not a satisfactory measure of manufactures' importance in the national economy.

TABLE X.4

VALUE ADDED PER PRODUCTION WORKER, 1909-63

(In Dollars)

1909	1,303	1933	2,420	1947	6,233
1919	2,817	1935	2,575	1954	9,459
1929	3,655	1937	2,938	1958	12,129
1931	3,018	1939	3,136	1962	14,781
				1963	15,448

TABLE X.5

VALUE ADDED AND NATIONAL

INCOME ORIGINATING IN MANUFACTURING, 1929-63

	Value Added	Income Originated in	Manufacturing
	(In Billions of Dollars)		Per Cent
1929	30.6	21.9	0.72
1939	24.5	18.1	0.74
1947	74.3	59.5	0.80
1954	117.0	94.6	0.81
1958	141.5	107.7	0.76
1960	164.0	125.8	0.77
1962	179.3	137.0	0.76
1963	190.4	143.8	0.76

Another measure is *value added by manufacture*, which is calculated by subtracting the cost of materials, supplies, containers, fuel, purchased electric energy, and contract work from the total value of shipments. Because value added avoids duplications contained in value of shipments, it is considered the best measurement of manufacturing activities.

The relationship between the value added by manufacture and the gross value of products in an industry depends on the relation of the cost of materials and supplies to the cost of manufacturing. In food industries, manufacturing adds, on the average, $1 value to each $2 in materials and supplies; in textiles, primary-metal industries, and some others, it adds $1 value to about $1.50. The ratio is about $1 to $4 in petroleum and coal-products industries, while in the industries of fabricated metal products, leather and leather products, and furniture and fixtures, it approaches a ratio of $1 to $1. In contrast, there are industries in which value added exceeds the cost of materials substantially—for example, in chemicals and allied products, machinery industries, and printing and publishing.

Value added per production worker increased between 1909 and 1962 as shown in Table X.4.

Value added by manufacture is generally larger than national income originated in manufacturing* (see Sec. 29); the relationship is rather stable (see Table X.5).

* Income originating in manufacturing is obtained by subtracting from the value of shipments not only the cost of materials but also depreciation   charges, state and local taxes, allowance for bad debts, insurance, advertising, patent fees, etc.

TABLE X.6

SHARE OF LARGEST MANUFACTURING COMPANIES
IN VALUE ADDED, 1947, 1954, AND 1958
(Per Cent)

	1947	1954	1958
Largest 50 companies	17	23	23
Largest 100 companies	23	30	30
Largest 150 companies	27	34	35
Largest 200 companies	30	37	38

The share of large companies* in total value added by manufacture increased between 1947 and 1954, but remained nearly stable between 1954 and 1958 (see Table X.6).

Capital expenditures for new plant and equipment by manufacturing industries amounted to $9.6 billion in 1958, $15.7 billion in 1963, $18.6 billion in 1964 and $22.5 billion in 1965. According to the 1958 Census of Manufactures, the 250,000 smaller establishments with 1–49 employees each, representing 84 per cent of all establishments, shared in the new

TABLE X.7

DISTRIBUTION OF NEW CAPITAL EXPENDITURES
BY SIZE OF ESTABLISHMENTS, 1958

Employees	Number of Establishments (In Thousands)	New Capital Expenditures by Employee-Size Class (Per Cent)
1- 4	106	3.2
5- 9	51	2.4
10- 19	47	3.8
20- 49	46	7.1
50- 99	22	6.7
100- 249	16	12.8
250- 499	6	12.4
500- 999	3	13.2
1,000-2,499	1	15.6
2,500 and over	a	22.8
TOTAL	298	100.0

[a]Less than 500.

capital expenditures only to the extent of 16.5 per cent; the 44,000 establishments with 50–499 employees, or 14.8 per cent of the total, spent nearly 32 per cent of the total new outlay, while the remaining few thousand giant enterprises, each employing 500 or more persons, accounted for more than 51 per cent (see Table X.7).

* A company may consist of one or more establishments at one or more locations, but each company is required to submit a separate report for each establishment at each location.

TABLE X.8

SALES AND PROFITS OF LARGEST
MANUFACTURING CORPORATIONS, 1948-64
(In Billions of Dollars)

	Total (177) Corporations			Durable Goods (99) Corporations		
	Sales	Profits		Sales	Profits	
		Before Taxes	After Taxes		Before Taxes	After Taxes
1948	56.1	7.9	4.9	32.8	4.4	2.6
1955	104.9	14.9	7.6	68.0	9.9	4.8
1960	123.9	13.5	7.2	76.5	8.0	3.9
1962	136.5	15.3	8.2	84.3	9.4	4.8
1964	157.6	18.8	10.5	98.4	11.9	6.4

In 1965, the combined new capital expenditures of industries producing petroleum, chemicals, metals, machinery, transportation equipment, and food amounted to more than 70 per cent of total industrial investment, $15.9 billion out of $22.5 billion. The petroleum industry led with nearly $4 billion and was followed by the machinery industry ($3 billion), and the industries of chemicals, metals, and transportation equipment, each spending about $2.6 billion.

Almost all the largest manufacturing firms are organized as corporations. Among these, 177 were the largest, each with sales of $150 million or more in 1957. Between 1948 and 1964, their sales rose from $56 billion to nearly $158 billion, and profits after taxes from $4.9 billion to $10.5 billion (see Table X.8).

TABLE X.9

SHARE OF LARGEST COMPANIES IN EMPLOYMENT, BY INDUSTRY, 1958
(Per Cent)

	4 Largest Companies	8 Largest Companies	20 Largest Companies
Telephone and telegraph equipment	92	97	99+
Computing and related machines	75	83	93
Tires and inner tubes	74	87	99
Motor vehicles and parts	70	74	85
Aircraft	58	82	99
Blast furnaces and steel mills	52	68	84
Electronic tubes	51	68	87
Aircraft engines	48	69	89
Shipbuilding and repairing	45	64	79
Inorganic chemicals n.e.c.	42	55	79
Motors and generators	41	51	69
Commercial printing	10	15	22
Lithographing	7	11	19
Plastics products n.e.c.	5	10	18
Women's suits, coats, and skirts	3	5	10
Dresses, unit price	2	3	6

The importance of these 177 corporations can be seen from the fact that their combined sales account for one-fourth of the GNP. Though they do not exercise monopolistic control over the manufactures, their expenditures for new plant and equipment importantly affect the national economy.

According to the Bureau of the Census, the 4 largest manufacturing companies in 1958 accounted for some 70 per cent of total employment in their industries and even for 92 per cent in some branches of manufacturing. In some industries, this proportion may have been as low as 2–5 per cent. The percentage of employment attributable to the 4, 8, or 20 largest companies of various industries in that year is shown in Table X.9.

59. Major Industries and Industrial Areas

The Census of Manufactures classifies industries in 20 major groups. In 1963, these industries engaged 17.1 million employees, including administrative and auxiliary personnel. Their total payroll approached $100 billion; total value added exceeded $190 billion, and total value of shipments amounted to $418 billion (see Table X.10 for data on individual industries in 1962).

TABLE X.10

MANUFACTURING INDUSTRIES IN THE UNITED STATES, 1962

Industry Group	All Employees	Production Workers	Total Payroll	Wages	Value Added	Cost of Materials	Value of Shipments[a]
	(In Thousands)			(In Billions of Dollars)			
Food and kindred products	1,682	1,119	8.6	5.1	20.9	46.0	66.9
Tobacco products	77	67	0.3	0.3	1.6	2.9	4.5
Textile mill products	878	785	3.4	2.7	6.1	9.2	15.2
Apparel and related products	1,237	1,087	4.2	3.2	7.2	9.0	16.1
Lumber and wood products	550	490	2.2	1.8	3.6	4.8	8.4
Furniture and fixtures	367	307	1.6	1.2	2.8	2.7	5.5
Paper and allied products	580	464	3.4	2.4	7.0	8.7	15.7
Printing and publishing	925	566	5.4	3.1	10.0	5.7	15.6
Chemicals and allied products	727	470	4.8	2.6	16.1	13.4	29.4
Petroleum and coal products	154	110	1.1	0.7	3.4	13.8	17.2
Rubber and plastics	398	314	2.2	1.6	4.3	4.3	8.5
Leather and products	346	308	1.3	1.0	2.1	2.2	4.3
Stone, clay, and glass products	574	464	3.1	2.3	6.6	5.0	11.5
Primary metal industries	1,133	921	7.5	5.7	13.7	19.9	33.9
Fabricated metal products	1,085	834	6.2	4.3	11.1	11.2	22.3
Machinery, except electrical	1,449	1,034	9.2	5.8	16.1	12.4	28.2
Electrical machinery	1,463	1,021	8.5	5.1	15.6	12.3	27.6
Transportation equipment	1,594	1,123	11.3	7.1	20.9	30.6	51.4
Instruments and related products	355	227	2.3	1.2	4.3	2.4	6.6
Miscellaneous manufacturing	588	419	3.3	1.9	5.7	4.8	10.4
Administrative and auxiliary	603	...	4.5	...	...	...	...
ALL MANUFACTURING ESTABLISHMENTS[b]	16,766	12,130	94.3	59.1	179.3	221.5	399.3

[a]Includes duplication arising from shipments between establishments in the same industry.
[b]Includes administrative personnel.

The following classification shows the comparative ranking of the 10 most important industrial groups by the size of employment, value of shipments, and value added:

Number of Employees	Value of Shipments	Value Added
1. Food	1. Food	1. Transportation equipment
2. Transportation equipment	2. Transportation equipment	2. Food
3. Electrical machinery	3. Primary metal industries	3. Machinery, except electrical
4. Machinery, except electrical	4. Chemicals and allied products	4. Chemicals and allied products
5. Apparel and related products	5. Machinery, except electrical	5. Electrical machinery
6. Primary metal industries	6. Electrical machinery	6. Primary metal industries
7. Fabricated metal products	7. Fabricated metal products	7. Fabricated metal products
8. Printing and publishing	8. Petroleum and coal products	8. Printing and publishing
9. Textile mill products	9. Apparel and related products	9. Apparel and related products
10. Chemicals and allied products	10. Paper and allied products	10. Paper and allied products

A comparison of this ranking of industries in 1962 with that in 1939 reveals many differences. For instance, in 1939, textile industries engaged more employees than any other group; in 1962, they ranked ninth in that classification, while the food industry was first and the industries pro-

TABLE X.11

PERCENTAGE DISTRIBUTION OF MANUFACTURING EMPLOYMENT
IN THE UNITED STATES, BY GEOGRAPHIC DIVISION, 1899-1963

Year	New England	Middle Atlantic	East North Central	West North Central	South Atlantic	East South Central	West South Central	Mountain	Pacific
1899	17.6	34.1	23.2	5.8	9.5	3.7	2.4	1.0	2.7
1909	16.0	33.8	23.3	5.9	9.7	3.9	3.0	1.1	3.3
1919	14.6	31.9	27.0	5.7	8.5	3.3	3.1	1.1	4.6
1929	12.3	29.8	29.1	5.6	10.1	4.1	3.3	1.1	4.6
1939	11.8	28.9	28.3	5.2	11.6	4.3	3.5	0.9	5.5
1947	10.3	27.6	30.2	5.5	10.7	4.4	3.9	1.0	6.4
1950	9.8	27.0	29.9	5.6	11.1	4.4	4.1	1.1	7.0
1955	8.9	25.6	29.0	5.8	11.3	4.7	4.6	1.3	8.9
1963	8.4	24.1	26.2	6.0	12.7	5.3	5.1	1.7	10.7

ducing transportation equipment had moved up to second place. In value of shipments, industries processing metals and producing instruments, transportation equipment and machinery, and chemicals crowded out many old industries; textiles, which had ranked fourth in 1939, disappeared from the list of the first 10.

However, this ranking of the 10 major industries somewhat obscures their real relationship in importance to the national economy. The pulse of the economy, so to speak, beats in the sector of manufactures represented by the industries producing machinery (both electrical and non-electrical), transportation equipment, and fabricated metal products; these, in turn, are based on the primary-metal industries—ferrous and nonferrous metals. Together, these 5 industrial groups produce durable, the so-called capital, goods, and employ more than 7 million people—about 45 per cent of total manufacturing employment; their payroll and value added exceed two-fifths of the national total. This block of industries, together with the chemical and oil-and-gas industries, represents the most dynamic sector of the U.S. economy.

Manufacturing is unevenly distributed throughout the United States. Historically, it once was concentrated in the East: New England, the birthplace of American industry, and the Middle Atlantic states and East North Central states; together, they accounted for three-fourths of all employment in manufactures in 1899. While New England has lost ground, though it remains one of the major industrial areas, the East North Central states have strengthened their position and have become a leading industrial region in terms of manufacturing employment and value added (see Table X.11). Today the industrial sinews of this country are largely concentrated in 10 states east of the Mississippi: New York, New Jersey, Pennsylvania, Ohio, Indiana, Illinois, Michigan, Wisconsin, Massachusetts, and Connecticut. Their combined industrial production represents about two-thirds of the total. Their manufactures provide jobs for almost 10 million persons, or six-tenths of all manufacturing employment, and account for $110 billion value added, out of the total $190 billion—almost 60 per cent (see Appendix Table XXIV). The maps in this chapter which illustrate the distribution of value added by different industries by state indicate clearly that the East is the heart of this country's industry. The new industrial center rising in the West, though important, only underscores the might of the East's industrial empire. Figure X.1 indicates the concentration of manufacturing employment in the East.

While manufacturing expanded throughout the nation during the war and postwar years—by 77 per cent between 1939 and 1963—not all regions experienced the same rate of growth. With an increase of only 26.9 per cent, New England lagged behind all other areas. The most significant growth was in the East North Central states, where more than 1.8 million employees were added to the payroll, exceeding all other areas in

FIGURE X.1

PER CENT OF EMPLOYED PERSONS IN MANUFACTURING
INDUSTRIES, BY STATE, 1960

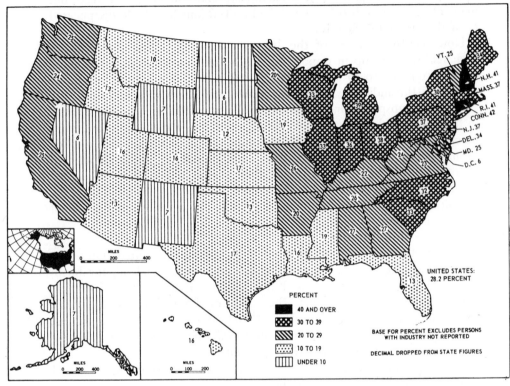

U.S. Department of Commerce, Bureau of the Census

TABLE X.12

INCREASE IN MANUFACTURING EMPLOYMENT,
BY GEOGRAPHIC DIVISION, 1939-63

| | Employment in Manufactures (In Thousands) | | Increase from 1939 to 1963 | |
	1939	1963	In Thousands	Per Cent
New England	1,128	1,432	304	26.9
Middle Atlantic	2,776	4,117	1,341	48.3
East North Central	2,711	4,480	1,769	65.2
West North Central	498	1,024	524	105.2
South Atlantic	1,121	2,148	1,027	91.6
East South Central	413	892	479	116.0
West South Central	335	860	525	156.7
Mountain	92	285	193	209.8
Pacific	545	1,828	1,283	235.4
UNITED STATES	9,622	17,065	7,443	77.4

TABLE X.13

GEOGRAPHIC DISTRIBUTION OF MANUFACTURES, BY VALUE ADDED, 1869-1963
(Per Cent)

	1869	1889	1909	1929	1939	1947	1958	1963
New England	23.9	17.5	14.3	10.4	9.8	9.2	7.4	7.0
Middle Atlantic	39.9	37.4	35.2	32.1	29.8	27.9	24.7	22.8
East North Central	18.1.	24.4	25.6	31.7	31.5	31.5	29.0	29.3
West North Central	6.7	7.0	6.4	5.7	5.5	5.5	6.3	6.2
South Atlantic	5.1	5.7	6.9	7.6	9.1	9.3	10.1	10.8
East South Central	2.7	2.9	3.4	2.8	3.4	3.9	4.5	4.7
West South Central	1.0	1.4	2.7	2.9	3.3	4.1	5.5	5.6
Mountain	0.6	0.7	1.5	1.1	1.1	1.1	1.6	1.8
Pacific	2.0	2.9	4.0	5.7	6.5	7.5	10.9	11.8
UNITED STATES	100.0	100.0	100.0	100.0	100.0	100.0	100.0	100.0

sheer numbers of new employees. Starting from a comparatively low level, the Mountain and Pacific states led all others in the rate of growth (see Table X.12).

The shift of manufactures from the East to the West and South is revealed by the changes in the share of different regions in the total value added by manufactures between 1869 and 1963, as illustrated by Table X.13.

Traditionally, apparel industries have dominated the manufacturing scene in New York and Pennsylvania, but the electrical- and nonelectrical-machinery industries now hold the lead. The textile industries, historically a feature of New England, have moved to the South Atlantic states. Metal industries are concentrated in the East North Central region, where machinery and automobile production is even more important. Together, these provide work for one-half of all manufacturing employment and six-tenths of all value added. Since World War II, new industrial centers have developed in the West, with those in California and Texas specializing in production of aircraft and electrical equipment.

60. Food, Beverages, Tobacco

The industry group producing food, beverages, and kindred products ranks first among all groups of manufactures in the number of persons employed, and the value of shipments. In value added by manufacturing, it ceded its rank for the first time in 1962 to the transportation-equipment industry and remains in this position, according to the 1963 Census of Manufactures.

In the food industry as a whole, plants are generally smaller than in many other industries. Nearly one-third of the establishments had 1–4 employees in 1958: 12,088 plants out of 41,619. It therefore accounts for a smaller share in total manufacturing employment than in manufacturing establishments: in 1958, the respective figures were 11 and 14 per cent. Various branches of the food industry differ in the average size of establishments—in 1958, there were 29 employees per establishment in dairies, 48 in bakeries, 56 in meat production, and 194 in sugar plants.

Food plants are spread throughout the United States, partly because some of the great variety of types of production are more suitable for one region than for others and partly because of the opportunities this industry presents to small enterprises catering to local markets. In the country as a whole, every tenth employee worked in the food industry in 1962, but the ratio varied from 5.3 per cent in New England and 12.6 per cent in the Pacific states to 19.6 per cent in the Mountain states and 21.5 per cent in the West North Central region. More than one-third of all employees in food industry are concentrated in New York, Illinois, and California.

The *meat-products* industry leads in the food industries by size of employment, payroll, and value of shipments (see Table X.14). Meat packing is the chief branch: the cost of its "materials" exceeded $10.5 billion in

TABLE X.14

FOOD, BEVERAGE, AND TOBACCO INDUSTRIES
IN THE UNITED STATES, 1963

	All Employees (In Thousands)	Production Workers	Payroll	Wages	Value Added
			(In Millions of Dollars)		
Meat products	299	238	1,633	1,206	2,832
Dairy products	258	118	1,389	583	3,345
Canned and frozen foods	239	208	930	716	2,609
Grain mill products	117	79	661	416	2,218
Bakery products	282	164	1,512	798	2,977
Sugar	32	26	188	145	593
Candy and related products	77	63	347	243	961
Beverages	205	108	1,224	602	3,459
Other food preparations	133	89	717	415	2,371
Tobacco products	76	67	328	269	1,678
TOTAL	1,718	1,161	8,930	5,393	23,042

1962 and was more than 6 times that for dairy products. Though there are many small meat plants—more than one-third employ 1–4 persons—a few establishments with 500 and more employees each, representing less than 3 per cent of the total number of plants, account for more than half the total value added by manufacturing. The North Central states, both East and West, are the center of this branch (see Figure X.2).

The manufacture of *dairy products* is characterized by a considerable overlapping of production; plants that primarily bottle and distribute fluid milk also produce large quantities of butter and ice cream. Every third employee in the dairy industry is engaged in delivering its products, chiefly fluid milk, from the central plant to retail and wholesale distributors, to company stores, or to households; the 1958 census found that 82,000 out of the total 211,500 employees were thus occupied. Fluid-milk production predominates, accounting for more than two-thirds of all employment and

FIGURE X.2

MEAT PRODUCTS (VALUE ADDED BY MANUFACTURE), BY STATE, 1958

in Millions of Dollars
100 and over
50 — 99
25 — 49
10 — 24
5 — 9
under 5

U.S. Department of Commerce, Bureau of the Census

value added by manufacturing in the dairy industry. Next in order, though considerably smaller, is the production of ice cream and frozen desserts. California, New York, Pennsylvania, Ohio, Wisconsin, Illinois, and Michigan are the main centers for dairy products as a whole.

About 40–54 per cent of all fluid milk is now produced by a centrally controlled system (a single operator controls the flow of milk through the various tanks, pipes, and other equipment by remote switches on a central panel). This percentage is expected to double within the next decade.

Canning and preserving establishments are usually located in the growing areas; they specialize in processing products raised in the vicinity of the plants. Large companies, concentrated mainly in California and Florida, produce a variety of products through ownership and operation of a number of establishments. Employment is characterized by sharp seasonal fluctuations, with a peak in harvest seasons. Canned fruit and vegetables have always been the most important branches, but they have to compete with a comparative newcomer—frozen fruit and vegetables, production of which has grown very rapidly from scratch: from $3.3 million value added in 1937 to $89 million in 1950, $324 million in 1958, and $429 million in 1962. Frozen concentrated milk and frozen bakery products are next in line.

The *bakery-products* industry accounts for many small plants: 2 out of

3 have fewer than 20 employees. Manufacture of bread and related products accounts for over 85 per cent of total employment and 80 per cent of the value added by manufacturing in this branch. Again, New York, California, Pennsylvania, Ohio, and Illinois are the main producing areas. Bakeries are of different types: wholesale bakeries, grocery-chain bakeries, home-service bakeries, and retail multi-outlet bakeries. Plants are distributed widely throughout the nation, but the most populous states lead.

In the manufacture of *grain-mill products*, prepared animal feeds account for about half of total employment and cost of materials but only about 40 per cent of the value added. Illinois, California, Iowa, and New York lead. Grain-mill products are centered in Kansas, Missouri, New York, Minnesota, Texas, and Illinois.

In the *beverage* industry, malt liquors and bottled and canned soft drinks combined account for eight-tenths of employment and seven-tenths of value added by manufacturing. The value added exceeds the cost of materials processed: $3.4 billion, as compared to slightly more than $3 billion. While production of nonalcoholic beverages is spread widely through nearly all states, production of malt liquors (ale, beer, etc.) is concentrated largely in New York, Wisconsin, New Jersey, Missouri, and California. Production of wine is centered in California, with New York in second place.

The *sugar* industry includes production and refining of both cane and beet sugar. Value added has been as follows: raw cane sugar, $22 million in 1958 and $31 million in 1962; refining of cane sugar, $185 million and $234 million, respectively; beet sugar, $130 million and $167 million, respectively.

In the *confectionary industry* (candy, chocolate, chewing gum, etc.), Illinois, New York, Pennsylvania, Massachusetts, and California are leading.

TABLE X.15

TOBACCO MANUFACTURE, BY TYPE OF PRODUCT,
1954, 1958, AND 1962
(Value Added in Millions of Dollars)

	1954	1958	1962
Cigarettes	677	1,059	1,248
Cigars	168	183	199
Chewing and smoking tobacco	80	86	76
Tobacco stemming and redrying	79	86	122
TOTAL	1,004	1,413	1,645

Tobacco manufacture comprises production of cigarettes, cigars, chewing and smoking tobacco, and also tobacco stemming and redrying. The cigarette industry towers over all other branches, accounting for more than three-fourths of total value added (see Table X.15).

FIGURE X.3.A

TOBACCO PRODUCTS (VALUE ADDED BY MANUFACTURE),
BY STATE: CIGARETTES

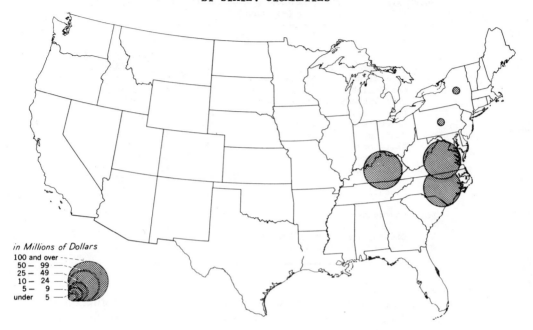

FIGURE X.3.B

TOBACCO PRODUCTS (VALUE ADDED BY MANUFACTURE),
BY STATE: CIGARS

U.S. Department of Commerce, Bureau of the Census

TABLE X.16

SHARE OF THE LARGEST COMPANIES IN THE VALUE OF
SHIPMENTS IN THE FOOD, BEVERAGE, AND TOBACCO INDUSTRIES, 1958
(Per Cent)

	4	8	20
	Largest	Companies	
Concentrated milk	50	60	73
Special dairy products	51	62	75
Cured fish	50	60	81
Cereal breakfast food	83	95	99+
Flour mixes	75	86	94
Biscuits and crackers	65	72	82
Cane-sugar refining	69	88	100
Beet sugar	64	94	100
Chocolate and cocoa products	71	84	98
Chewing gum	88	95	99+
Malt	50	70	95
Distilled liquor	60	77	94
Cigarettes	79	99+	100
Cigars	54	75	86
Chewing and smoking tobacco	57	82	98
Stemming and redrying tobacco	73	90	96

In cigarette production, North Carolina and Virginia are the chief producing states, accounting for some 60 and 20 per cent of the total, respectively; Kentucky is next. Pennsylvania and Florida rank first and second in the production of cigars, with respective shares of about 45 and 22 per cent (see Figures X.3A and X.3B). Because of the population growth in the smoking age groups, total output of tobacco is expected to continue to increase (according to the Bureau of Labor Statistics), despite the controversy over the health hazard of smoking.

Some branches of the food, beverage, and tobacco industries are highly concentrated, with a few companies dominating half or more than half of total production (see Table X.16).

TABLE X.17

TEXTILE-MILL AND APPAREL PRODUCTS IN THE UNITED STATES, 1962

	All Employees	Production Workers	Payroll	Wages	Value Added	Cost of Materials
	(In Thousands)		(In Millions of Dollars)			
Textile-mill products	878	785	3,353	2,718	6,098	9,198
Weaving mills	383	349	1,460	1,242	2,578	3,625
Knitting mills	221	197	767	607	1,326	1,783
Yarn-and-thread mills	104	96	358	303	638	1,277
Other textile goods	171	144	767	567	1,557	2,514
Apparel and related products	1,237	1,087	4,168	3,229	7,151	9,049
Men's and boys' clothing	422	379	1,347	1,120	2,161	2,739
Women's and misses' clothing	479	416	1,640	1,228	2,921	3,409
Millinery, hats, and caps	36	31	129	97	212	168
Children's outerwear	79	69	246	188	415	599
Miscellaneous apparel	222	192	805	595	1,442	2,134

61. *The Thread-and-Needle Industries*

The thread-and-needle industries comprise a great variety of products and processes: on the one hand, weaving and knitting of different fibers; textile finishing; yarn and thread; rugs and carpets; and miscellaneous other textile goods; and on the other, men's, women's, and children's apparel; fur goods; and miscellaneous fabricated textiles. In 1962, these industries employed more than 2.1 million persons, or 12.5 per cent of all employees in U.S. manufacturing plants; the value added by their work amounted to nearly $13.3 billion (see Table X.17).

TABLE X.18

EMPLOYMENT IN THREAD-AND-NEEDLE INDUSTRIES,
1958 AND 1962
(Per Cent of Total Employment)

	Textile Mills		Apparel and Related Plants	
	1958	1962	1958	1962
New England	8.9	7.3	6.3	6.3
Massachusetts	7.8	6.2	8.8	8.3
Rhode Island	24.6	20.6	3.7	3.6
Middle Atlantic	4.1	3.7	14.0	11.5
New York	3.1	3.1	17.9	17.3
New Jersey	4.2	3.4	9.5	9.0
Pennsylvania	5.5	5.0	11.3	12.3
South Atlantic	25.3	21.1	8.0	9.1
Virginia	13.5	12.3	8.3	9.3
North Carolina	45.9	43.0	6.4	7.9
South Carolina	56.8	51.1	10.9	13.2
Georgia	30.2	29.3	12.5	13.8
East South Central	9.8	9.0	13.0	13.5
Kentucky	1.6	1.5	11.0	11.9
Tennessee	10.5	9.7	13.5	15.6
Alabama	17.2	15.7	9.6	12.6
Mississippi	...	...	22.0	21.3
UNITED STATES	5.6	5.2	7.4	7.4

The ratio of employment in these industries to total employment was higher than the national average in New England and the Middle Atlantic States, and particularly in the South Atlantic region. In some of these states, textile mills provide more employment than any other branch of manufacturing; in others, the apparel industry is a substantial job producer (see Table X.18).

Both groups of thread-and-needle industries, but especially textile mills, are concentrated geographically. The Carolinas and Georgia account for more than half the total employment in textile-mill production and nearly half its value added. In South Carolina, textile mills provide the lion's

TABLE X.19

EMPLOYMENT IN TEXTILES AND
APPAREL INDUSTRY, BY STATE, 1962
(In Thousands)

	Total	Textiles	Apparel
New York	388	59	329
North Carolina	259	219	40
Pennsylvania	243	70	173
South Carolina	163	129	34
Georgia	141	96	45
Massachusetts	105	45	60
New Jersey	100	28	72
Tennessee	80	31	49
Alabama	67	37	30
California	65	7	58
Virginia	64	36	26
Other states	440	121	319
UNITED STATES	2,115	878	1,237

share of all employment in manufactures. New York, New Jersey, and Pennsylvania account for a little less than half the total employment in the apparel industry and for more than half the total value added.

The states listed in Table X.19 account for eight-tenths of employment in the textile and apparel industries combined.

Within the group of textile-mill products, the two most important branches are the weaving and knitting mills, in terms both of employment they provide and of value added by manufacturing. According to the last census, they engaged about 224,000 and 221,000 employees, respectively, and value added amounted to $1.3 million in each case. Figures X.4A and X.4B show the geographic distribution of value added for mills weaving cotton and synthetic fibers.

Despite the advances made by synthetic and mixed fabrics and the resulting decline in use of cotton, cotton still is king of the textile industry, far outdistancing the combined production of all other fabrics, except in the production of tire cord and fabrics. There man-made fibers have pushed out cotton almost completely in the short span of less than 2 decades (see Table X.20).

In the apparel industry, the so-called cutting-up and needle trades establishments are generally divided into 3 distinct types: regular factories, or "manufacturers"; apparel "jobbers"; and contract factories, or "contractors." The first purchase the fabrics, employ workers in their own plants, and produce and sell the final product. The jobbers buy the fabrics and other materials, prepare designs and samples, and arrange for manufacturing and selling the garments. Many jobbers cut the fabrics in their own plants, but cutting, sewing, and otherwise handling of fabrics is mostly done by the apparel contractor. Some establishments are mixed—that is,

FIGURE X.4.A

BROAD-WOVEN FABRICS (VALUE ADDED BY MANUFACTURE),
BY STATE: COTTON, 1958

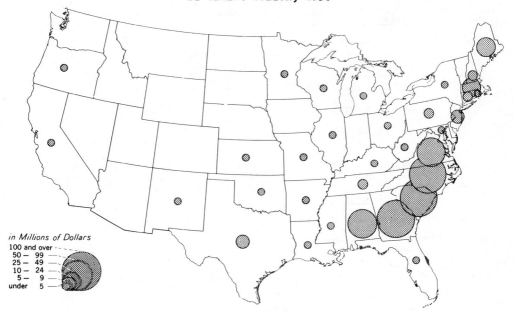

FIGURE X.4.B

BROAD-WOVEN FABRICS (VALUE ADDED BY MANUFACTURE),
BY STATE: MAN-MADE FIBER AND SILK, 1958

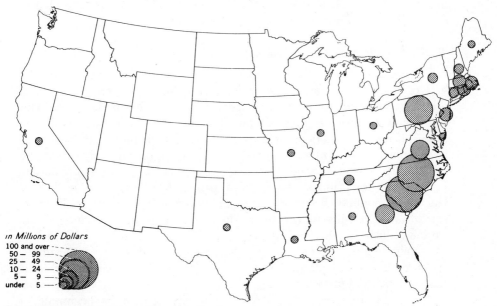

U.S. Department of Commerce, Bureau of the Census

TABLE X.20

COMPETITION OF COTTON AND MAN-MADE FIBERS
IN TEXTILE INDUSTRY, 1947-64[a]

Item	1947	1955	1960	1963	1964[c]
Broad-woven fabrics	12,371	13,119	12,056	12,104	12,630
Cotton woven goods[b]	9,817	10,175	9,366	8,759	8,855
Rayon and acetate	1,977	1,928	1,434	1,726	2,078
Woolen and worsted	516	318	286	284	260
Silk, nylon, glass, and other	62	699	970	1,335	1,435
Bleached, dyed, or printed goods	8,915	10,502	9,559	9,907	...
Cotton	6,944	8,144	7,440	7,546	...
Man-made fiber fabrics and silk	1,971	2,358	2,119	2,361	...
Tire cord and fabrics	565.3	524.4	417.4	424.2	468.9
Man-made fibers	214.6	456.1	387.4	411.3	458.6
Cotton	350.7	68.3	30.0	12.9	10.4

[a]Broad-woven fabrics and bleached, dyed, and printed goods in millions of linear yards; tire cord and fabrics in millions of pounds.
[b]Except tire fabrics.
[c]Preliminary.

they perform 2 of these operations, acting as both manufacturers and jobbers, or manufacturers and contractors.

Among the apparel and related products, the 2 outstanding industries are producers of women's and misses' outerwear (367,000 employees; $2.3 billion value added) and men's and boys' furnishings (298,000 employees; $1.4 billion value added).

Because of frequent changes in style, the apparel industry is expected to remain highly labor-intensive. Only minor modifications are expected to occur in the prevailing manufacturing system.

62. Chemicals and Allied Products

The group of chemicals and allied products includes a great number of heterogeneous industries, some of which produce basic chemicals while others manufacture products by predominantly chemical processes. This broad group is usually divided into 3 branches: (1) basic chemicals—acids, alkalies, salts, organic chemicals, etc.; (2) chemical products used in manufacture of synthetic fibers, plastics, dry colors, and pigments; and (3) finished chemical products—drugs, cosmetics, soaps, and products to be used in other industries, such as paints, fertilizers, and explosives. Chemical products are used for many different purposes: fertilizers in agriculture, dyestuffs in the textile industry, drugs in medicine, oils in various industries, etc. Some of the chemical branches are very old, such as the production of soap or candles; others are of recent origin—for example, synthetic fibers and plastics. Even the old branches, however, are using new methods and processes.

It is interesting that the chemical industry, even at its beginning, in

TABLE X.21

DEVELOPMENT OF THE CHEMICAL INDUSTRY, 1899-1963

Year	Establish- ments	All Employees (In Thousands)	Production Workers	Payroll	Wages	Value Added
				(In Millions of Dollars)		
1899	7,669	170	144	80	51	212
1909	10,280	235	185	144	82	401
1919	10,688	388	293	497	306	1,198
1929	9,327	382	307	550	352	1,737
1939	8,839	...	276	...	342	1,819
1949	10,019	626	440	2,092	1,319	5,848
1954	11,074	734	499	3,377	1,994	9,547
1958	11,309	699	476	4,091	2,339	12,645
1963	...	747	480	5,022	2,805	17,501

1899, when it was concerned mostly with the manufacture of candles, employed a relatively large number: 170,000 persons, as compared to some 747,000 in 1963; in contrast, the value added by manufacturing has in-

TABLE X.22

EMPLOYMENT IN THE CHEMICAL INDUSTRY,
BY GEOGRAPHIC DIVISION AND SELECTED STATES, 1962

	All Employees	Production Workers
New England	30,544	19,615
Middle Atlantic	191,554	118,785
New York	63,395	40,492
New Jersey	81,576	49,357
Pennsylvania	46,583	28,936
East North Central	155,580	96,137
Ohio	43,890	26,444
Illinois	46,983	28,056
Michigan	35,503	24,407
West North Central	36,296	23,229
South Atlantic	135,280	96,506
Virginia	33,662	24,616
West Virginia	21,546	15,928
North Carolina	13,622	9,449
South Carolina	17,438	10,856
Georgia	10,218	7,295
Florida	18,473	13,719
East South Central	62,750	42,309
West South Central	61,050	41,377
Mountain	7,392	4,467
Pacific	46,740	27,995
California	34,753	20,915
UNITED STATES	727,452[a]	469,995[a]

[a]Includes data not distributed by regions.

TABLE X.23

CHEMICAL INDUSTRY IN THE UNITED STATES, BY TYPE OF PRODUCT, 1963

	All Employees	Production Workers	Payroll	Wages	Value Added
	(In Thousands)		(In Millions of Dollars)		
Basic chemicals	238	156	1,766	1,055	6,054
Fibers, plastics, rubbers	148	104	992	614	2,980
Drugs	101	56	687	301	2,813
Cleaning and toilet goods	87	54	531	277	2,794
Paints and varnishes	62	34	403	183	1,055
Gum and wood chemicals	7	5	33	23	99
Agricultural chemicals	43	30	211	128	616
Other chemical products	63	42	400	224	1,089
TOTAL	747	480	5,022	2,805	17,501

creased 80 times during this period: $212 million in 1899, and $17.5 billion in 1963 (see Table X.21). Another way to characterize the great upsurge of the chemical industry in recent decades is by the growth of expenditures in new plant and equipment: from $376 million in 1945 to $1 billion in 1955, $2 billion in 1964, and $2.5 billion in 1965.

The chemical industry is a multibillion-dollar sector of U.S. manufactures: its payroll exceeded $5 billion and the value of its shipments approached $32 billion in 1963. Three geographic divisions—Middle Atlantic, East North Central, and South Atlantic—accounted for two-thirds of total employment in the industry, with New York, Newark, Philadelphia, and Chicago the most important centers of chemical production in this country (see Table X.22).

The industry's main subgroups—basic chemicals (industrial organic and inorganic); fibers, plastics, rubber; and drugs—together account for two-thirds of its employment and value added by manufacturing (see Table X.23). As in many other industries, production is located predominantly in the East and South (see Table X.24 and, for distribution by geographic division, Figures X.5A and X.5B).

The chemical industry is one of the most highly concentrated branches in manufactures. Its 4 largest companies dominate from 50 to 75 per cent of the production of many essential chemicals, and 80 per cent and more of the production of explosives and ammunition. The eight largest companies control the production of industrial oils, synthetic fibers, and acids almost completely (see Table X.25).

Except for the petroleum and coal industries, which themselves are largely chemical industries, the ratio of specialists and scientists to production workers in the chemical group is higher than in any other manufacturing industry. The number of engineers and scientists is close to

FIGURE X.5.A

CHEMICALS (VALUE ADDED BY MANUFACTURE),
BY STATE: INDUSTRIAL INORGANIC AND ORGANIC CHEMICALS, 1958

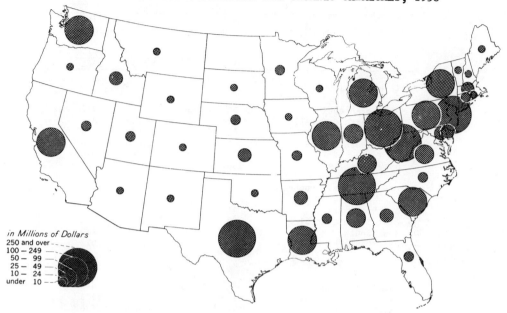

in Millions of Dollars
250 and over
100 — 249
50 — 99
25 — 49
10 — 24
under 10

FIGURE X.5.B

CHEMICALS (VALUE ADDED BY MANUFACTURE),
BY STATE: DRUGS, 1958

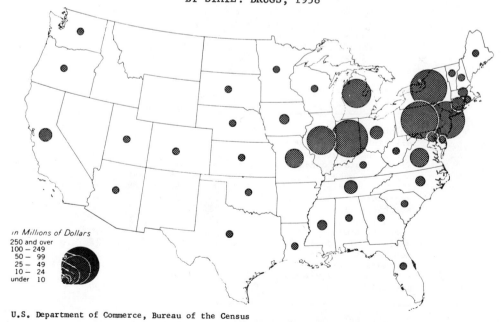

in Millions of Dollars
250 and over
100 — 249
50 — 99
25 — 49
10 — 24
under 10

U.S. Department of Commerce, Bureau of the Census

TABLE X.24

MAIN SUBGROUPS OF CHEMICAL INDUSTRY, BY EMPLOYMENT,
VALUE ADDED, AND LOCATION, 1958 AND 1962

	Employees (In Thousands)		Value Added by Manufacturing (In Millions of Dollars)	
	1958	1962	1958	1962
Basic chemicals				
Middle Atlantic	52	50	797	972
East North Central	43	43	658	841
South Atlantic	41	38	688	1,014
West South Central	39	41	1,029	1,436
Texas	25	27	748	1,070
UNITED STATES	238	235	4,260	5,673
Fibers, plastics, rubber				
South Atlantic	46	54	712	1,078
East South Central	23	23	329	462
West South Central	6	8	162	236
UNITED STATES	122	136	1,900	2,627
Drugs				
Middle Atlantic	44	46	1,096	1,475
East North Central	32	34	654	733
UNITED STATES	96	106	2,096	2,636

TABLE X.25

SHARE OF THE LARGEST COMPANIES IN THE VALUE OF
SHIPMENTS IN THE CHEMICAL INDUSTRY, 1958
(Per Cent)

	4	8	20	50
	Largest Companies			
Sulphuric acid	79	93	...	100
Alkalies and chlorine	64	89	100	0
Cyclic crudes (coal tar)	93	99	100	0
Intermediates, organic colors	54	72	89	98
Synthetic rubber	60	86	100	0
Plastic materials	40	56	79	92
Inorganic chemicals n.e.c.[a]	34	51	76	91
Synthetic fibers	78	96	100	0
Explosives	77	89	98	100
Organic chemicals	55	70	85	96
Biological products	44	59	84	97
Medical chemicals	64	77	89	98
Hardwood distillates	75	87	96	100
Softwood distillates	89	96	99	99+
Gum naval stores	52	77	99+	100

[a]N.e.c.: not elsewhere classified.

100,000, or almost 1 per 7 employees. The importance of research in the chemical industry can hardly be exaggerated; in the full sense of the term, research is its lifeblood. Capital investment per worker is the highest among manufacturing industries, with the same exception of the petroleum and coal industry. In 1963, new capital expenditures in the chemical industry amounted to nearly $2,000 per employee (cf. Sec. 96).

63. *The Metal Industries*

The U.S. Census of Manufactures divides the metal industries into two broad groups—primary products and fabricated products. Together, they employed more than 2.2 million persons in 1963, almost 13 per cent. of total manufacturing employment in this country; they added almost $27 billion to the cost of materials processed.

The establishments in the first group are engaged in smelting and refining ferrous and nonferrous metals from ore, pig, or scrap; in drawing and alloying metals of both types; manufacture of castings and forgings, nails, spikes, insulated wire, etc. The group of industries fabricating metal products covers a very wide variety of items ranging from pins and screws to structural steel for buildings and bridges, boilers and heating equipment (except electrical).

In individual states, the combined metal industries account for a high percentage of the state's manufacturing employment: 18 per cent in Michigan and Illinois and 22–26 per cent in Ohio, Alabama, Pennsylvania, and West Virginia, as compared to 13 per cent in the nation as a whole.

In 1963, 1.1 million persons were employed in the primary-metal industries; of these 7 out of 10 were engaged in various sections of iron and steel manufacturing; the others worked in nonferrous-metal mills (see Appendix Table XXV).

The iron and steel industry in the United States comprises over 275 companies, with plants located in 300 communities in 35 states. About

TABLE X.26

OUTPUT OF PIG IRON BY STATE, 1945-64
(In Millions of Short Tons)

	1945	1950	1955	1960	1963	1964
Pennsylvania	16.2	18.2	20.8	16.5	17.3	21.0
Ohio	11.3	12.5	15.4	11.8	12.8	15.4
Indiana	6.0	7.0	8.7	8.4	9.9	11.5
Michigan, Minnesota	1.9	2.8	4.0	5.0	6.5	7.4
Maryland, West Virginia[a]	4.3	6.7	7.8	8.0	8.7	10.6
New York	3.3	4.3	5.1	4.2	4.3	5.1
Illinois	5.0	6.0	6.5	5.3	4.5	5.6
Colorado, Utah, California	1.6	2.7	3.6	3.7	4.0	4.7
Alabama	3.6	4.3	4.9	3.5	3.9	4.4
PIG IRON, TOTAL	53.2	64.6	76.9	66.5	71.8	85.7

[a]Includes the small output of Kentucky, Tennessee, and Texas.

TABLE X.27

PRODUCTION OF STEEL AS PER CENT OF
INDUSTRY'S CAPACITY, 1930-60

	Capacity (In Millions of Short Tons)	Production (Per Cent of Capacity)
1930	71.0	57.3
1935	78.5	43.4
1940	81.6	73.3
1945	95.5	74.6
1950	100.0	86.5
1955	125.8	83.1
1960[a]	148.6	66.8

[a]Data on the industry's capacity after 1960 are not available.

a third of these companies make the raw steel required to produce their finished products. Most of the other companies are engaged in further rolling and drawing semifinished steel obtained from steel-ingot producers. Others produce pig iron (see also Sec. 54).

Blast furnaces are the backbone of the iron and steel industry, with half a million employees and half the total value added by manufacturing: $6.1 billion out of $11.7 billion in 1958; $6.6 billion out of $13.7 billion in 1962. Their capacity doubled between 1913 and 1960, rising from 48.4 million sh. t. to 96.5 million. Pennsylvania is the ranking producer of pig iron, followed by Ohio and Indiana (see Table X.26; cf. Figures IX.10A and IX.10B).

The capacity of steel mills more than tripled from the eve of World War I to 1960, rising from 42.7 million sh. t. to 148.6 million, but their production rarely approaches the upper limit of capacity (see Table X.27; cf. Figures IX.9 and IX.11).

Ownership and production are highly concentrated in the iron-and-steel industry; it is integrated both vertically and horizontally. Some giant corporations control production from beginning to end, owning and working the ore deposits and coal fields and operating the blast furnaces, steel mills, and factories that manufacture various steel products—even ships, bridges, and other large structures.

Large establishments are more dominant in some branches of the primary-metal industries than in others. Thus, of the 291 blast furnaces and steel mills, only 61, or about a fifth, employed fewer than 100 persons in 1958, and each of about as many establishments (62) employed 2,500 persons or more. In the primary-aluminum industry, 10 out of the existing 20 establishments had 500 employees or more, and the next 6 had 1,000–2,499 persons on the payroll; only 4 plants had fewer employees than 500. On the other hand, of the 955 establishments producing aluminum cast-

TABLE X.28

FABRICATED METAL PRODUCTS INDUSTRIES,
BY SIZE OF ESTABLISHMENT, 1958

	Establish-ments	All Employees (In Thousands)	Payroll	Value Added
			(In Millions of Dollars)	
Establishments with				
1- 4 employees	7,941	16.4	64	146
5- 9	4,177	28.2	124	225
10- 19	4,352	60.1	281	483
20- 49	4,246	131.7	640	1,084
50- 99	1,892	130.5	646	1,128
100- 249	1,375	213.5	1,085	1,895
250- 499	480	164.9	865	1,536
500- 999	231	156.6	849	1,523
1,000-2,499	74	97.9	537	919
2,500	14	58.2	323	474
TOTAL	24,782	1,058.0	5,412	9,412

ings, 329, or nearly one-third, employed only 1–4 persons and another third, 5–19 persons. Only 6 establishments had 500–999 employees, and only 1 plant reported a greater number.

In general, employment is more concentrated in the manufacture of nonferrous metals than in the iron and steel industry. In 1958, the 8 largest companies accounted for 99 per cent of the employment in the production of primary copper, 91 per cent in that of zinc, and all production of lead and aluminum.

TABLE X.29

SHARE OF THE LARGEST COMPANIES IN THE VALUE
OF SHIPMENTS IN THE FABRICATED-METAL
PRODUCTS INDUSTRY, 1958
(Per Cent)

	4	8	20	50
	Largest Companies			
Metal cans	80	89	97	99
Cutlery	54	64	77	91
Hand saws, saw blades	43	61	85	97
Metal plumbing fixtures	53	70	90	97
Safes and vaults	87	92	99	100
Collapsible tubes	53	85	100	-
Nonelectric heating equipment	17	26	42	60
Fabricated structural steel	22	26	34	46
Metal doors, sash and trim	8	13	23	38
Boiler shop products	29	38	50	64
Sheet-metal work	12	16	24	34
Screw-machine products	7	10	18	29
Bolts, nuts, washers, rivets	17	28	46	66
Metal stampings	13	18	28	42
Valves and pipe fittings	17	26	43	62
Fabricated pipe and fittings	19	30	49	70

TABLE X.30

INDUSTRIES OF FABRICATED-METAL PRODUCTS, BY STATE, 1962

	All Employees (In Thousands)	Value Added (In Millions of Dollars)
Illinois	123.7	1,304.0
Ohio	114.3	1,260.8
California	90.2	1,037.6
Pennsylvania	106.5	1,029.5
Michigan	85.2	916.7
New York	87.3	804.5
New Jersey	56.9	648.9
Indiana	41.5	402.7
Wisconsin	36.0	360.8
Missouri	24.3	240.6
Texas	30.3	269.2
Other	288.3	2,843.4
UNITED STATES	1,084.5	11,118.7

In 1963, the group of industries of fabricated metal products employed 1.1 million persons, paid over $6.4 billion in salaries and wages, and added value of $11.9 billion. Production is dispersed among thousands of small workshops employing, on the average, about 2 persons (7,941 shops with 16,411 employees in 1958). Only 319 establishments of the total 24,782 had each 500 persons or more on its payroll; they represented 1.3 per cent of all establishments, 30 per cent of all employees, and 31 per cent of total value added (see Table X.28).

With production of fabricated metal products spread throughout the country, there is less financial concentration than in the primary-metal industries. The 4 largest companies account for more than 50 per cent of production in only a few subgroups; in many branches, even the 50 largest companies produce less than half the value of the total output (see Table X.29).

The Middle Atlantic, East North Central, and Pacific states are the main centers of production. Illinois, Ohio, California, and Pennsylvania lead in these industries, followed by Michigan, New York, and New Jersey (see Table X.30).

64. The Machinery Industries

The Bureau of the Census divides production of machinery into 2 major groups—machinery except electrical, and electrical machinery. Together, they encompass the whole range of machinery produced in this country. The first group produces general industrial machinery, farm machinery and equipment, metal-working machinery, construction equipment, office and service machines, and machinery for individual industries, such as textile and woodworking machinery. Frequently, machinery is very complex and is produced to individual specifications, or as standard equipment. This group also produces parts, attachments, and accessories; in some cases, these items constitute a substantial part of an establishment's production. Though producers of parts are generally small enterprises, some larger plants are also producing such items. Often such establishments maintain machine shops, die-and-tool rooms, and even operate pattern shops, as well as other shops for metal processing, such as electroplating, plate fabrication, galvanizing, and the like.

Production of electrical machinery comprises primarily equipment and machinery for generation, storage, transmission, and utilization of electric energy, but also includes lighting and wiring devices, and goods for household consumption (ranges, water heaters, refrigerators and freezers, laundry equipment, radio and television sets, electric industrial apparatus, and electronic components). Some plants in this group produce electronic components, while others assemble components produced elsewhere; there are also establishments that both produce such components and assemble them as finished products.

In 1963, all machinery industries together employed about 2.9 million persons, and the value they added by manufacturing exceeded $33 billion (see Table X.31).

The East North Central and Middle Atlantic states are the backbone of this country's machinery industries, with Illinois, Ohio, and New York in the forefront. Together, these 2 geographic divisions accounted in

TABLE X.31

EMPLOYMENT AND VALUE ADDED BY MANUFACTURING
IN THE MACHINERY INDUSTRIES, 1958 AND 1963

Industry Group and Industry	Employees (In Thousands)		Payroll (In Millions of Dollars)		Value Added	
	1958	1963	1958	1963	1958	1963
Machinery, except electrical	1,348	1,463	7,305	9,581	12,393	16,897
Engines and turbines	96	85	552	600	1,068	1,078
Farm machinery and equipment	109	119	551	716	1,088	1,369
Construction and like equipment	200	212	1,073	1,380	2,055	2,667
Metal-working machinery	234	258	1,380	1,818	2,058	3,027
Special industry machinery	162	171	854	1,086	1,340	1,902
General industrial machinery	211	232	1,143	1,526	1,935	2,749
Office machines n.e.c.	122	141	667	1,005	971	1,417
Service industry machines	100	112	509	668	918	1,368
Miscellaneous machinery	116	133	575	781	960	1,322
Electrical machinery	1,122	1,472	5,606	8,850	10,395	16,333
Electric distribution products	134	140	724	880	1,339	1,627
Electric industrial apparatus	156	161	819	998	1,448	1,848
Household appliances	143	145	732	855	1,549	2,052
Lighting and wiring devices	123	142	564	756	1,177	1,637
Radio and TV receiving equipment	74	96	326	466	687	1,049
Communication equipment	215	414	1,204	2,870	2,038	4,556
Electronic components	198	283	854	1,497	1,434	2,459
Electrical products n.e.c.	78	91	383	526	724	1,105

TABLE X.32

SHARE OF THE LARGEST COMPANIES IN THE
VALUE OF SHIPMENTS IN THE MACHINERY INDUSTRIES, 1958
(Per Cent)

	4	8	20	50
	Largest Companies			
Steam engines and turbines	83	96	100	-
Internal-combustion engines	41	51	88	99
Computing machinery	75	83	93	99
Tractors	79	81	97	99
Electrical transformers	67	81	91	97
Telephone and telegraph equipment	92	97	99+	100
Sewing machines	90	94	97	99
Electric lamps (bulbs)	87	93	99	100
Vacuum cleaners	71	85	98	100
Phonograph records	64	77	88	98
Domestic laundry equipment	58	85	99	-

1962 for nearly two-thirds of the value added by all machinery-producing establishments. The combined share of New England and the Pacific divisions slightly exceeded one-fifth, with California alone accounting for almost as much as all the New England states (see Appendix Table XXVI).

Since production of heavy machinery and heavy equipment requires considerable capital, it is often in the hands of large companies. Production of many household appliances also is nearly monopolized by 32 large producers (see Table X.32).

Nevertheless, many machinery industries offer considerable opportunity for small enterprises, to judge by the substantial percentage of plants employing only 1–4 persons each in such fields as the production of metal-cutting machine tools and the manufacture of industrial patterns

TABLE X.33

MANUFACTURERS' SALES AND RETAIL VALUE
OF HOME APPLIANCES, 1950-64

Type of Appliance	Manufacturers' Sales of Electric Home Appliances (In Thousands of Units)			Retail Value (In Millions of Dollars)		
	1950	1960	1964	1950	1960	1964
Home laundry	4,591	4,775	6,089	855	1,148	1,320
Other major appliances	15,848	12,526	15,893	2,557	2,665	2,876
Electric housewares	32,234	43,652	65,105	733	949	1,221
Heating and cooling	4,581	7,857	10,002[a]	164	671	742[a]
Consumer electronics	17,313	20,926	25,689	2,669	2,191	3,028
Other appliances[b]	1,080	3,800	4,100	100	352	490
Lamp bulbs and tubes[c]	2,007	2,921	3,375	466	1,110	1,296

[a]1963.
[b]Incomplete.
[c]Millions of units.

and molds, food-producing machinery, or metal-working machinery attachments.

Considered as a whole, production of machinery is a multibillion-dollar industry; in 1963, the value of its shipments amounted to about $59 billion, divided nearly equally between nonelectrical and electrical products. Manufacturers' sales of electric, gas, and other home appliances (washing machines, dryers, refrigerators, freezers, dishwashers, water heaters, ranges, air conditioners, dehumidifiers, television sets, and hundreds of other items—in all, more than 119 million units in 1962 and 127 million in 1964) totaled almost $9 billion in retail value in 1962 and $11 billion in 1964 (see Table X.33).

65. *The Transportation-Equipment Industries*

This group of industries produces equipment for transportation of passengers and cargo by land, air, and water. It is dominated by the production of motor vehicles and parts and of aircraft, which together accounted for $20.6 billion out of this group's total value added of $22.7 billion in 1963—91 per cent of the total. The industry as a whole had about the same number of employees in 1963 as in 1958: 1,618,000 as compared to 1,558,000; but the value added by manufacturing increased over these 5 years from $15.3 billion to $22.7 billion, partly because of changes in the value of the dollar but mostly because of the greater productivity that resulted from technological innovations and increase in the available power per worker (see Table X.34).

Production of motor vehicles accounts for a much greater value added than that in the aircraft industry—$12.7 billion and $7.9 billion, respectively, in 1963. The composition and strength of their labor force differs in 2 respects: the aircraft industry has about as many employees as the

TABLE X.34

THE TRANSPORTATION-EQUIPMENT INDUSTRY,
1958 AND 1963

Industry	Employees (In Thousands)		Payroll (In Millions of Dollars)		Value Added	
	1958	1963	1958	1963	1958	1963
Motor vehicles and equipment	577	697	3,318	5,218	6,751	12,687
Aircraft and parts	765	691	4,720	5,371	6,924	7,929
Ships and boats	145	141	774	903	1,072	1,195
Railroad equipment	40	45	222	300	320	525
Motorcycles, bicycles, and parts	8	9	33	47	52	80
Transportation equipment n.e.c.	23	35	98	168	166	304
TOTAL	1,558	1,618	9,165	12,009	15,285	22,720

motor-vehicle industry but fewer among the aircraft employees are production workers. In 1963, 691,000 employees were engaged in aircraft production, as compared with 697,000 in making motor vehicles; corresponding figures for blue-collar workers among them were 386,000 and 573,000. Thus some 55 out of every 100 employees in the aircraft industry were production workers, as compared with 82 in the industry of motor vehicles.

About 95 per cent of the employment engaged in the production of motor vehicles and 97 per cent of the value added originated in the establishments producing passenger cars; the remaining small percentage related to the production of truck and bus bodies and truck trailers. Production of ships and boats, railroad equipment, motorcycles, etc., represents a small sector of the transportation-equipment industry.

Shipbuilding per se has experienced only 2 booms during this century, in both world wars, when it expanded tremendously. Between 1942 and 1946, the American shipyards built almost 5,000 ships, with 37 million gross registered tons. Many of them were lost during the hostilities, many sold afterward, some are still kept in mothballs. While other maritime nations whose fleets had been destroyed in war considered it among their first tasks to rehabilitate their merchant tonnage, the United States did not feel that need and, as a result, now finds itself with a good part of its merchant fleet overaged (see Sec. 73).

The entire merchant fleet, except 6 ships, has been built in domestic shipyards, which receive a construction subsidy for vessels to be used in foreign commerce, so as to enable American shipowners to construct vessels on a parity cost with their foreign competitors. The amount paid in 1963 was $92 million.

The transportation-equipment industry is perhaps the most heavily concentrated industry in the United States, both territorially and in organization. The East North Central states, Michigan in particular, are the home of motor-vehicle production; in the West, California and Washington specialize in aircraft production (see Figures X.6A and B). With a few exceptions, such as truck and bus bodies, trailers, ships, and boats, the 4 largest companies have the lion's share in both employment and value added (see Table X.35).

Nevertheless, many small plants share in the production of transportation equipment, especially in making parts and accessories. In 1958, one-third of all establishments in this group of industries had 1–4 employees, and almost as many had 5–19; only 7 per cent of all plants employed 500 persons or more. The largest establishments of all, each with 2,500 or more employees, represented 2 per cent of all plants but accounted for two-thirds of total employment and 60 per cent of total value added (see Table X.36).

FIGURE X.6.A

PRODUCTION OF MOTOR VEHICLES AND EQUIPMENT
(VALUE ADDED BY MANUFACTURE), BY STATE, 1958

FIGURE X.6.B

PRODUCTION OF AIRCRAFT AND PARTS
(VALUE ADDED BY MANUFACTURE), BY STATE, 1958

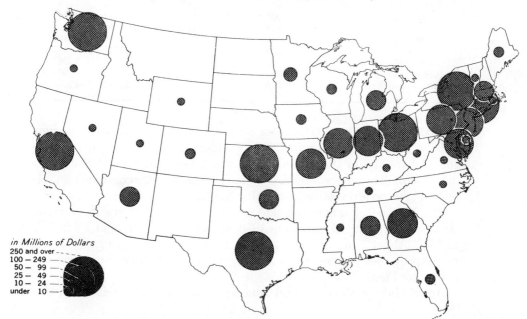

U.S. Department of Commerce, Bureau of the Census

TABLE X.35

SHARE OF THE LARGEST COMPANIES IN THE VALUE OF SHIPMENTS
IN THE TRANSPORTATION EQUIPMENT INDUSTRIES, 1958
(Per Cent)

	Employment				Value of Shipments			
	4	8	20	50	4	8	20	50
	Largest Companies				Largest Companies			
Motor vehicles and parts	70	74	85	91	99a	b	100a	-
Aircraft	58	82	99	99+	62	83	96	99
Aircraft engines	48	69	89	97	56	74	89	96
Aircraft propellers	97	99+	100	-	48	64	79	92
Shipbuilding and repairing	45	64	79	90	48	66	80	91
Locomotives and parts	93	98	99+	100	92	97	99	99+
Railroad and street cars	60	81	96	99+	54	73	91	99
Motorcycles and bicycles	57	79	96	100	52	75	95	99

aPassenger cars; value of shipments for motor vehicles contains a substantial
and unmeasurable amount of duplication.
bData withheld to avoid disclosing figures for individual companies.

TABLE X.36

PRODUCTION OF MOTOR VEHICLES BY
EMPLOYEE-SIZE OF ESTABLISHMENTS, 1958

	Number of Estab- lishments	All Employees (In Thousands)	Payroll	Value Added
			(In Millions of Dollars)	
ALL ESTABLISHMENTS				
With employees:	6,607	1,558	9,165	15,284
1- 4	2,099	4	16	33
5- 9	923	6	26	47
10- 19	923	13	58	97
20- 49	1,001	31	151	253
50- 99	528	37	180	297
100- 249	450	71	359	595
250- 499	225	78	419	651
500- 999	156	113	632	1,063
1,000-2,499	168	270	1,588	3,003
2,500 and over	134	935	5,735	9,244

Production of motor vehicles of all types increased spectacularly, from
4,192 in 1900 to 2.2 million in 1920; 4.5 million in 1940; 9.3 million in 1964
and 11.1 million in 1965. Throughout this period, the United States produced some 230 million vehicles—some 189 million passenger cars and 41
million commerical vehicles (see Table X.37).

The lifetime of motor vehicles is limited, and every year millions of
them are scrapped: 3.2 million in 1950, 4.8 million in 1960, and 5.9 million
in 1963. About 9 out of 10 scrapped vehicles are passenger cars. The rate
of scrappage for passenger cars is rising more rapidly than for trucks and
buses (see Figure X.7).

Automobile production is an American industry par excellence. In no

TABLE X.37

FACTORY SALES OF MOTOR VEHICLES, 1900-65

	Factory Sales (In Thousands)		Wholesale Value[a] (In Millions of Dollars)	
	Passenger Cars	Trucks and Buses	Passenger Cars	Trucks and Buses
1900	4	-	5	-
1910	181	6	215	10
1920	1,906	322	1,809	423
1930	2,787	575	1,644	391
1935	3,275	697	1,708	381
1940	3,717	755	2,371	569
1945	70	656	57	1,182
1950	6,666	1,337	8,468	1,708
1955	7,920	1,249	12,453	2,021
1960	6,675	1,194	12,164	2,156
1963	7,638	1,462	14,427	3,076
1964	7,752	1,540	14,837	3,224
1965[b]	9,306	1,752	18,400	3,900

[a]The value of bodies for a substantial number of trucks and buses not included. Value based on vehicles with standard equipment. Excludes federal excise taxes.

[b] Preliminary.

other country does the automobile play so decisive a role in everyday life or does the automobile industry exert such an outstanding role in the national economy as in the United States (see Sec. 41). This industry is the chief single consumer of steel, rubber, plate glass, and many other products; 44 per cent of U.S. produced radio sets in 1963 were auto sets.

FIGURE X.7

ANNUAL MOTOR VEHICLE SCRAPPAGE, 1935-63

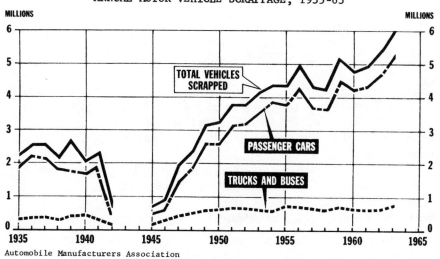

Automobile Manufacturers Association

TABLE X.38

WORLD PRODUCTION OF MOTOR VEHICLES, 1938-65
(In Thousands)

Country	1938	1950	1955	1960	1963	1964	1965
United States	2,509	8,004	9,069	7,869	9,101	9,308	11,137
Canada	166	391	454	397	633	671	·855
France	215	356	725	1,349	1,707	1,616	1,616
West Germany	...	301	907	1,055	2,668	2,910	2,976
Italy	71	128	269	645	1,181	1,090	1,134
Sweden	7	18	50	129	168	184	...
United Kingdom	545	783	1,237	1,811	2,012	2,342	...
U.S.S.R.	211	404	508	640	587	603	...
Japan	25	32	155	760	1,284	1,702	1,876

TABLE X.39

AIRCRAFT PRODUCTION AND SALES, 1929-63

Year	Aircraft Production		Sales[a]	Backlog[b]
	Total	Civil	(In Millions of Dollars)	
1929	6,193	5,516	91	...
1939	5,856	3,661	248	...
1940	12,813	6,785	370	...
1942	47,675	-	5,817	...
1944	95,272	-	16,047	...
1948	9,838	7,302	1,061	2,983
1952	10,640	3,509	6,495	17,653
1956	12,408	7,205	9,496	18,350
1960	10,237	8,181	10,997	15,452
1963	9,655	8,155	16,408	13,894

[a]1929-48: Value of products.
[b]December 31.

While this country still produces almost as many motor vehicles as the rest of the world taken as a unit, its share in the world production has been declining, as this industry expands in other countries (see Table X.38).

Like shipbuilding, the aircraft industry responded vigorously to war needs. In 1914, it produced 49 planes; in 1918, 14,020; similarly, it produced 5,856 planes in 1939; 95,272 in 1944. In the 8-year span 1940–47, it turned out 370,000 aircraft, averaging 46,000 a year and reaching peak production in 1944 (see Table X.39).

Of aircraft in operation on world civil airlines in 1958, 83 per cent were manufactured in the United States; in 1962, 74 per cent.

66. Paper, Printing, and Publishing

The industry of paper and allied products includes manufacture of pulp, primarily from wood but also from rags; conversion of pulp into

TABLE X.40

PRODUCTION OF WOOD PULP,
AND PAPER AND PAPERBOARD, 1899-1964
(In Millions of Short Tons)

	Wood Pulp	Paper and Paperboard
1899	1.2	2.2
1909	2.5	4.1
1919	3.5	6.0
1929	4.9	11.1
1939	7.0	13.5
1949	12.2	20.3
1959	24.4	34.0
1963	30.1	39.2
1964	31.7	41.3

TABLE X.41

PAPER INDUSTRY IN THE UNITED STATES, 1963

	All Employees	Production Workers	Payroll	Wages	Value Added
	(In Thousands)		(In Millions of Dollars)		
Pulp mills[a]	14	11	93	69	195
Paper mills, except building	131	107	881	684	1,876
Paperboard mills	64	52	433	331	1,186
Paper and paperboard products	167	130	917	636	1,847
Paperboard containers and boxes	201	159	1,110	770	1,877
Building paper and board mills[a]	12	17	118	95	249
PAPER AND ALLIED PRODUCTS[b]	589	470	3,508	2,552	7,295

[a]1962.
[b]Preliminary.

paper or board; and manufacture of paper and paperboard into bags, boxes, sanitary food and beverage containers, envelopes, etc. Some 99 per cent of all pulp is used for manufacturing paper and paperboard; only 1 per cent is used in making other products.

With the growth of the population and ever new uses of paper, production in this industry has been increasing every decade (see Table X.40).

Employment exceeds half a million: 554,000 in 1958; 589,000 in 1963. About one-third of the employees work in the pulp-and-paper mills; another third, in factories making various products of paper and paperboard (wallpaper, bags, envelopes, etc.), and the remaining third, in manufacturing paperboard containers and boxes. The value added by manufacture of paper and allied products amounted to $5.7 billion in 1958 and $7.3 billion in 1963 (see Table X.41).

Mills producing pulp, paper, and board are spread throughout the eastern and southern parts of the country, but Washington and Oregon,

TABLE X.42

PAPER INDUSTRY, PRINTING AND PUBLISHING IN THE UNITED STATES,
BY GEOGRAPHIC DIVISION AND STATE, 1962

	Paper and Allied Products		Printing and Publishing	
	Number of Employees (In Thousands)	Value Added (In Millions of Dollars)	Number of Employees (In Thousands)	Value Added (In Millions of Dollars)
New England	72	771	73	664
Massachusetts	37	349	44	402
Middle Atlantic	131	1,400	285	3,505
New York	64	626	186	2,511
New Jersey	28	323	33	361
Pennsylvania	39	452	66	633
East North Central	148	1,737	229	2,443
Ohio	37	429	63	660
Illinois	35	366	94	1,067
Indiana	12	116	23	206
Michigan	27	336	28	316
Wisconsin	36	491	21	195
West North Central	31	371	77	734
Missouri	12	120	27	265
Minnesota	13	185	21	191
South Atlantic	78	1,055	82	780
Maryland[a]	9	85	14	131
District of Columbia	...	...	14	170
Virginia	12	162	10	95
North Carolina	12	138	11	93
Florida	14	237	14	125
East South Central	32	440	31	257
Tennessee	9	140	14	123
West South Central	35	422	44	404
Texas	13	145	29	265
Mountain	3	48	22	185
Pacific	54	800	87	965
Washington	18	305	10	101
Oregon	7	127		...
California	28	364	70	789
UNITED STATES	580	7,044	925	9,996

[a]1961.

which have large forest resources, also participate importantly in these industries (see Table X.42 and Figures X.8A and B).

Two out of 5 paper-and-paperboard plants are small, employing 1–19 persons and, in all, fewer than 16,000 persons out of the total 555,398. At the other extreme, 213 mills, each with 500 employees or more, had some 205,000 persons on their payrolls. Concentration ratios are less than in some other important industries, though several branches are controlled by a few big companies (see Table X.43).

FIGURE X.8.A

PULP MILLS (VALUE ADDED BY MANUFACTURE),
BY STATE, 1958

in Millions of Dollars
50 and over
25 — 49
10 — 24
5 — 9
1 — 4
under 1

FIGURE X.8.B

PAPER MILLS (VALUE ADDED BY MANUFACTURE),
BY STATE, 1958

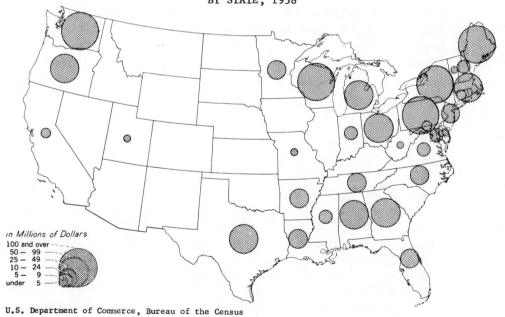

in Millions of Dollars
100 and over
50 — 99
25 — 49
10 — 24
5 — 9
under 5

U.S. Department of Commerce, Bureau of the Census

TABLE X.43

PAPER INDUSTRY: SHARE OF LARGEST COMPANIES IN EMPLOYMENT, 1958
(Per Cent)

	Employment			
	4	8	20	50
	Largest Companies			
Pulp mills	49	69	93	100
Paper and paperboard mills	21	33	52	69
Building paper and board mills	45	66	90	99
Envelopes	30	40	57	80
Paper bags	25	38	59	78
Paperboard boxes	14	23	37	51
Wallpaper	40	57	82	98

Printing and publishing establishments are engaged in printing by one or more common processes, such as letterpress, lithography, gravure, or screen. This heterogeneous group also includes plants for bookbinding, typesetting, engraving, and electrotyping, as well as for publishing newspapers, periodicals, and books and for printing business forms, greeting cards, etc. Employment is close to a million persons: 866,000 in 1958 and 926,000 in 1962.

More than half of all employees and about six-tenths of value added in this industry are concentrated in the Middle Atlantic and East North Central divisions (see Table X.42). The nation's most important center of printing and publishing is New York, accounting for one-fifth of total employment and one-fourth of value added by manufacture. Illinois ranks second, California third since it overtook Pennsylvania, which had occupied that position (see Figures X.9A and B).

In 1958, nearly half of all printing establishments (16,517 out of 35,456) were small, employing 1–4 persons, and accounted for only 4 per cent of total employment in the industry. Another 20 per cent of the plants had 5–9 employees each—in all, about 5 per cent of the industry's total. In contrast, the 220 largest plants, each engaging 500 employees or more, accounted for less than 3 per cent of establishments but reported almost one-third of total employment.

The largest single branch in this group is represented by the newspapers, with over 30 per cent of all employees and about the same ratio of value added in 1962. In general, there is little concentration in printing and publishing; rather, the scene is dominated by small enterprises of all kinds (see Table X.44).

In 1940, there were 1,878 newspapers in the United States with a net paid circulation of 41 million, and in 1964, 1,763 newspapers with 62 million circulation. In addition, there were 525 Sunday newspapers with net

FIGURE X.9.A

COMMERCIAL PRINTING (VALUE ADDED BY MANUFACTURE), BY STATE, 1958

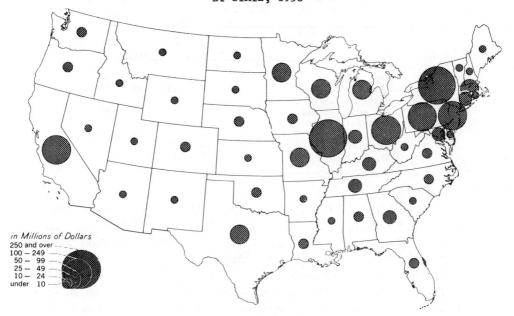

in Millions of Dollars
250 and over
100 — 249
50 — 99
25 — 49
10 — 24
under 10

FIGURE X.9.B

NEWSPAPERS: PUBLISHING (VALUE ADDED BY MANUFACTURE), BY STATE, 1958

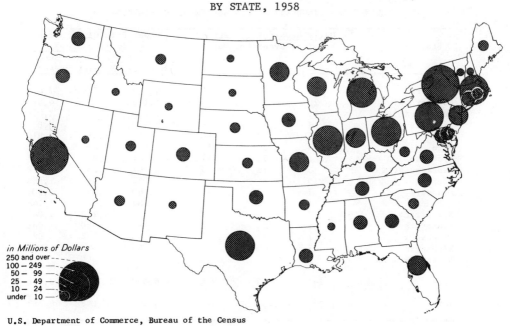

in Millions of Dollars
250 and over
100 — 249
50 — 99
25 — 49
10 — 24
under 10

U.S. Department of Commerce, Bureau of the Census

TABLE X.44

PUBLISHING: SHARE OF LARGEST COMPANIES IN EMPLOYMENT, 1958
(Per Cent)

	Employment			
	4	8	20	50
	Largest Companies			
Newspapers	15	20	29	43
Periodicals	21	33	43	59
Books, publishing and printing	20	31	49	65
Commercial printing	10	15	22	30
Greeting cards	47	62	76	90
Bookbinding	13	19	31	47
Typesetting	6	10	19	32

paid circulation of 32.4 million in 1940; 550 and 46.8 million, respectively, in 1964. Circulation per family in 1964 was 1.07 daily newspapers and 0.87 Sunday newspapers. A daily paper of 100,000 circulation or more had, on the average, 47 pages, and the Sunday issue, 154 pages.

In 1964, newspapers were distributed by state as shown in Table X.45.

There are few countries in the world in which the number of daily newspapers sold per 1,000 population exceeds that in the United States (see Table X.46).

TABLE X.45

NUMBER AND CIRCULATION OF NEWSPAPERS, BY STATE, 1964

State	Daily Newspapers		Sunday Papers	Net Paid Circulation (In Thousands)		
	Morning	Evening		Daily Newspapers		Sunday Papers
				Morning	Evening	
New York	21	65	17	4,270	3,675	7,461
California	20	112	32	2,143	3,360	4,533
Pennsylvania	26	96	11	1,309	2,771	3,076
Illinois	11	74	18	1,900	1,980	3,032
Texas	25	90	80	1,347	1,660	2,810
Ohio	8	88	16	855	2,495	2,126
Michigan	1	52	11	521	1,862	2,081
Massachusetts	6	43	9	1,007	1,331	1,572
Florida	15	32	30	1,052	667	1,584
Missouri	7	46	14	740	1,037	1,504
Indiana	11	78	18	484	1,236	1,148
New Jersey	7	23	6	441	1,213	1,040
Minnesota	5	24	7	384	680	988
Tennessee	7	22	11	500	572	821
Wisconsin	3	35	7	243	918	822
North Carolina	9	39	16	570	600	819
Other	141	532	258	6,599	11,991	12,966
TOTAL	323	1,452	561	24,365	38,048	48,383

TABLE X.46

NUMBER OF NEWSPAPERS SOLD PER 1,000 POPULATION, 1962
IN SELECTED COUNTRIES

United Kingdom	490	Canada	222	Brazil	53
Sweden	490	Israel	210	Peru	47
Japan	416	U.S.S.R.	181	Venezuela	45
New Zealand	400	Argentina	155	Turkey	45
Switzerland	378	Poland	144	Ceylon	37
Norway	378	Chile	134	Guatemala	31
Australia	375	Mexico	115	Bolivia	26
Finland	359	Italy	101	United Arab Republic	20
Denmark	347	Costa Rica	94	Tunisia	19
United States	321	Cuba	88	Philippines	16
West Germany	306	Union of South Africa	57	Iran	15
Belgium	285	Ecuador	56	Burma	9
France	257	Colombia	55	Pakistan	5
Austria	225			India	0.3[a]

[a]Refers to 354 dailies only.

In 1963, the apparent consumption of newsprint by newspapers amounted to 7.3 million t.; of this, 61 per cent was used for advertising content, 39 per cent for editorial writing. The newsprint consumption in the United States by far exceeds the combined consumption of the United Kingdom, France, West Germany, Italy, U.S.S.R., Japan, Canada, and Australia. On a per capita basis, the contrast is smaller (figures in lbs.): about 75 in the United States, 50 in the United Kingdom, 46 in Canada, 23 in France, 21 in West Germany, 17 in Japan, and 5 in the U.S.S.R.

Excluding government publications, subscription books, and some other categories, 11,622 new books were published in this country in 1950; 15,012 in 1960; and 20,542 in 1964. In addition, 7,909 new editions were printed in 1964, with substantial changes in text or format. The number of books published per 1,000 population doubled between 1880 and 1900, from 4 to 8 books but has since remained almost stable in this century: 8.5 books in 1940, 8.4 in 1960.

67. Rubber and Plastics Products

This group of industries covers manufacture of products from natural, synthetic, or reclaimed rubber; gutta-percha, and other materials—such products as tires, rubber footwear, fabricated rubber goods, and plastics products—while the manufacture of synthetic rubber and plastics materials are classified under the chemical industry (see Sec. 61).

In 1962, some 400,000 persons were occupied in the manufacture of rubber and plastics products. Production is heavily concentrated in the vicinity of the motor-vehicle industry, its chief outlet being in the eastern part of the country: the East North Central, the Middle Atlantic, and the New England states together account for three-fourths of total output. Ohio alone employs as many people as the Middle Atlantic states and exceeds them in value added. Geographically, rubber and plastics industries were distributed in 1962 as shown in Table X.47.

TABLE X.47

RUBBER AND PLASTICS INDUSTRIES, BY GEOGRAPHIC DIVISION AND STATE, 1962

	All Employees (In Thousands)	Payroll	Value Added
		(In Millions of Dollars)	
New England	67	350	666
Massachusetts	38	195	364
Middle Atlantic	79	421	802
New York	30	148	263
New Jersey	26	144	274
Pennsylvania	23	128	265
East North Central	148	903	1,623
Ohio	77	503	886
Illinois	25	136	248
Indiana	20	113	209
Michigan	17	105	188
West North Central	16	94	204
South Atlantic	26	120	239
East South Central	17	98	231
West South Central	10	56	141
Pacific California	28	163	309
UNITED STATES	398	2,250	4,316

Production of rubber and plastics goods has developed rapidly in recent decades: in 1929, it employed 172,000 persons; in 1963, 409,000. Value added by manufacture increased in this period from $539 million to $4,590 million. Per employee, value added was $3,100 in 1929; $9,200 in 1958; and nearly $11,000 in 1963.

TABLE X.48

RUBBER AND PLASTIC INDUSTRIES:
SHARE OF LARGEST COMPANIES IN VALUE OF SHIPMENTS, 1958
(Per Cent)

	4	8	20	50
	Largest Companies			
Tires and inner tubes	71	81	97	99
Rubber footwear	66	83	...	100
Rubber belts and belting	57	83	98	100
Sponge- and foam-rubber goods	47	69	89	97
Plastic dinnerware	31	46	68	89
Plastic pipe, hose	22	34	61	83
Molded plastic products	6	10	20	33
Fabricated plastic products n.e.c.	14	21	33	48

Rubber goods—tires, inner tubes, footwear, etc.—are produced in relatively larger plants than are plastics products, which can be manufactured even in small workshops. Thus, of 27 rubber-shoe establishments, only 1 plant is very small, engaging 5–9 employees, while 21, or three-fourths of the total, have more than 100 employees each, and 13 of these report more than 500. In contrast, of the 3,222 establishments manufacturing plastics products, 2,682, or more than 80 per cent, had fewer than 50 employees; only 22 plants, less than 7 per cent, reported more than 500 employees. The same tendency toward concentration is evident in the distribution of production by value of shipments (see Table X.48).

XI. *Construction and Housing*

68. *The Construction Industry*

Construction, including that of houses and other buildings, and of public facilities such as roads, schools, and military installations, is a key industry in the United States, employing large numbers of workers and consuming a wide range of materials and services. Construction activities are extremely sensitive to changes in business conditions; although they move broadly in the same direction as the general economy, except in wartime, their swings are much sharper and are likely to exercise considerable influence on the course of business cycles. Expansion in building may offset, at least temporarily, depression in other sectors of the economy, while contraction may accelerate depression and increase its severity, as it did in the early 1930's. Fluctuations in building activities are directly reflected in employment (see Table XI.1).

The Department of Commerce (OBE) estimates that about 5 million persons were engaged in construction activities in 1964: 3.1 million in contract construction (it exceeded 3 million for the first time in 1963), and 1.9 million self-employed contractors, nonconstruction firms, employees of manufacturing companies who install construction-type equipment (elevators, etc.), and builders who do not work on contract. This rise in employment is believed to have offset the reduced demand for labor caused by the increasing use of labor-saving equipment and prefabricated materials.

In the country as a whole, the construction industry accounts for 5.3 per cent of employment in nonagricultural establishments. The proportion is lower in such industrial states as New York (4.3 per cent) and Pennsylvania and Michigan (4 per cent). It is higher than the national average in agricultural states such as Minnesota (5.5), Nebraska (6.2), the Dakotas (8.2–8.3), Wyoming (10.1), and Nevada (11.4).

TABLE XI.1

EMPLOYMENT IN THE CONSTRUCTION INDUSTRY, 1919-65
(In Thousands)

1919	1,021	1934	862	1949	2,165
1920	848	1935	912	1950	2,333
1921	1,012	1936	1,145	1951	2,603
1922	1,185	1937	1,112	1952	2,634
1923	1,229	1938	1,055	1953	2,623
1924	1,321	1939	1,150	1954	2,612
1925	1,446	1940	1,294	1955	2,802
1926	1,555	1941	1,790	1956	2,999
1927	1,608	1942	2,170	1957	2,923
1928	1,606	1943	1,567	1958	2,778
1929	1,497	1944	1,094	1959	2,960
1930	1,372	1945	1,132	1960	2,885
1931	1,214	1946	1,661	1961	2,816
1932	970	1947	1,982	1962	2,909
1933	809	1948	2,169	1963	3,029
				1964	3,056
				1965	3,211

In absolute figures, California engages the largest number of construction workers—314,000 in 1963, followed by New York (267,000), and Texas (174,000). These 3 states together provide one-fourth of all jobs in construction. Illinois and Pennsylvania combined employ 300,000 persons; Ohio and Florida combined, some 250,000.

In the United States as a whole, about as many people as work in the construction industry may be employed in industries closely related to construction, such as the basic lumber industries; stone quarries; and the industries producing cement, brick, tile, structural steel, paint, wallpaper, and so on.

Employment in construction, in both the private and public sectors, usually fluctuates with the season; it is low in all parts of the country in January and February, begins to increase in March in the South and in April in the North, reaches a peak in June and July, and maintains this level through September and often through October, to decline during the winter. Except in periods marked by unusual weather conditions, the development of construction follows the same seasonal pattern.

The value of construction put in place in any single year represents the sum of all actual costs involved: the cost of materials incorporated and labor performed, a proportionate share of the equipment utilized, the contractors' profits, cost of architectural and engineering work, etc., but does not include cost of sales, or land cost, or speculative profits. In 1915, the value of new construction put in place in the United States slightly exceeded $3 billion; in the boom years of 1926–28, it reached the record high of some $12 billion, to plunge back to $3 billion at the bottom of the Great Depression. In the late 1930's, construction activities re-

TABLE XI.2

VALUE OF NEW CONSTRUCTION PUT IN PLACE, 1946-65
(In Millions of Dollars)

Type of Construction	1946	1949	1952	1955	1958	1961	1964	1965
Private construction	12,077	20,453	26,049	34,804	34,696	38,299	45,914	49,999
Residential buildings	6,247	12,428	15,803	21,877	19,789	21,680	26,507	26,689
New housing units	4,795	10,043	12,851	18,242	15,445	16,189	20,612	20,765
Nonresidential	3,362	3,383	5,014	7,611	8,675	10,734	12,998	16,521
Industrial	1,689	972	2,320	2,399	2,382	2,780	3,572	5,086
Commercial	1,153	1,182	1,137	3,218	3,589	4,674	5,406	6,704
Farm construction	1,161	1,570	1,614	1,385	1,355	1,300	1,221	1,195
Public utilities	1,255	2,994	3,533	3,770	4,688	4,335	4,850	5,178
All other private	52	78	85	161	189	250	338	416
Public construction	2,231	6,269	10,779	11,715	15,457	17,148	20,307	21,904
Residential buildings	374	359	654	266	846	842	474	464
Nonresidential	354	2,049	4,158	4,196	4,653	5,169	6,578	7,220
Military facilities	188	137	1,387	1,287	1,402	1,371	968	883
Highways	764	2,015	2,677	3,852	5,545	5,854	7,144	7,539
Sewer and water systems	194	619	790	1,085	1,387	1,581	2,281	2,470
Other	357	1,090	1,113	1,029	1,624	2,331	2,862	3,328
TOTAL NEW CONSTRUCTION	14,308	26,722	36,828	46,519	50,153	55,447	66,221	71,903

FIGURE XI.1

VALUE OF NEW CONSTRUCTION, 1920-63

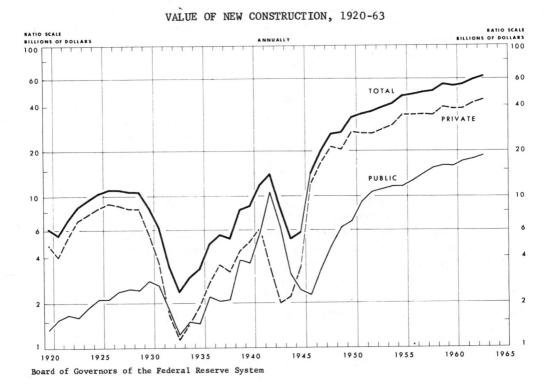

Board of Governors of the Federal Reserve System

covered gradually, but during World War II private construction shrank sharply, while the public sector expanded.

After the end of hostilities, the pressure of pent-up demand for housing for the millions of newly married couples and, generally, the growing population, on the one hand, and the savings accumulated during the war and rising incomes, on the other, pushed construction activities to record heights. The Federal Government's housing program for veterans also played an important role. As a result of all these and other factors, the value of new construction put in place surged from $14.3 billion in 1946 to $26.1 billion in 1948. It remained nearly stationary during the 1949 recession and then resumed its upward trend, reaching $62.8 billion in 1963 and then climbing up to $71.9 billion two years later (see Table XI.2 and Figure XI.1). Expressed in dollars of 1957–59, however, the increase in the value of new construction between 1946 and 1964 was less spectacular: not about 5 times, but only about 2 times. In addition to construction costs, $19–$20 billion is spent each year for maintenance and repair; of this, some $12 billion goes for residential upkeep and improvements.

Until the Great Depression, residential housing was in private hands; the Federal Government was not involved in it. But when private construction nearly collapsed, the Government entered the field to activate the stagnating economy. Between 1935 and 1945, nearly 4 million nonfarm dwelling units were started, mostly single-family structures and almost exclusively privately financed on the basis of U.S. Housing Authority loans to local housing authorities. These loans represented 90 per cent of the cost of construction. Two basic principles characterize the Federal housing policy: decent housing conditions for every American, and individual home ownership (its major goal).

The Federal Housing Authority has gone a long way since its creation in 1934. It has liberalized its policies, raised the term of loans for newly constructed homes from 20 to 25 years and the ratio of loans to value of existing homes from 78 to 90 per cent. The Veterans Administration, specifically concerned with homes for the veterans of World War II, has provided Federal Government guarantees of up to 50, and later up to 60, per cent of loans made by private lenders for the construction or purchase of homes by veterans, and has extended the maturity of a loan on a home from 25 to 30 years. In all, total outstanding debt on all housing properties amounted to $281 billion on December 31, 1963: $264 billion on nonfarm properties and nearly $17 billion on farm properties. In 1964, total debt was $310 billion. There have been comparatively few foreclosures for nonpayment.

A few hundred thousand nonfarm dwelling units were started each year in the 1930's (a start is the beginning of excavation for the footings or foundation of the building). In postwar years, this figure grew to a million or more units started each year; 1950 was the record year, with nearly 2

TABLE XI.3

NEW PRIVATE NONFARM HOUSING UNITS STARTED, 1945-65
(In Thousands of Units)

Year	Housing Units	Year	Housing Units
1945	326	1955	1,646
1946	1,023	1956	1,349
1947	1,268	1957	1,224
1948	1,362	1958	1,382
1949	1,466	1959	1,531
1950	1,952	1960	1,274
1951	1,491	1961	1,337
1952	1,504	1962	1,469
1953	1,438	1963	1,613
1954	1,551	1964	1,564
		1965	1,520

million units started. The number declined in subsequent years, fluctuating between 1.3 million and 1.6 million (see Table XI.3). It is believed that the data on starts are to some extent understated because of the difficulty of locating all construction projects. Nevertheless, this series is a good indicator of residential building activity and of the pulse of the economy as a whole; it is also considered a kind of guide in the formulation of national housing policy.

FIGURE XI.2

NEW PRIVATE HOUSING STARTS, 1920-63

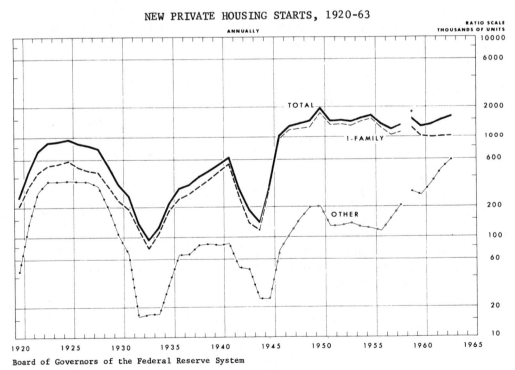

Board of Governors of the Federal Reserve System

TABLE XI.4

PUBLIC SECTOR IN NEW CONSTRUCTION PUT IN PLACE, 1915-65[a]
(Per Cent)

1915	22.0	1934	59.4	1952	29.3
1918	43.7	1937	44.2	1955	25.2
1921	26.0	1940	41.8	1958	30.8
1925	18.7	1943	76.2	1961	30.9
1928	21.3			1963	30.0
1931	41.4	1946	18.5	1964	30.3
		1949	23.5	1965	29.7

[a] Beginning 1946, revised figures, comparable
with earlier data only in general trend.

The median number of construction months required, from start to sale, is around 3 in summer and 4 in winter. At least two-thirds of the units are 1-family homes; recently there has been a growing tendency to build multiple-family structures: 102,000 in 1955; 237,000 in 1960; 556,000 in 1964 (see Figure XI.2).

The share of the public sector in the value of new construction put in place experiences considerable changes, skyrocketing in time of emergency such as depression and war, and contracting in peacetime and normalcy. On the average, the public sector represented about 20 per cent in the 1920's, about 40 per cent in the 1930's and 1940's, and approximately 30

TABLE XI.5

PUBLIC CONSTRUCTION, BY TYPE OF FUNDS, 1915-65
(In Millions of Dollars)

Year	Total	Federal Direct	Federal Grants-in-Aid[a]	State and Local
1915	719	71	...	648
1920	1,352	232	95	1,025
1925	2,138	100	89	1,949
1930	2,858	209	104	2,545
1935	2,233	814	567	852
1940	3,628	1,182	946	1,500
1945	2,398	1,737	99	562
1950[b]	6,866	1,624	454	4,788
1955	11,715	2,769	739	8,207
1960	15,863	3,622	2,267	9,974
1963	19,326	3,970		15,356[c]
1964	20,307	3,822		16,485[c]
1965	21,649	3,885		17,764[c]

[a] Construction programs currently receiving Federal
grants-in-aid cover highways, schools, hospitals,
airports, and miscellaneous community facilities.
[b] Beginning 1950, revised figures, not comparable
with earlier data.
[c] Includes Federal grants-in-aid.

TABLE XI.6

NEW PUBLIC CONSTRUCTION BY OWNERSHIP AND TYPE, 1955-64
(In Millions of Dollars)

	1955	1960	1963	1964
Federally owned	2,769	3,622	4,050[a]	4,172[a]
Military facilities	1,287	1,366		
Nonresidential buildings	802	736	1,070	1,237
Conservation and development	598	1,005	1,317	1,344
Other	82	515	340	290
State and locally owned	8,946	12,241	14,629	15,882
Highways	3,782	5,301	6,462	6,765
Educational buildings	2,436	2,798	3,017	3,305
Other	2,728	4,142	5,150	5,812

[a]Not available; estimate included in totals.

TABLE XI.7

INDEX OF CONSTRUCTION COSTS, 1946-65
(1957-59 = 100)

Year	Annual Average	January	April	August	November
1946	56	50	53	57	59
1950	77	73	74	79	79
1955	90	88	89	91	92
1960	103	103	103	104	104
1963	109	108	108	110	111
1964	112	111	112	112	113
1965	116	113	114	116	117

per cent since then. Within this 40-year period, there were record years when the share of public activity in total construction was as high as 59 per cent (1934) and even 76 per cent (1942–43) (see Table XI.4 and Figure XI.1).

The funds required for new public construction came from Federal, state, and local sources. Generally, the share of state and local authorities is substantially greater than that of the Federal Government, except in times of national emergency, when the reverse is true (see Table XI.5).

Of the expenditures for federally owned construction, the largest part of the funds is used for military facilities and for conservation and development; state and local funds are provided largely for construction of highways and educational buildings (see Table XI.6).

California ranks first in construction contracts, with $7 billion in 1963 and $6.6 billion in 1964. New York State follows with $3.6 billion and $3.3 billion, respectively. Construction contracts exceed $2 billion in several states: Texas, Illinois, Ohio. In 1964, the District of Columbia moved into this group.

A composite index of construction costs, prepared by the Department of Commerce, shows that on the average, construction costs doubled between 1946 and 1965 (1957–59=100) (see Table XI.7).

TABLE XI.8

OCCUPIED HOUSING UNITS IN THE UNITED STATES,
BY TENURE, COLOR OF OCCUPANTS, AND TYPE OF RESIDENCE,
1890-1960

Year	Total Units (In Thousands)	Per Cent									
		Occupants		White		Nonwhite		Nonfarm		Farm	
		Owners	Renters	Owners	Renters	Owners	Renters	Owners	Renters	Owners	Renters
1890	12,690	47.8	52.2	51.5	48.5	19.0	81.0	36.9	63.1	65.9	34.1
1900	15,964	46.7	53.3	49.8	50.2	23.6	76.4	36.9	63.1	64.4	35.6
1910	20,256	45.9	54.1	...	...	...	...	38.6	61.4	62.8	37.2
1920	24,352	45.6	54.4	48.2	51.8	23.9	76.1	40.8	59.2	58.1	41.9
1930	29,905	47.8	52.2	50.2	49.8	25.2	74.8	46.0	54.0	53.9	46.1
1940	34,855	43.6	56.4	45.7	54.3	23.6	76.4	41.1	58.9	53.2	46.8
1950	42,826	55.0	45.0	57.0	43.0	34.9	65.1	53.4	46.6	65.7	34.3
1960	53,024	61.9	38.1	64.4	35.6	38.4	61.6	61.0[a]	39.0[a]	73.8[a]	26.2[a]

[a]Not comparable with data for earlier censuses because of the changes in the definition of farm residence.

69. *Housing Conditions*

While some information on housing conditions is available as far back as 1890, the first regular census of housing, reporting on occupancy, structural characteristics of dwellings, plumbing and bathing facilities, etc., was taken in 1940. It has been repeated at 10-year intervals, most recently in 1960.

The 1960 census counted 58.3 million housing units in the United States, of which 53 million were occupied: 49.5 million nonfarm units and 3.6 million units on farms. Nearly two-thirds of the population (61 per cent) live in their own houses, either fully paid for or bought on long-term credit. The percentage of owner-occupied dwellings is even higher among farm people: 74 per cent in 1960. While 64 per cent of all white households live in owner-occupied dwellings, the figure for nonwhite families is only 38 per cent (see Table XI.8).

In general, the tendency to own one's home has always been stronger among farm people than among urban dwellers, but the percentage of renter-occupied dwellings on farms rose steadily between 1890 and 1950; since that year, it has tended to decline. Among city people, home ownership has shown a continuous upward trend since the 1920's, except for the depression years, when the movement out of the cities caused a drop in nonfarm ownership.

The proportion of owner-occupied housing units varies greatly from state to state. In 1960, families living in their own homes exceeded 70 per cent in Idaho, Indiana, Michigan, Minnesota, and Utah as compared with New York (44.8 per cent), Hawaii (41.1), and the District of Columbia (30 per cent). The contrast from state to state is even sharper in the ownership of housing units among the nonwhite population: on the one hand, less than 0.5 per cent are living in owned homes in Vermont, New Hampshire, and Maine and between 1 and 2 per cent in Minnesota, Iowa, North Dakota, Idaho, Oregon, Utah, Wisconsin, and Wyoming; and on the other, 25–30 per cent in Alabama, Oklahoma, and South Carolina, 44.1 per cent in the District of Columbia, and 64.1 per cent in Hawaii.

According to the Institute of Social Research, University of Michigan, almost half of families (45 per cent) with incomes under $2,000 own their homes; many of them have a retired head. On the other hand, over 84 per cent of families with current income of $10,000 or more own their homes.

Substantial progress in housing conditions in this country was achieved between the censuses of 1940 and 1960: in 1940, about 26 per cent of all housing units had no piped water inside the structure; in 1960, only 7 per cent. The corresponding figures for exclusive use of a flush toilet are 60 and 87 per cent; for exclusive use of bathtub or shower, 56 and 85 per cent; for gas as cooking fuel, 49 and 65 per cent; and for electricity as cooking fuel, 5 and 31 per cent (see Table XI.9). Despite this progress, in 1960 there still were more than 8 million deteriorating housing units

TABLE XI.9

SELECTED FEATURES OF HOUSING UNITS
IN THE UNITED STATES, 1940-60
(Per Cent)

	1940	1950	1960
Hot and cold water piped inside	} 74.2	{ 70.1	87.2
Only cold water piped		{ 12.7	5.7
No piped water inside structure	25.8	17.2	7.1
Flush toilet: exclusive use	59.7	71.4	86.8
shared use	5.0	4.1	3.0
Other toilet facilities or none	35.3	24.5	10.3
Bathtub or shower: exclusive use	56.2	69.3	85.2
shared use	4.7	3.9	2.9
No bathtub or shower	39.1	26.8	11.9
Heating equipment:			
Steam and hot water	21.8	23.5	21.8
Warm-air furnace; floor, wall, or			
pipeless furnace	20.3	26.9	42.7
Built-in electric units	...	...	1.3
Other means with flue	46.6	36.0	22.6
Other means without flue	...	12.3	10.0
Not heated	...	1.4	1.7
Cooking fuel:			
Utility gas	} 48.8	{ 51.6	51.5
Bottled, tank gas		{ 8.0	12.2
Electricity	5.4	15.0	30.8
Wood	23.6	9.9	2.7
Coal or coke	11.5	7.8	1.0
Fuel oil, kerosene, other fuel	10.3	7.5	1.2
No cooking fuel	0.4	0.3	0.5
Refrigerator:			
Electric	...	...	96.4[a]
Gas	...	...	2.4[a]
Range:			
Electric	...	...	34.6[a]
Gas	...	...	61.6[a]
Vacuum cleaner	...	...	72.3[a]
Radio[b]	82.8	95.7	91.5
No radio	17.2	4.3	8.5
Television	...	12.0	87.3
Automobile available: 1	...	...	56.9
2 or more	...	...	21.5
no automobile	...	...	21.5
With telephone	...	...	78.5
Without telephone	...	...	21.5
ALL HOUSING UNITS	100.0	100.0	100.0

[a]1963.
[b]Includes units with one radio or more; the same for television.

FIGURE XI.3

PERCENTAGE OF DWELLINGS WITH SELECTED HOUSING EQUIPMENT,
AND OF FAMILIES OWNING AUTOMOBILE, 1960

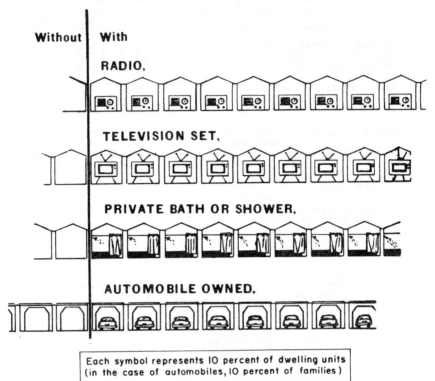

Each symbol represents 10 percent of dwelling units
(in the case of automobiles, 10 percent of families)

U.S. Department of Commerce, Bureau of the Census

and some 3 million dilapidated units. Of these, 1.5 million and 885,000, respectively, were occupied by nonwhite residents.

Of all occupied housing units in 1960, the residents in 73.7 per cent had a washing machine; in 79 per cent, a telephone and automobile; in 87 per cent, television; and in 92 per cent, radio. Percentagewise, occupants of urban housing had more telephones and television sets but fewer washing machines and freezers than those on farms. Most urban housing units have a flush toilet and private bath or shower; many farm dwellings do not. Nearly all units have electric lighting (see Figure XI.3).

The density of population per occupied unit declined from 5 persons in 1890 to 3.4 persons in 1960: for the white population, from 4.9 to 3.3; for the nonwhite, from 5.5 to 4.0.

At the time of the last housing census, about 28 per cent of all housing units were less than 10 years old; 15 per cent were 10–19 years old; the remaining units were older, many of them 30 years or more.

TABLE XI.10

HOUSING CONDITIONS IN SELECTED COUNTRIES, 1951-62[a]

Country	Number of Dwellings	Number of Dwellings Occupied	Average Number of Rooms per Dwelling	Per Cent of Dwellings with Rooms				Average Number of Persons per Room
	(In Thousands)			1-2	3-4	5-6	7	
United States, 1960								
Total	58,326	53,024	4.9	6.4	32.4	45.1	16.1	0.7
Urban	40,764	38,320	4.8	7.2	33.3	45.3	14.2	0.7
Canada, 1959								
Total	...	4,303	5.1	4.4	28.9	44.8	21.8	0.8
France, 1962								
Total	15,826	14,021	3.1	38.8	45.7	12.4	3.0	1.0
Urban	9,670	9,003	2.9	42.2	45.2	10.4	2.3	1.0
West Germany, 1960								
Total	15,564	...	4.1	10.0	60.5	23.2	6.2	0.9
Urban	6,199	...	...	...	...	...	...	...
United Kingdom, 1951								
Total	14,160	13,784	4.6	7.3	40.9	44.0	7.8	0.8
Urban	...	10,924	4.6	7.4	40.4	45.0	7.2	0.8
Australia, 1961								
Total	2,976	2,782	5.2	4.6	23.1	58.8	13.5	0.7
Urban	2,432	2,314	5.1	4.5	23.3	60.1	12.2	0.7

| Country | Per Cent of Dwellings with Persons per Room | | | | Per Cent of Dwellings with | | | | |
	Less Than 1.5	1.5 or more	2 or more	3 or more	Piped Water Inside	Outside	Gas	Elect- ricity	Bath	Flush Toilet
Canada, 1959										
Total	...	...	...	...	86.9	...	21.9	96.8	76.5	82.0
France, 1962										
Total	73.7	26.3	15.8	4.9	58.4	23.1	66.1	93.0	10.4	93.6
Urban	73.9	26.1	15.5	4.6	75.4	13.9	77.6	95.4	14.9	86.5
West Germany, 1960										
Total	91.5	8.5	2.5	0.2	96.7	...	48.5	99.4	51.9	75.3
Urban	...	...	...	...	99.2	...	75.8	99.7	61.8	93.9
United Kingdom, 1951										
Total	89.4	10.6	4.8	11.1	94.5	...	...	...	62.4	92.3
Urban	89.4	10.6	4.8	11.1	97.9	...	...	...	64.5	98.1
Australia, 1961										
Total	93.8	6.2	2.6	0.6	...	...	45.2	96.2	...	...
Urban	94.2	5.8	2.5	0.6	...	...	53.3	99.2	...	...

[a]Much more detailed data for the United States given in Table XI.9; data for piped water, gas, electricity, bath, and flush toilet in France, 1954; for per cent of dwellings with persons per room in Australia, 1954.

In 1960, four-fifths of all housing units and two-thirds of those occupied by nonwhite persons had more than 4 rooms. The median number of rooms per unit was 4.9 and 4.2, respectively. Nearly 9 out of 10 (88.7 per cent) of all occupied units had 1 person or less per room; of those occupied by nonwhite persons, 7 out of 10 (71.9 per cent).

More than 5 million housing units, about 10 per cent, are vacant. In 1963–64, the causes of vacancy were various: some were vacant seasonally, others had been held off the market; a few had been sold or rented and awaited occupancy; and the rest were offered either for rent only or for sale only and awaited claimants. On the whole, mobility of housing occupancy, or their "turnover," to use the term applied to the labor force, is perhaps no less or greater than the mobility of the American population and may be a logical concomitant of families changing places. In any event, the number of vacant housing units in the United States is larger than the total supply of units in Canada, or the supply of urban housing units in West Germany, and more than double that of all units in Australia.

Statistics on housing conditions in different countries are not fully comparable because of differences in methods of obtaining them, unequal accuracy, etc. Yet they provide some insight into the housing conditions and also into the customs of various countries, insofar as these are reflected in the available figures. The predominance of large housing units in the United States, Canada, Australia, and the United Kingdom is in sharp contrast to France, where 2 out of 5 units have only 1–2 rooms and only 1 out of 10 has 5–6 rooms; in Australia, in contrast, at least every second dwelling has 5–6 rooms. Contrasts in percentages of housing units with various conveniences are also noticeable (see Table XI.10).

XII. *Transportation and Communication*

70. We Travel on Land and on Water, in the Air and in Space—71. Railways—72. Highways and Motor Vehicles—73. Waterways—74. Airways and Outer Space—75. Our Many Ways to Communicate

70. *We Travel on Land and on Water, in the Air and in Space*

A real effort of imagination is required to visualize the tremendous development of transportation that has taken place in the United States within the last hundred years and to realize that hundreds of millions of people now living started their lives in a world that had no automobiles, no airplanes, no highways such as we know them now; and who could have anticipated the trips to the moon? At the beginning of the last century, the means of transport were the same as in the biblical times of King David—shanks' mare and draft animals on land, oar and sail on water. At its end, and in the first decades of our century, railways dominated the scene and seemed destined to perpetuate their monopoly in transporting people and goods overland. Then, in fast succession, new means of transportation emerged and opened unlimited vistas for future changes.

The railway era was ushered in on the day in October, 1829, when George Stephenson demonstrated that his Rocket steam engine could move a train 15 mi. per hr. In the following decades of the 1830's and 1840's, the United States built its first 2,800 mi. of railroad track; by 1850, it had raised the mileage to 9,021 (see Figure XII.1). Clippers carried freight and people on the sea, some at the rate of 12–15 mi. per hr. with favorable wind. They reached the pinnacle of their glory by the middle of the nineteenth century and went as far as China to pick up cargo bound for New York and London.

During the second half of the century, railways spread throughout the

335

FIGURE XII.1

THE FIRST RAILWAYS IN THE UNITED STATES, 1850

Association of American Railroads

United States, enabling traffic to expand with increasing speed and ever growing volume. By 1870, the nation's network reached 53,000 mi., and the first railroad to the Pacific Ocean had been constructed (see Figure XII.2). Not until the second decade of our century, less than 50 years ago, did motor vehicles make their sensational appearance in any number on U.S. roads. In all, however, there were fewer automobiles in this country in 1920–21 than are now produced weekly. The first flights also took place in those decades; 43 primitive airplanes were produced in 1913, 49 in 1914.

Turning from these modest beginnings to today's transportation picture in the United States, we see that the railways' monopoly has become a thing of the past, especially in passenger traffic; that the motor vehicle rules traffic on land; that ships of all kinds ply national and international waterways; that the airplane has become part and parcel of modern transport; that millions of miles of pipelines have been laid underground to move oil and natural gas, and that, on top of all this, the seeds have

FIGURE XII.2

THE RAILWAY NETWORK IN THE UNITED STATES, 1870

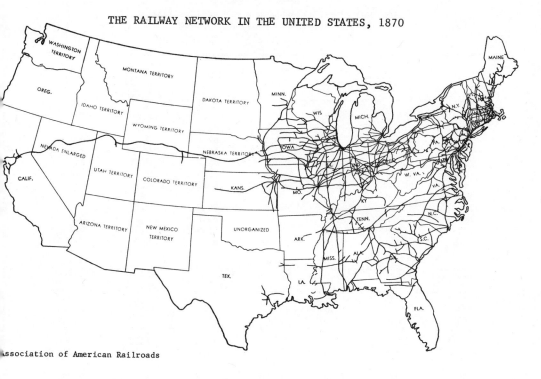

Association of American Railroads

been planted for a fantastic new adventure—travel in space. Moving with unprecedented ease on land, on water, and in the air, man now is bent on conquering extraorbital skies!

What has this rapid development of transportation meant for the U.S. economy? First, it has enabled each region in the country to specialize in the production for which it is best fitted and exchange its products for the goods of the other regions. It has made it possible for each industry to settle where costs of transporting the necessary raw materials are least onerous and the markets for its products most easily accessible. As effective and cheap transportation has become commonplace, it has helped to equalize prices in different parts of the country and to encourage mass production. It has diversified consumption, moving goods from remote parts of the country at reasonable expense and speed and making trade with foreign countries possible. And no less important, by enabling the population to move throughout the country and settle in every corner, it has promoted the sense of political, economic, social, and cultural unity. It has contributed to the growth of the cities by facilitating their supply of all the necessities of life. Nowhere in a country where a means of transport is within everybody's reach, is there any more room for the feeling of isolation.

TABLE XII.1

DOMESTIC INTERCITY PASSENGER AND FREIGHT TRAFFIC,
BY TYPE OF TRANSPORTATION, 1930-64

(Per Cent[a])

			PASSENGER-MILES		
Year	Total	Railroads[b]	Buses	Private Automobiles	Inland Waterways[c]	Airways[d]
1930	100.0	10.7	3.7	85.0	0.6	...
1935	100.0	7.1	3.8	88.4	0.6	0.2
1940	100.0	7.4	4.1	87.6	0.5	0.4
1945	100.0	29.3	9.0	59.9	0.7	1.1
1950	100.0	6.9	5.6	85.2	0.25	2.1
1955	100.0	4.3	3.8	88.2	0.3	3.4
1960	100.0	2.8	2.6	89.7	0.4	4.5
1961	100.0	2.7	2.6	90.0	0.3	4.5
1962	100.0	2.5	2.7	89.8	0.3	4.7
1963	100.0	2.2	2.6	89.8	0.3	5.1
1964	100.0	2.1	2.6	89.3	0.3	5.6

			TON-MILES		
Year	Total	Railroads[b]	Trucks	Pipelines	Inland Waterways[c]	Airways[e]
1930	100.0	74.3	3.9	5.3	16.5	...
1935	100.0	67.6	5.8	10.5	16.1	...
1940	100.0	63.2	9.5	9.1	18.1	0.002
1945	100.0	68.6	6.2	11.8	13.3	0.008
1950	100.0	57.4	15.8	11.8	14.9	0.029
1955	100.0	50.4	17.2	15.7	16.7	0.037
1960	100.0	44.3	22.2	17.0	16.4	0.057
1961	100.0	43.6	23.3	17.4	15.6	0.066
1962	100.0	43.7	23.6	16.9	15.8	0.083
1963	100.0	43.0	23.8	17.1	16.0	0.100
1964	100.0	42.9	23.8	17.2	16.0	0.100

[a]One passenger-mile = one passenger moved one mile;
one ton-mile = one ton moved one mile.
[b]Includes electric railways, express, and mail.
[c]Includes Great Lakes and Alaska for all years and Hawaii since 1959.
[d]Includes commercial revenue service, and private pleasure and business flying.
[e]Includes express, mail, and excess baggage.

With 5 basic means of transporting goods and 4 means of transporting people, competition is sharp. The carriers of each branch of transport—common, contract and private carriers, national and local carriers—try to capture as much of the existing traffic as possible and to generate new traffic opportunities. Their respective shares in the total volume of passenger and freight traffic, in terms of passenger-miles and ton-miles, have undergone considerable changes since 1930 (see Table XII.1).

Each type of transport has its advantages and its drawbacks. The railroads can operate virtually independent of weather conditions and thus are nearly always available—a feature of great importance in passenger traffic. In moving freight, they can handle bulky, heavy cargo in almost unlimited quantities just by making a train longer. The airplane's greatest advantage is speed, and this youngest, dynamic branch of transportation has utilized this feature in every imaginable way to court public favor. The motor vehicle seems to be the best means of land transportation in many respects, and it has cornered passenger traffic so successfully that any effective competition is apparently out of the question. The truck also has many advantages in offering services and conveniences in freight shipments that no other transport medium can match. Water transport, in turn, is feasible when time is not of prime importance but low rates are, and it is, of course, irreplaceable in moving heavy freight across the oceans. Dependence on weather and, therefore, a certain unreliability are the weaknesses of air traffic; when speed is of the essence, the automobile is not the answer; the railroads are too rigid and too expensive to outrun the flexibility and comparative cheapness of motor transport.

The list of advantages and disadvantages of each medium of transportation can be extended in both directions. Thus, the only certainty is that competition will continue unabated, forcing changes in policy and improvements in equipment to suit the final ruler—the consumer.

A concomitant of competition is the increasing capacity of the national transportation plant, which may possibly come to exceed public needs and demands. Thus, underutilization of available transportation facilities cannot be ruled out as a problem in national transportation policy.

71. Railways

The United States is the greatest railway builder in the world. Though some rail lines continue to be abandoned because they are unprofitable, the United States still has the largest rail network of any country in the world. It accounts for about one-fourth of the world's total railway mileage. Starting with short, disconnected lines, it put its first transcontinental railway into operation in 1869 and had completed the national railway network before World War I. In 1964, it was nearly 40,000 mi. shorter

TABLE XII.2

U.S. RAILWAY MILEAGE, 1840-1964
(In Thousands of Miles)

1840	2.8	1890	166.7	1940	233.7
1850	9.0	1900	193.3	1950	223.8
1860	30.6	1910	240.3	1955	220.7
1870	52.9	1920	252.8	1960	217.6
1880	93.3	1930	249.1	1963	214.4
				1964	213.8

FIGURE XII.3

U.S. RAILWAYS, 1965

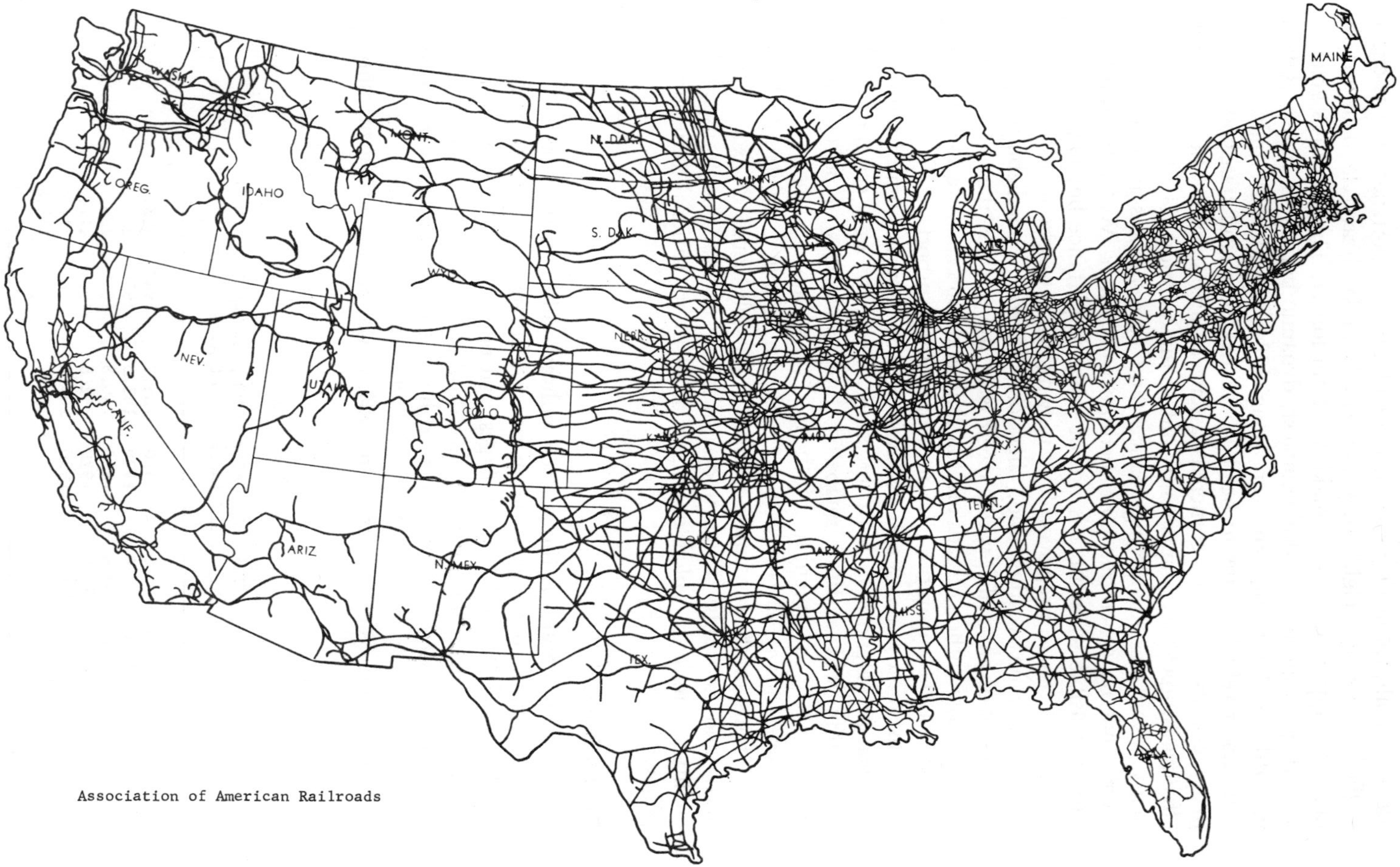

Association of American Railroads

TABLE XII.3

RAILWAY EQUIPMENT IN THE UNITED STATES, 1900-64

Item	1900	1910	1920	1930	1940	1950	1960	1964
Locomotives:								
Total	37,663	60,019	68,942	60,189	44,333	42,951	31,178	28,295
Steam	...	...	68,554	59,406	42,410	26,680	374	34
Electric	...	...	388	663	900	827	498	393
Diesel	...	...	...	77	967	15,396	30,240	27,837
Other	...	...	...	43	56	48	66	31
Average tractive effort (thousands of pounds)[a]	...	27.3	36.4	45.2	50.9	57.1	61.5	62.2
Freight-train cars (in thousands[b])	1,366	2,148	2,388	2,322	1,684	1,746	1,695	1,505
Average capacity per freight car (in tons)	...	35.9	42.4	46.9	50.0	52.6	55.4	58.2
Passenger-train cars	34,713	47,179	56,102	53,584	38,308	37,359	25,655	21,420
Air-conditioned cars[c]	...	...	...	...	...	16,747	11,787	10,423[d]

[a]For 1900-1950, average for steam locomotives only; Class I railroads, excluding terminal and switching companies. Operating railroads are classified on the basis of operating revenues: Class I have $3 million or more annual operating revenue; Class II, under $3 million. Before 1956, three classes were considered: Class I, with more than $1 million revenue; Class II, with $100,000 to $1 million; Class III, with less than $100,000 revenue.
[b]Class I railroads.
[c]Class I and Pullman Company.
[d]1963.

than 1920 but nonetheless covered the country (see Table XII.2 and Figure XII.3).

Though public aid to the railway companies was generous in land grants, tax exemption, guarantees of bonds, and subscriptions to capital stock, foreign capital played a great role in the construction of the American railroads. In many companies, foreign stockholding exceeded 50 per cent and in some reached 75 per cent: for example, 58 per cent in the New York Central Railroad, 65 per cent in the Illinois Central, and 75 per cent in the Louisville and Nashville. Only when construction was nearly completed did the American investors begin to repurchase foreign securities of the U.S. railways. The investment book value of all railroads amounted to $34.4 billion in 1962.

In equipment, American railroads reached their peak in the 1920's; since that time, the number of locomotives and cars, especially passenger cars, has been declining (see Table XII.3). The efficiency of locomotives, however, has increased by the shift from steam to dieselized equipment with much greater tractive power. Diesel-powered locomotives now account for more than 98 per cent of all U.S. railroad motive power, marking the end of the steam-locomotive era. The leading capacity of freight cars has also been substantially increased, and gigantic new freight cars are being introduced. Some can carry 100 tons of grain in a covered hopper; others take 30,000 gallons of oil in a tank (such cars are called "pregnant whales"). The area that has shown least progress is passenger-train cars. Most of them are 30 years old or more. Few new cars have been

TABLE XII.4

NUMBER OF RAILWAY EMPLOYEES, 1890-1964
(In Thousands)

1890	749	1940	1,046
1900	1,018	1945	1,439
1910	1,699	1950	1,237
1920	2,076	1960	781
1933	991	1963	680
		1964	665

installed: 1,324 between 1960 and 1964; this does not seem much in comparison with the airlines, which have re-equipped themselves between 1954 and 1964 and still continue ordering new type aircraft ($2.1 billion in 1965), and the bus industry, with equipment averaging 7 years in use at the end of 1962. However, about half of the passenger cars have been air-conditioned.

The number of railway employees increased from about 750,000 in 1890 to the record figure of 2.1 million in 1920, dropped to less than 1 million in 1933, and rose, under the impact of war, to 1.4 million in 1944-45. Since that time, the number of employees has declined uninterruptedly and now is smaller than it was in 1890 (see Table XII.4). The main reason for this decline is the contraction of rail activities; automation has also played an important role.

The decline in passenger traffic has been very sharp. In 1964, the volume of passenger miles was less than two-thirds of the annual average in 1926–30, and the number of revenue passengers was less than half, despite the fact that 70 million more people now populate the United States (see Table XII.5).

TABLE XII.5

PASSENGER TRAFFIC ON RAILROADS, 1926-64
(In Millions)

	Passengers Carried	Passenger-miles
1926-30 average	802	31,846
1931-35	481	18,375
1936-40	481	23,024
1941-45	772	71,713
1946-50	635	43,775
1951-55	458	31,642
1956	430	28,216
1958	382	23,295
1960	326	21,258
1962	313	19,926
1963	310	18,497
1964	313	18,248

TABLE XII.6

RAILROAD REVENUE FROM PASSENGER TRAFFIC, 1955-64

	1955	1960	1963	1964
Revenue from passenger traffic (in millions of dollars)	742.9	640.1	587.9	577.9
Commutation	101.4	122.4	130.0	134.2
Coach	427.6	376.1	353.4	349.0
Parlor and sleeping car	213.5	141.5	104.5	94.4
Revenue from each passenger (in dollars)	1.72	1.96	1.90	1.85
Commutation	0.41	0.60	0.67	0.68
Coach	2.56	3.29	3.25	3.18
Parlor and sleeping car	12.80	16.72	18.27	18.28
Average journey, per passenger (in miles)	66.1	65.2	59.7	58.3
Commutation	19.3	20.7	21.0	21.2
Coach	103.7	117.5	108.3	106.1
Parlor and sleeping car	386.1	430.6	456.5	467.9

The only sector of passenger traffic in which total revenue has been increasing is commutation; income from the 2 other sources, coach travel and parlor and sleeping-car travel, is on the decline, particularly from the latter (see Table XII.6).

Freight service has fluctuated less sharply within this period and is on a higher level than in 1926–30 (see Table XII.7).

Mining products represent half or more of revenue freight but provide less than one-fourth of gross freight revenue. In contrast, manufactured goods, though much less weighty, account for more than half of all freight revenue (see Table XII.8).

TABLE XII.7

RAILROAD FREIGHT SERVICE, 1926-64

	Revenue Tons Originated (In Millions)	Ton-Miles (In Millions)	Average Haul (Per Ton)
1926-30 average	1,279	427,234	315.3
1931-35	759	268,635	338.5
1936-40	931	339,328	346.1
1941-45	1,409	651,676	441.8
1946-50	1,398	599,941	411.2
1951-55	1,373	608,012	425.8
1956	1,521	651,188	428.1
1958	1,247	554,534	444.6
1960	1,301	575,360	442.1
1962	1,294	595,774	460.6
1963	1,285	621,737	464.0
1964	1,356	658,639	466.0

TABLE XII.8

FREIGHT ORIGINATED AND FREIGHT REVENUE OF
RAILROADS CLASS I, BY COMMODITY GROUP, 1950-63

	1950	1955	1960	1962	1963
Revenue freight originated (in millions of short tons)					
Agricultural products	129	134	150	155	161
Livestock and products	14	13	9	9	9
Mining products	747	762	649	635	662
Forest products	79	83	79	78	78
Manufactures, miscellaneous[a]	374	398	349	354	373
Less-than-carload freight	11	7	3	2	2
TOTAL	1,354	1,396	1,241	1,234	1,285
Gross freight revenue (in millions of dollars)					
Agricultural products	1,055	1,133	1,192	1,164	1,193
Livestock and products	276	294	229	210	205
Mining products	1,994	2,121	1,969	1,915	1,967
Forest products	581	687	651	647	661
Manufactures, miscellaneous[a]	3,888	4,421	4,207	4,348	4,460
Less-than-carload freight	353	281	153	100	75
TOTAL	8,146	8,938	8,402	8,385	8,561

[a]Including forwarder traffic.

Operating revenues originate largely from freight traffic, $8.5 billion out of the total $9.9 billion in 1964. Operating expenses consist of maintenance of way and structures, equipment repair and purchases, etc. The ratio of

TABLE XII.9

REVENUES AND EXPENSES OF CLASS I RAILWAYS, 1930-64
(In Millions of Dollars)

	1930[a]	1940[a]	1950	1960	1964
Operating revenue	5,536	4,335	9,473	9,517	9,857
Passenger revenue	731	418	813	640	578
Freight revenue	4,145	3,584	7,817	8,028	8,455
Mail	...	...	374	331	329
Other[b]	480	333	468	517	494
Operating expenses	3,994	3,132	7,059	7,566	7,738
Maintenance	1,754	1,335	2,995	2,952	2,990
Transportation, rail line	...	...	3,491	3,833	3,921
Other	...	...	573	781	827
Net revenue from railway operations	...	...	2,414	1,951	2,119
Tax accruals	349	396	1,195	999	871
Operating income	1,008	820	1,219	952	1,248
Less rent for equipment and joint facilities	...	...	179	367	430
Net operating income	874	691	1,040	585	818

[a]Class I, II, III.
[b]1930 and 1940: includes mail.

expense to revenue fluctuates at around 75–80 per cent. Revenues and expenses of the railways Class I have developed during recent decades as shown in Table XII.9.

With the shift of personal transportation and less weighty freight to motor vehicles, the percentage of total revenue derived from freight traffic has been increasing and that from passenger traffic falling (see Table XII.10).

In terms of cents per mile, on the other hand, railroads derive more than twice as much revenue from a passenger-mile than from a t.-mi. of freight, and this ratio has been increasing with the decline of passenger traffic (see Table XII.11 and Figure XII.4).

More than 99 per cent of freight handled is in volume shipments, so-called carloads, in contrast with that shipped by trucks, for which small shipments represent more than 25 per cent of the volume.

72. *Highways and Motor Vehicles*

For nearly 2 centuries, until 1790, Americans had practically no other roads on which to travel except Indian trails, some cut through dense forests and others worn into existence by pack horses and moving cattle. In 1797, the trip from Baltimore to Philadelphia took 5 days. The first turnpike—66 mi. from Philadelphia to Lancaster—was completed in 1794, and its immediate success called to life hundreds of turnpike companies; New York State alone had 137 chartered companies in 1811. Turnpikes

TABLE XII.10

PERCENTAGE DISTRIBUTION OF REVENUE FROM
PASSENGER AND FREIGHT TRAFFIC, 1909-64

	Total	Freight	Passenger	Other Sources
1909	100.0	67.8	22.8	9.4
1929	100.0	76.9	13.6	9.5
1939	100.0	81.4	10.3	8.3
1950	100.0	82.5	8.6	8.9
1960	100.0	84.3	6.7	9.0
1963	100.0	85.2	6.2	8.6
1964	100.0	85.7	5.9	8.3

TABLE XII.11

REVENUE PER UNIT OF TRAFFIC, 1953-64
(In Cents)

	Per Ton-Mile	Per Passenger-Mile
1953	1.478	2.660
1956	1.306	2.685
1959	1.459	2.955
1962	1.348	3.110
1963	1.310	3.179
1964	1.282	3.166

FIGURE XII.4
REVENUE PER PASSENGER-MILE AND TON-
MILE ON U₀S. RAILROADS, 1926-64
(In Cents)

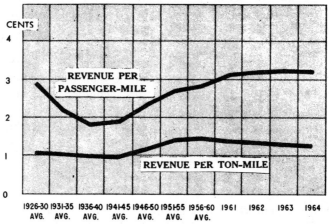

Association of American Railroads

were all-weather roads, but the tolls were prohibitive. Under pressure for a free road, the Federal Government built the "National Pike," the so-called Cumberland Road, a through road from the East to the Middle West. Started in 1811 in Cumberland, Md., it was completed in 1852, when it reached Illinois; it was 834 mi. long. It served for the great internal migration and as the first national post road. While the East had a system of highways in the first quarter of the nineteenth century, the West relied on only a few trails (see Figures XII.5A and B).

Just as turnpikes were approaching their apogee and their future seemed bright, railroads appeared on the scene and proved beyond doubt their superiority in land transportation (see Sec. 71). They were supreme for nearly a century until their monopoly was challenged by the motor vehicle. This latter brought about a resurgence of road building, and the motor vehicle became as characteristic a feature of the twentieth century as the railroad had been of the nineteenth.

Since the early 1890's, an increasing number of states have given financial aid to counties for improving and developing intercommunity roads. In 1916, Congress passed the Federal-Aid Highway Act, which provided for the sharing of highway-construction costs by the states and the Federal Government. Planning and developing the Federal-aid system began in 1921: its primary system connects all state capitals and nearly all cities with more than 50,000 population, county seats, ports, manufacturing centers, and other important traffic areas. The secondary system consists of feeders linking farms, factories, and markets, and of rural free-delivery mail routes, public-school bus routes, and the like. The National System of Interstate Highways, established in 1944, included at

FIGURE XII.5.A

MAIN HIGHWAYS IN THE EAST, 1820-30

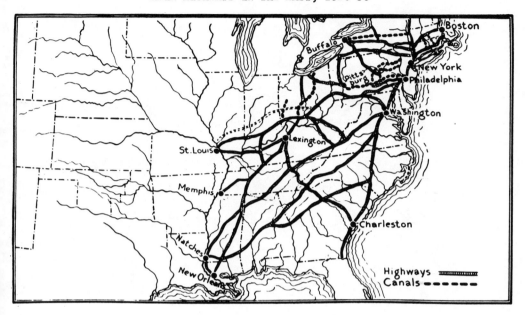

FIGURE XII.5.B

TRANSCONTINENTAL TRAILS IN THE UNITED STATES, 1820-30

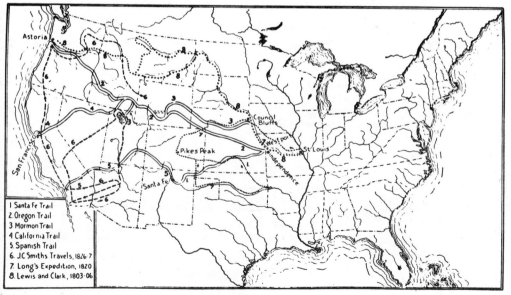

Courtesy of Thomas Y. Crowell Co.: G.R. Chatburn,
Highways and Highway Transportation (New York, 1923).

FIGURE XII.6

THE NATIONAL SYSTEM OF INTERSTATE AND DEFENSE HIGHWAYS
(Status of Improvement as of December 31, 1965)

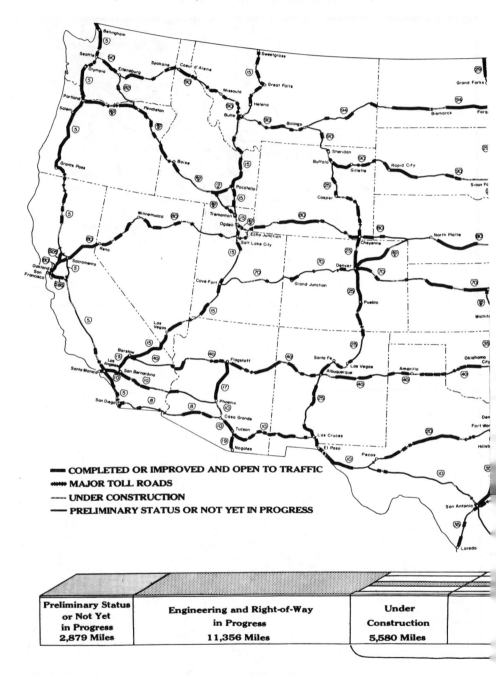

- ▬▬ COMPLETED OR IMPROVED AND OPEN TO TRAFFIC
- ⋘⋘ MAJOR TOLL ROADS
- ⋯⋯ UNDER CONSTRUCTION
- ▬ PRELIMINARY STATUS OR NOT YET IN PROGRESS

Preliminary Status or Not Yet in Progress 2,879 Miles	Engineering and Right-of-Way in Progress 11,356 Miles	Under Construction 5,580 Miles	

U.S. Department of Commerce, Bureau of Public Roads

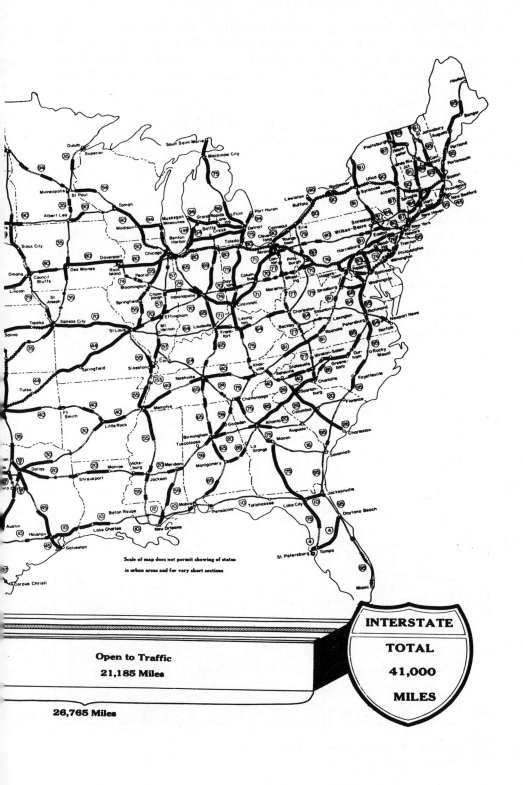

Scale of map does not permit showing of status
in urban areas and for very short sections

Open to Traffic
21,185 Miles

26,765 Miles

INTERSTATE

TOTAL

41,000

MILES

first 40,000 mi. but was later extended to 41,000 mi. Though this system represents a little more than 1 per cent of the country's total road mileage, it carries about one-fifth of all traffic. The Bureau of Public Roads estimates that by 1975, when the system will be completed, it will carry nearly 25 per cent of total traffic. In all, the Federal-aid highway system covered 887,000 mi. on December 31, 1965 (see Figure XII.6).

With the passage of the 1956 Federal-Aid Highway Act, Federal aid to road building increased rapidly, amounting to $14.5 billion for the years 1957–61, and $9.5 billion in 1962–64, mostly for work on the 41,000-mi. Interstate System.

By the end of 1964, roads and streets in the United States totaled more than 3.6 million mi., somewhat more than a mi. of road or street per sq. mi. of area. One-fourth of the total mileage is in nonsurfaced roads, which are almost exclusively county and local roads (see Figure XII.7). In many western states, such as Arizona, Wyoming, Montana, and Nevada, non-surfaced roads predominate, while in most eastern states they represent only a small percentage of total road mileage (see Table XII.12).

Surfaced roads, however, are of varying quality. More than half the surfaced rural roads are gravel, slag, and crushed stone; less than 30 per cent have a low-type bituminous surface and only 15–16 per cent, medium-

FIGURE XII.7

THE HIGHWAY MILEAGE IN THE UNITED STATES,
BY TYPE, 1900-1958

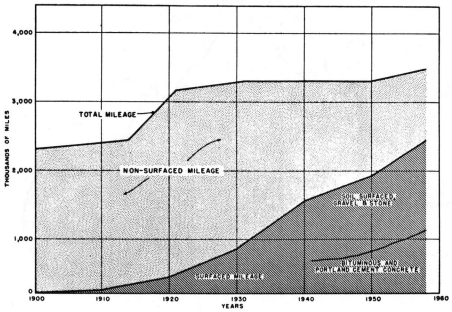

U.S. Department of Commerce, Bureau of Public Roads

TABLE XII.12

PERCENTAGE OF NONSURFACED ROADS IN THE UNITED STATES,
BY STATE, 1962

Maryland	1.0	North Carolina	13.7	Arkansas	39.1
Connecticut	1.4	Minnesota	14.9	Nebraska	40.6
Ohio	2.1	Vermont	16.0	Oregon	40.9
Virginia	2.2	Alabama	16.2	Georgia	42.7
Tennessee	3.1	Washington	18.7	North Dakota	43.0
Rhode Island	6.9	Michigan	20.9	South Carolina	43.8
Delaware	7.0	New Hampshire	22.2	South Dakota	44.6
Hawaii	8.1	Pennsylvania	22.8	Colorado	48.1
Wisconsin	8.2	Kentucky	24.2	Utah	50.6
Illinois	8.5	Louisiana	24.2	Montana	57.8
Massachusetts	8.9	West Virginia	34.5	Alaska	60.8
Indiana	9.0	Texas	37.1	Arizona	61.7
Iowa	9.1	Idaho	37.4	Mississippi	69.7
Missouri	9.9	Kansas	37.6	Nevada	70.4
New Jersey	11.4	Oklahoma	38.6	New Mexico	76.3
New York	12.6	California	38.6	Wyoming	79.5
Maine	13.6	Florida	39.0		

and high-type pavement. Rural roads account for nearly 87 per cent of total road mileage; the rest represents municipal roads or streets within incorporated places, towns and cities, and certain populous unincorporated areas. Yet municipal streets carry nearly three-fifths of all motor traffic.

Expenditures for highways—construction, land for right-of-way, other capital outlays, maintenance, etc.—are met by receipts from highway-user taxes: motor-fuel and motor-registration taxes, tolls, various state imports, Federal funds, receipts from bonds, etc. In 1965, total receipts by all agencies—Federal Government, state agencies, local rural governments, and municipalities—amounted to $14 billion; the estimate for 1966 is for $14.9 billion. Motor fuel, vehicle taxes, tolls, parking fees, and other imposts on highway users provide four-fifths of the total. Estimated expenditures of $14.1 billion in 1966 included $8.8 billion for capital outlay, about $3.5 billion for maintenance, and $1.8 billion for all other needs, excluding debt retirement ($0.8 billion).

Between 1914, when public concern for roads began to express itself, and today, nearly $170 billion has been spent in the United States for construction of public roads and streets. Some two-thirds of that enormous amount, or more, has been collected from highway users via different taxes. Maintenance of highways is increasingly costly since, with the growing volume and weight of traffic, the roads deteriorate rapidly. The estimated lifetime of the average road surface is 12 years.

The nation's highway system is administered by some 35,000 governmental units (in states, counties, townships, cities, towns, and small rural communities) that deal with traffic and maintenance of roads and streets. In addition to more than one-half million highway employees in government agencies and the contracting force of some 300,000, some 12 million people are connected with highway transportation. One out of every 7 workers has a job in this field: 8.5 million truck drivers and other employees of trucking companies; 2.4 million engaged in automotive sales and servicing; 650,000 in the manufacture of motor vehicles, tires, and parts; and more than 400,000 occupied in bus and taxi service and petroleum refining.

In 1964, licensed motor-vehicle operators numbered 94 million (57 million males and 37 million females). Of the more than 90 million motor vehicles registered in this country in 1965, 75 million were passenger cars and more than 15 million, trucks and buses (see Table XII.13).

The United States accounts for more than 55 per cent of all motor vehicles in the world; its motor fleet is almost twice as large as the combined fleet of all European countries together.

TABLE XII.13

FLEET OF MOTOR VEHICLES, BY TYPE, 1900-65
(In Thousands)

	Total	Passenger Cars	Buses	Trucks
1900	8	8	...	...
1910	469	458	...	10
1920	9,239	8,132	...	1,108
1930	26,750	23,035	41	3,675
1940	32,453	27,466	101	4,886
1950	49,162	40,334	224	8,604
1960	73,753	61,559	249	11,945
1963	82,748	69,027	298	13,423
1964	86,310	71,985	305	14,019
1965	90,497	75,400	15,097	

Motor-fuel consumption on highways increased from 2.7 million gal. in 1919 to 24 billion in 1940, dropped during the war to 16 billion, and has increased steadily since the end of the war. In 1964, it amounted to 68 billion gal. (see Figure XII.8). The average number of gal. consumed per vehicle was 680 in 1940 and 760 in 1963; the average for passenger cars in 1963 was 652 gal.; for buses, 2,813; and for trucks, 1,351 gal. Buses, however, accounted for only 1.3 per cent of 1963 fuel consumption; trucks, 28.1 per cent; and passenger cars, for 70.6 per cent.

In 1964, almost 4 out of 5 families in the United States owned 1 automobile; 1 out of 6 owned 2 cars or more. According to the Survey Research Center of the University of Michigan, 28 per cent of "spending units"* with income under $1,000 owned 1 car and 2 per cent of this group owned 2 cars or more; respective figures for the income group of $2,000–$2,999 were 59 and 6 per cent; for those with income of $6,000–$7,499, 71 and

---

* A spending unit consists of all persons related by blood, marriage, or adoption and living in the same dwelling who pool their income for major expenses. Some families contain 2 or more spending units.

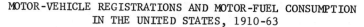

FIGURE XII.8

MOTOR-VEHICLE REGISTRATIONS AND MOTOR-FUEL CONSUMPTION
IN THE UNITED STATES, 1910-63

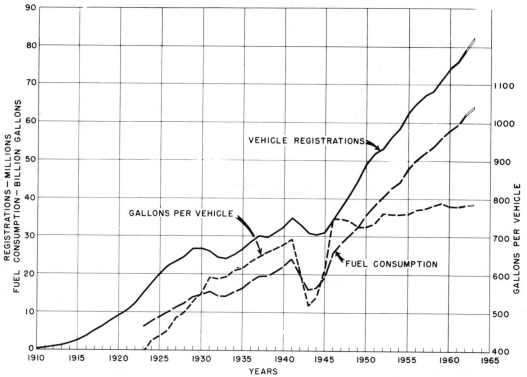

National Academy of Sciences and National Research Council

17 per cent (see Table XII.14). In age, the cars were distributed as follows: 11 per cent were less than 2 years old; 10 per cent, 2–3 years old; 32 per cent, 3–7 years old; and the remaining 47 per cent, 8 or more years.

The greatest use of passenger cars is for travel to and from work—almost one-half of all trips and one-fourth of the total mileage traveled. Seven workers out of 10 use a car for this purpose. The average car occupancy for such trips is 1.3 persons per vehicle; for all-purpose trips, 1.7 persons. About 90 per cent of all intercity travel is by motor vehicle: 89.7 per cent by car and 2.6 per cent by bus. In a typical city of 1 million population, about 87 per cent of trips start and end at home; half of these are work trips—to offices, stores, factories, schools, etc., largely outside the central business district (see Figure XII.9).

According to the Bureau of Public Roads, for every dollar the typical car owner spends for his vehicle, almost 28 cents goes for current operation: gasoline (excluding taxes), oil, garage, parking, etc.; 47 cents is for the initial cost and the upkeep (depreciation, repairs, maintenance, replacement of tires and tubes, accessories [excluding taxes]); 13 cents for

TABLE XII.14

PERCENTAGE DISTRIBUTION OF AUTOMOBILE OWNERS,
BY INCOME SIZE, 1964

	1 Automobile	2 Automobiles or more	None
All spending units	56	19	25
Money income before taxes:			
Under $1,000	28	2	70
$1,000-$1,999	32	3	65
$2,000-$2,999	59	6	35
$3,000-$3,999	58	8	34
$4,000-$4,999	62	10	28
$5,000-$5,999	66	19	15
$6,000-$7,499	71	17	12
$7,500-$9,999	63	31	6
$10,000 and more	51	45	4

FIGURE XII.9

PURPOSES OF INTRACITY TRIPS IN A TYPICAL CITY
OF ONE MILLION POPULATION, 1960
(Per Cent)

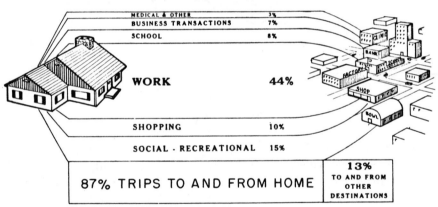

National Academy of Sciences, National Research Council

insurance; the remaining 12 cents goes for taxes; of these, 2 cents is used for government purposes other than highways (see Figure XII.10).

In terms of vehicle-miles, motor travel increased more than fourfold between 1929 and 1965, from 198 billion vehicle-mi. to 880 billion. More travel takes place on rural roads than on urban: 438 billion and 404 billion mi., respectively, in 1964.

Nearly 90 per cent of all intercity travel in this country is by private car, in terms of passenger-mi. (see Sec. 70).

The Bureau of Public Roads expects that motor-vehicle registration will exceed 100 million before 1971 and approach 114 million by 1976.

FIGURE XII.10

DISTRIBUTION OF COSTS OF OWNING AND OPERATING
A TYPICAL AUTOMOBILE PER DOLLAR SPENT

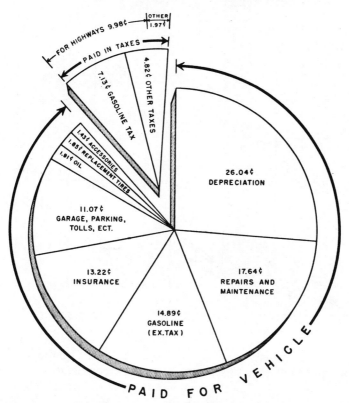

National Academy of Sciences, National Research Council

In terms of vehicle-mi., motor travel is projected to increase more than 55 per cent in the next 10 years, from 899 billion vehicle-mi. in 1966 to 1,051 billion in 1971, and 1,200 billion in 1976 (see Figure XII.11).

The Interstate Highway System is expected to absorb the largest part of the growth, as compared with rural roads and city streets.

Public motor carriers transport goods or passengers, or both; much property also is transported by private trucks. Trucks handle almost one-fourth of all intercity freight and are second only to the railroads in this respect. As late as 1959, they carried 90 per cent of all motor vehicles, but with the introduction of piggyback service by the railroads in 1955, this share began to decline, to 77 per cent in 1961 and 62 per cent in 1964. They deliver 90 per cent of livestock to the stockyards, 65 per cent of all fruit and vegetables to the leading markets.

Their operations are expanding (figures in billions of t.-mi.): 173 in

FIGURE XII.11

ESTIMATED MOTOR TRAFFIC IN 1966-76

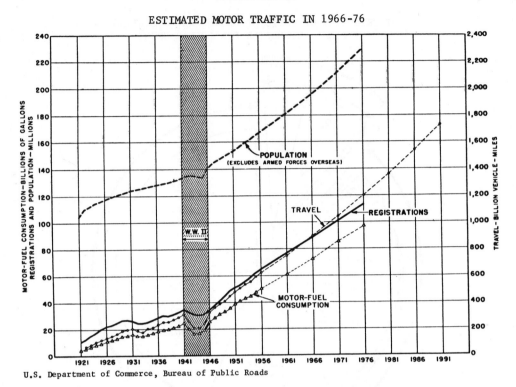

U.S. Department of Commerce, Bureau of Public Roads

1950, 226 in 1955, 298 in 1960, and 400 in 1965. On the average, the capacity of a single truck is 2.6 t.; of a truck combination, 12.6 t. The average length of the haul of a common motor carrier (Class I, with operating revenue of $1 million or more) was 263 mi. in 1963; of a contract carrier, 138 mi.

The 1963 Census of Transportation counted about 13 million private and commercial motor trucks. More trucks are used for agricultural purposes than for any other purpose; some 56 per cent of all trucks are used for a pickup. Some 87.0 per cent of all trucking firms consist of 1-truck operators; 8.2 per cent are in small fleets containing from 2 to 9 trucks; 3.1 per cent of fleets with 10–49 trucks; 0.8 per cent of fleets with 50–99 trucks, and 0.9 per cent of larger fleets.

The "heavy-heavy" trucks, consisting mostly of tractor-semitrailer combinations, are used more extensively than any other size class of trucks. Though they represented only 6 per cent of the truck population in 1963, they provided 21 per cent of total truck mileage in the United States and 67 per cent of truck mileage used "for hire."

The transit industry in the United States represents all local passenger transportation agencies, both privately and publicly owned, except taxicabs and suburban railroads, sightseeing and school buses. The industry comprises 14 electric railway and 14 trolley companies, and 1,129 motor bus companies. While the traffic by electric surface rail and trolley coach has been continuously declining, almost to the point of disappearing from the scene, that by motor bus, despite showing some decline, too, has become an important branch of the national transportation system. Thus the number of passengers on the electric surface rail was 7.3 billion in 1935, 1.2 billion in 1955 and 289 million in 1964; the respective figures for the trolley coach are: 95 million, 1.2 billion, and 349 million; for the motor bus; 2.6 billion, 7.3 billion, and 5.8 billion.

The industry as a whole employed 209,000 persons in 1935, but only 144,800 in 1964; despite this reduction in force, the annual payroll almost tripled between these two dates, from $321 million to $917 million. In 1964, the industry owned 10,624 railway cars; 1,865 trolley coaches, and more than 49,000 motor buses. Its total investment amounted to $4.1 billion; the 1964 operating revenue to $1.4 billion.

TABLE XII.15

PASSENGER FATALITIES BY TYPE OF TRAVEL, 1946-64
(Per 100 Million Passenger Miles)

	Railroads[a]	Intercity Buses	Automobiles[b]	Airlines[c]
1946	0.18	0.19	2.5	1.2
1950	0.58	0.18	2.9	1.5
1955	0.07	0.18	2.7	0.76
1960	0.16	0.13	2.2	1.01
1962	0.10	0.16	2.3	0.35
1963	0.07	0.23	2.3	0.12
1964	0.05	0.13	2.4	0.14

[a]Passenger trains.
[b]Private cars and taxis.
[c]Scheduled domestic airlines.

The 27,000 intercity buses served 459 million passengers in 1964 and accounted for 22.7 billion passenger-mi. Their operating revenues were $730 million; their expenses, $637 million; and operation taxes, $67 million. In addition to intercity buses, almost 50,000 local and suburban bus fleets accounted for about 1–1.5 billion vehicle-mi., as compared with 1.3 billion for intercity bus fleets. School-bus fleets comprise more than 175,000 buses, at least 20,000 station wagons, and many other small vehicles that transport pupils to and from schools. The average cost of intercity bus travel was 2.72 cents per mi. in 1963, as compared with 3 cents for rail coach and 5.62 cents for air coach. For thousands of small communities throughout the country, buses are the only means of public transportation.

The accident rate for bus service is comparable with that for railroads; passenger fatalities per 100 million passenger-mi. are heaviest in automobile travel; those in air travel are declining, but are still heavier than in rail travel (see Table XII.15).

In proportion to its population of over 400 million, Europe reports fewer road-traffic accidents than this country: 68,500 killed and 1.8 million injured in 1964, as compared with 47,700 and 1.7 million, respectively, in the United States. However, the index of traffic fatalities in European countries has been rising faster than in the United States: with 1959=100, the index for 1964 was 130 for West Germany, 138 for France, 142 for Great Britain, 153 for the Netherlands, 169 for Italy, 182 for Czechoslovakia, and 263 for Yugoslavia, as against 124 for the United States.

73. Waterways

Until the railroads gained supremacy in freight traffic during the second half of the nineteenth century, the inland waterways—rivers, lakes, and canals—were the chief avenues for the movement of goods. Today, waterways account for virtually all our trade with foreign countries, including a large part of the trade with Canada and Mexico, and for about one-third of our shipping in domestic commerce.

Water traffic consists of 3 types of operations: (1) Foreign commerce through the seaports and ports of the Great Lakes; (2) coastwise traffic between ports; and (3) traffic on rivers and canals. In recent years, somewhat more than 30 per cent of the total freight tonnage was in foreign commerce; about an equal amount was in traffic between the various Great Lakes ports and between them and seaports and inland waterways ports; the remainder was the traffic between ports and river ports, something less than 30 per cent, and between the outlying areas of the United States. The Maritime Administration has designated 34 trade routes as "essential" to the development, expansion, and maintenance of U.S. foreign commerce, some including the ports of the Great Lakes and St. Lawrence Seaway, and 3 essential services: Round-the-World-Westbound, Round-the-World-Eastbound, and Tri-Continent. There are specific sailing requirements for each route—these indicate the number of sailings per month for specified types of vessels (see Figures XII.12 and XII.13).

TABLE XII.16

U.S. MERCHANT MARINE OF THE UNITED STATES, 1930-64

	Number of Ships	Gross Registered Tons (In Millions)	
		Total	Steam and Motor
1930	25,214	16.1	13.8
1940	27,212	14.0	11.4
1945	29,797	32.8	30.2
1950	36,083	31.2	28.3
1955	39,242	30.0	26.8
1960	43,088	28.6	23.6
1963	44,077	25.7	20.1
1964	44,669	26.2	20.0

FIGURE XII.12

U.S. ESSENTIAL FOREIGN TRADE ROUTE NO.1:
BETWEEN U.S. ATLANTIC PORTS AND EAST COAST OF SOUTH AMERICA

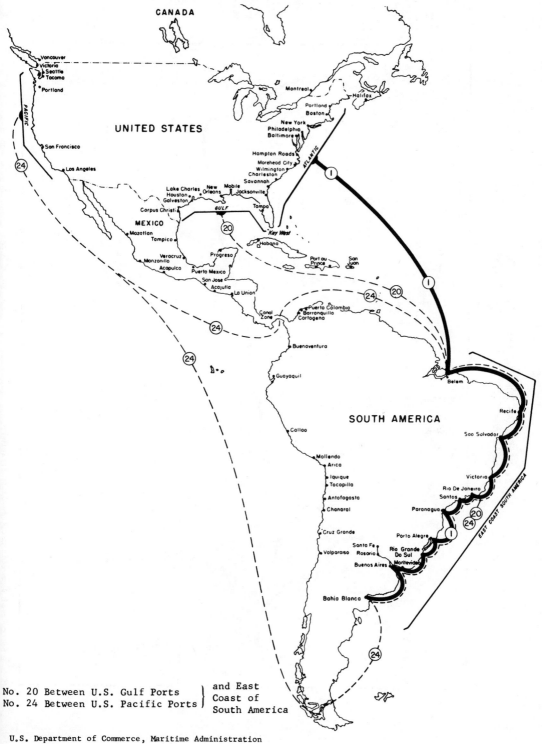

No. 20 Between U.S. Gulf Ports   } and East
No. 24 Between U.S. Pacific Ports }   Coast of
                                      South America

U.S. Department of Commerce, Maritime Administration

FIGURE XII.13

U.S. ESSENTIAL FOREIGN TRADE ROUTE NO. 12:
U.S. ATLANTIC PORTS AND THE FAR EAST

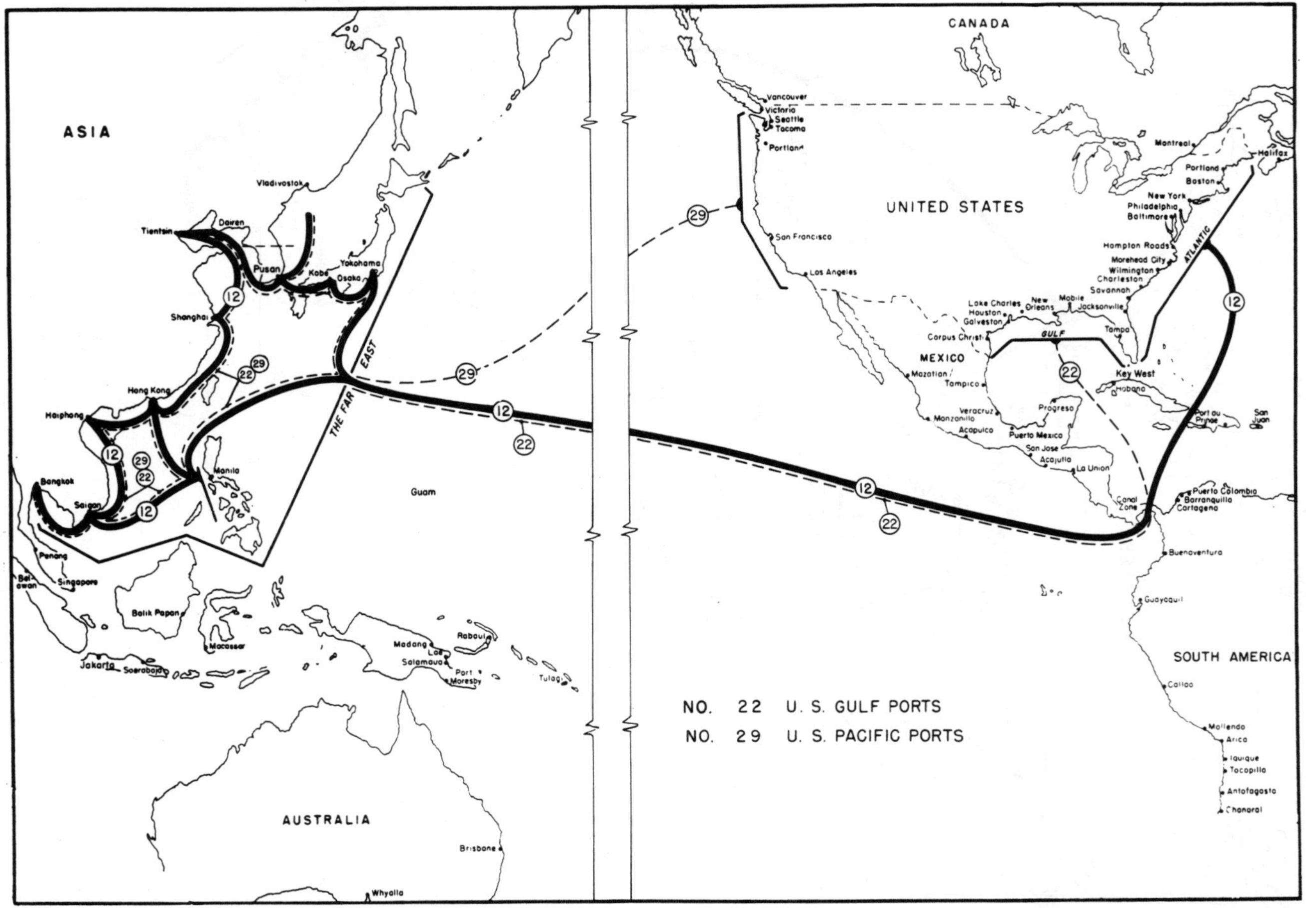

NO. 22   U. S. GULF PORTS
NO. 29   U. S. PACIFIC PORTS

U.S. Department of Commerce, Maritime Administration

In 1930, the U.S. merchant fleet consisted of 25,214 ships with 16.1 million gross registered t.; by 1964, it had increased to 44,669 vessels with 26.2 million t. (see Table XII.16).

Two-thirds of the present tonnage is used on the Atlantic coast, less than one-sixth on the Pacific, and the remainder on the northern lakes and western rivers. Only a small part of the fleet is in vessels of 1,000 gross registered t. or more—3,314 out of 44,669 ships—but their tonnage of 20.3 million represented nearly 80 per cent of the total in 1964.

The U.S. merchant fleet is larger than that of any country in the world, but its ships are considerably older, on the average, than those of most ranking maritime nations: 17.4 years, as compared with 9–10 years for the United Kingdom, France, West Germany, Norway, the Netherlands; Japan's fleet is still younger (8.4 years). Only the U.S.S.R. (15.5 years) and Italy (17 years) have about as old merchant vessels as does the United States. While nearly half of deadweight tonnage carrying the flags of Liberia, Panama, and Honduras is under effective U.S. control, many of these vessels, too, particularly tankers and freighters, are 15 years old and more (except Liberia's ships: 11.8 years).

In recent years, the replacement of the least efficient tankers by supergiant vessels has been achieved; many ships have been repaired or converted in the principal shipyards of the country. All in all, 411 ships, with 2.4 million gross registered t., have been launched from 1959 through 1964. Despite this, the total gross registered tonnage of the U.S. merchant marine decreased from 28.9 million in 1959 to 26.2 million in 1964. Its share in the world's tonnage declined from 22.6 to 14.7 per cent within this period.

Since no construction subsidy is given for vessels in domestic commerce (see Sec. 65), the Great Lakes fleet is now the smallest in 60 years. Other reasons for its decline are high cost of ship replacement, competition of the Canadian fleet (which receives government assistance), and relocation of industries since World War II.

The U.S. merchant marine participates to a much smaller extent in the country's foreign commerce than do the fleets of many other maritime or trading nations; it accounts for 8.5 per cent of our total foreign commerce, including government-sponsored cargoes, as compared with 42.7 per cent for Norway, 46.2 per cent for Japan, 52 for the United Kingdom, 58.7 per cent for France, etc. The participation of the U.S. flag in the nation's ocean-borne commerce has been declining. It was 26.5 per cent in 1937, 17.8 per cent in 1957, 10.6 per cent in 1960, and 9.9 per cent in 1964. As a matter of fact, more than half the tonnage of all U.S. ships has been inactive in the reserve fleet. At the end of 1964, of the 2,505 vessels of 1,000 gross t. and over, only 912 were on active duty: 617 in foreign trade, and 295 in domestic commerce.* In ownership, the merchant fleet com-

---

* Excludes vessels on inland waterways, Great Lakes, U.S. Army and U.S. Navy vessels, and special-type ships, such as cable ships, tugs, etc.

prised 1,566 government-owned vessels and 963 vessels in private hands; of the latter, 891 were active: 576 in foreign trade, 286 in domestic trade, and 29 in U.S. agency operations.

The ports of the Atlantic coast have played a very great role in the development of U.S. transportation and commerce. The coast, richly provided with excellent harbors, is a beehive of maritime activity. With time, channels have been widened and deepened, shorelines protected from erosion, possible obstructions beneath the water removed. Today, the coastwise and intercoastal traffic moves through 37 main Atlantic ports, about an equal number of Pacific ports, and some ports on the Gulf side. In foreign commerce, the most important ports are: New York, Philadelphia, and Baltimore on the Atlantic coast; Los Angeles and San Francisco on the Pacific; New Orleans on the Gulf.

TABLE XII.17

THE WATERBORNE COMMERCE OF THE UNITED STATES, 1940-63
(In Millions of Short Tons)

	1940	1945	1950	1955	1960	1962	1963
Foreign commerce	111	172	169	271	339	359	386
Through seaports: Imports	41	45	96	144	198	207	209
Exports	50	100	44	95	105	110	130
Great Lakes ports: Imports	4	7	6	9	13	16	18
Exports	17	21	24	23	23	25	29
Domestic commerce	497[a]	447[a]	651	745	761	771	788
Coastwise	157	91	183	196	209	215	214
Great Lakes, between ports	141	158	170	185	155	136	142
Local traffic[b]	98	98	107	113	104	102	99
Coastwise and river ports	70	87	191	252	292	316	332
TOTAL, FOREIGN AND DOMESTIC	608	619	821	1,016	1,100	1,129	1,174

[a]Approximate net totals.
[b]Seaports, Great Lakes ports, and waterways ports.

Cargo tonnage in waterborne commerce of the United States almost doubled between 1940 and 1963, as far as domestic commerce was concerned; in foreign commerce it more than tripled. Two-thirds of waterborne commerce is domestic (see Table XII.17). Atlantic ports, accounting for one-half of all U.S. waterborne trade, are the most important, in terms of tonnage, in foreign waterborne commerce; the Gulf ports come next. Imports and exports via the Pacific ports and the Great Lakes ports account for about the same tonnage in waterborne commerce as the Gulf ports.

Imports and exports through the most active U.S. ports are smaller, in terms of tonnage, than coastwise receipts and shipments; coastwise shipments through the southern ports exceed those through the Atlantic or Pacific ports (see Table XII.18).

TABLE XII.18

WATERBORNE COMMERCE OF SELECTED UNITED STATES PORTS, 1963
(In Millions of Short Tons)

	Foreign		Coastwise	
	Imports	Exports	Receipts	Shipments
Atlantic coast ports:				
New York	40	7	43	14
Portland, Me.	15	0.1	3	0.5
Baltimore	17	7	8	1
Boston	6	0.8	11	0.7
Gulf coast ports:				
Mobile, Ala.	7	2	0.4	3
New Orleans	5	16	1	19
Baton Rouge, La.	5	4	0.4	7
Houston	3	7	2	22
Corpus Christi	4	2	0.3	10
Beaumont	...	2	2	19
Port Arthur	0.2	3	3	18
Pacific coast ports:				
San Francisco	6	6	12	8
Los Angeles	6	3	4	7
Long Beach	3	3	1	2
UNITED STATES	209	130	214	215

The Maritime Administration estimates that exports of principal bulk commodities in U.S. oceanborne foreign trade (coal, grains, cotton, soybeans, scrap iron and steel) which amounted to 51 million l. t. in 1955 and 75 million in 1963, would increase to 113 million in 1970 and 124 million l. t. in 1975. Imports of principal bulk commodities (iron ore, bauxite,

TABLE XII.19

COMMERCE OF SELECTED GREAT LAKES PORTS[a]
(In Millions of Short Tons)

	Receipts				Shipments			
	1950	1955	1960	1963	1950	1955	1960	1963
Detroit	21.1	24.3	25.3	28.0	1.3	1.6	1.9	1.5
Duluth-Superior	10.1	7.4	5.2	4.5	53.0	61.2	37.5	37.0
Cleveland Harbor	17.4	19.7	17.1	16.6	0.4	0.4	0.5	0.2
Chicago	15.8	16.9	12.3	11.3	4.1	6.3	8.4	10.0
Buffalo	16.5	19.3	15.6	14.4	2.4	2.4	1.2	0.9
Ashtabula, Ohio	10.4	9.5	7.8	7.2	3.3	3.6	2.5	3.6
Indiana Harbor	10.4	13.7	12.1	12.7	5.2	6.4	7.1	4.8
Lorain Harbor, Ohio	8.2	5.6	5.0	3.6	3.3	2.3	1.7	1.1
Milwaukee	7.4	7.2	6.9	4.9	1.4	1.5	1.6	1.7
Toledo, Ohio	4.6	6.5	5.9	6.5	29.3	28.7	27.8	33.5
Two Harbors, Minn.	0.2	0.1	-	[b]	18.9	19.0	15.3	[b]
UNITED STATES	175.6	193.6	168.0	151.5	193.5	207.6	178.3	161.2

[a]Comprises foreign, lakewise, and coastwise shipping.
[b]Less than 500 tons.

other ores, petroleum products, and sugar), which amounted to 104 million
l. t. in 1955 and 168 million in 1963, would grow to 216 million and 246
million l. t., respectively.

The Great Lakes constitute the "fourth coastline" of the United States.
Together with the St. Lawrence Seaway, they handle a very large commercial tonnage and are, for all practical purposes, connected, through the
essential routes (Secs. 32–34), with all the great trading areas of the world.
The bulk of their traffic, however—about seven-tenths—is in domestic
commerce. The freight carried through their various ports has shown ups
and downs, some ports increasing their operations from year to year and
others experiencing a more uncertain course (see Table XII.19).

TABLE XII.20

FREIGHT CARRIED ON INLAND WATERWAYS, BY SYSTEM, 1940-63
(In Billions of Ton-Miles)

	1940	1945	1950	1955	1960	1962	1963
Atlantic coast rivers	1.9	1.0	6.5	27.0	28.6	29.4	30.1
Gulf coast rivers	0.6	0.3	1.2	13.9	16.9	17.9	19.9
Pacific coast rivers	1.2	1.6	1.7	4.7	6.0	6.4	6.5
Mississippi River System	13.9	19.6	33.6	52.0	69.3	79.3	82.3
Canals and connecting channels	4.8	7.2	8.6	...	...	...	...
Great Lakes System	95.6	113.0	111.7	118.8	99.5	90.0	95.3
TOTAL	118.1	142.7	163.3	216.5	220.3	223.1	234.2

Even in the atomic age, barges and towing vessels carry enormous quantities of bulk commodities over the inland waterways—rivers and canals.
Now many vessels are dieselized; barges have been developed to handle
various chemicals and related products; tank barges for moving petroleum
are in use; carfloats equipped to move 20 or more railroad cars are common. The Mississippi River system, comprising all the tributaries of the
Mississippi, Illinois, Missouri, and Ohio rivers, is next in importance to the
Great Lakes in domestic freight traffic (see Table XII.20). Exclusive of
the Great Lakes, the commercially navigable length of inland waterways
extends over 25,260 mi. More than half of the mileage has the 9-ft. or
greater depth considered standard for inland channels (see Figure XII.14).

The Panama Canal, about 50 mi. long, is the shortest route between
points on the Atlantic and Pacific coasts. The distance between New York
and San Francisco, via the Canal, is 5,262 miles, rather than the 13,135
miles via the Straits of Magellan, around South America. Part of the
Canal route is through Gatun Lake, the largest man-made lake in the
world. Today, the Canal is the center of controversy, because of Panama's
insistence of changing the original agreement, legally still in force. The
United States has declared its willingness to negotiate over changes in the

TABLE XII.21

PANAMA CANAL TRAFFIC, 1940-64

	Number of Transits	Net Registered Tons (In Millions)	Cargo Tonnage (In Millions of Long Tons)
1940	5,370	24.1	27.3
1945	1,939	8.4	8.6
1950	5,448	28.0	28.9
1955	7,997	38.6	40.6
1960	10,795	58.3	59.3
1963	11,017	64.4	62.2
1964	11,808	69.6	70.6

existing treaty. The Canal, though vitally important from the military and political points of view, is no longer fully satisfactory, since the modern gigantic ships cannot pass through it. Hence, studies are under way on its possible replacement by another canal to be built in Panama, Nicaragua, or Colombia.

Nevertheless, traffic on the Canal is still increasing, from 5,448 transits in 1950 to 7,997 in 1955 and 11,808 in 1964; cargo carried also has more than doubled within these years (see Table XII.21).

In 1964, traffic through the Panama Canal was distributed by nationality of vessels as shown in Table XII.22.

TABLE XII.22

PANAMA CANAL TRAFFIC, BY NATIONALITY OF VESSELS, 1964

	Number of Transits	Net Registered Tonnage of Vessels (In Millions)	Cargo Tonnage (In Millions of Long Tons)
United States	1,695	12.0	10.6
Norway	1,476	10.5	11.8
Great Britain	1,355	9.1	8.5
Germany	1,105	4.6	3.3
Japan	818	4.9	4.7
Liberia	914	7.1	10.1
Netherlands	754	3.2	2.9
Greece	597	4.3	6.1
Panama	548	1.7	1.8
Sweden	411	2.6	2.6
Denmark	280	1.7	1.6
Colombia	287	1.0	0.4
Honduras	269	0.4	0.2
Italy	180	1.3	1.0
Chile	131	0.8	0.9
France	167	0.8	0.7
Israel	64	0.3	0.2
Taiwan	73	0.5	0.6
Other	684	2.8	2.6

FIGURE XII.14

THE INLAND WATERWAYS OF THE UNITED STATES

The American Waterways Operators, Inc.

COMMERCIALLY NAVIGABLE
INLAND WATERWAYS
OF THE
UNITED STATES

CONTROLLING DEPTHS

9 FEET OR MORE
UNDER 9 FEET
PROPOSED EXTENSIONS

TABLE XII.23

OPERATIONS OF U.S. SCHEDULED PASSENGER
AND CARGO AIR CARRIERS, 1940-64

	1940	1950	1955	1960	1963	1964
Number of operators:						
Domestic	19	48	40	39	37	36
International	3	6	7	I0	8	8
Total employment:						
Domestic	15,984	61,903	95,548	134,546	143,112	153,243
International	6,067	20,883	26,655	30,098	32,327	34,695
Route miles in operation:						
Domestic	42,757	77,440	78,992	101,414	105,269	104,793
International	52,322	106,401	117,282	148,303	142,675	142,880
Aircraft in operation:						
Fixed wing	437	1,209	1,390	1,797	1,727	1,766
Helicopter	...	11	19	25	20	20
Available seats (average):						
Domestic	16.5	37.5	51.2	65.5	83.4	86.1
International	18.3	41.0	56.4	89.9	124.8	127.2
Average speed (miles per hour):						
Domestic	...	180	208	235	287	297
International	...	218	244	307	423	441
Revenue-miles flown (millions):						
Domestic	110	364	627	821	889	958
International	10	94	135	163	192	214
Revenue-passengers carried (thousands):						
Domestic	2,523	17,345	38,221	56,352	69,366	79,139
International	163	1,675	3,488	5,904	8,037	9,381
Revenue-passenger-miles flown (millions):						
Domestic	1,052	8,029	19,852	30,557	38,457	44,141
International	100	2,214	4,499	8,306	11,905	14,352
Express and freight, ton miles flown (millions):						
Domestic	3,473	152	230	387	604	744
International	...	61	96	192	296	395
Mail, ton-miles flown (millions):						
Domestic	10	48	89	136	174	190
International	...	26	53	103	181	181

74. Airways and Outer Space

Today scheduled air service is available in the United States to all cities with 100,000 population or more, to more than 75 per cent of the towns with 10,000 population, and to at least 50 per cent of the communities with 1,000 population or more. In all, more than 600 points receive scheduled airline service.

The network of air routes of the United States is longer than that of any

TABLE XII.24

PERSONNEL OF SCHEDULED AIR CARRIERS, 1940-63

	1940	1950	1960	1963
Domestic				
Pilots and copilots	1,939	5,787	11,460	12,137
Other flight personnel	18	776	3,144	3,182
Communications personnel	193	2,450	3,122	2,683
Pursers, stewards, stewardesses	914	3,372	8,923	10,829
Mechanics	4,054	15,788	28,067	28,592
Other hangar and field personnel	1,880	9,822	35,471	39,215
Office employees	5,855	21,894	27,819	29,225
All others	1,131	2,016	15,711	17,249
TOTAL	15,984	61,903	133,717	143,112
International				
Pilots and copilots	340	1,492	1,507	1,626
Other flight personnel	15	745	474	628
Communications personnel	...	953	1,044	1,018
Pursers, stewards, stewardesses	122	1,055	1,606	2,173
Mechanics	1,359	3,818	5,247	5,062
Other hangar and field personnel	2,397	2,434	7,097	8,944
Office employees	1,834	9,244	7,036	8,071
All others	...	1,142	5,043	4,805
TOTAL	6,067	20,883	29,054	32,327

other country. It consists of more than 105,000 mi. of domestic routes and almost 143,000 mi. of international routes (see Figure XII.15).

The striking feature of scheduled air transport is the small number of its aircraft and personnel. To service more than 88 million passengers, fly more than 371 million t.-mi. of mail, domestic and international, and more than a billion t.-mi. of express and freight in 1964 required only 1,766 aircraft and 188,000 employees. Between 1940 and 1964, the number of passengers multiplied about 30 times, that of personnel between 8 and 9 times, and of revenue passenger-mi. flown, more than 40 times (see Table XII.23).

The surprisingly small numbers of flight personnel, only a few thousand pilots and co-pilots, is supported by about an equal number of auxiliary flight personnel (see Table XII.24).

Planes do not fly in the boundless air as the pilots please. The Federal Airway System, with airways 10–30 mi. wide, constitutes the right-of-way for all users—the airlines, the many thousands of private civilian planes, and the military. Strict rules and regulations govern traffic in the atmosphere; pilots and planes must be certified and are guided through the entire flight. Just as the automobile driver pays for the use of highways via the gasoline tax, the airlines and other civilian users of the Federal Airway System pay for its use through the gasoline tax. Use of landing and other facilities is also subject to payment.

Since World War II, aircraft underwent great technical improvement, speed increased from 160 to 600 mi. per h.; seating capacity, from a maxi-

FIGURE XII.15

UNITED STATES AIR TRANSPORTATION SYSTEM
(ROUTES CERTIFICATED TO LOCAL SERVICE CARRIERS)
JUNE 30, 1964

Civil Aeronautics Board

NOTES: # Seasonal point

* Point authorized by temporary exemption

FIGURE XII.16

AIR AND SEA PASSENGER TRAVEL ON
U.S. FLAG CARRIERS, 1947-64

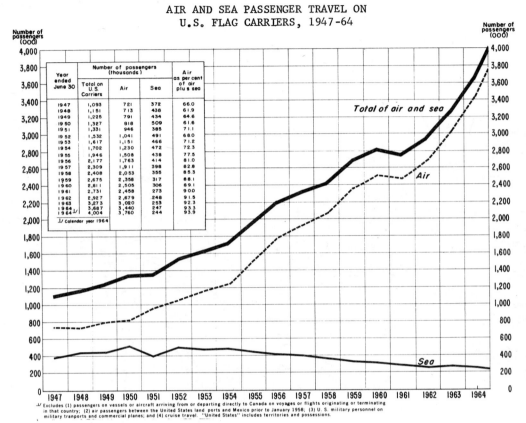

Year ended June 30	Number of passengers (thousands)			Air as per cent of air plus sea
	Total on U.S. Carriers	Air	Sea	
1947	1,093	721	372	66.0
1948	1,151	713	438	61.9
1949	1,225	791	434	64.6
1950	1,327	818	509	61.6
1951	1,331	946	385	71.1
1952	1,532	1,041	491	68.0
1953	1,617	1,151	466	71.2
1954	1,702	1,230	472	72.3
1955	1,946	1,508	438	77.5
1956	2,177	1,763	414	81.0
1957	2,309	1,911	398	82.8
1958	2,408	2,053	355	85.3
1959	2,675	2,358	317	88.1
1960	2,811	2,505	306	89.1
1961	2,731	2,458	273	90.0
1962	2,927	2,679	248	91.5
1963	3,273	3,020	253	92.3
1964 1/	3,687	3,440	247	93.3
1964	4,004	3,760	244	93.9

1/ Calendar year 1964

1/ Excludes (1) passengers on vessels or aircraft arriving from or departing directly to Canada on voyages or flights originating or terminating in that country; (2) air passengers between the United States land ports and Mexico prior to January 1958; (3) U. S. military personnel on military tranports and commercial planes; and (4) cruise travel. "United States" includes territories and possessions.

The American Waterways Operators, Inc.

mum of 21 persons to more than 100. The number of airports has risen, from 5,759 in 1948 to 9,940 in 1964.

Approximately 7.7 million passengers traveled by air between the United States and other countries in 1964, the greatest part of them moving across the Atlantic. Out of every 100 international passengers in 1964, 82 traveled by air. Among the factors contributing to the rapid increase of air travel are, on the one hand, rising incomes and lower fares, and on the other, go-now-pay-later travel opportunities, the growing number of charter flights, and other features appealing to the traveling public. Figure XII.16 illustrates the spectacularly growing air travel (from 66 per cent of total travel in 1947 to 94 per cent in 1964) and the steadily shrinking sea travel between this country and overseas on U.S. flag carriers from 1947 to 1964.

The main source of income is passenger travel; the main expense items are flying and ground costs (see Table XII.25).

TABLE XII.25

OPERATING REVENUES AND EXPENSES OF CERTIFIED AIR CARRIERS, 1955-64
(In Millions of Dollars)

	1955	1960	1962	1963	1964
Revenues, domestic	1,215	2,129	2,498	2,723	2,996
Passenger	1,065	1,860	2,168	2,374	2,615
Mail (incl. subsidy)	61	113	139	143	150
Express and freight	62	103	136	153	174
Excess baggage	12	21	20	18	17
Other	15	32	35	35	40
Expenses, domestic	1,091	2,091	2,408	2,565	2,733
Flying operations	328	601	659	701	736
Direct maintenance of flight equipment	138	258	496	523	561
Depreciation and amortization	93	184	293	299	306
Ground and indirect costs	532	1,048	960	1,042	1,130
Net operating income	124	38	90	158	263
Revenues, international	398	685	810	930	1,018
Passenger	300	528	595	693	763
Mail (incl. subsidy)	30	48	71	72	75
Express and freight	33	59	71	80	93
Excess baggage	7	10	10	12	11
Other	28	41	63	73	76
Expenses, international	380	639	724	799	854
Flying operations	115	180	193	217	225
Direct maintenance	37	58	114	118	129
Depreciation and amortization	29	66	92	95	91
Ground and indirect costs	200	336	325	369	409
Net operating income	18	45	86	131	164

Commercial aviation continues to grow by leaps and bounds. In 1963, the scheduled airlines offered the public more than 10,000 flights per day, all of which also carried some cargo—mail, express, freight. By the end of that year, giant "jet freighters" were in operation. A single such freighter can haul a load exceeding 40 t. of cargo nonstop across the continent or 35 t. nonstop from New York to Paris. It can be loaded or unloaded in 40 minutes and be converted to an all-passenger aircraft within a few hours. It represents a new challenge to other freight carriers of the country—for example, 100,000 head of calves were shipped from New York to Milan by air in the summer of 1964, at a speed which made it unnecessary to feed the calves underway.

General-aviation flying comprises all civil flying except public air carriers. In 1964, there were about 137,000 civil aircraft, including gliders, but only 91,000 of these were active; they used the existing airports and airfields for their operations, but their movements were tabulated on only 274 airports supplied with control towers of the Federal Aviation Agency. There are about 905,000 certified airplane pilots in this country: 26,545 in airline transport; 306,100 commercial pilots; and 572,610 private pilots. Other certified airmen, such as mechanics, parachute riggers, and instructors, exceed 171,000. The typical civil flying craft is fully equipped for flight under all but the most unfavorable weather conditions. In 1964, the pilots flew 2.2 billion miles; almost half the mileage was corporation and individual business transportation, not for hire; one-fifth was personal flying; the remainder comprised passenger and cargo transportation for hire, aerial service such as crop-dusting, spraying, seeding, and other work, on the one hand, and instructional flying, on the other. In all, general-aviation flying accounts for about two-thirds of all operations, local and itinerant, at airports with towers and for practically all at other airports; it also accounts for somewhat over one third of all flying hours.

In recent years, space vehicles have invaded the atmosphere. As of April 14, 1966, 238 spacecraft had been placed in orbit: 180 by the United States, 50 by the U.S.S.R., 2 by Canada, 2 by the United States and United Kingdom, 3 by France, and 1 by the United States and Italy. Of manned space flights, there had been 2 suborbital and 10 orbital by the United States and 8 orbital by the U.S.S.R. The longest flight by American pilots covered 206 orbits; by Russian, 81 orbits. There have also been many unmanned flights, and various spectacular achievements on both American and Russian sides.

Federal expenditures for space research and technology have grown

FIGURE XII.17

FEDERAL EXPENDITURES FOR SPACE RESEARCH
AND TECHNOLOGY, 1956-67

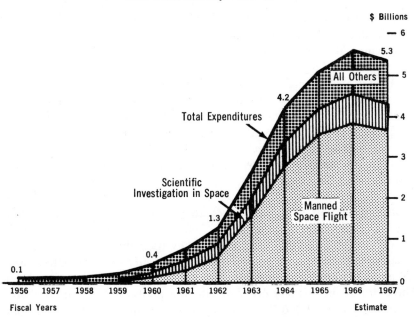

Executive Office of the President, Bureau of the Budget

rapidly: from $74 million in 1955 to $401 million in 1960, $4.4 billion in 1964 and $5.1 billion in 1965. The budgetary estimate for 1966 is $5.6 billion and for 1967, $5.3 billion (see Figure XII.17 and Sec. 75).

Much that concerns space travel is necessarily shrouded in military secrecy, but one thing is beyond any doubt: space is man's new frontier, and many technological advances made now for military aims will eventually be used for peacetime transportation and communication, just as many wartime technical achievements have been incorporated into the everyday economy. No matter how fantastic space travel now seems, it carries the promise that mail and freight transport, even passenger movement—perhaps controlled from the ground, at least in the beginning— will one day seem a matter of fact. Atomic energy, new fuels, space vehicles, missiles, rockets, weather satellites, Telstar, all are signposts crowded into the last 2 decades, a mere 2 decades as compared with man's slow groping on earth for thousands of years. Propulsed with such incredible speed, the space revolution may outdo the industrial revolution!

75. Our Many Ways to Communicate

Our communications system comprises several different branches— postal service, telephone and telegraph service, radio broadcasting, television. They originated at different times and each has developed in its own way, some slowly, others with extraordinary speed; some are maintained by the Federal Government, others are organized as independent businesses.

Although the postal service has grown from 7 billion pieces of mail handled in 1900 to 72 billion in 1965, the number of post offices in the country has declined within that period from 76,788 to 33,694 (and some 11,000 branches and stations) because of the increasing concentration of people in cities, where a single post office can service thousands of customers (see Table XII.26).

TABLE XII.26

U.S. POSTAL SERVICE, 1900-1964

	Number of Post Offices	Number of Pieces of Mail Handled (In Billions)	Sales of Postage Stamps and Other Stamped Paper (In Millions of Dollars)	Postage Paid and Permit[a]
1900	76,688	7.1	94	...
1910	59,580	14.9	202	4
1920	52,641	25.8[b]	380	13
1930	49,063	27.9	575	74
1940	44,024	27.7	522	177
1950	41,464	45.1	862	675
1960	35,238	63.7	1,243	1,701
1963	34,498	67.9	1,382	2,216
1964	34,040	69.7	1,504	2,475

[a]Second-, third-, and fourth-class mail.
[b]1925.

TABLE XII.27

REVENUES AND ACCRUED COSTS,
BY CLASS OF MAIL, 1926-65
(In Millions of Dollars)

Year	First-Class Mail		Domestic Air-mail		Second-Class Mail		Third-Class Mail		Fourth-Class Mail	
	Rev-enues	Accrued Costs	Rev-enues	Accrued Costs	Rev-enues	Accrued Costs	Rev-enues	Accrued Costs	Rev-enues	Accrued Costs
1926	321	247	...	...	34	117	69	71	144	147
1930	359	278	5	15	30	120	61	83	151	167
1935	343	229	6	12	20	106	54	75	112	133
1940	413	267	19	28	24	110	75	101	133	155
1945	615	373	81	49	29	144	76	99	232	232
1950	741	665	74	109	45	242	153	291	403	506
1955	967	905	130	121	65	298	269	441	595	593
1961	1,558	1,547	171	152	89	442	497	787	626	774
1962	1,615	1,605	185	163	94	456	510	787	634	787
1963	1,824	1,691	200	172	98	454	563	874	645	806
1964	2,109	1,814	216	181	108	481	612	899	659	815
1965	2,193	1,965	243	198	119	499	650	999	702	846

The U.S. Postal Service has always operated with a deficit, except in the 3 war years 1943–45. The only regular services providing surpluses have always been first-class mail and domestic airmail (in addition to government mail); some special services, such as certified and insured mail, also show small profits. The permanent source of deficit is second-, third-, and fourth-class mail. The postal deficit amounted to $657 million in 1963, $473 million in 1964, and $585 million in 1965 (see Table XII.27).

The number of pieces of mail received per capita has increased from 257 in 1945 to 349 in 1964 (see Table XII.28). The volume of mail is expected to reach 90 billion pieces by 1970 and 125 billion by 1980.

According to the Report of the Postmaster General, postal employees numbered 595,512 in 1965: 447,394 regular and 148,118 substitute. Among the full-time employees, there were 188,460 post-office clerks and mail handlers; 33,304 postmasters; 132,522 city carriers; and 30,981 rural carriers. Mail is shipped by rail, short-haul truck, star route, water, and air (via the domestic and international lines).

TABLE XII.28

PIECES OF MAIL RECEIVED PER CAPITA, 1945-64

	Total	First-Class and Airmail	Second-Class	Third-Class	Parcels
1945	257	166	42	41	8
1950	287	168	42	69	8
1955	324	184	41	92	7
1960	341	193	42	100	6
1963	347	199	44	98	6
1964	349	201	45	97	6

TABLE XII.29

TELEPHONES: AVERAGE DAILY CALLS, 1876-1964

	Number of Telephones (In Thousands)		Per 1,000 Population (Total System)	Average Daily Calls	
	Total	Bell Companies		Local Exchange[a]	Toll[a]
				(In Thousands)	
1876	3	3	0.1	...	...
1895	340	310	4.8	2,521	54
1915	10,524	5,968	103.9	43,719	1,101
1925	16,936	12,035	145.2	64,850	2,450
1935	17,424	13,845	136.4	73,440	2,560
1945	27,867	23,202	198.1	106,370	4,930
1955	56,436	48,028	336.9	205,270	8,852
1960	74,342	62,980	407.8	273,322	12,064
1963	84,440	71,151	442.5	314,682	14,184
1964	88,736	74,657	458.7	330,800	15,300

[a]A local call originates in and is completed within the same exchange area; a toll call originates in one exchange to reach another exchange, whether nearby or across the continent.

TABLE XII.30

THE DEVELOPMENT OF THE BELL TELEPHONE SYSTEM
AND INDEPENDENT TELEPHONE COMPANIES, 1940-64

	1940	1950	1955	1960	1963	1964
Bell Telephone System						
Miles of wire (millions)	91.3	144.3	201.2	307.9	368.6	394.4
Book value of plant (millions of dollars)	4,887	10,375	15,773	24,722	30,854	33,385
Depreciation and amortization reserves " " "	1,397	2,905	4,007	5,402	6,584	7,158
Operating revenues " " "	1,206	3,342	5,425	8,111	9,796	10,549
Operating expenses " " "	913	2,653	4,040	5,586	6,648	7,233
Federal income taxes " " "	64	248	644	1,172	1,455	1,477
Interest expense " " "	43	115	134	263	344	357
Net income " " "	226	370	701	1,279	1,557	1,744
Employees (number in thousands)	282	535	630	595	586	605
Independent telephone companies[a]						
All companies (number)	6,400	5,500	4,700	3,300	2,800	2,700
Telephones (number in thousands)	2,194	4,922	6,750	9,718	11,125	11,868
Miles of wire (millions)	...	9.2	15.2	28.6	35.0	40.0
Book value of plant (millions of dollars)	375	878	1,656	3,396	4,335	4,847
Depreciation reserves " " "	85	203	326	600	793	911
Operating revenues " " "	81	270	503	906	1,120	1,248
Operating expenses " " "	61	211	354	630	755	835
Federal income taxes " " "	...	19	61	107	138	154
Interest expenses " " "	6	12	22	58	78	88
Net income " " "	13	29	67	117	157	177
Employees (number in thousands)	...	63	72	85	86	90

[a]Data in the last two columns are for 1962 and 1963.

TABLE XII.31

HOUSEHOLDS WITH TELEPHONE,
AND TELEPHONES PER 100 POPULATION, BY STATE, 1962

State	Households with Telephone (Per Cent)	Telephones per 100 Population	State	Households with Telephone (Per Cent)	Telephones per 100 Population
District of Columbia	88	88.0	Florida	71	42.1
New York	87	54.5	New Hampshire	86	41.5
Connecticut	94	54.4	Hawaii	...	41.1
California	85	52.2	Oklahoma	74	40.7
New Jersey	90	51.9	Texas	71	38.8
Delaware	86	51.9	Montana	75	38.4
Illinois	87	51.6	Vermont	83	38.3
Massachusetts	92	50.2	North Dakota	83	37.1
Nevada	70	49.1	Maine	78	36.4
Pennsylvania	87	48.7	Virginia	71	35.7
Maryland	86	47.1	Idaho	74	35.6
Colorado	80	46.5	Arizona	64	35.4
Nebraska	88	45.6	Georgia	69	35.4
Missouri	84	45.5	Louisiana	72	35.0
Minnesota	92	44.8	South Dakota	74	34.5
Oregon	84	44.8	Tennessee	71	34.4
Michigan	88	44.6	New Mexico	64	34.0
Washington	81	44.5	West Virginia	71	32.4
Ohio	85	44.5	Alabama	65	31.2
Iowa	93	44.5	Kentucky	66	30.9
Rhode Island	85	44.4	North Carolina	64	29.6
Wyoming	78	44.3	Arkansas	59	28.9
Kansas	85	43.5	South Carolina	61	27.4
Indiana	85	43.3	Mississippi	50	23.3
Utah	84	42.9	Alaska	...	21.0
Wisconsin	87	42.3	UNITED STATES	81	44.4

In 1964, there were 88.7 million telephones in the United States. The telephone system spread slowly, from 3,000 telephones in 1876, the year when the patent was issued to Alexander Graham Bell, to 1 million instruments functioning across the country in 1899. The next peaks were reached in 1914, with 10 million telephones, and in 1929, with 20.1 million. The number of telephones per 1,000 population increased from 4.8 in 1895 to 198.1 in 1945 and 458.7 in 1964 (see Table XII.29).

Though the telephone system is largely in the hands of the Bell System, there are 2,700 other small telephone companies, mostly in rural areas. Practically all are interconnected with the Bell System, so that any of their subscribers can call anyone in the nationwide telephone system. The predominant position of the Bell System in relation to the independent companies is shown in Table XII.30.

In the country as a whole, 4 out of 5 households had telephone service at the residence in 1963, while in some states almost every household was included in the telephone system (90 per cent in New Jersey, 92 in Massachusetts, 93 in Iowa, and 94 in Connecticut); at the other extreme was Mississippi, where only 50 per cent of the households subscribed to telephone service. The District of Columbia stands out as the area with most telephones per 100 population: 88; even Connecticut, the state highest in the list of households with telephone service, had only 54.4 telephones per 100 population in 1963 (see Table XII.31).

A peak year for the number of domestic telegraph messages was 1937, with 207 million; a second peak was reached in 1945, with more than 236 million messages. Since that time, the number of messages has been declining: in 1964, it amounted to 97 million, or less than half the number in 1945. Competition comes from long-distance telephone service, airmail, and the telegraph business of the telephone company. In contrast, the number of international messages has been steadily increasing: from 7.7 million in 1940 to 12.3 million in 1964 by ocean cable and from 9 to 18.3 million, respectively, by radio-telegraph (see Table XII.32).

Nation-wide telegraph service is provided by Western Union in the United States; a few small independent companies serve some railroads and particular industries in limited areas. Telegraph cables link the country with other continents, and the invention of radio opened the way to wireless telegraph communications. The radio-telegraph circuits enable anyone anywhere in the United States to communicate with practically any place on the globe.

While Western Union is the single domestic carrier, 2 carriers provide international telegraph service. Ocean telegraph cables have been operated since 1963 by Western Union International, an independent company to which Western Union transferred its international operations, in compliance with the Communication Act. The second carrier is a French corporation that connects New York with France and England.

TABLE XII.32

DOMESTIC AND INTERNATIONAL MESSAGES, 1870-1964
(In Millions)

	Domestic Messages	International Messages	
		Cable	Radio
1870	9.2	...	...
1880	29.2	...	...
1890	55.9	...	...
1900	63.2	...	...
1910	75.1	5.8[a]	0.3[a]
1920	155.9	4.0	0.4
1930	212.0	15.3	5.2
1940	191.6	7.7	9.0
1945	236.2	10.5	10.5
1950	178.9	10.0	12.6
1955	153.9	10.7	15.0
1960	124.3	11.2	17.1
1962	112.5	11.3	17.3
1963	104.2	11.3	18.1
1964	97.4	12.3	18.3

[a]1912.

TABLE XII.33

TELEGRAPH OPERATIONS, 1950-63
(In Millions of Dollars)

	1950	1955	1960	1962	1963
Western Union					
Investment in plant and equipment	294.5	311.0	398.0	541.4	596.6
Depreciation and amortization reserves	128.2	135.8	168.6	183.1	198.9
Operating revenues	178.0	228.8	262.4	264.1	286.8
Operating expenses	167.3	206.0	246.8	257.1	266.7
Operating income	8.7	13.2	11.2	10.7	19.2
International carriers					
Ocean-cable					
Investment in plant and equipment	97.3	93.2	98.6	80.4	54.7
Depreciation and amortization reserves	63.9	58.0	57.7	43.1	34.5
Operating revenues	24.6	33.5	36.2	36.2	36.8
Operating expenses	22.3	29.2	34.7	35.3	35.3
Operating income	1.9	1.5	0.6	0.6	1.3
Radio-telegraph					
Investment in plant and equipment	38.9	42.0	65.2	82.9	98.8
Depreciation and amortization reserves	18.8	18.5	24.9	29.2	32.5
Operating revenues	25.7	34.6	50.8	56.2	61.0
Operating expenses	23.0	29.2	42.2	46.8	49.8
Operating income	1.9	2.0	5.0	5.6	7.8

Since World War II, telegraph operations have developed as shown in Table XII.33.

In 1964, the telephone service employed 695,000 persons; the domestic telegraph carrier, about 27,000; and the international carriers (ocean-cable and radio-telegraph together), about 9,000.

The licensing of radio broadcasting stations on a regular basis began in 1921, though there had been a few experimental transmissions previously; the first coast-to-coast hookup was made in 1927, the first round-the-world broadcast in 1930, and the first television license was issued in 1941.

In 1945, 936 stations were on the air; in 1965, 5,814. Of the latter, 3,972 were AM radio, 1,270 were FM radio, and 572 were television stations.

In 1922, about 60,000 families had radio sets; in 1926, 4.5 million; in 1930, 13.8 million. The number continued to grow fast: to 28.5 million in 1940 and 46.8 million in 1956. Long before that date, however, television sets appeared on the scene and grew in number with exceptional rapidity, from 8,000 in 1946 to 3.9 million in 1950 and 35 million in 1956.

TABLE XII.34

BROADCAST OPERATIONS, 1940-63

	1940	1950	1955	1960	1962	1963
All stations (number)	765	2,336	3,179	4,218	4,532	4,691
AM and AM-FM stations	765	2,143	2,704	3,470	3,668	3,832
FM (independent) stations	...	86	38	218	279	294
TV stations	...	107	437	530	555	565
Revenues (in millions of dollars)						
All stations	147	550	1,198	1,866	2,122	2,278
AM and AM-FM stations	147	443	452	592	627	670
FM (independent) stations	...	1	1	6	9	11
TV stations	...	106	745	1,269	1,486	1,597

More than 7 million television sets were produced in 1963; more than 8 million in 1964.

In May, 1964, 93 per cent of the households in the United States had 1 television set or more. The percentage was even higher in some states: 96 in the Northeast and North Central, 95 in the Middle Atlantic. The difference between urban areas and rural nonfarm areas was small: 95 versus 89 per cent; but in rural farm areas the percentage was 82. Of the households with television sets, every sixth had 2 sets or more.

Broadcast operations have expanded many times since 1940 (see Table XII.34).

There is only one radio spectrum, and all nations share in it. International agreements are therefore necessary on the allocation of frequencies for all the recognized radio services. No major frequency allocation can be made now by any nation without considering its world-wide usage; an international treaty determines the allocation of frequency bands. To distinguish the call signs of stations in different countries, alphabet letters and numbers are used. They identify the nationality and type of the station and are a kind of "license plate" for communication traffic on the radio highways. Since 1927, an international agreement has apportioned the alphabet for basic call-sign use among the nations.

In 1965, a new feature was established in the field of international communications with the installation of the Early Bird Satellite, 23,000 miles above the equator in the mid-Atlantic. So far, its operations are in the initial state but can be expected to develop to an important international communication medium.

XIII. *Trade and Finance*

The United States occupies a unique position in the world. It is the greatest trader, the largest producer, the greatest international banker, and the greatest investor among all the countries of the world. Its foreign trade reaches out to every area on this planet, and its products are used far and wide. But while its economy is closely associated with the world economy, its domestic market is so big that receipts from international transactions represent only a small part of its operations and activities.

76. *Our Exports and Imports*

The United States is the largest exporter and importer in the world. Before World War II, it was second to the United Kingdom in the value of imports, but after the war, it moved to the top of the list of importers also. Yet foreign trade accounts for a much smaller percentage of the national income of the United States than of most advanced countries, and this percentage, apart from occasional fluctuations, has been declining for more than a hundred years; it is one of the lowest in the world. The value of U.S. imports equaled 13.1 per cent of the national income in 1800; 9.5 per cent in 1900; 3.7 per cent in 1950; and 3.6 per cent in 1964. Corresponding percentages for the U.S. exports are: 10.2; 5.5; 4.3; and 5.2.

The per capita value of exports and imports of this country was $38 and $33, respectively, in 1926–30; $24 and $18 in 1936–40; $78 and $44 in 1946–50; $107 and $77 in 1956–60, and $134 and $96, respectively, in 1964. In contrast, corresponding figures for France in 1962 were $156 and $161; for the United Kingdom, $206 and $227; for West Germany, $244 and $224; for Sweden, $387 and $412; and for Canada, $329 and $325.

This position of the United States among the trading nations of the

TABLE XIII.1

FOREIGN TRADE OF THE UNITED STATES, 1791-1965
(In Millions of Dollars)

Year, Annual Average	Total	Exports[a]	Imports	Year, Annual Average	Total	Exports[a]	Imports
1791-1800	106	47	59	1916-1920	9,879	6,521	3,358
1801-1810	168	75	93	1921-1925	7,847	4,397	3,450
1811-1820	140	59	81	1926-1930	8,810	4,777	4,033
1821-1830	142	69	73	1931-1935	3,738	2,025	1,713
1831-1840	223	104	120	1936-1940	5,702	3,220	2,482
1841-1850	244	123	121	1941-1945	13,565	10,051	3,514
1851-1860	533	249	284	1946-1950	18,488	11,829	6,659
1861-1870	586	254	332	1951-1955	26,165	15,333	10,832
1871-1880	1,124	589	535	1956-1960	32,854	19,204	13,650
1881-1890	1,457	765	692	1960	35,232	20,578	14,654
1891-1900	1,789	1,025	764	1961	35,712	20,998	14,714
1901-1905	2,426	1,454	972	1962	38,080	21,700	16,380
1906-1910	3,124	1,779	1,345	1963	40,485	23,347	17,138
1911-1915	4,083	2,371	1,712	1964	45,173	26,489	18,684
				1965	48,712	27,346	21,366

[a]Exports of U.S. merchandise and re-exports.

world reflects not only the extent to which the growth of foreign trade
has been outstripped by the expansion of national output but also the
degree to which the diversification of domestic production has moved

FIGURE XIII.1

EXPORTS AND IMPORTS OF MERCHANDISE, 1955-64

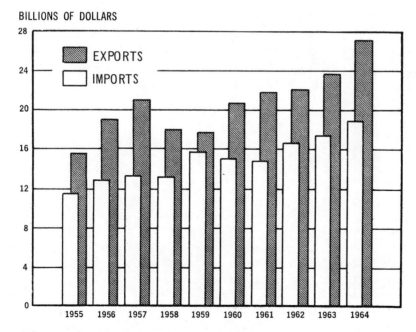

BILLIONS OF DOLLARS

U.S. Department of Commerce, Bureau of the Census

TABLE XIII.2

PERCENTAGE DISTRIBUTION OF U.S. EXPORTS AND IMPORTS BY ECONOMIC CLASS, 1840-1964

Year, Annual Average	Exports					Imports				
	Crude Materials	Crude Foodstuffs	Manu-factured Foodstuffs	Semi-manu-factures	Finished Manu-factures	Crude Materials	Crude Foodstuffs	Manu-factured Foodstuffs	Semi-manu-factures	Finished Manu-factures
1840	67.8	4.1	14.3	4.3	9.5	12.4	15.5	15.5	11.6	45.1
1866-1870	57.6	9.1	13.7	4.7	14.9	11.7	13.2	19.9	13.9	41.3
1886-1890	38.1	15.0	25.0	5.5	16.4	22.6	15.8	16.5	15.8	29.3
1896-1900	26.1	18.9	24.0	9.6	21.4	29.5	15.1	15.9	13.3	26.2
1901-1905	30.3	12.2	22.2	11.3	24.1	33.4	12.9	12.4	16.7	24.7
1906-1910	31.7	8.9	18.1	14.2	27.1	34.6	11.0	11.8	17.8	24.8
1911-1915	30.7	8.8	14.3	15.4	30.7	34.9	12.8	12.6	17.3	22.4
1916-1920	18.3	9.2	17.8	15.4	39.3	40.1	12.0	16.2	17.1	14.4
1921-1925	27.5	9.7	13.9	12.5	36.3	37.4	11.1	13.0	17.7	20.9
1926-1930	24.4	6.4	9.7	14.1	45.4	36.8	12.6	9.9	18.9	21.9
1931-1935	30.2	3.9	8.8	14.5	42.6	28.9	15.6	13.7	18.7	23.0
1936-1940	19.1	3.8	5.5	19.3	52.4	33.1	13.1	14.2	20.9	18.7
1941-1945	5.8	1.7	11.9	9.4	71.3	33.0	16.4	11.5	21.2	18.0
1946-1950	14.0	8.3	10.3	11.1	56.3	30.3	18.8	10.7	22.3	17.9
1951-1955	13.0	7.1	5.6	11.6	62.7	26.3	19.5	10.1	23.7	20.4
1956-1960	12.9	7.4	6.0	15.0	58.7	22.4	14.1	10.5	22.1	31.1
1960	12.7	8.1	5.5	17.3	56.4	20.6	11.7	10.7	21.1	35.9
1961	12.3	9.2	5.6	15.9	57.1	21.5	11.7	10.9	21.2	34.7
1962	10.4	9.4	6.4	14.2	59.6	20.6	10.9	11.0	20.9	36.6
1963	11.2	9.9	6.5	14.5	58.0	19.4	10.2	11.8	21.2	37.6
1964	11.1	9.7	6.5	15.6	57.1	18.5	10.9	9.7	21.4	39.4

this country toward self-sufficiency. Apart from its dependence on certain agricultural and mineral products (cf. Sec. 49 and Sec. 55), the bulk of its foodstuffs and of the raw materials used by its factories is produced domestically, and the largest part of its output is consumed within the country. The greatly developed regional specialization in this country plays, to some extent, the same role in its economy, which international division of labor has for other industrialized nations. Nevertheless, foreign outlets are of great importance to various branches of our economy and to our balance of international payments (see Sec. 77 and Sec. 78).

For the first hundred years of its existence, the United States depended heavily on foreign markets, both as sources of raw materials and manufactured goods and as outlets for its agricultural products. Not until the mid-1870's did its exports begin to exceed its imports; there was only one break in this pattern, from 1934 through 1940. Afterward, the previous trend was resumed, with exports exceeding imports (see Table XIII.1 and Figure XIII.1).

Changes in the composition of U.S. exports and imports reflect the development from an agricultural, semicolonial country to a great industrial power. Cotton and tobacco leaf predominated among the exports before the Civil War and paid for the imported goods, mainly machinery and other capital goods and luxury articles; in the last quarter of the past century, the importance of wheat and livestock products as export items began to increase. Since the beginning of the twentieth century, the United States has been exporting petroleum and its products, iron, steel, and copper, as well as machinery. The share of finished manufactured goods, other than foodstuffs, in merchandise exports rose from 24 per cent in 1901–5 to 63 per cent in 1951–55; in 1964, it was somewhat lower —57 per cent. In imports, the United States has shifted from manufactured foodstuffs and finished goods to crude materials—rubber, copper, tin, raw silk, and the like (see Table XIII.2; for the composition of our exports and imports in agricultural and mineral products, see Sec. 50 and Sec. 56).

U.S. export of machinery and motor vehicles represents nearly 40 per cent of the total value of exported goods. When some other manufactured goods, such as leather, manufactured cotton, wool and wood, paper, iron and steel products, chemicals, scientific instruments, and other manufactured products are included, the percentage rises to almost 60. In contrast, machinery and vehicles represent only some 10–12 per cent of the total value of imported goods, not much more than the share of coffee, tea, cocoa, sugar, and related products.

The percentage of our output exported varies from commodity to commodity. In 1962, the United States exported 20 per cent of its output of unmanufactured cotton, 27 per cent of that of leaf tobacco, 25 per cent

TABLE XIII.3

DOMESTIC EXPORTS IN RELATION TO OUTPUT, AND IMPORTS FOR CONSUMPTION
IN RELATION TO OUTPUT, SELECTED GOODS, 1962

Exports, Commodity Group	Millions of Dollars	Per Cent of Output	Imports, Commodity Group	Millions of Dollars	Per Cent of Output
Cotton-farm products	530	20	Bananas and plantains	79	100
Cash grains	2,194	23	Coffee, cocoa, tea	1,178	100
Leaf tobacco	372	27	Crude rubber, gums	232	100
			Finfish	123	34[a]
Bituminous coal and lignite	351	19	Shellfish	155	40[a]
Condensed and evaporated milk	115	10	Iron ore and concentrates	325	34
Flour and meal	228	10	Lead and zinc ores	62	28
Soybean-oil mill products	183	17	Bauxite, other aluminum ores	125	89
Synthetic rubber	170	21	Manganese ores, concentrates	66	94
Agricultural-insecticides			Uranium ores	252	65
chemicals and formulations	119	19	Crude petroleum	1,013	12
Fabricated plate work	156	11	Natural abrasives, except		
Internal combustion engines	202	15	sand	51	97
Farm machinery and equipment	264	12	Diamonds for gem stones	102	100
Construction and mining					
machinery	839	35	Raw cane sugar	519	70
Oil field machinery	143	26	Distilled liquor[b]	235	23
Metal-cutting machine tools	205	25	Textile goods, mainly jute		
Textile machinery	132	25	bagging, burlaps	181	80
Special industry machinery	211	20	Pulp-mill products	333	34
Pumps and compressors	157	14	Paper-mill products	727	19
Computing and related machines	271	17	Nonferrous refined metals,		
Aircraft and engines	720	15	mainly tin	309	56
Aircraft parts	634	17	Motor vehicles	504	2
Motor vehicles	1,309	6	Motorcycles, bicycles, parts	63	31
Pulp-mill products	169	26	Watches and clocks	68	14
Refined copper and alloys	202	32			
TOTAL EXPORTS	21,403		TOTAL IMPORTS	16,251	

[a]1961.
[b]Except brandy.

of metal-cutting machine tools, and 15 per cent of aircraft and engine output. Imports also include manufactured goods, some of which represent more than one-fourth of this country's new supply. Moreover, some articles are both exported and imported, among them motor vehicles, sewing machines, paper-mill and pulp-mill products, etc. (see Table XIII.3 and Figure XIII.2).

Using various complicated calculations, the Department of Labor has estimated employment in 1960 attributable to exports. It represented 3.1 million persons out of 52.9 million total employment. Of these 3.1 million, 1.5 million worked in industries producing directly for export or were otherwise involved in exporting their goods; 1.6 million worked in industries supporting production, transportation, or marketing of exported goods (see Table XIII.4).

The few big companies in which a substantial part of manufacturing in various fields is concentrated in this country (see Chapter X), also account for a large share of exports in their production. Thus the 4 largest U.S.

FIGURE XIII.2

U.S. COMMODITY IMPORTS AS RELATED TO OUTPUT, 1962

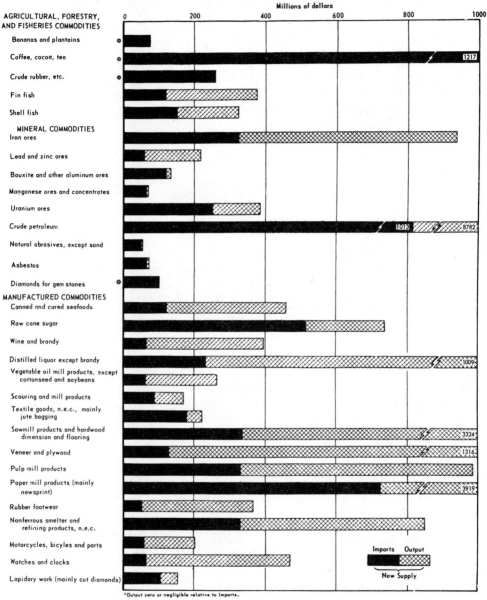

U.S. Department of Commerce, Bureau of the Census

TABLE XIII.4

EMPLOYMENT ATTRIBUTABLE TO EXPORTS, BY INDUSTRY, 1960

	Total (In Thousands)	Per Cent
Farm[a]	941.4	30.5
Nonfarm	2,140.3	69.5
Mining	89.9	2.9
Manufacturing	1,287.6	41.8
Machinery, except electrical	224.0	7.3
Electrical machinery	92.4	3.0
Primary metal industries	171.0	5.5
Chemicals and allied products	115.7	3.8
Transportation equipment	131.9	4.2
Other	552.6	18.0
Trade	198.6	6.4
Transportation, including U.S. ocean ships	213.5	6.9
All other	140.9	4.6
Employment attributable to replacement of plant and equipment consumed	210.0	6.8
TOTAL EMPLOYMENT[b]	3,081.7	100.0

[a]Includes farm operators, family workers, and employees.
[b]Excludes government employment; because of double job-holding, may exceed actual employment.

companies account for 44 per cent, and the 20 largest companies for 81 per cent of the value of exported paper and related products; for 59 and 93 per cent, respectively, of exported petroleum and coal products; for 51 and 86 per cent of transportation equipment, etc. (see Table XIII.5).

TABLE XIII.5

THE SHARE OF THE LARGEST COMPANIES IN THE U.S. VALUE OF EXPORTS,
BY SELECTED INDUSTRIES, 1963
(Per Cent)

Major Industry Group	Reported Exports		
	4 largest companies	8 largest companies	20 largest companies
Paper and allied products	44	60	81
Chemicals and allied products	29	40	58
Petroleum and coal products	59	71	93
Rubber and plastic products	47	59	73
Stone, clay, glass products	27	45	72
Primary-metal industries	36	54	76
Fabricated metal products	17	23	36
Machinery, except electrical	21	30	46
Electrical machinery	33	43	56
Transportation equipment	51	69	86
Instruments, and related products	41	50	68

77. *Our Foreign Markets*

Europe, taken as a whole, has always been the most important market for the United States. In 1880, 86 per cent of the value of U.S. exports went to it, but with every passing decade until recently, Europe's share in our exports declined: to 75 per cent in 1900, 54 per cent in 1920, and 41 per cent in 1940. Since 1950, its share has been stabilized at around 30 per cent of total exports. Europe's participation in U.S. imports has been smaller, percentagewise, than in exports: 56 per cent of total U.S. imports in 1880, 23 per cent in 1920, and 16 per cent in 1950. Gradually Europe's share began to increase and in 1960–64 amounted to about 28 per cent of the value of U.S. imports. The United Kingdom was the chief European customer of the United States throughout the nineteenth century but now accounts for only 6 per cent of U.S. exports and imports. In

TABLE XIII.6

THE SHARE OF EUROPE, THE UNITED KINGDOM, AND CANADA IN THE
VALUE OF U.S. EXPORTS AND IMPORTS, 1880-1964
(Per Cent of Total Exports and Imports)

Year	Exports To			Imports From		
	Europe[a]	United Kingdom	Canada	Europe[a]	United Kingdom	Canada
1880	86	54	3	56	32	5
1900	75	38	7	52	19	5
1920	54	27	15	23	10	12
1940	41	25	18	15	6	16
1950	31	5	20	16	4	22
1960	35	7	20	29	7	20
1964	32	6	19	28	6	23

[a]Includes United Kingdom.

contrast, Canada's share in our foreign trade has been growing consistently, from 3 per cent of exports in 1880 to 15 per cent in 1920 and 19–20 per cent in recent years; corresponding percentages for U.S. imports from Canada are 5, 12, and 20–23 (see Table XIII.6).

Western Europe generally takes about one-third of U.S. exports of agricultural commodities (tobacco, cotton, soybeans, grains and preparations, fruits, nuts, and vegetables), and also approximately one-third of our exports of chemicals and machinery, among other products. In turn, the United States acquires substantial amounts of machinery and transportation equipment, as well as iron-and-steel-mill products, textile yarns, fabrics, and other manufactured goods exported by Western Europe.

Canada's imports from the United States consist largely of machinery, motor vehicles, petroleum, and also agricultural products not adaptable to the Canadian climate—fruits, vegetables, soybeans, cotton, etc. The 2 most important groups of products supplied by Canada to us are pulp,

TABLE XIII.7

EXPORTS AND IMPORTS OF MERCHANDISE,
BY SELECTED COUNTRY OF DESTINATION AND ORIGIN, 1950-64

(In Millions of Dollars)

Country	Exports, Including Re-exports			General Imports		
	1950	1960	1964	1950	1960	1964
North America	3,448	5,382	6,791	3,101	4,429	5,883
Canada	2,010	3,709	4,747	1,960	2,901	4,241
Mexico	519	820	1,076	315	443	643
Panama	112	89	110	10	24	40
Cuba	461	224	...	406	357	...
Dominican Republic	42	41	114	38	110	128
South America	1,381	2,096	2,122	1,963	2,435	2,509
Colombia	232	246	246	313	299	280
Venezuela	401	551	600	324	948	956
Peru	75	143	221	49	183	213
Chile	71	195	180	160	193	218
Brazil	354	430	387	715	570	535
Argentina	144	350	261	206	98	111
Europe	3,006	6,481	8,157	1,411	4,245	5,287
Belgium-Luxembourg	270	439	628	140	364	420
France	345	580	802	132	396	495
West Germany	440[a]	1,068	1,310	104[a]	897	1,171
Sweden	99	300	300	71	170	203
Switzerland	130	253	341	110	198	255
United Kingdom	523	1,411	1,468	335	993	1,141
Greece	94	64	115	17	33	55
Spain	45	190	315	50	88	114
Italy	347	650	831	109	393	526
Turkey	62	126	164	61	60	69
Yugoslavia	42	86	145	19	41	56
Poland and Danzig	9	143	138	11	39	54
U.S.S.R.	1	38	145	38	23	20
Asia	1,478	3,646	5,226	1,638	2,721	3,617
Iran	35	117	131	24	51	75
Israel	93[b]	126	181	8[b]	27	56
India	217	641	955	259	228	304
Indonesia	82	86	68	156	216	170
Japan	417	1,341	1,908	182	1,149	1,769
Pakistan	31	170	376	31	36	40
Philippines	243	297	360	236	307	387
Hong Kong	103	123	188	5	139	250
Africa	369	766	1,218	494	534	917
South Africa	125	277	303	142	108	250
Oceania	146	475	738	208	266	440
Australia	111	387	626	141	142	280
New Zealand	29	75	87	65	119	150
GRAND TOTAL	10,275[c]	20,550[c]	26,438[c]	8,852	14,654	18,685[d]

[a]Includes East Germany.

[b]Includes Palestine.

[c]Includes exports of "special category" commodities not reported by country of destination, for security reasons.

[d]Includes imports from unidentified country.

paper, and paper products, on the one hand, and ores and metals, on the other. It is of greatest importance to the United States, both in peace and in war, that these vital products are so close to its frontiers. Latin America, too, has always been a very dependable area for exchange of goods in both directions. It is rich in many minerals and metals—silver, iron, copper, mercury, petroleum, etc.—and in tropical products—bananas, coffee, sugar, various fibers, and fruits and nuts. Trade with Asia and Africa consists mainly of exports of manufactured goods in exchange for raw materials.

Canada stands out as the greatest single market for U.S. goods. Until recently, the United Kingdom ranked next, but since 1961 Japan has occupied the second place. West Germany and the United Kingdom run almost neck and neck for the third place. Our exports to many of the industrialized countries of Europe and to Japan, as well as to the developing nations in Asia and Africa, exceed our imports from them. But with many Latin American countries from which we obtain such products as coffee (Brazil, Colombia, and others), and petroleum and iron ore (mainly Venezuela), the trade pattern is the reverse. The value of our imports from Venezuela, for example, is almost double that of exports (see Table XIII.7).

78. *Our International Accounts*

The *international accounts* of a country comprise its balance of international payments and its international investment position. The balance of payments includes all payments related to trade, rendering of services, and the transfer of assets between a country and the rest of the world during a specified period of time; the international investment position shows the value of a country's investments abroad and that of foreign investors in the country at a given time.

Apart from exports and imports of merchandise proper, international payments include the following principal items: (*a*) services, including such items as travel expenditures, government transactions, etc.; (*b*) transportation expenditures for moving people and cargo by American and foreign means of transport; (*c*) interest and dividends from American investments abroad and foreign investments in the United States, and personal remittances; (*d*) short- and long-term capital inflow and outflow; and settlements including: (*e*) gold movements; and (*f*) changes in official balances.

The value of goods exported and services rendered by the United States to foreign countries is listed in the U.S. balance of international payments as receipts or credits (+), because these items give rise to payments from abroad. Imports, services rendered by foreign countries, expenditures of American travelers abroad, remittances of immigrants to foreign countries, which represent payments to foreigners, are counted as debits (—).

The United States is not only the world's largest trader, but also the greatest single investor and international banker. The dollar is the most widely used currency in international transactions, and it also serves foreign countries as a means of holding monetary reserves. This combination of the roles of a trader, a banker, and an investor is reflected in the U.S. balance of payments and affects the world economy in many respects.

The United States has not always occupied this unique position in the world. Before World War I, it was a net debtor nation; just before the outbreak of that war, U.S. assets abroad amounted to $3.5 billion, as compared with $7.2 billion in European investments in this country. Though a debtor to Europe, the United States even then was a creditor in relation to the Western Hemisphere (Canada, Mexico and other Latin countries). During World War I and the 1920's, the great demand for American goods and services, financed largely by loans, resulted in large surpluses of exports over imports and changed the country's position from a debtor to creditor nation; until 1930, it remained an exporter of capital. Before the Great Depression, its foreign investments reached the level of $17.2 billion, but after 1932 it ceased to export capital, and after 1934 foreign capital began to move here—not for productive investment but to be held in safety in American banks and occasionally to be used for stock-exchange speculation. U.S. investments abroad shrank more and more, declining to $11.5 billion in 1939, while foreign investments in this country increased from $4 billion in 1919 to $9.6 billion by that time. Thus the net creditor position of the United States amounted to $1.9 billion. Almost all foreign investments in the United States were held by European countries, and the United States was again a debtor to Europe, though it continued to be a creditor to countries in the Western Hemisphere.

During World War II, the U.S. unilateral transactions under the Lend-Lease program resulted in transfer of goods and services amounting to some $49 billion ($31.6 billion to the United Kingdom, $11.1 billion to Soviet Russia, $3.3 billion to France, $1.6 billion to China, and various amounts to other countries). To some extent, the flow of goods to Europe was covered by the transfer of gold to this country, particularly early in the war and soon after its end, in 1946–50, on one hand, and by the liquidation of U.S. debts in Europe, on the other. There were also reverse Lend-Lease transactions, the obligations of the U.S. Government for military purchases and expenditures for our troops abroad; short-term debts, mainly in the form of foreign deposits in U.S. banks and other transactions. When all the wartime international operations are considered, it appears that the net debtor-creditor position of the United States changed little, although both its international assets and liabilities increased.

In 1946, the United States initiated a massive assistance program to European countries (see Sec. 78), providing nearly $23 billion in grants

TABLE XIII.8

U.S. BALANCE OF INTERNATIONAL PAYMENTS, 1925-64
(In Billions of Dollars)

Type of Transaction	1925	1935	1945[a]	1950[a]	1955	1960	1963	1964
Recorded payments:	6.6	2.8	19.0	17.8	22.3	31.2	36.0	39.8
Imports: Merchandise	4.3	2.5	5.2	9.1	11.5	14.7	17.0	18.6
Transportation	0.4	0.2	0.4	0.8	1.2	2.0	2.3	2.5
U.S. travel abroad	0.3	0.2	0.3	0.8	1.2	1.7	2.1	2.2
Military expenditures	0.04	0.04	2.4	0.6	2.9	3.0	2.9	2.8
Income on investments	0.2	0.2	0.2	0.4	0.5	0.9	1.2	1.3
Other services	0.02	0.03	1.6	0.4	0.5	0.8	0.9	0.9
Private remittances	0.4	0.2	0.5	0.4	0.4	0.5	0.6	0.5
Private capital outflow	0.9	-0.5	0.6	1.3	1.3	3.9	4.3	6.5
Government grants,pensions,other	0.03	0.02	6.6	3.6	2.0	1.9	2.2	2.2
Government capital outflow	-	0.01	1.1	0.5	0.7	1.7	2.6	2.4
Recorded receipts:	6.7	3.6	16.3	14.2	20.6	28.0	33.7	37.9
Exports: Merchandise	5.0	2.4	12.5	10.1	14.3	19.5	22.0	25.2
Transportation	0.3	0.1	1.3	1.0	1.4	1.7	2.1	2.3
Foreign travel in U.S.	0.08	0.1	0.2	0.4	0.7	0.9	0.9	1.1
Income on investments	0.9	0.5	0.6	1.6	2.4	3.3	4.5	5.2
Military transactions	-	-	-	-	0.2	0.3	0.7	0.8
Other services	0.02	0.1	1.7	0.6	0.8	1.4	1.9	2.1
Repayments on Government loans	0.03	0.01	0.1	0.3	0.4	0.6	1.0	0.7
Foreign capital other than liquid funds	0.3	0.3	-0.1	0.09	0.4	0.4	0.7	0.7
Unrecorded transactions, net[b]	-0.1	0.4	0.01	-0.02	0.5	-0.8	-0.3	-0.9
Balance of payments	-0.04	1.2	-2.7	-3.6	-1.1	-3.9	-2.6	-2.8

[a]Exports include "military transactions" not shown separately.
[b]Also called "errors and omissions." Believed to consist largely of unreported short-term capital flows.

and loans between 1946 and 1949. Beginning in 1946, this country returned to the position of a creditor nation to Europe; its assets and investments abroad doubled in 4 years, rising from $16.9 billion in 1946 to $32.5 billion in 1949. By then, the U.S. gold reserves had risen to nearly $25 billion, and its balance of payments showed a surplus throughout those years.

Since 1949, however, with the sole exception of 1957, our balance of payments has been negative and has fluctuated considerably: —$3.6 billion in 1950; —$1.1 billion in 1955; —$3.9 billion in 1960; and —$2.8 billion in 1964, dropping to —$1.3 billion in 1965 (see Table XIII.8).

The deficit in U.S. international transactions has not been caused, as often happens, by excess of imports over exports. On the contrary, our trade balance has remained active throughout this period, i.e., the value of exports from the United States has exceeded that of its imports. Indeed, the surplus of exports increased from $1 billion in 1950 to $6.6 billion in 1964, because of the expansion of the world economy, on the one hand, and the stability of American prices, the large foreign-aid shipments, and the high quality of U.S. products, on the other (see Sec. 76).

FIGURE XIII.3

FOREIGN TRAVEL EXPENDITURES
OF U.S. CITIZENS, 1953-63

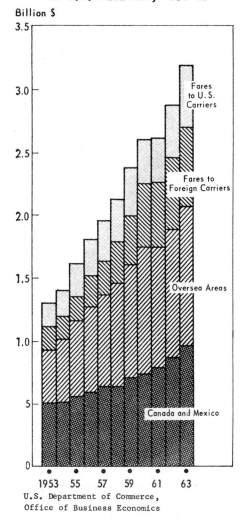

U.S. Department of Commerce,
Office of Business Economics

The stubborn deficit in the U.S. balance of payments must be attributed mainly to other factors:

(*a*) The enormous growth of U.S. Government expenditures abroad for military purposes, military grants, pensions, and other transfers. Military expenditures have acquired great importance, especially since the Korean War: from about $56 million in 1950, they increased to $1 billion in 1951, and $4.2 billion in 1953. After that, they declined, amounting to $1.5 billion in 1964; with the escalation of the war in Viet-Nam, however, they began to rise rapidly.

Military expenditures have been concentrated in Western Europe and Asia, with smaller amounts in other areas. Even in 1963 and 1964, more than half of all military spending was localized in Western Europe; in 1965, with the expansion of hostilities in Viet-Nam the center of gravity shifted to Asia.

(*b*) Economic aid to foreign countries has been another consequential factor (see Sec. 79). It has absorbed billions of. dollars during the last 15 years, and still takes about $3 billion a year.

(*c*) The expenditures of American travelers abroad have grown from $1.2 billion in 1955 to $2.1 billion in 1963 and $2.2 billion in 1964 (see Figure XIII.3).

(*d*) The large outflow of private capital in the form of direct investments, purchases of new issues of foreign securities, short-term bank loans, and other forms spurted to a total of $4.5 billion in 1963 and $6.5 billion in 1964. It is believed that there also has been a substantial unrecorded outflow of capital from the United States. To some extent, the key position of the U.S. dollar in the world as a reserve and trading currency may have contributed to the accumulation of private foreign dollar holdings as working balances and other assets.

The large outflow of private capital was made possible by the readily available and relatively cheap capital in the United States and the willingness of the American banks to provide substantial loans, both short-term and long-term, to accommodate the increased foreign demand for loans, which was stimulated by higher and rising interest rates and higher profits in major industrial countries. The persistent disequilibrium in our international accounts has become a serious concern for our government, and is also a major international issue. This country could restore the balance in its international payments by drastic restrictive measures, such as discontinuing foreign aid or sharply cutting its military and other expenditures abroad. Because of the unique position of the United States in the world, such measures would cause very severe repercussions in both the world economy and the world political situation and therefore would adversely affect the U.S. economy and policy as well. Thus it has been necessary to turn to other measures for restoring the balance of international transactions—by arrangements for substantial advance payments on loans made to various European countries; sales of special medium-term nonmarketable securities to foreign governments (as an alternative to accumulation of gold and shcrt-term liquid dollar holdings); the equalization tax, which raised the cost for foreign borrowings in this country; use of the International Monetary Fund facilities; appeal to domestic holders for voluntary return of dollar assets from abroad and reduction in directing U.S. money overseas. Some improvement has been noticeable so far, but imbalance in our international accounts has not been overcome, and further efforts to eliminate the deficit may be anticipated.

TABLE XIII.9

U.S. GOLD STOCK AND FOREIGN CURRENCY HOLDINGS, AND SHORT-TERM
LIABILITIES TO FOREIGNERS, 1955-64
(In Millions of Dollars)

	1955	1959	1960	1962	1963	1964[a]
Gold stock	21,753	19,507	17,804	16,057	15,596	15,471
Foreign currency holdings	...	...	...	99	212	432
Short-term liabilities to foreigners:	13,601	19,389	21,272	25,019	25,967	28,811
International and regional	1,881	3,158	4,012	5,145	4,637	4,974
Foreign:	11,720	16,231	17,260	19,874	21,330	23,837
Official[b]	6,953	9,154	10,212	11,963	12,467	13,222
Other	4,767	7,076	7,048	7,911	8,863	10,615
Foreign: Canada	1,032	2,198	2,439	3,349	2,988	2,983
Latin America	2,000	2,408	2,308	2,448	3,137	3,535
Asia	2,181	2,780	3,115	3,444	4,001	4,631
Europe	6,147	8,473	9,046	10,162	10,770	12,251
France	1,081	655	519	1,157	1,478	1,663
West Germany	1,454	1,987	3,476	2,730	3,041	2,010
Italy	785	1,370	877	1,384	803	1,621
Netherlands	164	485	328	248	360	367
Switzerland	757	969	678	908	906	1,370
United Kingdom	550	990	1,667	1,609	1,483	1,900
Other	1,355	2,017	1,501	2,126	2,699	3,321
Other regions	360	373	352	471	435	438

[a] December; for other years, averages.
[b] Liabilities to foreign central banks, foreign central governments and their agencies, Bank for International Settlements, and European Fund.

FIGURE XIII.4

U.S. SHORT-TERM LIABILITIES TO FOREIGNERS, 1935-64

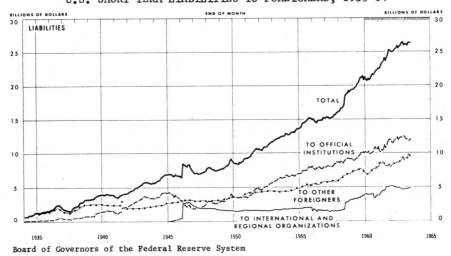

Board of Governors of the Federal Reserve System

U.S. short-term assets abroad amounted to $12.8 billion by the end of 1963 ($8.1 billion in private assets and $4.6 billion in government credits, claims, and foreign-currency holdings). Short-term obligations to foreigners amounted to $28.3 billion in March, 1965; $12.3 billion to official institutions; $5.1 billion to international and regional institutions such as the International Monetary Fund and the International Bank for Reconstruction and Development; and $10.9 billion to nonofficial holders.

This disequilibrium in short-term liabilities has been a matter of great concern, particularly since foreign holders can—and some do—require repayment in gold, and these holdings are substantial in comparison with the U.S. gold stock of $15.5 billion in December, 1964, and $14.6 billion in March, 1965 (see Table XIII.9 and Figure XIII.4).

In contrast, U.S. long-term investments and credits abroad are considerably larger than foreign investments and long-term assets in this country. By the end of 1964, private American long-term investments abroad totaled $64.7 billion, and long-term government credits and claims $18.8 billion—in all, $83.5 billion, as compared with $25 billion in long-term foreign investments and assets in the United States (see Table XIII.10 and Figure XIII.5 for the distribution of foreign and U.S. investments in 1950 and 1960 by type).

While U.S. investments abroad generate return movements of capital in the form of remitted profits and dividends on earnings and interest, a large part of the profits is usually reinvested abroad; sales by American investors abroad may displace exports from domestic producers, while their purchases abroad of needed materials and, especially, equipment may also deprive American industry of some business. Moreover, the payback from investments in foreign countries usually takes a long time to materialize, and several years may pass before returns from an investment

TABLE XIII.10

INTERNATIONAL INVESTMENT POSITION OF THE UNITED STATES, 1940-64, END OF YEAR
(In Billions of Dollars)

	1940	1950	1955	1960	1963	1964
U.S. long-term investments and assets abroad:	11.4	28.3	39.2	59.5	75.4	83.5
Private	11.3	17.5	26.8	45.4	58.3	64.7
Direct	7.3	11.8	19.4	32.8	40.7	44.3
Portfolio	4.0	5.7	7.4	12.6	17.6	20.4
U.S. Government	0.1	10.8	12.4	14.1	17.1	18.8
Foreign long-term investments and assets in the United States	8.1	8.0	13.4	18.4	22.7	25.0
Direct	2.9	3.4	5.1	6.9	7.9	8.4
Portfolio	5.2	4.6	8.3	11.5	14.8	16.6

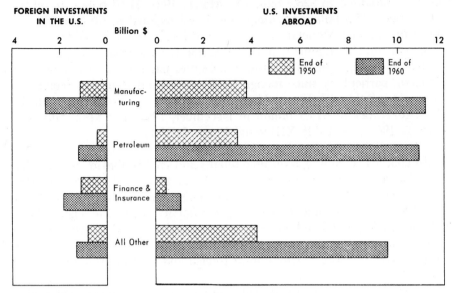

U.S. Department of Commerce, Office of Business Economics

abroad may become meaningful for the balance of international payments.

U.S. direct private investments abroad are concentrated in the Western Hemisphere and Europe: at the end of 1964, these 2 areas accounted for $36.2 billion out of the total of $44.3 billion. In recent years, the establishment of the European Common Market has activated U.S. direct investments in Common Market countries, largely for the purpose of getting behind the tariff wall but also for obtaining a foothold in both the Common Market and its overseas associate members.

Taken alone, Canada far exceeds any other country or region in attractiveness to American investors: almost one-third of all U.S. foreign investment is in Canada, as compared with somewhat less than one-fourth in all the rest of the Western Hemisphere and somewhat more than one-fourth of all of Europe.

About two-fifths of all U.S. investment abroad is in the development of natural resources and related processing installations. A single industry, petroleum, with $14.4 billion invested, has drawn one-third of total U.S. foreign investments (see Table XIII.11). However, manufacturing has become the largest activity of U.S. firms abroad in the 1960's. Investments of American manufacturing firms abroad for plant and equipment exceeded those for petroleum for the first time in 1961; respective figures for 1964 were: $3 billion and $2.1 billion; for 1965, $3.8 billion and $2.4 billion.

TABLE XIII.11
U.S. DIRECT INVESTMENTS ABROAD, BY AREA AND INDUSTRY, 1964
(In Millions of Dollars)

Area and Country	Total	Trade	Public Util-ities	Manufac-turing	Petro-leum	Mining and Smelt-ing	Other
ALL AREAS[a]	44,343	3,736	2,023	16,861	14,350	3,564	3,808
Canada	13,820	805	467	6,191	3,228	1,671	1,458
Latin America	8,932	951	568	2,340	3,142	1,098	832
Mexico	1,035	111	27	607	56	128	106
Brazil	994	153	41	673	51	34	42
Colombia	520	53	30	145	270	-	22[c]
Peru	460	46	22	65	56	241	31
Venezuela	2,808	200	18	219	2,162	-	209[c]
Other countries	3,114[d]	388	430	641	547	-	422
Other W.Hemisphere	1,386	89	49	166	569	250	263
Europe	12,067	1,472	53	6,547	3,086	56	854
France	1,437	189	22	893	281	9	43
Belgium-Luxembourg	452	73	1	296	66	-	16
West Germany	2,077	119	5	1,315	576	-	63
Italy	845	74	2	382	350	-	37
Netherlands	587	96	16	212	238	-	25
United Kingdom	4,550	384	4	3,015	905	-	239
Other countries	2,119	537	4	434	670	-	435
Asia: Middle East	1,331	11	4	39	1,238	2	36
Far East	1,731	227	52	496	775	31	150
Africa	1,629	93	2	225	830	356	122
Oceania	1,582	87	2	856	444	100	93
International[b]	1,865	-	827	-	1,038	-	-

[a]Detail does not add to totals because of rounding and adjustments.
[b]Includes shipping enterprises registered in Liberia and Panama but operating world-wide.
[c]Includes mining and smelting.
[d]Includes about $700 million in mining and smelting not assigned to individual countries.

Compared with U.S. investments abroad, foreign direct investments in this country look very small: $8.4 billion at the end of 1964. The United Kingdom has been traditionally the major investor. About 40 per cent of British investment is held in insurance and finance companies: some British companies, established in the United States for many years, particularly in the fire, marine, and casualty fields, have had world-wide prominence for a long time. The other important area of U.K. investment is in manufacturing (about 30 per cent) and the remainder is in petroleum. Canada ranks next. On the whole, foreign investments in this country predominate in manufacturing, which accounts for nearly two-fifths of the total; finance and insurance rank next; investment in petroleum companies is also important (see Table XIII.12).

Foreign capital played a significant role in the early development of American industry and transportation, contributing not only to the financing but also to the know-how and inventions on which many major U.S. industries are based. But present foreign investments differ from the earlier, when the investors often immigrated to settle in the United States, bringing machinery and, not seldom, skilled labor with them. Today there

TABLE XIII.12

DIRECT FOREIGN INVESTMENTS IN THE UNITED STATES, BY AREA AND INDUSTRY, 1963
(In Millions of Dollars)

Industry	All Areas	Canada	United Kingdom	Nether- lands	Switzer- land	Other Europe	Other Areas
Petroleum	1,513	213	480	772	-	54	...
Manufacturing	3,018	1,063	779	275	477	350	...
Finance and insurance	2,045	337	1,085	36	307	212	...
Other	1,368	570	321	51	41	251	...
TOTAL	7,944	2,183	2,665	1,134	825	867	269

is greater interest in portfolio investment than in ownership or control of industrial enterprises.

Among foreign direct investments in manufacturing, food industries and beverages now are favored, in contrast to the textile industries, which (together with the chemical industry) once were the major preferred industries but now are relegated to last place.

The over-all effect of foreign direct investment in the United States on our balance of payments is rather minor.

79. *U.S. Foreign Aid*

The United States has been a leader in initiating assistance to war-ravaged countries, assistance which has embraced not only allied and friendly countries but also wartime enemies. First came the Lend Lease, which was a part of the war effort, and the U.S. participation in the United Nations Relief and Rehabilitation Program (UNRRA). In the course of years, the assistance program has expanded greatly and has changed many times in form, content, and even name: the Marshall Plan and Economic Cooperation Administration (April, 1948–October, 1951); Mutual Security Agency (November, 1951–July, 1953); Foreign Operations Administration (August, 1953–June, 1955); International Cooperation Administration (July, 1955–November, 1961); and, finally, Agency for International Development (still in operation). There have been several additional programs: the Development Loan Fund, Food for Peace, Peace Corps, Alliance for Progress, participation in international assistance programs, and others.

With the recovery of the economy of Europe and Japan, the emphasis shifted to developing countries in Asia and Africa, and also to Latin American countries (Alliance for Progress). On the other hand, the Cold War, the dissolution of the colonial empires, and the political upheavals throughout the world caused a specific reorientation of policy in the foreign-aid policy. Military aid began to gain ground, at the expense of economic and technical assistance, for the support of governments believed to be friendly to the United States.

TABLE XIII.13

ECONOMIC AND MILITARY ASSISTANCE, BY GRANT AND LOAN, 1948-65

(In Millions of Dollars)

Year Ending June 30	Total Assistance[a]	Economic Assistance				Military Assistance			Additional Grants from Excess Stocks
		Total	Grants	Loans Total	Loans Development	Total	Grants	Loans	
1949 (15 mos.)	6,283	6,283	5,116	1,167	–	–	–	–	–
1950	3,670	3,614	3,451	163	–	56	56	–	33
1951	3,603	2,622	2,577	45	–	980	980	–	289
1952	3,466	1,985	1,784	201	–	1,481	1,481	–	191
1953	6,117	1,958	1,932	26	–	4,159	4,159	–	140
1954	5,524	2,228	2,114	114	–	3,296	3,296	–	107
1955	4,217	1,821	1,624	197	–	2,396	2,396	–	42
1956	4,434	1,506	1,298	208	–	2,928	2,920	8	106
1957	3,712	1,627	1,305	322	–	2,085	2,078	7	53
1958	3,984	1,620	1,203	417	267	2,363	2,325	39	257
1959	4,026	1,916	1,291	626	562	2,110	2,050	60	197
1960	3,584	1,866	1,302	564	522	1,718	1,697	21	289
1961	3,386	2,012	1,305	707	630	1,374	1,344	30	328
1962	3,956	2,508	1,178	1,331	1,087	1,448	1,427	21	248
1963	4,107	2,297	954	1,343	1,249	1,809	1,765	44	188
1964	3,633	2,136	808	1,328	1,253	1,498	1,415	83	125
1965	3,502	2,179	970	1,209	1,162	1,325	...	...	...
CUMULATIVE TOTAL, 1948-65	73,262	40,183	30,213	9,970	6,732	33,081	31,235[b]	521[b]	2,639[b]

[a]The difference between the sums of yearly data and the cumulative totals is the value of goods programmed but not delivered.
[b]Through 1964.

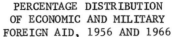

FIGURE XIII.6

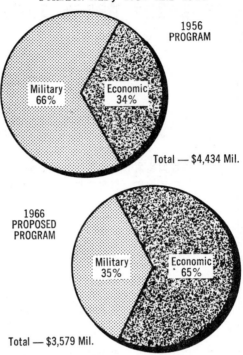

PERCENTAGE DISTRIBUTION
OF ECONOMIC AND MILITARY
FOREIGN AID, 1956 AND 1966

1956
PROGRAM

Military
66%

Economic
34%

Total — $4,434 Mil.

1966
PROPOSED
PROGRAM

Military
35%

Economic
65%

Total — $3,579 Mil.

U.S. Agency for International Development

The most successful program has been the Marshall Plan, which literally
saved Europe in the most critical postwar years. At that time, Europe was
on the brink of political and economic catastrophe, and the help from
across the ocean not only made physical reconstruction possible but also
restored the morale and hopes of the population. Its purpose fully
achieved, the Marshall Plan was terminated ahead of schedule.

From the beginning of the Marshall Plan through 1965, U.S. economic
assistance amounted to $40.2 billion ($30.2 billion in grants and $10.0 bil-
lion in loans). U.S. military assistance absorbed $31.8 billion ($31.2 billion
in grants and $0.5 billion in loans); additional military grants from excess
stocks not chargeable to appropriations amounted to $2.6 billion (see
Table XIII.13). However, the share of military aid has gradually declined,
from 68 per cent in 1953 to about 41 per cent in 1964. It continues to
decline in aid programs related to all countries except Viet-Nam,* where
military assistance programs have been increasing (see Figure XIII 6).

* Present expenditures for the war in Viet-Nam are outside the funds for foreign
assistance.

TABLE XIII.14

MAJOR U.S. ASSISTANCE, ECONOMIC AND TECHNICAL,
TO SELECTED COUNTRIES, JULY, 1945-DECEMBER, 1964
(In Millions of Dollars)

Country	Total	Country	Total	Country	Total
Europe	27,182	Latin America	4,931	Israel	813
United Kingdom	6,410	Brazil	1,517	Iran	680
France	4,443	Chile	634	Indonesia	686
West Germany	3,056	Mexico	365	Jordan	443
Italy	2,883	Argentina	389	Laos [a]	377
Yugoslavia	1,848	Colombia	383	Thailand	338
Greece	1,626	Bolivia	322	Cambodia [a]	255
Austria	1,088	Peru	222	Indochina [b]	109
Poland	985	Venezuela	111	Other	1,688
Spain	861	Guatemala	148		
Netherlands	830	Ecuador	106	Africa	2,818
Belgium-Luxembourg	664	Other	734	U.A.R. (Egypt)	956
Denmark	267	Near East, Far East,		Morocco	399
Norway	243	Pacific	25,060	Tunisia	337
Czechoslovakia	191	Korea	3,707	Libya	205
Ireland	132	India	4,299	Congo(Leopoldville)	197
Portugal	147	Japan	2,598	Ethiopia	107
Sweden	87	China (Taiwan)	2,070	Other	617
Finland	69	Pakistan	2,245		
Iceland	67	Viet-Nam [a]	2,031		
Other	1,285	Turkey	1,637		
		Philippines	1,084		
U.S.S.R.	399				

[a] Data for the period before 1954 for Viet-Nam, Laos, and Cambodia shown
together under Indochina.
[b] Figures for Viet-Nam, Laos, and Cambodia before 1954.

The main recipients of nonmilitary aid, in both grants and long-term
loans repayable in dollars, have been the United Kingdom, France, West
Germany, Italy, and other Marshall Plan countries in Europe; Japan, Korea,
India, Taiwan, Pakistan, and the Philippines in Asia. Compared with assistance to Europe and Asia, aid to all Latin America is small: $4.9 billion
in the entire postwar period, almost as much as France alone received from
the United States (see Table XIII.14).

In the 1950's, grants substantially exceeded loans, but since 1961 the
lion's share of economic assistance is provided in loans: in the 1962–64
period, the net obligations of the Agency for International Development
(AID) amounted to $6.9 billion, of which $4 billion, or 58 per cent of
the total, were loans. In general, emphasis shifted from assistance in
emergency situations to support of long-term economic and social development by so-called development loans and technical cooperation. In 1961,
such assistance accounted for less than 25 per cent of the total economic
and military program; in 1964, it constituted more than 45 per cent of the
total.

The U.S. foreign-aid program was at its peak in 1949, when it absorbed
almost 2 per cent of the gross national product. While economic assistance began to decline rapidly, military aid was introduced and in 1953–
54 reached a record-high level. Since then, it has moved down from about

FIGURE XIII.7

FOREIGN AID EXPENDITURES IN PER CENT OF
GROSS NATIONAL PRODUCT, 1949-65

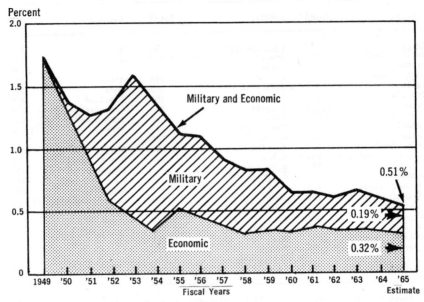

U.S. Agency for International Development

1.2 per cent of the GNP in 1953–54 to 0.19 per cent in 1965. The economic part of foreign aid represented 0.32 per cent of the GNP that year (see Figure XIII.7).

More than 80 countries receive assistance of one form or another from the United States. In 25 countries, the United States has major projects: in some, aid is provided in support of development policies of the host countries toward self-sustaining growth; in others, it is contingent on the adoption of more energetic self-help measures. Aid to 14 nations is considered transitional, because they are approaching the time when they will need no help from the United States. In some 40 countries, assistance is of a limited type, because they receive major aid from Western European countries or through international organizations.

In multilateral assistance to the developing nations, the United States has been not only leading financially but blazing the trail of foreign aid. Countries whose economies have been restored with the help of the Marshall Plan are now supporting, in their turn, the underdeveloped nations in their efforts to attain higher standards of living. Most of the advanced countries and several multilateral institutions (the World Bank, in the first place) have joined in aid consortia to finance the development needs of selected countries. The share of the United States in these consortia amounts to 45 per cent of funds pledged, but this country is no longer alone in these activities. In 1963 and 1964, India, Pakistan, and Turkey received pledges of $3.4 billion through consortia; the share of the United States was $1.5 billion in the form of long-term low-interest loans.

The range of U.S. foreign-aid operations is very broad and comprises a long line of projects adapted to the necessities of single countries: construction of all-weather roads, school buildings, health centers, and hospitals; training of the nationals of the developing countries in the United States and contracting American technicians for work in those countries; establishing savings and loan associations, credit unions, and banks and training the personnel for them; carrying out various projects in the fields of agriculture and public administration; building water systems and wells; etc. The Peace Corps has its own functions; Food for Peace under Public Law 480, provides surplus U.S. farm products for payment in local currency to countries not able to feed their populations from their farmers' work. A large part of this money is set aside as loans and grants for economic and social development in the receiving country (more than 80 per cent in India, for example). In emergencies, food is donated as in the present situation in India, where scores of millions face starvation (see Figure XIII.8). Alliance for Progress is a 10-year program linking the efforts of the United States with those of 19 Latin American countries for the improvement of economic and social conditions. The Export-Import

FIGURE XIII.8

FOOD FOR PEACE PROGRAM, 1960-65

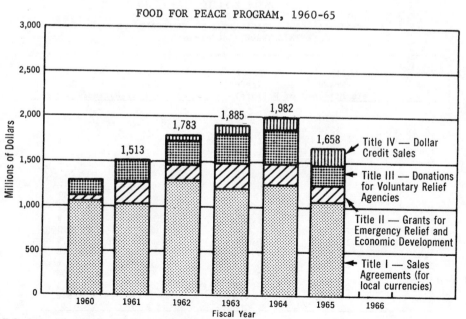

U.S. Agency for International Development

Bank provides loans for foreign purchases of U.S. goods. Private investments in developing countries are encouraged by issuance of government guaranties against losses through internal upheavals, war, or inconvertibility of currency. This list is far from complete . . .

It should not be overlooked that foreign aid, which began in 1945 and is expected to continue for an unknown number of years, is not alone a humanitarian activity and not only the key tool of U.S. foreign policy. It also plays an important role in this country's economy. A sizable part of our exports is financed by the aid programs; in 1964, for example, AID's expenditures for U.S. goods to be shipped abroad amounted to nearly $1 billion.

80. Wholesale Trade

Wholesale trade bridges the gap between manufacturing and retail trade, as an intermediate stage of the distributive process. National income originating in these two important branches of distribution services increased from some $9 billion in 1919 to $13 billion in 1929, dropped to $5.5 billion in 1933, and resumed the upward trend after the Depression. It crossed the $50 billion mark in 1950 and amounted to $82 billion in 1964 (see Table XIII.15). Percentagewise, the share of wholesale trade in national income was 4.9 per cent in 1929, slightly above 5 per cent in the 1930's, and 5.5 per cent in 1964.

TABLE XIII.15

NATIONAL INCOME ORIGINATING IN WHOLESALE AND
RETAIL TRADE, 1869-1964

Year	Wholesale Trade	Retail[a] Trade	Wholesale Trade	Retail Trade
	(In Millions of Dollars)		(Per Cent of National Income)	
1869	210	500	...	...
1879	220	560	...	...
1889	360	1,020	...	...
1899	810	1,340	...	...
1909	1,300	2,320	...	...
1919	3,130	5,920	4.2	8.0
1929	4,120	8,960	4.9	10.2
1933	1,781	3,704	4.4	9.2
1939	3,830	8,623	5.3	11.9
1946	10,393	24,024	5.7	13.3
1949	12,401	28,166	5.7	12.9
1959	23,454	43,114	5.8	10.8
1960	23,875	43,823	5.8	10.6
1962	26,190	47,605	5.7	10.4
1963	27,619	49,748	5.8	10.4
1964	28,512	49,616	5.5	9.6

[a] Includes automotive services.

The Census distinguishes 5 basic types of wholesale traders:

(1) Merchant wholesalers, who work on their own account, are the most important group within this field. They engage nearly two-thirds of total employment and account for more than 40 per cent of all sales. They buy and sell in the domestic market, specialize in foreign trade as exporters and importers, operate terminal grain elevators, and perform many other functions.

(2) Manufacturers' sales branches and sales offices are second to merchant wholesalers in the value of sales, accounting for about 30 per cent of the total. As a rule, they do not carry the goods produced by their companies, but keep an inventory of merchandise and ship the goods from the plant or the firm's warehouse.

(3) Petroleum bulk stations and terminals represent a special branch of wholesaling; they handle bulky and inflammable products with the use of large storage facilities. Some traders in this group are independent, others are affiliated with petroleum refineries or cooperatives.

(4) Merchandise agents and brokers buy and sell, or negotiate and arrange purchasing and sales for others. Compensation is usually in the form of commission or fee.

(5) Assemblers of farm products acquire such produce in small lots and sell it in large blocks in regional or central markets. They assemble the products, often sort and grade them, keep them if necessary in cold storage, or spray them to preserve freshness. Though they represent the smallest group among the wholesalers, they are very important in moving farm products into markets that handle dairy and milk products, fresh fruits, vegetables, etc. For the distribution of the wholesalers by type, as reported by the latest Census of Business for which data are available, see Table XIII.16.

As in family farming and in small workshops and stores, the proprietor of a small wholesale enterprise, together with unpaid family workers, does

TABLE XIII.16

WHOLESALE TRADE: ESTABLISHMENTS, EMPLOYEES, AND SALES, 1958 AND 1963

	Establishments (In Thousands)		Employees		Payroll (In Billions of Dollars)		Sales	
	1958	1963	1958	1963	1958	1963	1958	1963
Merchant wholesalers	190	209	1,843	2,064	8.3	11.5	122.1	157.4
Manufacturers' sales branches, offices	25	29	561	600	3.2	4.4	87.8	116.4
Petroleum bulk plants, terminals	31	31	140	144	0.7	0.8	20.3	21.5
Merchandise agents, brokers	27	25	149	170	0.7	1.0	46.6	53.2
Assemblers of farm products	14	14	115	111	0.3	0.4	9.0	9.8
WHOLESALE TRADE, TOTAL	287	308	2,808	3,089	13.2	18.1	285.7	358.4

TABLE XIII.17

WHOLESALE TRADE, BY SIZE OF ESTABLISHMENT AND
LEGAL FORM OF ORGANIZATION, 1958 AND 1963

	Establishments (In Thousands)		Sales (In Millions of Dollars)		Payroll	
	1958	1963	1958	1963	1958	1963
All establishments[a]	286.0	308.2	284,971	358,386	13,199	18,101
With paid employees:						
1	71.3	62.4	12,552	13,509	253	361
2	35.0	42.1	11,681	12,894	299	423
3	30.3	32.9	12,434	13,940	401	519
4-5	37.9	42.7	20,639	23,945	776	1,048
6-7	24.7	28.3	17,306	21,862	749	1,041
8-9	16.8	19.5	15,239	18,463	678	952
10-19	38.3	44.7	51,457	63,937	2,494	3,546
20-49	23.7	26.8	64,448	85,508	3,398	4,676
50-99	5.7	6.1	37,655	49,229	1,887	2,502
100 or more	2.4	2.6	41,559	55,099	2,263	3,035
Establishments by legal form:						
Individual proprietorships	78.4	...	24,335	...	977	...
Partnerships	37.6	...	25,625	...	904	...
Corporations	162.2	...	225,124	...	10,997	...
Cooperatives	7.0	...	9,002	...	285	...
Other legal form	0.8	...	885	...	36	...

[a]As of November 15. Data for 1958, as given in the 1963 Census report, slightly differ
from those in Table XIII.15.

much of the work himself. The majority of wholesale establishments engage only a few employees: nearly half, 48 per cent, had from 1 to 3
employees; on the other end of the scale, those establishments with 20–49
employees accounted for 8 per cent of the total number, and those with
50 or more employees, for only 2.8 per cent (see Table XIII.17).

More than half of the wholesalers operate as corporations; more than
one-fourth are individual proprietors; the remainder are partnerships,
cooperatives, or have other legal forms.

Wholesaling is a city business, even a metropolitan business. More than
two-thirds of all wholesale establishments are in metropolitan areas and
account for more than seven-tenths of all sales in these areas. The state of
New York is the greatest wholesale trade center, with the largest number
of establishments (40,160 in 1963), employees (412,175), and annual
sales of more than $66 billion, or 18.5 per cent of total wholesale sales in
the country. California follows next, though at a great distance, with sales
of $35 billion, or about 10 per cent.

The most important group among the wholesalers, the merchant wholesalers, represents three-fourths of the establishments and almost half
the sales of all wholesale trade in the state of New York. The largest
metropolitan areas, each with 1 million or more inhabitants, accounted for
one-tenth of the total U.S. population but for two-fifths of the value of
all sales. At the other end of the scale, the "remainder of the United
States" (areas not included in the Standard Metropolitan Statistical

TABLE XIII.18

ESTIMATED SALES OF MERCHANT WHOLESALERS, BY KIND OF
BUSINESS, 1960-64
(In Billions of Dollars)

Kind of Business	1960	1961	1962	1963	1964
Durable goods	56.8	56.9	60.3	62.9	69.0
Motor vehicles, automotive equipment	7.9	7.8	8.4	9.3	10.0
Electrical goods	8.7	8.6	9.1	9.4	10.3
Furniture, home furnishings	2.9	2.9	3.0	3.1	3.4
Hardware, plumbing, heating equipment	6.4	6.3	6.6	6.8	7.2
Lumber, construction materials	6.7	6.6	6.8	7.2	7.3
Machinery, equipment, supplies	14.3	14.4	16.2	16.6	18.6
Metals, metalwork (except scrap)	5.7	5.9	6.0	6.2	7.2
Scrap, waste materials	3.3	3.4	3.1	3.3	4.0
Jewelry	1.0	1.0	0.9	0.9	1.1
Nondurable goods	80.5	82.6	85.6	89.4	95.6
Groceries and related products	27.7	28.7	30.4	31.6	34.3
Beer, wine, distilled alcoholic beverages	7.4	7.6	8.0	8.5	9.2
Drugs, chemicals, allied products	5.4	5.5	5.7	5.9	6.2
Tobacco, tobacco products	4.2	4.3	4.5	4.6	4.8
Dry goods, apparel	6.7	6.8	7.3	7.2	8.0
Paper, paper products (excluding wallpaper)	4.2	4.3	4.4	4.5	4.9
Farm products (raw materials)	11.7	11.9	11.8	12.3	12.5
Other nondurable goods	13.3	13.6	13.5	14.6	15.6
ALL MERCHANT WHOLESALERS	137.3	139.5	145.9	152.3	164.6

Areas [SMSA]) comprised 28 per cent of the total population in 1963 and accounted for 25 per cent of the wholesale business in the country.

Data on sales and inventories are available for merchant wholesalers only; information on other kinds of wholesales exists only for the years when the Census of Business is taken. The merchant wholesalers increased their sales from about $137 billion in 1960 to some $165 billion in 1964. Nondurable goods account for the lion's share of sales, with groceries representing the largest single item (see Table XIII.18).

Inventories of merchant wholesalers are substantial. By the end of 1965, they amounted to nearly $18 billion ($10.1 billion were in durable goods and $7.8 billion in nondurables, exclusive of raw materials).

81. Retail Trade

National income originating in retail trade amounted to $0.5 billion in 1869, almost $9 billion in 1929, and approached $50 billion in 1964. But its percentage of national income has changed only slightly as compared with 1929: 9.6 per cent in 1964, 10.2 per cent in 1929 (see Table XIII.15).

Retail sales are related to personal consumption expenditures, but they

TABLE   XIII.19

RETAIL TRADE :   ESTABLISHMENTS,
EMPLOYEES, AND SALES, 1926-63

Year	Establish-ments	Employees Engaged	Sales (In Millions of Dollars)	Sales in Dollars Per Store	Per Employee
	(In Thousands)				
1929	1,476	5,721	48,329	32,745	8,450
1933	1,440	4,817	24,517	17,025	5,090
1939	1,770	6,436	42,041	23,750	6,530
1948	1,770	8,660	130,520	73,740	15,070
1954	1,722	8,890	169,967	111,660	19,120
1958	1,788	7,911	199,646	112,060	27,760
1963	1,708	8,410	244,202	143,000	29,000

do not include some of the major consumer expenditures such as rent, personal services, etc. Together with the wholesale-trade data, they are considered important indicators of economic conditions, reflecting the activities at the intermediate stage of distribution (wholesale trade) and at its final stage (retail trade).

The census classification of the retail trade comprises all establishments engaged in buying and selling merchandise, including the automotive dealers, gasoline service stations, nonstore retailers (mail-order houses), vending-machine operators and house-to-house sellers. It also includes liquor stores operated by state and local governments.

The 1963 Census of Business reported 1.7 million stores with 8.4 million paid employees and 1.5 million active sole proprietors of unincorporated businesses, and with $244 billion in sales (or $233 billion in establishments with payroll). On the average, sales amounted to $143,000 per store and $29,000 per employee. While the retail price index about doubled between 1929 and 1963, sales per paid employee more than tripled (see Table XIII.19).

TABLE XIII.20

RETAIL TRADE BY SINGLE UNIT AND MULTI-UNITS, 1958

	Establish-ments	Paid Employees, (In Thousands)	Sales (In Millions of Dollars)
All establishments	1,788,325	7,911	199,646
Single units	1,605,590	4,978	132,437
Multi-units	182,735	2,933	67,209
2 establishments	52,258	452	9,626
3 establishments	16,307	198	4,140
4 or 5 establishments	13,310	206	4,176
6-10 establishments	12,366	225	4,816
11-25 establishments	14,670	225	5,115
26-50 establishments	11,888	307	6,263
51-100 establishments	11,708	199	4,597
101 establishments and over multi-units	50,228	1,120	28,476

Unpaid family workers represent a considerable additional labor force in retail trade, particularly in grocery stores. For example, the 1958 Census of Business estimated their number at more than 930,000; in some lines of retailing, they accounted for half the total labor force.

Of the 1.8 million establishments reported in 1958, the latest census for which these and other detailed data are available, 1.6 million were single units and 183,000 were multi-units. Though the latter represented only about one-tenth of all establishments, they accounted for one-third of all sales and all employees. The big chain stores with 100 or more units represented less than 3 per cent of all establishments but handled some 14 per cent of all sales and employed about the same percentage of all paid workers (see Table XIII.20).

In contrast to wholesale trade, nearly 70 per cent of all retail stores belong to individual proprietors; corporations and partnerships account for almost all the remainder; the cooperatives and other types of stores represent only about one-half of 1 per cent.

The 2 largest groups among the retail establishments are the food stores and eating and drinking places: 319,433 and 334,481, respectively, in 1963. More than 100,000 retail stores are open only a part of the year, catering to seasonal business.

The distribution of retail establishments by the amount of annual sales similarly indicates the predominance of small shops throughout the nation. About 3 out of 5 stores had an annual turnover of less than $50,000; and 1 out of 5 had sales from $50,000 to $99,000; at the other extreme were

TABLE XIII.21

PERCENTAGE DISTRIBUTION OF RETAIL ESTABLISHMENTS, BY THE NUMBER
OF EMPLOYEES AND AMOUNT OF SALES, 1958

	Establishments	Paid Employees	Sales
All establishments operated entire year with:	100.0	100.0	100.0
No paid employees	35.9	...	6.7
1 paid employee	14.1	3.1	4.9
2 paid employees	13.0	5.8	6.3
3-5 paid employees	19.1	16.0	15.2
6-9 paid employees	8.5	13.6	12.3
10-19 paid employees	5.8	17.1	15.7
20-49 paid employees	2.9	19.1	19.4
50-99 paid employees	0.6	9.0	8.6
100 or more paid employees	0.2	16.3	10.9
All establishments operated entire year with annual sales of:	100.0	100.0	100.0
Less than $19,000	28.2	2.7	2.5
$20,000-$49,000	29.8	9.6	8.5
$50,000-$99,000	19.3	14.1	11.8
$100,000-$299,000	16.1	25.2	23.1
$300,000-$499,000	3.0	9.7	10.0
$500,000-$999,000	2.2	11.3	13.1
$1,000,000-$1,999,000	1.0	9.2	12.4
$2,000,000-$4,999,000	0.4	7.7	10.5
$5,000,000 and over	0.08	10.5	8.2

the gigantic establishments, a mere 0.08 of 1 per cent of all stores, each with $5 million or more in yearly sales (see Table XIII.21). More than one-third of retail stores had no paid employees.

Retail sales per capita of population are below the national average of $1,295 in the poor states of the South and much above it in the northern and western states, ranging from $918 in Mississippi and $908 in South Carolina to $1,316 in Connecticut; $1,485 in Delaware; $1,533 in Cal-

TABLE XIII.22

RETAIL SALES PER CAPITA OF POPULATION, BY GEOGRAPHIC DIVISION AND
STATE, 1958 AND 1963
(In Dollars)

State	Sales Per Capita 1958	1963	State	Sales Per Capita 1958	1963
United States	1,148	1,295	Virginia	951	1,119
			West Virginia	871	981
New England	1,219	1,379	North Carolina	877	1,039
Maine	1,092	1,202	South Carolina	758	908
New Hampshire	1,212	1,370	Georgia	927	1,084
Vermont	1,166	1,321	Florida	1,261	1,376
Massachusetts	1,246	1,403	East South Central	841	985
Rhode Island	1,083	1,262	Kentucky	872	1,015
Connecticut	1,269	1,316	Tennessee	922	1,070
Middle Atlantic	1,204	1,316	Alabama	812	964
New York	1,253	1,355	Mississippi	701	918
New Jersey	1,235	1,382	West South Central	1,078	1,167
Pennsylvania	1,114	1,218	Arkansas	890	1,043
East North Central	1,202	1,358	Louisiana	932	993
Ohio	1,131	1,295	Oklahoma	1,059	1,188
Indiana	1,130	1,355	Texas	1,167	1,243
Illinois	1,294	1,463	Mountain	1,222	1,351
Michigan	1,161	1,352	Montana	1,296	1,378
Wisconsin	1,159	1,275	Idaho	1,266	1,378
West North Central	1,214	1,344	Wyoming	1,321	1,434
Minnesota	1,200	1,335	Colorado	1,263	1,381
Iowa	1,243	1,411	New Mexico	1,098	1,183
Missouri	1,230	1,356	Arizona	1,184	1,330
North Dakota	1,259	1,350	Utah	1,099	1,246
South Dakota	1,177	1,237	Nevada	1,517	1,817
Nebraska	1,251	1,428	Pacific	1,298	1,488
Kansas	1,143	1,280	Washington	1,233	1,365
South Atlantic	1,018	1,166	Oregon	1,244	1,447
Delaware	1,346	1,485	California	1,341	1,533
Maryland	1,115	1,264	Alaska	912	1,154
District of Columbia	1,723	1,795	Hawaii	853	1,098

ifornia; and $1,817 in Nevada (see Table XIII.22). The 10 SMSA's ranking highest by amount of sales in 1963 were, in order given, New York; Los Angeles–Long Beach; Chicago; Philadelphia, Pa.–N.J.; Detroit; San Francisco–Oakland; Boston; Washington, D.C.–Md.–Va.; Pittsburgh; and St. Louis, Mo.–Ill. Yet because of the size of their population, the per capita retail sales do not rank as high, fluctuating from $1,200 to about $1,700, while 2 areas in Nevada—Las Vegas and Reno—top the list, with $3,014 and $2,297, respectively, in per capita sales.

The retail stores handle an enormous business, more than a quarter of a trillion dollars in 1964. Two-thirds of their business is in nondurable

TABLE XIII.23

SALES OF RETAIL STORES, BY KIND OF BUSINESS, 1960-64
(In Billions of Dollars)

Kind of Business	1960	1961	1962	1963	1964
Durable goods[a]	70.7	67.3	74.9	80.1	85.1
Automotive group	39.5	36.9	42.8	46.0	48.5
Furniture and appliance group	10.6	10.4	10.8	11.6	13.0
Lumber, building, hardware, farm equipment	14.8	14.1	15.1	15.5	15.6
Nondurable goods[a]	148.8	151.5	160.4	166.3	176.5
Apparel group	13.7	13.7	14.3	14.5	15.6
Drug and proprietary stores	7.5	7.7	8.0	8.2	8.6
Eating and drinking places	16.1	16.4	17.3	18.1	19.4
Food group	53.8	55.4	57.6	59.1	62.2
General-merchandise group	24.0	24.9	27.2	28.7	31.7
Liquor stores	4.9	4.9	5.4	5.7	6.0
Gasoline service stations	17.6	18.0	18.6	19.4	20.3
All retail stores	219.5	218.8	235.4	246.4	261.6

[a]Includes data not shown separately.

FIGURE XIII.9

SALES OF RETAIL STORES, BY KIND OF BUSINESS, 1964

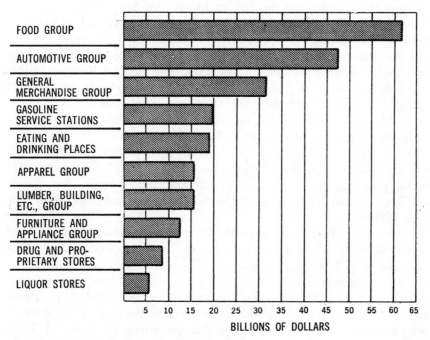

BILLIONS OF DOLLARS

U.S. Department of Commerce, Bureau of the Census

goods, of which the food group represents the most important part. In durable goods, the automotive group (comprising sales of passenger cars, tires, and other accessories) accounts for more than half of estimated sales (see Table XIII.23 and Figure XIII.9).

82. Banking and the Monetary System

The banking system of the United States goes back to the time less than 200 years ago when the first commercial bank was created with an initial capital of $10 million, of which $7 million was subscribed by foreigners. The long road to the banking system as we know it today has been strewn with failures, instances of mismanagement, suspension of payments, even frauds and panics, but has also been characterized by periods of competent operations and determined efforts to stabilize and create a strong, reliable system on which the country's economy could develop and grow. Many factors played a role in making this system different from the banking organizations in other advanced countries. Among the most consequential of these factors have been the size and great diversification of the economy, the state structure of the government, and the traditional opposition to concentration of power in a few financial centers. The U.S. banking system now consists of many thousands of institutions, some of which are chartered and supervised by an agency of the Federal Government while others are under the jurisdiction of state agencies.

The first important milestone in the development of the banking system in this country was the National Currency Act of 1863. Signed by President Lincoln, it authorized the incorporation of national banks, aimed at establishing uniform currency, and provided for supervision of bank operations by the Comptroller of the Currency. The second decisive step was the Federal Reserve Act of 1913. The Federal Reserve System started its operations in 1914; it includes all national banks, which were required to become its members (as is still required of each newly chartered national bank), and those state-chartered banks that joined it voluntarily.

The system consists of 12 regional Federal Reserve Banks and the Board of Governors—virtually bankers' banks. They serve commercial banks and, through them, the public, by facilitating the clearance and collection of checks, providing discount facilities, and furnishing currency for circulation. They regulate the growth of the money supply and bank credit (see Figure XIII.10).

Although the Federal Reserve Banks are not government banks and their stock is owned by member banks, the system operates as a public institution, similar to the central banks in other countries. The Federal Reserve Board acts as a fiscal agent for the U.S. Treasury Department through its agents. The member banks maintain their legal reserves with the Federal Reserve Banks of the respective districts; since 1959, member banks are also allowed to count a specified percentage of vault cash as reserves. The percentage of required reserves is set by the Federal Reserve

FIGURE XIII.10

THE FEDERAL RESERVE SYSTEM, 1964

——— Boundaries of Federal Reserve Districts
——— Boundaries of Federal Reserve Branch Territories
✪ Board of Governors of the Federal Reserve System
◉ Federal Reserve Bank Cities
• Federal Reserve Branch Cities

Federal Reserve Board

Board separately for demand and time deposits, and by class of bank. Present legal requirements are, for example, 16.5 per cent for demand deposits at reserve city banks. At the end of 1965, the reserves of all member banks with the Federal Reserve System amounted to $23 billion, slightly exceeding the required reserves. Reserve requirements for the nonmember banks are set by the states; they vary from state to state, but on the whole, they permit the banks to hold smaller cash resources in relation to deposits than those required of member banks. Originally, the chief purpose of reserve requirements was to assure the safety of deposits and the liquidity of the banking system. They now serve as a medium through which the volume of credit of member banks can be influenced by changing the reserve re-

TABLE XIII.24

NUMBER OF BANKS IN THE UNITED STATES, 1900-64

Year, Ending June 30	All Banks	Commercial Banks				Mutual Savings Banks
		Total	National	State	Nonmember	
1900	13,053	12,427	3,731	8,696	12,427	626
1910	25,151	24,514	7,138	17,376	24,514	637
1920	30,909	30,291	8,024	1,374	20,893	618
1930	24,273	23,679	7,247	1,068	15,364	594
1940	15,076	14,534	5,164	1,234	8,136	542
1950	14,676	14,146	4,971	1,911	7,264	530
1960	14,000	13,485	4,542[a]	1,675[a]	7,266[a]	515
1962	13,934	13,422	4,500	1,570	7,353	512
1964[b]	14,266	13,761	4,773	1,452	7,536	505

[a]June 15.
[b]December 31.

quirements; in other words, they serve as one of the principal instruments of monetary policy exercised by the Federal Reserve Board through its control over the volume of reserves.

The Federal Reserve System had 7,631 member banks in 1915; the number rose to 9,398 in 1920; then it declined—to 6,398 in 1940 and 6,225 at the end of 1964 (4,773 national banks and 1,452 state banks). Less than half the banks in this country are members of the Federal Reserve System, but their assets represent about 85 per cent of total deposits in all commercial banks.

FIGURE XIII.11

PER CENT OF DEPOSITS HELD BY THE
FIVE LARGEST BANKS IN EACH STATE

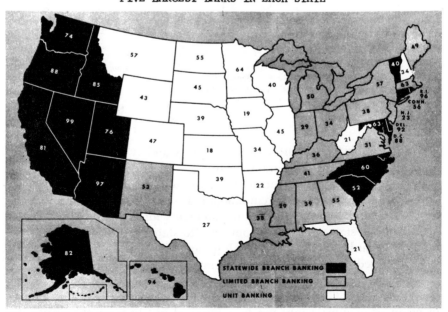

Federal Reserve Board

Today, the Federal Reserve Bank is in charge of conducting monetary policy for achieving the objectives of the Employment Act. It shares with the U.S. Treasury the responsibility of defending the international position of the dollar, has important regulatory functions in banking, and issues the bulk of our currency.

The Federal Deposit Insurance Corporation (FDIC), a Federally owned insurance corporation to insure bank deposits to a maximum of $5,000 (later raised to $10,000) per account, was established on a temporary basis in 1933 and made permanent in 1935. Insurance of bank deposits is obligatory for all member banks of the Federal Reserve System, and optional for others. In 1964, all commercial banks and mutual savings banks belonged to the FDIC, constituting about 97 per cent of all operating banks in the country. According to the FDIC, its maximum insurance per account ($10,000) fully covers some 98 per cent of all depositors, though only some 60 per cent of all deposits are insured, because the huge deposits of corporations account for a substantial part of total bank deposits.

The total number of banks in the United States was less than 2,000 in 1865; 50 years later, it was 28,017, and in 1922 it exceeded 31,000. These were the years of rapid industrial growth, of urbanization and improved transportation, of rising land and other prices, when more than 500 banks per year were chartered, on the average, between 1915 and 1922. Then, bank failures and mergers resulted in decreasing numbers, and the heaviest blow was inflicted by the Great Depression. Some 9,000 banks were closed, leaving whole communities without banking facilities. By the end of 1935, the banking structure, with about 15,000 banks and 3,000 branches, was back in operation. Since then, a slow decline has continued, but it has been caused less by bank failures than by the tendency among the banks to strengthen their competitive position through mergers. On December 31, 1964, there were 14,266 banks in the United States (see Table XIII.24).

In contrast, the number of branches has been on the rise; their number was 11,215 at the end of 1964. Branching is particularly prevalent in the western states, while unit banking predominates in the Middle West and some adjoining states. In most states of the East, branch banking is rather limited. Concentration of deposits is much greater in the states with branch banking than elsewhere (see Figure XIII.11).

Between 1940 and 1964, total assets of all banks (loans, investments, and cash), as well as total liabilities (deposits, borrowings, and capital accounts), more than quintupled; loans and investments increased more than sixfold, and deposits, five times. Loans and investments of all commercial banks represent about eight-tenths of their total assets. Of these, loans account for about 50 per cent; U.S. securities for some 30 per cent, and the remainder is in cash and various other securities (see Table XIII.25 and Figure XIII.12).

Commercial and industrial loans (loans to business for inventories, equipment, and other capital needs) have always been the main category of banking loans. In 1947, they represented almost half the amount of

TABLE XIII.25

BANKS IN THE UNITED STATES, BY PRINCIPAL ASSETS AND
LIABILITIES, 1900-64
(In Billions of Dollars)

Class of Bank	1900	1910	1920	1930	1940	1950	1960	1964
Total assets (or liabili-ties):								
All banks	11.4	22.9	53.1	74.3	79.7	191.3	298.1	401.2
Commercial banks	9.1	19.3	47.5	64.1	67.8	168.9	257.6	346.9
Federal Reserve member banks	...	...	33.6	47.4	62.7	144.7	216.6	289.1
Mutual savings banks	2.3	3.6	5.6	10.2	11.9	22.4	40.6	54.2
Loans and investments:								
All banks	8.6	17.6	42.2	59.1	51.3	148.0	238.6	329.7
Commercial banks	6.5	14.2	37.0	49.4	41.2	126.7	199.5	277.4
Federal Reserve member banks	...	...	25.5	34.9	37.1	107.4	165.6	228.5
Mutual savings banks	2.1	3.4	5.3	9.6	10.2	21.3	39.1	52.4
Deposits:								
All banks	8.9	18.0	41.8	60.4	70.9	163.8	266.2	356.3
Commercial banks	6.8	14.6	36.7	51.3	60.2	143.8	229.8	307.2
Federal Reserve member banks	...	...	...	37.0	56.4	133.1	193.0	255.7
Mutual savings banks	2.1	3.3	5.2	9.1	10.6	19.9	36.4	49.1

FIGURE XIII.12

PRINCIPAL ASSETS OF ALL COMMERCIAL BANKS, 1914-63

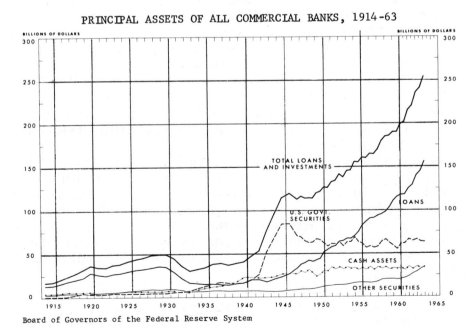

Board of Governors of the Federal Reserve System

TABLE XIII.26

LOANS OF INSURED COMMERCIAL BANKS BY CLASS OF BORROWER, 1947-64[a]
(In Billions of Dollars)

	1947	1955[b]	1962	1963	1964
Commercial and industrial	18.0	33.2	48.5	52.7	59.7
Agricultural	1.6	4.5	7.1	7.4	7.5
For purchasing or carrying securities	2.0	5.0	7.2	7.8	8.2
To financial institutions	0.1	0.6	11.0	13.0	14.2
Real estate	9.3	20.8	34.1	38.9	43.4
Other to individuals	5.7	17.2	30.4	34.4	39.6
Other	0.9	2.5	3.9	4.0	5.1
TOTAL LOANS	37.6	82.6	139.4	155.3	174.2

[a]December 31, except 1962 (December 28) and 1963 (December 20).
[b]Beginning 1955, figures for detailed loan items are shown gross (before deduction of valuation reserves). Total loans are shown net for all years.

total outstanding loans. But their share began to decline when two new groups of customers appeared in the field: consumers and mortgage lenders. Loans to consumers, classified in Table XIII.26 under "other to individuals" and used mostly for the purchase of durable goods and home repairs, skyrocketed from $5.7 billion in 1947 to $39.6 billion in 1964, when they accounted for almost one-fourth of total loan volume. Mortgage loans have also grown in importance, from $9 billion in 1947 to more than $43 billion in 1964. Together, these last two categories of loans now account for a greater part of bank lending than commercial and industrial business loans (see Table XIII.26).

Term loans, i.e., loans with an original maturity of one year or longer from the date it is taken down, represent the most substantial part of the business loan portfolios of banks. Statistical information on term loans is available from special surveys covering a specified group of leading banks. The Federal Reserve Board has made several surveys; its latest, in 1955, relates to 2,000 banks, which held 93 per cent of the business loans of member banks and some 87 per cent of the business loans of all commercial banks. According to this survey, term loans constituted one-third of all business loans.

In addition to commercial banks, there are many other credit institutions in the United States: mutual savings banks, savings and loan associations, credit unions, finance companies dealing primarily in installment sales financing, personal-loan companies, etc. The largest of these are the savings and loan associations. Their total assets amounted to only $6 billion in 1940, but they expanded rapidly in the 1950's, from $16.9 billion in 1950 to $71.5 billion in 1960, and again to nearly $120 billion in 1964. Their main assets are in mortgages ($101 billion in 1964); other assets consist of

TABLE XIII.27

ASSETS AND LIABILITIES OF SAVINGS AND LOAN ASSOCIATIONS, 1940-64
(In Billions of Dollars)

	1940	1945	1950	1955	1960	1962	1964
Number of associations	7,521	6,149	5,992	6,071	6,320	6,289	6,248
Total assets (or liabilities)	5.7	8.7	16.9	37.7	71.5	93.6	119.3
Assets: mortgages	4.1	5.5	13.7	31.4	60.1	78.8	101.3
U.S. Government securities, cash, other	1.6	3.2	3.2	6.4	11.4	14.8	18.0
Liabilities: savings capital	4.3	7.4	14.0	32.1	62.1	80.2	101.8
other[a]	1.4	1.4	2.9	5.5	9.3	13.4	17.4

[a]Includes loans in process, borrowed money, reserves and undivided profits, and other.

U.S. Government securities, cash, and other investments (see Table XIII.27).

About 85 per cent of all the coin and paper money issued by the U.S. Treasury and Federal Reserve Banks represents currency in circulation, the so-called currency outside the banks; the bank vaults hold the remaining cash. But the checkbook money, i.e., demand deposits at commercial banks, is used predominantly—and to a much greater extent than people use it in other countries—for most of our daily operations.

The money supply (currency outside banks and demand deposits) amounted to $26.2 billion in 1929; dropped to $19.2 billion in 1933, the worst Depression year; quintupled by 1945, at the peak of World War II, and exceeded $167 billion by the end of 1964. As shown by Table XIII.28, time deposits are rapidly approaching demand deposits.

TABLE XIII.28

MONEY SUPPLY AND TIME DEPOSITS IN THE UNITED STATES, 1940-64
(In Billions of Dollars)

Year [a]	Money Supply		Currency	Time Deposits Adjusted[c]
	Total	Demand Deposits Adjusted[b]		
1940	42.2	34.9	7.3	15.8
1945	102.4	75.9	26.5	30.1
1950	117.7	92.3	25.4	36.3
1955	138.2	109.9	28.3	48.4
1960	144.5	115.1	29.4	71.4
1961	150.6	120.5	30.1	82.1
1962	153.2	122.3	30.9	97.4
1963	158.1	124.6	33.5	110.8
1964	167.1	132.3	34.9	126.4

[a]Last Wednesday in December prior to 1960. Averages of daily figures thereafter.
[b]At all commercial banks, less cash items in process of collection; other than interbank and U.S. Government deposits.
[c]At all commercial banks other than those due to domestic commercial banks and U.S. Government.

TABLE XIII.29

CONSOLIDATED CONDITION STATEMENT OF THE MONETARY SYSTEM, 1929-64[a]
(In Billions of Dollars)

	1929	1933	1939	1945	1950	1960	1962	1964
Total assets, net (or lia-bilities and capital, net)	64.7	48.5	75.2	191.8	199.0	290.0	330.9	386.2
Assets:								
Gold	4.0	4.0	17.6	20.1	22.7	17.8	16.0	15.4
Treasury currency outstanding	2.0	2.3	3.0	4.3	4.6	5.4	5.6	5.4
Bank credit, total:	58.6	42.1	54.6	167.4	171.7	266.8	309.4	365.4
Loans, net	41.1	22.0	22.2	30.4	60.4	144.7	170.7	214.3
U.S.Government securi-ties, total	5.7	10.3	23.1	128.4	96.6	95.5	103.7	106.8
Other securities	11.8	9.9	9.3	8.6	14.7	26.6	35.0	44.3
Liabilities:								
Total deposits and currency	55.8	42.0	68.4	180.8	184.4	263.2	302.2	353.0
Capital, net[b]	8.9	6.4	6.8	11.0	14.6	26.8	28.7	33.2

[a]1929, 1933 and 1939, end of June; others, end of December.
[b]Includes miscellaneous accounts.

Assets and liabilities of the monetary system can be consolidated to avoid double counting. Table XIII.29, representing the consolidated statement of the banks and monetary system, shows that total net assets (as well as total liabilities and capital) approached $400 billion at the end of 1964 and were six times larger than in 1929. They experienced the most rapid growth during the 1940's, doubled in the war years, and again doubled between 1945 and 1964.

83. Insurance

Of the various types of private insurance, this chapter deals only with life, health, and property insurance; for social insurance, see Secs. 90–93.

Life insurance. The first life insurance company was established in 1759 and for some 10 years remained the only one in existence. Then other companies began to appear, but it was not until 1847, almost a century later, that the number of companies reached the figure of 25, and not until the twentieth century did the number of life insurance companies grow rapidly, from 84 in 1900 to 649 in 1950, skyrocketing to 1,550 in 1964. However, many life insurance companies are small (some have assets of less than $5 million); many are considered legal reserve only by their states and may not be so considered by all other states. Texas, Arizona, and Louisiana report the largest number of insurance companies: 261, 156, and 114, respectively. Only about one-tenth of all insurance companies in 1964 (157) were mutual companies owned by their policyholders; they accounted for about 60 per cent of the insurance in force and about

TABLE XIII.30

ASSETS OF U.S. LIFE INSURANCE COMPANIES, 1900-1964
(In Billions of Dollars)

Type of Assets	1900	1920	1930	1940	1950	1960	1964
Total	1.7	7.3	18.9	30.8	64.0	119.6	149.5
Mortgages	0.5	2.4	7.6	6.0	16.1	41.8	55.2
Bonds, total:	0.7	3.3	6.4	17.1	39.4	58.6	68.0
Industrial[a]	-	-	0.4	1.5	9.5	26.7	35.3
Public utility	-	0.1	1.6	4.3	10.6	16.7	17.2
U. S. Government	-	0.8	0.3	5.8	13.5	6.4	5.6
State and local government	-	0.4	1.0	2.4	1.5	4.6	5.6
Other	0.3	1.9	3.1	3.1	4.2	4.1	4.2
Stocks	0.1	0.1	0.5	0.6	2.1	5.0	7.9
Policy loans	-	0.9	2.8	3.1	2.4	5.2	7.1
Real estate	0.2	0.2	0.5	2.1	1.4	3.8	4.5
Miscellaneous	-	0.5	1.0	2.0	2.6	5.3	6.7

[a]Includes commercial bonds and other.

70 per cent of total assets of all U.S. companies. Twenty-two of them had been in insurance business for more than 100 years.

Total assets of life insurance companies have grown from $1.7 billion in 1900 to $18.9 billion in 1930; they more than tripled in the next 2 decades ($64 billion in 1950); and they approached $150 billion in 1964. More than one-third of the assets, 36.9 per cent, are in mortgages and about one-fourth, 23.7 per cent, in bonds of industrial and commercial firms; the remainder are spread among U.S. Government securities, bonds of state and local governments, stocks and bonds of railroad companies, real estate, and others (see Table XIII.30 and Figure XIII.13A).

FIGURE XIII.13.A

ASSETS OF U.S. LIFE INSURANCE COMPANIES, 1919-64

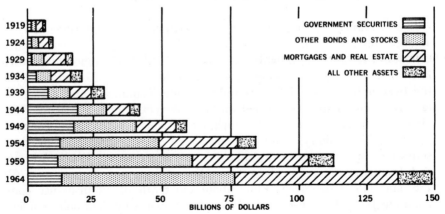

Institute of Life Insurance

FIGURE XIII.13.B

LIFE INSURANCE IN FORCE IN THE UNITED STATES, 1924-64

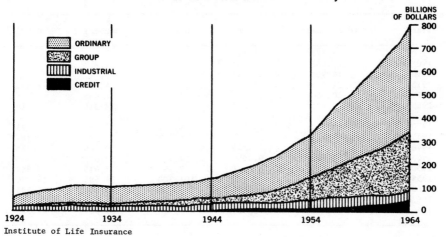

Institute of Life Insurance

Total life insurance in force with legal reserve companies in the United States was less than $8 billion in 1900 (sum total of the face amount outstanding at a given time), increased to $234 billion by 1950, and in 1964, with $800 billion, was more than 100 times larger than in 1900 (see Figure XIII.13B).

The basic type of life insurance, "ordinary" insurance, had $6 billion in force in 1900, $149 billion in 1950, and $458 billion in 1964. Industrial life insurance appeared next, to attract low-income groups who could not afford high single premiums but could pay small weekly or monthly installments. Premiums are usually collected at the home by the company's agent. This type of insurance reached its peak in 1957, with $40.1 billion, and began to decline afterward. It represents now about 5 per cent of all life insurance in force, as compared with 18 per cent in 1937, 3 decades before. The most consequential factor in this decline has been the spread of pension and retirement plans introduced in many industrial and commercial enterprises. Group life insurance has essentially the same purpose as industrial life insurance and has replaced it in time; premiums are paid in full or in part, by the employer. It is issued under a single master policy, but individual members of the group hold certificates for their coverage. It provides protection to a larger segment of the low-income population than industrial life insurance, which mainly covered the industrial labor force. From $100 million in 1915, it expanded rapidly and by the end of 1964 accounted for $252 billion. By 218,000 master contracts, it provided 54.5 million persons with life insurance certificates in 1964. Protection per certificate averaged $4,630.

The latest type of life insurance, so-called credit insurance, repays the outstanding debt or installment purchase, or other obligation to a lender

TABLE XIII.31

LIFE INSURANCE IN FORCE, 1900-1964
(In Millions of Dollars)

Year	Total Amount	Ordinary	Group	Industrial	Credit[a]
1900	7,573	6,124	...	1,449	...
1905	11,863	9,585	...	2,278	...
1910	14,908	11,783	...	3,125	...
1915	21,029	16,650	100	4,279	...
1920	40,540	32,018	1,570	6,948	4
1925	69,475	52,892	4,247	12,318	18
1930	106,413	78,576	9,801	17,963	73
1935	98,464	70,684	10,208	17,471	101
1940	115,530	79,346	14,938	20,866	380
1945	151,762	101,550	22,172	27,675	365
1950	234,168	149,071	47,793	33,415	3,889
1955	372,332	216,600	101,300	39,682	14,750
1960	586,448	340,268	175,434	39,563	31,183
1963	730,623	418,856	228,540	39,672	43,555
1964	799,977	458,029	252,182	39,833	49,933

[a]Insures borrower to cover loans in case of death.

in case the borrower should die. It began its operations in 1918 with the modest sum of $2 million and amounted to nearly $50 billion in 1964 (see Table XIII.31).

Life-insurance companies derive their income from 2 sources: premiums paid by policy-holders and earnings from their investments. In 1920, their total income was $1.8 billion; it more than tripled within the next 20 years, with $5.7 billion in 1940, about doubled by 1950, and again doubled by 1960. By the end of 1964, it amounted to $30.7 billion (see Table XIII.32).

TABLE XIII.32

INCOME OF U.S. LIFE INSURANCE COMPANIES, 1860-1964
(In Millions of Dollars)

Year	Total	Premiums	Investments	Other
1860	6.0	4.8	1.2	
1870	105.0	90.3	14.7	
1880	77.7	54.2	23.5	
1890	195.6	156.8	38.8	
1900	400.6	324.7	75.9	
1910	781.0	593.4	187.6	
1920	1,764	1,381	341	42
1930	4,594	3,517	891	186
1940	5,658	3,887	1,231	540
1950[a]	11,337	8,189	2,075	1,073
1955	16,544	12,546	2,801	1,197
1960	23,007	17,365	4,304	1,338
1962	26,000	19,373	5,044	1,583
1964	30,674	22,653	6,276	1,745

[a]Beginning with 1955, investment income is net of investment expenses.

TABLE XIII.33

LIFE INSURANCE BENEFIT PAYMENTS IN THE UNITED STATES, 1900-1964
(In Millions of Dollars)

Year	Total	Death Payments	Living Payments				
			Annuities	Matured Endowments	Surrender Values	Policy Dividends	Dis-ability
1900	169	101	4	18	23	23	-
1910	387	181	7	46	78	75	-
1920	745	350	9	101	119	158	8
1930	2,247	856	23	112	614	554	88
1940	2,664	995	177	269	652	468	104
1950	3,731	1,590	319	495	592	635	100
1960	8,119	3,346	722	673	1,633	1,620	124
1962	9,325	3,878	838	714	1,773	1,980	142
1964	10,758	4,534	961	899	1,834	2,370	161

Benefit payments by life-insurance companies consist of 2 principal types: living benefits to policy-holders and death payments to the survivors of policy-holders. The living benefits comprise annuities, matured endowments, surrender values, policy dividends, and disability payments. Total benefit payments increased from $2.7 billion in 1940 to $8.1 billion in 1960 and $10.8 billion in 1964. Living payments to policy-holders have fluctuated within 58–59 per cent of total payments; the remainder has been used for death payments (see Table XIII.33).

Property insurance. Property-insurance companies provide protection against fire, casualty, burglary, and the like. There are some 3,500 fire and casualty companies in the United States. In 1962, direct premiums obtained by them amounted to $24 billion, and direct losses incurred, to $15.5 billion. In contrast to life-insurance companies, they must hold a substantial part of their assets, half or even more, in a liquid form, to be able to handle large-scale catastrophes. Fire is one of the greatest risks insured: in 1963, losses from fire totaled $1.4 billion.

Automobile insurance has grown with the increase in the number of vehicle operators and the amount of motor traffic. Premiums written totaled $2.6 billion in 1950, $6.4 billion in 1960, and $7.3 billion in 1963. Losses paid on premiums written have also increased, from $1.1 billion in 1950 to $4.5 billion in 1963; the percentage of losses paid of premiums written rose in this period from 41 to 61—on all types of automobile insurance: damage to the car, damage to real property inflicted by the automobile, and bodily injury. These percentages fluctuated within narrow limits, ranging from 60.5 to 62.2 per cent in 1963.

Health insurance. Over 1,800 voluntary health-insurance organizations or plans existed in the United States in 1963. Plans differ in the type and extent of protection they accord policy-holders, and carrying several types of health insurance simultaneously is more frequent than with other types of insurance. The number of persons with hospitalization insurance increased from 12 million in 1940 to nearly 77 million in 1950 and 163 million by the end of 1964. Persons protected by surgical insurance numbered 152 million; and those with insurance providing for physicians' visits, mainly in the hospital, 113 million. Some had all these types of insurance, others carried 1 or 2, so that the figures are not additive.* At the end of 1963, it is estimated that more than two-thirds of the wage-earners and salary workers had some protection against the cost of hospitalization and surgery through employee-benefit plans. Most of the health plans cover dependents as well as the workers themselves. All in all, some 111 million workers and dependents had hospital protection at the end of 1963. According to the Social Security Administration, they represented four-fifths of all the persons covered by voluntary health insurance that year. It is estimated that by the end of 1964, 79 per cent of civilian population had some protection against hospitalization, 74 per cent some surgical-cost protection, and 57 per cent were protected to some degree against the cost of in-hospital medical visits.

Insurance coverage varies greatly among the states. Latest information indicates that in 6 states, less than 50 per cent of the population has hospital insurance; in 27 states, from 50 to 70 per cent of the population, and in 17 states, from 70 to 90 per cent of the population. Respective figures for surgical insurance are: 10, 30, and 40. The District of Columbia presents the apparent anomaly of having 169.1 per cent of its population insured; the explanation is that persons who live in Maryland or Virginia are enrolled in insurance or prepayment plans in the capital city.

Premiums written by the health-insurance companies amounted to $9 billion at the end of 1964, as compared with $1.3 billion in 1950; respective figures for benefit payments made by them are $7.8 billion and $75.5 million.

At this time, it is impossible to foresee how the legislation about the medical care for the aged enacted in July, 1965, and in operation since July 1, 1966, will affect private health insurance (cf. Sec. 93).

---

* A study, in which 42 leading insurance companies participated, revealed that, in 1960, duplication with respect to different types of private health insurance had reached 28 per cent.

XIV. *Public Finance*

The structure of the United States Government is extremely complex and consists of numerous public bodies and agencies, with varying degrees of power: Federal, state, county, municipal, and township governments and many districts, commissions, authorities, and other organizations. Great variations exist also from state to state. The 1962 Census of Governments reported 91,185 local government units: 3,043 counties; 17,997 municipalities; 17,144 townships; 18,323 special districts; and 34,678 school districts.

84. *The Budget of the Federal Government*

At the beginning of our national history, in 1789–91, a Federal budget of $4.4 million took care of all Federal Government activities and even provided a surplus of $150,000. In the 60 years between 1789 and 1849, total Federal receipts amounted to $1.16 billion, and total expenditures, to $1.09 billion, leaving a surplus of $70 million. In the period from 1850 to 1899, total cumulative receipts increased to $13.9 billion, while payments rose to $14.9 billion, resulting in a billion-dollar deficit. At the turn of the century, the Federal budget was still very modest; it did not reach the billion-dollar mark until 1917. The entrance of the United States into World War I necessitated large Federal expenditures, which jumped from $2 billion in 1917 to $12.7 billion in 1918 and $18.4 billion in 1919. In those 2 years, this country spent more than in the entire period of its existence from 1789 to 1917, nearly 130 years. The cumulative budget deficit of 1917–19 amounted to about $23 billion.

After the war, the deficit in the Federal budget disappeared, and in the 1920's the government spent less than it collected from the taxpayers. With the Depression, when receipts shrank and expenditures swelled, the

FIGURE XIV.1

BUDGET ESTIMATES FOR 1966 AND 1967

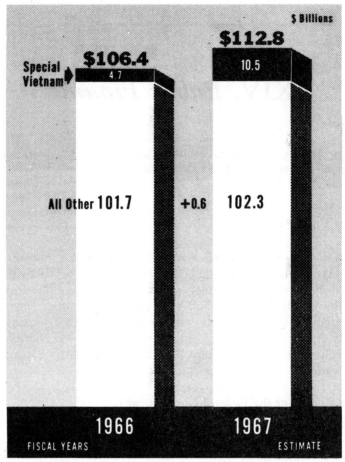

Executive Office of the President, Bureau of the Budget

deficit reappeared. World War II raised Federal expenditures to new heights, and subsequently the Cold War has kept defense expenditures on a very high level (see Table XIV.1). As a result, Federal expenditures in 1964 nearly matched those in the peak war year of 1945—$97.7 billion, as compared with $98.3 billion. The war in Viet-Nam, and particularly its escalation in 1966, has pushed upward the military and other defense expenditures. For the new budget presented by the President, Federal expenditures are estimated at $106.4 billion for 1966—about $10 billion higher than in 1965—and at $112.8 billion for 1967. Only time will tell whether these estimates are realistic, or will be exceeded, and by how much . . . (see Figure XIV.1).

Nevertheless, because of the continuous growth of the gross national

TABLE XIV.1

ADMINISTRATIVE BUDGET OF THE FEDERAL GOVERNMENT, 1789-1967
(In Millions of Dollars)

Fiscal Year	Receipts	Payments	Surplus (+) or Deficit (-)	Fiscal Year	Receipts	Payments	Surplus (+) or Deficit (-)
1789-1849	1,160	1,090	+70	1943	21,947	79,368	-57,420
1850-1899	13,895	14,932	-1,037	1944	43,563	94,986	-51,423
				1945	44,362	98,303	-53,941
1900	567	521	+46	1946	39,650	60,326	-20,676
1910	676	694	-18				
1917	1,100	1,954	-853	1950	36,422	39,544	-3,122
1918	3,630	12,662	-9,032	1955	60,209	64,389	-4,180
1919	5,085	18,448	-13,363	1959	67,915	80,342	-12,427
1920	6,649	6,357	+ 291	1960	77,763	76,539	+1,224
1925	3,598	2,881	+ 717				
1930	4,058	3,320	+ 738	1961	77,659	81,515	-3,856
1933	1,997	4,598	-2,602	1962	81,409	87,787	-6,378
1934	3,015	6,645	-3,630	1963	86,376	92,642	-6,266
1935	3,706	6,497	-2,791	1964	89,459	97,684	-8,226
				1965	93,072	96,507	-3,435
1940	5,137	9,055	-3,918	1966[a]	100,000	106,428	-6,428
1942	12,547	34,037	-21,490	1967[a]	111,000	112,847	-1,847

[a]Estimated.

product, estimated at over $700 billion for 1966, present Federal expenditures take a smaller bite out of it than during World War II: some 15–16 per cent instead of 45–46 per cent (see Figure XIV.2).

FIGURE XIV.2

FEDERAL BUDGET EXPENDITURES
AS PER CENT OF GROSS NATIONAL PRODUCT, 1942-67

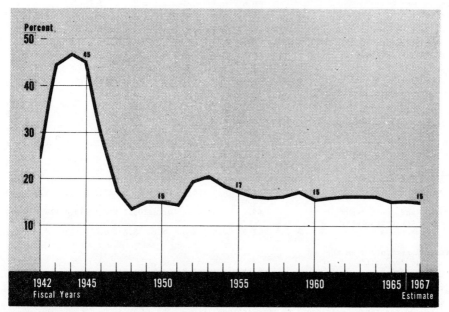

Executive Office of the President, Bureau of the Budget

TABLE XIV.2

PERCENTAGE DISTRIBUTION OF BUDGET RECEIPTS, 1939-67

	1939	1946	1950	1955	1960	1963	1964	1965	1966[a]	1967[a]
Total budget receipts	100.0	100.0	100.0	100.0	100.0	100.0	100.0	100.0	100.0	100.0
Individual income tax	20.5	40.6	43.2	47.7	52.4	55.1	53.7	52.4	51.4	50.6
Corporation (income and excess profits) taxes	22.8	29.8	28.7	29.7	27.6	25.0	26.8	27.4	29.7	31.0
Excise taxes	37.2	17.6	20.7	15.2	11.8	11.5	11.6	11.7	9.2	8.0
Customs	6.0	1.1	1.1	1.0	1.4	1.4	1.4	1.5	1.7	1.6
Net employment taxes[b]	2.6	0.5	0.7	1.0	0.4	...	...	...	...	...
Estate and gift taxes	7.1	1.7	1.9	1.5	2.1	2.5	2.6	2.9	2.9	3.0
Miscellaneous receipts	3.8	8.7	3.7	4.0	4.3	4.5	3.8	4.0	5.1	5.7

[a]Estimated.
[b]After deduction of appropriations to Federal old-age and survivors' insurance trust fund and railroad retirement account.

The largest revenue sources in the Federal budget are income taxes, individual and corporate; individual taxes produce roughly twice as much revenue as the corporate income tax. Though their rates were reduced

TABLE XIV.3

FEDERAL ADMINISTRATIVE-BUDGET AND TRUST-FUND RECEIPTS, 1955-67
(In Billions of Dollars)[a]

Item	1955	1957	1959	1961	1962	1963	1964	1965	1966	1967
A. Administrative budget funds										
Individual income taxes	28.7	35.6	36.7	41.3	45.6	47.6	48.7	48.8	51.4	56.2
Corporation income taxes	17.9	21.2	17.3	21.0	20.5	21.6	23.5	25.5	29.7	34.4
Excise taxes (net)	9.1	9.1	8.5	9.1	9.6	9.9	10.2	10.9	9.2	8.9
Employment taxes[b]	0.6	0.3	0.3	...	...	...	...	...	...	...
Estate and gift taxes	0.9	1.4	1.3	1.9	2.0	2.2	2.4	2.7	2.9	3.3
Customs	0.6	0.7	0.9	1.0	1.1	1.2	1.3	1.4	1.7	1.8
Other[c]	2.4	2.3	2.8	3.4	2.6	3.9	3.4	3.7	5.1	6.3
Total administrative-budget receipts	60.2	70.6	67.9	77.7	81.4	86.4	89.5	93.1	100.0	111.0
B. Trust funds										
Employment taxes	5.6	7.2	8.4	12.4	12.6	14.9	16.8	16.9	18.8	24.3
Unemployment-tax deposits by states	1.1	1.5	1.7	2.4	2.7	3.0	3.0	3.1	2.9	2.9
Excise taxes	...	1.5	2.1	2.8	2.9	3.3	3.5	3.7	3.9	4.4
Federal-employee and agency payments for retirement	0.5	1.2	1.5	1.7	1.8	1.9	2.0	2.2	2.2	2.2
Interest on trust funds	1.2	1.3	1.3	1.4	1.4	1.5	1.6	1.8	1.8	2.0
Veterans' life insurance premiums	0.4	0.5	0.5	0.5	0.5	0.5	0.5	0.5	0.5	0.5
Other[c]	0.7	1.1	1.2	2.3	2.4	2.7	2.8	3.0	3.4	5.3
Total trust-fund receipts	9.5	14.3	16.8	23.6	24.3	27.7	30.3	31.0	33.5	41.6
Budget and trust funds	69.7	84.9	84.7	101.3	105.7	114.1	119.8	124.1	133.5	152.6
Less intergovernmental transactions	1.9	2.8	3.0	4.1	3.8	4.4	4.3	4.3	4.5	5.5
Federal receipts from the public (consolidated cash statement)	67.8	82.1	81.7	97.2	101.9	109.7	115.5	119.8	129.0	147.1

[a]Actual data for 1955-65; estimate for 1966 and 1967.
[b]From 1961 on, less than one-half million dollars.
[c]Miscellaneous receipts, less interfund transactions.

by the Revenue Act of 1964, income taxes continue to be the mainstay of the tax structure. The individual income tax amounted to 20.5 per cent of the Federal budget in 1939, 43.2 per cent in 1950, 55.1 per cent in 1963, and is expected to decline to 51.4 per cent in 1966 and 50.6 per cent in 1967. The share of corporate tax increased comparatively less, from 22.8 per cent in 1939 to 27.4 per cent of the administrative budget in 1965 and is estimated to reach 29.7 per cent in 1966. The share of excise taxes fell from 37.2 per cent in 1939 to 11.7 per cent in 1965 and may be as low as 8 per cent in 1967 (see Table XIV.2).

According to the 1967 budget, individual taxes would provide $56.2 billion that year, or about twice the 1955 amount; corporation income taxes, $34.4 billion, also about twice the amount in 1955; while net excise taxes are expected to be slightly lower than in 1955 (see Table XIV.3).

TABLE XIV.4

FEDERAL EXPENDITURES FOR NATIONAL DEFENSE AND VETERANS BENEFITS
AND SERVICES, 1930-67[a]

Year	Total Expenditures	National Defense	Veteran's Benefits and Services	National Defense	Veteran's Benefits and Services
	(In Millions of Dollars)			(Per Cent of Total Expenditures)	
1930	3,320	734	821	22.1	24.7
1933	4,598	648	863	14.1	18.8
1935	6,497	711	607	10.9	9.3
1937	7,733	937	1,137	12.1	14.7
1939	8,841	1,075	560	12.2	6.3
1941	13,255	6,054	566	45.7	4.3
1943	79,368	63,216	606	79.6	6.8
1944	94,986	76,757	745	80.8	0.8
1945	98,303	81,277	2,095	82.7	2.1
1947	38,923	14,398	7,381	37.0	19.0
1949	39,474	12,926	6,725	32.7	17.0
1951	43,970	22,471	5,400	51.1	12.3
1953	74,120	50,442	4,368	68.1	5.9
1955	64,389	40,695	4,522	63.2	7.0
1957	68,966	43,368	4,870	62.9	7.1
1959	80,342	46,483	5,287	57.9	6.6
1961	81,515	47,494	5,414	58.3	6.6
1963	92,642	52,755	5,186	56.9	5.6
1965	96,507	50,163	5,495	52.0	5.7
1966[b]	106,428	56,560	5,122	53.2	4.8
1967[b]	112,847	60,541	5,721	53.7	5.1

[a]Administrative budget.
[b]Estimated.

Before World War II, veterans' benefits and services alone took a larger chunk from the Federal budget than national defense; in the 1930 budget of $3.3 billion, for example, expenditures for veterans exceeded those for defense: $821 million, as compared with $734 million. As war clouds began to gather over Europe in 1938-39, national defense took predominance over all other expenditures in the Federal budget and has maintained it ever since. In 1944, when defense absorbed more than 80 per cent of the budget, the military sector reached an unprecedented importance in the national economy (see Table XIV.4).

TABLE XIV.5

ADMINISTRATIVE-BUDGET AND TRUST EXPENDITURES BY FUNCTION, 1955-67[a]
(In Billions of Dollars)

Item	1955	1957	1959	1961	1962	1963	1964	1965	1966	1967
A. Administrative-budget funds										
National defense	40.7	43.4	46.5	47.5	51.1	52.8	54.2	50.2	56.6	60.5
International affairs and finance	2.3	3.3	4.8	4.0	4.3	4.2	3.7	4.3	3.9	4.2
Space research and technology[b]	...	...	...	0.7	1.3	2.6	4.2	5.1	5.6	5.3
Agriculture and agricultural resources[c]	4.3	3.2	5.5	3.7	4.4	5.3	5.5	4.9	4.3	3.4
Natural resources	1.2	1.3	1.7	2.0	2.1	2.4	2.6	2.8	2.9	3.1
Commerce and transportation	1.2	1.3	2.0	2.6	2.8	2.8	3.0	3.5	3.2	2.7
Housing and community development	0.1	-0.1	1.0	0.3	0.3	-0.1	-0.1	-0.1	-0.1	-0.1
Health, labor, and welfare	2.2	2.6	3.9	4.2	4.5	4.8	5.5	5.9	8.4	10.0
Education	0.4	0.4	0.7	0.9	1.1	1.2	1.3	1.5	2.3	2.8
Veterans' benefits and services	4.5	4.9	5.3	5.4	5.4	5.2	5.5	5.5	5.1	5.7
Interest	6.4	7.3	7.7	9.1	9.2	10.0	10.8	11.4	12.1	12.9
General government	1.2	1.7	1.5	1.7	1.9	2.0	2.3	2.4	2.5	2.6
Other[d]	-0.2	-0.5	-0.4	-0.7	-0.6	-0.5	-0.7	-0.9	-0.7	-1.1
Total administrative-budget funds	64.4	69.0	80.3	81.5	87.8	92.6	97.7	96.5	106.4	112.8
B. Trust funds										
National defense	0.2	0.1	0.2	0.2	0.4	0.7	0.5	0.8	0.9	0.9
Commerce and transportation	-0.1	0.9	2.5	2.5	2.7	2.9	3.5	3.9	3.8	3.9
Health, labor, and welfare	7.4	9.6	14.3	19.2	20.4	21.9	22.7	23.2	26.6	31.1
Veterans' benefits and services	0.6	0.6	0.7	0.8	0.7	0.8	0.7	0.6	0.6	0.7
Other	0.5	1.7	1.8	0.1	0.9	0.2	1.5	1.1	1.9	1.3
Total trust funds	8.6	12.9	19.5	22.8	25.1	26.5	28.9	29.6	33.8	37.9
Total expenditures by function	73.0	81.9	99.8	104.3	112.9	119.1	126.6	126.1	140.2	150.7

[a]Actual data for 1955-65; estimates for 1966 and 1967.
[b]Expenditures (in millions of dollars): 74 in 1955, 76 in 1957 and 145 in 1959. Almost exclusively NASA expenditures.
[c]Not including Food for Peace; by Public Law of October 8, 1964, Food for Peace is treated as part of the "International Affairs and Finance" function.
[d]Allowance for contingencies and interfund transactions.

National defense still absorbs the lion's share of the Federal budget: $50.2 billion, excluding special Viet-Nam costs, out of the total of $96.5 billion for the fiscal year 1965. This includes military assistance to allied countries and the activities of the Atomic Energy Commission, but not the space program of $5.1 billion, and not veterans' benefits and services using up another $5.5 billion. In 1966, these 3 items are expected to absorb $67.3 billion; in 1967, $71.5 billion (see Table XIV.5).

Military expenditures greatly influence our economy in many visible and invisible areas—in industrial production, employment, scientific work, development of new technology; in the field of communications; in imports and exports; in strategic stockpiling; etc.

Other large expenditure items in the Federal budget are interest on the public debt; research and technology; foreign aid; and health, education, welfare, and housing. Expenditures for general government—namely, the

FIGURE XIV.3

FEDERAL BUDGET FOR 1967

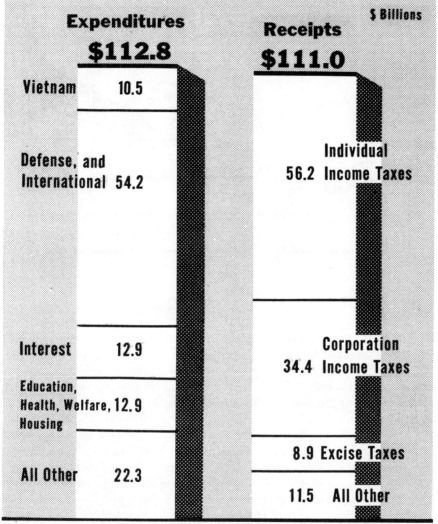

Executive Office of the President, Bureau of the Budget

legislative and judicial functions of the Federal Government and the general administrative, fiscal, and law-enforcement activities of the executive branch—take $2.2–$2.5 billion a year, or 2–3 per cent of total expenditures (see Table XIV.5, upper half, and Figure XIV.3).

So far we have discussed the so-called administrative budget, a traditionally used measure of all receipts and expenditures of government-owned funds. It has served as the basis of recommended legislation and as

FIGURE XIV.4

CONSOLIDATED CASH STATEMENT, 1942-67

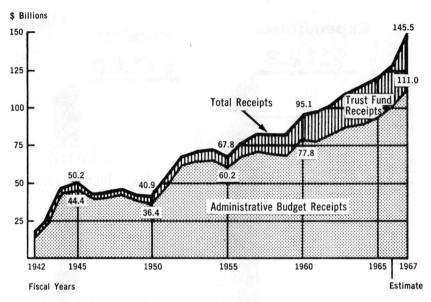

Executive Office of the President, Bureau of the Budget

the principal financial plan for government operations. As long as almost all Federal financial transactions were carried out with Federal funds, the administrative budget covered government operations quite adequately. In recent years, however, several significant government transactions have been carried out through special trust funds, such as social-security and highway trust funds. These have grown to such a size that the administrative budget, in which they are not represented, no longer shows the true flow of government operations. The measure that more fully represents cash transactions between the Federal Government and the public is the "consolidated cash statement" of Federal receipts and payments, which includes the transactions of trust funds.*

In recent years, receipts of the trust funds have equaled about one-third of the revenues from taxation and other sources in the administrative budget, or approximately one-fourth of the consolidated cash statement. They comprise employment taxes (federal old-age, survivors, and disability insurance; unemployment compensation; railroad-retirement taxes); excise taxes, which support the highway program; interest on trust funds; and others (see Table XIV.3, lower half, and Figure XIV.4).

When receipts and payments from the trust funds are included, the

---

* The consolidated cash statement excludes transactions between the budget and trust-fund accounts, because no exchange of cash with the public is involved in these operations.

TABLE XIV.6

CONSOLIDATED CASH STATEMENT AND
FEDERAL SECTOR OF THE NATIONAL INCOME ACCOUNTS, 1940-67
(In Billions of Dollars)

Year	Consolidated Cash Statement			Federal Sector of the National Income Accounts		
	Receipts	Payments	Surplus (+) or Deficit (-)	Receipts	Payments	Surplus (+) or Deficit (-)
1940	6.9	9.6	-2.7	7.6	9.1	-1.5
1942	15.1	34.5	-19.4	19.6	33.6	-14.0
1943	25.1	78.9	-53.8	28.9	76.8	-47.9
1944	47.8	94.0	-46.1	43.1	91.3	-48.1
1945	50.2	95.2	-45.0	43.0	98.2	-55.2
1950	40.9	43.1	-2.2	42.0	42.4	-0.5
1955	67.8	70.5	-2.7	67.2	67.3	-0.1
1959	81.7	94.8	-13.1	85.4	90.9	-5.5
1960	95.1	94.3	+0.8	94.8	91.3	+3.5
1961	97.2	99.5	-2.3	95.3	98.0	-2.7
1962	101.9	107.7	-5.8	104.2	106.4	-2.1
1963	109.7	113.8	-4.0	110.2	111.4	-1.2
1964	115.5	120.3	-4.8	115.1	117.1	-1.9
1965	119.7	122.4	-2.7	119.6	118.3	+1.2
1966[a]	128.2	135.0	-6.9	128.8	131.0	-2.2
1967[a]	145.5	145.0	+0.5	142.2	142.7	-0.5

[a]Estimated.

Federal budget looks bigger than the administrative budget, but the deficit appears smaller (see Table XIV.6).

The difference between the administrative budget and consolidated cash statement is illustrated by Figures XIV.5A and XIV.5B. They both show where the government dollar comes from and where it goes, but Figure XIV.5A demonstrates a dollar provided almost exclusively by taxes, while Figure XIV.5B shows the dollar coming from both taxes and trust funds. Percentagewise, expenditures for national defense loom smaller in the consolidated cash dollar—37 per cent (including international expenses) for the fiscal year 1967, instead of 48 per cent in the administrative dollar. On the other hand, the consolidated cash dollar also carries expenditures for social security and other trust obligations.

In addition to the concepts of the administrative budget and the consolidated cash account, a third measure is used in appraising the impact of government financial transactions on the nation's current flow of income and output, the so-called Federal sector of the national-income and products accounts. Like the consolidated cash statement, the national-income and products accounts include most of the transactions of the administrative budget and trust funds, but exclude all transactions which represent neither the production of current output nor incomes. On the other hand, they include some transactions which are not reflected in cash receipts or expenditures. Also, business taxes are recorded in the national-income accounts as they are accrued by the private sector, and not when they are collected by the Government; interest on savings bonds is treated

FIGURE XIV.5.A

THE GOVERNMENT DOLLAR IN THE ADMINISTRATIVE BUDGET, 1967

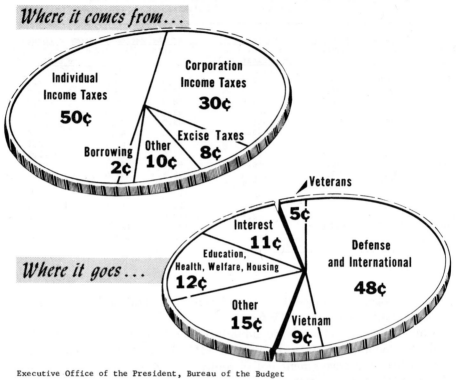

Where it comes from...

Individual Income Taxes **50¢**

Corporation Income Taxes **30¢**

Borrowing **2¢**

Other **10¢**

Excise Taxes **8¢**

Where it goes...

Veterans **5¢**

Interest **11¢**

Education, Health, Welfare, Housing **12¢**

Defense and International **48¢**

Other **15¢**

Vietnam **9¢**

Executive Office of the President, Bureau of the Budget

as an expenditure when the interest is accrued, not when it is actually paid out in cash. Though the conceptual difference between the consolidated cash statement and the Federal sector account is important, the difference in the final figures is not great (see Table XIV.6).

Today civilian employment in the Federal Government is slightly higher than it was in 1942: 2.5 million, as compared with 2.3 million. The peak year of Federal civilian employment was the last war year, 1945, when 3.8 million persons were on the payroll. After the end of the war, their number began to decline, with small occasional ups and downs. Federal employment dropped from 55 per cent of government employment on all levels in 1945 to 24.6 per cent in 1965; in relation to population, it declined from 27 per 1,000 population to 12.8 between these 2 benchmarks. In contrast, employment in state and local governments has more than doubled within the same period, rising from 3.1 million in 1945 to 7.7 million in 1965. One out of 4 public civilian employees works for the Federal Government, and the other 3 for state and local governments (see Table XIV.7 and Figure XIV.6).

FIGURE XIV.5.B

THE GOVERNMENT DOLLAR IN THE
CONSOLIDATED CASH STATEMENT, 1967

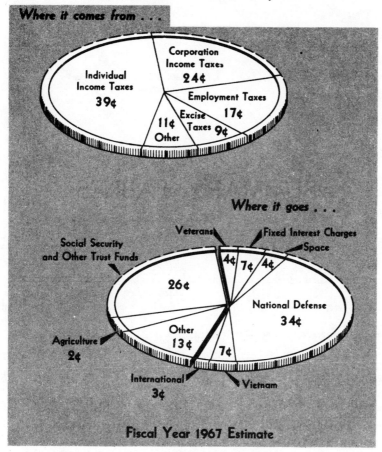

Executive Office of the President, Bureau of the Budget

TABLE XIV.7

FEDERAL, STATE, AND LOCAL EMPLOYMENT, 1942-67

Year	Government Employment		Federal Employment	
	Federal	State and Local	Per Cent of All	Per 1,000
	(In Thousands)		Government Employment	Population
1942	2,272	3,310	40.7	16.8
1945	3,787	3,104	55.0	27.0
1955	2,371	4,728	33.4	14.3
1960	2,371	6,073	28.1	13.1
1962	2,485	6,533	27.6	13.3
1964	2,469	7,236	25.4	12.9
1965	2,496	7,659	24.6	12.8
1966[a]	2,639	...	24.6	13.4
1967[a]	2,700	...	24.0	13.6

[a]Estimate.

FIGURE XIV.6

CIVILIAN EMPLOYMENT, BY LEVEL OF GOVERNMENT, 1942-65

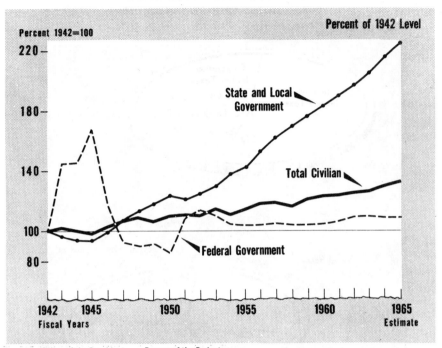

Executive Office of the President . Bureau of the Budget

Slightly more than 70 per cent of all Federal civilian employment is in 3 agencies—the Department of Defense, the Post Office, and the Veterans' Administration. The Post Office accounts for some 20 per cent of all Federal employment; the Departments of Agriculture; Interior; Treasury; and Health, Education, and Welfare for another 10 per cent. More than 50 other smaller government agencies share the remaining 17–18 per cent of all employees, some 440,000. The largest concentrations of Federal civilian employees are in the District of Columbia and 5 states: California, New York, Pennsylvania, Texas, and Illinois, in the order given (figures in thousands): 280, 251, 177, 132, 124, and 101, respectively. Military personnel exceeds the number of civilian employees—2.7 million and 2.5 million, respectively, in 1965.

85. State and Local Finances

Of the 91,185 local governments in the United States, 82,319 can impose taxes; the remaining 8,866 (independent public-housing authorities, the New York Port Authority, power and irrigation districts, etc.) cover expenditures by charging the public for their services or by receiving grants from other governmental or other nontax sources.

TABLE XIV.8

FINANCES OF STATE AND LOCAL GOVERNMENTS, 1902-63
(In Billions of Dollars)

	1902	1913	1922	1932	1938	1946	1952	1957	1963
State governments:									
Revenue	0.2	0.4	1.4	2.5	5.3	8.6	16.8	24.7	41.0
From state sources	0.2	0.4	1.2	2.3	4.6	7.7	14.3	20.7	32.8
From Federal government	a	a	0.1	0.2	0.6	0.8	2.3	3.5	7.8
From local governments	a	a	a	a	a	0.1	0.2	0.4	0.4
Expenditure	0.2	0.4	1.4	2.8	4.6	7.1	15.8	24.2	39.6
Intergovernmental	0.1	0.1	0.3	0.8	1.5	2.1	5.0	7.4	11.9
Direct	0.1	0.3	1.1	2.0	3.1	5.0	10.8	16.8	27.7
Local governments:									
Revenue	0.9	1.8	4.1	6.2	7.3	9.6	19.4	29.0	46.5
From local sources	0.9	1.7	3.8	5.4	5.6	7.4	14.1	21.4	33.8
From Federal government	a	a	a	a	0.2	0.1	0.2	0.3	0.9
From State governments	0.1	0.1	0.3	0.8	1.5	2.1	5.0	7.3	11.8
Expenditure	1.0	2.0	4.6	6.4	6.9	9.1	20.2	31.1	48.3
Intergovernmental[b]	...	...	...	...	...	...	0.2	0.3	0.2
Direct	1.0	2.0	4.6	6.4	6.9	9.1	20.1	30.8	48.1

[a]Minor amount.
[b]Minor payments to states not separated from "direct expenditure" in 1902-46.

Historically, local governments had an aggregate budget many times larger than that of state governments. In 1902, for which there are the first comparable data on the finances of all government levels in the United States, state-government revenue from all sources was only $192 million, as compared with the local governments' $914 million. Both state and local finances continued to expand rapidly: in 1932, the corresponding figures were $2.5 billion and $6.2 billion; in 1952, $16.8 billion and $19.4 billion; in 1963, $41.0 billion and $46.5 billion. Expenditures on both levels of government have shown about the same trend, at times exceeding revenue, at others holding the line (see Table XIV.8).

In 1963, the per capita general revenue of state and local governments combined was $399.3, of which $234.8 came from taxes, $52.4 from charges and miscellaneous receipts, $65.9 from insurance trust revenue and other revenues, and $46.2 from aid from the Federal Government. The distribution of outlays per capita was as follows: $131.3 for education; $59.9 for highways; $65.1 for public welfare, health, and hospitals; and the remainder for all other functions (police, fire protection, sanitation, financial administration, general control, etc.).

The Federal Government provides various kinds of aid to state and local governments. The rudiments of the present Federal-aid system date back to 1862, when land-grant colleges were established. Later, Federal assistance was extended to agriculture, highways, public health, and the like and in the Depression, to social-welfare needs. Today, Federal aid is counted in billions of dollars; the 1966 Federal budget (including the

FIGURE XIV.7

TOTAL FEDERAL AID AS A PER CENT
OF STATE AND LOCAL REVENUES, 1955-65

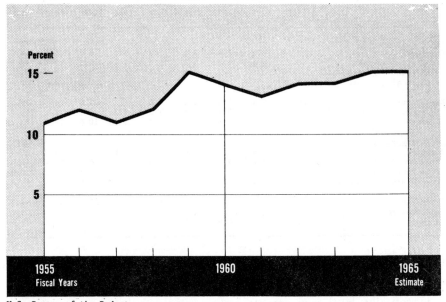

U.S. Bureau of the Budget

FIGURE XIV.8

FEDERAL AID TO STATE AND LOCAL GOVERNMENTS, BY PROGRAM, 1955-66

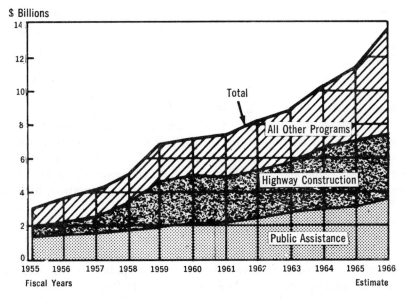

U.S. Bureau of the Budget

trust accounts) provides $13.6 billion for aid to state and local governments—$9.3 billion from the regular budget funds, and $4.3 billion from the highway and unemployment-insurance trust funds.

Federal financial assistance to state and local governments takes different forms, but the most consequential type of aid is in the form of direct grants. In the 1966 budget, $13.1 billion of the $13.6 billion provided, or 96 per cent of the total Federal assistance, is designated as grants-in-aid. Aid to state and local governments represented some 8 per cent of total Federal cash payments to the public in 1962 and is estimated at 11 per cent of the total in 1966; in the budget on the receiving side, taken as a whole, Federal payments represented 13.9 per cent in 1963 and were even more important in 1965 (see Figure XIV.7). This rate varies greatly among the states, ranging from less than 10 per cent for some (New York, 7.7 per cent, and New Jersey, 9.4 per cent) to 23.7–23.9 per cent for Vermont, Utah, and Arkansas; 34.9 per cent for Wyoming; and 35.5 per cent for Alaska.

Federal highway-construction grants have increased fivefold between 1956 and 1966—from $729 million to $3.9 billion, the largest increase in Federal aid for any purpose during that decade. Grants for public assistance have more than doubled, and in line with the new legislation, educational and other assistance will also be considerably greater in the 1966 budget year (see Figure XIV.8).

The different levels of government share among themselves the various sources of taxation: the Federal Government relies mainly on individual and corporate income taxes (see Sec. 84); the states depend on sales taxes; revenue from licenses and permits, and taxes on liquor stores and motor fuel; the counties and cities obtain revenue from property taxes, sales taxes, and public utilities. Of the total governmental revenue from taxes in 1963, $131.1 billion, the Federal Government obtained $86.8 billion, the states $22.1 billion, and local governments $22.2 billion (see Table XIV.9).

Expenditures of governmental units in the United States are distributed in accordance with their responsibilities. The Federal Government defrays all expenditures for national defense, postal service, foreign affairs, veterans' programs, interest on national debt, and a substantial part of expenditures on natural resources. State and local governments, including the school districts, carry the expenditures for education, police, fire protection, sanitation, public utilities, and the like.

Among the expenditures of government taken as a whole, national defense, space, and international relations account for some 30–31 per cent of all the outlays, with education following with 13 per cent. The share of these 2 most important expenditure items in the separate budgets of the Federal, state, and local governments reflects the structure of the governmental system, with its far-reaching division of responsibilities (see Table XIV.10).

TABLE XIV.9

GOVERNMENTAL REVENUE, BY LEVEL OF GOVERNMENT, 1963
(In Billions of Dollars)

Item	All Governments	Federal	State	Local
Revenue from own sources	181.2	114.6	32.8	33.8
General revenue from own sources	152.3	98.1	25.6	28.5
Taxes	131.1	86.8	22.1	22.2
Individual income	50.9	47.6	3.0	0.3
Corporation income	23.1	21.6	1.5	a
Property	20.1	-	0.7	19.4
Sales and gross receipts:	28.7	14.2	12.9	1.6
Custom duties	1.2	1.2	-	-
General sales and gross receipts	6.6	-	5.5	1.1
Selective sales and gross receipts:	20.9	13.0	7.3	0.5
Motor fuel	6.4	2.5	3.9	b
Alcoholic beverages	4.2	3.3	0.8	b
Tobacco products	3.3	2.1	1.1	0.1
Public utilities	1.9	1.1	0.4	0.3
Other	5.1	3.9	1.1	0.1
Motor vehicles and operators' licenses	1.9	-	1.8	0.1
Death and gift	2.8	2.2	0.6	b
All other	3.7	1.2	1.7	0.7
Charges and miscellaneous general revenue	21.2	11.3	3.5	6.4
Postal service	3.7	3.7	-	-
Education	2.5		1.3	1.2
Hospitals	1.2	b	0.3	0.8
Natural resources	3.0	2.8	0.1	0.1
Interest earnings	1.8	1.0	0.4	0.4
Other	9.0	3.8	1.4	3.9
Utility revenue	4.5	-	-	4.5
Liquor-store revenue	1.3	-	1.2	0.2
Insurance-trust revenue:	23.0	16.4	6.0	0.7
Unemployment compensation	3.3	0.2	3.2	b
Old-age, survivors' and disability insurance	14.2	14.2	-	-
Employee retirement	3.8	0.9	2.1	0.7
Other	1.7	1.1	0.7	-

aMinor amount included in individual income-tax figures.
bMinor amount.

The local governments are subdivided into many independent units, which obtain their revenue from different sources and also differ in the type of their expenditure. In 1963, school districts ranked first in their share of total local-government revenue and expenditure. Next were the municipalities and, at a considerable distance, the counties. Townships and special districts together accounted for less than one-tenth of the total (see Table XIV.11).

Employment by local governments is about 3 times that by state governments; education absorbs more than half of local and one-third of state employment.

TABLE XIV.10

GOVERNMENTAL EXPENDITURE BY TYPE, CHARACTER AND OBJECT, FUNCTION,
AND LEVEL OF GOVERNMENT, 1963
(In Billions of Dollars)

	All Governments	Federal	State	Local
Total expenditure	186.1	118.8	39.6	48.3
Intergovernmental expenditure	...	8.5	11.9	0.2
To states	...	7.6	-	0.2
To local governments	...	0.9	11.9	-
Direct expenditure	186.1	110.3	27.7	48.1
By type: General expenditure	156.8	92.0	22.5	42.3
Utility	4.9	-	-	4.9
Liquor stores	1.0	-	0.9	0.1
Insurance trust	23.3	18.3	4.3	0.7
By character and object:				
Current operation	104.1	57.7	12.4	33.9
Capital outlay	36.6	18.6	8.1	9.8
Construction	18.2	3.8	6.7	7.8
Equipment	15.8	14.3	0.4	1.1
Land and existing structures	2.5	0.6	1.0	1.0
Assistance and subsidies	11.8	8.0	2.1	1.7
Interest on debt	10.3	7.7	0.7	1.9
Insurance benefits and repayments	23.3	18.3	4.3	0.7
By function [a]				
General direct expenditure	156.8	92.0	22.5	42.3
National defense and international relations	54.6	54.6	-	-
All other functions	102.2	37.4	22.5	42.3
Postal service	4.4	4.4	-	-
Space research and technology	2.5	2.5	-	-
Education	24.8	0.8	5.0	19.1
Highways	11.3	0.2	7.4	3.7
Public welfare	5.6	0.1	2.7	2.8
Health and hospitals	6.7	2.0	2.3	2.4
Police protection	2.5	0.2	0.3	2.0
Natural resources	11.4	9.8	1.1	0.5
Interest on general debt	9.9	7.7	0.7	1.5
Other	23.1	9.7	3.0	10.3

[a]Federal expenditures for veterans' services are included under various headings
(education, health, hospitals, and other veterans' services not elsewhere classified).

86. *The Public Debt*

Public borrowing and debt management have called to life many sharp controversies among both practical and theoretical economists in this country, as well as among government officials in charge of U.S. fiscal policy and generally in charge of the national economic policy. Several times in its history, the United States has incurred large debts, always in times of war, especially the Civil War and World Wars I and II. Economic conditions such as the Depression of the 1930's also have affected the size of the public debt. In the past, with return of "normalcy," efforts have been made to refund and retire the public debt. But in World War II, the debt reached such gigantic proportions, on the one hand, and the Korean War and ever expanding Cold War have created so many obligations, on the other, that even partial retirement of the national debt has

TABLE XIV.11

REVENUE AND EXPENDITURE OF LOCAL GOVERNMENTS, BY TYPE OF GOVERNMENT, 1963
(In Millions of Dollars)

Item	All Local Governments	Counties	Munici-palities	Town-ships	School Districts	Special Districts
General revenue, total	41,218	9,067	14,032	1,699	15,336	1,949
Intergovernmental revenue	12,689	3,521	2,926	416	6,296	393
General revenue from own sources:	28,530	5,546	11,106	1,283	9,040	1,556
Tax Revenue	22,164	4,380	8,299	1,140	7,888	457
Property tax	19,401	4,095	6,014	1,069	7,766	457
Other taxes	2,764	285	2,285	71	122	-
Charges and miscel-laneous	6,365	1,165	2,807	143	1,152	1,098
Direct general expenditure, total	42,324	8,635	14,118	1,638	15,686	2,248
Education	19,058	1,153	2,088	541	15,210	67
Highways	3,710	1,565	1,651	385	-	109
Public welfare	2,769	1,941	726	101	-	-
Health and hospitals	2,351	1,078	980	23	-	271
Interest on general debt	1,478	174	545	37	476	246
All other	12,958	2,724	8,128	551	-	1,555

become more and more problematic. Moreover, the traditional belief in the desirability of rapid debt retirement has lost its strength among many economists.

In the early days of the Republic (*c.* 1791), the Federal Government carried a public debt of $75 million. With some fluctuations, it was gradu-

TABLE XIV.12

PUBLIC DEBT OF THE FEDERAL GOVERNMENT, 1791-1967

Year	PUBLIC DEBT			Year	PUBLIC DEBT		
	Total	Interest Paid	Per Capita		Total	Interest Paid	Per Capita
	(In Millions of Dollars)		(In Dollars)		(In Millions of Dollars)		(In Dollars)
1791	75	...	...	1940	42,968	1,041	325
1811	48	...	...	1945	258,682	3,617	1,849
1831	39	...[a]	...	1950	257,357	5,750	1,697
1851	68	2[a]	1	1955	274,374	6,370	1,660
1871	2,322	112	57	1960	286,331	9,180	1,585
1891	1,006	24	16	1961	288,971	8,957	1,573
1900	1,263	40	17	1962	298,201	9,120	1,598
1910	1,147	21	12	1963	305,860	9,895	1,616
1920	24,299	1,017	228	1964	311,713	10,765	1,623
1930	16,185	606	132	1965	317,864	11,435	1,633
1935	28,701	751	226	1966[b]	320,000	12,104	...
				1967[b]	321,680	12,854	...

[a]1855.
[b]Estimated.

FIGURE XIV.9

PUBLIC DEBT AS A PER CENT OF
GROSS NATIONAL PRODUCT, 1942-67

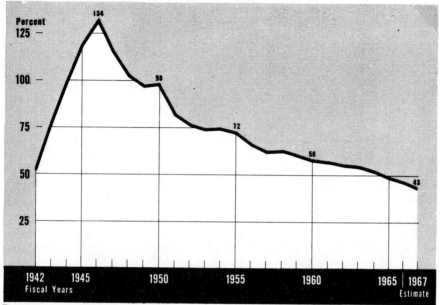

U.S. Bureau of the Budget

ally almost eliminated, and in the 1830's it amounted to only $39 million. In 1861, on the eve of the Civil War, it was close to the early amount—$90.6 million—but in the next few years it swelled to $2.7-$2.8 billion. Immediately after the war, the government's policy of refunding and retiring the debt cut it by half or more. At the turn of the nineteenth century, it amounted to $1.3 billion, and it remained more or less at that level until World War I, when heavy military expenditures shot it up to $12.5 billion in 1918 and again doubled it in the first peacetime years—$24.3 billion in 1923. The next push came with the Depression of the 1930's, and World War II raised it almost sixfold, from $43 billion in 1940 to $259 billion in 1945. During these war years, the public debt exceeded, for the first time in the history of this country, the annual national income and the aggregate private debt. Since the war, the public debt has continued to grow, though at a much slower pace, and in 1965 it amounted to $317.9 billion (see Table XIV.12). The per capita indebtedness was less than $12 in 1915; $226 in 1935; $1,849 in 1945; and $1,633 in 1965.

The Federal debt exceeded the gross national product only slightly in 1944, surpassed it by one-third in 1946, and started a declining curve—to 98 per cent of the GNP in 1950, 58 per cent in 1960, 49 per cent in 1965, and, according to estimates, 46 per cent in 1966 (see Figure XIV.9).

TABLE XIV.13

GOVERNMENTAL INDEBTEDNESS, BY LEVEL OF GOVERNMENT, 1902-63

Year	Total	Federal	State	Local	Federal	State	Local
	(In Millions of Dollars)				(Per Cent)		
1902	3.2	1.2	0.2	1.9	35.9	7.0	57.1
1913	5.6	1.2	0.4	4.1	21.2	6.7	72.1
1927	33.4	18.5	2.0	12.9	55.4	5.9	38.7
1934	46.0	27.1	3.2	15.7	58.8	7.1	34.1
1938	56.6	37.2	3.3	16.1	65.7	5.9	28.4
1942	91.8	72.4	3.3	16.1	78.9	3.5	17.5
1946	285.3	269.4	2.4	13.6	94.4	0.8	4.8
1954	310.9	271.3	9.6	29.3	87.4	3.1	9.5
1960	356.3	286.3	18.5	51.4	80.4	5.2	14.4
1962	379.5	298.6	22.0	58.8	78.7	5.8	15.5
1963	399.3	305.9	23.2	64.3	76.6	5.8	17.6

Of the $321.4 billion Federal debt outstanding on December 31, 1965, almost one half ($158.4 billion) was in the hands of private nonbank investors (private individuals, insurance companies, mutual savings banks, savings and loan associations, pension funds, nonprofit associations, nonfinancial corporations, nonbank dealers, etc.). Commercial banks held $60.3 billion, more than one-fifth of the total; Federal Reserve Banks, $40.8 billion; and the remaining $61.9 billion was held primarily in social security and unemployment trust funds, veterans' insurance funds, and Government employees' retirement funds. The largest single investor group in the Federal debt ownership consists of the individuals who buy the savings bonds, popular as a safe form for personal savings. The corporations consider the government securities convenient for the payment of taxes; state and local governments use the Federal securities as an investment outlet for capital temporarily idle.

Most of the time, state and local governments have surpassed the Federal Government in the amount of their indebtedness; actually, state debts were comparatively small, while those of local governments surpassed the Federal debt except in times of national emergency. In 1860, state debt was 4 times the amount of the Federal debt. At the opening of this century, the Federal debt amounted to a little more than one-third, and in 1913 to approximately one-fifth, of all government debt in the United States. The two world wars and the Great Depression changed the picture. In 1927, the Federal debt exceeded half the total public debt, and in 1946, it amounted to nearly 95 per cent. After World War II, the gap began to narrow slowly, and in 1964 the Federal debt was exceeding three-fourths of total public debt (see Table XIV.13).

Per capita indebtedness of state and local governments shows wide interstate variations—in 1963, from $99 in South Dakota and $187 in Iowa to $739 in Connecticut, $801 in Delaware, $887 in Washington, and $835 in New York. Apart from these 6 states, 12 states had a per capita in-

FIGURE XIV.10

NET PUBLIC AND PRIVATE DEBT, 1947-67

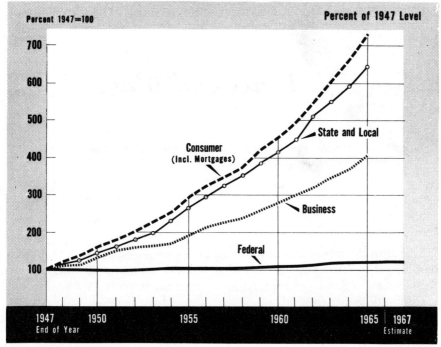

U.S. Bureau of the Budget

debtedness ranging from $200 to $300; 13 states, from $301 to $400; 14 states, from $401 to $500; and 6 states, from $501 to $725.

For comparisons of public and private debt, see Sec. 32 and Figure XIV.10.

XV. *Prices and Wages*

87. *Wholesale Prices*—88. *The Consumer Price Index*—89. *Hours of Work and Earnings*

Trends in the movement of prices and the degree of price stability represent one of the major barometers of a country's economy. In more recent years, price indexes have acquired great practical importance by wide use in negotiations between labor and management, or between business and government in long-term contracts. Not only do they reflect current economic conditions, but their use often affects the purchasing power of millions of people and thus the state of the national economy.

87. *Wholesale Prices*

Not until the end of the nineteenth century was there any real interest in studying and using the fluctuations of prices as one of the basic indicators of the state of the national economy. Though some scattered attempts to prepare unweighted price indexes had been registered at an earlier date, it was not until 1893 that the Senate Committee on Finance published a price index for 1840–90 on the basis of 230 quotations. In 1902, the Bureau of Labor Statistics (BLS) began publication of its index of wholesale prices, its oldest continuous statistical series.*

Since that time, this index has undergone several major revisions. Before 1952, it was based on quotations for about 900 commodities; between 1952 and 1960, on some 1,900 series and since 1961, on 2,200 price series selected to represent all commodities produced or imported for sale in the United States.

The *wholesale price index* is a measure of the price movements of single

* The indexes of the BLS were later carried backwards from 1890 to 1720 and then to 1700 by the efforts of the International Scientific Committee on Price History. These investigations had made it possible to obtain a historical perspective in the field of prices during the eighteenth and nineteenth century.

FIGURE XV.1

COMPOSITION OF THE WHOLESALE PRICE INDEX, 1965
(1957-59 = 100)

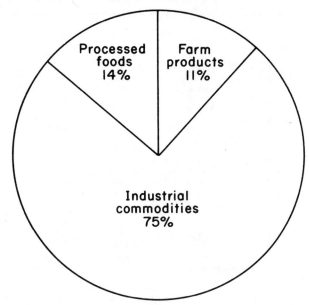

Processed foods 14%

Farm products 11%

Industrial commodities 75%

U.S. Department of Labor, Bureau of Labor Statistics

commodities and groups of commodities in primary markets for the first stable commercial transaction by the producer or the importer or such a transaction in a central market or a commodity exchange. "Wholesale" refers to sales in large lots, not to prices paid or received by wholesalers or distributors. Commodities at all stages of processing are included in the index, from raw materials to fabricated products, and weighted according to their relative importance in total sales in primary markets. Weights have varied over the years, as also have the base periods, lists of commodities, methods of computation, etc. However, great care has been exercised by the BLS to preserve comparability with previous indexes.

The current weights are derived from the latest (1958) Censuses of Manufactures and Mineral Industries,* and data from the Department of Agriculture; the present base period is 1957–59=100 (see Figure XV.1). Insofar as possible, identical qualities of commodities are used from period to period; the index is designed to measure the change in prices, not difference in quality. The wholesale price index excludes services, real estate, goods produced exclusively for the government, and those sold directly at retail by producers. Most price quotations are obtained directly from the sellers.

Historically, wholesale price indexes show a waving line, interrupted

* Data for the 1963 Censuses have not been published as yet.

TABLE **XV.1**

WHOLESALE PRICE INDEXES, 1890-1965

Year	All commod- ities	All Except Farm Products and Foods	Year	All commod- ities	All Except Farm Products
1926 = 100					
1890	56.2	...	1939	42.2	46.0
1895	48.8	...	1940	43.0	46.8
1900	56.1	...	1941	47.8	50.3
1905	60.1	...	1942	54.0	53.9
1910	70.4	...	1943	56.5	54.7
1914	68.1	66.4	1944	56.9	55.6
1917	117.5	114.2	1945	57.9	56.3
1919	138.6	128.8	1946	66.1	61.7
1924	98.1	99.7			
1929	95.3	91.6	1948	87.9	81.7
			1950	86.8	82.9
1957-59 = 100			1952	94.0	89.4
1914	37.3	37.4	1954	92.9	90.4
1915	38.0	38.4	1956	96.2	96.5
1916	46.8	49.8	1958	100.4	99.5
1917	64.3	64.8	1960	100.7	101.3
1918	71.7	70.1			
1919	75.8	72.9	1961	100.3	100.8
			1962	100.6	100.8
1924	53.6	56.4	1963	100.3	100.7
1929	52.1	51.7	1964	100.5	101.2
1933	36.1	40.2	1965	102.5	102.5

from time to time by sharp upswings followed by abrupt falls. The peaks correspond with the wars in which the United States has been engaged:

FIGURE XV.2

FLUCTUATIONS OF WHOLESALE PRICES, 1801-1963
(1957-59 = 100)

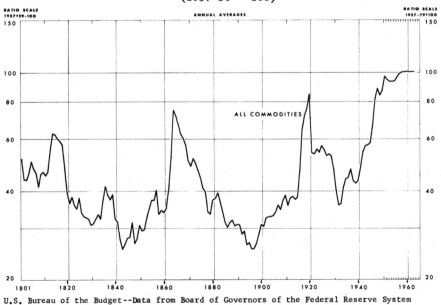

U.S. Bureau of the Budget--Data from Board of Governors of the Federal Reserve System

the war with Great Britain, in 1812–15; the Civil War, in 1861–65; World Wars I and II; the Korean War. An inflationary wartime rise in prices has usually been followed by several years of declining prices, and after postwar adjustments, prices have returned, more or less, to the prewar level. However, the behavior of prices during and since World War II has been in striking contrast to the experience of the Civil War and World War I. In the 2 earlier wars, prices nearly doubled, and each time it took them 10–12 years to regain the prewar level. The rise in prices during World War II was checked by price control, rationing, and other anti-inflationary measures. The rise during the war did not exceed 30–35 per cent, but elimination of price control after the war sent prices up about 50 per cent between 1945 and 1948 or to more than 100 per cent of the prewar level. Prices became more or less stabilized on that level except for the 3-year period 1955–58, when wholesale prices rose some 8 per cent. Since that time, over-all wholesale prices have been virtually at a standstill and have not responded to either the recent recessions or the recoveries that have followed them (see Table XV.1 and Figure XV.2).

TABLE XV.2

WHOLESALE PRICE INDEXES, BY COMMODITY GROUP, 1939-64
(1957-59 = 100)

Major Groups of Commodities	1939	1946	1953	1958	1960	1962	1963	1964
All commodities	42.2	66.1	92.7	100.4	100.7	100.6	100.3	100.5
Farm products	39.9	90.6	105.9	103.6	96.9	97.7	95.7	94.3
Processed foods	40.2	71.7	97.0	102.9	99.9	101.2	101.1	101.0
All commodities other than farm products and foods	46.0	61.7	90.1	99.5	101.3	100.8	100.7	101.2
Textile products and apparel	52.3	87.3	102.8	98.9	101.5	100.6	100.5	101.2
Hides, skins, leather and leather products	49.6	70.7	94.1	96.0	105.2	107.4	104.2	104.6
Fuels and related products and power	54.2	66.7	95.9	98.7	99.6	100.2	99.8	97.1
Chemicals and allied products	50.7	69.4	96.1	100.4	100.2	97.5	96.3	96.7
Rubber and rubber products	59.3	68.6	86.3	100.1	99.9	93.3	93.8	92.5
Lumber and wood products	26.1	49.7	99.4	97.4	100.4	96.5	98.6	100.6
Pulp, paper, and allied products	...	...	88.7	100.1	101.8	100.0	99.2	99.0
Metals and metal products	41.2	48.5	83.6	99.1	101.3	100.0	100.1	102.8
Machinery and motive products	43.7	53.6	82.2	100.1	102.4	102.3	102.2	102.9
Furniture and other household durables	53.2	67.8	92.9	100.2	100.1	98.8	98.1	98.5
Nonmetallic-mineral products	...	...	86.9	99.9	101.4	101.8	101.3	101.5
Tobacco products and bottled beverages	59.4	69.8	89.8	99.7	102.5	104.1	106.1	107.4
Miscellaneous products	...	...	105.4	101.5	99.3	107.3	110.4	109.2

FIGURE XV.3

WHOLESALE PRICE INDEX OF BEVERAGES AND CIGARETTES, 1953-62
(1957-59 = 100)

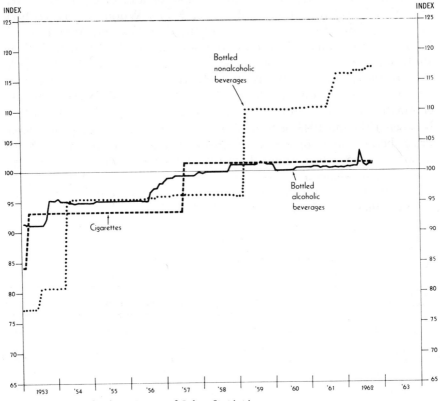

U.S. Department of Labor, Bureau of Labor Statistics

The wholesale price index is classified into 15 major commodity groups: farm products, processed foods, and 13 groups of industrial commodities that together are represented by the index of "all commodities other than farm products and processed foods" (see Table XV.2). Their movements show a great variation, from clearly downward trends to uncertain fluctuations up and down, or clearly upward tendencies, particularly in the intragroup variations. Wholesale prices of farm products continue a declining trend, supported by the exceptional growth of agricultural productivity (see Chapter VIII), a rather slow increase in total demand for foodstuffs despite the expanding population, and the decrease in the per capita consumption of nonfood farm products, due to competition from man-made products (synthetic fibers and rubber, waterbase paints, etc.).

Prices for processed foods as a group are somewhat above the base level of 1957–59, but within this group, cereal and bakery products followed an upward trend in the 1960's while prices for animal products dropped below that level. Similar variations can be observed within some

FIGURE XV.4

WHOLESALE PRICE INDEX OF NATURAL
AND SYNTHETIC RUBBER, 1953-62
(1957-59 = 100)

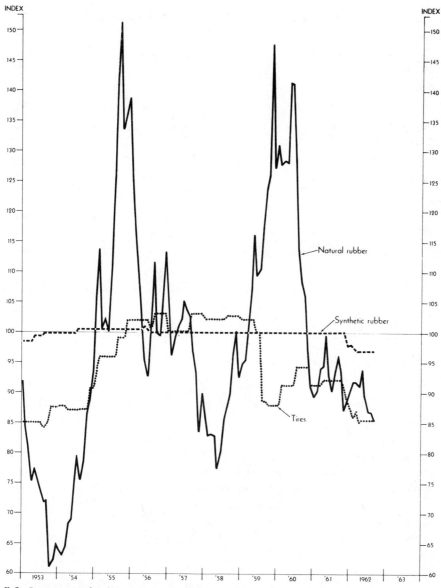

U.S. Department of Labor, Bureau of Labor Statistics

groups of industrial commodities. For example, within the group "fuels
and related products," prices for coal and crude petroleum were down in
1963 as compared with the base standard, but those for natural gas were

TABLE XV.3

WHOLESALE AND CONSUMER PRICE INDEXES IN SELECTED COUNTRIES, ALL ITEMS, 1962
(1958 = 100)

Country	Wholesale Index	Consumer Price Index	Country	Wholesale Index	Consumer Price Index
United States	100	105	Spain	110	118
			Sweden	107	112
Canada	105	104	Switzerland	102	107
Argentina	381	390	United Kingdom	100	110
Brazil	381	390	Yugoslavia	106	133
Colombia	125	124			
Chile	149	190	U.S.S.R.	...	99
Costa Rica	104	107			
Ecuador	103	109	China (Taiwan)	135	145
El Salvador	91	97	India	115	112
Guatemala	100	100	Iran	103	127
Mexico	109	111	Iraq	110	104
Paraguay	152[a]	152[a]	Israel	134[b]	121
Peru	147	136	Japan	101	118
Venezuela	110	105	Korea, South	152	129
			Pakistan	...	104
Austria	110	111	Philippines	116	111
Belgium	101	104	Syria	102	104
Denmark	105	115	Thailand	106	105
Finland	107	112	Turkey	137	142
France	113	119			
West Germany	103	109	Morocco	120	113
Greece	104	103	Tunisia	101	95
Ireland	105	108	South Africa	101	106
Italy	101	109	United Arab Republic	101	98
Netherlands	99	108	Uganda	...	108
Norway	104	111			
Portugal	103	109	Australia	100	108
			New Zealand	102	109

[a]1961.
[b]Building materials.

23 per cent above the base. Wholesale prices for furniture and other household durables, particularly household appliances and television, radio, etc. (as also the electrical machinery in the group of machinery and motive products) were below the average 1957–59, but household furniture evidenced price increases from year to year. Interestingly, prices for 1 group of products—tobacco products and bottled beverages—show a clear upward trend: in 1964, nonalcoholic beverages were 27 per cent above the base line (Appendix Table XXVII and Figure XV.3). While prices for synthetic rubber have been at a standstill, those for natural rubber have fluctuated wildly; tire prices have followed their own trend (see Figure XV.4).

In 1960–62, wholesale prices were stable in many countries, including the United Kingdom, Belgium, Italy, Switzerland, Japan, and the United Arab Republic. With the base 1958 = 100, their wholesale prices averaged between 100 (or even 98–99) and 102. The wholesale price index fluctuated between 102 and 105 in Denmark, West Germany, Greece, Ireland, Norway, Portugal, and Canada but was somewhat higher in Finland and

Sweden, with 107, and Austria and Spain, with 110. It showed an upward tendency in France, with 113 in 1962. In many Latin American countries, wholesale prices have reflected more or less stable economic conditions; the index ranged between 91–92 in El Salvador, 100 in Guatemala, and 104 in Costa Rica to 109–110 in Mexico and Venezuela. Inflation was evident in Colombia (125), Peru (147), Chile (149), while Argentina and Brazil, with 381, have been experiencing runaway inflation, in contrast to most other countries for which United Nations data are available (see Table XV.3).

88. *The Consumer Price Index*

The *consumer price index* is designed to measure the changes in prices of goods and services used by urban wage-earners and clerical workers. It plays a very important role in wage negotiations between labor and management, particularly since the introduction of the escalator clause in many labor contracts. It was estimated that as of January, 1965, about 2 million workers under major contracts were covered by cost-of-living escalator clauses.

The consumer price index differs from the wholesale price index in three respects: (1) It reflects changes in prices not only of food, clothing, household supplies, home furnishings, drugs, etc., but also in fees paid to physicians and lawyers and expenditures for shelter—rent, purchase of homes, repair costs, utilities. Dealing with prices paid by consumers, it includes sales and excise taxes, and real estate taxes on owned homes. (2) The variations in goods and services are weighted in accordance with their relative importance in the consumer budget, as established by special consumer-expenditure surveys. (3) It deals with prices paid by consumers in retail stores.

The BLS first published a consumer index roughly in its present form in 1921, with data carried back to 1913. Over the years, various changes have been introduced. The first comprehensive revision was accomplished in 1940; in the next basic revision, in 1953, small- and medium-sized cities were included, the purchase price of a house was introduced, and restaurant meals, home repair, maintenance, and other items were added. In January, 1962, the consumer price index, formerly calculated on the reference base 1947–49 = 100, was converted to a new base, 1957–59 = 100, in compliance with the recommendations of the Bureau of the Budget. Beginning with January, 1964, the index has reflected further changes: the "market basket" was expanded from 325 to 400 commodities; the number of priced cities was increased from 46 to 50 metropolitan areas and cities, including those in Alaska and Hawaii; single workers living alone were added. The weight structure has also been changed, following changes in consumer habits; the relative importance of food has been re-

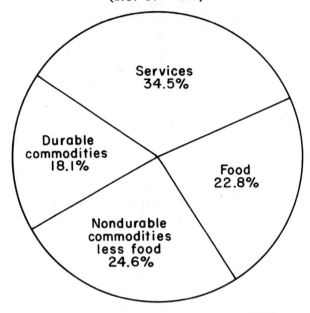

FIGURE XV.5

COMPOSITION OF THE CONSUMER PRICE INDEX
(1957-59 = 100)

RELATIVE IMPORTANCE IN 1965

U.S. Department of Labor, Bureau of Labor Statistics

duced from 28 to 22 per cent and that of the services increased as of December, 1963 (see Table XV.4 and Figure XV.5).

The current index, revised in January, 1964, and based on the survey of consumer expenditures in 1960–61, contains 5 major groups: food; housing; apparel; transportation; and health and recreation, which include medical care, personal care, reading and recreation, and other goods and services.

TABLE XV.4

OLD AND NEW SERIES OF THE CONSUMER PRICE INDEX, 1963
(Per Cent)

	Old Series	New Series
All items	100.00	100.00
All commodities	67.73	65.97
All food	28.18	22.43
All commodities less food	39.55	43.54
All durable commodities	17.53	18.78
All nondurable commodities other than food	22.02	24.76
All services	32.27	34.03
Rent	6.16	5.50
Services other than rent	26.11	28.53

Each major group covers both goods and services—for example, transportation includes expenditures for public transit, purchase of a new or used car, gasoline, tires, etc. The index does not include income taxes, luxury goods, foreign travel, consumption items for which there is no direct payment, or goods bought solely by rural people. Prices are collected monthly or quarterly by trained experienced interviewers who use precise specifications.

The index reflects the sharp rise of consumer prices during World War I, their much milder decline and near stabilization on a considerably higher level in the 1920's, their fall in the Depression years. During World War II, price control did not permit prices to jump as in the preceding war, but subsequent release of controls sent them up again, in contrast to the situation after World War I (see Table XV.5 and Figure XV.6). In 1958, consumer prices started to inch up, a little more than 1 point annually, but in 1966 they began to move upward more rapidly.

The consumer price index reveals a considerable disparity in price changes from city to city. Thus prices in Boston, New York, Scranton, Kansas City, and Seattle have risen more since 1960 than in many other metropolitan areas. The smallest advance in consumer prices was found in Detroit and Cleveland. It must be remembered that indexes for different cities show only that prices in one area have changed more or less than in others, and that the indexes do not measure differences among areas in price levels or living costs.

TABLE XV.5

CONSUMER PRICE INDEX IN THE UNITED STATES, ALL ITEMS, 1913-APRIL, 1966
(1957-59 = 100)

Year	Index	Year	Index	Year	Index
1913	34.5	1931	53.0	1949	83.0
1914	35.0	1932	47.6	1950	83.8
1915	35.4	1933	45.1	1951	90.5
1916	38.0	1934	46.6	1952	92.5
1917	44.7	1935	47.8	1953	93.2
1918	52.4	1936	48.3	1954	93.6
1919	60.3	1937	50.0	1955	93.3
1920	69.8	1938	49.1	1956	94.7
1921	62.3	1939	48.4	1957	98.0
1922	58.4	1940	48.8	1958	100.7
1923	59.4	1941	51.3	1959	101.5
1924	59.6	1942	56.8	1960	103.1
1925	61.1	1943	60.3	1961	104.2
1926	61.6	1944	61.3	1962	105.4
1927	60.5	1945	62.7	1963	106.7
1928	59.7	1946	68.0	1964	108.1
1929	59.7	1947	77.8	1965	109.9
1930	58.2	1948	83.8	1966, April	112.5

FIGURE XV.6

CONSUMER PRICE INDEX, 1913-63, ALL ITEMS
(1957-59 = 100)

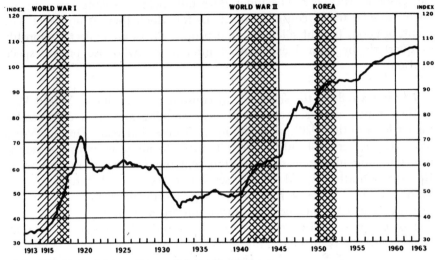

U.S. Department of Labor, Bureau of Labor Statistics

TABLE XV.6

CONSUMER PRICE INDEX, MAJOR GROUPS AND SELECTED ITEMS,
ANNUAL AVERAGES, 1953-64
(1957-59 = 100)

	1953	1955	1957	1959	1961	1962	1963	1964
All items	93.2	93.3	98.0	101.5	104.2	105.4	106.7	108.1
Food	95.6	94.0	97.8	100.3	102.6	103.6	105.1	106.4
Meats, poultry, fish	99.6	92.1	95.4	100.4	99.3	101.7	100.2	98.6
Dairy products	96.8	93.6	98.8	101.0	104.8	104.1	103.8	104.7
Fruits and vegetables	91.8	91.8	96.0	101.2	104.2	105.0	111.0	115.3
Housing	92.3	94.1	98.5	101.3	103.9	104.8	106.0	107.2
Rent	90.3	94.8	93.3	101.6	104.4	105.7	106.8	107.8
Home maintenance and repairs	87.1	90.6	98.4	101.7	105.0	105.8	107.2	109.4
Household furnishings and operation	98.8	97.3	99.4	100.7	101.4	101.5	102.4	102.8
Apparel and upkeep[a]	96.5	95.9	99.5	100.6	103.0	103.6	104.8	105.7
Transportation	92.1	89.7	96.5	103.8	105.0	107.2	107.8	109.3
Private	93.8	89.9	96.5	103.8	104.0	105.9	106.4	107.9
Public	81.0	89.0	96.0	103.5	111.7	115.4	116.9	119.0
Health and recreation[b]	89.7	91.4	97.0	102.8	107.3	109.4	111.4	113.6
Medical care	83.9	88.6	95.5	104.4	111.3	114.2	117.0	119.4
Hospital rates	74.8	83.0	94.5	105.5	121.3	129.8	138.0	144.9
Personal care	88.1	90.0	97.1	102.4	104.6	106.5	107.9	109.2
Reading and recreation	93.3	92.1	96.9	102.4	107.2	109.6	111.5	114.1
Newspapers	85.0	86.7	95.5	102.7	107.3	109.4	116.4	125.6
Television sets	106.6	93.9	98.4	101.5	99.5	94.6	92.2	90.1
Other goods and services	92.8	94.3	98.5	101.8	104.6	105.3	107.1	108.8
Tobacco products	90.5	92.1	96.7	103.6	108.0	108.8	112.2	114.8
Alcoholic beverages	93.9	95.9	99.7	100.6	102.5	102.9	103.9	104.7

[a]Includes laundry and drycleaning, formerly included in household operation.
[b]Revised grouping.

The increase in the cost of living, expressed by the consumer price index, is due to a great extent to the upward pressure exerted by the rapidly rising costs of services, which constitute over a third of the index. The impact of the continued postwar rise in costs of medical care, personal care, recreation, and other services has been substantial. The cost of medical care has advanced most of all—hospital rates have almost doubled, and the costs of hospitalization insurance have risen even more (cf. Secs. 19, 40, and 93). In contrast, prices for such durables as household appliances and home furnishings have exercised a somewhat restraining influence on the advancing index. Until 1965, prices for foodstuffs as a group increased only modestly because prices for such important items as meats, poultry, fish, and some other commodities had either fallen or increased only slightly (see Table XV.6). Food prices have gone up in 1966.

A comparison of consumer price indexes shows that in recent years prices have increased less in the United States than in most European countries. While this country, and two others, had the price index of 105 (1958 = 100), West Germany, Italy, Norway, Sweden, Austria, Portugal, and the United Kingdom had between 109 and 112; France had 119; Yugoslavia, 133. In 2 large Latin American countries, Argentina and Brazil, the index reflected wild inflation, like that of wholesale prices (see Table XV.3).

89. Hours of Work and Earnings

Prevailing working hours in a country depend on many factors—legislation, social custom, provisions of collective bargaining, changes in employment conditioned by the volume of business activities, etc. The concept of how long a workday or work week should be has changed with time; what seemed "normal" a hundred years ago would be totally intolerable today.

More or less reliable information on working hours in U.S. industries (including agriculture) goes back to the last part of the nineteenth century, but some earlier records indicate that in 1850 the work week had 70 hours, more than 11 hours per day for 6 days. By 1890–1900, the average work week was reduced to 60 hours and by 1909, to 51 hours, about 8½ hours per day for 6 days, though as late as 1913, the steel industry had a 66-hour week. The trend toward shorter hours continued, and a 48-hour week was established after World War I. In the Depression years, widespread part-time work brought the average work week down to 36–38 hours.

The most prevalent practice in U.S. manufacturing today is to work 8 hours a day for 5 days a week (see Table XV.7 and Figure XV.7), but the work week has been reduced, by collective agreements, to about 35–38 hours in coal mining and 39 hours in the building trades. Since many industries have longer weekly hours because of overtime work, the average

FIGURE XV.7

AVERAGE WEEKLY HOURS OF WORK, 1850-1960

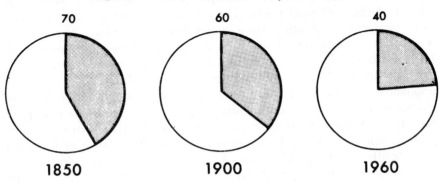

The circle represents a week, 168 hours.

U.S. Department of Labor, Bureau of Labor Statistics

TABLE XV.7

AVERAGE WEEKLY HOURS FOR PRODUCTION WORKERS IN U.S. MANUFACTURING INDUSTRIES, 1850-1965

Year	Average Weekly Hours	Year	Average Weekly Hours	Year	Average Weekly Hours
1850	70.0	1919	46.3	1949	39.1
1860	66.0	1924	43.7	1951	40.6
1865	64.2	1929	44.2	1953	40.5
1870	63.0	1931	40.5	1955	40.7
1875	61.8	1933	38.1	1957	39.8
1880	61.8	1935	36.6	1959	40.3
1885	61.8	1937	38.6	1961	39.8
1890	60.0	1939	37.7	1962	40.4
1895	59.5	1941	40.6	1963	40.5
1900	59.0	1943	45.0	1964	40.7
1905	57.7	1945	43.5	1965	40.7
1909	51.0	1947	40.4		
1914	49.4				

for all manufacturing has remained slightly above 40 hours per week in recent years. The average weekly hours in durable-goods industries exceed, more often than not, those in nondurable-goods industries: for example, a 41.1-hour week in 1950, 40.1 hours in 1960, and 42.0 hours in 1965 in durable-goods industries; and 39.7, 39.2, and 40.1, respectively, in non-durable-goods industries (see Table XV.8). In 1965, more than two-fifths of all employed workers had a regular 40-hour week; nearly one-third worked 8 or more hours of overtime a week, while another fifth—voluntary and involuntary part-timers—worked less than 35 hours. The average for all employed workers was 40.2 hours.

In agriculture, weekly hours fluctuate between 39 and 41 in winter and 48 or more in summer; because of a substantial number of part-time

TABLE XV.8

AVERAGE WEEKLY HOURS FOR PRODUCTION WORKERS IN U.S.,BY INDUSTRY, 1950-64

Industry	1950	1955	1960	1962	1963	1964
Mining: Metal mining	42.1	42.2	41.8	41.5	41.2	41.6
Coal mining[a]	...	...	35.5	36.9	38.8	39.0
Petroleum and natural gas	...	...	42.0	42.0	42.1	42.0
Nonmetallic mining and quarrying	43.8	44.3	43.7	44.3	44.5	44.7
Contract construction	37.4	37.1	36.7	37.0	37.3	37.2
Manufacturing: Durable goods	41.1	41.3	40.1	40.9	41.1	41.4
Nondurable goods	39.7	39.9	39.2	39.6	39.6	39.7
Transportation and public utilities[b]	40.8	41.9	41.7	42.6	42.9	43.5
Trade(except eating and drinking places)	41.0	39.9	39.1	38.7	38.6	38.4
Wholesale trade	40.7	40.7	40.5	40.6	40.6	40.7
Retail trade	41.1	39.6	38.5	37.9	37.8	37.4
Finance: Banking	...	...	37.1	37.2	37.3	37.4
Service and miscellaneous: Hotels [c]	...	...	39.9	39.1	39.0	38.6
Laundries[d]	...	...	38.8	38.9	39.0	38.7

[a]1962-64: 11-month average.
[b]Includes Class I railroads.
[c]1960-63: tourist courts and motels.
[d]Includes cleaning and dyeing plants.

seasonal workers, the average weekly hours are lower. Thus in 1964, two-thirds of agricultural workers averaged 35 or more hours per week; one-fifth worked from 15 to 34 hours weekly; and the remainder worked less than 15 hours. In retail trade, two-thirds of the employees had a regular 40-hour week; slightly more than one-fifth worked overtime; and others reported less than 40 hours weekly.

In earlier years, extra pay for overtime was exceptional, but now time-and-a-half is a permanent feature in most labor contracts. The statistical series on overtime work, which the Bureau of Labor Statistics started in 1956, shows that average overtime hours increased from 2.8 a week in 1956 to 3.1 hours in 1964 in manufacturing as a whole; from 3 to 3.3 hours in durable-goods industries, and from 2.4 to 2.9 hours in nondurable-goods industries. In single industries, overtime hours are considerably longer: for example, in 1964 in concrete and gypsum trades they averaged 5.5 hours a week; in the paperboard industries, 6.3 hours; in the grain-mill-products industry, 6.3 hours.

Since World War II, some reduction in actual work hours has come through the increasing prevalence of paid vacations. While varying from industry to industry, paid vacations average about 1.3–1.5 weeks a year. In combination with 6 or 7 paid holidays a year, the average time off is roughly equivalent to 2–2.5 hours a week.

Hours of work are somewhat longer in Europe than in this country. Thus, in 1962, the average weekly hours of paid-for work amounted in

Italy to 44.5, in West Germany to 44.7, in France* to 45.8, in the United Kingdom to 46.2, and in the Netherlands to 46.3. On the other hand, in Canada and New Zealand* they were about the same as in the United States: 40.7, 40.2, and 40.4, respectively. In Japan* the average weekly hours in manufacturing was 45.8; in South Africa, for white workers, 45.3.

Earnings of workers vary widely by occupation, industry, geographic area, and size of community. They depend on the relative importance of individual regions or localities (a big city, a rural community, an area of low wages or high wages, etc.), of individual companies, and of the prevailing size of the establishment; they depend also on the character of the industry (old and declining or young and dynamic), on the importance of incentive payments and of overtime work at premium pay, on the individual ability of workers, the composition of labor, seniority in service, sex, race, age of workers, predominance of skilled or unskilled labor, etc. Wage rates for highly qualified workers, such as tool- and diemakers, are higher than for unskilled workers; the average hourly earnings for any single industry are lower than those for its skilled workers, and higher than for the unskilled.

Weekly earnings are determined by prevailing hourly wages, on the one hand, and the average number of hours worked per week, on the other. Since the 1940's, a distinction has been made between weekly hours *worked* and weekly hours *paid for*. The widespread adoption of paid vacations and the increased number of paid holidays (and in some industries, paid travel time, lunch time, etc.) have raised the average weekly number of hours paid for above that of hours worked by increasing amounts. By 1962, working hours of production workers represented about 94 per cent of all paid hours in manufacturing; in bituminous-coal mining, in 1960, about 97 per cent of total hours paid for were working hours. Generally, weekly earnings are more sensitive to changes in business conditions than are hourly wages. Even if wage rates remain unchanged, weekly earnings tend to drop during a depression and to rise when business picks up. Actually, changes in economic activity frequently affect hours worked before they affect employment, and hours in manufacturing are therefore considered a telling business indicator.

Weekly earnings do not represent take-home pay, since they are subject to deductions for income and social security taxes, union dues, and other items. Annual earnings depend on prevailing weekly wages and continuity of employment. In industries with unstable employment, such as the building trades or coal mining, annual earnings may correspond to 30–35 times the usual weekly wage, while in white-collar occupations with steady employment they amount to 52 times the weekly wage.

Hourly earnings of production workers in manufacturing amounted to

* Includes salaried employees.

TABLE XV.9

GROSS EARNINGS OF PRODUCTION WORKERS ON MANUFACTURING PAYROLLS, 1909-64
(In Dollars)

Year	Manufacturing	Durable Goods	Nondurable	Manufacturing	Durable Goods	Nondurable
	Average Hourly Earnings			Average Weekly Earnings		
1909	0.19	...	...	9.74	...	...
1914	0.22	...	...	10.92	...	...
1919	0.47	...	...	21.84	...	...
1924	0.54	...	...	23.67	25.48	21.50
1929	0.56	...	...	24.76	26.84	22.47
1932	0.44	0.49	0.41	16.89	15.99	17.26
1933	0.44	0.47	0.42	16.65	16.20	16.76
1934	0.53	0.55	0.51	18.20	18.59	17.73
1935	0.54	0.57	0.52	19.91	21.24	18.77
1936	0.55	0.58	0.52	21.56	23.72	19.57
1937	0.62	0.67	0.57	23.82	26.61	21.17
1939	0.63	0.69	0.57	23.64	26.19	21.36
1941	0.73	0.80	0.63	29.48	33.56	24.39
1943	0.96	1.05	0.79	43.07	48.73	33.45
1945	1.02	1.10	0.89	44.20	48.36	37.48
1946	1.08	1.14	1.00	43.32	46.22	40.30
1948	1.33	1.40	1.25	53.12	56.36	49.50
1950	1.44	1.52	1.35	58.32	62.43	53.48
1952	1.65	1.75	1.51	67.16	72.63	59.95
1954	1.78	1.90	1.62	70.49	76.19	63.18
1956	1.95	2.08	1.77	78.78	85.28	70.09
1958	2.11	2.26	1.91	82.71	89.27	74.11
1960	2.26	2.43	2.05	89.72	97.44	80.36
1962	2.39	2.56	2.17	96.56	104.70	85.93
1963	2.46	2.64	2.22	99.63	108.50	87.91
1964	2.53	2.71	2.29	102.97	112.19	90.91

19 cents in 1909, in coal mining to 31 cents. On the eve of World War I, hourly earnings in manufacturing averaged 22 cents; weekly earnings $11. During that war, wages rose along with rising prices, and more than doubled by 1919. They continued to rise until 1929, the peak year, reaching 56 cents per hour and $25 per week. The drop during the Depression was abrupt—to 44 cents per hour and, even worse, to $16.7 per week (see Table XV.9). Earnings in durable-goods industries are normally higher than in nondurables, but in the Depression years they fell more sharply, because of greater contraction of demand for their products. Average weekly hours of work were also lower for durable goods, 32.5, in contrast to 41.9 for nondurable goods industries.

Since the middle of the 1930's, the average weekly earnings of production workers on manufacturing payrolls have increased uninterruptedly, except for 1944–46, when there was a slight reduction, due mostly to the drop in work hours from 45.2 in 1944 to 40.3 in 1946. Otherwise, the recurrent postwar recessions have not affected the average earnings of employed workers, despite the spread of unemployment in such periods (see Table XV.9).

TABLE XV.10

GROSS WEEKLY EARNINGS OF PRODUCTION WORKERS, BY INDUSTRY, 1962-64
(In Dollars)

Industry	1962	1963	1964	Industry	1962	1963	1964
Mining	110.4	114.5	118.0	Paper and allied			
Metal mining	117.5	118.7	122.7	products	102.0	105.9	109.6
Coal mining	113.1	120.0	126.7	Printing, pub-			
Petroleum, natural				lishing	108.0	110.7	114.4
gas	109.2	112.4	113.4	Chemicals	110.2	112.9	116.5
Quarrying	105.4	109.0	113.5	Petroleum refining,			
				related industries	126.9	131.8	133.8
Contract construction	122.5	127.2	132.1	Leather, leather			
				products	64.7	66.0	69.0
Manufacturing	96.6	99.6	103.0				
				Transportation, pub-			
Durable goods	104.7	108.5	112.2	lic utilities:			
Ordnance and				Railroads[a]	115.9	118.4	120.4
accessories	116.3	119.3	121.6	Motor freight	113.3	117.3	122.2
Furniture, fixtures	79.4	81.8	84.3	Pipeline	132.8	138.4	142.6
Stone, clay, glass	98.6	102.4	105.8	Telephone	99.0	102.4	105.1
Primary metals	119.8	124.6	130.0	Telegraph	107.8	110.9	116.1
Fabricated metal				Radio, television	127.2	134.0	140.7
products	104.8	108.1	111.8	Electric, gas,			
Machinery (except				sanitary services	116.9	121.5	125.7
electrical)	113.0	116.2	121.7				
Electrical equip-				Trade[b]	75.1	77.6	79.9
ment, supplies	97.4	99.1	102.3	Wholesale	96.2	99.5	102.6
Transportation				Retail	66.0	68.0	69.9
equipment	122.2	126.7	130.2				
Nondurable goods	85.9	87.9	90.9	Finance, insurance,			
Food	91.8	94.5	97.8	real estate	72.2	75.0	76.7
Tobacco products	71.4	74.1	76.4				
Textile-mill				Services	46.1	47.6	48.6
products	68.2	69.4	73.0	Hotels, motels[c]			
Apparel and re-				Laundries, cleaning,			
lated products	61.2	62.5	64.3	dyeing	50.6	51.9	55.7
				Motion pictures	123.3	131.6	136.1

[a]Class I.
[b]Except eating and drinking places; nonsupervisory workers.
[c]Money payments only; board, room, uniform, and tips excluded.

In 1964, weekly earnings ranged from $64–$69 in apparel and leather-products industries to $102–$134 in electrical-equipment plants, contract construction, and petroleum refining. In 1965, the respective earnings ranged from $67–$72 to $107–$138. In transportation and communication services, with higher skill requirements for work, earnings are generally considerably higher than in trade or other services (see Table XV.10).

Data on the earnings of construction workers are available only from 1947. Their hourly earnings amounted to $1.54 in 1947, $1.86 in 1950, $3.08 in 1960, and $3.69 in 1965. Corresponding figures for weekly earnings were $58.87, $69.68, $113.04, and $145.30.

Hourly earnings of nonsupervisory workers in retail trade, excluding eating and drinking places, were: 48 cents in 1939; 80 cents in 1946; $1.05 in 1950; $1.62 in 1960; and $1.87 in 1965. The respective data for weekly earnings of the same workers were: $21.01; $32.92; $43.16; $62.37; and $69.94.

TABLE XV.11

AVERAGE ANNUAL EARNINGS OF FULL-TIME WHITE AND NONWHITE WORKERS, 1939-63
(In Dollars)

Year	Male		Female	
	White	Nonwhite	White	Nonwhite
1939	1,419	639	863	327
1957	4,950	3,137	3,107	1,866
1959	5,456	3,339	3,306	2,196
1960	5,662	3,789	3,410	2,372
1963	6,277	4,104	3,723	2,368

Over the years, earnings of women have been, roughly speaking, about half those of men; earnings of Negro men, half those of white men; and of Negro women, half those of white women. This discrimination occurs not so much because there may be different wage rates for Negroes or women doing the same work as white men, but more because a fairly short list of jobs is open undiscriminately to both sexes or to white men and Negro men. There are fewer jobs for which employers take women, and there is a limited choice of jobs open to Negroes; very often they are

TABLE XV.12

WEEKLY EARNINGS OF PRODUCTION WORKERS IN MANUFACTURING INDUSTRIES,
BY STATE, 1960-64
(In Dollars)

State	1960	1963	1964	State	1960	1963	1964
United States	89.72	99.63	102.97	Maryland	90.63	100.44	103.38
				New York	89.61	98.78	102.44
Alaska	...	145.68	152.93	Pennsylvania	89.86	98.21	102.00
Michigan	112.00	128.27	135.11	Nebraska	87.41	97.96	101.93
Nevada	113.30	122.93	126.72	Missouri	87.57	98.41	101.32
Ohio	104.13	116.13	120.93	Texas	89.19	97.29	100.91
California	104.28	115.78	119.29	Idaho	90.00	96.56	99.50
Washington	101.78	112.50	115.92	Kentucky	83.92	94.77	98.66
Indiana	100.49	112.01	115.80	Oklahoma	85.47	93.75	98.23
Illinois	97.70	108.71	113.00	North Dakota	81.85	101.08	97.41
Colorado	98.25	109.34	112.34	Massachusetts	81.96	91.16	94.56
Oregon	97.04	106.90	112.01	New Mexico	82.58	92.84	90.91
Utah	98.89	109.21	111.91	Alabama	75.65	85.46	88.97
Kansas	95.82	107.54	111.24	Florida	76.07	85.28	87.78
Wisconsin	96.32	106.41	110.60	Vermont	76.59	83.22	86.32
Dist.of Columbia	97.61	108.38	110.45	Rhode Island	73.70	82.42	84.19
Iowa	93.68	105.47	109.90	Virginia	70.62	80.16	83.84
Montana	96.04	106.00	109.76	Tennessee	73.23	79.58	82.82
Arizona	90.14	107.87	109.62	Hawaii	...	77.52	82.18
Wyoming	95.25	102.49	108.57	Maine	71.15	79.56	81.60
Connecticut	93.26	104.90	108.47	New Hampshire	70.45	77.59	81.00
New Jersey	93.93	104.90	108.40	Georgia	65.40	73.38	77.95
Delaware	91.01	104.30	108.39	South Carolina	63.27	70.11	73.98
Minnesota	95.07	104.58	107.96	Arkansas	62.71	69.83	72.09
West Virginia	93.27	104.40	107.33	North Carolina	61.14	68.38	71.58
South Dakota	90.90	101.70	106.70	Mississippi	60.50	68.28	71.46
Louisiana	86.71	100.62	104.58				

offered jobs that white workers would not take at the existing wage. However, the gap has narrowed in recent years. In 1939, year-round full-time nonwhite male workers earned, on the average, about 41 per cent as much as whites; by 1963, 65 per cent; the corresponding percentages for nonwhite working women were about 38 and 64 per cent (see Table XV.11).

In 1963, the national average for weekly earnings of production workers in manufacturing was approaching $100; in 1964, $103; in 1965, $108. Many factors affect weekly earnings, and there is a great interstate variation in their level. Thus it may seem surprising to find New York State reporting average weekly earnings in manufacturing below the national average, and Louisiana with earnings above it; the explanation apparently is that New York State has mostly nondurable-goods industries, such as the apparel industry, while the chief manufacturing in Louisiana is in the petroleum industry, with its high percentage of skilled workers and higher wages. That Alaska ranks first, much above the northeastern industrialized states, must be due to scarcity in labor supply; because of its climate, it may be considered a hardship area. On the whole, however, and despite some exceptional cases, weekly earnings are generally above the national average in industrial states and considerably below it in the deep South (see Table XV.12).

XVI. *Social Security*

In the 30 years that have elapsed since the introduction of the social security system in the United States, it has grown from a puny seedling to a vigorous, full-blooded plant with branches stretching in many directions. The universe within which it operates has experienced many changes, too. One of the most consequential facts is the change in the composition of the population: in 1935, children under 14 and persons aged 65 years and over represented about one-third of the population; now they account for more than two-fifths. While there were 2 people in economically productive ages for each 1 of the very young and old when the Social Security Act was passed, today there is only 1½ to carry this responsibility.

90. *Old-Age, Survivors, and Disability Insurance*

Social security legislation was introduced in the United States much later than in most European countries. The different economic and psychological environment, with its almost unlimited opportunities, developed in Americans a great faith in their own ability to face life and overcome hardships. For generations, land was to be had for homesteading. Most people lived on farms and depended on themselves for nearly everything they needed; in a natural disaster or in sickness or a family difficulty, they counted on the neighbors to help them to withstand their troubles. The belief prevailed that only lazy people could not make a living in this rich and free land, and on the whole there was little sympathy for those who did not or could not.

At the beginning of this country's history as a nation, in 1800, only 6 per cent of population was urban, and the few large cities had less than 100,000 population. In 1860, barely 20 per cent of the population lived in urban places. Not until 60 years later, in 1920, did the Census of

Population report a slightly larger urban than rural population (see Sec. 8) But the development of industry and the money economy brought not only higher standards of living but also new social and economic conditions. The large self-sufficient farm family gradually gave way to the smaller city family, which lived in crowded dwellings, depended almost exclusively on wages or salaries, and was open to social stresses that weakened family ties. Communities found it necessary to provide some assistance to the poor and shiftless, the orphans and the sick. Usually such help was given after a means test that was often felt as a stigma of second-class citizenship.

Pension plans for various categories of public servants—teachers, policemen, firemen—date back to the last years of the nineteenth and the beginning of the twentieth centuries. Provisions for pension and medical and other benefits for the military personnel were introduced and substantially extended after World War I. Nevertheless, it was still not easy to break the spirit of "rugged individualism" in the country; even the trade unions opposed social security at the government level, though they did support the system of workmen's compensation—payments to a worker injured in connection with his job, or to his survivors if he was killed while at work.*

The Great Depression of the 1930's found the country unprepared; neither the states nor the private charitable organizations could cope effectively with the near universal misery. Federal action became imperative, and President Roosevelt asked Congress for the legislation signed on August 14, 1935, called the Social Security Act. It comprised 3 major social security programs: a Federal system of old-age insurance for the retired industrial and commercial workers 65 years and over; a Federal-state system of unemployment insurance; and Federal grants-in-aid for assisting the needy aged and blind, and children deprived of support and care by reason of the physical or mental incapacity, death, or absence from the home of a parent.

In 1939, the old-age insurance program was extended to members of the families of insured workers and, gradually, as time passed, was repeatedly broadened as to the size of the benefits and the coverage of additional groups—regularly employed farm and household employees and, later, farm operators, most self-employed professional people, state and local employees covered on an elective group basis, and members of the armed forces. Employees of nonprofit organizations were also covered on a voluntary group basis. In 1956, disability insurance for permanently and totally disabled workers was made a part of the system, which then became Old-Age, Survivors, and Disability Insurance (OASDI). The OASDI is self-supporting; it is based on social security taxes paid by employers, employees, and self-employed persons. All contributions are deposited into

* At the beginning of 1965, 48 million workers and employees, or almost four-fifths of the employed labor force, were covered by this type of insurance, domestic servants and agricultural and casual workers are not covered in many states.

FIGURE XVI.1

PER CENT OF WORKERS COVERED UNDER
PUBLIC RETIREMENT PROGRAMS, 1939-64

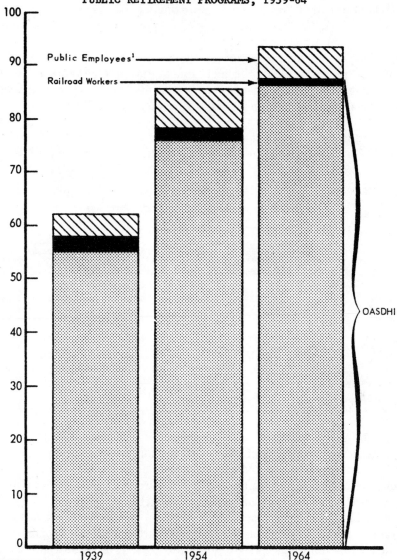

¹Covered exclusively by their own retirememt systems.

Social Security Administration

trust funds with the U.S. Treasury and can be used only to pay the benefits and the operating expenses of the program. The 1965 amendments
to the Social Security Act somewhat extended the coverage and included
provisions for the medical care to those aged 65 years and over, which
broadened the designation of the system to OASDHI (H standing for

health insurance). The railroad workers have their own retirement system, but until a railroad worker has 10 years of service, he is covered by the OASDI, and his wage credits are transferred to that system.

Today the basic OASDI covers approximately 90 per cent of all persons in paid jobs. At the beginning of 1965, 83 per cent of the population 65 years and over were drawing benefits or were eligible for benefits, and about 75 per cent of the paternal orphans under age 18 were benefiting under the program. With the inclusion of the railroad workers and the Federal, state, and local government employees, 94 per cent of the working population have retirement protection (see Figure XVI.1).

Registrations with the old-age and survivors insurance system started with about 37 million persons in 1937. In December, 1964, of the 72 million

TABLE XVI.1

COVERAGE STATUS UNDER OLD-AGE, SURVIVORS, AND
DISABILITY INSURANCE, 1940-64
(In Thousands)

Year	Paid Employment[a]	Covered by Law		Excluded from Coverage by Law				
		Total	Elective, Not Arranged	Total	Agriculture	Government[b]	Domestic	Others
1940	47,100	30,400	...	16,700	7,200	3,700	2,300	3,500
1945	57,300	38,900	...	18,400	5,800	5,400	1,600	5,700
1950	61,300	40,400	...	20,900	5,300	5,900	2,100	7,600
1955	65,700	59,400	3,400	6,300	1,300	2,200	900	1,900
1960	67,100	61,000	2,300	6,200	1,000	2,200	900	2,000
1962	69,200	63,100	2,400	6,100	800	2,400	1,000	2,000
1963	70,300	64,200	2,400	6,100	800	2,400	900	2,000
1964	72,000	65,800	2,400	6,200	800	2,400	1,000	2,100

[a]Includes self-employed persons.
[b]Federal, state, and local.

persons in paid employment, almost 66 million, or 91 per cent, worked in jobs covered by law for old-age, survivors, and disability insurance. Of these, 2.4 million were in jobs—mostly in state and local government—for which coverage has been authorized on an elective basis but not yet arranged. The jobs of the remaining 6.2 million persons were excluded from coverage either because the type of work performed was specifically excluded (some ministers, private physicians,* etc.), or because the workers did not meet tests of minimum earnings or regularity of work, such as domestic workers, persons engaged in casual labor, occasional farm workers, and low-income self-employed people (see Table XVI.1). Under disability protection, some 54 million workers are eligible for benefits if they become totally and permanently disabled. Independently of OASDI, the retirement protection for the Federal, state, and local government employees

* In 1965, self-employed physicians came under coverage of the program.

has grown from 2.5 million covered in 1935 to 7.8 million in 1964 (2.3 million Federal employees and 5.5 million other public employees), excluding military personnel, who are covered by their own retirement systems. The 800,000 railroad workers are protected by their own retirement system, closely connected with the OASDI.

The number of monthly beneficiaries under OASI was only 222,000 in 1940, the first year in which benefit payments were made: it multiplied more than 15 times by 1950, reaching 3.5 million; by 1960, under OASDI it more than quadrupled, to 14.8 million. In 1965, it exceeded 20.9 million, of whom 16.3 million were aged 62 or over, 1.0 million were disabled workers, 3.1 million were children of insured workers, and 0.5 million

TABLE XVI.2

NUMBER OF OASDI BENEFICIARIES AT END OF YEAR, 1940-65
(In Thousands)

Year	Total[a]	Total	Aged Retired Workers	Other[b]	Disabled Workers	Widowed Mothers	Children[c]
1940	222	147	112	35	—	20	55
1950	3,477	2,608	1,771	837	—	169	700
1954	6,886	5,454	3,775	1,679	—	272	1,161
1956	9,128	7,486	5,112	2,373	—	301	1,341
1958	12,430	10,215	6,921	3,294	238	354	1,624
1960	14,845	11,987	8,061	3,926	455	401	2,000
1962	18,053	14,313	9,738	4,575	741	452	2,547
1964	19,800	15,647	10,669	4,979	894	471	2,787
1965	20,867	16,315	11,101	5,214	988	472	3,093

[a]Includes duplicate accounts for beneficiaries receiving both old-age and wife's or husband's benefits.
[b]Wife or dependent husband of old-age or disability beneficiary, and aged widow or dependent widower; also aged dependent parent.
[c]All dependent children under 18 of old-age or disability beneficiary, and of a deceased worker.

were widowed mothers with the child of an insured worker in their care (see Table XVI.2 and Figure XVI.2).

All in all, about 3 out of 4 persons aged 65 years or over received old-age benefits in 1964. In addition, another 8 per cent of the aged were eligible for benefits but not receiving them, primarily because they or their spouses were still working (see Figure XVI.3).

More than half of the beneficiaries of old-age, survivors, and disability insurance in 1964 lived in 10 states: New York, California, Pennsylvania, Illinois, Ohio, Texas, Michigan, Florida, New Jersey, and Massachusetts (Table XVI.3).

Contribution rates to OASDI have been increased several times and are scheduled to increase gradually for the employer-employee each from the current 3.63 per cent to 3.85 per cent in 1966 to 3.9 per cent in 1967-68, 4.4 per cent in 1969-72, and 4.85 per cent in 1973 and after. The maximum annual earnings on which benefits are computed were $4,800, but

FIGURE XVI.2

SOCIAL SECURITY RECIPIENTS, 1939-65

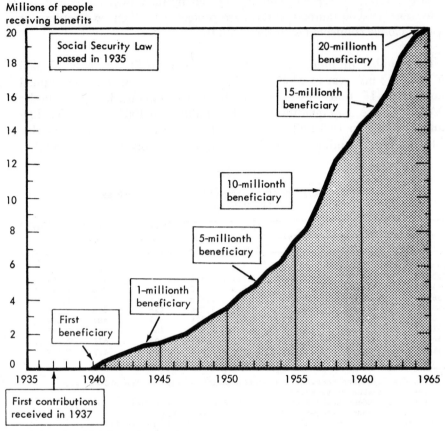

Social Security Administration

FIGURE XVI.3

PROPORTION OF THE POPULATION AGED 65 AND OVER RECEIVING CASH BENEFITS UNDER THE OASDHI PROGRAM AT END OF SELECTED YEARS, 1940-64

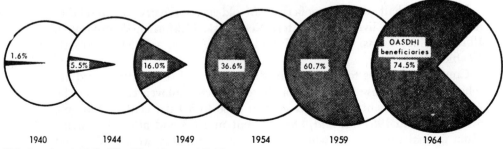

U.S. Department of Health, Education, and Welfare,
Social Security Administration

TABLE XVI.3

RANKING OF STATES BY NUMBER OF OASDI BENEFICIARIES AND
AMOUNT OF BENEFIT PAYMENTS, 1964

	Beneficiaries (In Thousands)			Benefit payments, (In Millions of Dollars)	
1.	New York	1,902	1.	New York	1,763
2.	California	1,601	2.	California	1,378
3.	Pennsylvania	1,299	3.	Pennsylvania	1,155
4.	Illinois	1,066	4.	Illinois	954
5.	Ohio	1,014	5.	Ohio	889
6.	Texas	892	6.	Michigan	735
7.	Michigan	808	7.	Texas	642
8.	Florida	751	8.	New Jersey	617
9.	New Jersey	669	9.	Florida	610
10.	Massachusetts	597	10.	Massachusetts	535
11.	Missouri	527	11.	Indiana	445
12.	Indiana	518	12.	Missouri	420
13.	Wisconsin	471	13.	Wisconsin	401
14.	North Carolina	459	14.	Minnesota	312
15.	Tennessee	387	15.	North Carolina	308
16.	Minnesota	386	16.	Iowa	275
17.	Kentucky	376	17.	Washington	272
18.	Virginia	376	18.	Virginia	270
19.	Georgia	374	19.	Kentucky	259
20.	Alabama	340	20.	Connecticut	259
21.	Iowa	338	21.	Tennessee	258
22.	Washington	313	22.	Georgia	249
23.	Louisiana	288	23.	Alabama	227
24.	Connecticut	274	24.	Maryland	219
25.	Maryland	265	25.	Louisiana	199
26.	Oklahoma	265	26.	Oklahoma	197
27.	West Virginia	249	27.	Kansas	196
28.	Kansas	246	28.	Oregon	190
29.	Mississippi	236	29.	West Virginia	189
30.	Arkansas	233	30.	Arkansas	150
31.	Oregon	222	31.	South Carolina	145
32.	South Carolina	221	32.	Mississippi	138
33.	Colorado	170	33.	Colorado	137
34.	Nebraska	168	34.	Nebraska	133
35.	Arizona	140	35.	Arizona	112
36.	Maine	122	36.	Maine	97
37.	Rhode Island	103	37.	Rhode Island	91
38.	South Dakota	79	38.	New Hampshire	66
39.	New Hampshire	77	39.	Utah	61
40.	Utah	74	40.	Montana	61
41.	Montana	73	41.	South Dakota	60
42.	New Mexico	72	42.	Idaho	56
43.	Idaho	70	43.	District of Columbia	52
44.	North Dakota	67	44.	North Dakota	51
45.	District of Columbia	65	45.	New Mexico	50
46.	Vermont	49	46.	Vermont	39
47.	Delaware	44	47.	Delaware	38
48.	Hawaii	43	48.	Hawaii	34
49.	Wyoming	30	49.	Wyoming	25
50.	Nevada	25	50.	Nevada	21
51.	Alaska	8	51.	Alaska	6

were raised to $6,600 as of January 1, 1966. Contribution rates of self-employed persons will also be gradually raised from the current rate of 5.4 per cent to 5.8 per cent in 1966 to 7 per cent in 1973 on the respective amounts of earnings.

TABLE XVI.4

RECEIPTS, EXPENDITURES, AND ASSETS OF THE OLD-AGE,
SURVIVORS, AND DISABILITY INSURANCE, 1937-64
(In Millions of Dollars)

Year	Receipts Contributions	Interest	Transfers[a]	Expenditures Benefit Payments	Adminis- trative Expenses	Assets at End of Period
	Old-Age and Survivors Insurance Trust Fund					
Cumulative, 1937-1964	131,617	8,487	-2,207	115,937	2,836	19,125
1940	325	43	-	35	26	2,031
1945	1,285	134	-	274	30	7,121
1950	2,671	257	-	961	61	13,721
1952	3,819	365	-	2,194	88	17,442
1954	5,163	447	21	3,670	92	20,576
1956	6,172	526	5	5,715	132	22,519
1958	7,566	552	-124	8,327	194	21,864
1960	10,866	516	-318	10,677	203	20,324
1961	11,285	548	-332	11,862	239	19,725
1962	12,059	526	-361	13,356	256	18,337
1963	14,541	521	-423	14,217	281	18,480
1964	15,689	569	-403	14,914	296	19,125
	Disability Insurance Trust Fund					
Cumulative, 1957-1964	7,905	389	-28	5,842	378	2,047
1957	702	7	-	6	3	649
1958	966	25	-	249	12	1,379
1960	1,010	53	5	568	36	2,289
1961	1,038	66	-5	887	64	2,437
1962	1,046	68	-11	1,105	66	2,368
1963	1,099	66	-20	1,210	68	2,235
1964	1,154	64	-19	1,309	79	2,047

[a]Transfers under financial interchange with railroad retirement account.

In 1945, total receipts of the trust funds, including interest, amounted to $1.3 billion; in 1956, to $6.7 billion; and in 1964, to $17.5 billion. With the exception of a few years, expenditures have been smaller than receipts. Expenditures exceeded income from both trusts by about $0.9 billion in 1962, and 1964 income exceeded expenditures by approximately $0.7 billion. At the end of 1964, the balance in the trust funds was $21.2 billion (see Table XVI.4).

The individual monthly benefit of a retired male worker in 1940 averaged $22.80 and of a female worker, $18.40; for a retired worker and wife, the average was $36.40. The corresponding figures for the end of 1964 were: $83.60, $64.30, and $130.10. A widowed mother and 2 children draw $193.40; and a disabled worker, with a wife and 1 or more children, $193.90.

Administrative expenses have never exceeded the 1941 figure of 9 per cent of contribution income and in recent years have been 2.2–2.3 per cent.

In conclusion, it seems appropriate to stress what is perhaps the most important feature of coverage under the OASDI system, namely, that it embraces all kinds of workers under one comprehensive system. In view of the great mobility of American labor, not only geographically but also on the social ladder, this broad type of coverage is essential. An unskilled worker of today may become a businessman or a skilled mechanic tomorrow. The broad coverage of OASDI protects his rights throughout all the changes during his working life.

The Western European countries devote a much larger percentage of their national income for social-insurance programs than the United States: about 9 per cent in Sweden, almost 11 per cent in the United Kingdom, and 12–14 per cent in countries of the Common Market, as compared with less than 5 per cent in the United States (before the introduction of the Medicare program). For one thing, those countries have elaborate sickness and maternity benefits; for another, almost all of them provide family allowances (absorbing in France, for example, 4.3 per cent of national income), which the United States does not have. However, if the expenditures for the type of programs which are designated in this country as OASDI are compared, the difference becomes much smaller: 3.6 per cent of national income in the United States; 3.9 per cent in France, 4.2 per cent in the United Kingdom, 4.7 per cent in Italy and Belgium, 5.1 per cent in the Netherlands. West Germany with 8.1 per cent is exceptional.

91. Unemployment Insurance

The Social Security Act of 1935 did not establish unemployment insurance, in the exact sense of the word, in the United States. What it did was to provide an inducement to the states to pass laws for unemployment insurance. The Federal Act levied a tax on the payrolls of employers with 8 or more workers in industrial and commercial enterprises and stipulated that if a state established unemployment insurance meeting certain minimum conditions, the employers subject to the state law could offset the state tax against 90 per cent of the Federal tax. Thus states without an unemployment insurance law would not be at a competitive advantage against states with such a law. Congress also authorized Federal grants to states to meet the full costs of administering the state systems. Very shortly, all states, including what then were the territories of Alaska and Hawaii, and the District of Columbia, had passed unemployment insurance laws. To assure the security of unemployment funds, each state was required to deposit the contributions it collected in the Unemployment Trust Fund in the U.S. Treasury, from which it could withdraw funds only to pay unemployment benefits. Unlike old-age, survivors, and disability insurance, state unemployment benefits are financed almost exclusively by the employers (except in Alabama, Alaska, and New Jersey).

Apart from certain Federal requirements concerning the financing and administration of the system, the states themselves decide about the coverage, contribution rates, eligibility, amount and duration of benefits, etc.

As has been the case with OASDI, the unemployment insurance program has been gradually extended—its coverage has been broadened, duration of payments extended, benefit amounts raised; the size-of-firm yardstick has been lowered to 4 workers instead of 8 and at the beginning of 1965, 20 states had size-of-firm provisions covering employers of 1 worker or more. The states have also arranged to pay benefits to workers who move across state lines.

The coverage of unemployment insurance is more limited than that of OASDI since in most states it includes only persons who work for wages for others, and excludes agricultural workers, domestic servants, state- and local-government employees, and those working for nonprofit institutions. In more than half the states, it also excludes jobs with employers of fewer than 4 workers. In 1964, there were 50.6 million workers in jobs covered by unemployment insurance, including railroad employees, Federal employees, and members of the armed forces. On the whole, 4 out of every 5 employed wage and salary workers are covered.

Most states compensate for a fraction of the full-time weekly wage, usually about 50 per cent, subject to a maximum amount. The duration of payment also varies, but most states also pay for 26 weeks of unemployment, after a 1-week waiting period. In recent recessions, the payment period has been extended under special legislation.

Unemployment insurance has been of great importance not only for the unemployed and their families during periods when they were without earnings but also for the national economy. The postwar recessions have been shorter and milder because the substantial purchasing power provided by unemployment insurance and OASDI has made the economy more resistant and stable. It has been estimated that unemployment-insurance payments have offset between one-fifth and one-third of the loss of income during the recent recessions. Because unemployment insurance is most sensitive to changing business conditions, it is considered one of the major devices in bolstering consumer expenditures during an economic downswing.

The total number of state beneficiaries under the state programs—that is, the number of first payments—was 5.2 million in 1940, 7.1 million in 1961, and 4.8 million in 1965. Insured unemployment in these years represented 5.6, 5.6, and 3.0 per cent of covered employment, respectively. In 1965, the insured joblessness rate was 1.3 per cent. The average weekly number of beneficiaries fluctuated between approximately 1.3 million in 1940, 2.5 million in 1958, and 1.3 million in 1965; the benefits paid, between $518.7 million, $3.5 billion, and $2.1 billion, respectively (see Table XVI.5).

TABLE XVI.5

UNEMPLOYMENT INSURANCE PROGRAMS, 1940-65

Year	All programs[a]		Benefits Paid, (In Millions of Dollars)[c]	State Programs		Benefits Paid (In Millions of Dollars)
	Covered Employment (In Thousands)	Insured Unemployment[b] (In Thousands)		Insured Unemployment Weekly Average, (In Thousands)	(As Per Cent of Covered Employment)	
1940	24,291	1,331	534.7	1,282	5.6	518.7
1941	28,136	842	358.8	814	3.0	344.3
1942	30,819	661	350.4	649	2.2	344.1
1943	32,419	149	80.5	147	0.5	79.6
1944	31.714	111	67.2	105	0.4	62.4
1945	30,087	720	574.9	589	2.1	445.9
1950	34,308	1,605	1,467.6	1,503	4.6	1,373.1
1955	40,018	1,395	1,560.2	1,254	3.5	1,350.3
1958	44,412	3,269	4,209.2	2,509	6.4	3,512.7
1959	45,728	2,099	2,803.0	1,682	4.4	2,279.0
1960	46,334	2,078	3,022.7	1,906	4.8	2,726.7
1961	46,264	2,994	4,358.1	2,290	5.6	3,422.7
1962	47,766	1,924	3,160.0	1,783	4.4	2,675.4
1963	48,435	1,973	3,025.9	1,806	4.3	2,774.7
1964	49,295	1,753	2,749.2	1,605	3.8	2,522.4
1965	...	1,450	2,260.0	1,328	3.0	2,070.0

[a]Includes programs for Federal employees, railroad employees, various ex-servicemen, and others.
[b]Weekly averages.
[c]Includes Federal and state programs for temporary extension of benefits from June, 1958, through June, 1962.

The ratio of benefits paid to contributions collected is a good indicator of the state of unemployment: when benefits represent only a small part of funds collected in a given year, it is evident that the number of unemployed beneficiaries is relatively small. On the other hand, when this ratio reaches the figure of 238.8, as it did in the recession year of 1958, the high level of unemployment in the country is beyond any doubt (see Table XVI.6). The average actual duration of benefits was less than 10 weeks in 1940, nearly 15 weeks in 1958, and 13 weeks in 1964.

The risk of unemployment varies among the states; the industrial composition of a state affects its benefit costs more than its provisions under the unemployment-insurance law. In 1964, 8 states (New York, California, Pennsylvania, New Jersey, Illinois, Massachusetts, Michigan, and Ohio) accounted for 61 per cent of all beneficiaries of the unemployment-insurance system; 2 of them—New York and California—accounted for more than 30 per cent. The next 12 states (Texas, North Carolina, Washington, Indiana, Missouri, Wisconsin, Connecticut, Maryland, Tennessee, Florida, Georgia, and Minnesota) accounted for an additional 21 per cent; the remaining 18 per cent was distributed among the other 30 states, the District of Columbia, and Puerto Rico.

The average weekly benefit payment was $10.56 in 1940, $20.76 in

1950, $32.87 in 1960, and $37.00 in 1965. There is a great variation in weekly checks from state to state. In 1964, the 3 highest weekly averages were provided in California, Colorado, and Wisconsin ($43.68, $42.76, and $42.60); the 4 lowest in North Carolina, West Virginia, Mississippi, and Maine ($23.15, $29.44, $24.54, and $24.16). In Puerto Rico, the weekly payments averaged only $15.48. Between these extremes, 17 states provided checks averaging $35–$40; 17 states, $30–$35; and the remainder, less than $30 a week.

92. Public Assistance

While the Social Security Act has provided a substantial measure of security against loss of income resulting from old age, disability, unemployment, and death of the family head, its public-assistance programs have aimed at assisting certain others who could not meet their immediate

TABLE XVI.6

STATE UNEMPLOYMENT INSURANCE PROGRAMS, BY
SELECTED FEATURES, 1960-64

Year	Contributions Collected (In Millions of Dollars)	Ratio of Benefits to Contributions	Final Payments (Exhaustions) (Millions of Claimants)	Funds Available for Benefits, End of Year (In Millions of Dollars)	Average Rate of Employer Contributions	Average Actual Duration of Benefits (In Weeks)
1940	854	60.7	2.6	1,817	2.7	9.8
1945	1,162	38.4	0.3	6,914	1.7	8.5
1950	1,191	115.2	1.9	6,972	1.5	13.0
1955	1,209	111.7	1.3	8,264	1.2	12.4
1958	1,471	238.8	2.6	6,953	1.3	14.8
1960	2,289	119.1	1.6	6,643	1.9	12.7
1961	2,450	139.7	2.4	5,802	2.1	14.7
1962	2,952	90.6	1.6	6,273	2.4	13.1
1963	3,019	91.9	1.6	6,648	2.3	13.3
1964	3,048	82.8	1.4	7,296	2.2	13.0

needs under the insurance provisions—the needy aged, blind, and needy dependent children. In the transition years after the enactment of the Social Security Act in 1935, these assistance provisions were of particular importance: public-assistance payments began in February, 1936, while the first monthly benefits under OASI were not payable until January, 1940. By 1940, Federal funds were used by 51 jurisdictions for old-age assistance, by 43 for the needy blind, and by 42 for helping needy families with dependent children. As OASI gained momentum and its provisions were improved, public assistance assumed a supplementary role, as had been originally planned. Until February, 1951, the number of persons aged 65 years and over receiving old-age assistance exceeded that of the aged who drew benefits under the OASI. By January, 1966, the 14.4 million insured aged beneficiaries outnumbered the 2.1 million assisted old people by a ratio of 7 to 1 (see Figure XVI.4).

FIGURE XVI.4

PERSONS AGED 65 YEARS AND OVER RECEIVING OASDI BENEFITS AND PUBLIC ASSISTANCE (OAA), 1940-64

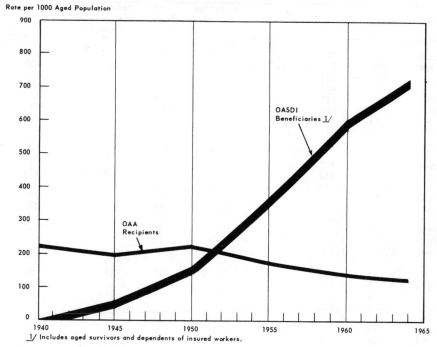

_1/_ Includes aged survivors and dependents of insured workers.

Social Security Administration

TABLE XVI.7

PERCENTAGE DISTRIBUTION OF SOURCES OF FUNDS FOR PUBLIC ASSISTANCE, 1936-65

Year	Total	Federal	State	Local
1936	100.0	13.4	51.4	35.2
1939	100.0	23.2	50.6	26.2
1942	100.0	38.2	43.4	18.4
1945	100.0	40.7	46.8	12.5
1948	100.0	43.9	45.5	10.6
1951	100.0	47.6	41.6	10.8
1954	100.0	50.6	37.4	12.0
1957	100.0	51.3	37.0	11.7
1960	100.0	51.7	36.4	11.9
1961	100.0	53.1	35.1	11.8
1962	100.0	54.4	34.4	11.2
1963	100.0	55.7	32.7	11.5
1964	100.0	55.0	33.2	11.7
1965	100.0	54.6	33.7	11.7

TABLE XVI.8

PUBLIC ASSISTANCE PAYMENTS, BY PROGRAM, 1936-64[a]
(In Millions of Dollars)

Year	Total[b]	Old-Age	Medical[c]	Dependent Children	The Blind	Permanently and Totally Disabled[d]	General Assistance[e]
1936	657	155	...	50	13	...	439
1937	804	310	...	71	16	...	407
1938	985	392	...	97	19	...	476
1939	1,049	431	...	115	21	...	483
1940	1,035	475	...	133	22	...	405
1941	990	542	...	153	23	...	273
1942	959	595	...	158	25	...	181
1943	930	653	...	141	25	...	111
1944	943	693	...	135	25	...	89
1945	990	727	...	150	27	...	87
1946	1,183	822	...	209	31	...	121
1947	1,486	990	...	295	36	...	165
1948	1,737	1,133	...	364	41	...	199
1949	2,187	1,380	...	475	49	...	282
1950	2,395	1,470	...	554	53	8	295
1951	2,395	1,475	...	562	56	58	195
1952	2,464	1,533	...	554	61	91	172
1953	2,547	1,597	...	562	66	115	151
1954	2,653	1,593	...	594	68	137	198
1955	2,757	1,608	...	639	71	157	214
1956	2,861	1,677	...	663	77	177	198
1957	3,099	1,773	...	755	84	201	213
1958	3,434	1,830	...	895	87	228	307
1959	3,680	1,883	...	1,003	91	260	344
1960	3,804	1,928	5	1,062	94	288	322
1961	4,115	1,890	113	1,237	93	317	356
1962	4,457	1,961	246	1,396	94	361	293
1963	4,736	2,029	330	1,477	96	417	280
1964	5,096	2,045	448	1,649	98	475	273

[a] Before 1943, excludes Hawaii and Alaska; since October, 1950, includes Puerto Rico and Virgin Islands; since July, 1959, includes Guam.
[b] Beginning October, 1950, total exceeds sum of columns because of inclusion of vendor payments for medical care from general assistance funds, from special medical funds and, for 1 state from October, 1950-June, 1954, and from funds for the special types of public assistance; data for such expenditures partly estimated for some states.
[c] Medical assistance established October, 1960.
[d] Aid to disabled initiated October, 1950.
[e] Excludes Idaho beginning September, 1957; Nebraska, September, 1952-December, 1953 and Indiana, January, 1962, for lack of data.

The public-assistance system embraces 6 categories of aid: old-age assistance, medical assistance for the aged (since 1960), aid to families with dependent children, aid to the blind, aid to the permanently and totally disabled (since 1950), and general assistance. The cost of the 6 programs has been shared by the Federal Government and state governments. However, Federal participation has not been uniform; it is larger for some programs and smaller for others. Thus while the Federal Government supplied 55 per cent for total public-assistance payments in 1964, its share was

64.9 per cent for the assistance to the aged, 48 per cent for the aid to the blind, 56.3 per cent for aid to families with dependent children, and so on. The Federal share was relatively small in the beginning of the public-assistance program: 13.4 per cent of total payments in 1936, as compared with 51.4 per cent carried by states and 35.2 per cent, by local governments. In the course of 2 decades, this relationship has been reversed. In 1954, the Federal share exceeded 50 per cent, and in 1965 it was 54.6 per cent as against 33.7 per cent for the states and 11.7 per cent for local governments (see Table XVI.7). State and local governments provide the so-called general assistance out of their own funds to needy persons who do not qualify under the Federally aided assistance programs.

Among the 6 programs of public assistance, old-age assistance and aid to families with dependent children account for the largest part of its expenditures. In 1964, for example, out of total payments of $5.1 billion, $2.0 billion and $1.6 billion were spent respectively for them (see Table XVI.8). The proportion of the population receiving public assistance varies greatly by the types of assistance, and also among the states, even the counties. The average ratio for the country as a whole per 1,000 population aged 65 years and over was, as of December, 1964: 119 for old-age assistance, 79 for aid to the blind, 45 for dependent children under 18, 18 for medical assistance, and 5 for general assistance.* In some southern states, the ratio for old-age assistance, for example, was several times that in the North; 499 per 1,000 in Louisiana, against 31 in New York; or 364 in Mississippi against 22 in New Jersey; 394 in Alabama against 37 in Delaware or 27 in Connecticut. But some states have high ratios reflecting relatively high standards in recognizing the need of certain groups of the population. California, for example, had a ratio of 176 receiving old-age assistance per 1,000 population aged 65 years and over, and Missouri, 196. Other programs of public assistance also present considerable deviations from state to state.

The number of recipients of public assistance differs by type of program. In 1936, at the start of the system, 1.1 million persons were receiving old-age assistance; in 1940, 2.1 million; the peak was reached in 1950 with 2.8 million; since then the number of recipients has been declining steadily and was 2.1 million by the end of 1965. Assistance to families with dependent children started with 162,000 recipient families and 404,000 children. Since 1950, the requirements of at least 1 parent or 1 adult relative have been considered in determining the help needed; in 1951, the total number of recipients in 593,000 families with 1.5 million dependent children increased to more than 2 million. Since 1961, Federal grants have also been available to help pay assistance costs to children in need because of their fathers' unemployment. In 1965, for example, public assistance aided in the support of 1.1 million families with some 3.4 million dependent children and total recipients of 4.5 million (see Table XVI.9 and Figure

* Some of these ratios are not calculated for all 50 states.

TABLE XVI.9

NUMBER OF RECIPIENTS OF PUBLIC ASSISTANCE,
BY PROGRAM, DECEMBER, 1936-65
(In Thousands)

Year	Old-Age	Medical Aid for the Aged	Families with Dependent Children			The Blind	Permanently and Totally Disabled	General Assistance (Cases)[b]
			Families	Total[a]	Children			
1936	1,108	...	162	...	404	45	...	1,510
1939	1,912	...	315	...	760	70	...	1,558
1942	2,230	...	348	...	849	79	...	460
1945	2,056	...	274	...	701	71	...	257
1948	2,498	...	475	...	1,214	86	...	398
1951	2,708	...	593	2,044	1,524	97	127	323
1954	2,565	...	604	2,174	1,640	102	224	351
1957	2,487	...	667	2,498	1,913	108	291	345
1960	2,332	15	806	3,080	2,377	108	374	431
1961	2,269	72	921	3,582	2,770	103	396	411
1962	2,226	110	943	3,823	2,870	100	437	353
1963	2,194	150	967	3,981	2,987	98	479	352
1964	2,159	227	1,030	4,289	3,218	96	528	346
1965	2,127	279	...	4,457	3,358	96	575	310

[a]Includes 1 parent or other adult relative in families in which the
requirements of at least 1 such adult were considered in determining
the amount of assistance.
[b]Partly estimated; excludes Idaho, Indiana, and Nebraska, for lack of
data. The number of recipients in 1960 was 1.2 million; in October,
1965, 630,000.

FIGURE XVI.5

PUBLIC ASSISTANCE RECIPIENTS, BY PROGRAM, 1960-65

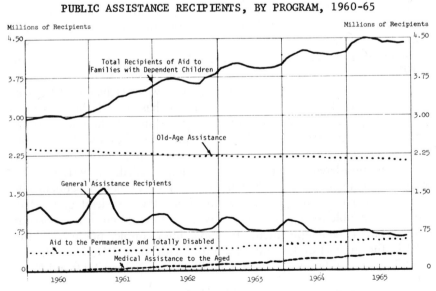

U.S. Department of Health, Education, and Welfare, Welfare Administration

XVI.5). There is also a great variation by state and county in both the rate of families with dependent children per 1,000 population and in the amount of monthly benefit. West Virginia has the highest average rate, 123 per 1,000 population, but some of its counties have a much higher rate. Even California, with a rate of 59, has large areas within the state with rates as high as in West Virginia. The lowest state rate is in New Hampshire. On the other hand, because of their lower economic conditions, states with highest rates of needy children provide lowest monthly payments.

More than half a million of permanently and totally disabled and almost 100,000 blind persons also obtain assistance under the Federally aided public-assistance program. Beyond this, the states themselves finance help to other needy persons, such as the temporarily or partially disabled. In 1936, they took care of 1.5 million cases where additional help was needed, but as the entire program of social security expanded more and more, the number of cases for general assistance has been steadily declining; in 1965, it was one-fifth of the initial number.

In December, 1964, the national average monthly payment was $79 for old-age assistance, $34 per recipient for families with dependent children, $86 for the blind, $81 for the disabled, and $195 for medical assistance to the aged. For individual states, these averages ranged widely: in old-age assistance, from $39 in Mississippi to $111 in Wisconsin; in aid to families with dependent children, from $10 per recipient in Mississippi to $52 in Minnesota; in aid for the blind, from $45 in Mississippi and $48 in West Virginia to $135 in California and $136 in Massachusetts; in aid to the disabled, from $43 in Mississippi and $46 in Alabama to $127 in New York, $160 in Massachusetts, and $132 in Hawaii; in medical assistance for the aged, from $25 in Kentucky to $366 in Michigan and $383 in Illinois.

TABLE XVI.10

EXPENDITURES PER INHABITANT FOR ALL TYPES OF
PUBLIC ASSISTANCE, BY STATE, 1964
(In Dollars and Cents)

Oklahoma	59.83	Mississippi	23.65	District of Columbia	18.69
Louisiana	51.46	Connecticut	23.43	Nevada	18.20
Colorado	43.51	Michigan	23.42	Arizona	18.08
California	41.01	Georgia	23.04	North Carolina	17.69
Massachusetts	35.23	Kansas	22.95	Alaska	17.41
Washington	34.01	Vermont	22.65	Florida	16.64
Alabama	32.66	North Dakota	22.48	Wyoming	16.46
Missouri	31.23	Texas	21.52	Hawaii	16.44
West Virginia	30.83	Oregon	20.92	New Hampshire	15.79
Arkansas	30.34	Utah	20.89	Tennessee	15.29
New York	29.34	Iowa	20.81	New Jersey	15.12
Minnesota	29.11	Pennsylvania	20.73	Nebraska	15.00
Illinois	26.06	Ohio	20.36	Maryland	14.35
Maine	25.87	Montana	20.24	South Carolina	12.37
New Mexico	25.60	Idaho	19.86	Delaware	11.18
Rhode Island	24.94	Wisconsin	19.28	Indiana	8.53
Kentucky	24.43	South Dakota	18.98	Virginia	7.05

FIGURE XVI.6

PUBLIC ASSISTANCE PAYMENTS PER INHABITANT, BY STATE, 1964

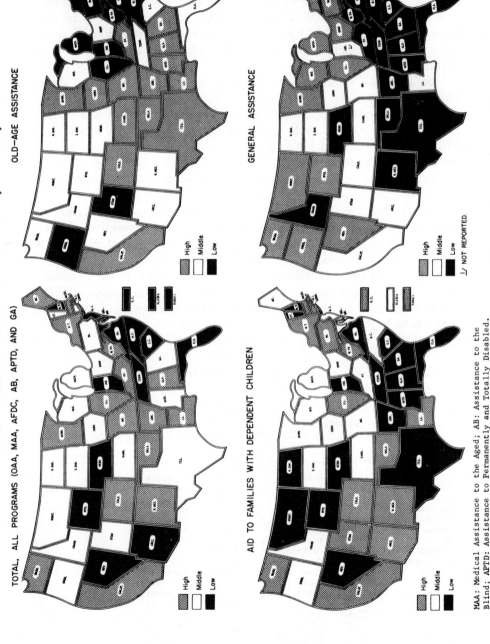

TOTAL, ALL PROGRAMS (OAA, MAA, AFDC, AB, APTD, AND GA)

OLD-AGE ASSISTANCE

GENERAL ASSISTANCE

AID TO FAMILIES WITH DEPENDENT CHILDREN

High
Middle
Low
1/ NOT REPORTED.

MAA: Medical Assistance to the Aged; AB: Assistance to the
Blind; APTD: Assistance to Permanently and Totally Disabled.
U.S. Department of Health, Education, and Welfare, Welfare

The pattern looks even more motley when the states are considered in terms of the amount expended per inhabitant in the total public-assistance program. The per capita amount depends not only on the state's affluence or poverty and its policies but also the composition of the population by race, age, place of residence, and various other factors. While the national average for the fiscal year ending June 30, 1964, was $25 per capita, the state averages ranged from $7.05 in Virginia to $59.83 in Oklahoma (see Table XVI.10). Figure XVI.6 shows the distribution of states by the amount spent per inhabitant for all assistance programs as a whole and for 3 types of assistance: old-age assistance (OAA), aid to families with dependent children (AFDC), and general assistance (GA).

93. Medical Care

No provisions for meeting medical costs of aid to the needy were included in the Social Security Act of 1935. However, if the states introduced the costs of medical care into the monthly payments for old-age assistance, or aid to the blind, or to dependent children, they could count on the Federal Government to share the costs within the limits of the Federal maximum for assistance payments. Still, when Federal participation was extended in 1939, 1946, and 1948, the financial help for medical care remained limited, and, as in other programs, it greatly varied among the states and even among counties of the same state.

In 1950, the amount of Federal funds for medical care available to the states was increased and payments directly to suppliers of such services (so-called vendor payments) were included. Medical care was also made available to the recipients of aid for the permanently and totally disabled. However, these vendor payments had to remain within the Federal maximum as it existed then. In the following years, the Federal share of medical-care costs increased; then, in 1960, a new type of assistance—medical assistance for the aged—was established to support states in helping aged people who have enough income to meet their ordinary expenses but cannot cover their medical expenses. In that program, the Federal Government was to share with states in the total cost of the program, without limitations either on the individual payment or total state expenditures. This program (under the Kerr-Mills legislation) developed rather slowly; by January, 1965, 44 jurisdictions (in 40 states, the District of Columbia, Guam, Puerto Rico, and the Virgin Islands) established varying services. About one-fifth of the aged population live in the jurisdictions that have this program, but because of variations in coverage and scope of benefits, about three-fifths of total expenditures were made in only 3 states.

Finally, in July, 1965, 2 major new contributory national health-insurance programs for the aged were enacted, along with an expanded Kerr-Mills medical-assistance program of Federal grants to states for greater medical help to the needy aged, blind, and disabled and to needy dependent children. The 3-layer system of health benefits is as follows:

(1) A *basic hospital* insurance program (with post-hospital extended care, home health services, and outpatient hospital diagnostic services) for persons aged 65 and over, financed through tax contributions to hospital insurance paid by employers, employees, and the self-employed.

(2) A *supplementary voluntary* health insurance program for the aged 65 and over, financed equally by the individual and by the treasury from general revenues. This program includes physicians' services in and out of hospital and some additional services not covered by the basic program (radiation therapy, ambulance services, psychiatric treatment, diagnostic tests, etc.).

(3) A *liberalized medical-assistance* program of Federal grants to help the states extend a Kerr-Mills–type medical assistance program to all recipients of Federally aided public-assistance programs and individuals and families who would, if needy, qualify for assistance under these programs.

According to the estimate of the Bill H.R. 6675 for medical care, 18.7 million persons would be eligible for hospital insurance on July 1, 1966, when this program becomes effective: 16.7 million persons aged 65 and over already eligible for social security or railroad retirement, and about 2 million additional persons who were aged 65 and over or would reach age 65 within the next few years, but for whom the cost would be paid from general revenues. A completely separate Hospital Insurance Trust Fund has been established, and all the payments of the Hospital Insurance tax must go to the Fund. Employers, employees, and self-employed persons each contribute the following percentages of taxable income up to $6,600: in 1966, 0.35; 1967–72, 0.5; 1973–75, 0.55; 1976–79, 0.6; 1980–86, 0.7; 1987 and after, 0.8. The combined rate for social-security and hospital insurance starts with 4.2 per cent each for the employers and employees on earnings up to $6,600, effective January 1, 1966, and the eventual maximum rate would be 5.65 per cent each in 1987 and after. The contribution rate for the self-employed will increase from the current 5.4 per cent to 7.8 per cent in 1987 and after. The basic hospital plan covers up to 90 days of hospital care for each duration of illness; the patient pays $40 deductible and $10 a day after the first 60 days.

Individuals who elect to join the supplementary health-insurance plan must pay a monthly premium of $3.00, deductible when possible from the benefits (of social security, railroad retirement, or civil-service retirement). The Federal Government will contribute an equal amount out of general revenues. This program is intended to be completely self-supporting from the contributions of insured individuals and the treasury. The premium rate is subject to change from time to time, in order to maintain the actuarial soundness of the system. The year 1968 has been selected for the first check to ascertain if adjustment of the premium is necessary. A separate Federal Supplementary Insurance Benefits Trust Fund has been established for the voluntary program; monthly premiums will flow to this Fund and the supplementary benefits will be paid out of it.

Much, however, will depend on the rate of participation, and the cost estimates for the program have been prepared on 2 bases—an assumed 80 per cent participation and a 95 per cent participation, both accepting that all state public-assistance agencies will "buy in" for their old-age assistance recipients. Only if participation should be at a very low level would the per capita cost rise substantially. Another consequential element is the benefit cost. Experience will indicate the need for changes, if any, and the soundness of the system as such.

By this program, the United States has taken a great step toward health insurance as it has existed in many industrial countries for a long time, for instance, in Germany before the end of the nineteenth century. Like other social security programs, this new program will undoubtedly contribute to the economic and social stability of our system. Like them, it will experience many difficulties and face many problems in the beginning of its operation but, as happened with the other programs, it will weather the difficulties and become a part of the American scene, of the "American way of life."

XVII. *The American Economy in an Age of Science and Technology*

Science and technology are the lifeblood of today's economy. Even the old, traditional industries, such as the textile or food industries, have been drawn into the stream of new processes, new materials, new equipment, while the young, dynamic, science-oriented industries are eager carriers of the electronics revolution. In the interest of defense and national security, the Federal Government, too, has become deeply involved in economic programs and projects of the highest scientific and technical sophistication.

94. *Science, Industry, Government*

Within the last 2 decades, science and technology have reached an unprecedented position in the nation's life and economy. They have made almost obsolete the traditional prerequisites for the location of an industry, such as the proximity to coal fields, or iron deposits, or water resources— or even markets. New products—plastics, electronics, antibiotics, synthetic rubber and diamonds, transistors, computers—can be produced almost anywhere. What is needed is scientific knowledge and technical skills; and human beings, unlike mineral deposits, are mobile. Thousands upon thousands of people work now in industrial plants making products unknown before World War II. Others work in laboratories searching for new knowledge about nature, without commitment to a specific need, or acquiring know-how and establishing a new process or a new apparatus for a given practical problem, or in special engineering complexes or plants where prototypes for new products are prepared. Some invent and make tools without which the prototypes cannot be produced; still others make and test the prototypes again and again, until they become operational. For example, until recently, assembly-line methods and mass production have characterized the aircraft and missile industry. Now its main feature is production of a small number of a large variety of highly complex flight and related devices, with strong emphasis on research and engineering. Sometimes success in producing some intricate mechanism depends on stored knowledge in related branches of technology or science. Specialized facilities are built for manufacturing procedures to stimulate environmental conditions for testing.

The increasing association of industrial production with advanced science and technology is one side of the story; the other is the impact of the Federal participation in scientific research and engineering on both private educational institutions and profit-making organizations. This impact has grown with the growth of the Federal program, from some $74 million in 1940 to more than $15 billion in 1965 (see Sec. 95).

Industrial research as such is not new in the United States. Several industries, especially the chemical and electrical-products industries, have a relatively long history of reliance on basic and applied science (see Sec. 53, Sec. 62, and Sec. 64). The chemical industry, for instance, had established its first laboratories by the turn of this century. Other industries likewise built research laboratories; these grew by the hundreds, and before World War II numbered several thousand. The last 2 or 3 decades have been especially productive: a host of new commodities has invaded the market—synthetics, antibiotics, plastics, detergents, insecticides, etc.

Nor have sciences been a stranger to the government in the United States, particularly the natural sciences—meteorology, oceanography, biology, etc. The Naval Observatory, U.S. Geological Survey, Bureau of Standards, Weather Bureau, experimental agricultural stations, Bureau of the Census, National Institute of Health, and other facilities speak for the long-standing association between the Federal Government and science.

Nevertheless, industry, government, and science in the past were strictly separate worlds. When industry turned to scientific research, it was for the purpose of finding commercially profitable processes or products; when universities expanded their laboratories or created new ones, it was in search of new knowledge. Today, business and universities work with the government, often as a team, usually on a contractual basis or grant. This close association of the 3 pillars of national life—largely in defense and space programs but also for peacetime national goals such as desalination of ocean water, conquest of cancer, utilization of nuclear energy, etc. —is a new and distinct feature, as is the undisputed predominance of technology in our economy. Never before has there been such massive concentration of all knowledge and skills, such a marshaling of all efforts and resources by industry and educational institutions, under the leadership of the Federal Government, on tasks of ultimate national importance. If the technological changes in the national economy can be considered a "new industrial revolution," as some economists call it, it differs from the Industrial Revolution of the past in being an *organized* revolution.

This revolution was born during World War II when this country realized that to overcome the technical advantages of the German blitz-krieg (with its submarines, rockets, and V-2's), much of the counterthrust had to come from science and technology: from the most potent catalyst of all—the human brain. The reason was simple: in the words of the National Academy of Sciences, "Europe, for the first time in American history, could no longer be relied upon to send over a sufficient stream of basic research results relevant to the rapidly changing frontiers of science and technology." Contemplating the wreck of Western Europe, Vannevar Bush, too, reported to President Roosevelt that "we cannot any longer depend upon Europe as a major source of . . . scientific capital." Fortunately for the United States in a time of national emergency, it still had help from outstanding European scientists who found themselves here for political reasons. As the National Academy of Science recognized: "But for the stimulus to American science created directly and indirectly by the inflow of refugees from Europe in the 1930's, it would not have been possible for us to do all that we did do during the war."

If the war and postwar achievements of American technology and science—nuclear power, radar, sonar, proximity fuses, antibiotics, masers and lasers, and many others—could have lulled this nation to complacency and overconfidence, Sputnik saved it from this error. From the day of Sputnik's appearance in the sky, organized efforts to gain leadership in the military field and aerospace began in earnest. Somehow the nation sensed, even if vaguely, that in our age of science, knowledge and technical skills are its greatest assets, even more important than its abundant natural resources.

These new activities, so-called research and development (currently abbreviated to R&D), comprise a great array of scientific and engineering fields: (*a*) *basic research*, which seeks to enlarge the body of knowledge of nature and man for its own sake, regardless of whether it would offer opportunities for practical utilization; (*b*) *applied research*, directed toward practical application of knowledge for specific commercial objectives; (*c*) *development*, the use of existing knowledge for the production of new materials, devices, systems, and methods, including the design and development of prototypes and processes. Though admittedly it is often difficult to distinguish where basic research ends and applied research begins, these definitions suggested by the National Science Foundation (NSF) have been widely accepted and used.

Created in 1950, the NSF, a government agency, supports research on a broad spectrum—in atmospheric sciences, high-energy physics, biology, and many other fields. In its surveys of R&D, begun in 1953, the NSF divides activities in research and development into 4 sectors: the Federal Government; industry; colleges and universities; and other nonprofit institutions (private research institutes, philanthropic research foundations, voluntary health organizations, etc.). The NSF examines the work of these 4 sectors from the following points of view: the type of activities performed (basic research, applied research, development, or mixed work); the sources that supply the funds for R&D; and the scientific and technical manpower used. Each of the 4 R&D sectors performs a different kind of work.

Major R&D efforts of the Federal Government have been concentrated in 3 areas—military, space, and nuclear power. Projects and tasks have been many, most of them of the highest technical complexity and novelty, such as antiballistic missiles, high-thrust boosters in space, missile-carrying submarines, means of communication over interplanetary distances, nuclear generation of power, human reaction to space flights, effect of nuclear radiation on living organisms, etc. Part of the R&D work has been performed intramurally—in government installations staffed by Federal personnel and in specially built Federal centers—while some has been administered by industrial firms and others by educational institutions, but removed from campuses and employing their own personnel; and other work has been done by plants for engineering experimentation and testing. But a much larger part of R&D work (and funds) has been transferred to industrial enterprises, and another, much smaller, part to educational institutions.

The great expansion of R&D has resulted in a huge increase of scientific and technical information. To collect and disseminate it, the Federal agencies have set up 250 information centers in addition to their regular facilities. Since to be cognizant of scientific and technical activities abroad is of the highest importance, various agencies have representatives stationed in foreign countries for this purpose. The allocation for these informational activities was estimated to exceed $200 million in 1965—two-thirds to be used intramurally, the remainder outside government offices.

Industry's participation in R&D is largely in engineering work and in developing prototypes, new tools, and materials. Company funds cover a part of the expenditures, more in some industries than in others, but the bulk of the support comes from the Federal Government (see Sec. 95). Only a small percentage of total R&D expenditures of profit organizations goes for research; 4 per cent was used in 1963 for basic research, the smallest proportion in any of the 4 sectors of R&D (see Figure XVII.1).

Colleges and universities are the major performers of basic research in this country, and the Federal Government is their major supporter in R&D work. They include agricultural experiment stations and associated schools of agriculture, and Federal research contract centers administered by them.

The last sector—other nonprofit institutions and private foundations—

FIGURE XVII.1

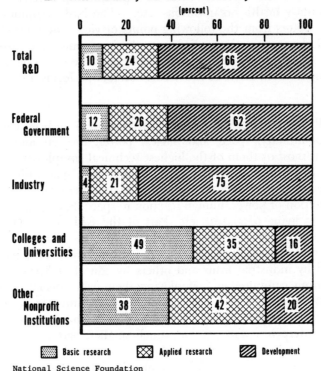

PERCENTAGE DISTRIBUTION OF FUNDS USED FOR
PERFORMANCE OF RESEARCH AND DEVELOPMENT
IN EACH SECTOR, BY TYPE OF WORK, 1963

National Science Foundation

pioneered in the past in supporting research and science by institutional grants and appropriations for individual projects. At times, they operated on the international scene and originated and led projects on a scale more appropriate for governmental or even international action, such as the world fight against yellow fever or hookworm. Today their financial contribution is overshadowed by the billions of dollars flowing from the Federal sources, but they retain their link with colleges and universities and are engaged predominantly in research.

The United States is not alone in the determined effort to raise the scientific and technical level of the national economy to new heights. In Western Europe, Japan, Canada, and other industrial countries there is evidence of rapid progress in both directions, and of concern for research and development, particularly in areas associated with defense. It is hardly necessary to mention Soviet Russia's mobilization of all its scientific and technical resources in sponsoring military and space industries.

In the United Kingdom, expenditures for R&D, when expressed as a percentage of gross national product, are closer to the ratio in the United States than to those of any other Western European country. Japan is developing its science-based industries forcefully; France is concentrating on nuclear programs. In most countries, the government finances R&D to a considerable degree, directing the bulk of the funds to industry for projects on a contractual basis. However, the proportion of funds provided by the governments for basic research is higher in most European countries than in the United States. It is estimated that worldwide expenditures for research and development, including the United States, Canada, Japan, Western Europe, and the U.S.S.R., may exceed $32–$35 billion a year; some seven-tenths of that amount may be spent in industry.

At official exchange rates, the United States spends about 4 times as much on R&D as Western Europe as a whole, and possibly as much as the U.S.S.R. But the Organization for Economic Cooperation and Development (OECD) uses a "research-exchange rate," instead of currency-exchange rate, for effective expenditure comparisons, to take account of the big differences in R&D costs between countries. In a special study on R&D in various countries, the OECD weighted many factors affecting the costs of R&D, such as personnel costs, costs of equipment, of operating and administering the laboratories, size and quality of research manpower, etc. At the OECD research-exchange rate, the United States spends about 2½ times as much as Western Europe taken as a whole, and perhaps only 20 per cent more than the U.S.S.R. About 60 per cent of this country's expenditure on R&D is for military and space research, as compared with 33 per cent in Western Europe.

95. Who Finances Research and Development?

According to more or less complete data on funds spent for R&D in this country from the beginning of World War II until 1953, when the National Science Foundation started its surveys, the Federal Government provided about $14.5 billion; industry, some $10 billion; and colleges and universities, about $0.5 billion—in all, a cumulative total of about $25 billion in a 12-year period.

Between 1953 and 1963, this country spent almost $120 billion on these activities: the Federal Government contributed $74.6 billion; industry, $41.8 billion; colleges and universities, about $2.1 billion; and other non-profit institutions, somewhat more than $1 billion (see Table XVII.1).

Data for 1964–67 are available only for the Federal Government, in the administrative budgets for the fiscal years 1966 and 1967: about $60 billion in these 4 years. On the assumption that industry and the 2 other nonprofit sectors would allocate about the same amounts for each of these years as they did in 1963, their shares can be roughly estimated at $22.3 billion, $1 billion, and $0.7 billion, respectively—in all, approximately $24 billion.

Thus, total national expenditures for R&D between 1940 and 1967 may

TABLE XVII.1

SOURCES OF FUNDS USED FOR RESEARCH AND DEVELOPMENT IN THE
UNITED STATES, BY SECTOR, 1940-63
(In Millions of Dollars)

Year	Total Cumulative	Total Annual	Federal Government	Industry	Colleges and Universities	Other Non-profit Organizations
1940-41	900	900	370	510	20	...
1941-42	1,970	1,070	490	560	20	...
1942-43	3,180	1,210	780	410	20	...
1943-44	4,560	1,380	940	420	20	...
1944-45	6,080	1,520	1,070	430	20	...
1945-46	7,860	1,780	910	840	30	...
1946-47	10,120	2,260	1,160	1,050	50	...
1947-48	12,730	2,610	1,390	1,150	70	...
1948-49	15,340	2,610	1,550	990	70	...
1949-50	18,210	2,870	1,610	1,180	80	...
1950-51	21,570	3,360	1,980	1,300	80	...
1951-52	25,320	3,750	2,240	1,430	80	...
1953	5,160	5,160	2,760	2,240	120	40
1954	10,820	5,660	3,120	2,365	130	45
1955	17,020	6,200	3,500	2,510	140	50
1956	25,390	8,370	4,820	3,330	155	65
1957	35,200	9,810	6,105	3,455	180	70
1958	46,010	10,810	6,840	3,700	190	80
1959	58,440	12,430	8,070	4,070	190	100
1960	72,060	13,620	8,770	4,540	200	110
1961	86,440	14,380	9,220	4,810	210	140
1962[a]	102,050	15,610	10,045	5,175	230	160
1963[a]	119,400	17,350	11,340	5,565	260	185

[a]Preliminary reports by the National Science Foundation, May, 1965.

TABLE XVII.2

FUNDS USED FOR RESEARCH AND DEVELOPMENT BY EACH PERFORMANCE SECTOR,
DISTRIBUTED BY SOURCE, 1953-63
(In Millions of Dollars)

	1953	1956	1959	1960	1961	1962[b]	1963[b]
Federal Government	1,010	1,090	1,730	1,830	1,890	2,220	2,400
Industry	3,630	6,610	9,620	10,510	10,910	11,540	12,720
Federal funds	1,430	3,330	5,640	6,080	6,240	6,520	7,340
Industry funds	2,200	3,280	3,980	4,430	4,670	5,020	5,380
Colleges and universities	420	530	840	1,000	1,200	1,400	1,700
Federal funds	260	330	570	720	890	1,050	1,300
Industry funds	20	20	40	40	50	55	65
College and university funds[a]	120	155	190	200	210	230	260
Other nonprofit institutions funds[a]	20	25	40	40	50	65	75
Other nonprofit institutions	100	140	240	280	380	450	530
Federal funds	60	70	130	140	200	255	300
Industry funds	20	30	50	70	90	100	120
Other nonprofit institutions[a]	20	40	60	70	90	95	110
Total funds used	5,160	8,370	12,430	13,620	14,380	15,610	17,350

[a]Includes state and local funds.
[b]Preliminary.

FIGURE XVII.2

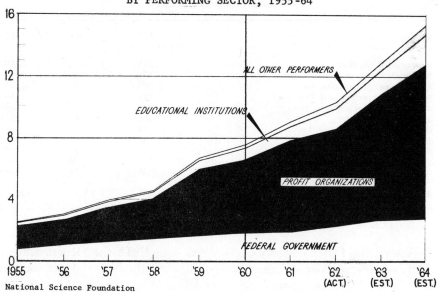

FEDERAL OBLIGATIONS FOR R&D FUNDS,
BY PERFORMING SECTOR, 1955-64

National Science Foundation

approach $229 billion: $149 billion by the Federal Government; more than
$74 billion by industry; $3.6 billion by colleges and universities; and $1.7
billion by other nonprofit institutions.

The Federal Government is the major source of funds for R&D. Its
allocations for these purposes have been growing uninterruptedly, except
for a short period of demobilization when all Federal expenditures dropped
drastically, from $95 billion in 1945 to $33 billion in 1948. As a percentage of the total Federal budget, expenditures for R&D rose from 0.8
per cent in 1940 to 1.6 per cent in 1945, 4.2 per cent in 1953, and 10.1
per cent in 1960, and are estimated to exceed 15 per cent in 1964–66.

The Federal Government provides two-thirds of all R&D funds ($11.4
billion out of $17.4 billion in 1963); industry as a whole, nearly one-third
($5.5 billion); and educational and other nonprofit institutions together,
the remaining part ($445 million) (see Table XVII.2). Out of its budget
for this purpose, the Federal Government uses about one-fifth for intramural work, and transfers two-thirds to profit organizations, one-tenth to
colleges and universities, and the small remainder to other nonprofit institutions. The lion's share of Federal money is directed toward engineering work—in 1964, some $9.3 billion out of $15.1 billion, or about six-tenths
—and this work is largely performed by industrial firms on a contractual
basis. The remainder is used for research, and appropriations for it are
divided between applied and basic research in a ratio of approximately 2 to
1, with deviations in both directions (see Figure XVII.2).

TABLE XVII.3

DISTRIBUTION OF FEDERAL FUNDS FOR R&D, BY AGENCY,
1964-66
(In Millions of Dollars)

Agency	1964	1965	1966
Department of Defense	7,516	7,222	6,880
National Aeronautics and Space Administration[a]	4,171	4,900	5,100
Atomic Energy Commission	1,503	1,569	1,556
Health, Education and Welfare	791	805	942
National Science Foundation	197	208	266
Agriculture	182	236	256
Commerce	71	89	91
Interior	98	116	129
Aviation	70	105	81
Veterans Administration	36	43	46
Other	39	63	97
TOTAL	14,674	15,355	15,445

[a]Total NASA funds are considered R&D

Among the Federal agencies connected with R&D, the Department of
Defense towers above all others; next in line are the National Aeronautics
and Space Administration (NASA) and the Atomic Energy Commission
(AEC). These three agencies together account for some 90 per cent of
total Federal funds for R&D. The Department of Health, Education, and
Welfare (HEW) obtains about 5 per cent of the total, mainly for medical
and health-related research (four-fifths of it goes to the National Institute
of Health). The NSF, the Departments of Agriculture and Interior, and

TABLE XVII.4

FEDERAL FUNDS OBLIGATED FOR RESEARCH AND DEVELOPMENT,[a] 1959-64
(In Millions of Dollars)

	1959	1960	1962	1963	1964
Total	6,468	7,358	10,046	12,723	15,081
Basic research	484	585	1,085	1,395	1,782
Applied research	906	1,342	1,892	2,850	4,003
Development	5,078	5,431	7,069	8,478	9,296
Total research	1,390	1,927	2,977	4,245	5,785
Life sciences: biological	88	106	152	205	266
medical	268	342	598	740	841
agricultural	64	68	71	76	86
Psychological sciences	24	38	56	67	97
Physical science proper	288	421	988	1,249	1,537
Mathematics	16	24	69	117	168
Engineering	461	861	830	1,565	2,570
Social sciences	31	35	62	72	106
Other sciences	150	33	151	155	113

[a]Federal expenditures differ from obligations in any given year, because not all
funds obligated are expended during that year.

TABLE XVII.5

SOURCE OF FUNDS SPENT BY INDUSTRY IN PERFORMING R&D, 1953-63
(In Millions of Dollars)

Year	Total	Federal Government	Company
1953	3,630	1,430	2,200
1954	4,070	1,750	2,320
1955	4,640	2,180	2,460
1956	6,610	3,330	3,280
1957	7,730	4,330	3,400
1958	8,390	4,760	3,630
1959	9,620	5,640	3,980
1960	10,510	6,080	4,430
1961	10,910	6,240	4,670
1962[a]	11,540	6,520	5,020
1963[a]	12,720	7,340	5,380

[a]Preliminary reports by the National Science Foundation, May, 1965.

all other agencies share the remaining small percentage, as shown in the administrative budget of the Federal Government (see Table XVII.3).

Under "other expenditures" are included small allocations for foreign performers of R&D. Such funds come partly from regular appropriations to agencies but also from funds provided by Public Law 480, that is, from excess currencies obtained from the sales of our surplus commodities in various countries. Europe is the primary recipient of support to foreign performers for R&D, with the major portion going to the United Kingdom from the Department of Defense. The largest receivers in Asia are India and Japan. Israel receives a substantial part of the R&D funds destined for the Near East, mostly from the Departments of Agriculture and Health, Education, and Welfare.

Physical sciences, including engineering research, take the largest portion of Federal funds for research; life sciences get 20–25 per cent; and only crumbs are left for the social sciences, humanities, and other disciplines (see Table XVII.4).

While the Federal Government supplies the largest part of the cost of R&D, private industry does most of the work, to a great extent on Federal money. Federal funds for that purpose transferred to industry between 1953 and 1963 approached $50 billion (see Table XVII.5).

NSF surveys cover virtually the entire industrial sector of the economy; it is estimated that firms not covered account for less than 1 per cent of the nation's dollar volume of R&D.

In 1961, 11,800 companies were engaged in R&D activities, of which 10,300 were in manufacturing and 1,500 in nonmanufacturing.* Of these

* For this survey, the NSF classified crude petroleum and communication companies as manufacturing industries.

companies, only 359 and 32, respectively, were employing 5,000 or more persons; 9,200 and 1,400, respectively, had fewer than 1,000 employees; and the remaining companies were in the middle bracket, with 1,000–4,999 employees. The largest 391 companies accounted for 86 per cent of total R&D funds, and the smallest—9,200 manufacturing and 1,400 nonmanufacturing—for only 5 per cent. About the same relationship was valid for 1963, though there were some changes within both groups: 89 and 5 per cent, respectively. In some industries, including aircraft and missiles and some transportation-equipment industries, 96–97 per cent of the Federal funds for R&D performance were exhausted at the level of the largest companies in the classification above. Five industries—aircraft and missiles, electric equipment and communication, chemicals, motor vehicles, and machinery—accounted for 84 per cent of the total for R&D performance by industry as a whole.

The rationale of this extreme concentration of R&D industrial activities has been that the largest companies possess more modern and better-equipped laboratories and installations, have outstanding scientific and technical personnel, are generally more dependable as to terms and quality of performance, etc. However, many independent scientists and engineers question the superiority of big companies and affirm that reliable small industrial companies have many advantages in using less time, money, and manpower per individual project than do larger establishments, and in attracting specialists with inventive minds who feel freer in smaller plants.*

In all, 11.3 million employees were in companies performing R&D as of March, 1961, divided by size of company as follows: 7.9 million in companies with 5,000 employees or more; 1.9 million in middle-sized companies; and 1.4 million in those with fewer than 1,000 employees. On the average, total R&D funds per employee amounted to $970, while company-financed R&D costs were $410. For the largest companies, the corresponding expenditures were $1,180 and $470; for middle-sized companies, $490 and $310; data for smallest companies are incomplete.

A similar relationship appears with regard to R&D annual performance costs per scientist or engineer: the largest companies report average costs of $38,200; middle-sized companies, $26,100; and small companies, $18,000. Of course, costs vary from industry to industry: the highest costs, of the largest companies in the aircraft and missile industry, reached $45,000, as contrasted with the lowest, $14,900, in the paper, wood, and furniture industries; in between are chemicals, petroleum refining and extraction, primary metals, machinery, and electrical equipment and communication, with costs per R&D scientists or engineer ranging from $34,000 to $36,000 per year.

* These and similar assertions have been emphasized in the hearings of various Congressional committees (on Small Business and on Antitrust and Monopoly, for example).

TABLE XVII.6

DISTRIBUTION OF FEDERAL GOVERNMENT AND INDUSTRY FUNDS FOR R&D,
BY INDUSTRY GROUP, 1963
(In Millions of Dollars)

Industry Group	Total	Federal Government	Company
Food and kindred products	135	a	a
Textiles and apparel	34	2	32
Lumber, wood products, furniture	a	a	a
Paper and allied products	71	-	71
Chemicals and allied products	1,253	264	989
Petroleum refining and extraction	315	20	295
Rubber products	146	39	107
Stone, clay, glass products	122	a	a
Primary metals	191	12	179
Fabricated metal products	162	29	133
Machinery	977	264	713
Electrical equipment and communication	2,483	1,562	921
Motor vehicles, other transportation equipment	1,103	289	814
Aircraft and missiles	4,835	4,371	464
Professional and scientific instruments	497	232	265
Other industries	388	a	a
TOTAL	12,723	7,345	5,378

[a]Not separately available but included in total.

Generally speaking, industries which place relatively greater emphasis on research have lower R&D costs per scientist or engineer than those engaged primarily in development projects. In industries of the former type, the largest expense is normally for the payroll of the personnel: development projects, on the other hand, require large supporting manpower, expensive testing and other equipment, and usually have high overhead expenses.

Company-financed R&D is naturally concentrated in the largest companies, which account for 80 per cent of all company funds; middle-sized companies account for 13 per cent and the small enterprises, with less than 1,000 employees, for 7 per cent. While Federal funds predominate in industries connected with defense and space, some peacetime industries, including paper and allied products and petroleum refining and extraction, carry on research and development largely with company funds (see Table XVII.6).

While the Federal Government financed nearly three-fifths of R&D performed by industry as a whole, only aircraft and missiles and electric equipment and communication had the lion's share of their R&D performance supported by Federal funds in 1957–63 (90 per cent in aircraft and missiles in 1963). However, in 1963, funds of the industry producing scientific instruments exceeded Federal Funds.

The home of basic research is in the colleges and universities. They devote 80–85 per cent of their own R&D funds for it, using the remainder

FIGURE XVII.3

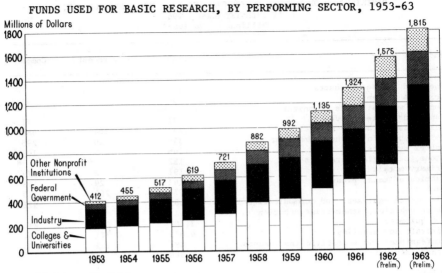

FUNDS USED FOR BASIC RESEARCH, BY PERFORMING SECTOR, 1953-63

National Science Foundation

for applied research. Their major supporter is also the Federal Government, which, in 1963, contributed $1.3 billion, or about three-fourths of all funds at the disposal of these institutions for R&D. Of this Federal $1.3 billion, the allocation for basic research was $530 million; colleges and universities used $220 million of their own funds, industry added $30 million, and other nonprofit organizations supplied $60 million, bringing the universities' total for basic research to $840 million (including a small undetermined amount from state and local governments) (see Figure XVII.3).

On the national scale, basic research, with $1.8 billion, represented about 10 per cent of total R&D funds in 1963; applied research accounted for 24 per cent; and some 66 per cent was used for development. The Federal Government contracts many scientific projects with educational institutions, supports various research centers administered by universities, and facilitates training of new cadres of scientists and engineers by its grants, fellowships, and loans.

As is true for the largest industrial companies, the Federal Government tends to concentrate research tasks in a few universities and a few states. Of 2,000 colleges and universities in this country, of which 681 offer graduate courses, the top 100 received nearly 80 per cent of total Federal research funds for this sector, i.e., over $1.3 billion out of $1.7 billion in 1963. Ten institutions (University of California, Stanford, Harvard, MIT, Columbia, Cornell, and the Universities of Chicago, Michigan, and Minnesota) received 38 per cent. Concentration in a few states is even greater: California received 28.6 per cent of the Federal funds; Massachusetts, 11.7

per cent; and New York, 8.5 per cent—in all, 48.8 per cent for their 6 universities. In many institutions, Federal funds represent a very sizable part of their regular budget: in Stanford, Princeton, Johns Hopkins, and the University of Alaska, they account for almost half the budget; in some middle-sized institutions, Federal funds carry almost the entire research effort.

While the nation undoubtedly benefits from the substantial support of science by the Federal Government, the question has been raised in scholarly quarters whether the essential functions of colleges and universities— teaching and basic research—have not become somewhat overshadowed by the unusual and attractive opportunities to expand university research into promising new adventures. The Government and universities have entered into a new and unforeseen relationship. Only the future will show whether the university world will be strong enough to maintain the integrity of its main purpose under the shower of ever increasing Federal funds . . .

Compared with the 2 giants, the Federal Government and industry, the fourth sector in R&D—other nonprofit institutions—seems very small indeed. These institutions spend $75 million of their own funds on basic research and obtain $105 million for that purpose from the Federal Government and $20 million from industry, thus using $200 million in performing projects in basic research. Out of these funds, they also support basic research in colleges and universities and participate in national R&D activities.

In summary, it is worth noting that relative allocations of funds for basic research and for applied research and development over the past years have been fairly consistent, reflecting a certain internal adherence to priorities in national programs: funds allocated for the pursuit of knowledge amount to about one-half of those used for the development of materials, systems, and methods, or to one-third of total R&D expenditures. Thus out of the total R&D funds of $17,350 million in 1963, $5.9 billion was spent on research and $11.4 billion on development.

96. Scientific and Technical Personnel

Scientific and technical manpower represents only a small proportion of the nation's labor force, but it is one of the fastest growing occupational groups: while professional, technical, and kindred workers increased from 1.2 million in 1900 to 8.3 million in 1963, or some 7 times, the number of engineers increased within the same period from 41,000 to 950,000, or 23 times. The rate of increase for the scientists is even more impressive.

Data on scientific and technical manpower come from several sources, such as the censuses of population, the National Register of Scientific and Technical Personnel, the Civil Service Commission, BLS surveys conducted annually for the NSF, etc. While there now exists a substantial

TABLE XVII.7

NUMBER OF ENGINEERS AND SCIENTISTS IN THE UNITED STATES, 1930-63

Year	Total	Engineers	Scientists	Number of Workers per Engineer	Number of Engineers per 100,000
	(Figures Given in Thousands)				Civilian Labor Force
1930	263	217	46	230	436
1940	389	297	92	187	534
1950	713	543	170	116	861
1954	850	650	200	89	1,008
1960	1,185	850	335	83	1,204
1963	1,360	950	410	77	1,302

body of knowledge of various occupational groups within this broad universe, this chapter is primarily concerned with engineers and scientists and the technicians supporting their work—more specifically, with those of them who work on R&D.

The BLS surveys cover engineers and scientists engaged in R&D, as reported by their employers in private industry. Because of differences in definitions, concepts, time of inquiry, and methods used in obtaining the data, the results offered by various collecting agencies are not fully comparable. However, the over-all figures are not too far apart.

According to NSF, 263,000 engineers and scientists were employed in the United States in 1930; 713,000 in 1950; and 1,185,000 in 1960. Three years later, the number had increased to 1,365,000.

About 3 out of 4 engineers and every second scientist were employed in industry. Government was the second largest employer of engineers; colleges and universities, of scientists.

As the number of engineers in industrial enterprises increased, that of the industrial workers per engineer declined, while the rate of engineers per 100,000 civilian labor force was rising (see Table XVII.7).

In 1962, according to the BLS, 852,000 engineers and scientists worked in industrial establishments. Very small firms and self-employed persons were excluded from the survey. Of this industrial manpower, 685,000, or 80 per cent, were engineers; 136,000, or 16 per cent, physical scientists; and some 27,000, or 3 per cent, life scientists (biological, agricultural, and medical); about 5,000 were unclassified.

Industry as a whole employed 69 technicians for every 100 engineers and scientists, with the ratio ranging from 62 technicians in manufactures to 86 in nonmanufacturing industries. Ratios varied greatly from industry to industry: 25 technicians per 100 scientists in the drug and pharmaceutical industry, as compared with 98 per 100 in industries fabricating metal products. The high ratio of technicians to engineers and scientists in nonmanufacturing is largely due to the very high ratio in service industries, some of which report 120 technicians per 100 engineers. About three-fifths of all technicians in nonmanufacturing industries work in

FIGURE XVII.4

SCIENTISTS AND ENGINEERS EMPLOYED BY THE FEDERAL GOVERNMENT
IN R&D, BY AGENCY, OCTOBER, 1962

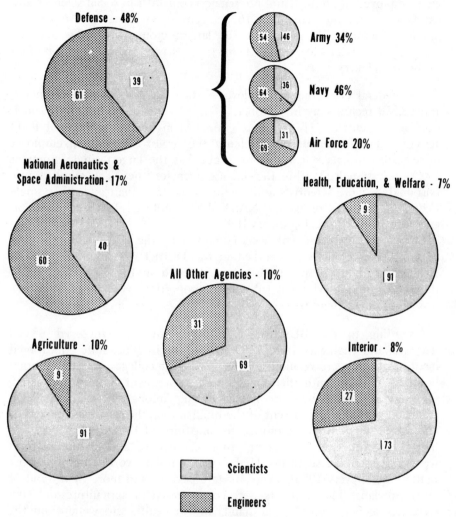

National Science Foundation and Civil Service Commission

engineering and architectural firms, under the supervision of architects, who are left out of the count.

The 1961 survey of colleges and universities revealed that they employed 176,000 scientists and engineers.* Faculty members represented over three-fifths of the total, and nonfaculty, almost one-fifth. Graduate students

* It is estimated that 5–10 per cent of personnel of this type were employed in institutions that did not answer the questionnaire.

working part-time accounted for one-fifth of the personnel; students who worked full time were counted with nonfaculty professional personnel. Scientists predominated among the faculty members; about two-thirds were employed in physical and life sciences, one-fifth in social sciences and psychology, and the remaining 16 per cent in engineering. Among the physical scientists, chemists were the largest group, while the so-called clinical scientists (M.D.'s and D.D.S.'s) represented the largest proportion in the life sciences.

The Federal Government employed 76,620 scientists, 67,500 engineers, and 93,350 technicians in October, 1962.* Nearly one-third of the engineers and scientists (51,000) were employed in Federal intramural R&D activities. The Department of Defense, the largest Government employer of scientific and technical personnel, also has the largest single group of R&D professionals. Within the defense agencies, the Navy employs proportionately more scientists and engineers in R&D than any other single Federal department or agency. NASA alone employed 9,000 scientists and engineers in R&D (see Figure XVII.4).

Of the scientists and engineers employed by the Federal Government in 1960, only 19 per cent worked in the District of Columbia. Almost 100,000, or about 70 per cent, were employed in the 50 states; several thousands, among whom a substantial proportion were social scientists, worked in foreign countries.

According to the BLS study, state governments employed 48,000 scientists and engineers and 55,500 technicians in 1962; state educational institutes, which are counted in the surveys of colleges and universities, hospitals affiliated with them, agricultural experiment stations and extension services, and others are not included. Among the engineers, civil engineers made up 88 per cent of the total; among the scientists, biologists, and agriculturists, each accounted for one-third of the group. More than half the technicians were engineering technicians, and about one-third were draftsmen and surveyors. Highways and public works employed more than 9 out of every 10 engineers on state payrolls and more than 8 out of 10 technicians. The scientists were concentrated in agriculture and conservation agencies, on the one hand, and in health and welfare, on the other: 54 and 36 per cent, respectively, of the total.

Nationwide data on the employment of engineers and scientists by local governments are not available. However, a pilot study of the BLS, conducted at the request of the NSF in 6 states (Connecticut, Pennsylvania, South Carolina, Wisconsin, Colorado, and Oregon) and covering almost 1,000 counties, municipalities, townships, and school and other special districts indicates that roughly 30,000 scientists and an equal number of engineers were employed by local governments in 1960.

* Data of the Civil Service Commission. Personnel of CIA and national security agencies omitted.

Nonprofit organizations employed 7,145 scientific and engineering personnel and about 2,000 technicians in 1960. By 1962, the number of scientists increased to 9,400.

The NSF has estimated the recent over-all trends in employment of R&D personnel in 1954, 1958, and 1961. It used the concept of full-time equivalent for part-time employees in R&D as an indicator of total manpower input. In 1961, the total number of engineers and scientists employed full-time in R&D was 411,000, as compared with 223,200 in 1954, an increase of 84 per cent (see Table XVII.8).

Because of the concern for the future requirements for scientific and technical manpower and its availability, various attempts have been made to estimate the long-run demand. The most recent estimate has been prepared by the BLS for the NSF. In its study, the BLS used the so-called "segmental method," i.e., a careful examination of employment

TABLE XVII.8

DISTRIBUTION OF FULL-TIME EQUIVALENT NUMBER OF R&D SCIENTISTS
AND ENGINEERS, 1954-61

Level of Employment	1954	1958	1961	Per Cent Increase 1954-61
TOTAL	223,200	326,200	411,100	84
Federal Government	29,500	40,400	44,500	51
Industry[a]	164,100	238,400	306,100	87
Colleges and universities	25,200	42,000	52,500	108
Other nonprofit institutions[b]	4,400	5,400	8,000	82

[a]Excludes social scientists and psychologists
[b]Includes professional R&D personnel employed at Federal contract research
centers administered by organizations in the sector.

trends for such manpower within each economic sector: each industrial segment in private industry, each level of government—Federal, state, and local—employing such personnel, and in colleges and universities and non-profit organizations. Certain assumptions were made with respect to general economic conditions, and census projections of the total population and other projections concerning the total labor force and the growth of the GNP were used. Various other methods were applied and intensive investigation conducted. The latest estimate based on the completed study on this country's total requirements in scientific and technical manpower in 1970 indicates a 10-year increase of almost 70 per cent in the number of needed scientists and engineers over 1960 levels, bringing the employment level of such personnel in 1970 to slightly under 2 million.

Definitions of "scientists" and "engineers" vary in different countries; in some, full academic qualifications are required for the designation of "engineer" and particularly "scientist"; in others, the difference between a "technician" and an "engineer," is rather vague. Another limiting factor in international comparisons of the size of manpower engaged in R&D is that some of the professionals working on R&D combine this work with other activities, while the majority do it as a full-time occupation. Despite these and various other difficulties in attempting to appraise the size of international manpower involved in work on R&D, the OECD study has ventured to make the estimate for Western Europe (United Kingdom, France, Germany, Belgium, and the Netherlands), the U.S.S.R., and the United States on the basis of available data. According to that estimate, more than 3 million professional people were engaged in this work in 1962: 1.2 million in the United States, 1.5 million in the U.S.S.R., and slightly more than half a million in Western Europe. No doubt considerable numbers are occupied with R&D in Japan and Canada; probably some work in this field is done in various other industrially developed countries. Also, the size of R&D manpower has increased since 1962 in the United States; it is reasonable to assume that this may have happened also in the U.S.S.R.

An interesting sideline feature of our scientific and engineering manpower is that it comprises a certain percentage of fresh immigrants from Europe, attracted by a greater allocation of resources to R&D, better laboratories, and higher salaries. The OECD study estimates that between 1955 and 1962, immigration of Western European engineers and scientists into the United States has been the equivalent of about 3 per cent of the U.S. new domestic supply of graduate scientists and engineers, or about 5.5 per cent of the Western European output.

97. Impact of Research and Development
Activities on the Nation's Economy

Research and development has become one of the most important industries in the United States; its product is knowledge. Though the value

TABLE XVII.9

R&D EXPENDITURES IN RELATION TO GROSS NATIONAL PRODUCT AND
TOTAL NATIONAL INVESTMENT, 1953-64

| Year | Gross National Product | Investment | | | R&D Expenditures | R&D as per cent of: | |
| | | Total | Government | Business | | GNP | National Investment |
		(In Billions of Dollars)					
1953	364.6	69.1	32.5	36.6	5.2	1.4	7.5
1954	364.8	63.1	29.6	33.5	5.7	1.6	9.0
1955	398.0	72.2	27.1	45.1	6.2	1.6	8.6
1956	419.2	79.3	29.6	49.7	8.4	2.0	10.6
1957	441.1	82.7	33.6	49.1	9.8	2.2	11.9
1958	447.3	72.7	34.7	38.6	10.8	2.4	14.9
1959	483.7	85.9	36.2	50.4	12.4	2.6	14.5
1960	503.8	84.4	33.7	50.7	13.6	2.7	16.1
1961	520.1	85.2	37.6	47.6	14.4	2.8	16.9
1962	560.3	94.2	38.6	55.6	15.6	2.8	16.6
1963	589.2	96.6	39.8	56.8	17.4	3.0	17.0
1964	628.7	101.6	39.9	61.7	19.0	3.0	18.7

FIGURE XVII.5

R&D IN THE UNITED STATES AS PER CENT OF
GROSS NATIONAL PRODUCT, 1958-63

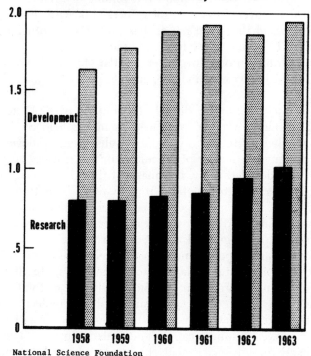

National Science Foundation

of this product is not as measurable as that of other industrial products and its goods and services are not sold in the market, the money spent on it sometimes yields future returns representing many times the initial outlays.

The importance of R&D in our economy can be measured by the relation of expenditures for it to the gross national product. While the GNP increased by 60 per cent between 1953 and 1963, R&D expenditures more than tripled; compared with the increase in GNP, they more than doubled during this period (see Table XVII.9 and Figure XVII.5).

In 1961, the NSF offered a yardstick for measuring the part of R&D in the national economy: the concept of a "total national investment," which consists of all gross domestic business investment, less residential construction, plus Government investment, i.e., Government purchases of durable goods and public construction. These items roughly conform to our concepts of capital formation. The argument is that since R&D may potentially stimulate new developments and activities, it promotes long-term production; in this sense, it performs the same function as investment and can be considered a capital expenditure. This attitude was forcefully expressed by Sumner H. Slichter at the Conference of the NSF on the impact of R&D on the economy: "In an age of research, the capacity of the economy to discover investment opportunities depends in the main (1) upon the fund of knowledge that has been accumulated and that is available to be drawn upon, and (2) upon the volume of resources devoted to the industry of discovery," as he called R&D. Likewise, Fritz Machlup, writing of R&D, said that "the nation has probably no other field of investment that yields results of [so high an] order."

In relation to total national investment, outlays for R&D represented 7.5 per cent in 1953, 14.9 per cent in 1958, and 18.7 per cent in 1964.

There is no way to measure directly the impact of R&D activities on the national economy. Much of this work is in the field of defense and space, and whether there is or will be a substantial spillover into the peacetime economy is a matter of speculation. Nevertheless, technological changes are the order of the day, and many of these have been inspired by the massive R&D effort to penetrate the mysteries of nature and create new dimensions of our knowledge, new approaches, new processes. Some spillover from defense and space work can already be observed.

The control system originated and perfected in the aerospace program is widely used in various peacetime industries. New instrumentation, computers, electronic processing of data, automatic devices, etc., have become a feature of the American economic scene. By the use of totally new techniques, new understanding has been gained of the molecular structure, which has fertilized the development of new materials for agriculture, textile industries, power, communication, and space industries. The discovery of biological activities of nucleic acid, the genetic material, has made possible the combined work of chemists and biologists on the gene at the molecular level. This work of great scientific and practical promise could not have been done without the government's assistance, because it requires extremely complex and expensive equipment of all kinds. On the industrial side, a considerable proportion of our exports of manufactures comes from the science-based industries, producing computers, specialized instruments, power-generating and data-processing equipment, new types of aircraft, etc. Measured by foreign payments of about half a billion dollars a year for royalties, licensing agreements, and management fees, the export of technical knowledge is more than 5 times the U.S. payments of this type to all other countries. The "technological balance of payments," as the OECD study calls the paid exchange of know-how from country to country, has been persistently in favor of the United States during the last decade. In electrical machinery and electronics, the U.S. receipts from Western European countries were 30 times as big as the payments to them; in other machinery, 22 times; in vehicles, 11 times; and in other transport equipment, 6 times. The lead of the United States is less marked in chemicals, particularly in exchange with Germany, famous for the high level of her chemical industry. Most Western European countries have a heavy and growing technological deficit with the United States: two-thirds of the total French deficit and half the total German deficit came from their buying American patents, licenses, and other forms of know-how.

The BLS study *Technological Trends in 36 Major American Industries* summarizes the extent to which new processes and new instrumentation have affected those industries. The electronics industry, the very symbol of the technological revolution, has expanded vigorously. The BLS expects that its shipments will nearly double in value between 1961 and 1970, from $10.8 billion to about $20 billion, in constant dollars of 1960. Despite the high degree of mechanization, this industry's employment is expected to grow from 778,000 in 1963 to more than 1 million by the end of the decade. Computers have revolutionized the engineering field, particularly the aerospace industry, where they made it possible to make thousands of test flights in simulated laboratories. In the electric-power industry, computers are standard equipment in the new plants and are being installed in old establishments. Production of synthetic fibers and rubber is completely computerized; the petroleum industry is striving toward that goal. The paper industry, printing and publishing, and even ice-cream manufacture have introduced computer control. Traffic in the sky is coming under that control. Banks, insurance companies, and other service establishments are also using computers. Thus the 1962 survey of the Federal Reserve, which covered 1,000 commercial banks, each with deposits of at least $25 million, found that 2 out of 5 either operated computers or were about to install them. The 1963 poll among smaller banks revealed that many were obtaining computer services from other banks or special bureaus or through cooperative arrangements. On June 30, 1963, the Federal Government had 1,248 computers, not counting those used in certain areas of the Department of Defense. The Budget Bureau expected that the number might reach 2,100 by June 30, 1966. In the meantime, computers themselves have grown in complexity and power; the latest models are several times faster than the earlier computers. It is estimated that about 25,000 computers are being used, and additional thousands are on order.

On the other hand, many innovations have come from the science-oriented peacetime economy. The invention of transistors not only led to the establishment of a transistor industry but also affected all industries producing and using electronic equipment. In the drug industry, roughly seven-tenths of current sales are made from products which did not exist only a decade ago.

The list of technological changes in the American economy can be prolonged, but it is important to bear in mind that it may be too early to evaluate all the effects of R&D on the national economy, some beneficial, others adverse. Many questions need study, such as the effect of automation on employment, of the not always effective utilization of the not inexhaustible supply of scientific and technical manpower, of insufficient support of basic research, of the reasons why the spillover from the military uses of new processes and products is slower now than it was after the world wars. These and many other questions are beyond the field of this study, but some conclusions on the new industry in the United States —research and development—and its product, knowledge, seem appropriate here:

1. Whether government and private funds are always spent efficiently, the fact remains that never before has this country made so great an investment in human resources, in increasing the cadres of scientific and technical manpower, and in upgrading its labor force.

2. Concomitant with this fact has been this country's strengthened awareness of the importance of science and technology for national security, for its leadership position in the world, for its own well-being and its people, for its industrial and commercial success.

3. Research and development have become institutionalized as a part of the national scene and an unquestioned part of government activity.

4. The body of knowledge in various sciences has been enormously expanded, in many fields beyond human imagination only a decade or even a few years ago. The frontier of science has been opened wide . . .

XVIII. *Government of the People*

98. Election of the President—99. Congress

Different procedures determine the types of elections held in a country: compulsory or voluntary voting, proportional representation or majority vote, one slate of candidates or several, and various other conditions. One feature, however, characterizes free elections only: that is, the outcome of an election remains uncertain until the last moment, no matter how strong the probability in favor of one or the other candidate, one or the other slate. When the surprise is discounted in advance and government nominees are in fact elected before the votes are counted, then even 99.9 per cent of "yes" votes is totally unconvincing. Despite all the polls taken and their predictions, surprises happen in this country, though more rarely in Presidential elections than in congressional or gubernatorial.

98. *Election of the President*

In the words of President Woodrow Wilson, the President is "the only national voice" in the United States. Despite this, he and the Vice President are the only elective officials who are not elected directly by the people but are elected by the so-called Electoral College. Every 4 years, on the first Tuesday in November, the people of every state in the Union elect as many electors as their state has members in both Houses of Congress. The electors vote in December, each in their respective states, and their votes are counted in the presence of the members of both Houses on January 6 of the next year, when the election of the President of the United States is made official. Of course, this is only a formality denuded of any real importance, yet this institution established by the Constitution has survived numerous attempts to liquidate it. In 3 cases, however, the electors voted against the popular majority: in 1824, 1876, and 1888.

All citizens 21 years of age, except inmates of mental and penal institutions, are potential voters.* But the universal franchise has been limited

* The voting age is 18 in Georgia and Kentucky, 19 in Alaska, and 20 in Hawaii.

by residence requirements, varying between 6 months in 12 states and 1 year in 38 states (Mississippi requires 2 years of residence) and different rules for registration. The residence requirement might not have been much of a hindrance to potential voters in older times, but today, when the American people have acquired almost nomadic habits, it often disfranchises particularly mobile citizens. Not all states permit absentee voting, though there is a tendency in several states to adjust their residence requirements to changing conditions.

Much more restrictive have been the poll tax and the literacy test, effectively used in barring the Negroes from registration. The poll tax has been gradually outlawed in various states, but until the Twenty-fourth Amendment to the Constitution was adopted in 1964, 5 southern states (Alabama, Arkansas, Virginia, Texas, and Mississippi) still had it on their books. This Amendment now enables inhabitants of any state to vote in Presidential elections without paying the poll tax.

The literacy test has been used and incredibly abused. Coupled with all sorts of discrimination and intimidation, it has effectively prevented the Negroes from exercising their citizens' right of participation in national life. The South has fought to the finish every law intended to eliminate such practices as unconstitutional: the Constitution leaves it to the states to determine the qualifications for voting (rules for registration, voting age, literacy and residence requirements, etc.). The 1965 Voting Act was intended to take care of all the loopholes and evasions used to bar the Negro from voting.

TABLE XVIII.1

CIVILIAN POPULATION OF VOTING AGE AND VOTE CAST FOR
PRESIDENTIAL ELECTORS, 1920-64

Year	Population of Voting Age (In Millions)	Vote Cast (In Millions)	(Per Cent)
1920	61.5	26.7	43.5
1924	66.2	29.1	43.9
1928	71.0	36.8	51.9
1932	75.7	39.7	52.5
1936	80.1	45.6	57.0
1940	84.3	49.9	59.2
1944[a]	90.6	48.0	52.9
1948	94.9	48.7	51.3
1952	98.3	61.6	62.6
1956	103.2	62.0	60.1
1960[b]	107.6	68.8	64.0
1964	112.5	70.6	62.8

[a]Includes armed forces abroad. Civilian population was 81 million; vote cast by civilians, 45.3 million; per cent, 55.9.
[b]Includes Alaska which voted for Representatives in November, 1958, although it became a state in January, 1959; for Hawaii includes 1959 population of voting age and the vote cast in the July, 1959 elections.

TABLE XVIII.2

POPULATION OF VOTING AGE AND POPULAR VOTE CAST FOR
PRESIDENTIAL ELECTORS, BY STATE, 1960 AND 1964

State	Population of Voting Age (In Thousands)			Popular Vote for Presidential Electors (In Thousands)		(Per Cent)	
	Total 1960	Negro	Total 1964	1960	1964	1960	1964
United States	107,597	9,972	112,549	68,838	70,644	64.0	62.8
Alabama	1,828	480	1,901	570	690	31.2	36.3
Alaska	103	4	108	61	67	59.2	62.2
Arizona	741	23	866	398	481	53.8	55.5
Arkansas	1,041	191	1,113	429	560	41.1	50.4
California	9,583	488	10,684	6,507	7,058	67.9	66.1
Colorado	1,027	22	1,114	736	777	71.7	69.7
Connecticut	1,587	59	1,690	1,223	1,219	77.1	72.1
Delaware	263	33	278	197	201	74.5	72.5
District of Columbia	501	237	507	-	199	-	39.2
Florida	3,086	464	3,447	1,544	1,854	50.0	53.8
Georgia	2,354	588	2,541	733	1,139	31.2	44.8
Hawaii	313	2	345	185	207	58.9	60.0
Idaho	373	1	382	300	292	80.6	76.5
Illinois	6,220	572	6,333	4,757	4,703	76.5	74.3
Indiana	2,776	147	2,823	2,135	2,092	76.9	74.1
Iowa	1,658	14	1,639	1,274	1,185	76.8	72.3
Kansas	1,294	50	1,299	929	838	71.8	66.0
Kentucky	1,859	131	1,932	1,124	1,046	60.5	54.1
Louisiana	1,790	507	1,870	808	896	45.1	47.9
Maine	570	2	569	422	381	74.0	66.9
Maryland	1,810	274	1,958	1,055	1,116	58.3	57.0
Massachusetts	3,212	63	3,268	2,469	2,345	76.9	71.7
Michigan	4,564	393	4,638	3,318	3,203	72.7	69.1
Minnesota	2,001	12	2,024	1,542	1,554	77.1	76.8
Mississippi	1,162	417	1,228	298	409	25.7	33.3
Missouri	2,665	216	2,672	1,934	1,818	72.6	68.0
Montana	387	1	391	278	279	71.7	71.2
Nebraska	851	16	864	613	584	72.1	67.6
Nevada	176	7	237	107	135	61.0	57.1
New Hampshire	369	1	391	296	288	80.2	73.8
New Jersey	3,860	295	4,113	2,773	2,848	71.8	69.2
New Mexico	482	9	501	311	329	64.5	65.4
New York	10,897	861	11,303	7,291	7,166	66.9	63.4
North Carolina	2,528	529	2,689	1,369	1,425	54.1	53.0
North Dakota	352	1	350	278	258	79.1	73.8
Ohio	5,837	441	5,952	4,162	3,969	71.3	66.7
Oklahoma	1,404	81	1,470	903	932	64.3	63.5
Oregon	1,072	10	1,126	776	786	72.4	69.8
Pennsylvania	7,085	490	7,077	5,007	4,823	70.7	68.1
Rhode Island	524	9	548	406	390	77.3	71.1
South Carolina	1,230	360	1,334	387	525	31.4	39.3
South Dakota	389	1	399	306	293	78.8	73.4
Tennessee	2,086	311	2,219	1,052	1,144	50.4	51.6
Texas	5,452	629	5,805	2,311	2,627	42.4	45.3
Utah	475	2	520	375	401	78.9	77.3
Vermont	230	a	240	167	163	72.9	67.9
Virginia	2,241	419	2,428	771	1,042	34.4	42.9
Washington	1,676	26	1,725	1,242	1,258	74.1	73.0
West Virginia	1,076	48	1,055	838	792	77.9	75.1
Wisconsin	2,352	37	2,392	1,729	1,692	73.5	70.7
Wyoming	189	1	192	141	143	73.9	74.5

a Less than 500.

Since Federal lists of voters do not exist in this country, the number of potential voters can only be estimated by using the number of people aged 21 years or more (with adjustments for the few states where voting starts at earlier ages, and the number of aliens), as the number of those qualified to vote. There is no way to correct this figure for restrictions on voting rights but this should not affect the result to any substantial degree. In 1964, 70.6 million votes were cast in the Presidential election out of an estimated 112.5 million possible votes. The difference of 42 million comprises those who did not vote for personal reasons and persons excluded from voting by restrictive laws and discriminatory administrative practices.

The percentage of voter participation in Presidential elections has shown ups and downs but, on the whole, it has been increasing, from 43.5 per cent in 1920 to 62.8 per cent in 1964 (see Table XVIII.1). Still, the range of annual fluctuations is much smaller than are the contrasts among the states. In 1964, for example, the range was between 33.3 per cent of the vote cast by the population of voting age in Mississippi and by 36.3 per cent in Alabama and more than 75 per cent in Idaho, Minnesota, and Utah (see Table XVIII.2).

Because the Negroes have larger families and more minors than have the white population, their percentage of potential voters is smaller than that

TABLE XVIII.3

VOTE CAST PER PRESIDENTIAL ELECTOR, BY STATE, 1964
(In Thousands)

State	Vote	State	Vote
Alabama	69	Montana	70
Alaska	23	Nebraska	117
Arizona	96	Nevada	45
Arkansas	92	New Hampshire	72
California	176	New Jersey	168
Colorado	129	New Mexico	82
Connecticut	152	New York	167
Delaware	67	North Carolina	110
District of Columbia	66	North Dakota	65
Florida	132	Ohio	153
Georgia	95	Oklahoma	119
Hawaii	52	Oregon	131
Idaho	73	Pennsylvania	166
Illinois	181	Rhode Island	98
Indiana	161	South Carolina	66
Iowa	132	South Dakota	74
Kansas	123	Tennessee	104
Kentucky	116	Texas	105
Louisiana	90	Utah	100
Maine	95	Vermont	54
Maryland	112	Virginia	87
Massachusetts	168	Washington	140
Michigan	153	West Virginia	113
Minnesota	155	Wisconsin	141
Mississippi	58	Wyoming	48
Missouri	152		

of the total population. In 1960, the Negroes represented 10.5 per cent of the country's total population but 9.3 per cent of the voting-age population; in 1964, the respective figures were 11.8 and 9.3. In the discriminatory states in the South, the contrast is much sharper: respective figures for Mississippi were 42 and 35.9 per cent; in South Carolina, 34.8 and 29.1 per cent.

The size of popular vote cast per Presidential elector varies from state to state. In 1964, it amounted to 45,000 votes in Nevada; 48,000 in Wyoming; and 54,000 in Virginia; as compared with 168,000 votes in Massachusetts and 181,000 in Illinois. Alabama, Mississippi, and South Carolina together cast 1.6 million votes and had 25 electoral votes; Michigan, with 3.2 million votes, or twice that many, had 21 electoral votes. On the whole, rural states, thinly populated states in the West, and discriminatory states in the South are favored in this respect in comparison with the industrial, heavily populated states (see Table XVIII.3).

The electoral laws in this country, which require single-member constituencies and a majority vote in Presidential elections, favor the 2-party system. Chances of a "third" party are slim. Any substantial split in the ranks of the 2 major parties, Republican and Democratic, is likely to bring

TABLE XVIII.4

POPULAR VOTE FOR PRESIDENTIAL ELECTORS, BY PARTY AFFILIATION, 1888-1964
(In Thousands)

Year	Total Vote	Republican Candidate	Votes	Democrat Candidate	Votes	Independent Party	Votes	Socialist Votes	Other Votes[a]
1888	11,381	Harrison	5,444	Cleveland	5,540	Union Labor	147	-	250
1892	12,044	Harrison	5,191	Cleveland	5,554	Populist	1,027	-	271
1896	13,813	McKinley	7,036	Bryan	6,468	Populist	132	36	142
1900	13,968	McKinley	7,218	Bryan	6,357	Populist	56	128	209
1904	13,521	T.Roosevelt	7,628	Parker	5,084	Nat. Democrats	117	434	259
1908	14,884	Taft	7,675	Bryan	6,412	Populist	108	435	254
1912	15,037	Taft	3,487	Wilson	6,297	Progressive[b]	4,119	929	206
1916	18,531	Hughes	8,534	Wilson	9,128	Progressive	49	599	221
1920	26,748	Harding	16,143	Cox	9,130	Farm-Labor	334	952	189
1924	29,086	Coolidge	15,718	Davis	8,385	Farm-Labor[c]	4,853	36	95
1928	36,812	Hoover	21,392	Smith	15,016	Farm-Labor	74	289	41
1932	39,732	Hoover	15,759	F.Roosevelt	22,810	Farm-Labor	63	915	185
1936	45,643	Landon	16,675	F.Roosevelt	27,753	Union	897	200	118
1940	49,891	Willkie	22,321	F.Roosevelt	27,308	Progressive	44	114	104
1944	47,969	Dewey	22,015	F.Roosevelt	25,607	[d]	146	126	75
1948	48,691	Dewey	21,970	Truman	24,106	States Rights	2,343	169	103
1952	61,551	Eisenhower	33,936	Stevenson	27,315	[d]	176	50	73
1956	62,027	Eisenhower	35,590	Stevenson	26,023	[d]	325	46	42
1960	68,839	Nixon	34,108	Kennedy	34,227	[d]	410	48	46
1964	70,644	Goldwater	27,178	Johnson	43,130	[d]	269	45	23

[a]Votes for Prohibition and minor party candidates; 1924-40, includes votes for the Communist party.
[b]Theodore Roosevelt.
[c]La Follette.
[d]Miscellaneous small independent parties.

FIGURE XVIII.1

POPULAR VOTE CAST FOR PRESIDENT BY MAJOR PARTIES, 1900-1964

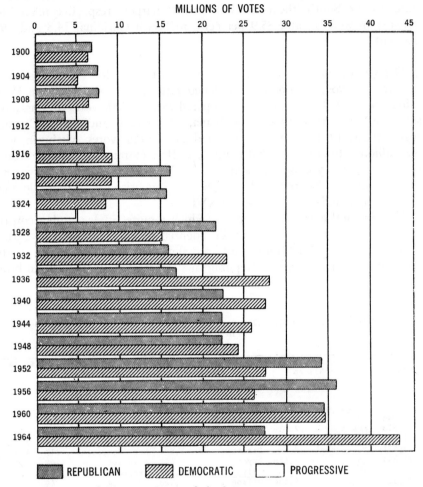

U.S. Department of Commerce, Bureau of the Census

victory to the rival party. Thus in 1912, the candidacy of Theodore Roosevelt against William Howard Taft, the regular nominee of the Republican party, resulted in, or at least greatly contributed to, the election of Woodrow Wilson by dividing the 7.6 million total Republican votes into two parts, each smaller than the 6.3 million received by Wilson. The practical result of the La Follette campaign in 1924 was to split the vote cast for the Democratic ticket and possibly to lessen the total vote for it (see Table XVIII.4 and Figure XVIII.1).

Because of the 2-party system, elections in the United States may often be decided by a shift of a comparatively small number of votes, particularly if this occurs in strategic voting districts. In the 1960 elections, the difference in total popular vote received by the 2 leading candidates was exceedingly small: 34,227,000 votes for Kennedy and 34,107,646 votes for Nixon. Thus less than 115,000 votes out of 68.8 million, or less than two-tenths of 1 per cent, decided the election results. But Kennedy's majority in 7 pivotal states (New York, Pennsylvania, Illinois, Massachusetts, Michigan, Texas, and New Jersey) represented 180 electoral votes; 16 other states provided 123 votes—in all, 303 electoral votes. Among the 27 states that went for Nixon, only 2 large states (California and Ohio, with 57 electoral votes) gave him a majority of the popular vote.

In single states, too, a small number of votes may affect the results one way or another. For example, some 9,000 votes in Illinois, or less than half of 1 per cent of the votes cast in that state, were sufficient to turn the state to the Democrats in 1960. On the other hand, an extra 36,000 votes in California, or just above 1 per cent of the popular vote, assured Nixon's victory in that state.

In 1964, the situation was different. Only 1 state, Arizona, the home of the candidate Goldwater, split the votes almost equally: 242,900 for Goldwater and 238,100 for Johnson. Almost everywhere else, except for the South, the Democratic ticket won a substantial majority of the popular vote.

V. O. Key, Jr. distinguishes 3 types of Presidential elections in this country: maintaining, developing, and realigning.

The maintaining election is one in which the pattern of party attachment persists so that one party is repeatedly voted to the occupancy of the White House. In this sense, many, if not most, Presidential elections during the last 100 years or more have been of the maintaining type. In recent years, the 1948 elections were an example of a maintaining election, something of a fifth Roosevelt term.

In the developing election, basic party loyalties are not seriously affected, but the party in power experiences a temporary defeat that interrupts its long period of holding the Presidency. To Key, such developing elections were the elections of Cleveland and Wilson, and, in recent times, the elections of Eisenhower. Such elections do not change the basic party pattern and represent a rather temporary reversal in the country's political attitude.

In realigning elections, the popular feelings are so intense that they change the attachment to the dominant party in the country and crystallize a new party pattern. Such shifts are not frequent; in our time, the realigning election came in 1932, during the Great Depression, which changed the political climate in the country. The election of Franklin D. Roosevelt was one such realigning election; the elections of 1960 and 1964 were, in this sense, maintaining elections.

99. Congress

The Congress of the United States is composed of 100 Senators and 435 Representatives. The Senators, 2 from each state, are elected for 6 years. One-third of them is elected every 2 years. The Constitution provides that "Representatives shall be apportioned among the several States according to their respective numbers." Each state must have at least 1 representative, regardless of the size of its population. Members of the House are elected for 2-year terms; all terms cover the same period.

Because of the great mobility of the American people, shifts in the population among the states result in changes in the size of the House membership and the distribution of members among the states. In 1790, the number of representatives was 106; in 1890, it was more than 3 times as large (357); it has remained constant since 1912 at 435, except for the short period when, as new states, Alaska and Hawaii were allotted 1 representative each before the 1962 elections.

Some states that have been growing very rapidly have increased their number of seats in the House. For example, California started with 2 representatives in 1850, increased their number to 11 by 1910, and 38 in 1960. Other states with slight changes in population have maintained their strength of representation but could not increase it: Wisconsin, to name one, has had 10 representatives since 1890 (see Table XVIII.5 and Figure XVIII.2, showing changes in House membership after the reapportionment following the 1960 Census).

The vote for Congressional representation is usually lighter than for the election of the President, and is still lighter in the off-years. The percentage of voters in 1932, for example, was 52.5 for the President and 49.8 for the Representatives; in the following elections (1934), only 41.4 per cent of the voting-age population cast their votes. In 1960, the respective figures were 64.0 and 59.9 per cent; in 1962, 46.7 per cent; in 1964, 62.8 and 58.7 per cent.

As in Presidential elections, a Congressional candidate must have the support of a major party to be elected. Occasionally, an independent and popular politician may challenge the party nominees and at times may even win, but, on the whole, such rare cases only underscore their infrequency.

While the national party committees can influence the local organizations, they cannot control them. Local issues play a much more important role in Congressional than in Presidential elections.

The composition of Congress by party affiliation does not necessarily reflect itself in its voting record. Officially, only 2 parties, Democratic and Republican, are represented in Congress; independents or members of any other party are rather an exception than a rule. But there is no party discipline, such as exists in many European parliaments, to force party members to vote as a bloc. In our Congress, votes needed for passing

TABLE XVIII.5

APPORTIONMENT OF MEMBERSHIP IN HOUSE OF REPRESENTATIVES,
BY STATE, 1790-1960

State	1790	1810	1830	1850	1870	1890	1910	1930	1950	1960
Total membership	106	186	242	237	293	357	435	435	437[a]	435
Alabama	-	1	5	7	8	9	10	9	9	8
Alaska	-	-	-	-	-	-	-	-	1[b]	1
Arizona	-	-	-	-	-	-	1	1	2	3
Arkansas	-	-	1	2	4	6	7	7	6	4
California	-	-	-	2	4	7	11	20	30	38
Colorado	-	-	-	-	1	2	4	4	4	4
Connecticut	7	7	6	4	4	4	5	6	6	6
Delaware	1	2	1	1	1	1	1	1	1	1
Florida	-	-	-	1	2	2	4	5	8	12
Georgia	2	6	9	8	9	11	11	10	10	10
Hawaii	-	-	-	-	-	-	-	-	1[b]	2
Idaho	-	-	-	-	-	1	2	2	2	2
Illinois	-	1	3	9	19	22	25	27	25	24
Indiana	-	1	7	11	13	13	13	12	11	11
Iowa	-	-	-	2	9	11	11	9	8	7
Kansas	-	-	-	-	3	8	8	7	6	5
Kentucky	2	10	13	10	10	11	11	9	8	7
Louisiana	-	1	3	4	6	6	8	8	8	8
Maine	-	7	8	6	5	4	4	3	3	2
Maryland	8	9	8	6	6	6	6	6	7	8
Massachusetts	14	13	12	11	11	13	16	15	14	12
Michigan	-	-	1	4	9	12	13	17	18	19
Minnesota	-	-	-	2	3	7	10	9	9	8
Mississippi	-	1	2	5	6	7	8	7	6	5
Missouri	-	-	2	7	13	15	16	13	11	10
Montana	-	-	-	-	-	1	2	2	2	2
Nebraska	-	-	-	-	1	6	6	5	4	3
Nevada	-	-	-	-	1	1	1	1	1	1
New Hampshire	4	6	5	3	3	2	2	2	2	2
New Jersey	5	6	6	5	7	8	12	14	14	15
New Mexico	-	-	-	-	-	-	1	1	2	2
New York	10	27	40	33	33	34	43	45	43	41
North Carolina	10	13	13	8	8	9	10	11	12	11
North Dakota	-	-	-	-	-	1	3	2	2	2
Ohio	-	6	19	21	20	21	22	24	23	24
Oklahoma	-	-	-	-	-	-	8	9	6	6
Oregon	-	-	-	1	1	2	3	3	4	4
Pennsylvania	13	23	28	25	27	30	36	34	30	27
Rhode Island	2	2	2	2	2	2	3	2	2	2
South Carolina	6	9	9	6	5	7	7	6	6	6
South Dakota	-	-	-	-	-	2	3	2	2	2
Tennessee	1	6	13	10	10	10	10	9	9	9
Texas	-	-	-	2	6	13	18	21	22	23
Utah	-	-	-	-	-	1	2	2	2	2
Vermont	2	6	5	3	3	2	2	1	1	1
Virginia	19	23	21	13	9	10	10	9	10	10
Washington	-	-	-	-	-	2	5	6	7	7
West Virginia	-	-	-	-	3	4	6	6	6	5
Wisconsin	-	-	-	3	8	10	11	10	10	10
Wyoming	-	-	-	-	-	1	1	1	1	1

[a] Includes 1 member each assigned to Alaska and Hawaii after apportionment.
[b] Seated in 1959.

FIGURE XVIII.2

GAIN OR LOSS OF MEMBERSHIP IN HOUSE OF
REPRESENTATIVES, BY STATE, 1960

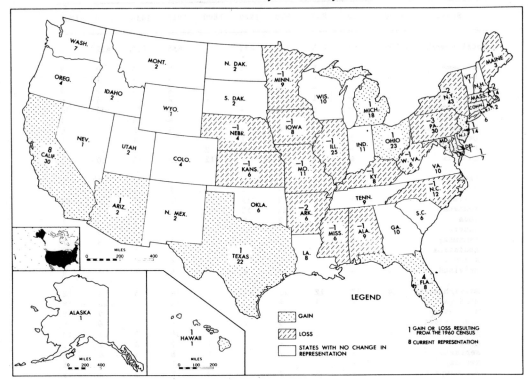

U.S. Department of Commerce, Bureau of the Census

one or another controversial measure (and almost all of them are controversial) can only be achieved when the majority party obtains support
from some members within the minority party—be it by persuasion, pressure, influence of the White House, promises of patronage, even threats.
Yet despite the frequent shifts in voting from one party to another, the
Congress remains the basic framework of political life in this country.

It is not seldom that the voters choose a member of one party for the
White House but do not provide him with a majority of his own party
in Congress. President Wilson, for example, faced a Congress in which the
Republicans were in the majority (240 Republicans as against 190 Democrats in the House; 49 against 47, respectively, in the Senate). Both President Truman and President Eisenhower were in a similar situation (see
Table XVIII.6).

All in all, despite the shifts in popular vote and variations from state to
state, there is, in the long run, a certain rhythm, a certain stability in the
American political life. From 1828 through 1964, the period covering

TABLE XVIII.6

COMPOSITION OF CONGRESS, BY PARTY AFFILIATIONS, 1917-65

Year[a]	Party and President[b]	Majority Party	House Principal Minority Party	Other[c]	Majority Party	Senate Principal Minority Party	Other[c]
1917	Wilson(D)	D - 216	R - 210	6	D - 53	R - 42	-
1919	Wilson(D)	R - 240	D - 190	3	R - 49	D - 47	-
1921	Harding(R)	R - 301	D - 131	1	R - 59	D - 37	-
1923	Coolidge(R)	R - 225	D - 205	3	R - 51	D - 43	2
1925	Coolidge(R)	R - 247	D - 183	4	R - 56	D - 39	1
1927	Coolidge(R)	R - 237	D - 195	3	R - 49	D - 46	1
1929	Hoover(R)	R - 267	D - 167	1	R - 56	D - 39	1
1931	Hoover(R)	D - 220	R - 214	1	R - 48	D - 47	1
1933	F. Roosevelt(D)	D - 310	R - 117	5	D - 60	R - 35	1
1935	F. Roosevelt(D)	D - 319	R - 103	10	D - 69	R - 25	2
1937	F. Roosevelt(D)	D - 331	R - 89	13	D - 76	R - 16	4
1939	F. Roosevelt(D)	D - 261	R - 164	4	D - 69	R - 23	4
1941	F. Roosevelt(D)	D - 268	R - 162	5	D - 66	R - 28	2
1943	F. Roosevelt(D)	D - 218	R - 208	4	D - 58	R - 37	1
1945	F. Roosevelt(D)	D - 242	R - 190	2	D - 56	R - 38	1
	Truman(D)	D - 242	R - 190	2	D - 56	R - 38	1
1947	Truman(D)	R - 245	D - 188	1	R - 51	D - 45	-
1949	Truman(D)	D - 263	R - 171	1	D - 54	R - 42	-
1951	Truman(D)	D - 234	R - 199	1	D - 49	R - 47	-
1953	Eisenhower(R)	R - 221	D - 211	1	R - 48	D - 47	1
1955	Eisenhower(R)	D - 232	R - 203	-	D - 48	R - 47	1
1957	Eisenhower(R)	D - 233	R - 200	-	D - 49	R - 47	-
1959	Eisenhower(R)	D - 283	R - 153	-	D - 64	R - 34	-
1961	Kennedy(D)	D - 263	R - 174	-	D - 65	R - 35	-
1963	Kennedy(D)	D - 258	R - 177	-	D - 67	R - 33	-
	Johnson(D)	D - 258	R - 177	-	D - 67	R - 33	-
1964[d]	Johnson(D)	D - 255	R - 178	-	D - 67	R - 33	-
1965	Johnson(D)	D - 295	R - 140	-	D - 68	R - 32	-

[a]First session of each Congress, except 1964: beginning of second session
[b]D - Democratic; R - Republican.
[c]Except vacancies.
[d]At beginning of session, 2 vacancies in House of Representatives.

almost the entire American political history, the Presidential office has been shared nearly equally between the Republicans and the Democrats.

The Republicans held the Presidency during 72 years, or 18 terms, and the Democrats during 68 years, or 17 terms.

Appendix Tables

TABLE I

CLIMATIC CONDITIONS IN SELECTED POINTS OF THE UNITED STATES
(Average Data for 30 Years)

Climatic Region and City	Elevation of Station (Feet)	Temperature (In Fahrenheit Degrees)					Total Precipitation (In Inches)	Average Snowfall (In Inches)	Average Relative Humidity[a] (In Per Cent)
		Normal Mean			Highest (On Record[a])	Lowest			
		January	July	Annual					
Humid East									
Portland, Me.	61	21.8	68.1	45.0	100	-39	42.9	71.7	71
New York, N.Y.	10	32.2	76.8	54.5	106	-15	42.4	29.7	65
Atlanta, Ga.	1,054	44.8	78.8	61.6	94	- 3	47.1	1.7	69
Chicago, Ill.	610	26.0	75.6	50.8	104	-15	33.2	37.0	69
Miami, Fla.	8	66.9	81.8	75.1	98	32	59.8	0.0	73
Subhumid Interior									
Minneapolis-St. Paul, Minn.	830	12.4	72.3	43.7	99	-32	24.8	41.5	72
Oklahoma City, Okla.	1,254	37.0	82.5	60.3	107	- 4	30.8	9.3	70
Dallas, Tex.	487	45.9	84.9	65.8	103	8	34.6	2.0	67
Sioux Falls, S.D.	1,420	15.2	74.3	45.7	108	-31	25.2	42.6	67
Omaha, Neb.	978	22.3	78.5	51.5	107	-15	27.6	32.7	69
Wichita, Kan.	1,321	32.0	80.9	57.1	113	-12	28.4	16.6	67
Great Plains									
Cheyenne, Wyo.	6,131	25.4	70.0	45.9	96	-27	15.1	55.5	44
Denver, Colo.	5,221	28.5	72.9	49.5	100	-25	14.8	59.1	39
Arid West									
Boise, Ida.	2,842	29.1	75.2	51.0	111	-17	11.4	20.4	50
Phoenix, Ariz.	1,083	49.7	89.8	69.0	114	20	7.2	b	27
Pacific Region									
Seattle, Wash.	14	41.2	65.6	53.2	100	11	34.1	8.1	70
Los Angeles, Calif.	312	55.8	73.0	64.4	110	28	14.7	b	51

[a]Length of record from 1 to 65 years.
[b]Trace.

TABLE II

IMMIGRATION INTO THE UNITED STATES,
BY COUNTRY OF ORIGIN, 1820-1964[a]
(In Thousands)

Country	1820-1840	1841-1860	1861-1880	1881-1900	1901-1920	1921-1940	1941-1964	1820-1964
Germany	160	1,386	1,506	1,958	485	526	801	6,823
Italy	3	11	68	959	3,155	523	311	5,030
Ireland[b]	262	1,695	873	1,044	485	234	107	4,699
Great Britain[c]	103	691	1,155	1,079	867	360	413	4,668
Austria	} -	-	81	946	3,042	{ 37	97 }	4,283
Hungary						39	42	
Russia (U.S.S.R.)	-	1	42	719	2,519	63	2	3,345
Norway	} 1	35 {	167	272	257	73	41	846
Sweden			154	618	345	101	40	1,257
France	55	154	108	81	135	62	109	704
Greece	-	-	-	18	352	60	73	503
Poland[d]	-	1	15	149	5	245	43	458
Denmark	1	4	49	138	107	35	20	355
Netherlands	3	19	26	80	92	34	87	341
Switzerland	8	30	52	113	58	36	35	331
Portugal	1	2	17	45	159	33	39	295
Spain	5	12	12	13	97	32	23	193
Belgium	-	10	14	38	75	21	35	193
Turkey in Europe	-	-	-	5	135	15	6	161
Romania	-	-	-	19	66	72	3	160
Czechoslovakia	-	-	-	-	3	117	10	130
Bulgaria	-	-	-	-	62	4	1	67
Rest of Europe	-	-	-	1	12	104	42	162
EUROPE	602	4,050	4,338	8,296	12,513	2,826	2,380	35,004
Canada[e]	16	101	538	397	921	1,033	743	3,749
Mexico	11	6	7	3	269	482	548	1,326
West Indies	16	24	23	62	231	90	261	708
Other American countries	2	6	3	4	87	72	423	594
AMERICA	45	137	571	466	1,506	1,677	1,975	6,377
China	-	41	188	77	42	35	32	415
Japan	-	-	-	28	215	35	65	342
Turkey in Asia	-	-	-	29	157	20	2	208
Other Asian countries	-	-	-	6	22	23	164	217
ASIA	-	41	188	140	436	113	263	1,182
Africa	-	-	1	1	16	8	29	55
Australia and New Zealand[f]	-	-	11	17	26	12	43	108
Nonspecified-countries	103	82	19	15	35	-	13	267
ALL COUNTRIES	751	4,311	5,127	8,934	14,531	4,636	4,705	42,995

[a]Prior to 1906, data refer to the country from which the immigrants came; thereafter, to the country of last permanent residence. Because of boundary changes in the list of countries reported separately, data for certain countries not comparable throughout. Dash indicates less than 1,000.
[b]Includes Northern Ireland.
[c]Includes 798,177 immigrants who arrived from United Kingdom but are not specified.
[d]Between 1899 and 1919, Poland was included with Austria-Hungary, Germany, and Russia.
[e]Includes Newfoundland.
[f]Includes Pacific Islands.

TABLE III

POPULATION OF THE UNITED STATES
BY GEOGRAPHIC DIVISION AND STATE, 1960

Geographic Division and State	Total (In Thousands)	Per Square Mile	Geographic Division and State	Total (In Thousands)	Per Square Mile
New England	10,509	166.5	North Carolina	4,556	92.9
Maine	969	31.3	South Carolina	2,383	78.7
New Hampshire	607	67.3	Georgia	3,943	67.7
Vermont	390	42.0	Florida	4,952	91.3
Massachusetts	5,149	654.5			
Rhode Island	859	812.4	East South Central	12,050	67.0
Connecticut	2,535	517.5	Kentucky	3,038	76.2
			Tennessee	3,567	85.4
Middle Atlantic	34,168	340.1	Alabama	3,267	64.0
New York	16,782	350.1	Mississippi	2,178	46.1
New Jersey	6,067	806.7			
Pennsylvania	11,319	251.5	West South Central	16,951	39.5
			Arkansas	1,786	34.0
East North Central	36,225	148.0	Louisiana	3,257	72.2
Ohio	9,706	236.9	Oklahoma	2,328	33.8
Indiana	4,662	128.9	Texas	9,580	36.5
Illinois	10,081	180.3			
Michigan	7,823	137.2	Mountain	6,855	8.0
Wisconsin	3,952	72.2	Montana	675	4.6
			Idaho	667	8.1
West North Central	15,394	30.2	Wyoming	330	3.4
Minnesota	3,414	42.7	Colorado	1,754	16.9
Iowa	2,758	49.2	New Mexico	951	7.8
Missouri	4,320	62.5	Arizona	1,302	11.5
North Dakota	632	9.1	Utah	891	10.8
South Dakota	681	8.9	Nevada	285	2.6
Nebraska	1,411	18.4			
Kansas	2,179	26.6	Pacific	21,198	23.6
			Washington	2,853	42.8
South Atlantic	25,972	97.0	Oregon	1,769	18.4
Delaware	446	225.6	California	15,717	100.4
Maryland	3,101	314.0	Alaska	266	0.4
District of Columbia	764	12,523.9	Hawaii	633	98.6
Virginia	3,967	99.6			
West Virginia	1,860	77.3	UNITED STATES	179,323	50.5

TABLE IV

POPULATION OF THE UNITED STATES BY REGION AND DIVISION, 1790-1964[a]

(In Thousands)

Year	United States	The North				The South			The West	
		New England	Middle Atlantic	East North Central	West North Central	South Atlantic	East South Central	West South Central	Mountain	Pacific
1790	3,929	1,009	959	-	-	1,852	109	-	-	-
1800	5,308	1,233	1,403	51	-	2,286	335	-	-	-
1810	7,240	1,472	2,015	272	20	2,675	709	78	-	-
1820	9,638	1,660	2,700	793	67	3,061	1,190	168	-	-
1830	12,866	1,955	3,588	1,470	140	3,646	1,816	246	-	-
1840	17,069	2,235	4,526	2,925	427	3,925	2,575	450	-	-
1850	23,192	2,728	5,899	4,523	880	4,679	3,363	940	73	106
1860	31,443	3,135	7,459	6,927	2,170	5,365	4,021	1,748	175	444
1870	39,905	3,488	8,811	9,125	3,857	5,854	4,404	2,030	315	675
1880	50,156	4,011	10,497	11,207	6,157	7,597	5,585	3,334	653	1,115
1890	62,948	4,701	12,706	13,478	8,932	8,858	6,429	4,741	1,214	1,888
1900	75,995	5,592	15,455	15,986	10,347	10,443	7,548	6,532	1,675	2,417
1910	92,228	6,553	19,316	18,251	11,638	12,195	8,410	8,785	2,634	4,449
1920	106,022	7,401	22,261	21,476	12,544	13,990	8,893	10,242	3,336	5,878
1930	123,203	8,166	26,261	25,297	13,297	15,794	9,887	12,177	3,702	8,622
1940	132,165	8,437	27,539	26,626	13,517	17,823	10,778	13,065	4,150	10,229
1950[b]	151,326	9,314	30,164	30,399	14,061	21,182	11,477	14,538	5,075	15,115
1960	179,323	10,509	34,168	36,225	15,394	25,972	12,050	16,951	6,855	21,198
1963[c]	188,616	10,939	35,674	37,259	15,669	27,764	12,535	17,987	7,508	23,282
1964[c]	191,334	11,070	36,055	37,619	15,751	28,311	12,678	18,263	7,697	23,891

[a] Includes armed forces abroad.
[b] Includes Alaska and Hawaii.

TABLE V

RURAL AND URBAN POPULATION
IN THE UNITED STATES, 1790-1960

Inhabitants	1790	1840	1880	1900	1920	1930	1940	Previous Definition 1950	1960	Current Definition 1950	1960
					(IN MILLIONS)						
Rural	3.7	15.2	36.0	45.8	51.6	53.8	57.2	60.9	66.3	54.2	54.1
Urban, total	0.2	1.8	14.1	30.2	54.2	69.0	74.4	89.7	113.1	96.5	125.3
In places with:											
2,500-10,000	0.1	0.5	3.3	6.1	9.4	'0.6	11.7	13.4	15.7	22.6[a]	27.9[b]
10,000-100,000	0.1	0.8	4.6	9.9	17.4	22.0	24.7	31.8	46.5	29.6	46.5
100,000-1,000,000	-	0.5	5.0	7.8	17.3	21.3	22.1	27.1	33.4	26.9	33.5
1,000,000 or more	-	-	1.2	6.4	10.1	15.1	15.9	17.4	17.5	17.4	17.5
UNITED STATES	3.9	17.1	50.2	76.0	105.7	122.8	131.7	150.7	179.3	150.7	179.3
					(PER CENT)						
Rural	94.9	89.4	71.8	60.3	48.8	43.8	43.5	40.4	37.0	36.0	30.1
Urban, total	5.1	10.6	28.2	39.7	51.2	56.2	56.5	59.6	63.0	64.0	69.9
In places with:											
2,500-10,000	2.3	2.9	6.6	8.0	8.8	8.6	8.9	8.9	8.7	15.0[a]	15.6[b]
10,000-100,000	2.8	4.7	9.2	13.0	16.5	17.9	18.8	21.2	25.9	19.6	25.8
100,000-1,000,000	-	2.9	10.0	10.3	16.4	17.3	16.7	18.1	18.6	17.9	18.7
1,000,000 or more	-	-	2.4	8.5	9.6	12.3	12.1	11.5	9.8	11.5	9.8
UNITED STATES	100.0	100.0	100.0	100.0	100.0	100.0	100.0	100.0	100.0	100.0	100.0

[a]Includes 7.9 million population (5.3 per cent) in unincorporated parts of urbanized areas and urban places under 2,500.
[b]Includes 10.6 million population (5.9 per cent) in areas defined in note[a].

TABLE VI

RELIGIOUS AFFILIATION OF THE POPULATION
OF THE UNITED STATES, 1957[a]

Religion	Total	White Male	Female	Nonwhite Male	Female	North-east	North Central	South	West
				NUMBER OF PERSONS (In Thousands)					
Protestant	78,952	32,320	36,155	4,851	5,626	13,225	24,025	30,249	11,453
Baptist	23,525	7,822	8,450	3,354	3,899	...	...	...	...
Lutheran	8,417	4,084	4,301	17	15	...	...	...	...
Methodist	16,676	6,788	7,821	968	1,099	...	...	...	...
Presbyterian	6,656	3,000	3,549	57	50	...	...	...	...
Other Protestant	23,678	10,626	12,034	455	563	...	...	...	...
Roman Catholic	30,669	14,396	15,499	361	413	14,106	8,587	4,254	3,722
Jewish	3,868	1,860	1,999	1	8	2,671	460	299	438
Other religion	1,545	688	676	88	93	647	410	269	219
No religion	3,195	2,051	730	306	108	358	1,024	1,108	705
Not reported	1,104	476	511	72	45	257	319	372	156
TOTAL	119,333	51,791	55,570	5,679	6,293	31,264	34,825	36,551	16,693
				PERCENTAGE DISTRIBUTION					
Protestant	66.2	62.4	65.1	85.4	89.4	42.3	69.0	82.8	68.6
Roman Catholic	25.7	27.8	27.9	6.4	6.6	45.1	24.7	11.6	22.3
Jewish	3.2	3.6	3.6	-	-	8.5	1.3	0.8	2.6
Other religion	1.3	1.3	1.2	1.5	1.5	2.1	1.2	0.7	1.3
No religion	2.7	4.0	1.3	5.4	1.7	1.1	2.9	3.0	4.2
Not reported	0.9	0.9	0.9	1.3	0.7	0.8	0.9	1.0	0.9
TOTAL	100.0	100.0	100.0	100.0	100.0	100.0	100.0	100.0	100.0

[a]Aged 14 years and over.

TABLE VII

DISTRIBUTION OF MEN AND WOMEN IN URBAN AND RURAL AREAS
IN THE UNITED STATES, BY AGE GROUPS, 1960

Age Groups[a]	Urban			Rural Nonfarm			Rural Farm		
	In Thousands		Men per 100 Women	In Thousands		Men per 100 Women	In Thousands		Men per 100 Women
	Men	Women		Men	Women		Men	Women	
Under 5 years	7,148	6,914	103.4	2,511	2,415	104.0	680	653	104.1
5-14 years	11,984	11,679	102.6	4,495	4,272	105.2	1,572	1,473	106.7
15-24 years	7,922	8,584	92.3	3,056	2,685	113.8	1,004	840	119.5
25-34 years	8,040	8,452	95.1	2,552	2,575	99.1	582	621	93.7
35-44 years	8,390	8,985	93.4	2,550	2,516	101.4	799	836	95.6
45-54 years	7,072	7,576	93.3	2,162	2,067	104.6	907	843	107.6
55-64 years	5,278	5,920	89.1	1,557	1,574	98.9	734	645	113.8
65-74 years	3,400	4,239	80.2	1,147	1,192	96.2	476	395	120.5
75 years and over	1,485	2,215	67.0	599	675	88.7	202	182	111.0
ALL AGES	60,719	64,565	94.0	20,628	19,969	103.3	6,957	6,488	107.2

[a]Because the statement of age is often inaccurate as to the exact year, data on population by age are usually tabulated in 5- or 10-year groups, to minimize the effect of errors.

TABLE VIII

SEX RATIO IN SELECTED COUNTRIES
(Latest Data Available)

Country, Year	Sex Ratio	Country, Year	Sex Ratio
United States, 1960	97.1	Poland, 1960	93.6
1964	96.4	Portugal, 1960	91.9
Canada, 1961	102.2	Romania, 1956	94.6
Mexico, 1960	94.7	Spain, 1960	94.2
Guatemala, 1964	102.7	Sweden, 1960	99.5
Cuba, 1953	105.0	Switzerland, 1960	96.3
Argentina, 1960	100.6	United Kingdom, 1961	93.7
Colombia, 1957	98.9	Yugoslavia, 1961	95.1
Chile, 1960	96.2		
Bolivia, 1950	96.2	Burma, 1953	104.0
Brazil, 1950	99.3	Ceylon, 1956	111.5
Ecuador, 1962	100.0	India, 1961	106.2
Peru, 1961	99.1	Indonesia, 1961	97.3
Venezuela, 1961	103.3	Israel, 1961	103.1
		Japan, 1960	96.5
Austria, 1961	88.1	South Korea, 1960	100.8
Belgium, 1961	95.8	Taiwan, 1957	104.1
Bulgaria, 1956	97.4	Thailand, 1960	100.4
Czechoslovakia, 1961	95.2	Turkey, 1960	104.2
Finland, 1960	93.0	Pakistan, 1961	111.1
France, 1962	94.6		
West Germany, 1961	89.4	Algeria, 1954	101.6
East Germany, 1957	81.3	United Arab Republic, 1960	100.4
Greece, 1961	95.7	Morocco, 1960	99.9
Hungary, 1960	93.2	Nigeria, 1953	95.7
Ireland, 1961	101.1	Sudan, 1956	102.2
Italy, 1961	96.0	Tunisia, 1956	107.2
Netherlands, 1960	99.2	South Africa, 1960	101.6
Norway, 1960	99.3		
		Australia, 1961	102.2
U.S.S.R., 1959	81.9	New Zealand, 1961	100.9

TABLE IX

AGE AND SEX DISTRIBUTION OF THE POPULATION
OF THE UNITED STATES, 1870-1960

Sex and Age	Number (In Thousands)						Per Cent of Total Population					
	1870	1890	1910	1930	1950	1960	1870	1890	1910	1930	1950	1960
ale												
nder 5 years	2,797	3,885	5,381	5,834	8,277	10,330	14.3	12.1	11.4	9.4	11.0	11.7
-9 years	2,437	3,830	4,924	6,408	6,747	9,504	12.5	11.9	10.4	10.3	9.0	10.8
0-14 years	2,436	3,575	4,602	6,091	5,685	8,524	12.5	11.1	9.7	9.8	7.6	9.7
5-19 years	1,990	3,249	4,527	5,780	5,342	6,634	10.2	10.1	9.6	9.3	7.1	7.5
0-24 years	1,836	3,105	4,580	5,371	5,647	5,272	9.4	9.7	9.7	8.6	7.5	6.0
5-34 years	2,789	5,124	7,901	9,469	11,662	11,179	14.3	16.0	16.7	15.2	15.5	12.7
5-44 years	2,169	3,706	6,153	8,847	10,640	11,755	11.1	11.6	13.0	14.2	14.2	13.3
5-54 years	1,580	2,627	4,489	6,828	8,688	10,093	8.1	8.2	9.5	10.9	11.6	11.4
5-64 years	877	1,630	2,674	4,383	6,687	7,536	4.5	5.1	5.6	7.0	8.9	8.5
5-69 years	251	526	864	1,422	2,431	2,931	1.3	1.6	1.8	2.3	3.0	3.3
0-74 years	173	364	562	994	1,633	2,185	0.9	1.1	1.2	1.6	2.1	2.5
5 years and over	155	344	560	917	1,748	2,387	0.8	1.1	1.2	1.5	2.2	2.7
ot reported	4	104	114	52	-	-	-	0.3	0.2	0.1	-	-
LL AGES	19,494	32,068	47,332	62,395	75,187	88,331	100.0	100.0	100.0	100.0	100.0	100.0
emale												
nder 5 years	2,717	3,750	5,251	5,665	7,927	9,991	14.3	12.3	11.8	9.3	10.4	11.0
-9 years	2,377	3,744	4,837	6,253	6,485	9,187	12.5	12.3	10.8	10.3	8.5	10.1
0-14 years	2,351	3,459	4,505	5,957	5,459	8,249	12.3	11.3	10.1	9.8	7.2	8.9
5-19 years	2,050	3,309	4,437	5,811	5,329	6,586	10.7	10.8	10.3	9.5	7.0	7.2
0-24 years	1,912	3,091	4,477	5,547	5,903	5,528	10.0	10.1	10.0	9.1	7.8	6.1
5-34 years	2,849	4,682	7,251	9,557	12,162	11,639	15.0	15.3	16.2	15.7	16.0	12.8
5-44 years	2,085	3,346	5,501	8,402	10,863	12,326	11.0	10.9	12.3	13.8	14.3	13.5
5-54 years	1,367	2,431	3,881	6,227	8,688	10,393	7.2	8.0	8.7	10.3	11.5	11.4
5-64 years	779	1,500	2,380	4,035	6,627	8,036	4.0	4.9	5.3	6.7	8.8	8.8
5-69 years	234	484	816	1,354	2,578	3,327	1.2	1.6	1.8	2.2	3.4	3.7
0-74 years	171	338	552	959	1,783	2,554	0.9	1.1	1.2	1.6	2.3	2.8
5 years and over	170	361	596	998	2,111	3,176	0.9	1.2	1.3	1.6	2.8	3.5
ot reported	1	59	55	42	-	-	-	0.2	0.1	0.1	-	-
LL AGES	19,065	30,554	44,690	60,807	75,864	90,992	100.0	100.0	100.0	100.0	100.0	100.0

TABLE X

DISTRIBUTION OF FAMILIES BY SIZE AND RACE, 1960

Type and Race of Family	Total	Number of Family Members						Average per Family
		2	3	4	5	6	7 or More	
IN THOUSANDS								
White								
Urban	28,711	9,744	6,427	5,958	3,619	1,729	1,235	3.51
Rural nonfarm	9,109	2,823	1,895	1,839	1,243	686	622	3.73
Rural farm	3,053	972	618	552	400	247	264	3.80
All families	40,873	13,540	8,939	8,349	5,262	2,662	2,121	3.58
Nonwhite								
Urban	3,229	978	654	509	380	273	436	4.07
Rural nonfarm	747	184	123	99	85	74	183	4.83
Rural farm	279	54	38	33	30	28	97	5.60
All families	4,256	1,216	815	641	494	375	715	4.31
All families								
Urban	31,940	10,722	7,081	6,467	3,999	2,002	1,671	3.56
Rural nonfarm	9,856	3,008	2,018	1,938	1,328	760	805	3.81
Rural farm	3,332	1,026	656	585	430	276	361	3.96
TOTAL	45,128	14,756	9,754	8,990	5,756	3,037	2,836	3.65
PER CENT								
White								
Urban	100.0	33.9	22.4	20.8	12.6	6.0	4.3	...
Rural nonfarm	100.0	31.0	20.8	20.2	13.6	7.5	6.8	.‹.
Rural farm	100.0	31.8	20.2	18.1	13.1	8.1	8.6	...
All families	100.0	33.1	21.9	20.4	12.9	6.5	5.2	...
Nonwhite								
Urban	100.0	30.3	20.2	15.8	11.8	8.4	13.5	...
Rural nonfarm	100.0	24.7	16.5	13.2	11.4	9.8	24.4	...
Rural farm	100.0	19.2	13.7	11.8	10.6	10.2	34.6	...
All families	100.0	28.6	19.2	15.1	11.6	8.8	16.8	...
All families								
Urban	100.0	33.6	22.2	20.2	12.5	6.3	5.2	...
Rural nonfarm	100.0	30.5	20.5	19.7	13.5	7.7	8.2	...
Rural farm	100.0	30.8	19.7	17.6	12.9	8.3	10.8	...
TOTAL	100.0	32.7	21.6	19.9	12.8	6.7	6.3	...

TABLE XI

PERCENTAGE DISTRIBUTION OF WOMEN AGED 45-49 YEARS, EVER MARRIED,
BY NUMBER OF CHILDREN EVER BORN, 1910-60

Children Ever Born	Total				White				Nonwhite			
	1910	1940	1950	1960	1910	1940	1950	1960	1910	1940	1950	1960
None	9.5	16.7	20.4	18.1	9.6	16.1	19.5	17.1	8.7	23.4	28.1	27.1
1 child	10.3	16.2	19.8	19.5	10.4	16.4	20.1	19.5	9.5	14.2	17.9	19.3
2 children	12.1	19.1	21.7	24.7	12.5	19.6	22.6	25.9	8.3	13.4	13.7	14.0
3 children	11.3	14.7	13.8	15.8	11.7	15.1	14.2	16.5	7.6	10.9	10.3	9.8
4 children	10.7	10.3	8.7	8.9	11.0	10.5	8.8	9.1	7.9	8.8	7.3	7.1
5 and 6 children	17.3	12.2	8.4	7.8	17.6	12.1	8.3	7.6	13.8	13.0	9.4	9.4
7 to 9 children	17.6	7.7	5.0 ⎫	5.3	17.4	7.4	4.6 ⎫	4.4	18.8	10.2	8.3 ⎫	13.3
10 or more children	11.2	3.1	2.2 ⎭		9.8	2.8	1.9 ⎭		25.4	6.3	4.9 ⎭	
TOTAL	100.0	100.0	100.0	100.0	100.0	100.0	100.0	100.0	100.0	100.0	100.0	100.0

TABLE XII

BIRTH RATE PER 1,000 POPULATION IN SELECTED COUNTRIES

Country and Year	Birth Rate	Country and Year	Birth Rate
United States, 1964	27.2	Romania, 1964	15.2
Canada, 1964	23.8	Spain, 1964	22.2
Mexico, 1964	45.2	Sweden, 1964	16.0
Brazil, 1960	46.0	Switzerland, 1963	19.1
Chile, 1963	33.7	United Kingdom, 1964	18.7
Guatemala, 1963	47.7	Yugoslavia, 1964	26.8
Argentina, 1964	21.5		
		Israel, 1964	25.7
Austria, 1964	18.5	Japan, 1964	17.7
Belgium, 1963	17.1	India, 1961	21.0
Bulgaria, 1964	16.1		
Czechoslovakia, 1964	17.1	U.S.S.R., 1962	22.4
Denmark, 1964	17.6		
Finland, 1964	17.6	Tunisia, 1964	45.1
France, 1964	18.1	South Africa, 1962: White	24.0
West Germany, 1964	18.2	Colored	46.3
Ireland, 1964	22.5	Asiatic	46.8
Italy, 1964	20.0		
Netherlands, 1964	20.7	Australia, 1964	20.6
Norway, 1964	17.9	New Zealand, 1964	24.1
Poland, 1964	18.1		
Portugal, 1964	23.7		

TABLE XIII

PERCENTAGE DISTRIBUTION OF THE POPULATION OF THE UNITED STATES,
AGED 14 YEARS AND OVER, BY MARITAL STATUS, SEX AND AGE, 1930-60

Marital Status and Age	Male				Female			
	1930[a]	1940	1950	1960	1930[a]	1940	1950	1960
Single	35.8	34.8	26.4	24.9	28.4	27.6	20.0	19.0
14 years	99.9	99.9	99.1	99.4	99.6	99.7	99.3	98.9
15-19 years	98.0	98.3	96.7	96.1	86.8	88.1	82.9	83.9
20-24 years	70.8	72.2	59.1	53.0	46.0	47.2	32.3	28.4
25-29 years	36.7	36.0	23.8	20.8	21.7	22.8	13.3	10.5
30-34 years	21.2	20.7	13.2	11.9	13.2	14.7	9.3	6.9
35-39 years	15.4	15.3	10.1	8.8	10.4	11.2	8.4	6.1
40-44 years	13.1	12.6	9.0	7.3	9.5	9.5	8.3	6.1
45-49 years	11.9	11.2	8.7	7.1	9.0	8.6	7.9	6.5
50-54 years	10.9	11.0	8.3	7.6	9.2	8.7	7.7	7.6
55-59 years	10.3	10.8	8.3	8.2	9.0	8.7	7.7	8.2
60-64 years	9.9	10.5	8.6	7.6	8.9	9.3	8.2	7.7
65-69 years	9.3	10.3	8.7	7.7	8.4	9.4	8.4	7.9
70-74 years	8.6	9.9	8.3	7.8	8.4	9.5	9.0	8.4
75-79 years		9.5	8.1	7.9		9.2	9.4	8.8
80-84 years	7.0	8.7	7.4	7.4	7.3	9.2	9.4	9.5
85 and over		7.9	7.7	7.1		8.0	9.7	9.6
Married	58.4	59.7	67.5	69.6	59.5	59.5	65.8	66.0
14 years	0.1	0.1	0.6	0.6	0.4	0.3	0.7	1.1
15-19 years	1.7	1.7	3.1	3.8	12.6	11.6	16.7	15.7
20-24 years	28.1	27.4	39.9	45.9	51.6	51.3	65.6	69.5
25-29 years	61.3	62.7	74.2	77.2	74.3	74.1	83.3	86.2
30-34 years	76.0	77.2	84.3	85.7	81.5	80.4	86.2	88.7
35-39 years	81.0	81.6	86.8	88.3	82.3	81.5	85.5	88.1
40-44 years	82.1	83.2	87.1	89.1	80.6	80.6	83.1	85.9
45-49 years	82.1	83.6	86.2	88.5	77.6	78.3	79.8	82.5
50-54 years	81.0	81.9	85.0	87.0	72.3	73.3	75.0	77.0
55-59 years	79.5	79.9	83.1	84.8	66.2	67.2	69.1	69.9
60-64 years	76.2	76.7	79.3	82.9	56.9	58.0	60.1	61.4
65-69 years	71.5	71.9	74.0	79.4	46.6	46.5	48.9	51.6
70-74 years	64.7	64.9	67.5	73.1	38.0	34.3	36.6	39.1
75-79 years		56.1	59.0	64.7		23.0	34.7	27.4
80-84 years	50.4	45.8	48.2	53.7	18.2	13.5	14.2	16.2
85 and over		33.0	33.6	38.7		6.7	7.0	8.2
Widowed	4.5	4.2	4.1	3.4	10.8	11.3	11.8	12.2
14 years	...	...	0.2	...	...	...	0.1	...
15-19 years	...	...	0.1	...	0.2	0.1	0.1	0.1
20-24 years	0.3	0.1	0.2	0.1	1.0	0.6	0.4	0.3
25-29 years	0.8	0.4	0.3	0.2	2.1	1.3	0.9	0.7
30-34 years	1.3	0.7	0.4	0.3	3.3	2.5	1.6	1.2
35-39 years	2.0	1.3	0.7	0.5	5.3	4.6	2.7	2.2
40-44 years	3.0	2.1	1.2	0.8	8.0	7.3	5.0	4.0
45-49 years	4.3	3.2	2.1	1.4	11.6	10.7	8.6	6.7
50-54 years	6.3	5.1	3.7	2.3	16.9	15.9	13.9	11.1
55-59 years	8.4	7.4	5.9	3.8	23.4	22.4	20.5	17.9
60-64 years	12.4	11.1	9.6	6.5	33.1	31.3	29.7	27.6
65-69 years	17.8	16.2	15.0	10.2	44.1	43.1	41.1	37.9
70-74 years	25.4	23.8	22.2	16.7	55.9	55.3	53.3	50.4
75-79 years		33.3	31.4	25.3		67.3	65.1	62.2
80-84 years	41.5	44.7	43.3	37.2	73.9	77.1	75.9	73.1
85 and over		58.5	57.9	52.8		85.1	82.9	81.4

(continued)

TABLE XIII (continued)

Marital Status and Age	Male				Female			
	1930[a]	1940	1950	1960	1930[a]	1940	1950	1960
Divorced	1.1	1.2	2.0	2.1	1.3	1.6	2.4	2.9
14 years	...	...	0.1	...	...	...	...	...
15-19 years	...	...	0.1	0.1	0.2	0.1	0.3	0.3
20-24 years	0.4	0.3	0.9	1.0	1.1	0.9	1.7	1.8
25-29 years	1.0	0.9	1.7	1.8	1.8	1.8	2.5	2.6
30-34 years	1.4	1.4	2.1	2.2	1.9	2.4	3.0	3.1
35-39 years	1.5	1.8	2.4	2.4	1.9	2.8	3.5	3.6
40-44 years	1.6	2.0	2.7	2.7	1.8	2.7	3.7	4.0
45-49 years	1.7	2.0	2.9	3.0	1.7	2.4	3.6	4.3
50-54 years	1.6	2.0	3.0	3.1	1.5	2.0	3.3	4.2
55-59 years	1.6	1.9	2.7	3.1	1.3	1.7	2.7	3.9
60-64 years	1.5	1.7	2.5	3.0	1.0	1.4	2.1	3.3
65-69 years	1.3	1.6	2.3	2.7	0.8	1.0	1.5	2.7
70-74 years	1.1	1.3	1.9	2.4	0.5	0.7	1.1	2.1
75-79 years	⎱	1.1	1.5	2.1 ⎱	⎧	0.4	0.7	1.5
80-84 years	10.8 ⎰	0.8	1.1	1.7 ⎰	0.3 ⎨	0.3	0.5	1.1
85 and over	⎰	0.6	0.8	1.4 ⎰	⎩	0.2	0.4	0.8

[a]Includes persons with marital status not reported, not shown separately.

TABLE XIV

MARRIAGE RATES IN SELECTED COUNTRIES
(Per 1,000 Marriageable Males or Females)

Country and Year	Males	Females	Country and Year	Males	Females
United States, 1960	73.5	72.4	Poland, 1949-51	96.2	63.9
Canada, 1955-57	69.1	72.6	Portugal, 1949-51	54.1	43.1
Mexico, 1949-51	50.7	39.2	Spain, 1949-51	46.1	36.4
Costa Rica, 1949-51	50.5	49.3	Sweden, 1949-51	52.6	49.5
Guatemala, 1949-51	15.4	15.4	Switzerland, 1949-51	54.1	42.1
Honduras, 1949-51	18.1	17.8	United Kingdom, 1950-52	70.2	51.6
Argentina, 1946-48	42.3	47.0	Yugoslavia, 1952-53	85.1	66.6
Bolivia, 1949-51	57.2	47.7			
Chile, 1951-53	54.4	49.9	Japan, 1954-56	61.9	52.5
Colombia, 1950-52	34.4	32.8	Ceylon, 1952-54	33.1	42.9
Peru, 1939-41	17.9	15.5	Israel, 1945-47	93.2	113.7
Venezuela, 1949-51	23.6	23.5	Philippines, 1956-57	52.9	48.1
			Thailand, 1946-48	11.5	11.4
Austria, 1950-52	69.3	44.2			
Belgium, 1946-48	71.4	63.6	Algeria, 1953-55:		
Bulgaria, 1945-47	103.4	100.7	Moslems	95.7	110.5
Czechoslovakia, 1946-48	83.3	68.1	Europeans	70.7	50.2
Denmark, 1949-51	68.8	62.5	Tunis, Europeans	48.0	43.8
Finland, 1949-51	65.4	47.3	Union of South Africa:		
France, 1953-55	57.0	42.2	White, 1950-52	86.8	83.9
Germany, Federal Rep., 1949-51	83.5	56.0	Colored, 1946-47	62.0	64.8
Greece, 1950-52	48.1	41.3	Bantu, 1946-47	18.5	20.3
Hungary, 1948-50	89.8	69.6	Asians, 1946-47	55.8	75.0
Italy, 1950-52	49.9	42.2			
Netherlands, 1946-48	72.5	67.3	Australia, 1953-55	63.9	66.3
Norway, 1949-51	55.2	50.5	New Zealand, 1955-57	69.0	68.5

TABLE XV

DEATH RATES FROM SELECTED CAUSES OF DEATH, 1910-64
(Per 100,000 Population)

Causes of Death	1910	1920	1940	1950	1960	1962	1963	1964
Conquered causes of death								
Pneumonia and influenza	156	207	70	31	37	32	37.	31
Tuberculosis	154	113	46	23	6.1	5.1	4.9	4.2
Diarrhea, enteritis, a.o.	115	54	10	5.1	4.4	4.4	4.4	4.1
Diphtheria	21	15	1.1	0.3	0.0	0.0	0.0	0.0
Typhoid and								
paratyphoid fever	23	8	1.1	0.1	0.0	0.0	0.0	0.0
Measles	12	9	0.5	0.3	0.2	0.2	0.2	0.2
Whooping cough	12	13	2.2	0.7	0.1	0.0	0.1	0.1
Syphilis	14	17	14	5.0	1.6	1.5	1.4	0.4
Total	507	426	145	66	49	43	48	40
Unconquered causes of death								
Diseases of heart	137	160	293	357	369	370	375	367
Vascular lesions of								
central nervous system	107	93	91	104	108	106	107	105
Malignant neoplasms	76	83	120	140	149	150	151	152
Diabetes mellitus	15	16	27	16	17	17	17	17
Certain diseases of								
early infancy	73	69	39	41	37	35	33	31
Accidents[a]	84	70	73	61	52	52	53	54
Suicide and homicide	11	17	11	17	15	16	16	16
Total	503	508	654	736	748	747	752	742
All other causes	458	365	277	162	158	155	162	159
ALL CAUSES	1,468	1,299	1,076	964	955	945	962	941

[a]Including motor vehicle accidents: 23 in 1950, 21 in 1960, 22 in 1962 and 23 in 1963.

TABLE XVI

LIFE EXPECTANCY IN SELECTED COUNTRIES

Country and Year		At the Age of							
		0	1	10	20	40	60	65	70
United States, 1963	M	67.5	68.2	59.6	50.1	31.6	19.9	12.8	10.2
	F	74.4	74.8	66.2	56.4	37.3	14.6	16.0	12.5
Canada, 1960-62	M	68.4	69.5	61.0	51.5	33.0	16.7	13.5	10.7
	F	74.2	75.0	66.4	56.7	37.5	19.9	16.1	12.6
France, 1963	M	67.2	67.8	59.3	49.7	31.3	15.5	12.4	9.6
	F	74.1	74.5	65.9	56.1	37.1	19.6	15.6	12.0
West Germany, 1960-62	M	66.9	68.3	59.9	50.3	31.4	15.5	12.4	9.6
	F	72.4	73.5	64.9	55.2	36.1	18.5	14.6	11.1
Sweden, 1962	M	67.5	70.5	62.5	52.9	34.0	17.0	13.5	10.4
	F	70.7	73.5	65.5	55.8	36.6	18.9	15.1	11.1
United Kingdom, 1961-63	M	68.0	68.6	60.0	50.4	31.4	14.9	11.8	9.1
	F	73.9	74.3	65.0	55.8	36.5	18.9	15.1	11.6
India, 1951-60	M	41.9	48.4	45.2	37.0	22.1	11.8	9.8	8.1
	F	40.6	46.0	43.8	35.6	22.4	13.0	11.1	9.3
Israel, 1963 (Jewish	M	70.9	71.7	63.1	53.6	34.6	17.5	14.1	11.2
population)	F	73.0	73.5	64.9	55.2	35.9	18.5	14.9	11.7
Japan, 1963	M	67.2	68.0	59.7	50.1	31.8	15.4	12.1	9.2
	F	72.3	72.9	64.5	54.7	35.9	18.5	14.7	11.3

TABLE XVII

JOB CHANGING BY SEX, AGE, EMPLOYMENT PATTERN,
AND REASON FOR CHANGING JOBS, 1961

Sex, Employment Pattern, and Reason for Changing Jobs	Total	14-17 Years	18-19 Years	20-24 Years	25-54 Years	55-64 Years	65 Years and Over
Male workers (in thousands):							
Total	49,854	2,926	1,946	4,507	30,806	6,768	2,901
Changed jobs	5,509	261	457	1,101	3,319	271	100
Per cent:	100.0	100.0	100.0	100.0	100.0	100.0	100.0
Worked at 2 jobs only	62.7	70.1	64.6	62.8	62.1	59.0	65.0
Lost no work between jobs	31.5	28.0	26.3	30.2	34.0	20.7	22.0
Lost work between jobs	31.2	42.1	38.3	32.5	28.0	38.4	43.0
Did not look for work	5.8	20.7	12.0	6.6	3.2	4.4	19.0
Looked for work	25.4	21.5	26.3	25.9	24.9	33.9	24.0
1-14 weeks	21.8	17.2	24.1	23.2	20.9	29.2	20.0
15 weeks or more	3.6	4.2	2.2	2.7	3.9	4.8	4.0
Worked at more than 2 jobs	37.3	29.9	35.4	37.2	37.9	41.0	35.0
Reasons for changing jobs (per cent)							
Total	100.0	100.0	100.0	100.0	100.0	100.0	100.0
Job loss	37.5	18.2	27.0	32.0	41.1	56.2	41.0
Improvement in status	33.7	20.0	30.9	33.5	37.5	18.1	13.3
Termination of temporary job	10.9	30.9	14.5	11.6	7.6	14.6	21.0
Other reasons[a]	18.0	30.9	27.5	22.9	13.8	11.1	24.6
Female workers (in thousands[b]):							
Total	30,433	2,044	1,789	3,476	17,995	3,782	1,347
Changed jobs	2,612	118	397	568	1,348	156	25
Per cent:	100.0	100.0	100.0	100.0	100.0	100.0	100.0
Worked at 2 jobs only	75.2	82.2	70.8	75.0	76.5	71.8	...
Lost no work between jobs	30.7	29.7	28.2	32.7	31.2	28.2	...
Lost work between jobs	44.5	52.5	42.6	42.3	45.3	43.6	...
Did not look for work	15.3	31.4	9.8	13.7	15.4	17.3	...
Looked for work	29.2	21.2	32.7	28.5	29.8	26.3	...
1-14 weeks	25.7	21.2	32.2	25.9	24.7	23.1	...
15 weeks or more	3.5	-	0.5	2.6	5.1	3.2	...
Worked at more than 2 jobs	24.8	17.8	29.2	25.0	23.5	28.2	...
Reasons for changing jobs (per cent)							
Total	100.0	100.0	100.0	100.0	100.0	100.0	...
Job loss	20.6	13.9	18.2	17.5	22.4	27.9	...
Improvement in status	30.1	14.4	31.0	29.9	32.9	18.9	...
Termination of temporary job	17.1	32.7	17.0	17.7	13.6	29.3	...
Other reasons[a]	32.2	39.1	33.8	34.9	31.6	23.9	...

[a]Illness, household or school responsibilities, fired, retired, reasons not reported.
[b]Breakdown for female workers ends at 55 years and over.

TABLE XVIII

DISTRIBUTION OF FAMILIES AND THEIR FAMILY PERSONAL INCOME,
BY INCOME LEVEL, 1947-62

Income Group, Before Income Taxes (In Dollars)	Number of Families (In Millions)				Aggregate Family Personal Income (In Millions of Dollars)			
	1947	1955	1959	1962	1947	1955	1959	1962
Under 2,000	6.4	3.9	3.5	3.2	8,388	4,890	4,254	3,905
2,000-2,999	6.7	3.8	3.2	2.9	16,967	9,636	8,020	7,313
3,000-3,999	7.9	5.9	4.4	3.8	27,503	20 703	5,506	13,491
4,000-4,999	5.5	6.6	5.2	4.6	24,444	29,609	23,326	20,715
5,000-5,999	3.4	5.9	5.3	5.1	18,375	32.599	29,673	27,918
6,000-7,499	3.1	6.7	7.4	7.5	20,288	44,843	49,667	50,436
7,500-9,999	2.1	5.1	7.5	8.7	18,085	43,292	64,365	75,057
10,000-14,999	1.2	3.0	5.2	6.9	14,009	36,136	61,712	82,956
15,000-19,999	0.4	0.9	1.7 ⎫		6,411 ⎧	14,805	29,102 ⎫	
20,000-24,999	0.2	0.4	0.6 ⎬	4.1	3,568 ⎨	8,140	12,809 ⎬	100,424
25,000-49,999	0.1	0.4	0.6 ⎭		6,636 ⎩	14,596	20,255 ⎭	
50,000 and over	0.04	0.1	0.2		4,666	9,690	'4,253	
TOTAL	37.0	42.7	44.8	46.9	169,340	268,939	332,942	382,215

PERCENTAGE DISTRIBUTION

Under 2,000	17.3	9.1	7.8	6.9	5.0	1.8	1.3	1.0
2,000-2,999	18.2	8.9	7.1	6.2	10.0	3.6	2.4	1.9
3,000-3,999	21.3	13.8	9.8	8.2	16.2	7.7	4.7	3.5
4,000-4,999	14.8	15.7	11.6	9.8	14.4	11.0	7.0	5.4
5,000-5,999	9.1	13.8	12.0	10.8	10.8	12.1	8.9	7.3
6,000-7,499	8.3	15.7	16.5	16.0	12.0	16.7	14.9	13.2
7,500-9,999	5.8	11.9	16.7	18.6	10.7	16.1	19.3	19.7
10,000-14,999	3.2	7.0	11.6	14.8	8.3	13.5	18.5	21.7
15,000-19,999	1.0	2.1	3.8 ⎫		3.8 ⎧	5.5	8.7 ⎫	
20,000-24,999	0.4	0.9	1.3 ⎬	8.7	2.1 ⎨	3.0	3.9 ⎬	26.3
25,000-49,999	0.5	0.9	1.4 ⎭		3.9 ⎩	5.4	6.1 ⎭	
50,000 and over	0.1	0.2	0.4		2.8	3.6	4.3	
TOTAL	100.0	100.0	100.0	100.0	100.0	100.0	100.0	100.0

TABLE XIX

PERCENTAGE DISTRIBUTION OF EXPENDITURES FOR CURRENT
CONSUMPTION OF URBAN FAMILIES AND SINGLE CONSUMERS,
BY INCOME CLASS, 1950 AND 1960-61

1950

	Total	1,000-1,999	2,000-2,999	3,000-3,999	4,000-4,999	5,000-5,999	6,000-7,499	7,500-9,999	10,000-14,999	15,000 and Over
Food and beverages	31.4	36.3	34.7	32.8	31.1	30.2	29.1	28.9	26.4	24.5
Tobacco	1.8	2.0	2.1	2.0	1.9	1.7	1.6	1.4	1.2	1.0
Housing: shelter	11.5	15.7	12.7	11.5	10.9	10.3	10.3	9.9	10.7	10.7
utilities	4.1	6.1	4.8	4.3	4.0	3.7	3.5	3.4	3.0	2.8
household operations	4.7	4.6	4.2	4.1	4.2	4.5	4.6	5.4	7.2	9.0
furnishings and equipment	6.9	4.9	6.4	6.6	7.4	7.2	7.2	6.4	7.4	8.4
Clothing	11.5	9.2	10.3	10.8	11.4	12.3	12.8	13.5	13.8	14.1
Transportation	13.4	7.9	10.9	13.3	14.4	15.5	15.6	15.4	14.1	12.8
Personal care	2.2	2.4	2.4	2.3	2.2	2.2	2.1	2.1	2.0	1.9
Medical care	5.2	5.4	5.3	5.5	5.0	4.8	5.0	5.2	4.4	4.1
Recreation, reading, education	5.9	3.7	4.7	5.7	6.3	6.3	6.9	6.9	7.6	7.8
Other expenditures	1.4	1.6	1.4	1.1	1.2	1.4	1.4	1.3	2.2	2.9
ALL EXPENDITURES	100.0	100.0	100.0	100.0	100.0	100.0	100.0	100.0	100.0	100.0

1960-61

	Total	1,000-1,999	2,000-2,999	3,000-3,999	4,000-4,999	5,000-5,999	6,000-7,499	7,500-9,999	10,000-14,999	15,000 and Over
Food	24.3	29.8	28.4	25.9	25.3	25.0	24.2	24.0	22.2	19.1
Beverages	1.7	1.1	1.2	1.5	1.6	1.6	1.7	1.8	1.9	1.9
Tobacco	1.8	1.8	2.1	2.1	2.1	2.0	1.9	1.7	1.3	1.0
Housing: shelter	13.9	21.6	18.5	15.7	14.5	14.1	13.5	12.5	11.7	12.5
utilities	4.5	7.3	5.8	4.9	4.7	4.8	4.5	4.2	3.8	3.3
household operations	5.9	6.5	5.9	6.0	5.7	5.5	5.6	5.5	6.1	8.5
furnishings and equipment	5.1	3.6	3.9	4.7	4.9	5.3	5.5	5.4	5.4	5.3
Clothing	10.4	6.1	8.2	9.0	9.7	9.9	10.3	11.1	11.9	12.3
Personal care	2.9	2.9	3.3	3.1	3.0	3.0	2.8	2.9	2.7	2.4
Medical care	6.6	8.0	8.1	7.3	6.3	6.5	6.5	6.3	6.1	6.2
Recreation, reading, education	6.0	3.4	4.1	4.8	5.1	5.2	6.0	6.5	8.0	8.3
Transportation	14.7	5.4	8.6	13.1	15.4	15.4	15.3	16.0	16.4	14.2
Other expenditures	2.2	2.4	1.9	1.7	1.8	1.7	2.1	2.0	2.6	5.0
ALL EXPENDITURES	100.0	100.0	100.0	100.0	100.0	100.0	100.0	100.0	100.0	100.0

TABLE XX

NUMBER, ACREAGE, AND VALUE OF FARMS IN THE UNITED STATES
BY GEOGRAPHIC DIVISION, 1940, 1950, AND 1959

Item and Year	United States	New England	Middle Atlantic	East North Central	West North Central	South Atlantic	East South Central	West South Central	Mountain	Pacific
Land in farms (In Millions of Acres)										
1940	1,065	13.4	33.6	113.7	274.4	92.6	77.1	200.5	191.9	68.0
1950	1,161	12.5	31.9	112.1	284.3	102.2	79.6	211.5	250.2	77.2
1959	1,124	9.3	26.7	103.4	282.0	83.3	68.3	205.8	264.4	80.2
Number of farms (In Thousands)										
1940	6,103	135	348	1,006	1,091	1,019	1,023	964	233	283
1950	5,339	103	297	885	983	959	913	780	195	274
1959	3,711	57	198	666	795	592	563	491	149	200
Average acreage per farm										
1940	174	99	97	113	252	91	75	208	822	231
1950	216	122	107	127	289	107	87	271	1,284	279
1959	303	164	135	155	355	141	121	419	1,774	401
Average value per farm (In Thousands of Dollars)										
1940	5.5	5.5	5.9	7.3	8.1	3.1	2.3	4.4	7.6	11.7
1950	14.0	11.8	11.7	16.6	19.4	7.5	5.7	13.6	28.3	31.2
1959	34.8	24.9	24.7	37.1	38.7	21.7	14.0	37.3	73.0	89.6
Average value per acre (In Dollars)										
1940	31.7	55.4	60.6	64.5	32.1	34.1	30.2	21.1	9.3	50.8
1950	65.0	97.4	109.4	131.2	67.0	70.1	65.0	50.3	22.0	112.2
1959	115.1	151.8	182.5	239.3	109.0	154.0	115.0	89.0	41.1	223.3

TABLE XXI

ACREAGE, PRODUCTION, YIELD PER ACRE, AND
FARM VALUE OF SELECTED FIELD CROPS, 1931-64

rop	Harvested Acreage (In Millions)			Production (In Millions of Units Indicated[a])			Yield per Acre (In Units Indicated[b])			Farm Value (In Millions of Dollars)		
	1936-40	1956-60	1964	1936-40	1956-60	1964	1936-40	1956-60	1964	1936-40	1956-60	1964
'heat	57.7	50.0	49.2	796	1,179	1,290	13.8	23.5	26.2	614	2,142	1,774
orn[c]	77.3	67.0	57.1	2,091	3,442	3,549	26.8	51.2	62.1	...	3,798	4,051
ats	34.8	30.6	20.4	1,053	1,210	882	30.2	39.7	43.2	329	752	552
arley	11.0	14.3	10.7	243	430	403	22.0	30.1	37.8	113	381	374
orghum[c]	4.7	15.3	11.9	61	506	490	13.0	32.4	41.1	32	471	520
oybeans[d]	3.4	22.4	30.7	62	520	700	18.1	23.2	22.8	53	1,075	1,836
otton lint	27.1	14.3	14.1	14	13	15	239	434	524	647	2,022	2,357
ay	68.8	69.7	67.9	85	115	116	1.2	1.7	1.7	790	2,282	2,691
obacco	1.6	1.2	1.1	1,492	1,864	2,230	909	1,591	2,066	278	1,075	1,307
ice, rough	1.1	1.5	1.8	24	49	73	2,256	3,265	4,095	39	233	361
eanuts	1.8	1.4	1.4	1,352	1,646	2,167	764	1,137	1,551	46	170	243
rish potatoes	2.9	1.4	1.3	213	252	243	73.4	182.6	185.8	238	476	786
laxseed	1.7	4.0	2.8	14	32	24	8.5	8.1	8.6	22	92	69
ottonseed	...	...	...	6	5	6	...	...	...	132	243	297

heat, corn, oats, barley, sorghum, soybeans, flaxseed in millions of bushels; cotton lint, in millions
f bales; hay and cottonseed in millions of short tons; tobacco and peanuts in millions of pounds; rice
nd Irish potatoes in millions of cwt.

ield of wheat, corn, oats, barley, sorghum, soybeans, and flaxseed in bushels; cotton lint, tobacco,
eanuts, and rice in pounds; hay in short tons; Irish potatoes, in cwt.

or grain.

or beans.

TABLE XXII

PRODUCTION OF ENERGY FROM MINERAL FUELS AND
WATER POWER IN THE UNITED STATES, 1900-1964

| | Production (In Trillions of BTU[a]) | | | | | Percentage Distribution | | | | |
Year	Total	Coal[b]	Crude Petroleum	Natural Gas, Wet	Water Power	Total	Coal	Crude Petroleum	Natural Gas, Wet	Water Power
1900	7,893	7,020	369	264	250	100.0	88.9	4.7	3.2	3.2
1910	15,375	13,074	1,215	547	539	100.0	85.1	7.9	3.5	3.5
1920	21,365	17,175	2,569	883	738	100.0	80.4	12.0	4.1	3.5
1930	22,119	14,011	5,208	2,148	752	100.0	63.4	23.5	9.7	3.4
1940	25,088	13,380	7,849	2,979	880	100.0	53.3	31.3	11.9	3.5
1945	32,333	16,529	9,939	4,423	1,442	100.0	51.1	30.7	13.7	4.5
1950	34,510	14,647	11,449	6,841	1,573	100.0	42.4	33.2	19.8	4.6
1955	38,900	12,839	14,410	10,204	1,447	100.0	33.0	37.1	26.2	3.7
1960	41,844	11,364	14,935	13,822	1,723	100.0	27.2	35.7	33.0	4.1
1961	42,295	11,001	15,206	14,336	1,752	100.0	26.1	35.9	33.9	4.1
1962	43,926[c]	11,463	15,522	15,004	1,937	100.0[c]	26.1	35.3	34.2	4.4
1963	46,296[c]	12,488	15,966	15,941	1,901	100.0[c]	26.9	34.5	34.5	4.1
1964	48,012[c]	13,045	16,270	16,679	2,018	100.0[c]	27.2	33.8	34.7	4.2

[a]British Thermal Unit represents the amount of heat required to raise the temperature of one pound of water one degree Fahrenheit. The unit heat value used in the calculation by the Bureau of Mines is as follows: 12,700 BTU per 1 pound anthracite; 13,100 BTU per pound bituminous coal and lignite; 5.8 million BTU per barrel petroleum. More complicated calculations have been used for energy provided by natural gas and water power.

[b]Bituminous coal, lignite, and anthracite. Alaska included for all years.

[c]Includes energy from nuclear power (0.1 of 1 per cent of total).

TABLE XXIII

CONSUMPTION OF ENERGY FROM MINERAL
FUELS AND WATER POWER IN THE UNITED STATES, 1920-64

Year	Total	Coal[a]	Crude Oil	Petroleum Products, Net[b]	Natural Gas, Dry	Natural Gas, Liquids	Water-Power
			(In Trillions of British Thermal Units)				
1920	19,782	15,504	3,027	-393	827	42	775
1925	20,899	14,706	4,641	-485	1,212	124	701
1930	22,288	13,639	6,148	-496	1,969	243	785
1935	19,107	10,634	5,799	-300	1,974	169	831
1940	23,908	12,535	7,662	-175	2,726	243	917
1945	31,541	15;972	10,199	-580	3,973	491	1,486
1950	34,153	12,913	12,304	+402	6,150	783	1,601
1955	39,956	11,603	15,956	+372	9,232	1,196	1,497
1960	44,960	10,414	17,172	+1,436	12,736	1,427	1,775
1961	45,705	10,213	17,372	+1,617	13,228	1,498	1,777
1962	47,760[c]	10,523	17,853	+1,809	14,027	1,605	1,943
1963	49,725[c]	11,083	18,434	+1,828	14,843	1,688	1,910
1964	51,676[c]	11,660	18,742	+1,965	15,648	1,769	1,858
			(Percentage Distribution)				
1920	100.0	78.4	15.3	-2.0	4.2	0.2	3.9
1925	100.0	70.4	22.2	-2.3	5.8	0.6	3.3
1930	100.0	61.2	27.6	-2.2	8.8	1.1	3.5
1935	100.0	55.7	30.4	-1.6	10.3	9.9	4.3
1940	100.0	52.4	32.1	-0.7	11.4	1.0	3.8
1945	100.0	50.7	32.3	-1.8	12.6	1.5	4.7
1950	100.0	37.8	36.0	+1.2	18.0	2.3	4.7
1955	100.0	29.3	39.0	+0.9	23.1	3.0	3.8
1960	100.0	23.2	38.2	+3.2	28.3	3.2	3.9
1961	100.0	22.4	38.0	+3.4	28.9	3.3	3.9
1962	100.0[c]	22.0	37.3	+3.8	29.4	3.4	4.1
1963	100.0[c]	22.3	37.0	+3.7	29.8	3.4	3.8
1964	100.0[c]	22.5	36.5	+3.8	30.1	3.4	3.6

[a]Bituminous, lignite and anthracite.

[b]Exports (-); Imports (+).

[c]Includes energy from nuclear power (0.1 of 1 per cent of total).

TABLE XXIV

MANUFACTURING INDUSTRIES IN THE UNITED STATES,
BY STATE, 1963[a]

State	All Employees (In Thousands)	Production Workers (In Thousands)	Payroll (In Millions of Dollars)	Wages (In Millions of Dollars)	Value Added by Manufacture (In Millions of Dollars)
Maine	100	84	436	333	778
New Hampshire	87	71	389	279	653
Vermont	34	26	169	115	318
Massachusetts	681	485	3,760	2,246	6,340
Rhode Island	113	89	530	363	948
Connecticut	417	293	2,568	1,553	4,360
New York	1,877	1,271	11,239	6,241	19,633
New Jersey	840	583	5,177	3,056	10,371
Pennsylvania	1,400	1,030	8,042	5,099	13,459
Ohio	1,251	893	8,138	5,251	15,250
Indiana	610	463	3,809	2,616	7,660
Illinois	1,222	861	7,544	4,664	14,385
Michigan	930	693	6,674	4,515	13,039
Wisconsin	467	342	2,798	1,836	5,365
Minnesota	252	169	1,507	878	2,872
Iowa	179	127	1,045	687	2,285
Missouri	394	277	2,242	1,363	4,277
North Dakota	6	4	31	20	69
South Dakota	13	10	72	48	148
Nebraska	66	48	352	230	757
Kansas	114	84	682	461	1,403
Delaware	59	31	432	160	635
Maryland	264	189	1,551	960	2,973
District of Columbia	22	11	148	65	260
Virginia	306	242	1,441	998	3,013
West Virginia	119	91	719	490	1,787
North Carolina	539	448	2,150	1,539	4,298
South Carolina	262	221	1,032	782	2,094
Georgia	357	293	1,501	1,070	3,165
Florida	218	151	1,096	625	2,347
Kentucky	181	139	938	687	2,446
Tennessee	335	269	1,489	1,031	3,317
Alabama	246	199	1,162	845	2,270
Mississippi	130	109	490	368	1,008
Arkansas	114	96	437	331	952
Louisiana	142	106	774	528	1,909
Oklahoma	94	62	525	288	983
Texas	510	363	2,870	1,746	6,811
Montana	20	16	108	82	245
Idaho	30	24	159	114	348
Wyoming	7	5	38	25	77
Colorado	94	64	590	368	1,126
New Mexico	16	10	82	48	144
Arizona	57	39	364	212	618
Utah	54	34	329	183	716
Nevada	7	5	44	30	107
Washington	225	151	1,474	869	2,922
Oregon	146	118	813	612	578
California	1,426	911	9,621	5,208	17,498
Alaska	6	5	40	30	81
Hawaii	25	18	105	66	298
UNITED STATES	17,065	12,325	99,725	62,162	190,395

[a]Preliminary data of the 1963 Census of Manufactures. Includes employment and payroll at administrative offices and auxiliary units.

TABLE XXV

METAL INDUSTRIES IN THE UNITED STATES, 1958 AND 1963

Industry Group	Employees (In Thousands)		Payroll (In Millions of Dollars)		Value Added	
	1958	1963	1958	1963	1958	1963
A. Primary metal industries	1,096	1,119	6,303	7,669	11,671	14,949
Steel rolling and finishing	578	561	3,571	4,111	6,863	8,350
Iron and steel foundries	182	202	886	1,238	1,322	1,994
Primary nonferrous metals	47	48	266	318	700	978
Secondary nonferrous metals	14	15	76	92	147	232
Nonferrous rolling and drawing	160	167	885	1,095	1,726	2,126
Nonferrous foundries	62	69	319	411	471	644
Primary metal industries n.e.c.[a]	52	58	301	404	442	625
B. Fabricated metal products	1,059	1,096	5,416	6,447	9,413	11,865
Metal cans	54	53	304	379	669	808
Cutlery, hand tools, hardware	136	138	657	807	1,202	1,695
Plumbing and nonelectric heating	72	70	357	404	672	812
Structural metal products	341	328	1,807	1,913	2,963	3,248
Screw-machine products and bolts	85	95	441	588	755	1,056
Metal stampings	126	134	646	779	1,049	1,366
Metal services n.e.c.[a]	52	67	224	336	362	553
Fabricated wire products n.e.c.	55	55	261	297	440	529
Fabricated metal products n.e.c.	137	155	715	945	1,300	1,799

[a]N.e.c.: not elsewhere classified

TABLE XXVI

MACHINERY INDUSTRIES IN THE UNITED STATES,
BY GEOGRAPHIC DIVISION AND SELECTED STATES, 1962

Geographic Division or State	All Employees	Production Workers	Payroll	Wages	Value Added
	(In Thousands)		(In Millions of Dollars)		
New England	330	233	1,882	1,152	3,346
Massachusetts	175	119	1,013	599	1,742
Connecticut	105	77	609	387	1,145
Middle Atlantic	728	500	4,534	2,644	7,619
New York	325	212	2,057	1,107	3,312
New Jersey	180	126	1,148	706	1,937
Pennsylvania	224	162	1,329	832	2,371
East North Central	1,057	780	6,643	4,380	12,180
Ohio	278	205	1,784	1,178	3,387
Indiana	145	113	872	613	1,633
Illinois	342	246	2,083	1,316	3,715
Michigan	166	128	1,117	770	2,050
Wisconsin	128	90	802	508	1,411
West North Central	165	117	944	576	1,828
Minnesota	34	21	207	108	372
Iowa	50	35	294	183	617
Missouri	49	35	271	174	469
South Atlantic	134	92	725	411	1,482
Maryland	31	19	198	99	370
East South Central	78	61	404	272	924
Kentucky	36	29	207	143	483
Tennessee	27	20	133	84	308
West South Central	90	45	493	303	999
Texas	63	44	358	210	727
Mountain	16	16	104	54	170
Arizona	6	4	42	21	65
Pacific	277	178	1,859	1,025	3,180
California	258	165	1,748	952	2,982
UNITED STATES	2,912	2,055	17,733	10,948	31,662

TABLE XXVII

WHOLESALE PRICE INDEXES, BY SELECTED COMMODITY, 1950-64
(1957-59 = 100)

	1950	1955	1960	1961	1962	1963	1964
Farm products	106.4	97.9	96.9	96.0	97.7	95.7	94.3
Livestock and live poultry	115.0	88.0	96.0	92.5	96.2	88.8	84.7
Fluid milk	93.3	96.4	103.2	103.9	101.2	100.6	102.0
Eggs	113.4	114.6	103.2	99.0	95.2	94.0	90.8
Processed foods	92.6	94.3	100.0	100.7	101.2	101.1	101.0
Cereal and bakery products	83.9	98.5	103.2	105.1	107.6	107.3	107.8
Meats, poultry, and fish	102.6	85.7	97.8	95.4	99.1	93.3	90.8
Dairy products and ice cream	84.0	94.0	105.0	107.5	106.9	107.5	107.8
Canned and frozen fruits and vegetables	92.8	98.1	99.5	101.7	98.0	103.9	104.8
Sugar and confectionery	85.1	96.3	101.8	101.2	102.2	118.4	111.8
Animal fats and oils	106.3	100.4	86.6	94.4	88.4	83.9	95.4
Textile products and apparel	104.8	100.7	101.5	99.7	100.6	100.5	101.2
Cotton products	110.3	101.4	104.4	100.4	101.7	100.3	99.6
Wool products	108.6	100.7	98.2	97.1	99.1	100.9	103.0
Man-made fiber textile products	117.5	106.8	97.5	93.4	93.9	93.9	95.8
Silk products	85.8	106.4	105.7	113.2	125.9	139.9	117.3
Hides, skins, leather, and leather products	99.9	89.5	105.2	106.2	107.4	104.2	104.6
Fuels and related products, and power	90.2	94.5	99.6	100.7	100.2	99.8	97.1
Coal	86.1	85.0	98.8	97.7	96.8	96.9	96.9
Gas fuels[a]	...	...	116.6	118.6	119.2	122.8	121.3
Electric power[a]	...	...	101.9	102.4	102.8	102.0	101.1
Crude petroleum	82.0	91.1	92.2	97.5	97.7	97.3	96.9
Chemicals and allied products	87.5	96.9	100.2	99.1	97.5	96.3	96.7
Rubber and rubber products	83.2	99.2	99.9	96.1	93.3	93.8	92.5
Tires and tubes	76.3	97.4	93.0	92.4	87.1	90.1	89.0
Pulp, paper, and allied products	77.1	91.1	101.8	98.8	100.0	99.2	99.0
Paper	74.7	91.1	102.0	102.2	102.6	102.4	103.6
Metals and metal products	72.7	90.0	101.3	100.7	100.0	100.1	102.8
Iron and steel	66.9	83.2	100.6	100.7	99.3	99.1	100.5
Nonferrous metals	77.8	106.7	103.9	100.4	99.2	99.1	105.9
Machinery and motive products	72.6	85.8	102.4	102.3	102.3	102.2	102.9
Furniture and other household durables	85.6	94.3	100.1	99.5	98.8	98.1	98.5
Household furniture	85.4	92.5	101.6	102.8	103.8	104.6	105.3
Household appliances	97.1	101.8	97.0	95.2	94.0	91.8	91.3
T.V., radio, phonographs	103.2	99.1	97.3	95.3	91.1	88.6	87.2
Tobacco products, and bottled beverages	80.5	94.6	102.5	103.2	104.1	106.1	107.4
Tobacco products	83.1	93.4	101.9	102.0	102.1	104.5	106.0
Alcoholic beverages	84.6	95.2	100.3	100.6	101.0	101.0	100.7
Nonalcoholic beverages	65.5	95.4	110.3	112.8	116.9	122.6	127.0

[a] January, 1958 = 100

List of Tables

CHAPTER V

CHAPTER VII

CHAPTER VIII

CHAPTER IX

CHAPTER X

CHAPTER XI

CHAPTER XII

CHAPTER XIV

CHAPTER XV

CHAPTER XVI

CHAPTER XVII

CHAPTER XVIII

APPENDIX TABLES

List of Figures

CHAPTER III

CHAPTER IV

CHAPTER V

CHAPTER IX

CHAPTER X

CHAPTER XI

CHAPTER XII

CHAPTER XIII

CHAPTER XVII

CHAPTER XVIII

Sources

Only the most important sources used in the preparation of this book are listed below. They are enumerated in the following order: (1) publications of international organizations, (2) publications of U.S. governmental agencies, (3) publications of private organizations and of individual authors. Within each group, the sources are listed alphabetically. Two basic publications of the Bureau of the Census, Statistical Abstract of the United States (various years; last edition used: 1965) and Historical Statistics of the United States: Colonial Times to 1957 (Washington, D.C., 1960), have been used throughout the entire book. Because of this, the reference to them in each chapter has been omitted.

Current statistical publications often revise their data in following issues; usually such revisions amount to minor changes. To give one example: the 1966 edition of the Statistical Abstract of the United States, released while this book was in the printer's hands, published revised data on the percentage of federally owned land by state (see Table I.3), with 98.3 per cent for Alaska, instead of 98.8 per cent as in previous editions. The difference amounts to less than two-tenths of one per cent, and is much smaller for other states. However, there is always a cut-off time after which neither "revisions" nor new data can be introduced into a book. The cut-off time for this book was the middle of 1966.

CHAPTER I

Sections 1 and 2

UNITED NATIONS, STATISTICAL OFFICE: *Statistical Yearbook*, New York, various years.

U.S. DEPARTMENT OF AGRICULTURE: *Agricultural Land Resources*, Washington, D.C., Government Printing Office (GPO), 1962; *Climate and Man: Yearbook of Agriculture, 1941*, GPO, 1941.

Section 3

U.S. DEPARTMENT OF AGRICULTURE: *Land Use and Its Patterns in the United States* (Agricultural Handbook No. 153), GPO, 1958; *Report of the Administrator of Soil Conservation Service* (annual), GPO, various years.

U.S. DEPARTMENT OF HEALTH, EDUCATION, AND WELFARE: *Clean Water: A Chart Book of America's Water Needs, 1900–1980*, GPO, 1960; *New Directions in Health, Education, and Welfare*, GPO, 1963; *Report of the Committee on Environmental Health Problems*, GPO, 1962.

U.S. DEPARTMENT OF THE INTERIOR: *Report of the Secretary* (annual), GPO, various years; *Resources for Tomorrow* (1961 report), GPO, 1962.

CHAPTER II

Section 4

U.S. Department of Commerce, Bureau of the Census: *United States Census of Population, 1960* (Vol. I: *Characteristics of the Population;* Part 1: *United States Summary*), GPO, 1964.

Section 5

U.S. Department of Justice, Immigration and Naturalization Service: *Annual Report,* GPO, 1965.

Sections 6, 7, and 8

U.S. Department of Agriculture: *Recent Population Trends in the United States, with Emphasis on Rural Areas,* GPO, 1963.

U.S. Department of Commerce, Bureau of the Census: *Census of Population, 1960,* Vol. I, Part 1.

Taeuber, Conrad and Irene B.: *The Changing Population of the United States,* New York, Wiley & Sons, 1958.

Section 9

U.S. Department of Commerce, Bureau of the Census: *Census of Population, 1960,* Vol. I, Part 1.

Woytinsky, W. S. and E.'S.: *World Population and Production: Trends and Outlook* (hereafter cited as *World Population and Production*), second edition, New York, Twentieth Century Fund, 1955.

Sections 10 and 11

United Nations, Statistical Office: *Demographic Yearbook,* New York, various years.

U.S. Department of Commerce, Bureau of the Census: *Census of Population, 1960,* Vol. I, Part 1.

U.S. Department of the Interior, Bureau of Indian Affairs: *Indian Population and Land,* GPO, 1964.

Sections 12 and 13

United Nations, Statistical Office: *Demographic Yearbook,* various years.

U.S. Department of Commerce, Bureau of the Census: *Census of Population, 1960,* Vol. I, Part 1.

Bogue, Donald J.: *The Population of the United States,* Chicago, Ill., Free Press of Glencoe, 1959.

Sheldon, Henry D.: *The Older Population of the United States at Mid-Century,* New York, Wiley & Sons, 1958.

Woytinsky, W. S. and E. S.: *World Population and Production.*

CHAPTER III

Section 14

U.S. DEPARTMENT OF COMMERCE, BUREAU OF THE CENSUS: *Current Population Reports* (Series P-20), GPO, various issues.

U.S. DEPARTMENT OF HEALTH, EDUCATION, AND WELFARE, PUBLIC HEALTH SERVICE: *Vital Statistics of the United States* (annual) (Vol. I: *Natality*), GPO, various years.

Sections 15 and 16

UNITED NATIONS, STATISTICAL OFFICE: *Demographic Yearbook,* various years.

U.S. DEPARTMENT OF COMMERCE, BUREAU OF THE CENSUS: *Census of Population, 1960,* Vol. I, Part 1; *Current Population Reports* (Series P-20), various issues.

U.S. DEPARTMENT OF HEALTH, EDUCATION, AND WELFARE, PUBLIC HEALTH SERVICE: *Monthly Vital Statistics Reports* (monthly and annual summary), GPO, various years; *Vital Statistics of the United States* (Vol. II: *Mortality,* Parts A and B), various years.

Sections 17 and 18

UNITED NATIONS, STATISTICAL OFFICE: *Demographic Yearbook,* various years.

U.S. DEPARTMENT OF COMMERCE, BUREAU OF THE CENSUS: *Current Population Reports* (Series P-25), various issues.

U.S. DEPARTMENT OF HEALTH, EDUCATION, AND WELFARE, PUBLIC HEALTH SERVICE: *Monthly Vital Statistics Report, Annual Summary,* GPO, various years; *Vital Statistics of the United States* (Vol. II: *Mortality,* Section 5, Parts A and B), various years; *Life Tables* (Vol. II, Part A, Section 5), GPO, various years.

CHAPTER IV

Section 19

UNITED NATIONS, STATISTICAL OFFICE: *Demographic Yearbook,* various years.

U.S. DEPARTMENT OF HEALTH, EDUCATION, AND WELFARE: *Health, Education, and Welfare Indicators* (monthly) (hereafter cited as *Indicators*), GPO, various months; *Health, Education, and Welfare Trends* (annual supplement to *Indicators*) (hereafter cited as *Trends*), GPO, various years; PUBLIC HEALTH SERVICE: *Health Statistics* (Series B), GPO, various years; *Medical Care, Health Status, and Family Income, United States,* GPO, 1964; *Patients in Mental Institutions* (Parts I and II), GPO, 1963.

HEALTH INSURANCE INSTITUTE: *Source Book of Health Insurance Data* (annual), New York, 1965.

WOYTINSKY, W. S. and E. S.: *World Population and Production.*

Sections 20 and 21

UNITED NATIONS, STATISTICAL OFFICE: *Statistical Yearbook*, 1964.

U.S. DEPARTMENT OF COMMERCE, BUREAU OF THE CENSUS: *Census of Population, 1960*, Vol. I, Part 1.

U.S. DEPARTMENT OF HEALTH, EDUCATION, AND WELFARE, OFFICE OF EDUCATION: *Digest of Educational Statistics*, GPO, various years; *Fall 1964 Enrollment of Public School Systems*, GPO, 1965; *Fall 1964 Statistics of Public Schools*, GPO, 1965; *Projections of Educational Statistics to 1973–74*, GPO, 1964.

CHAPTER V

Sections 22 and 23

U.S. PRESIDENT: *Manpower Report of the President and a Report on Manpower Requirements, Resources, Utilization, and Training by the United States Department of Labor* (hereafter cited as *Manpower Report*), GPO, 1963 and 1965.

PRESIDENT'S COMMISSION ON THE STATUS OF WOMEN: *American Women*, GPO, 1963.

U.S. DEPARTMENT OF COMMERCE, BUREAU OF THE CENSUS: *Current Population Reports* (Series P-50 and P-57), various issues.

U.S. DEPARTMENT OF LABOR, BUREAU OF LABOR STATISTICS: *Employment and Earnings Statistics for the United States, 1909–62*, GPO, 1963; *Special Labor Force Report*, Nos. 4, 14, 23, 31, 39.

Sections 24, 25, and 26

U.S. PRESIDENT: *Manpower Report*, 1963 and 1965.

U.S. DEPARTMENT OF LABOR, BUREAU OF LABOR STATISTICS: *Employment and Earnings* (monthly), GPO, various months; *Employment and Earnings Statistics for the United States, 1909–62*; *Manpower and Training: Trends, Outlook, and Programs* (hereafter cited as *Manpower and Training*) ("Manpower Research" Bulletin No. 2), revised edition, GPO, 1963; *Mobility and Worker Adaptation to Economic Change in the United States* ("Manpower Research" Bulletin No. 1), revised edition, GPO, 1963.

WOYTINSKY, W. S.: *Three Aspects of Labor Dynamics*, Washington, D.C., Social Science Research Council, 1942.

Section 27

U.S. PRESIDENT: *Manpower Report*, 1963 and 1965.

U.S. DEPARTMENT OF LABOR, BUREAU OF LABOR STATISTICS: "Labor Force Projections 1970–80: Special Labor Force Report," *Monthly Labor Review*, February, 1965; *Manpower and Training*, 1963.

CHAPTER VI

Sections 28 and 29

BUREAU OF THE BUDGET, OFFICE OF STATISTICAL STANDARDS: *1964 Supplement to Economic Indicators: Historical and Descriptive Background* (hereafter cited as *1964 Supplement to Economic Indicators*), GPO, 1964.

COUNCIL OF ECONOMIC ADVISERS: *Economic Indicators* (monthly), GPO, various months; *Economic Report of the President* (annual), GPO, various years.

U.S. DEPARTMENT OF COMMERCE, OFFICE OF BUSINESS ECONOMICS: *Survey of Current Business* (monthly), GPO, various months; *U.S. Income and Output* (supplement to *Survey of Current Business*), GPO, 1958.

Sections 30 and 31

COUNCIL OF ECONOMIC ADVISERS: *Economic Indicators,* various months; *Economic Report of the President,* various years.

SECURITIES AND EXCHANGE COMMISSION: "Volume and Composition of Individuals' Saving" (a quarterly series), *Statistical Bulletin* (monthly), GPO, various months.

MILLER, HERMAN P.: *Income of the American People,* New York, Wiley & Sons, 1955.

Section 32

COUNCIL OF ECONOMIC ADVISERS: *Economic Indicators,* various months; *Economic Report of the President,* various years.

FEDERAL RESERVE SYSTEM, BOARD OF GOVERNORS: *Federal Reserve Bulletin* (monthly), various months.

SECURITIES AND EXCHANGE COMMISSION: "Volume and Composition of Individuals' Saving," *Statistical Bulletin,* various months.

U.S. DEPARTMENT OF COMMERCE, OFFICE OF BUSINESS ECONOMICS: *Survey of Current Business,* various months.

SURVEY RESEARCH CENTER: *Survey of Consumer Finances* (annual), Ann Arbor, Mich., University of Michigan Press, various years.

Section 33

U.S. DEPARTMENT OF COMMERCE, OFFICE OF BUSINESS ECONOMICS: *Personal Income by States Since 1929,* GPO, 1956: *Survey of Current Business,* various months; *U.S. Income and Output,* 1958.

Section 34

U.S. CONGRESS, JOINT ECONOMIC COMMITTEE, SUBCOMMITTEE ON ECONOMIC STATISTICS: *Hearings, Measuring the Nation's Wealth* (89th Cong., 1st sess.), GPO, 1965.

GOLDSMITH, RAYMOND W.: *The National Wealth of the United States in the Postwar Period,* Princeton, N.J., Princeton University Press, for the National Bureau of Economic Research, 1962.

CHAPTER VII

Section 35

U.S. DEPARTMENT OF AGRICULTURE: *Farm Family Spending in the United States*, GPO, 1958; *Spending Patterns of Rural and Urban Families*, GPO, 1964.

U.S. DEPARTMENT OF LABOR, BUREAU OF LABOR STATISTICS: *Cost of Living in the United States* (Bulletin No. 357), GPO, 1924; *Money Disbursements of Wage Earners and Clerical Workers, 1934–36* (Bulletin No. 638), GPO, 1941; *Survey of Consumer Expenditures and Income, 1960–61*, GPO, 1964–65.

UNIVERSITY OF PENNSYLVANIA, WHARTON SCHOOL OF FINANCE AND COMMERCE: *Study of Consumer Expenditures, Income, and Savings: Statistical Tables, Urban U.S., 1950* (hereafter cited as *Wharton School Survey of Consumer Expenditures*), Philadelphia, University of Pennsylvania Press, 1959–60.

Section 36

UNITED NATIONS, STATISTICAL OFFICE: *Statistical Yearbook*, 1964, 1965.

U.S. DEPARTMENT OF COMMERCE, OFFICE OF BUSINESS ECONOMICS: *Survey of Current Business*, various months; *U.S. Income and Output*, 1958.

Sections 37, 38, and 39

U.S. DEPARTMENT OF AGRICULTURE: *Agricultural Statistics* (annual), GPO, 1965; *Farm Family Spending in the United States*; *Spending Patterns of Rural and Urban Families*; *Trends and Patterns in U.S. Food Consumption*, GPO, 1961.

U.S. DEPARTMENT OF COMMERCE, OFFICE OF BUSINESS ECONOMICS: *Survey of Current Business*, various months.

U.S. DEPARTMENT OF LABOR, BUREAU OF LABOR STATISTICS: *How American Buying Habits Change*, GPO, 1959; *Survey of Consumer Expenditures and Income, 1960–61*.

UNIVERSITY OF PENNSYLVANIA: *Wharton School Survey of Consumer Expenditures*.

WOYTINSKY, W. S. and E. S.: *World Population and Production*.

Section 40

U.S. DEPARTMENT OF COMMERCE, OFFICE OF BUSINESS ECONOMICS: *Survey of Current Business*, various months.

U.S. DEPARTMENT OF HEALTH, EDUCATION, AND WELFARE: *Trends*, 1964; PUBLIC HEALTH SERVICE: *Medical Care, Health Status, and Family Income, United States*; SOCIAL SECURITY ADMINISTRATION: *Social Security Bulletin* (monthly), GPO, various months.

U.S. DEPARTMENT OF LABOR, BUREAU OF LABOR STATISTICS: *Survey of Consumer Expenditures and Income, 1960–61*.

HEALTH INSURANCE INSTITUTE: *Source Book of Health Insurance Data*, 1965.

Section 41

U.S. DEPARTMENT OF COMMERCE, OFFICE OF BUSINESS ECONOMICS: *National Income Supplement*, GPO, 1954; *Survey of Current Business*, various months; *U.S. Income and Output*, 1958.

U.S. DEPARTMENT OF LABOR, BUREAU OF LABOR STATISTICS: *How American Buying Habits Change*; *Survey of Consumer Expenditures and Income, 1960–61*.

CHAPTER VIII

Sections 42 and 43

UNITED NATIONS, FOOD AND AGRICULTURE ORGANIZATION: *Production Yearbook*, Rome, various years.

U.S. DEPARTMENT OF AGRICULTURE: *Agricultural Statistics*, various years; *Farm Employment, 1950–57* (Statistical Bulletin No. 236), GPO, 1958; *The Farm Index* (monthly), GPO, various months; *Farm Production: Trends, Prospects, and Programs*, GPO, 1961.

U.S. DEPARTMENT OF COMMERCE, BUREAU OF THE CENSUS: *United States Census of Agriculture, 1959* (Vol. II: *General Report*), GPO, 1962.

WOYTINSKY, W. S. and E. S.: *World Population and Production*.

Sections 44 and 45

U.S. DEPARTMENT OF AGRICULTURE: *Agricultural Statistics*, various years; *Census of Agriculture, 1959* (Vol. V: *Special Reports*; Part 6: *A Graphic Summary of Farm Tenure*); *Farm Employment* (Statistical Bulletin No. 236); *Farm Production: Trends, Prospects, and Programs*; *Handbook of Agricultural Charts* (annual), GPO, 1965; *The Hired Farm Working Force of 1960*, GPO, 1962; *A Statistical Summary of Farm Tenure, 1954*, GPO, 1958; *The Tenure Status of Farm Workers in the United States*, GPO, 1960.

U.S. DEPARTMENT OF COMMERCE, BUREAU OF THE CENSUS: *Census of Agriculture, 1959*, Vol. II.

Section 46

U.S. DEPARTMENT OF AGRICULTURE: *Agricultural Finance Outlook* (annual), GPO, various years; *The Balance Sheet of Agriculture* (annual), GPO, various years; *The Farm Income Situation* (quarterly), GPO, various years; *Farm-Mortgage Lending* (semiannual), GPO, various years.

U.S. DEPARTMENT OF COMMERCE, BUREAU OF THE CENSUS: *Census of Agriculture, 1959*, Vol. II.

Sections 47 and 48

U.S. DEPARTMENT OF AGRICULTURE: *Agricultural Statistics*, various years; *Crop Production* (annual), GPO, various years; *Crop Values* (annual), GPO, various years; *Farm Income: State Estimates, 1949–64*, GPO, 1965; *Farm Production: Trends, Prospects, and Programs*.

WOYTINSKY, W. S. and E. S.: *World Population and Production*.

Sections 49 and 50

U.S. DEPARTMENT OF AGRICULTURE: *Agricultural Statistics,* various years; *The Farm Income Situation,* various years; *U.S. Foreign Agricultural Trade by Countries,* GPO, 1965; COMMODITY CREDIT CORPORATION: *Report of Financial Conditions and Operations* (quarterly), GPO, various years; *Summary of 30 Years Operations of the Commodity Credit Corporation, with Report of the President of the Corporation,* GPO, 1964.

U.S. DEPARTMENT OF COMMERCE, BUREAU OF THE CENSUS: *Quarterly Summary of Foreign Commerce of the United States,* GPO, various years; *U.S. Commodity Exports and Imports as Related to Output, 1962 and 1961,* GPO, 1964.

CHAPTER IX

Sections 51 and 52

UNITED NATIONS, STATISTICAL OFFICE: *Statistical Yearbook,* 1964.

U.S. DEPARTMENT OF COMMERCE, BUREAU OF THE CENSUS: *United States Census of Mineral Industries, 1958,* GPO, 1961; *United States Census of Mineral Industries, 1963* (*General Summary,* Series MC63 [P]-1, -2, -3), GPO, 1965.

U.S. DEPARTMENT OF THE INTERIOR, BUREAU OF MINES: *Minerals Yearbook* (Vol. I: *Metals and Minerals Except Fuels*), GPO, various years.

WOYTINSKY, W. S. and E. S.: *World Population and Production.*

Section 53

U.S. DEPARTMENT OF COMMERCE, BUREAU OF THE CENSUS: *Census of Mineral Industries, 1958; Census of Mineral Industries, 1963,* Vol. I, Series MC63 [P]-1, -2, -3.

U.S. DEPARTMENT OF THE INTERIOR, BUREAU OF MINES: *Minerals Yearbook* (Vol. II: *Fuels*), various years; "Petroleum and Natural Gas," *Mineral Facts and Problems,* GPO, 1965.

AMERICAN GAS ASSOCIATION: *Gas Facts* (annual), New York, various years.

AMERICAN PETROLEUM INSTITUTE: *Petroleum Facts and Figures* (biennial), New York, various years.

WOYTINSKY, W. S. and E. S.: *World Population and Production.*

Sections 54 and 55

U.S. DEPARTMENT OF THE INTERIOR, BUREAU OF MINES: *Minerals Yearbook* (Vol. I), various years.

U.S. DEPARTMENT OF THE INTERIOR, BUREAU OF THE CENSUS: *Census of Mineral Industries, 1958; Census of Mineral Industries, 1963, General Summary,* Series MC63 [P]-1, -2, -3.

Section 56

U.S. DEPARTMENT OF COMMERCE, BUREAU OF THE CENSUS: *U.S. Commodity Exports and Imports as Related to Output, 1962 and 1961.*

U.S. DEPARTMENT OF THE INTERIOR, BUREAU OF MINES: *Minerals Yearbook* (Vol. I), various years.

Section 57

FEDERAL POWER COMMISSION: *Hydroelectric Power Resources of the United States, Developed and Undeveloped, January 1, 1964*, GPO, 1965; *National Power Survey* (two parts), GPO, 1964.
WOYTINSKY, W. S. and E. S.: *World Population and Production.*

CHAPTER X

Sections 58 and 59

UNITED NATIONS, STATISTICAL OFFICE: *Statistical Yearbook*, 1964.
U.S. DEPARTMENT OF COMMERCE, BUREAU OF THE CENSUS: *Annual Survey of Manufactures, 1962*, GPO, 1964; *Concentration Ratios in Manufacturing Industry, 1958* (prepared for the Senate Subcommittee on Antitrust and Monopoly, 87th Cong., 2d sess.), GPO, 1962; *United States Census of Manufactures, 1958*, GPO, 1961; *United States Census of Manufactures, 1963* (Series MC63 [P], GPO, 1965.

Sections 60, 61, 62, 63, 64, 65, 66, and 67

UNITED NATIONS, STATISTICAL OFFICE: *Statistical Yearbook*, various years.
U.S. DEPARTMENT OF COMMERCE, BUREAU OF THE CENSUS: *Annual Survey of Manufactures, 1962; Census of Manufactures, 1958; Census of Manufactures, 1963* (Series MC63 [P]); *Census of Population, 1960*, Vol. I, Part 1; *Concentration Ratios in Manufacturing Industry, 1958; Current Industrial Reports* (Series M221 and M22S), GPO, various years.
WOYTINSKY, W. S. and E. S.: *World Population and Production.*

CHAPTER XI

Sections 68 and 69

UNITED NATIONS, STATISTICAL OFFICE: *Statistical Yearbook*, 1964.
HOUSING AND HOME FINANCE AGENCY: *Eighteenth Annual Report, 1964*, GPO, 1965.
U.S. DEPARTMENT OF COMMERCE, BUREAU OF THE CENSUS: *Construction Reports* (monthly), GPO, various months; *Value of New Construction Put in Place, 1946–63*, revised edition, GPO, 1965.
U.S. DEPARTMENT OF COMMERCE and U.S. DEPARTMENT OF LABOR: *Construction Volume and Costs, 1915–56*, GPO, 1958.
U.S. DEPARTMENT OF LABOR, BUREAU OF LABOR STATISTICS: *Construction During Five Decades: Historical Statistics, 1907–52* (Bulletin No. 1146), GPO, 1954.
INSTITUTE FOR SOCIAL RESEARCH: *1964 Survey of Consumer Finances*, Ann Arbor, Mich., University of Michigan, 1965.

CHAPTER XII

Section 70

INTERSTATE COMMERCE COMMISSION: *Transport Economics* (monthly), GPO, various months; *Transport Statistics in the United States* (annual; issued separately for each type of transportation), GPO, various years.

NATIONAL ACADEMY OF SCIENCES and NATIONAL RESEARCH COUNCIL: *U.S. Transportation: Resources, Performance, and Problems*, Washington, D.C., 1962.

U.S. DEPARTMENT OF COMMERCE, BUREAU OF CENSUS: *United States Census of Transportation, 1963* (Series TC63 [A]-P4, -P5, -T61), GPO, 1965.

U.S. SENATE, COMMITTEE ON COMMERCE: *Hearings, National Transportation Policy* (87th Cong., 1st sess.), GPO, 1961.

WOYTINSKY, W. S. and E. S.: *World Commerce and Governments: Trends and Outlook* (hereafter cited as *World Commerce and Governments*), New York, Twentieth Century Fund, 1955.

Section 71

INTERSTATE COMMERCE COMMISSION: *Annual Report on Transport Statistics in the United States*, GPO, various years.

ASSOCIATION OF AMERICAN RAILROADS: *Statistics of Railroads, Class I, 1954–64*, Washington, D.C., 1965.

Section 72

U.S. DEPARTMENT OF COMMERCE, BUREAU OF PUBLIC ROADS: *Highway Statistics* (annual), GPO, various years; *Highway Progress* (annual), GPO, various years.

AUTOMOBILE MANUFACTURERS ASSOCIATION: *Automobile Facts and Figures* (annual), Detroit, Mich., various years.

NATIONAL ASSOCIATION OF MOTOR BUS OWNERS: *Bus Facts* (annual), Washington, D.C., various years.

NATIONAL SAFETY COUNCIL: *Accident Facts* (annual), Chicago, various years.

Section 73

INTERSTATE COMMERCE COMMISSION: *Annual Report on Transport Statistics in the United States* (Part V: *Carriers by Water*), various years.

U.S. DEPARTMENT OF THE ARMY, CORPS OF ENGINEERS: *Waterborne Commerce of the United States* (annual) (Part V: *National Summaries*), GPO, various years.

U.S. DEPARTMENT OF COMMERCE, MARITIME ADMINISTRATION: *Essential United States Foreign Trade Routes*, GPO, 1963; *United States Sea Ports* (two parts), GPO, 1963.

THE AMERICAN WATERWAYS OPERATORS: *Inland Waterborne Commerce Statistics* (annual), Washington, D.C., various years; *Big Load Afloat*, 1965.

Section 74

CIVIL AERONAUTICS BOARD: *Annual Report*, GPO, various years.

FEDERAL AVIATION AGENCY: *Statistical Handbook of Aviation* (annual), various years.

U.S. PRESIDENT: *United States Aeronautics and Space Activities, 1963* (message from the President, 88th Cong., 2d sess.), GPO, 1965.

AEROSPACE INDUSTRIES ASSOCIATION OF AMERICA: *Aerospace Facts and Figures* (annual), Washington, D.C., various years.

AIR TRANSPORT ASSOCIATION OF AMERICA: *1965 Fact and Figures*, Washington, D.C., 1965.

Section 75

FEDERAL COMMUNICATIONS COMMISSION: Annual Report, GPO, various years; *Statistics of Communications Common Carriers* (annual), GPO, various years.

U.S. POST OFFICE DEPARTMENT: *Annual Report of the Postmaster General*, GPO, various years.

CHAPTER XIII

Sections 76 and 77

U.S. DEPARTMENT OF COMMERCE, BUREAU OF THE CENSUS: *Quarterly Summary of Foreign Commerce of the United States*, GPO, various years; *Survey of the Origin of Exports of Manufactured Products*, GPO, 1963 and 1965; *U.S. Commodity Exports and Imports as Related to Output, 1962 and 1961.*

U.S. DEPARTMENT OF LABOR, BUREAU OF LABOR STATISTICS: *Domestic Employment Attributable to U.S. Exports*, GPO, 1960.

Section 78

REVIEW COMMITTEE FOR BALANCE OF PAYMENTS STATISTICS: *The Balance of Payments Statistics of the United States: A Review and Appraisal*, GPO, 1965.

U.S. CONGRESS, JOINT ECONOMIC COMMITTEE: *The United States Balance of Payments: Perspectives and Policies*, GPO, 1965.

U.S. DEPARTMENT OF COMMERCE, OFFICE OF BUSINESS ECONOMICS: *Balance of Payments—Statistical Supplement* (supplement to *Survey of Current Business*), GPO, 1958 and 1963; *Foreign Business Investments in the United States*, GPO, 1962; *Foreign Grants and Credits by the United States Government*, GPO, 1963; *Survey of Current Business*, various months.

SALANT, WALTER, et al.: *The United States Balance of Payments in 1968*, Washington, D.C., Brookings Institution, 1963.

WOYTINSKY, W. S. and E. S.: *World Commerce and Governments*.

Section 79

U.S. PRESIDENT: *Annual Report to Congress*, GPO, various years.

U.S. DEPARTMENT OF COMMERCE, OFFICE OF BUSINESS ECONOMICS: *Foreign Grants and Credits by the United States Government*, 1963.

U.S. DEPARTMENT OF STATE, AGENCY FOR INTERNATIONAL DEVELOPMENT: *The Aid Program*, GPO, 1964; *The Foreign Assistance Program*, GPO, 1966;

Operations Report (annual), GPO, various years; *U.S. Economic Assistance Programs, 1948–64*, GPO, 1965.

U.S. DEPARTMENT OF STATE and U.S. DEPARTMENT OF DEFENSE: *Proposed Mutual Defense and Development Programs, FY 1966*, GPO, 1965.

Section 80

BUREAU OF THE BUDGET, OFFICE OF STATISTICAL STANDARDS: *1964 Supplement to Economic Indicators.*

U.S. DEPARTMENT OF COMMERCE, BUREAU OF THE CENSUS: *Monthly Wholesale Trade Report*, various months; *United States Census of Business, 1958: Wholesale Trade*, GPO, 1961; *United States Census of Business, 1963: Wholesale Trade* (Series BC63-WAi), GPO, 1965; OFFICE OF BUSINESS ECONOMICS: *Survey of Current Business*, various months.

Section 81

BUREAU OF THE BUDGET, OFFICE OF STATISTICAL STANDARDS: *1964 Supplement to Economic Indicators.*

U.S. DEPARTMENT OF COMMERCE, BUREAU OF THE CENSUS: *Census of Business, 1958: Retail Trade; Census of Business, 1963: Retail Trade Summary Statistics*; Series BC63-RA1 and -[A]RS7A); OFFICE OF BUSINESS ECONOMICS: *Survey of Current Business*, various months.

Section 82

FEDERAL DEPOSIT INSURANCE CORPORATION: *Annual Report*, GPO, various years.

FEDERAL RESERVE SYSTEM, BOARD OF GOVERNORS: *All-Bank Statistics, United States, 1896–1955*, GPO, 1959; *Annual Report*, GPO, various years; *Federal Reserve Bulletin*, various months.

U.S. DEPARTMENT OF COMMERCE, OFFICE OF BUSINESS ECONOMICS: *Survey of Current Business*, various months.

U.S. DEPARTMENT OF TREASURY, OFFICE OF THE COMPTROLLER OF THE CURRENCY, DEPARTMENT OF BANKING ECONOMIC RESEARCH: *Banking and Monetary Studies*, ed. DEANE GARSON, GPO, 1963.

Section 83

U.S. DEPARTMENT OF COMMERCE, OFFICE OF BUSINESS ECONOMICS: *Survey of Current Business*, various months.

U.S. DEPARTMENT OF HEALTH, EDUCATION, AND WELFARE, SOCIAL SECURITY ADMINISTRATION: *The Extent of Health Insurance Coverage in the United States* (Research Report No. 10), GPO, 1965.

HEALTH INSURANCE INSTITUTE: *Source Book of Health Insurance Data*, various years.

INSTITUTE OF LIFE INSURANCE: *Life Insurance Fact Book* (annual), New York, various years.

THE SPECTATOR: *Insurance Yearbook*, Philadelphia, various years.

CHAPTER XIV

Sections 84 and 85

BUREAU OF THE BUDGET: *The Budget of the United States Government* (annual), GPO, various years.

COUNCIL OF ECONOMIC ADVISERS: *Economic Report of the President*, various years.

U.S. CONGRESS, JOINT ECONOMIC COMMITTEE: *The Federal Tax System: Facts and Problems*, GPO, 1964.

U.S. DEPARTMENT OF COMMERCE, BUREAU OF THE CENSUS: *United States Census of Governments, 1962* (Vol. I: *Governmental Organization;* Vol. VI: *Historical Statistics on Governmental Finances and Employment*), GPO, 1963–64; OFFICE OF BUSINESS ECONOMICS: *Survey of Current Business*, various months.

Section 86

BUREAU OF THE BUDGET: *The Budget of the United States Government*, various years.

U.S. DEPARTMENT OF COMMERCE, BUREAU OF THE CENSUS: *Census of Governments, 1962* (Vol. IV: *Governmental Finance, 1963*).

U.S. DEPARTMENT OF THE TREASURY: *Annual Report of the Secretary*, GPO, various years.

STUDENSKI, PAUL, and H. E. KROOSS: *Financial History of the United States*, New York, McGraw-Hill, 1952.

WOYTINSKY, W. S. and E. S.: *World Commerce and Governments*.

CHAPTER XV

Sections 87 and 88

INTERNATIONAL LABOR OFFICE: *Yearbook of Labor Statistics*, Geneva, various years.

BUREAU OF THE BUDGET, OFFICE OF STATISTICAL STANDARDS: *1964 Supplement to Economic Indicators*.

COUNCIL OF ECONOMIC ADVISERS: *Economic Indicators*, various months.

U.S. DEPARTMENT OF LABOR, BUREAU OF LABOR STATISTICS: *Consumer Price Index* (monthly), GPO, various months; *Consumer Prices in the United States* (monthly and annual) (Bulletins No. 1165 and 1256), GPO, 1959; *Monthly Labor Review*, various months; *Prices: A Chartbook, 1953–62* (Bulletin No. 1351), GPO, 1962; *Prices: A Chartbook, 1953–62, Supplement* (Bulletin No. 1351-1), GPO, 1963; *Wholesale Prices and Price Indexes* (monthly and annual) (Bulletin No. 1376), GPO, 1963.

Section 89

COUNCIL OF ECONOMIC ADVISERS: *Economic Indicators*, various months.

U.S. DEPARTMENT OF COMMERCE, BUREAU OF THE CENSUS: *Current Population Reports* (Series P-60: "Consumer Income"; No. 43).

U.S. Department of Labor, Bureau of Labor Statistics: *Current Wage Developments* (monthly), GPO, various months; *Deferred Wage Increases and Escalator Clause, 1952–63*, GPO; *Employment and Earnings* (monthly), GPO, various months; *Employment and Earnings Statistics for the United States, 1902–62* (Bulletin No. 1312–1), GPO, 1963; *Wage Indexes* (Bulletin No. 1427), GPO, 1965.

Woytinsky, W. S., and Associates: *Employment and Wages in the United States*, New York, Twentieth Century Fund, 1953.

CHAPTER XVI

Section 90

U.S. Congress, Joint Economic Committee: *European Social Security System* (89th Cong., 1st sess.), GPO, 1965.

U.S. Department of Health, Education, and Welfare: *The Social Security Act: Its First Twenty-Five Years*, GPO, 1965; *State Data and State Rankings in Health, Education, Welfare* (annual supplement to *Indicators*), GPO, various years; *Social Security Programs in the United States*, GPO, 1964; *Welfare in Review* (monthly), GPO, various months; Social Security Administration: *Social Security Bulletin*, various months.

Section 91

Bureau of the Budget, Office of Statistical Standards: *1964 Supplement to Economic Indicators*.

U.S. Department of Health, Education, and Welfare: *New Directions in Health, Education, and Welfare*, 1963; *The Social Security Act: Its First Twenty-Five Years*; *Trends*, various years; Social Security Administration: *Social Security Bulletin*, various months; *Social Security Programs in the United States*.

U.S. Department of Labor, Bureau of Employment Security: *Unemployment Insurance Statistics* (monthly), GPO, various months.

Woytinsky, W. S., and Associates: *Employment and Wages in the United States*.

Sections 92 and 93

U.S. Department of Health, Education, and Welfare: *Indicators*, various months; *New Directions in Health, Education, and Welfare*, 1963; *The Social Security Act: Its First Twenty-Five Years*; *State Data and State Rankings in Health, Education, Welfare*, various years; *Trends*, various years; *Welfare in Review*, various months; Social Security Administration: *Social Security Bulletin* (annual statistical supplement), various years; *Summary of Major Provisions of Social Security Amendments of 1965, as Reported Out by the Conference Committee*, GPO, 1965.

CHAPTER XVII

Section 94

ORGANIZATION FOR ECONOMIC CO-OPERATION: *Country Reports of the Organization of Scientific Research, United States,* by Mary E. Corning, Paris, 1963; *The Research and Development Effort in Western Europe, North America, and the Soviet Union,* by C. Freeman and A. Young (hereafter cited as *Research and Development Effort*), Paris, 1965.
NATIONAL ACADEMY OF SCIENCES: *Basic Research and National Goals,* Washington, D.C., 1965.
NATIONAL ACADEMY OF SCIENCES and NATIONAL RESEARCH COUNCIL: *Federal Support of Basic Research in Institutions of Higher Learning,* Washington, D.C., 1964.
NATIONAL SCIENCE FOUNDATION: *American Science Manpower,* 64–11 (publication year–publication number); *Basic Research—A National Resource,* 57–35; *Federal Funds for Research, Development, and Other Scientific Activities,* 64–11; *Proceedings of a Conference on Academic and Industrial Basic Research,* 61–39; *Research and Development in Industry,* 64–9; *Science, the Endless Frontier,* by Vannevar Bush (originally published in 1945 as A *Report to the President on a Program for Postwar Scientific Research*), GPO, 1960.
MACHLUP, FRITZ: *The Production and Distribution of Knowledge in the United States,* Princeton, N.J., Princeton University Press, 1962.

Section 95

BUREAU OF THE BUDGET: *The Budget of the United States Government,* 1967.
NATIONAL ACADEMY OF SCIENCES: *Basic Research and National Goals.*
NATIONAL ACADEMY OF SCIENCES and NATIONAL RESEARCH COUNCIL: *Federal Support of Basic Research in Institutions of Higher Learning.*
NATIONAL SCIENCE FOUNDATION: *Federal Funds for Research, Development, and Other Scientific Activities,* 64–11; *Review of Data on Research and Development* (monthly), various months; *Review of Data on Science Resources* (monthly), various months.

Section 96

ORGANIZATION FOR ECONOMIC CO-OPERATION: *Research and Development Effort.*
NATIONAL SCIENCE FOUNDATION: *American Science Manpower,* 64–16; *Engineering Manpower in Profile* (a report of Engineers Joint Council), 1964; *Review of Data on Science Resources,* various months; *Scientific and Technical Manpower Resources,* 64–28.
U.S. DEPARTMENT OF COMMERCE, BUREAU OF THE CENSUS: *Census of Population, 1960,* Vol. I, Part 1.

Section 97

ORGANIZATION FOR ECONOMIC CO-OPERATION: *Research and Development Effort.*

NATIONAL SCIENCE FOUNDATION: *Basic Research—A National Resource,* 57–35; *Proceedings of a Conference on Academic and Industrial Basic Research,* 61–39; *Proceedings of a Conference on Research and Development and Its Impact on the Economy,* 58–36.

U.S. CONGRESS, SELECT COMMITTEE ON SMALL BUSINESS: *The Role and Effect of Technology in the Nation's Economy* (88th Cong., 1st sess.), GPO, 1963.

U.S. DEPARTMENT OF LABOR, BUREAU OF LABOR STATISTICS: *Technological Trends in Major American Industries* (Bulletin No. 1474), GPO, 1966; *Technological Trends in Thirty-Six Major American Industries,* GPO, 1964.

TERLECKYJ, N. E.: *Research and Development: Its Growth and Composition* ("Studies in Business Economics"), New York, National Industrial Conference Board, 1964.

MACHLUP, FRITZ: *The Production and Distribution of Knowledge in the United States.*

CHAPTER XVIII

Sections 98 and 99

U.S. CONGRESS OF THE HOUSE OF REPRESENTATIVES, CLERK OF THE HOUSE: *Statistics of the Presidential and Congressional Election Year,* GPO, various years.

U.S. DEPARTMENT OF COMMERCE, BUREAU OF THE CENSUS: *Current Population Reports* (Series P-20, No. 143); *Voter Participation in the National Election, November, 1964,* GPO.

KEY, V. O., JR.: *Politics, Parties, and Pressure Groups,* 5th ed., New York, Thomas Y. Crowell, 1964.

WOYTINSKY, W. S. and E. S.: *World Commerce and Governments.*

Index

Because this book is concerned with the United States as a whole, rather than with single states or regions, this is essentially a subject index. Data concerning all states or several states are referred to under the heading: "State Data"; concerning regions and geographic divisions, under the heading: "Regional and Geographic Data." References to other countries appear when comparative data are used and are included under the title: "International Data."

ABOUT THE AUTHOR

Forty years ago in Germany, the now famous husband-and-wife team of Wladimir and Emma Woytinsky published the pioneering seven-volume work, *Die Welt in Zahlen (The World in Figures)*. In 1935, the Woytinskys came to the United States and began distinguished careers of government service. Mrs. Woytinsky served with the Committee on Social Security of the Social Science Research Council, the Board of Economic Warfare (later the Foreign Economic Administration), and the Department of State. In the 1950's, the Woytinskys produced two monumental works, *World Population and Production* and *World Commerce and Governments*. Together they made lecture tours of the Far East (for the Department of State and the Indian Ministry of Education) and of Latin America (for the Department of State).

Mrs. Woytinsky's memoir, *Two Lives in One*, which warmly recalls her four decades of marriage to and fruitful collaboration with her late husband, was published in 1965.